The New Reality of Municipal Finance

The New Reality of Municipal Finance

The Rise and Fall of the Intergovernmental City

Robert W. Burchell

James H. Carr
Richard L. Florida
James Németh

with

Michael Pawlik
Felix R. Barreto

CENTER
FOR URBAN
POLICY RESEARCH

Published in the United States of America
by the Center for Urban Policy Research
Building 4051—Kilmer Campus
New Brunswick, New Jersey 08903

Library of Congress Cataloging in Publication Data
Main entry under title:

The new reality of municipal finance.

  Bibliography: p. 4 33
  Includes index.
  1. Revenue sharing—United States. 2. Municipal
finance—United States.   3. Intergovernmental fiscal
relations—United States.   I. Burchell, Robert W.
HJ9145.N45   1984   336 '.014 '73   83–7377
ISBN 0-88285-091-1

Contents

List of Exhibits

Preface

AT MID-DECADE, THE PROCESS of painful review of urban, fiscal and service strategies is now under way. The level of guides available, however, is all too inadequate for what gives every evidence of being a long, drawn-out effort. The procedures of accommodating growth have long dominated the learned literature—but have often proven to be elusive in practice. No-growth, and more so, decline represent even more mysterious and difficult terrain.

To a very substantial degree, however, one does not have to invent the future. The observations incorporated in this study indicate that the reshaping processes are already at work. What is evident from both the secondary data, as well as conversations with municipal administrators, is that over a period of time what conventional accounting wisdom viewed as variable costs, i.e., costs associated with specific caseload and the like, growing with the latter and retreating with it as well, had become largely entrenched in the municipal fabric. In part, this process was fortified by unionization, by civil service, and, perhaps even more noticeably, by habit.

Encouraged and nurtured by transfer payments, the municipal budget burgeoned even while the physical reality of cities tended to decline, particularly in terms of population. The selective migration from central cities meant that own-source revenues, which were largely linked to resident wealth and spending power—with even realty values over the long term obviously reflective of this base—have tended to shrink. At the same time, however, the burdens of poverty have remained, if not in absolute numerical growth, then certainly as a proportion of total.

A strong case can be made that the flow of external funds may well have been a mixed blessing. On the one hand, in many cases, it addressed—in a most useful fashion—immediate problems of the municipalities. On the other hand, however, in a much less salubrious way, it encouraged a weight of staffing and of bureaucratic overhead which may have yielded little in the way of effective service while raising the overall ambient costs of municipal services.

To paraphrase Samuel Johnson, there's nothing like the sight of a noose to concentrate one's thinking. The rumblings of potential reduction, if not in the absolute level, then in the growth of transfer payments, have long been heard. The recurring examples of New York City's fiscal crises have sharpened the focus of municipal administrators. In turn, there has been a significant effort to reduce costs both in operations secured by own-source funds as well as those underwritten by transfers.

The long-term impact of these elements upon the ecology of municipalities is still far from evident. In many cases, significant cutbacks in expenditure and staffing have yet to result in much in the way of noticeable loss of service and amenities.

There is some indication, however, that this has been accomplished at the cost of longer-term maintenance and reconstruction.

In general, declining, fiscally dependent, *intergovernmental* cities are older and their physical plants suffer from all of the geriatric diseases. User charges have been inadequate and now, in several cases, the very user base has been attenuated. Although not directly in our study, a principal prototype would be the New York City mass transit system, put into operation for a city of eight million people, projected to encompass nine million—and now supported by a base of only seven million—and that shrinking!

The more complex the infrastructure, the more costly and demanding are both the operating and maintenance charges associated with it. To use the biological analogy, the more specialized an organism, the more vulnerable it is to major changes in its context. Within that concept, there evidently is a much greater level of adaptation available to newer cities, predicated on the technology of the present rather than the past, with much less in the way of antique infrastructure—and perhaps even more strikingly, of antique patterns of behavior and operation.

Intergovernmental cities have learned to live with markedly less. The problems of attrition in own-source revenues are difficult enough to encompass, much less the major downward step functions as transfer payments were cut. Non-intergovernmental cities on the other hand, in general, have had much more modest patterns of total expenditure. Further, more of it was dedicated to current and future need. They represent, at least in part, the advantage of coming last, carrying with them much less of the burden of things past. By offering a much more privatized, atomized, and in some cases reduced sets of services, they are not quite so vulnerable to City Hall's functioning and vigor for their futures.

But what is the future of these agglomerations of people and functions in the levels of concentration which we call cities? It is evident that the more blessed among the municipalities discussed here are those which have generated a meaningful, post-industrial level of competence and pulling power; cities whose functions no longer depend on manufacturing, but rather on information processing or face-to-face contact. The least fortunate are those dependent on those relatively perilous areas of blue-collar employment which is fast shrinking. But even in the former case, clearly what has evolved is a city-within-a-city phenomenon: a relatively small core dominated by office buildings and central city hotels sometimes coupled with major entertainment and recreational elements. In very large part, the differentiation as we view it in the future between the city of dependency and the city as a relative independent entity lies within the relationship of the pulling power and potency of tax base generated by its post-industrial sectors versus the levels of expenditure and frictions engendered by its older "conventional" sectors. And once again, both of these must be viewed within the pattern of service delivery costs and infrastructure requirements that are a function of history and habit.

In retrospect, the fiscal crises of New York and other cities marked a turning point in the perception of municipal finance. While part of the lesson was obscured by the panic-driven levels of coping with inflation, and further muted by the last flows of new transfer payments, à la CETA and countercyclical measures, which were introduced to the central city, the new calculus of relationships with municipal employees became evident.

The requirements of cutting fiscal expenditures to meet a largely municipally self-derived purse have been under way. The issues are not merely what services the city should provide but also how they are to be provided. Although the utilization of private vendors is still much more discussed than implemented, certainly a very substantial beginning has been made in using external sources of public services. This, in turn, has significance both in light of potential and direct cost savings, and perhaps even more so, as a yardstick of performance for those directly provided and administered by the city.

But this is the more positive side of the coin. The issues of how we get from the past day to a more efficient and realistic future for the intergovernmental city present some ominous elements. Clearly much will be required in the way of state alleviation. Continuous reordering of function and division of responsibilities, not only with the statehouse but also with the federal government, will be essential as well.

As of this writing, the financial exigencies required by domestic economic stability and deficit reduction clearly have national priority. Once these have been attained, given a sustained halt of inflation and interest rates, a time for consolidation of central cities and a measured restoration of essential infrastructure should be forthcoming.

But these measures must be viewed within the context of a substantial reduction in function of all but a very few of the cities in question. *Although certainly growth should be supported wherever possible, the first order or priority must be stabilization and a careful reappraisal by municipal leaders of the services that they are offering, levels of priority that should be accorded them, and wherever possible, the restoration of self-generated revenues.*

The remerchandizing of the cities currently involves drastic reappraisals of user fees and internal investment procedures commensurate with the multipliers of growth and reinvigoration. Balancing these new priorities with the sustenance requirements of the poor and the helpless, of sustaining the basic safety net at the same time, will require leadership, flexibility, and, hopefully, some measure of outside support as well.

George Sternlieb
Director
Center for Urban Policy Research
Summer, 1984

Acknowledgments

The New Reality of Municipal Finance is the result of a two-year research effort commissioned by the U.S. Department of Housing and Urban Development (HUD), Office of Policy Development and Research. The study was undertaken during the first term of the Reagan Administration and made ready for publication as a decision on the Administration's second term was put before the electorate.

HUD's governmental technical representatives were Dr. Howard Sumka and Mr. Samuel Hodges III. The patience and support of Mr. Hodges and the foresight of Dr. Sumka allowed this study to take its final form.

The Rutgers University Center for Urban Policy Research (CUPR) provided additional funding to extend the number of sites of investigation and also to provide essential analyses of the emergence and dismantling of intergovernmentalism. We thank Dr. George Sternlieb, director of CUPR, for his willingness to extend and broaden the study.

Our colleagues at CUPR, David Listokin, Robert W. Lake, W. Patrick Beaton, William Dolphin, and Edward E. Duensing, are a continuous delight as a source of insight and assistance. David Listokin drafted Chapter 9; Edward Duensing compiled the bibliography; William Dolphin assembled the data for the computer and ran the required statistical tests; Robert W. Lake and W. Patrick Beaton provided directional insight and allowed their own work to take lower priority when CUPR's full effort had to be directed to this study.

Mary Picarella, CUPR administrative officer and publications director, maintained financial control of the research project and prepared the final manuscript for publication. The form and structure of the work are largely a tribute to her efforts. Joan Frantz maintained the payroll, supervised chapter drafts, and maintained chapter files. Lydia Lombardi almost single-handedly completed several drafts of manuscript typing. Arlene Pashman typed the tabular material and proofed the various stages of the evolving book. Barry Jones designed the book's interior. Judith Hancock edited the manuscript and prepared the index. This volume is dedicated to, and clearly reflects, the competency and diligence of CUPR's administrative staff.

Graduate students from the Rutgers Urban Planning and Policy Development program completed 200 Newark landlord interviews, 400 New Jersey tenant interviews, and 200 property inspections.

A great deal of time has been spent to ensure accuracy and representativeness of the data provided here. Although many contributed, we alone remain responsible for any errors or omissions.

Robert W. Burchell
James H. Carr
Richard Florida
James Németh
Summer, 1984

Introduction

THE STUDY which follows is an analysis of the growth and decline of a special class of cities in the United States. These are cities which became dependent upon a variety of revenues, primarily from federal and state governments, to support an array of local public services which were basic to the needs of their citizens.

The term used to describe this category of cities is "intergovernmental." Intergovernmental cities are those locations where revenue raising is substantially shared by multiple levels of government. Direct revenue transfers are made from state and federal governments to the general fund of local governments to augment insufficient revenues. Further, indirect revenues flow to the residents of these cities and then to local economic entities in the form of social security, unemployment, food stamp payments, etc., which further bolster the economies of these geographic areas.

It is important to isolate the phenomenon of intergovernmentalism, to trace its growth, and specify its magnitude. For twenty years, until the beginning of the 1980s, intergovernmental cities became significantly dependent upon revenue transfers. They spent much more money on local public services than did most other cities of their size. And more than half of what they spent was composed of revenue transfers from other levels of government. The public employees of intergovernmental cities formed two pools, those supported by hard (local) and those financed or paid for by soft (intergovernmental) money, and separate budget strategies had to be developed for each. In effect, these cities became wards of external levels of government interest and programs.

To say that these cities arrived at this condition because of mismanagement or dereliction of duty is to understand neither their social and economic structure nor the thrust of domestic public policy for the previous two decades. To say also that these cities do not have a problem, in terms of sustained intergovernmental support, is to misinterpret the thrust of current and future public policy.

Intergovernmental cities are for the most part large, old, declining, Northeast and North Central communities whose industries and businesses have left and whose populations have become increasingly poverty-stricken. Most social and economic indicators put these cities at the bottom of any list of criteria of municipal vigor. Their residents are poor, frequently out of work, and poorly educated. They have and continue to experience ill health, higher-than-average rates of crime, and live in housing and neighborhoods where structure abandonment is visibly present. The local tax bases of these communities have been eroded both relative to their suburban and other metropolitan neighbors, and even absolutely, in terms of previously existing tax base levels. The revenues which flow from these taxing foundations are also diminished because the cities are reluctant to tax existing residences and businesses for fear they will leave for neighboring areas.

The problem of revenue shortfalls in these locations has been dealt with in the past through a policy of increasing federal and state fiscal intervention. An array of federal programs was developed to supplement income, provide access to basic levels of nutrition and health, assist in community and regional development, encourage education, training and employment, and subsidize transportation, public works, and other capital outlays.

From 1960 to 1980, these programs increased public spending on human resources and community development by a factor of ten-to-one—a rate double the growth of the federal budget as a whole. In 1980 dollars, intergovernmental transfers went from $460 per capita in 1960 to over $1,000 per capita in 1980. A situation emerged where the distinction between minimal threshold public services and general public responsibility could no longer be made.

Further, as the ability to target programs through hardship indices of one type or another improved, intergovernmental cities increasingly became the recipients of both categorical and broad-based grants. Ratios of the receipt of large grants in the areas of income security, community and regional development, education, training, employment, social services, health, transportation, state and local assistance, favored intergovernmental versus other cities by ratios of two-to-three to one. These grants became not special purpose, external to the local treasury, but operational and absolutely vital to local solvency. Over the period 1960 to 1980, state and federal aid in intergovernmental cities grew from 20 percent of all general revenues to over 50 percent. State and federal transfer payments were meeting more local expenditures than were local revenues.

These programs, which state governments provided at twice the funding level of the federal government, yet which grew in the federal sector at twice the state rate, had undeniable impacts on the various areas of cities' economic, social, and physical hardship. State basic education aid contributed to narrowing the gap in educational services in poor and affluent school districts. Community health centers took medical services to the heart of some of the nation's most adversely affected and poorly served neighborhoods. The Job Corps program provided youths with almost insurmountable personal problems with marketable skills. Community Development funds were a major source of central city economic redevelopment, and so on.

Currently, however, there is broad-base support for limiting the growth of public spending support based upon disillusionment with the cost–benefit relationships that evolved and the impact of this spending on national economic growth. And whether it takes the form of federal cutbacks encouraged by the executive branch or by state statutes controlling expenditures and revenues spawned by populist movements, the mood for curtailment is definitely present.

Cutbacks have taken place at the federal level through redefinition of programs, changes in eligibility requirements, and either actual cuts in existing or reduction of growth in future budget authority. Examples include the reduction through consolidation of the various Job Corps programs, the reduction through eligibility requirement changes of food stamps, school lunch and breakfast, Medicare and Medicaid programs, the reduction through direct cuts of EDA, EPA and UMTA programs, and finally, the reduction through growth cuts in AFDC, unemployment, and supplemental security benefits. At the state level, Propositions 13 and 2½ have limited revenue growth to minimal levels in California and Massachusetts, respectively, and similar controls have had comparable effects on expenditures in New Jersey and Illinois. Some kind of limiting mechanism is currently in effect in four out of five states nationally.

How have intergovernmental cities responded? The answer, though far from complete, is already at hand. Cities have cut back—first across the board through natural attrition, then more selectively by priority of public service. Via retrenchment management, they decreased both the quality of most and the quantity of many public services. Staff provided by revenue transfers were the first to go; these were joined by reductions in staff supported by locally raised revenues. A core of essential services and a method for the delivery of these services emerged. Cities looked toward sharing and contracting out of services not provided publicly. Taxes rose, tax exemptions decreased, and both user charges and fees and permits grew significantly.

Initially state government has provided a buffer. Experiencing inordinately good economic times towards the mid-1980s and with treasuries buoyed up by pension and gaming revenues, state governments have softened the blow of federal withdrawal. However, there have been few new state initiatives, and little in the way of additional long-term state aid has been structured. Basically, the intergovernmental city became less intergovernmental, more self-sufficient and more interrelated with both the business sector and other communities. The city readjusted to what upper-level intergovernmental priorities remained, while at the same time looked to local private-public partnerships for future mutually beneficial endeavors. The adjustment process was not easy. Those cities most dependent on intergovernmental transfers were those most affected and also those least able to generate own-source revenues. Regardless of whether there were short-run "fixes," the onus of change was upon these cities. City managers of intergovernmental cities were constantly reappraising the mix of costs and services. Issue by issue, they were called upon to decide if there was a public responsibility and if so, to what degree. Both the former and the latter were consistently influenced by the availability of local public resources to finance such objectives.

This work is intended to provide some perspective on who these cities are and the changes they have undergone given the drastic shifts in national domestic spending.

1
Conceptual Framework of the Intergovernmental City

THIS CHAPTER establishes a conceptual framework from which to evaluate the emergence of the intergovernmental city. It contends that the intergovernmental city was the product of prolonged and concentrated urban economic decline. It begins by outlining various theories of urban economic decline or disinvestment. It continues with a discussion of the effects of disinvestment on the economy of the city. It concludes with a statement of the relationship between economic decline, fiscal stress, and intergovernmentalism. In so doing, this chapter serves as a conceptual preview to the empirical work which follows.

Background

The intergovernmental city is defined as an older, economically-declining, industrial city that is characterized by acute levels of federal and state revenue transfer. Over the past two decades, the intergovernmental city has lost a substantial part of its industry and with it both retail trade and population. Its housing stock typically has been significantly diminished; its economic base and revenue-producing capabilities, sorely depleted.

Plagued by a shrinking tax base and burdened with escalating demands for public services, the intergovernmental city has and will face the overwhelming pressures of municipal fiscal stress. With market actors abandoning key sectors of the local economy, the municipal government of the intergovernmental city is increasingly forced to assume once-private entrepreneurial functions, and to do so under the most adverse conditions. Stripped of its revenue-generating capacity, this under-capitalized local government is thrust into a position of virtual dependence upon federal and state transfers as a way to provide routine public services.

Many of the problems currently facing the intergovernmental city stem, primarily, from tremendous reductions in private investment in its economic base. Put quite simply, private investors abandoned the older core city for more lucrative endeavors elsewhere. Disinvestment in the intergovernmental city involved the transfer of productive activities and capital out of the older industrial sectors of these manufacturing cities, into new activities in different geographic areas of the same metropolitan region or in different metropolitan regions. In the intergovernmental city, the macroeconomic processes of increased capital mobility and heightened investment

1

shifts underlie the more visible problems of central city economic decline and the rise of fiscal dependency. Private disinvestment — its causes and consequences, as well as the public responses to it — thus forms the crux for our theoretical understanding of the intergovernmental city.

The Causes of Disinvestment in the Intergovernmental City

In large measure, the forces shaping the overall process of disinvestment, undercutting central city economies, and in turn, motivating the emergent trend toward intergovernmentalism lie well beyond the domain of city hall or local economic factors. These forces are enmeshed within political-economic structures and institutions which transcend local, state, and even national boundaries, and which may be truly global in scope.[1] What literature exists on the central city decline largely sidesteps this issue, focusing exclusively on the city-specific costs of doing business or upon the mismanagement of particular local programs or budgets. Little attention is paid to the structural processes underlying the decline of manufacturing cities and their attendant dependence upon federal transfers for day-to-day operations. True understanding of the intergovernmental city requires factoring out the salient linkages between the macroeconomics of disinvestment and its local geographic impact, and the emergence of intergovernmental dependence. In essence, understanding the intergovernmental city means understanding the relationship between the causes of private disinvestment and the historical forms of public response.

In the conventional literature, near-exclusive focus is placed on the negative impacts that rapid technological progress holds for the aging city. According to this view, technological innovation — particularly recent advances in communications and transportation technology — deprive the manufacturing city of many of its former locational advantages. With the advent of motor and air transport, proximity to rail or water lines is no longer essential for most productive activities (Baumol, 1981).* The aging built environment of manufacturing locations becomes obsolete (Sternlieb and Hughes, 1975). As capital is freed from its past spatial ties, both the technical opportunities and the economic incentives for relocation are provided.

Overemphasis upon the microeconomics of factor cost disadvantage is the central deficiency of this literature. While the shifting locational prerogatives of technological change are certainly important, other non-technical forces, such as unionization, wage rates, local government responsiveness to business, and flows of federal aid, all exert varying degrees of influence over the life.cycle of aging economic centers. These factors cannot be ignored.

Recent research documents the importance of many of these factors. Higher wage rates in the manufacturing cities are seen to effect patterns of plant relocation (Perry and Watkins, 1978). Other studies point to the conclusion that higher rates of unionization and increased patterns of strike activity are what prompt the flight of capital from the intergovernmental city (Gordon, 1978). Social turmoil, such as crime, fire, and rioting, also forces industry to move (Matz, 1979). Local government programs

*Citations in parentheses refer the reader to further sources of information. Full citations are provided under References.

which place serious dollar demands on the municipal fisc, and which result in higher tax burdens or poor service provision for businesses, further work against the declining city (Academy for Contemporary Problems, 1978). The relative non-responsiveness of city hall to business interests, and the political activities involved in granting tax abatements or zoning variances, or in putting together economic stimulus packages are lesser but nonetheless added disadvantages of the intergovernmental city (Mollenkopf, 1981).

Further, both the tremendous increase in conglomerate takeover and the heightened rates of market control witnessed over the past fifteen years, effect the shift in investment out of the intergovernmental city. Here, large corporations often use their acquired plant and equipment in older areas as "cash cows," milking the resources from these aging assets and using this cash to bankroll new investments in different geographic locations (Drucker, 1970; Bluestone and Harrison, 1980).

Recession likewise holds serious consequences for the older city. With the onset of economic contraction, corporations typically idle their oldest plants and equipment assemblages. Over the course of expansion and recovery, these older plants may be left closed, while investment is shifted to the construction of new facilities (Harris, 1983). Finally, imbalance in intrametropolitan and regional flows of federal contracts often work against the older core city (Fainstein and Fainstein, 1978). These policies combine with national tax incentives for investment in new plant and equipment, and help to push private economic activity out of the aging city, hastening the onset of increased intergovernmental dependence.

The Consequences of Disinvestment in the Intergovernmental City

The geographic and social consequences of disinvestment are mirrored in the political economy of the intergovernmental city. Disinvestment is not only the structural macroeconomic process shaping its long-term economic decline, but its overriding characteristic as well. The liquidation of major investment in the intergovernmental city causes plant closures, secondary business bankruptcies, heightened unemployment, and significant property abandonment and tax nonpayment. Capital flight also carries with it the affluent and middle-income workers of the city. The intergovernmental city is left with an increasingly impoverished and welfare-dependent population. Rates of crime, fire, and property damage shoot upward. Spiralling inflation and the increasing wage demands of public employees push the costs of providing necessary municipal services even higher. With its revenue base depleted by the relinquishment of investment, and facing escalating expenditure demands, a severe revenue-expenditure mismatch develops within the regular operational budget of the intergovernmental city. Much-needed social services are cut back and their quality declines. Infrastructure deteriorates. Education, police and fire protection services get worse. Over the past two decades, federal aid has increasingly been called upon to fill the social and economic gaps.

The costs of private disinvestment to date have required public revenue transfers to interimly maintain the viability of the declining, divested city. But once the cumulative forces of capital flight, demographic shift, and fiscal strain are set in motion, there is seemingly little the local polity can do to concretely remedy the consequences of disinvestment. At this point, federal and state resources are viewed as absolutely necessary; the only way for the local government to continue to provide services, yet remain fiscally solvent.

Thus, the relinquishment of private economic activity in the city, plus the onset of governmental policy aimed at mediating the social consequences and political conflicts brought on by disinvestment, work together to condition long-term fiscal strain and sustained transfer dependency. Denied a revenue-generating base, incapable of attracting private investment back to the city, unable to obtain private financing, and forced to support its impoverished residents, the local government of the intergovernmental city goes the route of "government public assistance." Its economic development marred by the wholesale liquidation of capital commitments —its own redevelopment strategies sorely constrained by a lack of resources and the poverty of residents—the local government undergoes a prolonged state of acute budgetary stress and increased intergovernmental dependency.

Industrial Disinvestment

Industrial disinvestment in the intergovernmental city is the single most important factor shaping its overall economic decline. The abandonment of industrial investment involves both overall reductions in new capital expenditure for plant and equipment in the intergovernmental city and the closure of existing plants and transfer of older equipment out of these areas. Industrial disinvestment, quite obviously, reduces employment opportunities, lowers rates of labor force participation, and dilutes the tax base. Perhaps, most significantly, an extremely rapid rate of disinvestment in the manufacturing sector of the local economy seriously alters the industrial structure and the sectoral composition of the labor market.[2]

There are three general trends, national, regional, and intrametropolitan, which make up the overall picture of industrial disinvestment in the intergovernmental city. At the national level, recessions occurring throughout the 1970s and early 1980s caused average annual investment in new plant and equipment to slow significantly over the course of this period (Lake, 1979). Direct foreign investment by multinationals has taken capital, investment, and jobs out of the country (Bluestone and Harrison, 1982). Increased automation in the manufacturing sectors of the macroeconomy has contributed to a further decrease in national manufacturing employment (Bluestone and Harrison, 1982). Moreover, not only are national rates of investment and employment showing signs of significant slowdown, both the industrial structure and the sectoral composition of the labor market are changing at the national level. Generally speaking, low-skill, high-paying, manufacturing jobs are being lost. High-skill, high-credential jobs, which generally preclude residents of the intergovernmental city, and low-skill, low-paying jobs, in the service sector, are their only replacements (Browne, 1983). In sum, shifts witnessed at the national level mean less investment and employment in the manufacturing sectors of the macroeconomy. These hit hardest at the manufacturing-dominated economy of the older intergovernmental city.

At the regional level, the Northeast and North Central areas, locales with the highest concentrations of intergovernmental cities, are losing significant amounts of investment and employment to the South and West. From 1960 to 1976, the capital stock of the South grew at nearly twice the rate of the Northeast (Glickman, 1980).

Over the same 16-year period, the Northeast and North Central regions lost nearly one million manufacturing jobs, while the Sunbelt gained over 1.5 million (Sternlieb and Hughes, 1978). Current research indicates that the great bulk of investment and job loss in the Frostbelt results not so much from the transfer of plants between regions, but rather from rates of birth, death and expansion of plants in places which are locationally static (Birch, 1979; Harris, 1983). Other studies show that what regional transfers do exist impact most seriously upon the older, manufacturing cities of the northern regions (James 1981; Thompson and Thompson, 1983.) Overall, while the growth centers of the Sunbelt have witnessed steady expansion in the manufacturing and service sectors of their economies, the declining cities of the Frostbelt have lost significant amounts of manufacturing investment and employment. And, even though substantial growth is taking place in the service sectors of many of these older cities, the service boom has neither been rapid enough, nor has it generated the kinds of jobs necessary to counter such devastating losses in manufacturing (Harrison and Hill, 1977).

The intergovernmental city is perhaps most severely impacted by the shift in investment and employment to its neighboring suburbs (Sternlieb and Hughes, 1975). While cities across the country have been losing jobs and money to their suburbs, the older manufacturing cities of the Northeast and North Central regions have experienced the most severe suburban losses. And while the aging intergovernmental city has traditionally lost only manufacturing jobs to suburban competition, retaining most service-based industries and jobs, today, even this trend is changing. Banks, insurance companies and corporate headquarters are all leaving the intergovernmental city to relocate either to the suburbs or to freestanding cities in other regions (Mollenkopf, 1981).

Thus, national, regional and intrametropolitan trends in investment and employment have all impacted adversely upon the older, manufacturing-based, economy of the intergovernmental city. Slowdowns in national levels of investment and employment, have hit key sectors of the local economy. Regional trends have pulled additional jobs and capital away. City-to-suburban shifts have left little of the urban core.

Beneath these absolute shifts, however, lie the more important changes in both the industrial structure and labor market composition of the intergovernmental city which rapid patterns of disinvestment have brought about. The traditional employment base of the intergovernmental city — the high-paying but low-skill factory jobs that provided steady work for the great bulk of its immigrants and minority populations — is now almost totally gone (Magaziner and Reich, 1982). And, what few jobs are being created in the intergovernmental city are either very poorly matched to the skill levels of its residents, or provide only very low wages.

The good jobs opening up in the intergovernmental city are for higher-skilled professionals: lawyers, accountants, managers and physicians. These jobs require a substantial amount of formal education and training, and for a variety of socio-economic reasons, go disproportionately to commuters who continue to reside in the suburbs (Harrison and Hill, 1977). For the residents of the intergovernmental city the employment picture is not so rosy: low-skill manufacturing jobs become harder and harder to find and only low-pay, in some cases temporary, service positions are available. Recent research supports the conclusion that the rapid growth occupations in the intergovernmental city for keypunchers, clerks, waitresses and store-

hands provide only about one-half of the income of stable manufacturing employment. These new positions are typically part-time and subject to frequent layoff
(Jacobson, 1983).

Moreover, the loss of manufacturing jobs and the growth of service-oriented
employment mean that male workers are being displaced and that women are, by
and large, moving disproportionately into newly established positions. Formerly
high-paid men find little incentive to retrain for lower-paying service jobs and frequently wind up on a community's welfare rolls (Thurow, 1980). Compounding this
very serious problem, much of the manufacturing employment left in the intergovernmental city provides low wages and irregular patterns of work that are quite
similar to those in the low-skill end of the service sector. Finally, the small-scale,
labor-intensive manufacturing firms of the intergovernmental city being relatively
seasonal in operation and highly sensitive to recession, also frequently force workers
to regularly use unemployment benefits (Harrison, 1979). Thus, the very structure
of the labor market of the intergovernmental city — itself produced by rapid patterns of private disinvestment — exerts a strong impact upon the rates and regularity
of return to public dependency. In the end, a resident population characterized by
rapidly diminishing potentials for advancement, that barely survives from day-to-
day on varying combinations of welfare and irregular wages, is left alone to bear the
brunt of rapid capital flight.

The labor market of the intergovernmental city is thus changing quite dramatically. While it was once a regional center for manufacturing employment, today it is
characterized by a high concentration of poorly paid, irregular jobs necessarily supplemented by unemployment compensation and welfare transfers. In other words,
the good jobs that had traditionally been available in the intergovernmental city are
fading. The intergovernmental city and its residents are getting less and less of a
shrinking investment and employment pie. (These themes are picked up with much
greater detail in Chapter three.)

In short, industrial disinvestment infers less jobs in the city and lower per capita
income levels as well. Along with directly depleting the revenue-generating capabilities of the intergovernmental city, the flight of industry leaves widespread unemployment, poverty, and increasing demand for public services in its wake. The process of industrial disinvestment affects both the revenue and expenditure side of the
city fisc. This is the reality that many local governments perceive when they find
themselves increasingly in a position of intergovernmental dependency.

Financial Disinvestment

The problem of financial disinvestment in the older, manufacturing city, seriously
aggravates the outmigration of industrial capital there. When neither venture capital
nor equity financing can be found, new businesses cannot be started. Established
enterprises are forced to close down. At the same time that large firms are fleeing the
intergovernmental city, private reinvestment by smaller, spin-off or support firms
becomes impossible. Compounding this problem, public redevelopment is also
limited, as the private market for qualitatively downgraded municipal bonds strongly disfavors the government of the intergovernmental city.

As with the liquidation of private industrial commitments, financial disinvestment is a national problem accelerated in its geographical impact by local and regional factors. In an era characterized by high interest rates, both venture capital, which is used to finance new business, and equity financing, necessary to expand established enterprises, are quite difficult to obtain, and extremely expensive when they are available. A recent study shows the seriousness of this national problem. While in 1972, there were 418 private underwritings for companies with a net worth of less than $5 million dollars, in 1977 there were only four (Small Business Administration Survey, cited in Academy for Contemporary Problems, 1978).

In the older declining intergovernmental cities of the Frostbelt, these national trends are much more pronounced. Some private investment firms simply look at citywide rates of bankruptcy and foreclosure, deem the economic geography of the intergovernmental city a bad risk, and refrain from investment. Similarly, new businesses may be refused the venture capital necessary for start-up. Even the most established firms with proven track records, find equity financing difficult to obtain. Moreover, the transfer of ownership of viable enterprises becomes impossible when financing cannot be garnered. When an owner dies, or wants to sell his business, termination will result if there is no capital to underwrite a buyout (Schwartz, 1981). Similarly, community-based organizations are denied the ability to purchase and retain "footloose" plants in the absence of private investment.

Compounding the difficulties facing private reinvestment in the intergovernmental city is the unavailability of capital to finance its public redevelopment. The local government of the intergovernmental city is effectively closed out of the private market for general obligation municipal bonds. Recent studies show, quite conclusively, that while the aging intergovernmental city faces perhaps the greatest need for private financing of all jurisdictions — both to reconstruct its infrastructure and to redevelop its economic base — its local government is either totally excluded from participation in the tax-exempt municipal bond market, or forced to pay exceedingly high rates of interest (J. E. Petersen, 1981). Private investment houses are very reluctant to issue bonds, and investors even more reluctant to purchase them, where severely deteriorating economic and fiscal problems spell potential repayment difficulties. As a result, credit ratings for the economically declining intergovernmental city worsen. Its costs for borrowing skyrocket (G. Peterson, 1981). Indeed, some commentators speak of a two-tiered market for municipal bonds, one characterized by low credit cost, and high degrees of liquidity for growth cities, the other distinguished by the unavailability and high cost of credit for declining cities. (The municipal bond market is dealt with in much greater depth in Chapter seven.)

The loss of economic function and the fiscal strain that accompanies it, thus lead directly to a rescinding of private financial commitment to the intergovernmental city. With large enterprises abandoning the city at a rapid rate, those smaller firms that remain, that might make a difference, are denied sorely needed capital. And, there develops a similar void in sources of private credit for the municipal government. At the same time that private investment stops, public redevelopment of the intergovernmental city is simultaneously unable to take place.

The Demographic Impacts of Capital Flight

The demographic shifts affecting the population mix of the intergovernmental city stem largely from the structural processes of industrial and financial disinvestment. Far-reaching relocations of investment, production facilities, and jobs, carry population with them. Those households that can afford to, follow the capital outflow from the aging manufacturing cities of the North, to growth centers in the suburbs and in the Sunbelt. A process of selective depopulation thus lies at the heart of the demographics of the intergovernmental city (Lake, 1979). The outmigration of an affluent, educated population leaves behind it largely those unable to move. And, the remaining residents—the impoverished, the undereducated, the elderly, and the emotionally and physically handicapped—hit hard at the city's fisc.

A plethora of studies document the movement of population from city to suburb. Here, shifts in private investment decisions plus federal policy directives combine to shape the rapid process of suburbanization. If mass consumption of the automobile provided the mechanism, federally subsidized highway construction afforded the pathway (Tobin, 1976). Federally backed mortgages added the affordable single family house (Aaron, 1971; Stone, 1980). A tradition of local home rule, plus sophisticated manipulation of zoning regulations, provided the final touch: the protected suburb was created — the ultimate escape from a more intense and dense urban life. And, it worked: from 1950 to 1970, the key movement of population centered about the emptying of the northeastern cities into their surrounding suburbs and beyond (Sternlieb and Hughes, 1975).

By the 1970s, the demographics of central city population loss began to take on an added dimension. Over that decade, the southern and western regions of the country started to draw population out of the northern tier (Sternlieb and Hughes, 1975; 1978). With the Sunbelt growing at a rate more than double the national average, the older central cities of the North lost over 7 million persons between 1970 and 1975, a rate four times greater than that of the previous decade. Today the intergovernmental city is losing population in the form of both suburban and regional shifts. Moreover, for the first time in history, greater numbers of black households are leaving the city than are coming in (Salant, 1982).

Patterns of intrametropolitan and regional demographic shift thus combine to bring about the selective depopulation of the intergovernmental city. Both black and white residents, who are able, vacate the city. A population characterized by extreme impoverishment results. Current research indicates that during the first half of the 1970s, such migratory patterns were responsible for the outflow of nearly $10 billion per year in aggregate income from the older central cities (Berry and Gillard, 1977). Rapidly falling income levels mean decreased aggregate demand, declining revenue-generating capabilities and heightened fiscal strain. Moreover, a resident structure comprised mainly of below poverty level, and many female-headed households spells more crime, more fires, and increased social turmoil in general (Sternlieb and Hughes, 1981). A reputation for criminal activity and danger comes to characterize the core city.[3] Alongside the serious economic problem of capital flight, and the fiscally deleterious population shifts which it activates, the myriad socioeconomic costs of poverty become highly concentrated and highly visible in the intergovernmental city, further eroding potentials for its public or private redevelopment. (The social problems facing intergovernmental cities are the subject of Chapter four.)

Residential Disinvestment

The housing market of the intergovernmental city functions within the bounds set down by the flight of private capital from those areas. While residential disinvestment can be understood as one aspect of the overall relinquishment of capital commitment in the intergovernmental city, demographic shifts also undercut the operation of the local housing market (Dodge/Sweets, 1983). The nonavailability of investment capital in the intergovernmental city thus shapes the overall problem of residential disinvestment. The process of selective depopulation reduces real money demand for housing in the intergovernmental city and, in so doing, aggravates the abandonment of the private real estate commitment there. (Housing in the intergovernmental city is considered in Chapter five.)

Both the lethargy of private financial institutions and the reductions in citywide demand thus underlie the actual liquidation of residential investment in the intergovernmental city. These structural processes work together to motivate the stage-like occurrence of residential disinvestment. At the first stage, the citywide loss of industrial and financial commitments establishes an overall economic climate of instability and uncertainty in the intergovernmental city; this is quickly transferred to the local housing market. Second, the process of selective depopulation reduces per capita income and causes real money demand for rental and owned housing to erode. During this stage, citywide rent levels and property values decline significantly, and positive rates of return from property investment become increasingly difficult to attain. Also, during this stage, the stored equity or dollar value of real estate investment starts to slip both because rental income levels are increasingly insufficient to support profitable ownership and because mortgage capital is becoming difficult to obtain (Lake, 1979; Listokin and Casey, 1980).

The next stage of residential disinvestment occurs within this context of prolonged market failure and continued institutional non-participation. During this stage, all of the problems faced in the previous stage deepen. Real estate investors face simultaneously the serious problems of insufficient income, vanishing equity, low liquidity and rising operating costs, each a significant problem in itself. At this point, the decision to consciously "milk" the building may be made (Sternlieb and Burchell, 1972). Maintenance expenditures are reduced, tax payments are not made (Lake, 1979), individual and corporate shells are sought. Eventually when delinquent taxes approach a significant proportion of the dollar value of the property, or when real income is reduced to a trickle, outright abandonment ensues. Finally, abandoned residences are vandalized or invaded by squatters, and either demolished or boarded and sealed by the city government.

Such a cycle of residential disinvestment is brought on both by the overriding failure of the local housing market, and by the cessation of function of once-reliable support institutions. The progression of this cycle accelerates and reinforces its existence: residential abandonment promotes increased housing market failure, heightening the rate of relinquishment of property ownership in the city and spurring yet another round of capital flight. In the end, the local government of the intergovernmental city is left with the abandoned properties of disillusioned investors—by this time moderate-income, minority investors. City hall subsequently becomes the main provider of housing for its residents, and, it does so at high cost and with great difficulty (Lake, 1979).[4] The failure of the local housing market, a cause and a consequence of private disinvestment, leaves local government to fill the gaps.

Social Welfare and Public Service
Provision in the Face of Capital Flight

The flight of private capital from the intergovernmental city takes with it the provision of most necessary goods and services. The demographics of selective depopulation simultaneously leave the intergovernmental city with an increasingly impoverished and high service-consuming population. Although revenue-generating capacities decline rapidly, the need for sound infrastructure, adequate police and fire protection, good housing, and quality education remain. As a result, the responsibility both for replacing withdrawn private goods and services and for providing more efficient and a greater range of public services to severely impoverished residents rests increasingly with the local public sector. If one dimension of private disinvestment lies in the geographic concentration of economic and social costs brought on by capital flight, another dimension centers about local government's possibilities for ameliorating them.

Adequate levels of public service provision are important both to accomplish economic redevelopment and to ensure the well-being of the city's residents. Deteriorated infrastructure and housing not only contribute significantly to the flight of capital from the intergovernmental city, but impede short-run public redevelopment in the process. Services, particularly the provision of police protection and primary/secondary education, also effect the inducement of private reinvestment or the undertaking of government-sponsored revitalization (Matz, 1979; Muller, 1981). Most importantly, the abdication of private service production and the inadequacy of public service provision in the intergovernmental city impact quite adversely upon the health, safety and welfare of its residents.

The quality of education in the intergovernmental city is declining at a rapid rate. Schools that are deteriorated and facilities that are outmoded are not replaced. Teachers function ever increasingly as disciplinarians rather than educators. Moreover, the economically disadvantaged school population of the intergovernmental city requires additional training if barriers to success are to be overcome. Special programs for skill development and linguistic improvement are essential here. Yet, fiscal stress in the intergovernmental city means that educational expenditures are being continuously cut back. As a result, facilities worsen. Student-teacher ratios climb. Marginal students are passed from grade to grade and even then, dropout rates steadily increase. The rate of educational illiteracy presses dangerously upward.[5]

Health-care provision is likewise inadequate in the intergovernmental city (Alford, 1975). Rates of infant mortality are significantly higher there than elsewhere. Adults die younger, and rates of disease contraction are higher. Fiscal retrenchment means that city-run hospitals and clinics are being closed down and that doctors are in insufficient supply and if available, of inferior quality. Often these publicly administered institutions and in-house physicians are the only contact that inner city residents have with the medical profession. Good health and decent medical care are thus totally dependent on what funds and personnel can be attracted to these facilities.

Poverty and the deterioration of infrastructure in the intergovernmental city also mean higher rates of crime and fire there. A number of studies show the positive relationship of poverty to rates of crime and fire (Sternlieb and Burchell, 1973; Muller, 1981). Income poverty motivates some to make a living through illegal activity (Harrison, 1980). Others become entangled within a culture of crime, delinquency and violence, which is alleged to develop in economically declining areas (Banfield, 1974). Additionally, the problem of residential disinvestment in the intergovernmental city influences higher rates of crime and fire. Abandoned buildings are places where criminal activity can occur (Sternlieb and Burchell, 1973). They are also the origin of serious fires, that often destroy the housing stock of entire neighborhoods. Heating by gas burner or open oven when the oil runs out, or even setting indoor fires — common practices in the intergovernmental city — lead to still higher rates of fire, further contribute to reduced levels of overall protection, and compound all of the above trends.

Even in the face of severe fiscal retrenchment and significant population loss, expenditures for local service provision in the intergovernmental city are rising rapidly (Schefter, 1977). Deteriorating infrastructure makes heightened capital expenditure necessary for its improvement. Public redevelopment projects both to attract business back to the city and to put local residents to work, even though publicly funded, do require substantial local commitment. Widespread residential abandonment means that the municipal government must continually rehabilitate and look for subsidies to construct housing for its low-income residents. Severe impoverishment causes local welfare assistance payments to rise. Acute income poverty also implies that costs for traditionally provided public services such as police, fire, and education will increase substantially as requirements for their provision escalate.

Just as importantly, the successful unionization of municipal employees over the past fifteen years has combined with miniscule improvements in the productivity of local service provision to force the costs of public services still higher (Baumol, 1972). Taking into account all of these factors, recent research indicates that annual expenditures for municipal services in older cities have risen by nearly sixty percent over the past decade (Muller, 1981). On a per capita basis, central city costs for common municipal functions are twice suburban rates. Abandoned by private capital, left with a severely deteriorated infrastructure and faced by the dire poverty of its residents, the local government of the intergovernmental city is forced to provide divested private services (i.e. housing), and to increase levels of traditional public services as well. And, as inflation, capital flight, and the dilution of revenue-generating capacity hit hard at the city fisc, it is left increasingly incapable of directing its own affairs.

Fiscal Stress and the Intergovernmental
Impacts of Disinvestment

The most ominous consequence of private disinvestment is the onset of severe fiscal stress in the older, declining intergovernmental city and the emergence of its characteristically high degree of fiscal dependency. The liquidation of investment commitments in the intergovernmental city depletes its revenue-generating base. The socioeconomic costs of disinvestment place greater and greater upward pressure on its expenditures. Such a local revenue-expenditure mismatch very quickly develops into acute budgetary strain, outlining, at least, the contours of fiscal collapse (Stanley, 1980). Shunned by most private investment houses, and facing fiscal insolvency, the local government is forced to obtain resources from the only place left — federal and state revenue transfers.

Economic flight from the city thus combines with local political fragmentation to shape the budgetary problems of the intergovernmental city. Suburban municipalities are jurisdictionally independent from the older city. This means that the intergovernmental city must generate all of its revenues within its own geographical boundaries (Hill, 1978; Walker, 1980). Since the property tax is the main revenue-generating mechanism for local governments, jurisdictional fragmentation makes the fiscal operation of the intergovernmental city dependent solely upon the viability of its private economic base. With investment fleeing the intergovernmental city, little revenue can be generated from the property tax. And, as this levy ceases to function adequately, the intergovernmental city is left to the insurmountable task of meeting rapidly mounting expenditure demands with nonexistent revenues. A period of acute budgetary pressure and potential fiscal collapse sets in. (Expenditure and revenue patterns in the intergovernmental city are the topic of Chapter seven.)

By the late 1960s, public policy was beginning to address the fiscal problems of the older, declining city. State governments moved to formulate property tax relief measures. Cities were, for the first time, allowed to levy their own sales and income taxes. Regional tax base sharing plans were introduced in some areas to deal with political fragmentation (Beaton, 1981). Direct aid was granted by many states to those municipalities with the most serious revenue-generating problems.

Both state and federal programs to aid fiscal stress have increased massively over the past two decades. Between 1968 and 1975, when state aid to cities doubled, federal aid increased more than fourfold (Walker, 1980). During this time, new programs were created (Markusen et al., 1981), many existing programs were expanded (Walker, 1981), and more overall federal dollars were provided. (Federal policy towards the intergovernmental city is the subject of Chapter 6.) Facing budgetary collapse, many city governments simply made the city more open to them: they joined the intergovernmental bandwagon.

In the decade of the 1970s, with private disinvestment and fiscal stress a fact of life in many urban political economies, federal and state assistance was seen as the sole route to fiscal stability. Interestingly enough, current macroeconomic trends and government directives seem to indicate that the golden era of intergovernmentalism has come to a close. A new age of municipal soul-searching, resource conservatism, and fiscal solvency is upon the city. In the absence of the upper-level public assistance, local governments will undergo continued streamlining and cutbacks and as never before, a local private–public partnership must emerge. A more thorough-going self-evaluation by affected municipalities will be undertaken. (The future of older intergovernmental cities is discussed in Chapters eight and nine.)

The next chapter empirically documents the scenarios of change which character-ized the emergence of the intergovernmental city. Subsequent chapters cover with more detail the component dimensions of economic, social, and physical decline.

NOTES

1. The debate over the causes of locational biases in flows of federal funds is as lengthy as it is complex. It is not the central issue at stake in this paper. Suffice to say here, that one school of thought looks at federal funding via policy analysis, finding that eligibility determined by formula leads to slight but insig-nificant locational biases. The other behavioral or political school looks at the determination of these eligibility formulas in the Congress as the important point. For a representation of these points of view see, Thomas Anton, Jerry Cawley, and Kevin Kramer, "Federal Spending in States and Regions: Pat-terns of Stability and Change," and Ann Markusen, A. Saxenian, and Marc Weiss, "Who Benefits from Federal Transfers?," both articles in Robert W. Burchell and David Listokin (eds.), *Cities Under Stress*, New Brunswick, NJ: Center for Urban Policy Research, 1981.

2. For more information on labor market sectors and industrial structure, see Glen C. Cain, "The Challenge of Segmented Labor Market Theories to Orthodox Theory: A Survey," *Journal of Economic Literature*, December 1976 or Richard Edwards, Michael Reich and David Gordon (eds.), *Labor Market Segmentation*, Lexington, MA: Lexington Books, 1975.

3. Matz presents data which show that crime rates influence patterns of industrial relocation. On the social and economic aspects of crime, and its impact upon the flight of capital from older urban areas, see D.B. Matz, *Central City Business — Plans and Problems*, Joint Economic Committee, U.S. Congress, January 1979.

4. For an interesting interpretation of the role of local government in the face of residential disinvest-ment, see Robert W. Lake, *Real Estate Tax Delinquency: Private Disinvestment and Public Response*, New Brunswick, NJ: Center for Urban Policy Research, 1979.

5. On the related topic of recreation in declining cities, see Thomas Muller, "Changing Expenditure and Service Demand Patterns of Stressed Cities," Burchell and Listokin (eds.), *Cities Under Stress, op. cit.*

REFERENCES

Aaron, Henry. *Shelter and Subsidies: Who Benefits From Federal Housing Policy?* Washington, D.C.: The Brookings Institution, 1971.

Academy for Contemporary Problems. *Revitalizing the Northeast.* Monograph prepared for the U.S. Department of Commerce, 1978.

Alford, Robert. *Health Care Politics: Ideological and Interest Group Barriers to Reform.* Chicago, IL: University of Chicago Press, 1975.

Anton, Thomas, Jerry Cawley and Kevin Kramer. "Federal Spending In States and Regions: Patterns of Stability and Change," in Robert W. Burchell and David Listokin, *Cities Under Stress.* New Bruns-wick, NJ: Center for Urban Policy Research, 1981.

Banfield, Edward. *The Unheavenly City Revisited.* Boston: Little, Brown and Company, 1974.

Baumol, William. "Technological Change and the New Urban Equilibrium," in Robert W. Burchell and David Listokin (eds.), *Cities Under Stress.* New Brunswick, NJ: Center for Urban Policy Re-search, 1981.

_____. "The Macroeconomics of Unbalanced Growth." *American Economic Review.*

Berry, Brian and Quentin, Gillard. *The Changing Shape of Metropolitan America.* Cambridge, MA: Ballinger, 1977.

Birch, David. *The Job Generation Process.* Cambridge, MA: MIT Neighborhood Redevelopment Proj-ect, 1979.

Bluestone, Barry and Bennett Harrison. *The Deindustrialization of America*. New York: The Free Press, 1982.

Browne, Lynne. "Can High Tech Save the Great Lake States." *New England Economic Review*. Nov.–Dec. 1983.

Burchell, Robert W. and David Listokin (eds.). *Cities Under Stress*, New Brunswick, NJ: Center for Urban Policy Research, 1981.

Cain, Glen W. "The Challenge of Segmented Labor Market Theories to Orthodox Theory: A Survey." *Journal of Economic Literature*, December 1976.

Clark, Thomas. *Blacks in the Suburbs*. New Brunswick, NJ: Center for Urban Policy Research, 1979.

Dodge/Sweets, *Construction Outlooks 1984*. New York, McGraw-Hill, 1984.

Drucker, Peter. "New Markets and the New Capitalism," in Daniel Bell and Irving Kristol (eds.), *Capitalism Today*. New York: Mentor Books, 1970.

Edwards, Richard, David Gordon and Michael Reich (eds.). *Labor Market Segmentation*. Lexington, MA: Lexington Books, 1975.

Glickman, Norman. "The International Trade, Capital Mobility, and Economic Growth: Some Implications for American Cities and Regions in the 1980s." *Working Paper #32*. *Working Papers in Regional Science and Transportation*, University of Pennsylvania, 1980.

Harris, Candee. "Plant Closings and the Replacement of Manufacturing Jobs — 1978–1982." Washington, D.C. The Brookings Institution, 1983. (unpublished).

Harrison, Bennett. "Welfare Payments and the Reproduction of Low-Wage Workers and Secondary Jobs." *Review of Radical Political Economy*, Fall 1979.

_____ and Edward Hill. "The Changing Structure of Jobs in Older and Younger Cities." Joint Center Working Paper #58. Cambridge, MA: 1979.

Hill, Richard Child. "Fiscal Crisis and Political Struggle in the Decaying U.S. Central City." *Kapitalistate*, Nos. 4–5, Summer 1976.

James, Franklin. "Economic Distress in Central Cities," in *Cities Under Stress, op. cit.*

Kemp, Jack. *An American Renaissance: A Strategy for the 1980s*. New York: Harper & Row Publishers, 1978.

Lake, Robert W. *Real Estate Tax Delinquency: Private Disinvestment and Public Response*. New Brunswick, NJ: Center for Urban Policy Research, 1979.

Levine, Charles. *Managing Fiscal Stress: The Crisis in the Public Sector*. Chatham, NJ: Chatham House Publishers, 1980.

Listokin, David and Stephen Casey. *Mortgage Lending and Race*. New Brunswick, NJ: Center for Urban Policy Research, 1980.

Magaziner, Ira C. and Robert D. Reich. *Minding America's Business: The Decline and Rise of the American Economy*. New York: Harcourt-Brace, 1982.

Markusen, Ann, Annalee Saxenian and Marc Weiss. "Who Benefits from Intergovernmental Transfers?" in *Cities Under Stress, op. cit.*

Matz, D.B. "Central City Business: Plans and Problems." U.S. Congress, Joint Economic Committee, 1979.

Mollenkopf, John. "The Post-War Politics of Urban Development." *Politics and Society*, Vol. 5, No. 3, 1975.

_____. "Paths Toward the Post-Industrial Service City," in *Cities Under Stress, op. cit.*

Perry, David and Alfred Watkins (eds.). "The Rise of the Sunbelt Cities." *Urban Affairs Annual Review*, Vol. 14. Beverly Hills, CA: Sage, 1977.

Petersen, John E. "Big City Borrowing and Credit Quality," in *Cities Under Stress, op. cit.*

Peterson, George E. "Transmitting the Municipal Fiscal Squeeze to a New Generation of Taxpayers: Pension Obligations and Capital Investment Needs," in *Cities Under Stress, op. cit.*

Salant, Walter S. "The American Economy in Transition." *The Journal of Economic Literature*, June 1982.

Schefter, Martin. "New York City's Fiscal Crisis: The Politics of Inflation and Retrenchment." *The Public Interest*, No. 48, Summer 1977.

Schwartz, Gail G. (ed.), *Advanced Industrialization in the Inner Cities*. Lexington Books, Lexington, MA, 1981.

Sternlieb, George. "The City as Sandbox." *The Public Interest*, Fall 1971.

_____ and Robert W. Burchell. *Residential Abandonment: The Tenement Landlord Revisited*. New Brunswick, NJ: Center for Urban Policy Research, 1972.

Sternlieb, George and James Hughes. *Post-Industrial America: Metropolitan Decline and Interregional Job Shifts*. New Brunswick, NJ: Center for Urban Policy Research, 1975.

_____. "New Economic Geography of America," in Sternlieb and Hughes (eds.), *Revitalizing the Northeast*. New Brunswick, NJ: Center for Urban Policy Research, 1978.

_____. "New Dimensions of the Urban Crisis," in *Cities Under Stress, op. cit.*

_____. *Demographic Trends and Economic Reality*. New Brunswick, NJ: Center for Urban Policy Research, 1982.

Stone, Michael. "Housing and the American Economy," in P. Clavel, J. Forester, and W. W. Goldsmith (eds.), *Urban and Regional Planning in an Age of Austerity*. Elmsford, NY: Pergamon Press, 1980.

Thompson, Wilbur R. and P. R. Thompson. "High-Tech Industry and High-Tech Places." *REI Review*, Nov. 1983.

Thurow, Lester. *The Zero-Sum Society: Distribution and the Possibilities for Economic Change*. New York: Basic Books, 1980.

_____. "How to Rescue a Drowning Economy." *The New York Review*, April 11, 1982.

Tobin, Gary. "Suburbanization and the Development of Motor Transportation," in Barry Schwartz (ed.), *The Changing Face of the Suburbs*. Chicago, IL: University of Chicago, 1976.

Walker, David B. "The New System of Intergovernmental Relations: More Fiscal Relief and More Governmental Intrusions." *Governmental Finance*, November 1978.

2
Empirical Isolation
of the Intergovernmental City

HE PREVIOUS CHAPTER sought to describe the conceptual framework for the emergence and growth of the intergovernmental city. Discussed were the macro and micro forces impacting on the economics of the central city, and the public sector's reaction to these forces. A rationale was given for the rise of a class of economically fragile cities that spent heavily to deliver public services and, in so doing, were dependent upon regular financial support from state and federal governments. Dependence in this context is defined as recurring, necessary revenue augmentation for the provision of routine or specialized public services.

The Nature of Intergovernmentalism

This class of cities is herein labeled *intergovernmental*, a term adapted from the Census of Governments.[1] The term is defined as "of or between governments"; the Census of Governments uses it as an adjective to describe those general fund revenues originating primarily from other than own local sources. As used here, an intergovernmental city is a community which must use the resources of other governments to meet its own fiscal obligations. The majority of the costs associated with the provision of local police, fire, public works, and other services are paid for with state or federal money.*

In the previous chapter, a number of reasons were also tendered as to why intergovernmentalism or fiscal dependency could occur. These were: (1) a change in the spatial locus of significant economic activities; (2) the growth of national and international as well as regional consumer markets; (3) disproportionate inter- or intraregional growth; (4) unbalanced, differential effects of cyclical recession; (5) changes in transportation modes and routes, deemphasizing the importance of centrality; (6) technological obsolescence of older cities' capital infrastructure; (7) unequal city wages and levels of unionization, and so on.

---

*A small share of a city's intergovernmental revenues come from other local (city) jurisdictions. This income is primarily for services rendered and represents no more than two percent of cities' intergovernmental revenue nationally. As such, for the remainder of this study intergovernmental revenue will be viewed as those funds flowing to local governments predominantly from *state* and *federal* governments.

17

These situations occasion "city hardship"— a phrase which has grown to mean significant, economic, social, and physical impaction. In most instances "hardship" is viewed as a precondition to fiscal dependency. Those cities that were *unable* to raise their own money looked first to the revenues of other governments. And while the term intergovernmental in the context of fiscal dependency is relatively new, the usual precondition, "hardship," has had a considerable history of analysis.[2]

It is the purpose of this chapter to first define and empirically isolate American cities which are characterized by intergovernmentalism. Second, these cities, once selected, will be compared to additional independent selections for "hardship." It is the intent of this dual selection process to demonstrate that while intergovernmentalism might be a relatively new conceptual way to group cities, these same cities have largely been identified before under one hardship categorization or another.

Subsequent chapters use the distinction between "intergovernmental" and "non-intergovernmental" cities to view socioeconomic impaction in detail as well as to trace the rise of intergovernmentalism. The latter group of cities are locations which spend both relatively low amounts of money and mostly their own, to finance local public services.

Municipal Revenues and Intergovernmental Transfers

The general revenues of a local government are its aggregate sources of income. They include: taxes, charges, miscellaneous revenues, and intergovernmental transfers.* General revenues represent the municipal purse from which disbursements are made to pay the cost of the financial obligations of a city: salaries, supplies/equipment, contracted services, etc. Taxes, charges and miscellaneous revenues are termed "own-source" revenues which means they are raised *locally* by the municipal/school jurisdiction. Rates are set, charges are levied, and special assessments made, according to local priorities and need.[3]

Intergovernmental transfers are revenues received from other governments, either in the form of grants-in-aid or as reimbursements for performance of general government activity and/or special services. Intergovernmental revenue typically comes from three sources: the federal government, the host state government or other local governments. In the first two instances, intergovernmental revenues from federal and state governments, revenues are primarily of the grant-disbursement type. In the latter, revenues flow usually as a payment performed for services. Only the former are considered here. Intergovernmental revenue from the federal government includes only that which is received directly. Federal aid channeled through state governments is excluded. Intergovernmental revenue from the state government includes revenue received from the state government, including amounts originally from the federal government but channeled through the state.

Depending upon the nature of the transfer, intergovernmental revenues may be used to support general expenditures or be targeted to specific activities. In the former case, "block" grants may be used for numerous purposes under very broad guidelines affecting use. In the latter, "categorical" grants are usually earmarked

*They do not include income from utilities, liquor stores or trusts.

for special purposes and must be expended according to specific program directives.[4]

In the course of annual city budget preparation, intergovernmental transfers and revenues from user charges and fees/permits are projected into the future and compared to anticipated expenditures. The unmet gap between the sum of these sources and total expenditures is made up through the application of taxing levies of one type or another to a taxing base (income, sales, property), at a rate necessary to raise the required revenues. In a developed community, fees/permits and user charges are relatively stable from year to year. In order to maintain low property, sales and/or income tax rates, intergovernmental transfers have been eagerly sought by the electorate and city managers/finance officers as well, to meet rising expenditures within the confines of shrinking tax bases.

Accounting for Intergovernmental Transfers

Documenting the flow of intergovernmental revenues is particularly difficult. This is even more acute in national comparisons where local accounting procedures often differ from state to state. Local quasi-public agencies, such as the economic development authority, that are strong and well-funded in one city, may receive funds directly which may not enter the general fund of that city. On the other hand, where the agency is small or weak, the money may go directly to the city's general fund for subsequent disbursement to the economic development authority.

Further, grants of a capital nature often do not appear as general revenue operating funds. Yet increasingly, the definition of capital funding has been operationalized to include significant expenditures for routine maintenance. Regardless of *disbursement* acceptability, funds *received* for this purpose may or may not be considered part of the local general fund.

Finally, several government subsidies require the establishment of a separate trust fund so that federal and local funds are not comingled. It is unclear at this writing whether this is consistently counted as part of a locality's general fund.

Notwithstanding these difficulties, the following sections attempt to empirically specify the high proportion of intergovernmental transfers within a certain class of cities. In this exercise, intergovernmental transfers will not be divided by source. It is assumed that while a share of federal revenues will probably be undercounted because it is passed through the state government, state transfers (including this share) will be overcounted by the same margin. By combining the two sources of aid, this persistent measuring difficulty will not be allowed to alter the general specification of a community's "other-than-local" revenue dependency.

Meeting the Definition of Intergovernmentalism

The specific intergovernmental and non-intergovernmental cities examined by this study for detailed analysis were selected on the basis of their: (1) population size, (2) direction of population change, and (3) dependence on other than local intergovernmental revenue transfers.

Why Large Cities?

In order to study the phenomenon of intergovernmentalism in American cities, the largest cities of the United States were chosen as the laboratory for investigation. This was done for several reasons. First, they represent the backbone of the United States economy. The vast bulk of jobs and residences are located there: 40 percent of the U.S. employment base and 30 percent of the housing units of the United States are found in the approximately sixty cities nationally that are in excess of 250,000 in population. Second, large cities have had historic significance as a base for the emergence of basic sectors of the United States's economy: first manufacturing, then growing proportions of retail/wholesale and finance/insurance/real estate, then service, high technology, and so on.

Third, they have been the originators of, and currently exhibit, some of the most advanced public service systems in the United States. Public services originated in early city governments when owners of business properties in Philadelphia and Boston were tithed a share of their income to pay for street leveling and raking. In Detroit, early city governments had to raise revenues to inspect mattresses for reasons of public health. Much more recently, Boston, New York, and Los Angeles have been laboratories for highly advanced police dispatch, traffic light systems, sanitation equipment experiments, bridge and tunnel design, recreation and cultural user studies, etc.

Finally, large cities provide a depth and array of public services that are: (1) relatively comparable by functional area, and (2) able to be analyzed through standard Census of Governments categories.

Why Specific Cities?

The selection of cities was an iterative process. In order to have a pool of approximately fifty large cities remaining after subsequent elimination for special cases, cities over 220,000 in population (1980) were selected for study. This initial sift isolated sixty-four cities throughout the United States (Exhibit 2.1).

When expenditure and revenue profiles of large cities were viewed, it became quite apparent that because of their international, national, and state roles, the very largest and special case cities expended significantly larger amounts of money on public services. In order not to have these cities dominate any group measure of central tendency and thus dominate the revenues spent for essentially local services by slightly smaller cities, the very largest cities were eliminated. A 1980 population size of 1,000,000 was selected as an upper threshold above which larger cities would be eliminated. This was the point of a significant jump in per capita expenditures between large and very large cities. Cities over or close to 1,000,000 which were excluded consisted of: New York, Chicago, Los Angeles, Philadelphia, Houston, Detroit and Dallas. Washington, D.C. and Honolulu were also removed because of significant ties to the federal and state governments respectively. In these two cities the linkage to other levels of government also occasioned significant local expenditures for essentially non-local purposes.

This sifting narrowed the cities remaining to approximately fifty-five. At this point cities were grouped by direction of population change over the past decade. Population change encompassed households rather than raw population counts as the important variable. This was done to separate communities that had lost households and resultantly support for public services from those where support was sustained by an equivalent number of housing units being occupied by smaller, possibly unbundled, households. The household count variable was the basis for categorizing the fifty-five cities as either declining, stable, or growing (see Exhibit 2.2).

Three declensions of household growth were chosen. Those cities where there was a loss of households were categorized as "declining"; those where household growth was between 0 and 10 percent were categorized as "stable"; and those where household growth exceeded 10 percent were considered "growth" communities. Percentage change ranges, while chosen arbitrarily, reflect a definite intuitive logic. The ranges define respectively: household loss, some positive household gain, and significant positive household gain.

As mentioned previously, household loss indicates that in addition to a shrinkage of household size that has probably caused total population to decline locally, there has also been an absolute decrease in households. Households are leaving this type of city, and housing demand is potentially down here. This is a far different situation than in many other political subdivisions where there may have been absolute population loss due to household size shrinkage, yet there was positive household growth due to new households being formed to fill available housing.

This latter situation is approximated by the second grouping of cities, wherein almost all cities experienced absolute population decline simultaneous with some slight increase in the number of households. These are essentially stable locations wherein the local population adjustment occasions relatively constant housing demand even though the socioeconomic characteristics and household size of the occupants of local housing may change over time.

The final category contains cities whose households have increased by more than 10 percent in number. These are locations of significant population increase—in excess of household growth—and thus sites of significant net new demand for housing.

Residential growth usually takes place in the presence of nonresidential growth, and in this last category of cities, significant ratables are added to the local tax base. Revenue-raising capacity is linked to tax base, thus three distinctly different revenue-raising capacity scenarios are represented by the three declensions of household change — i.e., cities which, if expenditures remain constant, must respectively: (1) find other revenues, (2) keep the existing revenue picture intact, or (3) reduce revenues. Thus, the presence of intergovernmentalism (i.e., the augmentation of local revenues with revenues from other levels of government) is potentially greater in the first grouping than it is in the second or third. This will be tested in the next section.

Intergovernmentalism and Household Decline

When cities are classified by 1970 to 1980 household change groupings, the distribution of cities among groups is quite symmetrical. Of the fifty-five cities, twenty-two were found to be declining, ten stable, and twenty-three to be growing. Except

EXHIBIT 2.1. — *Large Cities in the United States by 1980 Census Population Rank*[1]

Rank 1980	City and State	1980 Census	1970 Census	Percent Change, 1970-80	Rank 1970
1	New York, NY	7,071,030	7,895,563	-10.4	1
2	Chicago, IL	3,005,072	3,369,357	-10.8	2
3	Los Angeles, CA	2,966,763	2,811,801	5.5	3
4	Philadelphia, PA	1,688,210	1,949,996	-13.4	4
5	Houston, TX	1,594,086	1,233,535	29.2	6
6	Detroit, MI	1,203,339	1,514,063	-20.5	5
7	Dallas, TX	904,078	844,401	7.1	8
8	San Diego, CA	875,504	697,471	25.5	14
9	Phoenix, AZ	789,704	584,303	35.2	20
10	Baltimore, MD	786,775	905,787	-13.1	7
11	San Antonio, TX	785,410	654,153	20.1	15
12	Indianapolis, IN	700,807	736,856	-4.9	11
13	San Francisco, CA	678,974	715,674	-5.1	13
14	Memphis, TN	646,356	623,988	3.6	17
15	Washington, D.C.	637,651	756,668	-15.7	9
16	San Jose, CA	636,550	459,913	38.4	29
17	Milwaukee, WI	636,212	717,372	-13.3	12
18	Cleveland, OH	573,822	750,879	-23.6	10
19	Columbus, OH	564,871	540,025	4.6	21
20	Boston, MA	562,994	641,071	-12.2	16
21	New Orleans, LA	557,482	593,471	-6.1	19
22	Jacksonville, FL	540,898	504,265	7.3	26
23	Seattle, WA	493,846	530,831	-7.0	22
24	Denver, CO	491,396	514,678	-4.5	24
25	Nashville-Davidson, TN	455,651	426,029	7.0	32
26	St. Louis, MO	453,085	622,236	-27.2	18
27	Kansas City, MO	448,159	507,330	-11.7	25
28	El Paso, TX	425,259	322,261	32.0	45
29	Atlanta, GA	425,022	495,039	-14.1	27
30	Pittsburgh, PA	423,938	520,089	-18.5	23
31	Oklahoma City, OK	403,213	368,164	9.5	37

Source: See bottom of next page.

EXHIBIT 2.1. (Continued)

32	Cincinnati, OH	385,457	453,514	-15.0	30
33	Fort Worth, TX	385,141	393,455	-2.1	33
34	Minneapolis, MN	370,951	434,400	-14.6	31
35	Portland, OR	366,383	379,967	-3.6	36
36	Honolulu, HA	365,048	324,871	12.4	44
37	Long Beach, CA	361,334	358,879	0.7	40
38	Tulsa, OK	360,919	330,350	9.3	43
39	Buffalo, NY	357,870	462,768	-22.7	28
40	Toledo, OH	354,635	383,062	-7.4	34
41	Miami, FL	346,931	334,859	3.6	42
42	Austin, TX	345,496	253,539	36.3	56
43	Oakland, CA	339,288	361,561	-6.2	39
44	Albuquerque, NM	331,767	244,501	35.7	58
45	Tucson, AZ	330,537	262,933	25.7	53
46	Newark, NJ	329,248	381,930	-13.8	35
47	Charlotte, NC	314,447	241,420	30.2	60
48	Omaha, NE	311,681	346,929	-10.2	41
49	Louisville, KY	298,451	361,706	-17.5	38
50	Birmingham, AL	284,413	300,910	-5.5	48
51	Wichita, KS	279,272	276,554	1.0	51
52	Sacramento, CA	275,741	257,105	7.2	55
53	Tampa, FL	271,523	277,714	-2.2	50
54	St. Paul, MN	270,230	309,866	-12.8	46
55	Norfolk, VA	266,979	307,951	-11.3	47
56	Virginia Beach, VA	262,199	172,106	52.3	77
57	Rochester, NY	241,741	295,011	-18.1	49
58	Akron, OH	237,177	275,425	-13.9	52
59	St. Petersburg, FL	236,893	216,159	9.6	61
60	Corpus Christi, TX	231,999	204,525	13.4	62
61	Jersey City, NJ	223,532	260,350	-14.1	54
62	Anaheim, CA	221,847	166,408	33.3	81
63	Baton Rouge, LA	220,486	165,921	32.3	82
64	Richmond, VA	220,214	249,332	-12.1	57

[1]Final counts as published in 1980 Census Advance Reports by State, Series PHC80-V. Includes revisions of 1970 Census counts.

Source: U.S. Census of Population and Housing, 1980.

EXHIBIT 2.2. — *Population Change Groupings of Cities*
220,000 to 1,000,000 in Population (n = 55)
(1970–1980)

GROUP I[1] Declining (Any Loss of Households) (n = 22)		GROUP II[1] Stable (0-10 Percent Growth in Households) (n = 10)		GROUP III[1] Growing (More than 10 Percent Growth in Households) (n = 23)	
Kansas City*	(- 8.8)	Birmingham	(+7.0)	Tulsa	(+18.8)
St. Louis	(-25.2)	Denver	(+9.3)	Virginia Beach	(+80.8)
Atlanta	(- 4.1)	Fort Worth	(+3.5)	Austin	(+56.6)
Jersey City	(-12.0)	Portland	(+4.6)	Anaheim	(+52.8)
Richmond	(- 1.1)	Long Beach	(+1.3)	Sacramento	(+15.0)
Pittsburgh	(-12.6)	Tampa	(+6.0)	San Jose	(+55.9)
Boston	(- 6.0)	Toledo	(+2.3)	Oklahoma City	(+15.9)
Louisville*	(-10.0)	Omaha	(+0.0)	Nashville-Davidson	(+15.6)
Cleveland*	(-17.4)	New Orleans	(+7.8)	Wichita	(+10.4)
Cincinnati*	(- 8.7)	Indianapolis	(+3.1)	Baton Rouge	(+41.1)
Akron*	(- 5.2)			Corpus Christi	(+20.3)
Minneapolis*	(- 3.0)			Columbus	(+19.2)
St. Paul*	(- 1.8)			San Antonio	(+27.6)
Milwaukee*	(- 1.6)			Tucson	(+21.0)
Newark*	(-12.6)			Miami	(+11.7)
Baltimore*	(- 7.8)			Jacksonville	(+21.0)
Rochester*	(-10.4)			San Diego	(+33.8)
Buffalo*	(-15.1)			St. Petersburg	(+15.7)
Oakland*	(- 3.4)			Albuquerque	(+57.0)
San Francisco*	(- 3.5)			Memphis	(+16.2)
Norfolk	(- 3.3)			El Paso	(+37.6)
Seattle	(- 1.4)			Phoenix	(+48.4)
				Charlotte	(+45.1)

General Revenues Per Capita

$1,048	$892	$708

*Group I significantly different from II and III at
0.05 Level (Duncan Multiple Range Test).*

Intergovernmental Revenue Per Capita

$552	$394	$324

*Group I significantly different from II and III at
0.05 level (Duncan Multiple Range Test).*

Notes: *Meets initial sorting criteria for "Intergovernmental" status
a) >$1,000 in general revenues per capita
b) >50 percent provided through intergovernmental transfers

[1]a) *Declining Cities* - those that had any loss of households
from 1970 to 1980
b) *Stable cities* - those that had from 0 to 10 percent
household gain from 1970 to 1980
c) *Growing cities* - those that had more than 10 percent
household gain from 1970 to 1980

Source: U.S. Census of Population and Housing 1970, 1980; U.S. Census of
Governments.

in the case of a few cities, there were also clear gaps between groupings. All cities at the low end of the decline grouping fell in excess of 1 percent decline whereas the low end of the stable group evidenced most cities above 3 percent growth — a 4 percent gap between decline and stable categories. Similarly, while the upper end of the stable grouping was 9 percent growth, except for one city, the lower end of the growth grouping was 15 percent*—a 6 percent spread between these two city groupings.

Once categorized by direction of household population change, intergovernmentalism, measured by both significant revenue-raising requirements and a large share of revenues from federal and state governments, was viewed within the three city groupings. As a first sort, intergovernmentalism within cities was defined as per capita general revenues (municipal and school) in excess of $1,000 with approximately one-half of this sum paid for via intergovernmental transfers.** Within the twenty-two declining cities, fourteen or 64 percent could be categorized as intergovernmental; within the ten stable cities, and within the twenty-three growing cities, not a single city met the definition of intergovernmentalism posed above (Exhibit 2.2).

Overall, for declining cities, general revenues per capita (school and municipal) averaged approximately $1,050, of which $550 or about 52 percent was contributed to by intergovernmental transfers. Stable cities raised $892 in general revenues per capita of which less than $400 or 44 percent was supported by intergovernmental transfers. Finally, growing cities raised only $708 in general revenues of which $324 or 44 percent was contributed to by intergovernmental transfers. Both the level of general revenues and the share supported by intergovernmental transfers between declining cities and either stable or growing cities were found to be significantly different at the .05 level (Duncan Multiple Range Test).

Thus, stable and growing cities display significantly smaller levels of both revenue raising and intergovernmental support than is the case for declining cities. Total revenues, reflecting obligated expenditures, and intergovernmental transfers are largest in declining cities and lowest in cities which are experiencing growth. Declining cities largely reflect the presence of intergovernmental revenue transfer; growing and stable cities are more often characterized by its lesser importance.

Intergovernmental and Non-Intergovernmental Cities

From the two extreme population change categories, growing and declining, ten cities representing respectively, those most and least intergovernmentally dependent, were chosen. These cities are listed in Exhibit 2.3. Intergovernmental cities are those which, for the most part, raise more than $1,150 per capita in general revenues, 55 percent of which is contributed to by intergovernmental transfers. These cities are:

*Again, except for one or two cities.
**A section of Appendix I Methodology deals with tabulation of both educational and municipal revenues for local governments. It details the separation of dependent and independent school districts as well as the aggregation of multiple school districts in the same municipality.

EXHIBIT 2.3.—*General Revenue*[1] *and Intergovernmental Transfer Levels in Intergovernmental and Non-Intergovernmental Cities—1980*

Intergovernmental Cities (I)[2]	Mean Intergovernmental City Fiscal Indices	Non-Intergovernmental Cities (II)[2]	Mean Non-Intergovernmental City Fiscal Indices
AKRON		ANAHEIM	
BALTIMORE	Per Capita General Revenues[1]	AUSTIN	Per Capita General Revenues
BUFFALO	$1160	BATON ROUGE	$843
CINCINNATI		COLUMBUS	
CLEVELAND	Per Capita Intergovernmental Transfers	NASHVILLE-DAVIDSON	Per Capita Intergovernmental Transfers
LOUISVILLE	$630	OKLAHOMA CITY	$340
MILWAUKEE		SAN JOSE	
MINNEAPOLIS		TULSA	
NEWARK	Percent Intergovernmental Transfers	VIRGINIA BEACH	Percent Intergovernmental Transfers
ROCHESTER	55%	WICHITA	39%

[1]Includes Municipal and School.
[2]Group I significantly different from Group II at .01 level (Duncan Multiple Range Test).
Source: U.S. Census of Governments, *City Government Finances 1979–1980; School District Finances, 1979–1980.*

Akron	Louisville
Baltimore	Milwaukee
Buffalo	Minneapolis
Cincinnati	Newark
Cleveland	Rochester

Non-intergovernmental cities raise only 75 percent of the revenues needed by intergovernmental cities to support public services ($843), of which only 40 percent is supported by intergovernmental transfers. These cities are:

Anaheim	Oklahoma City
Austin	San Jose
Baton Rouge	Tulsa
Columbus	Virginia Beach
Nashville-Davidson	Wichita

The absolute dollar level of intergovernmental transfers is close to twice the level ($630 versus $340) in intergovernmental versus non-intergovernmental cities.

How Large Are the Differences?

Because school district and municipal revenues are almost equivalent in magnitude, they were included in the tally of both total revenues and intergovernmental assistance per capita in all prior comparisons of groupings of cities. Yet, a significant share of school district intergovernmental assistance is targeted to the physically and mentally handicapped, and the incidence rate of those of school age with these handicaps is not noticeably different in intergovernmental versus non-intergovernmental cities. This leads to closer parity of this form of aid in these two types of locations. Thus, school district near-equivalency in intergovernmental assistance tends to dampen the differences in overall magnitude and proportions of intergovernmental assistance between the two groups of cities.

In Chapter 7, both municipal expenditures and municipal intergovernmental assistance are teased out separately. When this is done, much greater differences appear in both the magnitude and the percentage share of revenue transfers in intergovernmental versus non-intergovernmental cities. Here, municipal revenues raised in intergovernmental cities are almost one and one-half times the level of municipal expenditures in non-intergovernmental cities ($695 versus $482), and the level of intergovernmental transfers is two and one-half times as high ($351 versus $136). The proportion of intergovernmental transfers as a percent of all municipal revenues in intergovernmental cities is over 50 percent; in non-intergovernmental cities, it is under 30 percent. The difference in the proportion of non-local to general revenues is almost two to one.

In a prior section, statistically significant differences were found in the revenue levels and intergovernmental transfer percentages in three groups of cities: declining, stable and growing. Subsequently, cities from the growing and declining group were selected and viewed separately; greater differences in revenue levels and sources of revenue were found between these two sets of communities. Yet, in overall magnitude and percentage terms, these differences may still not appear convincing. The aforementioned analysis shows that even greater differences appear if municipal intergovernmentalism is viewed separately. Additionally, it must be reemphasized that of the twenty-two declining cities, fourteen—or two-thirds—experienced high revenue-raising requirements whose majority share came from non-local sources. Of the thirty-three stable or growing communities, not one met the combined test of high revenue-raising requirements and funding from intergovernmental sources.

Cities characterized by high revenue-raising requirements and significant dependence on state and federal aid are cities of declining household growth. Those which require less revenues and raise most of what they require locally are those with relatively stable or growing numbers of households.

What Are Intergovernmental Cities and What Is Their Importance?

Intergovernmental cities are both high-expenditure cities as well as those whose expenditures are heavily supported by external aid flows. The isolation of cities and the assignment of the term "intergovernmental" is obviously one of degree. All cities, in some measure, are intergovernmental — i.e., they spend more for the provision of public services, a portion of which has not come from the resources of their own jurisdictions. Further, there may be some measure of local impaction that has occasioned one resource transfer or another to flow to them from upper-level governments. Notwithstanding the continuum of intergovernmental revenue determinacy, there remains a class of cities that depends more heavily than others on recurring revenue from the state or federal governments. These cities are, for the most part, aging industrial cities whose household populations are declining. As will be shown in subsequent chapters, they are locations of serious economic and social downturn whose problems have been buoyed up in the past by significant amounts of state and federal monetary assistance.

Initial dependence caused subsequent dependence. Sustained dependence structured the nature of spending, i.e., in accordance with substantive areas of federal and state funding. It also determined the types of personnel to be hired — part- versus full-time, summer versus work-year, etc. — again, according to the funding structure of the grantor.

Intergovernmental cities approached each year's budgetary cycle in terms of viewing local revenues as deficits to be made up after "regular" intergovernmental revenues were accounted for. Local economic development strategies called for "active grantsmanship," i.e., the securing of extralocal funding, as a key activity of successful urban revitalization. These cities often disputed U.S. Census population counts because population size would affect the amount of funds that would be distributed locally.

The intergovernmental city, had the philosophy continued, would have been a public city where multi-governmental transfer payments signaled both local public service priorities as well as the agenda for their delivery.

As was indicated in the introduction to this chapter, the grouping and categorization of cities by the rubric intergovernmental/non-intergovernmental is being introduced here. The importance of this grouping mechanism, however, is not the careful, statistical slotting of one city or another. There are some additional cities which could be included in the grouping; there also may be several cities for which the categorization is too restrictive. Rather, it is the isolation of a set of cities that is more dependent upon the revenue transfers of other governments from another set which is less dependent. This is true largely because the former group's populations are characterized by socioeconomic distress and deteriorated housing, and their parent cities are unable to raise the revenues necessary to support the range and quality of services that had once been available in the past.

Thus, the inclusion of one city or the lack of inclusion of another is far less important for the analysis which follows, than the identification of two groups of cities, recognizably distinct from one another both in terms of their distress and the fiscal reactions to this distress. It is the thesis of this study that cities under stress have been able to draw upon intergovernmental assistance for close to two decades. Further, as computer politics was added to normal political lobbying, and the distress in these locations was verified by the computer, these cities increasingly became the beneficiaries of "free" intergovernmental revenue. Unable to raise their own revenue and with dependent populations to serve, they became dependent on a vast array of other-than-local revenue streams.

The following section describes the computer isolation of these cities via hardship criteria and the closeness of fit between the cities segregated as previously needing funds and those which are now listed as fiscally dependent or intergovernmental.

Urban Distress Measures

Interest in measuring the level of city distress or hardship heightened during the late 1960s and 1970s.[5] In part, this effort was fueled by the idea that public support as a replacement for private disinvestment was at least the short-run answer to the problems of urban areas and the major question was only how to best pair money and need. These considerations led a group of researchers to develop what they believed to be "empirically based" city hardship rankings. A selected group of the more prominent measures are listed in Exhibit 2.4 and are described below.

The Brookings Institution's two indices — Intrametropolitan Hardship and Intercity Hardship — were the first distress measures and are still cited as evaluations of municipal distress.[6] The goal of both indices was to provide a *relative* rating of "city hardship." The Intrametropolitan index compared cities to surrounding suburbs; the Intercity index compared one city to other cities. Operationally, both indices started by assembling data on various local characteristics, i.e., educational attainment, income, poverty incidence, and housing condition. Ratios were then derived for each of the local variables. The ratios were city-to-city in the case of the Intercity index, city-to-suburb for the Intrametropolitan measure. These ratios were further expressed in standard value form and the average value of these standardized scores used to rank distress (Exhibit 2.5).

The Brookings ranking was followed by several later efforts, most encompassing a broader array of variables and utilizing more sophisticated statistical approaches (see Exhibit 2.4). To illustrate, the Congressional Budget Office (CBO) Urban Need Index encompassed social, economic, and fiscal need.[7] Each of these three dimensions was scrutinized by examining appropriate local variables, i.e., social and economic need could be determined by considering changes in income, population char-

EXHIBIT 2.4.—*Characteristics of Selected City Hardship Measures*

Index	Source/Author	Year	Distress Measure	Data Considered (Examples)
Intrametropolitan Hardship	Brookings Institution	1976	City-to-suburb relative hardship	Unemployment, social dependency, education, income level, crowded housing, poverty
Intercity Hardship	Brookings Institution	1976	See Intrametropolitan Hardship	Brookings' measures, density, aged housing, and changes in employment and per capita income
Urban Need	Congressional Budget Office	1978	Social, economic, and fiscal need	Population change, aged households, minority share, economic variables, e.g. employment, retail sales
Community Need	U.S. Department of Housing and Urban Development	1979	Stress related to three dimensions: "age and decline," "density," and "poverty,"	Age of housing, unemployment, poverty, growth lag
UDAG Rank Weighted	U.S. Department of Housing and Urban Development	1979	Stress as indicated by UDAG qualification criteria	Broad array of "public service requirements" (e.g., health, transportation, safety as indicated by death rate, poverty, other data) and fiscal indicators
Evaluation	Institute for the Future	1975	Socioeconomic need/municipal fisc status	
Fiscal Strain	U.S. Department of the Treasury	1978	Municipal fisc posture	Income, own-source revenue, local tax rate
Economic Performance	Urban Institute	1980	Economic stress	Unemployment, population, per capita income

Source: See text.

EXHIBIT 2.5. — *Brookings Institution Intercity Hardship Index (53 Cities)*

City	Hardship Index	Hardship Rank	City	Hardship Index	Hardship Rank
Newark	85.5	1	Boston	45.8	28
St. Louis	75.5	2	New York	45.3	29
New Orleans	72.6	3	Akron	43.4	30
Gary	70.0	4	Norfolk	43.4	31
Miami	62.5	5	Ft. Worth	42.8	32
Birmingham	61.8	6	Milwaukee	42.2	33
Youngstown	60.3	7	San Jose	41.9	34
Baltimore	60.0	8	Toledo	41.4	35
Cleveland	59.6	9	Syracuse	40.8	36
Detroit	58.6	10	Indianapolis	40.3	37
Buffalo	57.2	11	Phoenix	40.1	38
Jersey City	56.6	12	Kansas City, Mo.	38.9	39
Hartford	56.2	13	Houston	38.2	40
Louisville	55.9	14	Los Angeles	37.9	41
Cincinnati	53.5	15	Portland, Ore.	37.7	42
Providence	52.7	16	Omaha	35.3	43
Springfield, Mass.	52.0	17	Columbus	34.9	44
Tampa	50.9	18	San Diego	33.2	45
Sacramento	50.4	19	Dallas	32.6	46
Grand Rapids	50.3	20	Denver	30.0	47
Atlanta	50.1	21	Allentown	29.1	48
Philadelphia	50.0	22	Memphis	28.9	49
Chicago	49.3	23	San Francisco	28.8	50
Pittsburgh	47.1	24	Seattle	28.5	51
Dayton	46.9	25	Greensboro	28.2	52
Rochester	46.3	26	Ft. Lauderdale	24.0	53
Richmond	46.2	27			

Source: Richard P. Nathan and Charles Adams, "Understanding Central City Hardship," *Political Science Quarterly*, Vol. 91, No. 1 (Spring 1976).

acteristics and employment; fiscal need, by examining the property tax base and tax effort. A composite score for each of the three need dimensions (social, economic, and fiscal) was derived by converting all of the local indicator variables into standard scores and an overall average measure secured. A city's composite score was then used to rank its relative distress — the most severely impacted attained the highest scores and were therefore accorded the most severe hardship designations (Exhibit 2.6). In short, CBO utilized a quantitative technique almost identical to Brookings but applied it to a wider range of data.

At the end of the 1970s, several of the distress measures turned to more sophisticated statistical aggregation routines. The Community Need Index developed by HUD in 1979 is illustrative.[8] The measure first gathered over twenty local socioeconomic variables, incorporating elements of demography, poverty, economic activity and social trauma (i.e., population change, unemployment, and crime rates). This data assemblage was then reduced into a smaller group of three dimensions by the use of factor analysis. The three factors comprised city "age and decline," "density," and "poverty." Standardized scores for each of these factor groups were then derived and statistically aggregated to yield a single index of community need. The aggregate need scores and hardship rankings for fifty-eight cities with populations over 250,000 are shown in Exhibit 2.7.

There were several other distress measures also developed at the conclusion of the 1970s:[9]

1. HUD-UDAG Index — In addition to the Need Index described above, in 1979 HUD developed a ranking system based on the Urban Development Action Grant (UDAG). The UDAG-derived ordering consisted of a twofold measure. First categories were ordered according to the number of six UDAG qualifying criteria they satisfied: (1) age of housing, (2) per capita income growth lag, (3) population growth lag, (4) unemployment, (5) employment, and (6) poverty. A community could thus score from zero to six. Second, cities were further ranked by a specially devised impaction ranking system encompassing standardized scores of city poverty, population, and other decline indicators. The distress ranking of thirty cities according to the UDAG-based measure is shown in Exhibit 2.8.

2. Treasury-Fiscal Strain Index[10] — This index measured stress on the municipal fisc as indicated by changes in long-term debt, property tax base, and own-source (as opposed to intergovernmental) taxes and other charges. The statistical construction of the Fiscal Strain Index was analogous to CBO's Urban Need Index. The distress ranking of thirty cities according to the fiscal strain measure is shown in Exhibit 2.8.

3. Urban Institute-Economic Performance Index[11] — As its title implies, this index focused on local economic "hardship." Economic performance, in turn, was gauged by numerous city characteristics such as employment level and per capita income growth. These indicator data were expressed in standardized terms which were then summed.

In summary, the hardship measures differed in their substantive focus (social, economic, or fiscal), data selection (i.e, specifically which economic, social, housing, or municipal expenditure variables were referred to), and statistical treatment of their data inputs (deriving a simple average versus utilizing a more sophisticated statistical treatment).[12] These variations, however, should not obscure the measures' conceptual kinship — the quantitative ranking of distress. The measures also possessed generic similarities. While, as noted, there were differences in emphasis, data

EXHIBIT 2.6. — *Congressional Budget Office Economic Need Index (45 Cities)**

City	Index Score	Rank	City	Index Score	Rank
Newark	84	1	Los Angeles	57	23
(New York)	(80)	(2)	Kansas City, Mo.	56	24
Jersey City	78	3	(Washington, D.C.)	(54)	(25)
Cleveland	78	4	New Orleans	53	26
Buffalo	77	5	Louisville	51	27
Chicago	76	6	Columbus	51	28
St. Louis	74	7	San Bernadino	49	29
Boston	74	8	Atlanta	45	30
Paterson	72	9	Birmingham	45	31
Pittsburgh	71	10	San Diego	43	32
Rochester	70	11	Sacramento	43	33
Philadelphia	70	12	Miami	42	34
San Francisco	68	13	Denver	41	35
Seattle	66	14	Norfolk	40	36
Detroit	66	15	Indianapolis	37	37
Cincinnati	65	16	Dallas	35	38
Akron	64	17	Oklahoma City	34	39
Milwaukee	64	18	Anaheim	31	40
Baltimore	63	19	El Paso	30	41
Minneapolis	62	20	Tampa	29	42
Albany	59	21	Houston	26	43
Gary	58	22	San Jose	24	44
			Phoenix	16	45

*Actually, forty-three cities were used in this analysis; New York City and Washington, D.C. were excluded.

Source: Congressional Budget Office, City Need and the Responsiveness of Federal Grants Programs (1978).

EXHIBIT 2.7.—*HUD (1979) Need Scores and Need Rankings for Cities with Populations Over 250,000*

City	Need Score	Need or Distress Rank	City	Need Score	Need or Distress Rank
Newark	1.448	1	Kansas City	.042	30
New Orleans	1.166	2	Los Angeles	.017	31
St. Louis	1.022	3	Denver	-.030	32
Cleveland	.782	4	Fort Worth	-.117	33
Birmingham	.777	5	St. Paul	-.134	34
Baltimore	.764	6	Sacramento	-.142	35
Washington	.663	7	Portland	-.160	36
Detroit	.626	8	Columbus	-.165	37
Atlanta	.590	9	Toledo	-.168	38
Boston	.556	10	Baton Rouge	-.178	39
Cincinnati	.543	11	Long Beach	-.202	40
Oakland	.524	12	Seattle	-.221	41
Chicago	.521	13	Oklahoma City	-.242	42
Buffalo	.513	14	Dallas	-.249	43
New York	.507	15	Charlotte	-.260	44
Philadelphia	.495	16	Jacksonville	-.331	45
Louisville	.485	17	Houston	-.356	46
Pittsburgh	.484	18	Wichita	-.363	47
San Antonio	.467	19	Albuquerque	-.365	48
Miami	.459	20	Omaha	-.389	49
Norfolk	.341	21	Austin	-.399	50
El Paso	.322	22	Tucson	-.435	51
Memphis	.316	23	Honolulu	-.476	52
Rochester	.299	24	San Diego	-.510	53
San Francisco	.219	25	Tulsa	-.517	54
Tampa	.155	26	Nashville-Davidson	-.556	55
Milwaukee	.060	27	Phoenix	-.564	56
Minneapolis	.059	28	Indianapolis	-.567	57
Akron	.048	29	San Jose	-.892	58

Source: Harold L. Bunce and Robert L. Goldberg, City Need and Community Development Funding (Washington, D.C.: Government Printing Office, January 1979), U.S. Department of Housing and Urban Development, Office of Policy Development and Research, Division of Evaluation.

EXHIBIT 2.8. — *Distress Criteria Rankings and Intergovernmental City Status*

CITY	CITY STATUS *Intergovernmental or Non-Intergovernmental*	Distress Ranking (1 = most severe distress) (30 = least severe distress) INDIVIDUAL RANKINGS					MEAN RANKING
		UDAG (Rank-Weighted)	*BROOKINGS (Intercity)*	*CBO (Economic)*	*HUD (Need)*	*TREASURY (Fiscal Strain)*	
St. Louis		1	2	5	3	11	4.4
Newark	Intergovernmental	2	1	1	1	2	1.4
Cleveland	Intergovernmental	3	7	3	4	5	4.4
Pittsburgh		4	17	8	16	18	12.6
New Orleans		5	3	22	2	20	10.4
Cincinnati	Intergovernmental	6	11	14	10	16	11.4
Buffalo	Intergovernmental	7	9	4	12	4	7.2
Rochester	Intergovernmental	8	18	10	19	21	15.2
Boston		9	19	6	9	8	10.2
Philadelphia		10	15	9	14	17	13.0
Chicago		11	16	7	11	6	10.2
Detroit		12	8	12	7	7	9.2
Baltimore	Intergovernmental	13	6	17	6	27	13.8
New York		14	20	2	13	1	10.0
Louisville		15	10	23	15	15	15.6
Akron		16	21	15	24	23	19.8
Atlanta		17	14	25	8	14	15.6
San Francisco		18	29	11	20	13	18.2
Birmingham		19	5	26	5	19	14.8
Milwaukee	Intergovernmental	20	23	16	22	26	21.4
Kansas City		21	24	19	25	12	20.2
Columbus		22	26	24	29	24	25.0
Los Angeles		23	25	20	26	3	19.4
Minneapolis	Intergovernmental	24	28	18	23	9	20.4
Seattle		25	30	13	30	10	21.6
Denver		26	27	21	27	29	26.0
Norfolk		27	22	29	18	28	24.8
Tampa		28	12	30	21	25	23.2
Sacramento		29	13	27	28	22	23.8
Miami		30	4	28	17	30	21.8

Source: See Robert W. Burchell and David Listokin, "Measuring Urban Distress" in Burchell and Listokin (editors), Cities Under Stress (New Brunswick, N.J.: Center for Urban Policy Research, Rutgers - The State University, 1981), p. 159.

inputs, and statistical handling, there were strong similarities in the rankings' basic format and construction (see Exhibit 2.4). Some of the measures were even more closely connected: CBO's Social Need Index, for example, was derived from the Brookings Intercity and Intrametropolitan indices.

Most importantly, the measures shared a similarity of results — city distress ranks accorded by the different approaches were found to be in reasonably close agreement. The consistency is shown in Exhibit 2.8 which presents the hardship ranks assigned by five different distress measures to a common set of thirty cities. The five yield a very similar ordering. To illustrate, Newark is ranked the most distressed by three of the measures (Brookings-Intercity, CBO Economic Hardship, and HUD Need) and second most distressed by the remaining two indices (HUD-UDAG and Treasury-Fiscal Strain). While the rank assignments are not as close for some of the other thirty cities, differences in ranking were not found to be statistically significant. Tests conducted by the Rutgers University Center for Urban Policy Research concluded:[13]

> Findings show that the urban distress measures have a high level of consistency in ranking the hardship of a common set of cities. Despite some differences in their variable selection/expression and statistical treatment, the distress measures are similar in their practical operation or throughput, namely the ordering of urban distress. City hardship therefore appears to be largely independent of the mechanism from which it is determined.

Distress Measures and Intergovernmental Versus Non-Intergovernmental Cities

Across the various distress indices there was an essentially fundamental agreement in the ordering of hardship. They pointed to a constellation of communities that appeared impacted, and also to a grouping of cities which seemed to be in much better condition. Such differentiation was, in fact, the forerunner of this study's classification of cities into older, declining intergovernmental cities and newer, more robust, non-intergovernmental jurisdictions. The very isolation of these cities by distress criteria meant that funds distributed by the agency, that directly or indirectly developed the index, would ultimately flow to the distressed jurisdiction. Thus, a "distressed" city would ultimately be the recipient of intergovernmental transfers; a healthy city would not. Since most indices produced similar results, a distressed city most likely would be the recipient of considerable intergovernmental transfers. The parallels between both city classification efforts — the hardship ranking and intergovernmental or non-intergovernmental approaches — are further evident by the strong similarity in their categorization of specific cities. To an overwhelming extent, those communities classified as intergovernmental in 1980 were assigned the most severe distress rankings in the 1970s. Conversely, those cities designated as least impacted have been subsequently classified as non-intergovernmental due to minimal levels of intergovernmental transfer.

Exhibit 2.8 displays how five different hardship measures evaluate a common set of thirty cities. Included in this group of the "top thirty most distressed" are eight of ten intergovernmental cities selected by this study. None of the ten non-intergovernmental cities is found in the listing of the thirty communities. The near-full inclusion of high distress cities as intergovernmental contrasts sharply with the universal absence of non-intergovernmental communities under these designation mechanisms. Exhibit 2.8, listing the average city hardship rank assigned by the five indices to the thirty cities, points more specifically to the parallelism of distress and intergovernmentalism. For example, Newark's average rank is 1.4. In other words, the hardship measures, on average, considered Newark to be midway between the first and second most impacted city. Cleveland, another intergovernmental city, was fourth most distressed; Cincinnati seventh; Baltimore ninth; and so on.

More complete evidence reveals the relatively severe hardship of the intergovernmental cities, as opposed to their non-intergovernmental counterparts. Exhibit 2.9 lists the hardship ranks accorded by four distress measures to the ten intergovernmental versus ten non-intergovernmental cities. The four indices are: Brookings-Intercity, CBO-Economic Need, HUD-Need, and Urban Institute-Economic Performance. These four were chosen because they cover the range of distress measures as far as substantive focus, data inputs, and statistical treatments are concerned (see Exhibit 2.8). The four measures are also comprehensive, examining a large, rather than an abbreviated group of cities. This latter characteristic is important for it allows the ranking of the non-intergovernmental cities—a group typically omitted in the shorter lists of distressed communities.

In Exhibit 2.9, distress is shown by rank — the *lower* the number, the higher the level of distress. The ten intergovernmental cities have much lower distress ranks than the non-intergovernmental communities. Results from the CBO Economic Need index are illustrative. The median Economic Need rank for the intergovernmental cities is close to 10; for non-intergovernmental jurisdictions the median is approximately 40, four times greater than for the intergovernmental group. A similar disparity is shown by the HUD Need Index. The median rank for the ten intergovernmental cities is 15.5 — one-third of the 47.0 rank for the non-intergovernmental group. Results from the Brookings Intercity Hardship ordering display a similar greater hardship designation for intergovernmental cities. The Urban Institute-Economic Performance Index shows a fourfold difference between intergovernmental and non-intergovernmental cities, a difference equivalent to that reported by the CBO Economic Need Index. In this case, the median rank for intergovernmental cities is 29.5, compared to 127.0 for non-intergovernmental cities.

Summary

Intergovernmental cities are locations where the major portions of significant outlays for local public services were paid for by other levels of government. They have had to raise more revenues to cover local expenditures than other comparably sized cities and to do so from ever-shrinking property tax bases. As this situation was faced by these groups of cities, they turned to the revenue resources of other governments. Service delivery and staffing were no longer exclusively determined locally but rather were a reflection of the priorities of these other governments.

Non-intergovernmental cities, on the other hand, spent significantly less money to finance public services, the vast majority of which came from their own resources. Non-intergovernmental cities were growth nodes, seldom enumerated under any index of impaction or hardship.

EXHIBIT 2.9. — *Distress Rankings of Intergovernmental Versus Non-Intergovernmental Cities*

	SELECTED DISTRESS MEASURES (1 = most severely distressed)			
	BROOKINGS[1] (Intercity Hardship)	CBO[2] (Economic Need)	HUD[3] (Need)	URBAN INSTITUTE[4] (Economic Performance)
INTERGOVERNMENTAL				
Akron	–	–	29	37
Baltimore	8	–	6	30
Buffalo	11	5	14	5
Cincinnati	15	16	11	29
Cleveland	9	4	4	21
Louisville	14	–	17	53
Milwaukee	33	18	27	45
Minneapolis	–	20	28	76
Newark	1	1	1	1
Rochester	26	11	24	16
MEDIAN	14.5	11.0	15.5	29.5
NON-INTERGOVERNMENTAL				
Anaheim	–	40	–	129
Austin	–	–	–	128
Baton Rouge	–	–	39	111
Columbus	44	28	37	54
Nashville-Davidson	–	–	55	112
Oklahoma City	51	39	42	69
San Jose	–	44	58	127
Tulsa	–	–	54	126
Virginia Beach	–	–	–	143
Wichita	–	–	47	142
MEDIAN	47.5	39.5	47.0	127.0

Notes: [1] 53 Cities were ranked.
         [2] 45 Cities were ranked.
         [3] 58 Cities were ranked.
         [4] 147 Cities were ranked.

Source: See text and Exhibits 2.5-2.7.

These two types of cities, each represented by ten examples, are scrutinized and compared for the remainder of the study. The growth and character of the dependent, intergovernmental city are carefully analyzed through constant comparison to the more independent, and healthier, non-intergovernmental city.

In the chapters which follow, certain caricatures of physical, economic, and social health will be associated with intergovernmental and non-intergovernmental cities. It will also be shown that over the more recent period, these two groups of cities differed in their levels of receipt of federal and state aid. It is not the intent of these comparative analyses to imply that public assistance either caused physical, economic and social problems or hastened their rate of development. What will be shown here is that one group of cities, as opposed to another, encountered a severe, socioeconomic downturn. Public policy sought to address this problem with direct, public monetary intervention. This situation ultimately occasioned a recurring, large domestic outlay. National priorities changed, the deficit grew, and the scale of this outlay could not be maintained into the future. The city of transfer payments, in full bloom during the 1970s, fell in the 1980s. The following chapters seek to document the events which led to this occurrence.

NOTES

1. See, for example, U.S. Department of Commerce, Bureau of Census, *Finances of Municipalities and Township Governments* (1957 Census of Governments), Vol. III-3, pp. 454.

2. *Webster's New Collegiate Dictionary*. Springfield, MA: G. & C. Merriam Company, 1976.

3. Burchell, Robert W. and David Listokin. *The Fiscal Impact Handbook*. New Brunswick, NJ: Center for Urban Policy Research, 1978, pp. 434.

4. U.S. Office of Management and Budget, *Catalog of Federal Domestic Assistance*. Washington, DC: Government Printing Office, 1981.

5. Richard P. Nathan, et al., *Block Grants for Community Development* (Washington, DC: U.S. Department of Housing and Urban Development, 1976); Richard P. Nathan, et al., "Cities in Crisis: The Impact of Federal Aid," *Current Focus*; Richard P. Nathan and Charles Adams, Jr., *Revenue Sharing: The Second Round* (Washington, DC: The Brookings Institution, 1977); Richard P. Nathan and Charles Adams, Jr., "Understanding Central City Hardship," *Political Science Quarterly*, Vol. 91, No. 1 (Spring 1976); Richard P. Nathan and Paul R. Dommel, *Federal Aid for Cities: A Multiple Strategy* (Washington, DC: The Brookings Institution, 1976); Richard P. Nathan and Paul R. Dommel, "Federal-Local Relations Under Block Grants," *Political Science Quarterly*, Vol. 93, No. 3 (Fall 1978), p. 421.

6. Subcommittee on the City of the Committee on Banking, Finance and Urban Affairs, House of Representatives, *City Need and the Responsiveness of Federal Programs*.

7. Harold L. Bunce and Robert L. Goldberg, *City Need and Community Development Funding* (Washington, DC: Government Printing Office, January 1979). See also, Harold L. Bunce, *An Evaluation of the Community Development Block Grant Program* (Washington, DC: U.S. Department of Housing and Urban Development, 1976); Harold L. Bunce, "The Community Development Block Grant Formula: An Evaluation," *Urban Studies Quarterly*, Vol. 14, No. 4 (June 1979), p. 443.

8. Ibid.

9. U.S. Department of the Treasury, Office of State and Local Finance, *Report on the Fiscal Impact of the Economic Stimulus Package on 48 Large Urban Governments*. Washington, DC: Treasury, January 1978.

10. Harvey A. Garn and Larry C. Ledebur, "The Economic Performance and Prospects of Cities," in Arthur Solomon (ed.), *The Prospective City*. Cambridge, MA: MIT Press, 1980, p. 204.

11. See Robert W. Burchell and David Listokin, "Measuring Urban Distress," in Burchell and Listokin (ed.), *Cities Under Stress*. New Brunswick, N.J.: Center for Urban Policy Research, 1981.

12. Ibid.

13. Ibid.

3

Economic Hardship in Intergovernmental and Non-Intergovernmental Cities

THE DYNAMICS of urban economics are not fully understood. Theories explaining the rapid and substantial exodus of people and jobs from densely populated, primarily northeastern and north-central regions, range from orthodox models to conspiracy arguments. At present, all of these interpretations of the determinants of urban growth and decline are deficient in some respects.

Although the forces influencing business and personal location decisions have not been completely documented, the outcomes of such decisions are clear. Massive spatial redistribution of economic activity and population from the older industrial heartlands to new service-oriented communities has resulted in high rates of unemployment, depressed housing markets, stagnating business environments and a multiplicity of social and fiscal difficulties for the intergovernmental city. Moreover, the financial instability of the intergovernmental city, brought about by numerous, interwoven and mutually reinforcing long-term economic trends, as well as cyclical business fluctuations, resulted in mounting concern with regard to its ability to service existing debts and to meet future obligations.

Having empirically verified the intergovernmental/non-intergovernmental city phenomenon in the previous chapter, this chapter will examine the relative performances of the resource base of both sets of cities. The extensive economic decline of intergovernmental cities and the concomitant growth and expansion of non-intergovernmental cities is documented. To accomplish this task, several studies involving the measurement of urban economic conditions have been reviewed, and variables most frequently employed in these studies are identified and selected as an evaluative framework. Chapters 4 and 5 will analyze the social needs and fiscal pressures which not only accompany but also are manifestations of the economic deterioration discussed here.

Economic Indicators

A congressional sub-committee report on city needs observed that communities with weak economies could be identified by either: (1) the outcomes of factors responsible for poor economic performance, i.e., declines in population, employment,

41

earnings or value of output, or (2) the presence of the factors themselves, such as outmoded plants and equipment, lack of developable land; and the extent to which the economic base is composed of declining industries.[1] A review of several studies on urban economic decline indicates that most researchers evaluate the level of a city's economic health by the former method, that is, by analyzing the actual performance of a community's resource base with respect to key economic indicators.[2]

This chapter reviews the economic status of both intergovernmental and non-intergovernmental cities based on four performance indicators: population, employment, unemployment and per capita income. Additionally, employment is disaggregated into manufacturing, selective services, retail sales, and wholesale trade and is further analyzed by subsets of industrial base including: total establishments, employment and sales, receipts and value of production. Although employment trends are the most frequently accepted and most often employed indicator of urban economic performance, a comparison of cities based solely on one indicator can be misleading since cities differ considerably in their economic resources and patterns of performance.[3] Further insight into the economic performance of intergovernmental and non-intergovernmental cities is provided through the documentation of new private investments and manufacturing capital expenditures as well as through the growth of local housing markets.

In outline format, the analysis in this chapter will proceed in the following manner:

I. Primary Economic Indicators

    Population Trends
    Employment Levels
    Unemployment Rates
    Income Patterns

II. Industrial Base Characteristics

    Establishments
      Manufactures
      Selected Services
      Retail Trade
      Wholesale Trade
    Employment
      Manufactures
      Selected Services
      Retail Trade Trends

      Wholesale Trade Trends
    Sales and Receipts
      Selected Services
      Retail Trade
      Wholesale Trade
    Value of Production
      Manufactures

III. Private Investments

    Manufacturing
      New Capital
      Expenditures
    Housing
      New Units Authorized
      Total Housing Units
      Median Housing Value
      Median Gross Rent

All data will be confined to an end-state period of the late 1970s. This represents the height of intergovernmentalism in American cities. The median for each period, indicated in the exhibits which follow, is the value of the $\frac{n+1}{2}$ case. Percent change in medians is the difference between the two derived median values for the time periods under observation.

Economic Performance Comparison: Primary Indicators

Population Trends

Changes in a community's population are an important and frequently employed indicator of urban economic performance. Population growth implies a growing labor supply, expanding markets, improved employment opportunities, and an attractive residential environment. Retail sales, consumer-oriented services, and financial institutions are all directly affected by shrinking consumer markets and reduced disposable income, both of which accompany population outmigration. To the extent that the most frequent types of households abandoning declining cities are younger, better educated, and of higher income, relatively minor reductions in population can have significant repercussions on an area's economic resource base.

With regard to the local fisc, loss of population translates into fewer tax ratables from the structures they occupy and support and, thus, reduced local revenue sources. Unfortunately for declining cities, the demand for and cost of municipal services does not decrease in proportion to population outmigration and, in many instances, actually increases. The result of this phenomenon is clear; cities must often maintain or increase public expenditure levels with dwindling resource bases.

Shifts in population offer a clear indication of the overall magnitude of the intergovernmental city's decline. As early as the 1960s, intergovernmental cities were already experiencing significant population losses (Exhibit 3.1). While the nation as a whole increased by 13.3 percent in total population between 1960 and 1970, the average intergovernmental city lost 10 percent of its population. With an average population of 493,000 persons in 1960, the intergovernmental city category began the decade of the Seventies with 49,000 fewer individuals, for a median population of 444,000. During that same ten-year period, the average non-intergovernmental city increased its population by 119,000, or 51.7 percent. Climbing from a 1960 count of 230,000, the non-intergovernmental city category had a median population of 349,000 by 1970.

Buffalo and Cleveland were the major losers in absolute intergovernmental city population, registering decade declines of 69,000 and 125,000, respectively. Cleveland was also the largest percentage loser, with a loss of 14.3 percent. Newark, on the other hand, performed relatively well compared to other intergovernmental cities. Newark retained in 1970, 94.6 percent of its 1960 population level. As for the growing non-intergovernmental cities, San Jose was the principal gainer in both absolute and percentage terms, increasing by 256,000 or 125.5 percent during the decade of the Sixties.

For the intergovernmental cities, the 1970s were especially damaging with regard to population outflows. Indeed, population loss in the average intergovernmental city was almost double its 1960–1970 decrease. For the intergovernmental city, this loss represented a full 80,000 or an 18.0 percent absolute reduction in population. The average intergovernmental city population loss was 45.0 percent greater during the 1970s than it was throughout the Sixties. Cleveland maintained its dubious distinction as front-runner in population loss, entering the 1980s with 177,000 or 23.5 percent fewer city residents than it had in 1970. Newark again trailed the

EXHIBIT 3.1. — *Population Trends, 1960–1980 (Thousands)*

	1960	1970	1980	CHANGE					
				1960–1970 Absolute	1960–1970 Percent	1970–1980 Absolute	1970–1980 Percent	1960–1980 Absolute	1960–1980 Percent
INTERGOVERNMENTAL									
AKRON	290	275	237	- 15	- 5.2	- 38	- 13.8	- 53	- 18.3
BALTIMORE	939	906	787	- 33	- 3.5	- 119	- 13.1	- 152	- 16.2
BUFFALO	532	463	358	- 69	- 13.0	- 105	- 22.7	- 174	- 32.7
CINCINNATI	502	454	385	- 48	- 9.6	- 69	- 15.2	- 117	- 23.3
CLEVELAND	876	751	574	- 125	- 14.3	- 177	- 23.5	- 302	- 34.5
LOUISVILLE	390	362	298	- 28	- 7.2	- 64	- 17.7	- 92	- 23.6
MILWAUKEE	741	717	636	- 24	- 3.2	- 81	- 11.3	- 105	- 14.2
MINNEAPOLIS	483	434	370	- 49	- 10.1	- 64	- 14.7	- 113	- 23.4
NEWARK	405	382	329	- 22	- 5.4	- 53	- 13.9	- 76	- 18.7
ROCHESTER	318	295	242	- 23	- 7.3	- 53	- 18.0	- 76	- 23.9
MEDIAN	493	444	364	- 49	- 9.9	- 80	- 18.0	- 129	- 26.2
NON-INTERGOVERNMENTAL									
ANAHEIM	104	166	222	+ 62	+59.6	+ 56	+ 33.7	+118	+113.5
AUSTIN	187	253	346	+ 66	+35.3	+ 93	+ 36.7	+159	+ 85.0
BATON ROUGE	152	166	219	+ 14	+ 9.2	+ 53	+ 31.9	+ 67	+ 44.0
COLUMBUS	471	540	565	+ 69	+14.6	+ 25	+ 4.6	+ 94	+ 20.0
NASHVILLE-DAVIDSON	171	426	456	+ 55	+32.2	+ 30	+ 7.0	+285	+166.7
OKLAHOMA CITY	324	368	403	+ 44	+13.6	+ 35	+ 9.5	+ 79	+ 24.4
SAN JOSE	204	460	637	+256	+125.5	+177	+ 38.5	+433	+212.3
TULSA	262	330	361	+ 68	+30.0	+ 31	+ 9.4	+ 99	+ 37.8
VIRGINIA BEACH	NA	172	262	NA	NA	+ 90	+ 52.3	NA	NA
WICHITA	255	277	279	+ 22	+ 8.6	+ 2	+ 0.7	+ 24	+ 9.4
MEDIAN	230	349	382	+119	+51.7	+ 33	+ 9.5	+152	+ 66.1
U.S. Total (Mil)	179.3	203.2	226.5	+23.9	+13.3	+23.3	+ 11.5	+47.2	+26.3

Sources: U.S. Department of Commerce, Bureau of the Census, Census of Population, 1960 and 1970; U.S. Department of Commerce, Bureau of the Census, 1980 Census of Population for Cities of 100,000 and Over by Rank Order; "Final Counts as Published in 1980 Census Advance Reports by State, Series PHC80-V." Changes calculated by the Center for Urban Policy Research.

median intergovernmental city, losing an additional 13.9 percent of its 1970 population.

Viewing the 1960 to 1980 period in aggregate demonstrates the severity of the population decline in the intergovernmental city (Exhibit 3.1). During that time span, the average intergovernmental city lost over one-fourth of its population, or 129,000 people. The average intergovernmental city thus underwent two decades of population change in which it decreased by 6,500 persons annually. In sharp contrast, the average non-intergovernmental city welcomed total new residents at a rate of 7,600 persons per year. At the extremes of these trends were Cleveland, losing 15,100 in population per year, and San Jose gaining 21,700 annually.

Employment Trends

As basic measures of economic performance, employment trends are the most widely accepted indicator of the viability of a municipality's economic foundation. Total employment levels may, however, mask job trends in individual industrial sectors which can more clearly explain and accurately indicate a city's long-term, as well as short-term, economic prospects. Nevertheless, total employment data, over time, reflect an aggregate measure of change in a city's overall job base.

Similar to total population trends, employment levels in the intergovernmental city spiraled consistently downward while the non-intergovernmental city experienced dramatic rates of increase (Exhibit 3.2). Between 1960 and 1977, national employment increased by 24.7 million, or fully 37.5 percent. This new growth markedly favored non-intergovernmental cities. In fact, over this 17-year period, only one intergovernmental city, Louisville, experienced any net new jobs. In 1977, the average intergovernmental city had 225,000 employees, down 45,000 or 16.7 percent from its 1960 level. The average non-intergovernmental city, which in 1960 had approximately 90,000 jobs, increased its total employment by 92,000 to 182,000 in 1977.

At the start of the Sixties, the average intergovernmental city enjoyed a substantial margin in absolute employment over the average non-intergovernmental city, employing 108,000 more workers. Restated, in 1960, on average, intergovernmental cities employed three times the number of persons employed by the non-intergovernmental cities. By 1977, this gap was reduced to an intergovernmental city lead of 19.1 percent, or only 43,000 jobs. More currently (1982), the two categories of cities are essentially even in aggregate job levels. Nationally, 12.8 million new jobs were created during the 1960s. These new positions were of little consequence to intergovernmental cities; on average, they lost over 10 percent of their employment base by 1970. During that same ten years, the average non-intergovernmental city grew by 23,000 jobs, or 25.6 percent.

The 1970 to 1977 period was one of weak national economic performance; the national pool of jobs increased by a mere 15.1 percent. In terms of employment growth, the non-intergovernmental city was impervious to the nationwide economic slowdown; its 1970 to 1977 rate of expansion was more than double its growth increment for the previous ten years. And, for every 10 jobs gained by the average non-intergovernmental city, the average intergovernmental city lost 2.5.

Newark proved to be less successful in retaining jobs than it was in maintaining its population. While the average intergovernmental city employment base declined by

EXHIBIT 3.2.—*Total Employment, 1960–1977 (Thousands)*

| | 1960 | 1970 | 1977 | CHANGE | | | | | |
				1960–1970 Absolute	1960–1970 Percent	1970–1977 Absolute	1970–1977 Percent	1960–1977 Absolute	1960–1977 Percent
INTERGOVERNMENTAL									
AKRON	137	128	118	- 9	- 16.6	-10	- 7.8	- 19	- 13.9
BALTIMORE	425	405	362	-20	- 4.7	-43	-10.6	- 63	- 14.8
BUFFALO	262	220	183	-42	- 16.0	-37	-16.8	- 79	- 30.2
CINCINNATI	278	262	252	-16	- 5.8	-10	- 3.8	- 26	- 9.4
CLEVELAND	508	443	371	-65	- 12.8	-72	-16.3	-137	- 27.9
LOUISVILLE	177	204	207	+27	+ 15.3	+ 3	+ 1.5	+ 30	+ 16.9
MILWAUKEE	356	320	280	-36	- 10.1	-40	-12.5	- 76	- 21.3
MINNEAPOLIS	285	272	243	-13	- 4.6	-29	-10.7	- 42	- 14.7
NEWARK	224	196	168	-28	- 12.5	-28	-14.3	- 56	- 25.0
ROCHESTER	205	207	181	+ 2	+ 1.0	-26	-12.6	- 24	- 11.7
MEDIAN	270	241	225	-29	- 10.7	-16	- 6.6	- 45	- 16.7
NON-INTERGOVERNMENTAL									
ANAHEIM	35	82	131	+47	+134.3	+49	+59.8	+ 96	+274.3
AUSTIN	75	113	182	+38	+ 50.7	+69	+61.1	+107	+142.7
BATON ROUGE	70	82	NA	+12	+ 17.1	NA	NA	NA	NA
COLUMBUS	216	260	273	+44	+ 20.4	+13	+ 5.0	+ 57	+ 26.4
NASHVILLE-DAVIDSON	NA	183	NA	NA	NA	NA	NA	NA	NA
OKLAHOMA CITY	155	215	259	+60	+ 38.7	+44	+20.5	+104	+ 67.1
SAN JOSE	90	135	169	+45	+ 50.0	+34	+25.2	+ 79	+ 87.8
TULSA	120	154	207	+34	+ 28.3	+53	+34.4	+ 87	+ 72.5
VIRGINIA BEACH	NA	48	NA	NA	NA	NA	NA	NA	NA
WICHITA	89	107	136	+18	+ 20.2	+29	+27.1	+ 47	+ 52.8
MEDIAN	90	113	182	+23	+ 25.6	+64	+56.7	+ 92	+102.2
U.S. Total (Mil)	65.8	78.6	90.5	+12.8	+ 19.5	+11.9	+15.1	+ 24.7	+37.5

Sources: U.S. Department of Commerce, Bureau of the Census, Census of Population, Subject Reports, "Journey to Work," 1960 and 1970; U.S. Department of Commerce, Bureau of the Census, County and City Data Book, 1972. Changes calculated by the Center for Urban Policy Research.

16.7 percent, from 270,000 to 225,000, Newark's rate of job loss was 8.3 percentage points higher, or 25.0 percent. Still, Newark was not the worst performing city in either absolute or percentage terms. Cleveland lost a full 137,000 jobs, while Buffalo retained, in 1977, only 68.8 percent of its 1960 level of employment.

Unemployment Rates

Rates of unemployment are used as critical indicators of weakness in local and regional employment demand. As evidenced by the data presented here, however, unemployment rates can be as high in growing cities as they are in declining communities. In the former instance, the high rates of unemployment often reflect an over-supply of labor due to migration; in the latter, the abundance of labor supply is predominantly composed of long-term residents. In some cases, a high unemployment rate in expanding communities may reflect a mismatch between available job opportunities and the skill or educational levels of those persons who are initially attracted there. In declining areas, high rates of unemployment generally reflect more serious and long-term structural problems of the local economy's ability to support the area's labor force. For instance, when local unemployment levels rise relative to national economic fluctuations during cyclical downturns, it may reflect an area's overreliance on businesses excessively vulnerable to national setbacks.

Reaction to business cycles provides a measure of capacity to change. In declining cities, unemployment rates can be expected to soar during periods of poor national economic performance. Moreover, declining cities tend to recover at much slower rates than growth cities. Whereas in growing areas, economic downturns cause temporary sluggish performance by local businesses, older cities often face permanent plant closures or other business failures, resulting in prolonged high unemployment rates. These trends are clear in the data which follow.

In 1963, the national unemployment rate was 5.7 percent, reflecting a healthy but nevertheless lackluster nationwide performance (Exhibit 3.3). With rates of unemployment ranging from a low of 3.3 percent to a high of 6.1 percent, the average non-intergovernmental city, at 4.6 percent, ranked approximately one percentage point better than the national unemployment rate. The average intergovernmental city had an unemployment rate approximately one-half point inferior to the national rate. In the midst of stronger national economic performance by 1967, the national rate of unemployment dropped to 3.9 percent bettering both intergovernmental and non-intergovernmental cities by one-half percentage point.

Still recovering from the first recession of the Seventies, national unemployment in 1972 increased one full percentage point from its 1967 level. And, while the non-intergovernmental city again did not perform as well as the nation as a whole, the sharp decline in economic performance from 1971 to 1977 revealed the extreme fragility of the intergovernmental city. In 1972, the percentage of persons temporarily out of work had risen to 4.9 percent nationally. That rate was 1.9 percent lower than the non-intergovernmental city's unemployment statistic and a full 5.4 percent below the intergovernmental city unemployment rate. The average intergovernmental city during the early 1970s experienced unemployment at a rate twice the national average.

EXHIBIT 3.3. — *Unemployment Rates, 1963–1977 (Percent)*

	1963	1967	1972	1977
INTERGOVERNMENTAL				
AKRON	6.0	4.9	10.4	7.0
BALTIMORE	6.5	4.6	10.1	7.6
BUFFALO	8.5	6.0	14.7	10.3
CINCINNATI	5.9	4.8	10.6	6.4
CLEVELAND	7.5	5.2	11.5	6.8
LOUISVILLE	6.2	4.6	8.5	5.5
MILWAUKEE	4.6	4.1	10.0	5.1
MINNEAPOLIS	4.3	3.8	7.8	3.8
NEWARK	8.2	6.5	17.7	12.0
ROCHESTER	5.9	4.3	9.3	7.1
MEDIAN	6.1	4.6	10.3	6.9
NON-INTERGOVERNMENTAL				
ANAHEIM	4.6	5.8	8.1	5.3
AUSTIN	3.3	3.2	4.1	3.6
BATON ROUGE	6.1	4.6	5.7	6.1
COLUMBUS	5.4	3.8	7.9	5.3
NASHVILLE-DAVIDSON	4.8	3.4	6.8	4.1
OKLAHOMA CITY	3.8	3.3	8.1	3.7
SAN JOSE	4.0	6.5	10.3	6.7
TULSA	4.3	4.6	6.4	3.7
VIRGINIA BEACH	NA	3.3	NA	NA
WICHITA	4.8	7.2	5.6	3.3
MEDIAN	4.6	4.2	6.8	4.1
UNITED STATES AVERAGE	5.7	3.9	4.9	7.0

Source: U.S. Department of the Commerce, County and City Data Book, 1977; U. S. Department of Labor, forthcoming; U. S. Department of Commerce, Statistical Abstract of the United States: 1980.

An enormous disparity was *not* present between the national unemployment rate and that of the intergovernmental city in 1977, despite the fact that the nation was recovering from an even deeper recession than it had undergone in the early 1970s. During the intervening period 1972 to 1977, massive federal anti-recessionary fiscal assistance helped to stabilize the intergovernmental city's weak economy and to keep the rate of persons seeking work to within 0.1 percent of the national unemployment rate. Non-intergovernmental cities during this period had 3 percent lower average unemployment rates than the national average.

With the second highest rate of unemployed persons in 1963 and the highest rate of unemployment for the following three consecutive periods, Newark was by far the most distressed intergovernmental city in terms of persons seeking unemployment.

Income Flows

Briefly stated, income is an index of the standard of living of a community's
population. Levels of per capita and household incomes reflect the size and strength
of local purchasing power, a factor bearing directly on the health of consumer-
oriented industries. Retail sales and housing, for example, are especially influenced
by the purchasing power of the resident population. With respect to the local fisc,
income levels are important since lower incomes translate into fewer own-source
revenues generated principally from local property, income and sales taxes.

When income levels are coupled with population trends, they allow for a more
comprehensive analysis of the implications of outmigration on declining cities. To
the extent that higher income households are the most mobile and first to leave less
desirable locations, small population losses or even stable population counts can
have significant local purchasing-power implications.*

It should be noted that income levels, in addition to serving as an economic indicator, are perhaps the single most significant measure of social need. The health
condition, illiteracy rates and crime levels which have come to characterize declining
urban areas, are in large part manifestations of the significant poverty of these
areas. Therefore, while the data below document the decline of income levels in intergovernmental cities in a general fashion, the following chapter probes this phenomenon in much more detail, as well as estimating its social implications.

While the nation as a whole experienced a convergence of income levels between
wealthy and poor regions since the 1930s, the intergovernmental/non-intergovern-
mental city pattern of income disparity moved in the opposite direction. As early as
1960, the intergovernmental city, on a per capita basis, was the less wealthy of the
two sets of cities (Exhibit 3.4). With a per capita income of $1,890, the average in-
tergovernmental city's income per person was 95.4 percent of the non-
intergovernmental city's level. Since 1960, the non-intergovernmental city income
level has grown at an increasing rate while the intergovernmental city's income has
fallen behind. Between 1960 and 1977, the income per intergovernmental city resident increased by $3,872 while the equivalent for the non-intergovernmental city
resident rose $4,236. The average intergovernmental city increase was 8.6 percent
less than the average non-intergovernmental city increase. The net result was that by
1977, intergovernmental city per capita income had dropped to 92.7 percent of that
of the non-intergovernmental city.

The disparity between the highest per capita income averages in non-intergovernmental cities and the lowest per capita income averages in intergovernmental cities
reflects much more dramatic income differentials. In 1960, the average per capita income level of the poorest intergovernmental city was 78 percent of the level of the
wealthiest non-intergovernmental city. By 1977, this margin was even more pronounced: the poorest intergovernmental city had an average per capita income of
58.1 percent of that of the wealthiest non-intergovernmental city. Newark, which
represented the poorest intergovernmental city in 1977, performed poorly even when
compared to other intergovernmental cities. Whereas Newark's income per capita in

*Negative income shifts within a static population can be of substantial magnitude.

EXHIBIT 3.4. — *Per Capita Income, 1960-1977*

				CHANGE					
	1960	*1970*	*1977*	*1960-1970 Absolute*	*1960-1970 Percent*	*1970-1977 Absolute*	*1970-1977 Percent*	*1960-1977 Absolute*	*1960-1977 Percent*
INTERGOVERNMENTAL									
AKRON	2124	3274	5760	+1150	+54.1	+2486	+75.9	+3636	+171.2
BALTIMORE	1866	2876	5242	+1010	+54.1	+2366	+82.3	+3376	+180.9
BUFFALO	1913	2877	4942	+964	+50.4	+2065	+71.8	+3029	+158.3
CINCINNATI	2043	3132	5763	+1089	+53.3	+2631	+84.0	+3720	+182.1
CLEVELAND	1856	2821	4914	+965	+52.0	+2093	+74.2	+3058	+164.8
LOUISVILLE	1764	2949	5835	+1185	+67.2	+2886	+97.9	+4071	+230.8
MILWAUKEE	2104	3183	5826	+1079	+51.3	+2643	+83.0	+3722	+176.9
MINNEAPOLIS	2046	3483	6569	+1437	+70.2	+3086	+88.6	+4523	+221.1
NEWARK	1792	2492	4038	+700	+39.1	+1546	+86.3	+2246	+125.3
ROCHESTER	2072	3239	5533	+1167	+56.3	+2294	+70.8	+3461	+167.0
MEDIAN	1890	3066	5762	+1176	+62.2	+2696	+87.9	+3872	+204.8
NON-INTERGOVERNMENTAL									
ANAHEIM	2255	3787	6633	+1532	+67.9	+2846	+75.2	+4378	+194.1
AUSTIN	1688	2998	5766	+1310	+77.6	+2768	+92.3	+4078	+241.6
BATON ROUGE	1855	2846	5813	+991	+53.4	+2967	+104.3	+3958	+213.4
COLUMBUS	1885	3025	5441	+1140	+60.5	+2416	+79.9	+3556	+188.6
NASHVILLE-DAVIDSON	1258	3003	5879	+1715	+133.2	+2876	+95.8	+4591	+356.4
OKLAHOMA CITY	1981	3236	6217	+1255	+63.1	+2981	+92.1	+4236	+213.8
SAN JOSE	2205	3394	6462	+1189	+53.9	+3068	+90.4	+4257	+193.1
TULSA	2298	3492	6950	+1194	+52.0	+3458	+99.0	+4652	+202.4
VIRGINIA BEACH	NA	3088	6070	NA	NA	+2982	+96.6	NA	NA
WICHITA	2082	3259	6344	+1177	+56.5	+3085	+94.6	+4262	+204.7
MEDIAN	1981	3236	6217	+1255	+63.4	+2981	+92.1	+4236	+213.8

Sources: U.S. Department of Commerce, Bureau of the Census, Census of Population, Vol. I., "Characteristics of the Population," 1960 and 1970; U.S. Department of Commerce, Bureau of the Census, Current Population Reports, Series P.25, 1977. Changes calculated by the Center for Urban Policy Research.

1960 was 94.8 percent of that of the average intergovernmental city, by 1977, its per capita income had dropped to 74.1 percent of the average intergovernmental city's level.

The key significance of income trends is their effect on buying power, i.e., the amount of income which is actually available for consumer goods and services after taxes, fees and other income encumbrances. An index of effective buying income has been developed by *Sales and Marketing Management Magazine* which offers a bulk measurement of market potential.[4] The effective buying income index reflects personal income, including wages, salaries, and other labor income, minus personal tax/non-tax payments, and personal contributions for social security insurance.*

Using the index of effective buying income, the 1963 median household income for the intergovernmental city was $7,200; slightly less than the non-intergovernmental city equivalent of $7,300 (Exhibit 3.5). By 1967, the effective buying income of the average intergovernmental city had grown to $8,700, an increase of approximately 20 percent. This growth was outdistanced by a one-third higher (27 percent) rise in non-intergovernmental cities. Between 1967 and 1973, the percent gain in average non-intergovernmental city effective buying income also decreased from the previous period, but at 10.2 percent, remained four times above the intergovernmental city rate and twice above the national effective buying income growth rate of 5.6 percent. Following national surges, nominal income for both intergovernmental and non-intergovernmental cities soared from 1973 to 1977 with the latter experiencing a 60.8 percent gain compared with the former's increase of 53.9 percent. Between 1977 and 1980, the average non-intergovernmental city continued to lead in effective buying income growth, increasing at almost double (36.5 percent) the rate of intergovernmental cities (20.1 percent) during this four-year period.

Reviewing aggregate growth over the 1963–1980 time period dramatizes the explosive growth of household income in non-intergovernmental cities. During that period, the average non-intergovernmental city's nominal effective buying income rose from $7,300 to $21,300, representing close to a tripling of household income. The average non-intergovernmental city family increased its effective buying power by 25 percent or $4,500 more than the average intergovernmental city family.

The product of total households and median household effective buying income yields a citywide measure of effective purchasing power. Although the average non-intergovernmental city's combined resident buying income was greater in 1960 than that of the intergovernmental city, significantly greater population in the average intergovernmental city resulted in citywide purchasing power almost twice as large in the intergovernmental city as in the non-intergovernmental city (Exhibit 3.6). Within 10 years, however, the non-intergovernmental/intergovernmental city margin had been reduced to only 8.3 percent; this convergence emphasized the significance of both income turgidity and population declines on the retail support bases of older, urban areas.

With an effective resident purchasing power of more than $2.3 billion, average non-intergovernmental city growth outpaced that of the intergovernmental city, in

---

*The resulting income index is synonymous with disposable income, not adjusted for inflation.

EXHIBIT 3.5.—*Effective Buying Income:* Median Household
By City, 1963-1980 (thousands)

| | | | | | | CHANGE | | | | | | | | |
| | | | | | | 1963-67 | 1963-67 | 1967-73 | 1967-73 | 1973-77 | 1973-77 | 1977-80 | 1977-80 | 1963-80 | 1963-80 |
	1963	1967	1973	1977	1980	Absolute	Percent	Absolute	Percent	Absolute	Percent	Absolute	Percent	Absolute	Percent
INTERGOVERNMENTAL															
AKRON	7.4	9.0	9.7	15.1	18.3	+1.6	+21.6	+0.7	+7.8	+5.4	+55.7	+13.2	+21.2	+10.9	+147.3
BALTIMORE	7.4	8.2	8.0	12.2	15.4	+0.8	+10.8	-0.2	-2.4	+4.2	+52.5	+13.2	+26.2	+8.0	+108.1
BUFFALO	7.1	8.2	8.5	14.6	15.1	+1.1	+15.5	+0.3	+3.7	+6.1	+70.8	+0.5	+3.4	+8.0	+112.6
CINCINNATI	6.3	8.4	8.3	12.7	16.1	+2.1	+33.3	-0.1	-1.2	+4.4	+53.0	+3.4	+26.8	+9.8	+155.6
CLEVELAND	6.4	8.0	8.9	13.2	15.9	+1.6	+25.0	+0.9	+11.3	+4.3	+48.3	+2.7	+20.5	+9.5	+148.4
LOUISVILLE	6.6	8.2	8.9	14.4	16.8	+1.6	+24.2	+0.7	+8.5	+5.5	+61.8	+2.4	+16.7	+10.2	+154.5
MILWAUKEE	7.3	9.0	9.5	14.9	18.1	+1.7	+23.3	+0.5	+5.6	+5.4	+56.8	+3.2	+21.5	+10.8	+147.9
MINNEAPOLIS	7.6	9.2	9.3	13.1	18.0	+1.6	+21.1	+0.1	+1.1	+3.8	+40.9	+4.9	+37.4	+10.4	+136.8
NEWARK	6.2	8.9	7.6	11.8	14.8	+2.7	+43.5	-0.3	-14.6	+4.2	+55.3	+3.0	+25.4	+8.6	+138.7
ROCHESTER	7.7	9.5	9.5	14.3	18.8	+1.8	+23.4	-0-	-0-	+4.8	+50.5	+4.5	+31.5	+11.1	+144.2
MEAN	7.2	8.7	8.9	13.7	16.5	+1.5	+20.8	+0.2	+2.3	+4.8	+53.9	+2.8	+20.4	+9.3	+129.2
NON-INTERGOVERNMENTAL															
ANAHEIM	8.3	10.6	11.7	17.4	24.5	+2.3	+27.7	+1.1	+10.4	+5.7	+48.7	+7.1	+40.8	+16.2	+195.2
AUSTIN	7.2	8.5	9.0	15.5	19.7	+1.3	+18.1	+0.5	+5.9	+6.5	+72.2	+4.2	+27.1	+12.5	+173.6
BATON ROUGE	7.3	9.7	9.9	15.9	21.3	+2.4	+32.8	+0.2	+2.1	+6.0	+60.6	+5.4	+34.0	+14.0	+191.7
COLUMBUS	9.6	8.5	9.7	14.7	18.1	-1.1	-11.5	+1.2	+14.1	+5.0	+51.5	+3.4	+23.1	+8.5	+88.5
NASHVILLE/DAVIDSON	6.1	8.1	9.5	16.4	19.7	+2.0	+32.8	+1.4	+17.3	+6.9	+72.6	+3.3	+20.1	+13.6	+223.0
OKLAHOMA CITY	6.5	7.9	8.7	14.1	21.0	+1.4	+21.5	+0.8	+10.1	+5.4	+62.1	+6.9	+48.9	+14.5	+223.7
SAN JOSE	7.8	10.5	11.8	19.6	28.1	+2.7	+34.6	+1.3	+12.4	+7.8	+66.1	+8.5	+43.4	+20.3	+260.3
TULSA	7.5	8.8	9.2	15.6	22.1	+1.3	+17.3	+0.4	+4.5	+6.4	+69.6	+6.5	+41.7	+14.6	+194.7
VIRGINIA BEACH	NA	9.2	10.1	16.0	19.7	NA	NA	+0.9	+9.8	+5.9	+58.4	+3.7	+23.1	NA	NA
WICHITA	7.0	8.9	9.7	15.5	22.8	+1.9	+27.0	+0.8	+9.0	+5.8	+59.8	+7.3	+47.1	+15.8	+225.7
MEAN	7.3	8.8	9.7	15.6	21.3	+1.5	+20.5	+0.9	+10.2	+5.9	+60.8	+5.7	+36.5	+14.0	+191.8
U.S. MEDIAN	7.1	9.0	9.5	15.0	19.1	+1.9	+26.8	+0.5	+5.6	+5.5	+57.9	+4.1	+27.3	+12.0	+169.0

*Unadjusted for inflation.

Sources: Sales and Marketing Management, "Effective Buying Income by City," 1964, 1968, 1974, 1978 and 1981. Change calculated by the Center for Urban Policy Research.

EXHIBIT 3.6.—*Effective Buying Income.* Total By City,[1]
1963–1980 ($ millions)*

						CHANGE									
						1963-67 Absolute	1963-67 Percent	1967-73 Absolute	1967-73 Percent	1973-77 Absolute	1973-77 Percent	1977-80 Absolute	1977-80 Percent	1963-80 Absolute	1963-80 Percent
INTERGOVERNMENTAL	1963	1967	1973	1977	1980										
AKRON	677.3	847.9	1191.4	1492.2	1844.8	+170.6	+25.2	+343.5	+40.5	+300.8	+25.2	+352.6	+23.6	+1167.5	+172.4
BALTIMORE	2038.8	2254.0	3150.5	4127.6	4977.5	+215.2	+10.6	+896.5	+39.8	+977.1	+31.0	+849.9	+20.6	+2938.7	+144.1
BUFFALO	1157.6	1258.3	1685.3	2105.0	2497.3	+100.7	+8.7	+427.0	+33.9	+419.7	+24.9	+392.3	+18.6	+1339.7	+115.7
CINCINNATI	1168.5	1366.4	1843.3	2373.8	3075.6	+197.9	+16.9	+476.9	+34.9	+530.5	+28.8	+701.8	+29.6	+1907.1	+163.2
CLEVELAND	1717.6	2047.6	2566.8	3252.9	3834.8	+330.0	+19.2	+499.2	+36.5	+706.1	+27.7	+581.9	+17.9	+2117.2	+123.7
LOUISVILLE	818.0	996.2	1464.9	2044.1	2412.3	+178.2	+21.8	+468.7	+47.0	+579.2	+39.5	+368.2	+18.0	+1594.3	+194.9
MILWAUKEE	1745.0	2139.9	2872.1	3669.8	4805.3	+394.9	+22.6	+732.2	+34.2	+797.7	+27.8	+1135.5	+30.9	+3060.3	+175.4
MINNEAPOLIS	1237.8	1545.8	1973.8	2261.0	3500.3	+308.0	+24.9	+428.0	+27.7	+287.2	+14.6	+1239.3	+54.8	+2262.5	+182.8
NEWARK	768.8	1106.2	1292.1	1613.9	1963.6	+337.4	+43.9	+185.9	+16.8	+321.8	+24.9	+349.7	+21.7	+1194.8	+155.4
ROCHESTER	785.6	930.7	1179.4	1670.9	2043.4	+145.1	+18.5	+248.7	+26.7	+491.5	+41.7	+372.5	+22.3	+1257.8	+160.1
MEDIAN	1163.1	1312.4	1764.3	2183.0	2786.5	+149.3	+12.8	+451.9	+34.4	+418.7	+23.7	+603.5	+27.6	+1623.4	+139.6
NON-INTERGOVERNMENTAL															
ANAHEIM	332.9	482.3	936.8	1459.5	2187.3	+149.4	+44.9	+454.5	+94.2	+522.7	+55.8	+727.8	+49.9	+1854.4	+557.0
AUSTIN	421.5	563.6	1155.5	2035.1	3291.3	+142.1	+33.7	+591.7	+105.0	+879.8	+76.2	+1256.2	+61.7	+2869.8	+680.8
BATON ROUGE	331.1	484.7	719.3	1280.6	2089.8	+153.6	+46.4	+234.6	+48.4	+561.3	+78.0	+809.2	+63.2	+1758.7	+531.2
COLUMBUS	1075.6	1472.7	2406.2	3170.6	4511.9	+397.1	+36.9	+933.5	+63.4	+764.4	+31.8	+1341.3	+42.3	+3436.3	+319.5
NASHVILLE/DAVIDSON	463.1	621.5	1974.0	3063.1	3932.0	+158.4	+34.2	+1352.5	+117.6	+1089.1	+55.2	+868.9	+28.4	+3468.9	+749.1
OKLAHOMA CITY	774.2	1014.8	1670.0	2429.3	4069.4	+240.6	+31.1	+655.2	+64.6	+759.3	+45.5	+1460.1	+67.5	+3295.2	+425.6
SAN JOSE	709.4	1209.6	2423.8	3956.1	6550.2	+500.2	+70.5	+1214.2	+100.4	+1532.3	+63.2	+2594.1	+65.6	+5840.8	+823.3
TULSA	708.8	915.8	1617.4	2348.9	3741.4	+207.0	+29.2	+701.6	+76.6	+731.5	+45.2	+1392.5	+59.3	+3032.6	+427.8
VIRGINIA BEACH	NA	347.8	779.6	1278.6	2046.8	NA	NA	+431.8	+124.2	+499.0	+64.0	+768.2	+60.1	NA	NA
WICHITA	597.5	809.0	1345.4	1732.4	2906.1	+211.5	+35.4	+536.4	+66.3	+387.0	+28.8	+1173.7	+67.7	+2308.6	+386.4
MEDIAN	597.5	809.0	1617.4	2348.9	3741.4	+211.5	+35.4	+808.4	+99.9	+731.5	+45.2	+1392.5	+59.3	+3143.9	+526.2
U.S. TOTAL (bil)	339.7	537.2	880.7	1303.6	1814.2	+197.5	+58.1	+343.5	+63.9	+422.9	+48.0	+511.2	+39.2	+1474.5	+434.1

*Unadjusted for inflation.

[1]Total households x median household effective buying income.

Sources: Sales and Marketing Management, "Effective Buying Income by City," 1964, 1968, 1974, 1978 and 1981. Changes calculated by the Center for Urban Policy Research.

absolute terms, by 1977. The intergovernmental city's effective purchasing power lagged behind that of the non-intergovernmental city by 7.1 percent. And by 1980, three years later, citywide effective purchasing power for the average inter-governmental city fell to only 74.5 percent of that of the non-intergovernmental city.

The combination of Newark's low nominal buying income and sizable population loss resulted in an extremely poor showing in terms of effective purchasing power. In 1963, Newark's citywide purchasing power by the criteria cited above was only 66.1 percent of the median intergovernmental city, and through 1980, it remained at approximately this comparative level. With regard to non-intergovernmental cities, Newark's citywide purchasing power was approximately 50 percent of the average of this group's level in 1980.

Summary: Primary Economic Indicators

The intergovernmental city, relative to the non-intergovernmental city, experienced significant losses in population and employment, a decline in per capita income and higher rates of unemployment. On average, between 1960 and 1980, the intergovernmental city lost over one-quarter of its population while the average non-intergovernmental city expanded by two-thirds. Rates of employment decline in intergovernmental cities, from 1960 to 1977, were less than the rates of population loss in those cities, while the exact opposite trend occurred in non-intergovernmental cities. Rates of change in non-intergovernmental city employment were one and one-half times as great as their rates of population increase. Moreover, these employment gains were nearly triple the national average job growth.

Unemployment rates in intergovernmental cities, although only slightly above national averages, were consistently half-again higher than equivalent rates for non-intergovernmental cities. Unadjusted citywide purchasing power in intergovernmental cities rose by a full 140 percent, but nevertheless lagged significantly behind both non-intergovernmental cities and the nation as a whole by rates of 3.8 to 1 and 3.1 to 1, respectively. By 1980, the average intergovernmental city was clearly in an inferior economic position compared with average national growth and non-intergovernmental city growth across multiple economic indicators.

Industrial Base Characteristics

As indicated previously, where a city is disproportionately composed of industries extremely vulnerable to national economic swings, low economic growth or recessions can produce an inordinate level of stress on the local economy. Moreover, to the extent that a community's industrial base consists principally of businesses with only limited prospects for future growth and expansion, and the locality is simultaneously unable to attract or generate new industries, the long-term outlook is not favorable. These conditions aptly describe the economic plight of the intergovernmental city. Representative of the older industrial community, the economy of the intergovernmental city has historically been predicated on a solid manufacturing base. Historically, the intergovernmental city's reliance on manufacturing was responsible for its initial impressive growth and prosperity. However, the downturn in manufacturing activity nationally, in the decade of the 1970s, resulted in manufacturing becoming an intergovernmental city liability.

Establishments By Sector

Establishment data are infrequently employed as indicators of economic condition; employment figures are more often relied upon to demonstrate the overall condition of various industries. This study, however, reviews both employment and establishment trends. Although the direction of change between the two indicators is similar, their magnitudes differ substantially as do the implications of their changes.

Total establishment data has direct implications for a municipality's property tax base which is not conveyed by employment data. For example, between 1963 and 1977, intergovernmental city retail trade employment fell by 7.3 percent, but its loss of firms was a full 34.7 percent. Not only does this high rate of establishment loss imply greater own-source revenue reductions which are masked by employment data, it also indicates that smaller businesses were experiencing difficulty in their operations in intergovernmental cities.

Finally, establishment data offer a clearer picture of the diversity of a city's economy. This view is important since an economic base which is highly dependent on a relatively small set of large firms is more vulnerable to fiscal stress resulting from either regional, national or international economic trends or fluctuations, strains which adversely affect that particular industry. Cities whose economies are extremely dependent on industries such as steel or automotive manufacturing are clear examples of this dilemma.

Manufacturing

During the four-year period from 1963 to 1967, all ten intergovernmental cities experienced absolute declines in total manufacturing facilities (Exhibit 3.7). These reductions ranged from a loss of four firms in Akron to a decrease of 287 manufacturing firms in Newark. In percentage terms, this amounted to declines of one percent and 16.9 percent, respectively. And, while the average intergovernmental city suffered an 8.0 percent reduction of manufacturing facilities for the period ending in 1967, that figure rose to nearly 10 percent from 1967 to 1972. During this latter five-year period, Newark sustained a near 25 percent loss of manufacturing firms for an aggregate decline of 352 establishments. On an annual basis, this translates to an attrition of more than 70 manufacturing firms annually.

In the final period for which data are analyzed, 1972 to 1977, the average intergovernmental city continued to lose manufacturing facilities, albeit at a lower rate than that of the two previous time spans. Over the fourteen-year period, 1963 to 1977, the average intergovernmental city lost slightly over one-fifth of its 1963 manufacturing firms. Newark, during that time, lost one out of every two firms or 46.7 percent of its 1963 base. Although two intergovernmental cities, Louisville and Minneapolis, did experience a growth in manufacturing firms from 1972 to 1977,

EXHIBIT 3.7. — *Manufactures: All Establishments, 1963-1977*

| | 1963 | 1967 | 1972 | 1977 | CHANGE | | | | | | | |
					1963-1967 Absolute	1963-1967 Percent	1967-1972 Absolute	1967-1972 Percent	1972-1977 Absolute	1972-1977 Percent	1963-1977 Absolute	1963-1977 Percent
INTERGOVERNMENTAL												
AKRON	415	411	391	376	- 4	- 1.0	- 20	- 4.9	- 15	- 3.8	- 39	- 9.4
BALTIMORE	1515	1396	1237	1099	- 119	- 7.9	- 159	- 11.4	- 138	- 11.2	- 416	- 27.5
BUFFALO	984	942	786	725	- 42	- 4.3	- 156	- 16.6	- 61	- 7.8	- 259	- 26.3
CINCINNATI	1112	1052	960	942	- 60	- 5.4	- 92	- 8.7	- 18	- 1.9	- 170	- 15.3
CLEVELAND	2821	2537	2336	2099	- 284	- 10.1	- 201	- 7.9	- 237	- 10.1	- 722	- 25.6
LOUISVILLE	644	606	567	586	- 38	- 5.9	- 39	- 6.4	+ 19	+ 3.4	- 58	- 9.0
MILWAUKEE	1525	1394	1237	1192	- 131	- 8.6	- 157	- 11.3	- 45	- 3.6	- 333	- 21.8
MINNEAPOLIS	1283	1150	1027	1046	- 133	- 10.4	- 123	- 10.7	+ 19	+ 1.9	- 237	- 18.5
NEWARK	1700	1413	1061	906	- 287	- 16.9	- 352	- 24.9	- 155	- 14.6	- 794	- 46.7
ROCHESTER	762	719	644	621	- 43	- 5.6	- 75	- 10.4	- 23	- 3.6	- 141	- 18.5
MEDIAN	1198	1101	993	924	- 97	- 8.1	- 108	- 9.8	- 69	- 6.9	- 274	- 22.9
NON-INTERGOVERNMENTAL												
ANAHEIM	262	283	400	762	+ 21	+ 8.0	+117	+41.3	+362	+ 90.5	+500	+190.8
AUSTIN	223	204	269	371	- 19	- 8.5	+ 65	+31.9	+102	+ 37.9	+148	+ 66.4
BATON ROUGE	130	148	182	212	+ 18	+ 13.8	+ 34	+23.0	+ 30	+ 16.5	+ 82	+ 63.1
COLUMBUS	754	695	741	793	- 59	- 7.8	+ 46	+ 6.6	+ 52	+ 7.0	+ 39	+ 5.2
NASHVILLE/DAVIDSON	501	636	766	829	+135	+ 26.9	+130	+20.4	+ 63	+ 8.2	+328	+ 65.5
OKLAHOMA CITY	594	594	642	772	-0-	-0-	+ 48	+ 8.1	+130	+ 20.2	+178	+ 30.0
SAN JOSE	396	400	451	661	+ 4	+ 1.0	+ 51	+12.8	+210	+ 46.6	+265	+ 66.9
TULSA	514	560	706	901	+ 46	+ 8.9	+146	+26.1	+195	+ 27.6	+387	+ 75.3
* VIRGINIA BEACH	21	32	53	NA	+ 11	+ 52.4	+ 21	+65.6	NA	NA	NA	NA
WICHITA	431	424	449	483	- 7	- 1.6	+ 25	+ 5.9	+ 34	+ 7.6	+ 52	+ 12.1
MEDIAN	431	424	451	762	- 7	- 1.6	+ 27	+ 6.4	+311	+ 69.0	+331	+ 76.8
U.S. TOTAL (000)	311.9	311.1	320.7	359.9	-0.8	- 0.3	+ 9.6	+ 3.1	+39.2	+ 12.2	+48.0	+ 15.4

*Not included in media calculation.

Sources: U.S. Department of Commerce, Bureau of the Census, <u>Census of Manufactures</u>, "Geographic Area Series" (For Years Indicated). Changes calculated by the Center for Urban Policy Research.

these new firms were not enough to compensate for the losses sustained during the previous two periods. Even these cities recorded fourteen-year net manufacturing firm losses of 9.0 percent and 18.5 percent, respectively.

From 1963 to 1977, the average non-intergovernmental city increased its share of manufacturing firms at a rate of five times the national rate. The average non-intergovernmental city did not experience a decline in manufacturing establishments for any of the periods under study, including 1963 through 1967, when the nation as a whole experienced a net drop of 0.3 percent.

Small Manufacturing Firms

A study, currently under detailed scrutiny by the field, indicates that some share of new employment opportunities is created by firms with fewer than 20 employees.[5] To the extent that this observation proves reasonably accurate, it is interesting to note that the loss of a substantial proportion of the intergovernmental city's manufacturing sector coincides with its faltering ability to attract or generate new small manufacturing facilities.

In 1963, the average intergovernmental city dominated the non-intergovernmental city in total small (less than 20 employees) manufacturing firms by a ratio of 2.5 to 1 (Exhibit 3.8). Between 1963 and 1977, the non-intergovernmental city added new small manufacturing plants at a rate five times the national average. During that same time span, intergovernmental cities lost, on average, thirty percent of their small manufacturing establishments. The end result was that, by 1977, the average non-intergovernmental city had surpassed the average intergovernmental city in total small manufacturing plants. Newark's poor performance during this period is noteworthy; the city, once one of the nation's pioneering manufacturing hubs, lost fully one-half of its small manufacturing firms. Compared with the average intergovernmental city, in 1963 Newark had over 50 percent more small firms; by 1977 it retained its lead but by less than 10 percent.

Selected Services

Since the 1950s, service establishments grew more rapidly than manufacturing firms (Exhibit 3.9). Nationally, between 1963 and 1977, selected services increased by 773,000 firms or nearly 73 percent, compared to manufacturing expansion for this same time span of 48,000 firms or 15 percent. This significant growth in the service industries largely bypassed declining intergovernmental cities, however. The rise in service establishments favored the non-intergovernmental city more so than any other single industrial sector. For the full fourteen-year period 1963 to 1977, the average non-intergovernmental city expanded its base by close to 2,400 service firms, for an increase of nearly 140 percent. By contrast, the intergovernmental city added less than 400 new firms for an increase of just over 12 percent. Looking at the interim periods shows that the vast majority of the intergovernmental city's growth, on average, took place between 1967 and 1972, when it received more than its proportional share of the national growth rate. The 1972 to 1977 period shows intergovernmental cities losing significant service sector businesses.

EXHIBIT 3.8.—*Manufactures: Firms with Fewer Than 20 Employees, 1963-1977*

| | 1963 | 1967 | 1972 | 1977 | CHANGE | | | | | | | |
					1963-1967 Absolute	1963-1967 Percent	1967-1972 Absolute	1967-1972 Percent	1972-1977 Absolute	1972-1977 Percent	1963-1977 Absolute	1963-1977 Percent
INTERGOVERNMENTAL												
AKRON	263	241	230	237	- 22	- 8.4	- 11	- 4.6	+ 7	+ 3.0	- 26	- 9.9
BALTIMORE	1215	771	695	670	-444	- 36.5	- 76	- 9.9	- 25	- 3.6	-545	- 44.9
BUFFALO	630	551	470	454	- 79	- 12.5	- 81	- 14.7	- 16	- 3.4	-176	- 27.9
CINCINNATI	634	590	554	575	- 44	- 6.9	- 36	- 6.1	+ 21	+ 3.8	- 59	- 9.3
CLEVELAND	1813	1530	1489	1334	-283	- 15.6	- 41	- 2.7	-155	-15.0	-479	- 26.4
LOUISVILLE	342	315	286	329	- 27	- 7.9	- 29	- 9.2	+ 43	+15.0	- 13	- 3.8
MILWAUKEE	972	825	735	707	-147	- 15.1	- 90	-10.9	- 28	- 3.8	-265	- 27.2
MINNEAPOLIS	789	671	613	657	-118	- 15.0	- 58	- 8.6	+ 44	+ 7.2	-132	- 16.7
NEWARK	1079	855	644	539	-224	- 20.8	-211	-24.7	-105	-16.3	-540	- 50.0
ROCHESTER	497	446	422	414	- 51	- 10.3	- 24	- 5.4	- 8	- 1.9	- 83	- 16.7
MEDIAN	712	631	584	497	- 81	- 11.4	- 47	- 7.4	- 87	-14.9	-215	- 30.2
NON-INTERGOVERNMENTAL												
ANAHEIM	167	169	245	521	+ 2	+ 1.2	+ 76	+45.0	+276	+112.6	+354	+212.0
AUSTIN	173	152	204	279	- 21	- 12.1	+ 52	+34.2	+ 75	+ 36.8	+106	+ 61.3
BATON ROUGE	82	96	120	149	+ 14	+ 17.1	+ 24	+25.0	+ 29	+ 24.2	+ 67	+ 81.7
COLUMBUS	472	429	439	511	- 43	- 9.1	+ 10	+ 2.3	+ 72	+ 16.4	+ 39	+ 8.3
NASHVILLE/DAVIDSON	278	361	487	584	+ 83	+ 29.9	+126	+34.9	+ 97	+ 19.9	+306	+110.1
OKLAHOMA CITY	440	432	446	554	- 8	- 1.8	+ 14	+ 3.2	+108	+ 24.2	+114	+ 25.9
SAN JOSE	276	262	318	500	- 14	- 5.1	+ 56	+21.4	+182	+ 57.2	+224	+ 81.2
TULSA	370	377	488	638	+ 7	+ 1.9	+111	+29.4	+150	+ 30.7	+268	+ 72.4
VIRGINIA BEACH	18	27	43	69	+ 9	+50.0	+ 16	+59.3	+ 26	+ 60.5	+ 51	+283.3
WICHITA	300	279	298	324	- 21	- 7.0	+ 19	+ 6.4	+ 26	+ 8.7	+ 24	+ 8.0
MEDIAN	289	271	308	506	- 18	- 6.2	+ 37	+13.7	+198	+ 64.3	+217	+ 75.1
U.S. TOTAL (000)	209.6	200.8	206.5	241.2	- 8.8	- 4.2	+ 5.7	+ 2.8	+ 34.7	+ 16.8	+ 31.6	+ 15.1

Sources: U.S. Department of Commerce, Bureau of the Census, Census of Manufactures, "Geographic Area Series" (For Years Indicated). Changes calculated by the Center for Urban Policy Research.

EXHIBIT 3.9. — *Selected Services: All Establishments, 1963–1977*

	1963	1967	1972	1977	CHANGE 1963-1967 Absolute	1963-1967 Percent	1967-1972 Absolute	1967-1972 Percent	1972-1977 Absolute	1972-1977 Percent	1963-1977 Absolute	1963-1977 Percent
INTERGOVERNMENTAL												
AKRON	1831	1649	1909	1939	- 182	- 9.9	+ 260	+15.8	+ 30	+ 1.6	+ 108	+ 5.9
BALTIMORE	5000	5121	5920	5572	+ 121	+ 2.4	+ 799	+15.6	-348	- 5.9	+ 572	+ 11.4
BUFFALO	3143	3033	3518	3020	- 110	- 3.5	+ 485	+16.0	-498	-14.2	- 123	- 3.9
CINCINNATI	3143	3064	4025	3898	- 79	- 2.5	+ 961	+31.4	-127	- 3.2	+ 755	+ 24.0
CLEVELAND	5500	4990	6022	5126	- 510	- 9.3	+1032	+20.7	-896	-14.9	- 374	- 6.8
LOUISVILLE	2669	2674	3090	3171	+ 5	+ 0.2	+ 416	+15.6	+ 81	+ 2.6	+ 502	+ 18.8
MILWAUKEE	3781	3692	4841	4792	- 89	- 2.4	+1149	+31.1	- 49	- 1.0	+1011	+ 26.7
MINNEAPOLIS	3217	3226	4276	4704	+ 9	+ 0.3	+1050	+32.5	+428	+10.0	+1487	+ 46.2
NEWARK	2760	2373	2270	1853	- 387	-14.0	- 103	- 4.3	-417	-18.4	- 907	- 32.9
ROCHESTER	2192	2269	2567	2463	+ 77	+ 3.5	+ 298	+13.1	-104	- 4.1	+ 271	+ 12.4
MEDIAN	3143	3049	3772	3535	- 94	- 3.0	+ 723	+23.7	-237	- 6.2	+ 392	+ 12.5
NON-INTERGOVERNMENTAL												
ANAHEIM	774	1107	1543	2141	+333	+43.0	+ 436	+39.4	+598	+38.8	+1367	+176.6
AUSTIN	1316	1637	2914	3774	+321	+24.4	+1277	+78.0	+860	+29.5	+2458	+186.8
BATON ROUGE	834	1146	1834	2108	+312	+37.4	+ 688	+60.0	+274	+14.9	+1274	+152.8
COLUMBUS	2848	2948	4424	4698	+100	+ 3.5	+1476	+50.1	+274	+ 6.2	+1850	+ 65.0
NASHVILLE/DAVIDSON	1849	2867	4034	4916	+ 812	+55.1	+1167	+40.7	+882	+21.9	+3067	+165.9
OKLAHOMA CITY	2495	3307	4583	4755	+ 812	+32.5	+1276	+38.6	+172	+ 3.8	+2260	+ 90.6
SAN JOSE	1772	2215	3515	5177	+ 443	+25.0	+1300	+58.7	+1662	+47.3	+3405	+192.2
TULSA	1867	2683	4018	4515	+ 816	+43.7	+1335	+49.8	+497	+12.4	+2648	+141.8
VIRGINIA BEACH	441	602	901	1407	+ 161	+26.7	+ 299	+49.7	+506	+56.2	+ 966	+219.0
WICHITA	1728	2190	2526	2968	+ 462	+26.7	+ 336	+15.3	+442	+17.5	+1240	+ 71.8
MEDIAN	1750	2203	3215	4145	+ 453	+25.9	+1012	+45.9	+930	+28.9	+2395	+136.8
U.S. TOTAL (000)	1061.7	1187.8	1590.2	1834.7	+ 126.1	+11.9	+402.4	+33.9	+244.5	+15.4	+773.0	+72.8

Sources: U.S. Department of Commerce, Bureau of the Census, Census of Selected Service Industries, "Geographic Area Series" (For Years Indicated).
Changes calculated by the Center for Urban Policy Research.

In absolute numbers of firms, the average intergovernmental city, in 1963, contained nearly 1,400 more service firms than the average non-intergovernmental city. By 1972, this margin had been cut severely as non-intergovernmental cities trailed intergovernmental cities by a mere 560 firms. As of 1977, strong and consistent growth in non-intergovernmental cities allowed the average non-intergovernmental city to surpass the average intergovernmental city by more than 600 firms or 17.3 percent. The population difference between these two city groupings was only 10 percent in 1980.

Newark, again, performed below the level of the average intergovernmental city. From 1963 through 1977, Newark recorded a net decline of nearly one-third of its service base. That percentage loss accounted for 907 service industry firms. Newark experienced, by far, the largest loss of service industries; by comparison the second largest rate of decline was Cleveland's 6.8 percent, representing 374 firms.

Retail Trade

Retail trade is typically locally based and is therefore highly susceptible to population fluctuations and their implied income-loss consequences. Reduced purchasing power is translated directly into reduced consumer markets and, thus, decreased retail sales. As population has flowed away from intergovernmental cities and as income levels have failed to keep pace with inflation, retail establishments have been forced to terminate their businesses or to relocate to more profitable suburban locations. One commentator has also attributed loss of retail sales in large northern cities to the exodus of manufacturing and wholesale trades, stating that typically 20 percent of retail store purchases are made by other local businesses.[6] Finally, the significance of crime cannot be ignored when analyzing trends in the movement of retail sales establishments. The fear on the part of customers, as well as the cost of thefts, robberies and vandalism to proprietors can act to significantly curtail retail activities to a point where certain locations are no longer profitable to continue to operate.

Following the steady declines in population, income, manufacturing and wholesale trade, the intergovernmental city, between 1963 and 1977, experienced a net loss of retail trade establishments (Exhibit 3.10). On an annual basis, the average intergovernmental city lost over 115 firms per year over this fourteen-year period. For Newark, retail establishments either ended operations or abandoned the city for new locations at an annual rate of more than 175 firms per year, for an aggregate fourteen-year decline of more than 50 percent of its retail base.

Retail firms nationally also experienced sluggish growth between 1963 and 1977. With a rate of growth of only 8.6 percent, retail sales establishments grew at the slowest rate of any industrial category. This low rate of growth, however, did not significantly affect non-intergovernmental cities; this group of cities added new retail facilities over the fourteen-year period at a rate of 57.7 percent, or nearly seven times the national average.

EXHIBIT 3.10.—*Retail Trade: All Establishments, 1963-1977*

| | 1963 | 1967 | 1972 | 1977 | CHANGE | | | | | | | |
					1963-1967 Absolute	1963-1967 Percent	1967-1972 Absolute	1967-1972 Percent	1972-1977 Absolute	1972-1977 Percent	1963-1977 Absolute	1963-1977 Percent
INTERGOVERNMENTAL												
AKRON	2239	2101	2117	1855	-138	- 6.2	+ 16	+ 0.7	- 262	-12.4	- 384	-17.2
BALTIMORE	8661	7963	7006	5595	-698	- 8.1	- 957	-12.0	-1411	-20.1	-3066	-35.4
BUFFALO	5332	4902	4047	3181	-430	- 8.1	- 855	-17.4	- 866	-21.4	-2194	-41.1
CINCINNATI	4555	4232	3799	3265	-323	- 7.1	- 433	-10.2	- 534	-14.1	-1290	-28.3
CLEVELAND	8177	7008	6178	4839	-1169	-14.3	- 830	-11.8	-1339	-21.7	-3338	-40.8
LOUISVILLE	3726	3435	3057	2689	-291	- 7.8	- 378	-11.0	- 368	-12.0	-1039	-27.8
MILWAUKEE	6699	6303	5732	4911	-396	- 5.9	- 571	- 9.1	- 821	-14.3	-1788	-26.7
MINNEAPOLIS	3974	3810	3529	2898	-164	- 4.1	- 281	- 7.4	- 631	-17.9	-1076	-27.1
NEWARK	4760	3869	2626	2304	-891	-18.7	-1243	-32.1	- 322	-12.3	-2456	-51.6
ROCHESTER	3055	2928	2509	2017	-127	- 4.2	- 419	-14.3	- 492	-19.6	-1038	-34.0
MEDIAN	4658	4051	3664	3040	-607	-13.0	- 387	- 9.6	- 624	-17.0	-1618	-34.7
NON-INTERGOVERNMENTAL												
ANAHEIM	1027	1471	1537	1728	+444	+43.2	+ 66	+ 4.5	+191	+12.4	+ 701	+68.3
AUSTIN	1761	2077	2755	3124	+316	+18.0	+ 678	+32.6	+369	+13.4	+1363	+77.4
BATON ROUGE	1285	1505	1761	1817	+220	+17.1	+ 256	+17.0	+ 56	+ 3.2	+ 532	+41.4
COLUMBUS	3826	3832	4403	3917	+ 6	+ 0.2	+ 571	+14.9	-486	-11.0	+ 91	+ 2.4
NASHVILLE/DAVIDSON	2419	3338	4136	3745	+919	+38.0	+ 798	+24.0	-391	- 9.5	+1326	+54.8
OKLAHOMA CITY	2982	3851	3986	3752	+869	+29.1	+ 135	+ 3.5	-234	- 5.9	+ 770	+25.8
SAN JOSE	2205	2761	3471	3690	+556	+25.2	+ 710	+25.7	+219	+ 6.3	+1485	+67.3
TULSA	2304	3155	3516	3546	+851	+36.9	+ 361	+11.4	+ 30	+ 0.8	+1242	+53.9
VIRGINIA BEACH	550	744	1074	1373	+194	+35.3	+ 330	+44.4	+299	+27.8	+ 823	+149.6
WICHITA	2286	2811	2813	2708	+525	+23.0	+ 2	+ 0.1	-105	- 3.7	+422	+18.5
MEDIAN	1983	2836	3142	3127	+853	+43.0	+ 306	+10.8	- 15	- 0.4	+1144	+57.7
U.S. TOTAL (000)	1707.9	1763.3	1780.3	1855.1	+ 55.4	+ 3.2	+ 17.1	+ 1.0	+ 74.7	+ 4.2	+ 147.2	+ 8.6

Sources: U.S. Department of Commerce, Bureau of the Census, Census of Retail Trade, "Geographic Area Series" (For Years Indicated).
Changes calculated by the Center for Urban Policy Research.

Wholesale Trade

Historically, wholesale trade establishments have been located in close proximity to manufacturing establishments. Moreover, the reasons for wholesale firms abandoning cities, generally, are similar to the shift of manufacturing firms to outlying areas. Good access to highways and interchanges, the need for large amounts of inexpensive land, and lower construction costs outside the central city have all contributed to the decline of wholesale firms in the intergovernmental city. Wholesale operations are closely linked to retail businesses, and together they form a self-perpetuating force which leads them away from population-loss locations. As retail establishments leave the intergovernmental city, wholesalers who once ordered, stored and, in some cases, repackaged goods for these businesses are encouraged to follow.

Interim period observations add little to the aggregate 1963–1977 picture of intergovernmental wholesale establishment declines. By 1977, the average intergovernmental city retained approximately two-thirds of the number of manufacturing firms that it held in 1963 (Exhibit 3.11). While Cleveland led intergovernmental cities in total firms lost, Newark was hardest hit in percentage terms, losing more than one-half of its wholesale businesses.

In sharp contrast to the intergovernmental cities were the non-intergovernmental cities which gained wholesale facilities at a percentage slightly below the national (urban and suburban) growth rate. However, wholesale trade establishments represent the slowest expanding industrial category of non-intergovernmental cities. Over the entire period 1963–1977, the average non-intergovernmental city gained only 120 new wholesale facilities, for a fourteen-year growth of less than 9 establishments per year.

Employment By Sector

Manufacturing

The intergovernmental city, representative of the older industrial city, exhibits a job base which is dominated by manufacturing employment. In 1963, manufacturing in the average intergovernmental city accounted for over 45,000 more jobs than the second highest industrial category, which was retail sales. In percentage terms, manufacturing firms in intergovernmental cities employed 150 percent more persons than its nearest industrial competitor (Exhibit 3.12). By 1977, the manufacturing sector of the average intergovernmental city continued to employ more persons than any other sector. During the intervening years, 12,500 workers or 16.7 percent of the manufacturing labor force lost jobs in the average intergovernmental city. And, the intergovernmental city's large percentage gain (30 percent) in service sector employees during this same time period could not compensate for this loss of manufacturing jobs; service sector gains represented less than 6,000 net new jobs.

From 1963 to 1967, manufacturing employment, nationally, increased by 13.9 percent. During this time, intergovernmental cities were still adding to their manufacturing employment base, although at a substantially lower rate than the nation as a

EXHIBIT 3.11. — *Wholesale Trade: All Establishments, 1963–1977*

| | | | | | CHANGE | | | | | | | |
	1963	1967	1972	1977	1963-1967 Absolute	1963-1967 Percent	1967-1972 Absolute	1967-1972 Percent	1972-1977 Absolute	1972-1977 Percent	1963-1977 Absolute	1963-1977 Percent
INTERGOVERNMENTAL												
AKRON	539	523	425	408	- 16	- 3.0	- 98	- 18.7	- 17	- 4.0	- 131	- 24.3
BALTIMORE	1906	1700	1400	1162	-206	-10.8	-300	- 17.6	-238	-17.0	-744	- 39.0
BUFFALO	1360	1192	995	763	-168	-12.4	-197	- 16.5	-232	-23.3	-597	- 43.9
CINCINNATI	1564	1474	1237	1102	- 90	- 5.9	-237	- 16.1	-135	-10.9	-462	- 29.5
CLEVELAND	2561	2239	1783	1451	-322	-12.6	-456	- 20.4	-332	-18.6	-1110	- 43.3
LOUISVILLE	954	903	856	825	- 51	- 5.3	- 47	- 5.3	- 31	- 3.6	-129	- 13.5
MILWAUKEE	1688	1450	1243	1077	-238	-14.1	-207	- 14.3	-166	-13.4	-611	- 36.2
MINNEAPOLIS	1730	1529	1360	1225	-201	-11.6	-169	- 11.1	-135	- 9.9	-505	- 29.2
NEWARK	1331	1119	783	644	-212	-15.9	-336	- 30.0	-139	-17.8	-687	- 51.6
ROCHESTER	848	822	711	663	- 26	- 3.1	-111	- 13.5	- 48	- 6.8	-185	- 5.7
MEDIAN	1462	1321	1116	951	-141	- 9.6	-205	- 15.5	-165	-14.8	-511	- 35.0
NON-INTERGOVERNMENTAL												
ANAHEIM	165	223	290	502	+ 58	+35.2	+ 67	+ 30.0	+212	+73.1	+337	+204.2
AUSTIN	333	338	419	500	+ 5	+ 1.5	+ 81	+ 24.0	+ 81	+19.3	+167	+ 50.2
BATON ROUGE	345	411	467	530	+ 66	+19.1	+ 56	+ 13.6	+ 63	+13.5	+185	+ 53.6
COLUMBUS	888	873	980	1078	- 15	- 1.7	+107	+ 12.3	+ 98	+10.0	+190	+ 21.4
NASHVILLE/DAVIDSON	793	887	1071	1183	+ 94	+11.9	+184	+ 20.7	+112	+10.5	+390	+ 49.2
OKLAHOMA CITY	1045	1049	1161	1318	+ 4	+ 0.4	+112	+ 10.7	+147	+12.7	+263	+ 25.2
SAN JOSE	433	412	530	611	- 21	- 4.8	+118	+ 28.6	+ 81	+15.3	+178	+ 41.1
TULSA	805	870	982	1191	+ 65	+ 8.1	+112	+ 12.9	+209	+21.3	+386	+ 48.0
VIRGINIA BEACH	39	68	122	214	+ 29	+74.4	+ 54	+ 79.4	+ 92	+75.4	+175	+448.7
WICHITA	669	679	713	731	+ 10	+ 1.5	+ 34	+ 5.0	+ 18	+ 2.5	+ 62	+ 9.3
MEDIAN	551	546	622	671	- 5	- 0.9	+ 76	+ 13.9	+ 49	+ 7.9	+120	+ 21.8
U.S. TOTAL (000)	308.1	311.5	369.8	382.8	+ 3.4	+ 1.1	+ 58.3	+ 18.7	+ 13.0	+ 3.5	+ 74.7	+ 24.2

Sources: U.S. Department of Commerce, Bureau of the Census, *Census of Wholesale Trade,* "Geographic Area Series" (For Years Indicated). Changes calculated by the Center for Urban Policy Research.

EXHIBIT 3.12. — *Manufactures: All Employees, 1963-1977 (Thousands)*

	1963	1967	1972	1977	CHANGE							
					1963-1967 Absolute	1963-1967 Percent	1967-1972 Absolute	1967-1972 Percent	1972-1977 Absolute	1972-1977 Percent	1963-1977 Absolute	1963-1977 Percent
INTERGOVERNMENTAL												
AKRON	58.7	62.0	50.5	44.4	+ 3.3	+ 5.6	- 11.5	- 18.5	- 6.1	- 12.1	- 14.3	- 24.4
BALTIMORE	103.9	106.7	91.2	72.9	+ 2.8	+ 2.7	- 15.5	- 14.5	- 18.3	- 20.1	- 31.0	- 29.8
BUFFALO	57.0	66.7	53.2	46.4	+ 9.7	+17.0	- 13.5	- 20.2	- 6.8	- 12.8	- 10.6	- 18.6
CINCINNATI	76.6	84.5	68.2	64.4	+ 7.9	+10.3	- 16.3	- 19.3	- 3.8	- 5.6	- 12.2	- 15.9
CLEVELAND	168.9	171.3	131.0	120.8	+ 2.4	+ 1.4	- 40.3	- 23.5	-10.2	- 7.8	- 48.1	- 28.5
LOUISVILLE	58.0	64.0	60.2	61.0	+ 6.0	+10.3	- 3.8	- 5.9	+ 0.8	+ 1.3	+ 3.0	+ 5.2
MILWAUKEE	119.3	118.6	106.3	91.4	- 0.7	- 0.6	- 12.3	- 10.4	-14.9	- 14.0	- 27.9	- 23.4
MINNEAPOLIS	67.0	69.2	57.9	52.0	+ 2.2	+ 3.3	- 11.3	- 16.3	- 5.9	- 10.2	- 15.0	- 22.4
NEWARK	73.7	68.5	47.3	38.6	- 5.2	- 7.1	- 21.2	- 30.9	- 8.7	- 18.4	- 35.1	- 47.6
ROCHESTER	97.3	114.2	89.9	86.5	+16.9	+17.4	- 24.3	- 21.3	- 3.4	- 3.8	- 10.8	- 11.1
MEDIAN	75.2	76.9	64.2	62.7	+ 1.7	+ 2.3	- 12.7	- 16.5	- 1.5	- 2.3	- 12.5	- 16.7
NON-INTERGOVERNMENTAL												
ANAHEIM	45.8	18.9	30.4	39.5	-26.9	-58.7	+ 11.5	+ 60.8	+ 9.1	+ 29.9	- 6.3	- 13.8
AUSTIN	5.1	5.2	7.7	11.5	+ 0.1	+ 2.0	+ 2.5	+ 48.1	+ 3.8	+ 49.4	+ 6.4	+125.5
BATON ROUGE	6.2	11.0	13.0	11.4	+ 4.8	+77.4	+ 2.0	+ 18.2	- 1.6	- 12.3	+ 5.2	+ 83.9
COLUMBUS	65.9	65.4	62.1	55.5	- 0.5	- 0.8	- 3.3	- 5.0	- 6.6	- 10.6	- 10.4	- 15.3
NASHVILLE/DAVIDSON	34.0	46.8	45.9	48.4	+12.8	+37.6	- 0.9	- 1.9	+ 2.5	+ 5.4	+ 14.4	+ 42.4
OKLAHOMA CITY	24.4	26.3	33.8	35.1	+ 1.9	+ 7.8	+ 7.5	+ 28.5	+ 1.3	+ 3.3	+ 10.7	+ 43.9
SAN JOSE	24.2	31.1	30.6	38.4	+ 6.9	+28.5	- 0.5	- 1.6	+ 7.8	+ 25.5	+ 14.2	+ 58.7
TULSA	18.1	22.2	34.8	43.3	+ 4.1	+22.6	+ 12.6	+ 56.8	+ 8.5	+ 24.4	+ 25.2	+139.2
VIRGINIA BEACH	0.2	0.5	1.1	NA	+ 0.3	+150.0	+ 0.6	+120.0	NA	NA	NA	NA
WICHITA	16.2	NA	23.3	28.9	NA	NA	NA	NA	+ 5.6	+ 24.0	+ 12.7	+ 78.4
MEDIAN	24.3	24.3	32.2	39.0	-0-	-0-	+ 7.9	+ 32.5	+ 6.8	+ 21.1	+ 14.7	+ 60.5
U.S. TOTAL (Mil)	17.0	19.3	19.0	19.6	+ 2.4	+13.9	- 0.3	- 1.5	+ 0.6	+ 3.0	+ 2.6	+ 15.5

Sources: U.S. Department of Commerce, Bureau of the Census, Census of Manufactures, "Geographic Area Series" (For Years Indicated). Changes calculated by the Center for Urban Policy Research.

whole. Between 1967 and 1972, the average intergovernmental city experienced a sharp decline in manufacturing employment, equal to 12,700 jobs, or 16.5 percent of its 1967 manufacturing employment level. Between 1972 and 1977, the average intergovernmental city continued to experience losses in manufacturing employment. But in absolute terms, the intergovernmental city cut its rate of manufacturing job loss significantly from the preceding period. Newark's percentage of manufacturing job losses was more than double those of the average intergovernmental city: 47.6 percent of its 1963 manufacturing employees had lost their jobs by 1977.

Manufacturing was also the single largest employment sector in the average non-intergovernmental city in 1967. But rather than losing employees, non-intergovernmental cities gained, by 1977, close to 15,000 new manufacturing jobs, an increase of over 60 percent from the 1967 base. As the nation as a whole added only 15 percent to its manufacturing employment levels, the average non-intergovernmental city's manufacturing employment base expanded at almost four times the percentage rate of national manufacturing employment growth.

Selected Services

For the past three decades, service industries have been growing at rates unmatched by any other sector of the economy. Between 1963 and 1977, the nation added over 3 million workers to the service industry, amounting to a near doubling of its service workers (Exhibit 3.13). While intergovernmental cities added to their service sector employment during that time, their average rate of increase was far below the national average.

Service sector growth has clearly been a non-intergovernmental phenomenon. Expanding at a rate of 152.4 percent during the 1963 to 1977 time period, the average non-intergovernmental city increased its service sector employment from 6,300 to 15,900. While in 1963, the average intergovernmental city employed 9,800 more service sector workers than the typical non-intergovernmental city, by 1977 this margin had closed to 5,800 employees. The average non-intergovernmental city gained fully 300 more service sector jobs annually throughout this period than the average intergovernmental city.

The service sector of Newark was the only intergovernmental service sector to experience a net loss in employment. In fact, the only period in which the city of Newark actually gained in service sector jobs was during the nationally expansive period, 1963 to 1967. This interim period of 6.4 percent growth, however, was not enough to offset the losses sustained during the following two periods. Newark, in 1977, employed nearly 15 percent fewer service sector workers than it did in 1963.

Retail Sales

As consumer markets shift with the geographical redistribution in income, retail sales establishments adjust to the changing market conditions through relocation. This fact is evidenced by the trends in retail employment. Between 1963 and 1967,

EXHIBIT 3.13. — *Selected Services: Paid Employees, 1963-1977 (Thousands)*

| | 1963 | 1967 | 1972 | 1977 | CHANGE | | | | | | | |
					1963-1967 Absolute	1963-1967 Percent	1967-1972 Absolute	1967-1972 Percent	1972-1977 Absolute	1972-1977 Percent	1963-1977 Absolute	1963-1977 Percent
INTERGOVERNMENTAL												
AKRON	5.8	6.8	8.4	8.5	+1.0	+17.2	+1.6	+23.5	+0.1	+1.2	+2.7	+46.6
BALTIMORE	24.9	27.8	34.7	31.1	+2.9	+11.6	+6.9	+24.8	-3.6	-10.4	+6.2	+24.9
BUFFALO	12.6	14.0	17.5	16.2	+1.4	+11.1	+3.5	+25.0	-1.3	-7.4	+3.6	+28.6
CINCINNATI	16.4	18.8	22.8	25.4	+2.4	+14.6	+4.0	+21.3	+2.6	+11.4	+9.0	+54.9
CLEVELAND	26.8	32.1	36.8	33.4	+5.3	+19.8	+4.7	+14.6	-3.4	-9.2	+6.6	+24.6
LOUISVILLE	12.2	12.9	14.9	18.0	+0.7	+5.7	+2.0	+15.5	+3.1	+20.8	+5.8	+47.5
MILWAUKEE	18.0	19.7	25.5	27.2	+1.7	+9.4	+5.8	+29.4	+1.7	+6.7	+9.2	+51.1
MINNEAPOLIS	20.9	21.9	27.4	27.1	+1.0	+4.8	+5.5	+25.1	-0.3	-1.1	+6.2	+29.7
NEWARK	15.7	16.7	15.5	13.5	+1.0	+6.4	-1.2	-7.2	-2.0	-12.9	-2.2	-14.0
ROCHESTER	9.7	10.7	12.8	13.3	+1.0	+10.3	+2.1	+19.6	+0.5	+3.9	+3.6	+37.1
MEDIAN	16.1	17.8	20.2	21.7	+1.7	+10.6	+2.4	+13.5	+1.5	+7.4	+5.6	+34.8
NON-INTERGOVERNMENTAL												
ANAHEIM	4.9	8.2	11.9	16.4	+3.3	+67.3	+3.7	+45.1	+4.5	+37.8	+11.5	+134.7
AUSTIN	5.2	8.0	9.6	13.1	+2.8	+53.8	+1.6	+20.0	+3.5	+36.5	+7.9	+51.9
BATON ROUGE	3.8	5.0	8.4	12.2	+1.2	+31.6	+3.4	+68.0	+3.8	+45.2	+8.4	+221.1
COLUMBUS	13.7	15.9	25.6	26.5	+2.2	+16.1	+9.7	+61.0	+0.9	+3.5	+12.8	+93.4
NASHVILLE/DAVIDSON	8.2	11.2	16.3	21.7	+3.0	+36.6	+5.1	+45.5	+5.4	+33.1	+13.5	+164.6
OKLAHOMA CITY	11.0	12.9	16.0	20.3	+1.9	+17.3	+3.1	+24.0	+4.3	+26.9	+9.3	+84.5
SAN JOSE	6.2	8.6	10.8	15.3	+2.4	+38.7	+2.2	+25.6	+4.5	+41.7	+9.1	+146.8
TULSA	7.6	9.0	14.7	18.2	+1.4	+18.4	+5.7	+63.3	+3.5	+23.8	+10.6	+139.5
VIRGINIA BEACH	1.1	1.7	3.7	6.5	+0.6	+54.5	+2.0	+117.6	+2.8	+75.7	+5.4	+390.9
WICHITA	6.4	7.4	9.5	12.1	+1.0	+15.6	+2.1	+28.4	+2.6	+27.4	+5.7	+89.1
MEDIAN	6.3	8.4	11.4	15.9	+2.1	+33.3	+3.0	+35.7	+4.5	+39.5	+9.6	+152.4
U.S. TOTAL (Mil.)	3.3	3.8	5.3	6.3	+0.6	+17.8	+1.5	+38.1	+1.0	+19.5	+3.1	+94.3

Sources: U.S. Department of Commerce, Bureau of the Census, Census of Selected Service Industries, "Geographic Area Series" (For Years Indicated). Changes calculated by the Center for Urban Policy Research.

the median intergovernmental city experienced a meager one percent growth in retail employment (Exhibit 3.14). For the following two periods, the intergovernmental city lost 5.0 percent and 3.5 percent respectively for a net decrease in retail employment of over 7 percent. Thus, while the nation as a whole added 55 percent to its retail employment, the average intergovernmental city lost 7.3 percent (2,200) of its retail workers.

Non-intergovernmental cities were the major recipients of higher income flows and population, along with major growth in services, wholesale trade and manufacturing. Since these trends represent the requisite ingredients for retail expansion, the non-intergovernmental city was the primary benefactor in this industrial category as well. From 1963 to 1977, retail employment doubled in the average non-intergovernmental city. Representing over 15,000 new employment positions, the retail trade sector was the single largest absolute employment gainer. In contrast to 14,600 persons employed in retail sales in 1963, the average non-intergovernmental city had close to 30,000 retail jobs by 1977. Viewing the interim period, non-intergovernmental city retail employment performance reveals increasing levels, as well as rates of growth, during each consecutive time span.

Newark consistently has been the major intergovernmental city employer loser. In retail sales, Newark lost a full 11,000 more retail jobs than the average intergovernmental city. Relatively, Newark lost six retail jobs for every one job lost by the average intergovernmental city.

Wholesale Trade

Reflecting establishment data for wholesale trade, the average intergovernmental city experienced the loss of a significant proportion of its wholesale employment, while in the typical non-intergovernmental city wholesale employment increased dramatically. Similar to retail trade employment, intergovernmental cities, on average, experienced a small gain in wholesale employment during the initial period reported, 1963–1967, followed by two consecutive periods of decline (Exhibit 3.15). The net result was the loss of 3,600 jobs and a 20 percent reduction in wholesale employment from the 1963 level. While Newark sustained a substantial employment loss, 7,400 jobs, Minneapolis was the largest net employment loser, having had its wholesale job market reduced by close to 9,000 positions. In percentage terms, Newark was the front-runner in the loss column: 43.5 percent of its wholesale employment was eliminated.

At a rate of 122 percent of the 1963 base, non-intergovernmental cities, on average, added to their wholesale trade employment, a total of 4,000 employees. For every one wholesale employee in 1963, there were 2.2 employees in 1977. On an annual basis, non-intergovernmental cities gained new wholesale employees during the 1963–1977 time span at a rate of approximately 300 employees per year. As in every other labor sector, the non-intergovernmental city experienced rates of growth substantially greater than the national average.

EXHIBIT 3.14. — Retail Trade: Paid Employees, 1963–1977 (Thousands)

	1963	1967	1972	1977	CHANGE							
					1963-1967 Absolute	1963-1967 Percent	1967-1972 Absolute	1967-1972 Percent	1972-1977 Absolute	1972-1977 Percent	1963-1977 Absolute	1963-1977 Percent
INTERGOVERNMENTAL												
AKRON	16.0	17.4	16.7	18.4	+1.4	+8.8	-0.7	-4.0	+1.7	+10.2	+2.4	+15.0
BALTIMORE	57.2	56.4	52.4	43.7	-0.8	-2.1	-4.0	-7.1	-8.7	-16.6	-13.5	-23.6
BUFFALO	28.9	28.3	26.9	23.5	-0.6	-2.1	-1.4	-4.9	-3.4	-12.6	-5.4	-18.7
CINCINNATI	31.1	32.2	30.6	31.8	+1.1	+3.5	-1.6	-5.0	+1.2	+3.9	+0.7	+2.3
CLEVELAND	47.0	47.2	41.4	36.9	+0.2	+0.4	-5.8	-12.3	-4.5	-10.9	-10.1	-21.5
LOUISVILLE	24.2	25.7	24.6	23.8	+1.5	+6.2	-1.1	-4.3	-0.8	-3.3	-0.4	-1.7
MILWAUKEE	42.2	46.1	42.6	45.5	+3.9	+9.2	-3.5	-7.6	+2.9	+6.8	+3.3	+7.8
MINNEAPOLIS	36.8	38.6	35.7	33.5	+1.6	-4.3	-2.9	-7.5	-2.2	-6.2	-3.3	-9.0
NEWARK	27.5	22.7	18.5	14.3	-4.8	-17.5	-4.2	-18.5	-4.2	-22.7	-13.2	-48.0
ROCHESTER	22.9	23.0	19.8	15.4	+0.1	+0.4	-3.2	-13.9	-4.4	-22.2	-7.5	-32.8
MEDIAN	30.0	30.3	28.8	27.8	+0.3	+1.0	-1.5	-5.0	-1.0	-3.5	-2.2	-7.3
NON-INTERGOVERNMENTAL												
ANAHEIM	10.0	11.0	11.4	14.8	+1.0	+10.0	+0.4	+3.6	+3.4	+29.8	+4.8	+48.0
AUSTIN	11.3	13.8	21.4	29.7	+0.5	+2.5	+7.6	+7.6	+8.3	+38.8	+18.4	+62.8
BATON ROUGE	10.1	12.6	15.2	19.9	+2.5	+24.8	+2.6	+20.6	+4.7	+30.9	+9.8	+97.0
COLUMBUS	29.5	31.5	40.0	47.6	+2.0	+6.8	+8.5	+27.0	+7.6	+19.0	+18.1	+61.4
NASHVILLE/DAVIDSON	16.2	25.1	32.3	35.3	+8.9	+54.9	+7.1	+28.3	+3.0	+9.3	+19.1	+117.9
OKLAHOMA CITY	NA	NA	29.6	34.6	NA	NA	NA	NA	+5.0	+16.9	NA	NA
SAN JOSE	14.6	19.5	24.9	33.2	+4.9	+33.6	+5.4	+27.7	+8.3	+33.3	+18.6	+127.4
TULSA	15.8	20.6	24.1	30.2	+4.8	+30.4	+3.5	+17.0	+6.1	+25.3	+14.4	+91.1
VIRGINIA BEACH	2.9	4.9	8.2	13.7	+2.0	+69.0	+3.3	+67.3	+5.5	+67.0	+10.8	+372.4
WICHITA	15.4	18.4	19.6	24.9	+3.0	+19.5	+1.2	+6.5	+5.3	+27.0	+9.5	+61.7
MEDIAN	14.6	18.4	21.4	29.7	+3.8	+26.0	+3.0	+16.3	+8.3	+38.8	+15.1	+103.4
U.S. TOTAL	8.4	9.4	NA	13.0	+1.0	+11.5	NA	NA	NA	NA	+4.6	+55.1

Sources: U.S. Department of Commerce, Bureau of the Census, Census of Retail Trade, "Geographic Area Series" (For Years Indicated). Changes calculated by the Center for Urban Policy Research.

EXHIBIT 3.15.—Wholesale Trade: Paid Employees, 1963-1977 (Thousands)

	1963	1967	1972	1977	CHANGE 1963-1967 Absolute	1963-1967 Percent	1967-1972 Absolute	1967-1972 Percent	1972-1977 Absolute	1972-1977 Percent	1963-1977 Absolute	1963-1977 Percent
INTERGOVERNMENTAL												
AKRON	6.4	7.2	6.7	5.9	+0.8	+12.5	-0.5	- 6.9	- 0.8	-19.4	-0.5	- 7.8
BALTIMORE	26.6	25.5	23.9	19.0	-1.1	- 4.1	-1.6	- 6.3	- 4.9	-20.5	-7.6	- 28.6
BUFFALO	15.3	16.4	13.0	9.8	+1.1	+ 7.2	-3.4	-20.7	- 3.2	-24.6	-5.5	- 35.9
CINCINNATI	20.2	21.3	19.8	19.6	+1.1	+ 5.4	-1.5	- 7.0	- 0.2	- 1.0	-0.6	- 3.0
CLEVELAND	33.2	32.6	27.8	25.8	-0.6	- 1.8	-4.8	-14.7	- 2.0	- 7.2	-7.4	- 22.3
LOUISVILLE	14.0	13.9	14.4	13.5	-0.1	- 0.7	+0.5	+ 3.6	- 0.9	- 6.3	-0.5	- 3.6
MILWAUKEE	19.5	21.0	15.9	15.9	+1.5	+ 7.7	-5.1	-24.3	- 0-	- 0-	-3.6	- 18.5
MINNEAPOLIS	27.7	25.6	21.6	18.8	-2.1	- 7.7	-4.0	-15.6	- 2.8	-13.0	-8.9	- 32.1
NEWARK	17.0	16.4	12.0	9.6	-0.6	- 3.5	-4.4	-26.8	- 2.4	-20.0	-7.4	- 43.5
ROCHESTER	9.2	11.2	8.8	7.2	+2.0	+21.7	-2.4	-21.4	- 1.6	-18.2	-2.0	- 21.7
MEDIAN	18.3	18.7	15.2	14.7	+0.4	+ 2.1	-3.5	-18.7	- 0.5	- 3.3	-3.6	- 19.7
NON-INTERGOVERNMENTAL												
ANAHEIM	1.8	3.2	3.4	5.9	+1.4	+77.8	+0.2	+ 6.3	+ 2.5	+73.5	+4.1	+227.8
AUSTIN	3.0	3.9	5.1	5.6	+0.9	+30.0	+1.2	+30.8	+ 0.5	+ 9.8	+2.6	+ 86.7
BATON ROUGE	3.2	4.7	5.5	7.1	+1.5	+46.9	+0.8	+17.0	+ 1.6	+29.1	+3.9	+121.9
COLUMBUS	12.7	14.1	15.2	NA	+1.4	+11.0	+1.1	+ 7.8	NA	NA	NA	NA
NASHVILLE/DAVIDSON	11.4	13.7	16.6	NA	+2.3	+20.2	+2.9	+21.2	NA	NA	NA	NA
OKLAHOMA CITY	NA	NA	NA	17.7	NA	NA	NA	NA	NA	NA	NA	NA
SAN JOSE	5.8	6.1	6.9	8.2	+0.3	+ 5.2	+0.8	+13.1	+ 1.3	+18.8	+2.4	+ 41.4
TULSA	8.3	9.8	10.9	14.9	+1.5	+18.1	+1.1	+11.2	+ 4.0	+36.7	+6.6	+ 79.5
VIRGINIA BEACH	0.2	0.6	1.1	1.9	+0.4	+100.0	+0.5	+83.3	+ 0.8	+72.7	+1.7	+850.0
WICHITA	7.0	7.9	8.2	9.9	+0.9	+12.9	+0.3	+ 3.8	+ 1.7	+20.7	+2.9	+ 41.4
MEDIAN	3.2	4.7	5.5	7.1	+1.5	+46.9	+0.8	+17.0	+ 1.6	+29.1	+3.9	+121.9
U.S. TOTAL (Mil)	3.1	3.5	4.0	4.4	+0.4	+13.9	+0.5	+14.4	+ 0.4	+29.1	+1.3	+ 42.3

Sources: U.S. Department of Commerce, Bureau of the Census, Census of Wholesale Trade, "Geographic Area Series" (For Years Indicated). Changes calculated by the Center for Urban Policy Research.

Sales and Value of Production

Sales and value of production are indicators which directly measure the relative strength of industries across labor markets. Retail sales, primarily, as well as a significant proportion of service receipts are strongly linked to the economic characteristics of the resident population. Where a population is declining and its income levels dwindling, retail sales and service receipts will experience considerably slower growth rates or even absolute declines. Since wholesale trade principally serves other businesses, its sales also fluctuate with changing business climates.

Value of production, also referred to as value added, is used as an equivalent measure for manufacturing industries. Derived by subtracting the total cost of materials from the value of the finished product, value added is also instrumental in determining productivity of different sectors of the manufacturing industry.

Retail Trade Sales

Reflecting strong growth in retail establishments from 1963 to 1977, retail sales in non-intergovernmental cities experienced tremendous growth (Exhibit 3.16). Sales in intergovernmental cities were also up, but at rates far below the national average. During that period, retail sales in the average intergovernmental city grew by close to $460 million, or 61 percent, considerably lower than the nation's growth rate of nearly 200 percent. Non-intergovernmental cities expanded by 1.4 times the rate of national growth, improving their retail sales by a healthy 272.6 percent. In absolute dollars, the average non-intergovernmental city sold almost $1.2 billion more retail goods in 1977 than it marketed in 1963. In 1963, average intergovernmental city retail sales were 177.1 percent of sales in non-intergovernmental cities. By 1977, non-intergovernmental cities were selling $1.3 million in retail goods for every $1 million of goods sold in the intergovernmental city. The net result was that by 1977, average intergovernmental city total retail sales were only 75 percent of those for the average non-intergovernmental city.

Of all intergovernmental cities, Newark was the only city to experience a net decline in retail sales over the entire 1963–1977 period. And, this loss is not easily explained, since during that same time period, Newark's citywide purchasing power grew by more than 155 percent, while median household buying income expanded by 138.7 percent. Newark's largest decline in retail sales was recorded during 1963–1967. Interestingly, that was the period in which the city's effective buying income increased at the greatest rate, climbing $337.4 million, or nearly 44 percent.

Wholesale Trade Sales

Between 1963 and 1977, wholesale trade sales more than tripled nationally (Exhibit 3.17). In similar fashion, non-intergovernmental cities accounted for far more than their share of national growth, increasing their sales over this same period of time by just under $1.2 billion, representing a rate increase of significantly over 300 percent. Intergovernmental cities during that same time span raised their sales of

EXHIBIT 3.16. — *Retail Trade: Sales, 1963–1977 ($ millions)*

	1963	1967	1972	1977	1963-1967 Absolute	1963-1967 Percent	1967-1972 Absolute	1967-1972 Percent	1972-1977 Absolute	1972-1977 Percent	1963-1977 Absolute	1963-1977 Percent
INTERGOVERNMENTAL												
AKRON	422	497	649	960	+ 75	+17.8	+152	+ 30.6	+311	+ 47.9	+ 538	+127.5
BALTIMORE	1317	1539	1811	2089	+222	+16.9	+272	+ 17.7	+278	+ 15.4	+ 772	+ 58.6
BUFFALO	701	796	853	950	+ 95	+13.6	+ 57	+ 7.2	+ 97	+ 11.4	+ 249	+ 35.5
CINCINNATI	800	948	1030	1378	+148	+18.5	+ 82	+ 8.6	+348	+ 33.8	+ 578	+ 72.3
CLEVELAND	1278	1333	1397	1640	+ 55	+ 4.3	+ 64	+ 4.8	+243	+ 17.4	+ 362	+ 28.3
LOUISVILLE	625	733	892	1107	+108	+17.3	+159	21.7	+215	+ 24.1	+ 482	+ 77.1
MILWAUKEE	1076	1275	1426	1961	+199	+18.5	+151	+ 11.8	+535	+ 37.5	+ 885	+ 82.2
MINNEAPOLIS	861	994	1050	1314	+133	+15.4	+ 56	+ 5.6	+264	+ 25.1	+ 453	+ 52.6
NEWARK	665	644	634	643	- 21	- 3.2	- 10	- 1.6	+ 9	+ 1.4	- 22	- 3.3
ROCHESTER	602	725	733	775	+123	+20.4	+ 8	+ 1.1	+ 42	+ 5.7	+ 173	+ 28.7
MEDIAN	751	872	961	1211	+121	+16.1	+ 89	+ 10.2	+250	+ 33.3	+ 460	+ 61.3
NON-INTERGOVERNMENTAL												
ANAHEIM	289	365	440	793	+ 76	+26.3	+ 75	+ 20.5	+353	+ 80.2	+ 504	+174.4
AUSTIN	267	399	768	1454	+132	+49.4	+369	+ 92.5	+686	+ 89.3	+1187	+344.6
BATON ROUGE	284	419	639	1091	+135	+47.5	+220	+ 52.5	+452	+ 70.7	+ 807	+284.2
COLUMBUS	790	1003	1540	2272	+213	+27.0	+537	+ 53.5	+732	+ 47.5	+1482	+187.6
NASHVILLE/DAVIDSON	445	790	1283	1817	+345	+77.5	+493	+ 62.4	+658	+ 51.3	+1496	+236.2
OKLAHOMA CITY	473	733	1126	1817	+260	+55.0	+393	+ 53.6	+691	+ 61.4	+1344	+284.1
SAN JOSE	460	705	1114	1986	+245	+53.3	+409	+ 58.0	+872	+ 78.3	+1526	+331.7
TULSA	429	647	963	1706	+218	+50.8	+316	+ 48.8	+743	+ 77.2	+1277	+297.7
VIRGINIA BEACH	89	155	346	733	+ 66	+74.2	+191	+123.2	+387	+111.8	+ 644	+723.6
WICHITA	418	534	744	1241	+116	+27.8	+210	+ 39.3	+497	+ 66.8	+ 823	+196.9
MEDIAN	424	591	866	1580	+167	+39.4	+275	+ 46.5	+714	+ 82.4	+1156	+272.6
U.S. TOTAL (Bil)	244.2	310.2	457.4	723.1	+ 66.0	+27.0	+147.2	+ 47.5	+265.7	+ 58.1	+ 478.9	+196.1

Sources: U.S. Department of Commerce, Bureau of Labor Statistics, Census of Retail Trade, "Geographic Area Series" (For Years Indicated). Changes calculated by the Center for Urban Policy Research.

EXHIBIT 3.17. — *Wholesale Trade: Sales, 1963–1977 ($ millions)*

| | 1963 | 1967 | 1972 | 1977 | CHANGE | | | | | | | |
					1963-1967 Absolute	1963-1967 Percent	1967-1972 Absolute	1967-1972 Percent	1972-1977 Absolute	1972-1977 Percent	1963-1977 Absolute	1963-1977 Percent
INTERGOVERNMENTAL												
AKRON	853	1205	1001	1285	+352	+41.3	-204	-16.9	+284	+28.4	+432	+50.6
BALTIMORE	2682	2824	3498	4910	+142	+5.3	+674	+23.9	+1412	+40.4	+2228	+83.1
BUFFALO	2101	2250	1910	2025	+149	+7.1	-340	-15.1	+115	+6.0	-76	-3.6
CINCINNATI	3150	3980	4263	6618	+830	+26.3	+313	+7.9	+2355	+55.2	+3468	+110.1
CLEVELAND	4475	4529	5137	6000	+54	+1.2	+608	+13.4	+863	+16.8	+1525	+34.1
LOUISVILLE	1348	1707	2687	3469	+359	+26.6	+980	+57.4	+782	+29.1	+2121	+157.3
MILWAUKEE	2397	3025	3212	4830	+628	+26.2	+187	+6.2	+1618	+50.4	+2433	+101.5
MINNEAPOLIS	3949	3808	3953	5408	-141	-3.6	+145	+3.8	+1455	+36.8	+1459	+36.9
NEWARK	1865	1785	1991	2683	-80	-4.3	+206	+11.5	+692	+34.8	+818	+43.9
ROCHESTER	901	1324	1315	1214	+423	+46.9	-9	-0.7	-101	-7.7	+313	+34.7
MEDIAN	2249	2537	2950	4150	+288	+12.8	+413	+16.3	+1200	+40.7	+1901	+84.5
NON-INTERGOVERNMENTAL												
ANAHEIM	370	467	674	1542	+97	+26.2	+207	+44.3	+868	+128.8	+1172	+316.8
AUSTIN	211	306	494	837	+95	+45.0	+188	+61.4	+343	+69.4	+626	+296.7
BATON ROUGE	236	441	562	1333	+205	+86.9	+121	+27.4	+771	+137.2	+1097	+464.8
COLUMBUS	1140	1466	1945	NA	+326	+28.6	+479	+32.7	NA	NA	NA	NA
NASHVILLE/DAVIDSON	951	1376	2320	NA	+425	+44.6	+944	+68.6	NA	NA	NA	NA
OKLAHOMA CITY	NA	NA	NA	5381	NA	NA	NA	NA	NA	NA	NA	NA
SAN JOSE	504	667	932	1994	+163	+32.3	+265	+39.7	+1062	+113.9	+1490	+295.6
TULSA	831	1158	1787	3893	+327	+39.4	+629	+54.3	+2106	+117.9	+3062	+368.5
VIRGINIA BEACH	23	64	198	387	+41	+178.2	+134	+109.4	+189	+95.5	+364	+1582.6
WICHITA	655	880	674	1542	+225	+34.4	-206	-23.4	+868	+128.8	+887	135.4
MEDIAN	370	441	674	1542	+71	+19.2	+233	+52.8	+868	+128.8	+1172	+316.8
U.S. TOTAL (Bil)	358.3	495.5	695.2	1258.4	+101.2	+28.2	+235.7	+51.3	+563.2	+81.0	+900.1	+251.2

Sources: U.S. Department of Commerce, Bureau of the Census, Census of Wholesale Trade, "Geographic Area Series" (For Years Indicated). Changes calculated by the Center for Urban Policy Research.

wholesale goods, on average, $1.9 billion, or 85 percent. Thus, while intergovernmental cities lagged behind non-intergovernmental cities in their rate of growth, their absolute growth was 58.3 percent greater.

Faster rates of growth in non-intergovernmental cities has led to a convergence, in these two classes of cities, in the sale of wholesale goods. From a 1963 ratio of 6.0 to 1, to a 1977 ratio of 2.7 to 1, non-intergovernmental cities have made significant steps toward narrowing the gaps in wholesale trade vis-à-vis intergovernmental cities. Another way to view the magnitude of growth by non-intergovernmental cities is as follows: for every $1 million in wholesale goods sold in 1963, the average non-intergovernmental city sold over four times that amount by 1977. The average intergovernmental city in 1977 sold only $1.8 million of wholesale products for every $1 million sold in 1963.

There was substantial variation in wholesale trade sales among the intergovernmental cities. Ranging from a low of a loss of nearly four percent in Buffalo, intergovernmental cities experienced 1963 to 1977 growth rates as high as 157.3 percent in Louisville. Newark, which had consistently performed below the level of other intergovernmental cities across most economic indices, made wholesale trade sales no exception. Newark's rate of growth in sales of wholesale products was only one-half the rate of that for the average intergovernmental city.

Selected Service Receipts

Despite literally hundreds of studies, conferences and congressional hearings on urban economic growth and decline, the selection of southern and western regions by service industries for their recent explosive growth has never been fully explained. However, as new establishments begin operations in these regions and as employment in these industries grows, their relative success is reflected in the rising monetary value of their transactions.

From 1963 to 1977, non-intergovernmental cities increased their volume of selected service receipts by 433 percent, or a rate more than two and one-half times the intergovernmental city growth rate (Exhibit 3.18). In absolute value, however, the gain in non-intergovernmental city receipts was on a par with that for intergovernmental cities. Throughout the entire fourteen-year period, intergovernmental cities led non-intergovernmental cities in total receipts but, over the years, there has been some level of convergence between the two city groupings. In 1963, the ratio of intergovernmental city to non-intergovernmental city receipts was 2.7 to 1. By 1977, the ratio was reduced by over 50 percent, to 1.3 to 1.

Only one city, Minneapolis, experienced a rate of growth lower than that of Newark's. And, Akron alone, increased its actual dollar amount of service receipts at an amount less than Newark's aggregate absolute growth level.

Value of Manufacturing Production

In 1963, the ratio of the average intergovernmental city's value of manufacturing production to that of the equivalent non-intergovernmental city was 2.6 to 1 and by

EXHIBIT 3.18. — *Selected Services: Receipts, 1963–1977 ($ millions)*

| | 1963 | 1967 | 1972 | 1977 | CHANGE | | | | | | | |
					1963-1967 Absolute	1963-1967 Percent	1967-1972 Absolute	1967-1972 Percent	1972-1977 Absolute	1972-1977 Percent	1963-1977 Absolute	1963-1977 Percent
INTERGOVERNMENTAL												
AKRON	64.1	85.5	142.4	203.9	+ 21.4	+33.4	+ 56.9	+ 66.5	+ 61.5	+43.2	+139.8	+218.1
BALTIMORE	296.2	467.2	599.8	725.1	+171.0	+57.7	+132.6	+ 28.4	+125.3	+20.9	+428.9	+144.8
BUFFALO	144.4	180.5	302.9	374.3	+ 36.1	+25.0	+122.4	+ 67.8	+ 71.4	+23.6	+229.9	+159.2
CINCINNATI	213.3	285.5	424.3	658.1	+ 72.2	+33.8	+138.8	+ 48.6	+233.8	+55.1	+444.8	+208.5
CLEVELAND	387.7	482.2	788.1	903.6	+ 94.5	+24.4	+305.9	+ 63.4	+115.5	+14.7	+515.9	+133.1
LOUISVILLE	126.8	164.4	278.4	414.6	+ 37.6	+29.7	+114.0	+ 69.3	+136.2	+48.9	+287.8	+227.0
MILWAUKEE	224.9	281.9	468.0	619.6	+ 57.0	+25.3	+186.1	+ 66.0	+151.6	+32.4	+394.7	+175.5
MINNEAPOLIS	343.9	384.6	556.3	725.0	+ 40.7	+11.8	+171.7	+ 44.6	168.7	+30.3	+381.1	+ 68.5
NEWARK	170.5	197.3	317.7	387.3	+ 26.8	+15.7	+120.4	+ 61.0	+ 69.6	+21.9	+216.8	+127.2
ROCHESTER	124.1	174.1	280.3	377.4	+ 50.0	+40.3	+106.2	+ 61.0	+ 97.1	+34.6	+253.3	+204.1
MEDIAN	191.9	239.6	371.0	517.1	+ 47.7	+24.8	+131.4	+ 54.8	+146.1	+39.4	+325.2	+169.5
NON-INTERGOVERNMENTAL												
ANAHEIM	68.8	119.6	241.6	470.8	+ 50.8	+73.8	+122.0	+102.0	+229.2	+95.0	+402.0	+584.3
AUSTIN	45.5	88.2	179.6	332.6	+ 42.7	+93.8	+ 91.4	+103.6	+153.0	+85.2	+287.1	+631.0
BATON ROUGE	37.9	58.3	133.6	281.0	+ 20.4	+53.8	+ 75.3	+129.2	+147.4	+110.3	+243.1	+641.4
COLUMBUS	137.7	186.7	458.9	666.3	+ 49.0	+35.6	+272.2	+145.8	+207.4	+45.2	+528.6	+383.9
NASHVILLE/DAVIDSON	92.2	157.2	328.7	595.6	+ 65.0	+70.5	+171.5	+109.1	+266.9	+81.2	+503.4	+546.0
OKLAHOMA CITY	124.4	167.7	296.9	501.2	+ 43.3	+34.8	+129.2	+ 77.0	+204.3	+68.8	+376.8	+302.9
SAN JOSE	75.3	126.3	225.9	436.0	+ 51.0	+67.7	+ 99.6	+ 78.9	+210.1	+93.0	+360.7	+479.0
TULSA	93.7	128.0	311.9	507.2	+ 34.3	+36.6	+183.9	+143.7	+195.3	+62.6	+413.5	+441.3
VIRGINIA BEACH	14.6	25.4	60.5	147.3	+ 10.8	+74.0	+ 35.1	+138.2	+ 86.8	+143.5	+132.7	+908.9
WICHITA	64.7	93.2	180.0	301.7	+ 28.5	+44.0	+ 86.8	+ 93.1	+121.7	+67.6	+237.0	+366.3
MEDIAN	72.1	123.0	203.0	384.3	+ 50.9	+70.6	+ 80.0	+ 65.0	+181.3	+89.3	+312.2	+433.0
U.S. TOTAL (Bil)	44.6	60.5	113.0	179.5	+ 15.9	+35.7	+ 52.5	+ 86.5	+ 66.5	+58.8	+134.9	+302.5

Sources: U.S. Department of Commerce, Bureau of the Census, Census of Selected Service Industries, "Geographic Area Series" (For Years Indicated). Changes calculated by the Center for Urban Policy Research.

1967, this ratio had grown to 3.9 to 1 (Exhibit 3.19). By the end of the Sixties, manufacturing production in the intergovernmental city was almost fourfold that of the non-intergovernmental city. From 1967 to 1977, however, value of production increases in the average non-intergovernmental city outpaced intergovernmental cities by a rate of nearly 3 to 1. Yet despite higher rate increases in non-intergovernmental cities, by 1977 the intergovernmental city maintained its absolute lead in value added by a margin of 1.8 to 1.

Compared with the national rate of growth in manufacturing value added, the average intergovernmental city rate was approximately 20 percent less; the non-intergovernmental city rate was about 40 percent in excess of the national average.

Summary: Industrial Base Characteristics

Intergovernmental cities relative to non-intergovernmental cities and to national averages from 1963 to 1977 are characterized by absolute percent decreases in both employment and establishments in three of four standard industrial categories: manufacturing, retail and wholesale trade. In selected services, intergovernmental cities' employment and establishments experienced percentage increases but at a lower rate than for non-intergovernmental cities or for the nation as a whole. Across all SIC categories analyzed previously, non-intergovernmental cities either equalled or far exceeded national rates of growth.

Wholesale and retail sales, selected service receipts and value of manufacturing production showed percentage increases in both intergovernmental and non-intergovernmental cities. In most instances, intergovernmental cities lagged national averages by 50 percent whereas non-intergovernmental cities exceeded national averages by this same percentage.

Private Investments

Private sector investment is the most vital component of urban economic growth. While public subsidies can be useful in stimulating and encouraging certain economic development ventures, the amount of funds necessary to build a healthy economy are far beyond the reach of the public purse. Moreover, private spending represents a vote of confidence by the private sector with regard to a locality's prospects for a viable business future.

Private investments also add directly to the resource base of a community. When industrial equipment is upgraded and improved, increased municipal revenues are obtained as a result of taxes on the expanding personal income of workers and rising property values of businesses and residents. Linkages between businesses further imply gains by other sectors of the economy when one industry experiences growth and expansion.

EXHIBIT 3.19. — *Manufactures: Value Added, 1963–1977 ($ millions)*

	1963	1967	1972	1977	1963-1967 Absolute	1963-1967 Percent	1967-1972 Absolute	1967-1972 Percent	1972-1977 Absolute	1972-1977 Percent	1963-1977 Absolute	1963-1977 Percent
INTERGOVERNMENTAL												
AKRON	613.1	805.1	929.5	906.4	+192.0	+ 31.3	+124.4	+15.5	- 23.1	- 2.5	+ 293.3	+ 47.8
BALTIMORE	1292.5	1521.0	1859.3	2565.7	+228.5	+ 17.7	+338.3	+22.4	+ 706.4	+38.0	+1273.2	+ 98.5
BUFFALO	734.2	940.7	1052.1	1445.1	+106.5	+ 14.5	+111.4	+11.8	+ 393.1	+37.4	+ 710.9	+ 96.8
CINCINNATI	769.4	1040.1	1052.8	1653.0	+270.7	+ 35.2	+ 12.7	+ 1.2	+ 600.2	+57.0	+ 883.6	+114.8
CLEVELAND	1997.0	2370.6	2455.1	3523.5	+373.6	+ 18.7	+ 84.5	+ 3.6	+1070.4	+43.6	+1526.5	+ 76.4
LOUISVILLE	944.8	1221.0	1434.2	2551.8	+276.2	+ 29.3	+213.2	+17.5	+1117.6	+77.9	+1607.0	+ 70.1
MILWAUKEE	1401.2	1612.0	1898.1	2736.6	+210.8	+ 15.4	+286.1	+17.7	+ 838.5	+44.2	+1335.4	+ 95.3
MINNEAPOLIS	725.4	852.4	958.3	1318.4	+127.0	+ 17.5	+105.9	+12.4	+ 360.1	+37.6	+ 593.0	+ 81.7
NEWARK	798.3	936.7	803.8	1058.0	+138.4	+ 17.3	-132.9	-14.2	+ 254.2	+31.6	+ 259.7	+ 32.5
ROCHESTER	1393.0	2081.6	2393.3	3456.1	+688.6	+ 49.4	+311.7	+15.0	+1062.8	+44.4	+2063.1	+148.1
MEDIAN	783.9	1130.6	1243.5	2102.4	+346.7	+ 44.2	+112.9	+99.8	+ 858.9	+69.1	+1318.5	+168.2
NON-INTERGOVERNMENTAL												
ANAHEIM	594.7	278.0	672.7	1179.9	-316.7	- 53.2	+394.7	+142.0	+507.2	+75.4	+ 585.2	+ 98.4
AUSTIN	41.7	48.1	94.2	278.2	+ 6.4	+ 15.3	+ 46.1	+ 95.8	+184.0	+195.3	+ 236.5	+567.1
BATON ROUGE	100.0	288.0	394.6	552.3	+188.0	+ 88.0	+106.6	+ 37.0	+157.7	+40.0	+ 88.0	+ 88.0
COLUMBUS	740.4	875.2	1161.6	1732.3	+134.8	+ 18.2	+286.4	+ 32.7	+570.7	+49.2	+ 991.9	+134.0
NASHVILLE/DAVIDSON	330.7	579.2	792.4	1193.9	+248.5	+ 75.1	+213.4	+ 36.8	+401.5	+50.7	+ 863.2	+261.0
OKLAHOMA CITY	278.4	296.0	662.0	1047.7	+ 17.6	+ 6.3	+326.0	+110.4	+385.7	+58.2	+ 769.3	+276.3
SAN JOSE	326.0	483.3	570.3	1141.9	+157.3	+ 48.3	+ 87.0	+ 18.0	+571.6	+100.2	+ 815.9	+250.3
TULSA	166.7	243.8	533.0	1197.9	+ 77.1	+ 46.3	+289.2	+118.6	+664.9	+124.7	+1031.2	+618.6
VIRGINIA BEACH	1.2	3.8	16.0	NA	+ 2.6	+116.7	+ 12.2	+321.1	NA	NA	NA	NA
WICHITA	157.5	NA	426.1	799.7	NA	NA	NA	NA	+373.6	+87.7	+ 642.2	+507.7
MEDIAN	302.2	292.0	616.2	1160.9	- 10.2	- 3.3	+324.2	+111.0	+544.7	+88.3	+ 858.7	+284.2
U.S. TOTAL (Bil)	192.0	262.0	354.0	585.0	+ 70.0	36.5	+ 92.0	+ 35.1	+231.0	+65.3	+ 393.0	+204.7

Sources: U.S. Department of Commerce, Bureau of the Census, Census of Manufactures, "Geographic Area Series" (For Year Indicated). Changes calculated by the Center for Urban Policy Research.

New Capital Expenditures

The rates, as well as the absolute levels of manufacturing capital expenditures, provide the backdrop for the continued decline of manufacturing facilities in intergovernmental cities and the complementary growth of new facilities in non-intergovernmental cities. As non-intergovernmental city manufacturers invest heavily in new and technologically-advanced plants and equipment, the value of their products rises in comparison to the cost of production. On the other hand, in intergovernmental cities, with relatively low levels of private investment, the value of their products decreases. As facilities become older, production processes tend to be outmoded and products are more expensive to produce.

In 1963, intergovernmental city manufacturers invested substantially more money in new facilities and machinery than those of non-intergovernmental cities (Exhibit 3.20). In fact, during that year, intergovernmental cities' new capital expenditures of manufacturers averaged $43.3 million, almost three times the amount invested by non-intergovernmental city manufacturers. For the last period recorded, however, non-intergovernmental cities led intergovernmental cities in terms of the level of new capital expenditures by 7.4 percent, or $91.7 million to $85.4 million. The investment ratio between intergovernmental and non-intergovernmental city manufacturing businesses in 1963 was 2.9 to 1; by 1977 that ratio had fallen to 0.9 to 1. Given the enormous disparity in expenditure levels in 1963 between intergovernmental cities and non-intergovernmental cities, it was necessary for non-intergovernmental cities to expand their expenditure levels at rates significantly greater than those of intergovernmental cities in order to surpass them by 1977. The rates of growth between the two city sets are striking. From 1963 to 1977, non-intergovernmental cities increased their manufacturing plant and equipment expenditures at a rate of close to 600 percent. The intergovernmental city rate of increase was only 16.9 percent of the non-intergovernmental city rate of growth or less than a doubling over the fourteen-year monitoring period.

Growth rates of new capital expenditures in intergovernmental cities ranged from a low in Cleveland of 38.4 percent to a high of 218.9 percent in Rochester. Newark's rate of increase was less than half of that for the average intergovernmental city and only 7.1 percent of the average non-intergovernmental city. Tulsa, Austin, and Baton Rouge were notable non-intergovernmental city gainers, with rate increases of nine to tenfold each. Not including Virginia Beach, for which data are unavailable, the weakest performing non-intergovernmental city in terms of new capital expenditures was Columbus, at a rate of nearly 100 percent increase over the fourteen-year period.

Another way of viewing capital additions is expenditures per establishment. This method of expenditure analysis indicates that while non-intergovernmental cities lagged behind intergovernmental cities by 4.3 percent in terms of new capital expenditures in 1963, by 1967, non-intergovernmental cities were investing in new plants and equipment at a rate of 1.2 to 1 compared to intergovernmental cities. By 1977, non-intergovernmental cities invested more in manufacturing facilities than intergovernmental cities by a ratio of 1.3 to 1. It is interesting to note that between 1967 and 1972, both non-intergovernmental cities and intergovernmental cities experienced decreased expenditure levels for new capital facilities, while the nation as a

EXHIBIT 3.20. — *Manufactures: New Capital Expenditures, 1963-1977 ($ millions)*

	1963	1967	1972	1977	1963-1967 Absolute	1963-1967 Percent	1967-1972 Absolute	1967-1972 Percent	1972-1977 Absolute	1972-1977 Percent	1963-1977 Absolute	1963-1977 Percent
INTERGOVERNMENTAL												
AKRON	41.2	60.5	72.4	73.2	+19.3	+ 46.8	+11.9	+ 19.7	+ 0.8	+ 1.1	+ 32.0	+ 77.7
BALTIMORE	58.9	79.3	130.9	140.2	+20.4	+ 34.6	+51.6	+ 65.1	+ 9.3	+ 7.1	+ 81.3	+138.0
BUFFALO	32.3	73.4	47.2	79.7	+41.1	+127.2	-26.2	- 35.7	+32.5	+ 68.9	+ 47.4	+146.7
CINCINNATI	26.7	48.1	56.2	79.5	+21.4	+ 80.1	+ 8.1	+ 16.8	+23.3	+ 41.5	+ 52.8	+197.8
CLEVELAND	107.7	182.5	102.0	149.1	+74.8	+ 69.5	-31.6	- 17.3	+42.1	+ 46.2	+ 41.4	+ 38.4
LOUISVILLE	45.3	72.7	66.9	91.1	+27.4	+ 60.5	- 5.8	- 8.0	+24.2	+ 36.2	+ 45.8	+101.1
MILWAUKEE	59.1	93.3	97.5	182.2	+34.2	+ 57.9	+ 4.2	+ 4.5	+84.7	+ 86.9	+123.1	+208.3
MINNEAPOLIS	40.8	42.6	44.2	60.6	+ 1.8	+ 4.4	+ 1.6	+ 3.8	+16.4	+ 37.1	+ 19.8	+ 48.5
NEWARK	36.3	90.1	35.6	51.2	+53.8	+148.2	-54.5	- 60.5	+15.6	+ 43.8	+ 14.9	+141.0
ROCHESTER	70.0	174.5	124.9	223.2	+104.5	+149.3	-49.6	- 28.4	+98.3	+ 78.7	+153.2	+218.9
MEDIAN	43.3	76.4	69.7	85.4	+33.1	+ 76.4	- 6.7	- 8.7	+15.7	+ 22.5	+ 42.1	+ 97.2
NON-INTERGOVERNMENTAL												
ANAHEIM	26.1	11.1	27.6	67.6	-15.0	- 57.5	+16.5	+148.6	+40.0	+144.9	+ 41.5	+159.0
AUSTIN	1.8	8.0	7.0	20.8	+ 6.2	+344.4	- 1.0	- 16.7	+14.8	+111.4	+ 19.0	+955.6
BATON ROUGE	10.1	66.9	94.5	102.0	+56.8	+562.4	+27.6	+ 41.3	+ 7.5	+ 7.9	+ 91.9	+909.9
COLUMBUS	44.7	89.3	57.6	86.6	+44.6	+ 99.8	-31.7	- 35.5	+29.0	+ 50.3	+ 41.9	+ 93.7
NASHVILLE/DAVIDSON	14.4	58.0	58.3	96.8	+43.6	+302.8	+ 0.3	+ 0.5	+38.5	+ 66.0	+ 82.4	+472.2
OKLAHOMA CITY	18.0	15.2	30.2	61.7	- 2.8	- 15.6	+15.0	+ 98.7	+31.5	+104.3	+ 43.7	+242.8
SAN JOSE	15.3	56.9	33.9	125.3	+41.6	+271.9	-23.0	- 40.4	+91.4	+269.6	+ 11.0	+719.0
TULSA	9.2	12.4	27.7	103.1	+ 3.2	+ 34.7	+15.3	+123.4	+75.4	+272.2	+ 93.9	+1020.7
VIRGINIA BEACH	0.1	0.3	0.8	NA	+ 0.2	+100.0	+ 0.5	+166.7	NA	NA	NA	NA
WICHITA	6.4	NA	25.3	50.3	NA	NA	NA	NA	+25.0	+ 98.8	+ 43.9	+685.9
MEDIAN	14.9	36.1	32.1	91.7	+21.2	+142.3	- 4.0	- 11.1	+59.6	+185.7	+ 76.8	+575.4
U.S. TOTAL (Bil)	11.4	21.5	24.1	47.5	+10.1	+ 88.6	+ 2.6	+ 12.1	+23.4	+ 97.1	+ 36.1	+316.7

Sources: U.S. Department of Commerce, Bureau of the Census, Census of Manufactures, "Geographic Area Series" (For Years Indicated). Changes calculated by the Center for Urban Policy Research.

whole increased expenditures by 12.1 percent. In net growth, however, the average non-intergovernmental city rate of increase was over 80 percent greater than the national average, while the intergovernmental city rate was 70 percent less than the nation as a whole.

Housing Construction

While serving as an indicator of population growth in an area, housing development is also a principal economic stimulus. The construction of housing units involves financial institutions, contractors, electricians, plumbers, engineers, as well as a host of building material concerns and appliance or furniture retailers. Moreover, for large-scale residential projects, architects, planners and attorneys also participate heavily in the development process. These linkages and others allow the building of housing to have a significant effect on both regional and local economies.

As an indicator of urban economic condition, new private housing implies population growth and a stimulus and regeneration of the tax base of an area. On the other hand, net declines in housing units are usually associated with significant out-migration of population, a stagnating housing market and a generally unpopular and unstable residential environment. These assumptions are borne out in the inter-governmental–non-intergovernmental city comparison which follows.

In terms of planned construction, reflected in authorized building permit data, both intergovernmental and non-intergovernmental cities experienced a net decline in the rate of new housing construction between 1965 and 1976. A generally weak economy, two recessions, and consistently high interest rates, had a staggering effect on the building of new housing units nationally during this period.

Despite this overall gloomy housing picture, non-intergovernmental cities have performed exceedingly well compared to intergovernmental cities. In 1965, the ratio of new housing units authorized in the average non-intergovernmental city (Exhibit 3.21) versus the equivalent intergovernmental city was 2.8 to 1. By 1976, this ratio had increased dramatically by 140 percent to 6.7 to 1. In terms of actual building permits, these ratios represented a 1965 figure of 1,423 authorized building permits in the typical intergovernmental city and 3,933 authorizations in the representative non-intergovernmental city. Authorized permits in 1976 were a mere 467 in the average intergovernmental city and fully 3,152 in the non-intergovernmental city equivalent. In other words, the average non-intergovernmental city authorized a full 2,685 more building permits or nearly six times the level of new residential authorizations for the average intergovernmental city.

The year of highest new authorizations for both city sets from the data presented is the national building boom year, 1970–1971. In that year, 2,090 units were authorized for construction in the average intergovernmental city while 6,082 units were approved for development in the equivalent non-intergovernmental city.

Relatively low levels of new construction combined with major reductions in the existing housing stock, culminated in a net decrease of nearly 6 percent (10,000 units) in the intergovernmental city between 1960 and 1980. On average, the non-intergovernmental city housing stock grew from approximately 70,000 to 177,000

EXHIBIT 3.21. — *Housing: New Private Units Authorized By Building Permits, 1965-1976*

	1965	1971	1975	1976	CHANGE							
					1965-1971 Absolute	1965-1971 Percent	1971-1975 Absolute	1971-1975 Percent	1975-1976 Absolute	1975-1976 Percent	1965-1976 Absolute	1965-1976 Percent
INTERGOVERNMENTAL												
AKRON	1094	1932	408	299	+ 838	+ 76.6	-1524	-78.9	- 109	- 26.7	- 795.	-72.7
BALTIMORE	2097	2533	1295	1539	+ 436	+ 20.8	-1238	-48.9	+ 244	+ 18.8	- 558	-26.6
BUFFALO	360	235	35	201	- 125	- 34.7	- 200	-85.1	+ 166	+474.3	- 159	-44.2
CINCINNATI	2411	3829	803	807	+1418	+ 58.8	-3026	-79.0	+ 4	+ 0.5	-1604	-66.5
CLEVELAND	1134	1573	370	394	+ 439	+ 38.7	-1203	-76.5	+ 24	+ 6.5	- 740	-65.3
LOUISVILLE	1711	2247	369	216	+ 536	+ 31.3	-1878	-83.6	- 153	- 41.5	-1495	-87.4
MILWAUKEE	3106	3625	735	1920	+ 519	+ 16.7	-2890	-79.7	+1185	+161.2	-1186	-38.2
MINNEAPOLIS	1898	1823	372	769	- 75	- 4.0	-1451	-79.6	+ 397	+106.7	-1129	-59.5
NEWARK	447	226	355	539	- 221	- 49.4	+ 129	+57.1	+ 184	+ 51.8	+ 92	+20.6
ROCHESTER	558	2586	176	24	+2028	+363.4	-2410	-93.2	- 152	- 86.4	- 534	-95.7
MEDIAN	1423	2090	371	467	+ 667	+ 46.9	-1719	-82.2	+ 96	+ 25.9	- 956	-67.2
NON-INTERGOVERNMENTAL												
ANAHEIM	2218	2296	1696	2781	+ 78	+ 3.5	- 600	-26.1	+1085	+ 64.0	+ 563	+25.4
AUSTIN	4596	7324	2032	3075	+2728	+ 59.4	-5292	-72.3	+1043	+ 51.3	-1521	-33.1
BATON ROUGE	3130	5638	2465	3792	+2508	+ 80.1	-3173	-56.3	+1327	+ 53.8	+ 662	+21.2
COLUMBUS	5580	12072	2300	3971	+6492	+116.3	-9772	-80.9	+1671	+ 72.7	-1609	-28.8
NASHVILLE/DAVIDSON	4559	6819	1955	3461	+2260	+ 49.6	-4864	-71.3	+1506	+ 77.0	-1098	-24.1
OKLAHOMA CITY	3895	9373	1692	2719	+5478	+140.6	-7681	-81.9	+1027	+ 60.7	-1176	-30.2
SAN JOSE	7377	10645	4683	7337	+3268	+ 44.3	-5962	-56.0	+2654	+ 56.7	- 40	- 0.5
TULSA	3971	5251	1719	3091	+1280	+ 32.2	-3532	-67.3	+1372	+ 79.8	- 880	-22.2
VIRGINIA BEACH	2587	6526	2137	3213	+3939	+152.3	-4389	-67.3	+1076	+ 50.4	+ 626	+24.2
WICHITA	1426	1134	2386	2591	- 292	- 20.5	+ 1252	+110.4	+ 205	+ 8.6	+1165	+81.7
MEDIAN	3933	6082	2085	3152	+2149	+ 54.6	- 3997	-65.7	+1067	+ 51.2	- 781	-19.9

Source: U.S. Department of Commerce, Bureau of the Census, *County and City Data Book*, 1977. Changes calculated by the Center for Urban Policy Research

units, accounting for a net increase of close to 160 percent. The result of these trends was that whereas in 1960 the intergovernmental city had 2.5 times the number of residences of the non-intergovernmental city, by 1980 the intergovernmental city had nearly 10 percent fewer residential units (Exhibit 3.22).

Not all intergovernmental cities experienced small net losses in housing units over the twenty-year period. Newark, Buffalo, and Cleveland during this twenty-year period, lost between 10 and 15 percent of their residential stock. Akron, Baltimore, and Louisville actually gained 2.5 to 5 percent in additional residential units.

Housing disinvestment translates directly into reduced rent revenues, decreasing home values and a diminished local tax base. Although the data for 1978 are incomplete for non-intergovernmental cities, they do show a trend toward lower rents and home prices as a result of declining housing demand in the intergovernmental city.

From 1960 to 1978, median single-family housing value in the intergovernmental city increased 116.5 percent from its 1960 level of $12,700 to a 1978 figure of $27,500 (Exhibit 3.23). By comparison, the average non-intergovernmental city house value rose from $11,600 in 1960 to $39,000 in 1978, a net increase of 236.2 percent. While, in the average intergovernmental city, single-family housing value in 1960 was approximately 10 percent greater than that in its non-intergovernmental city equivalent, by 1978 it was over 40 percent less. Surprisingly, Newark has been able to maintain relatively high housing value compared with other intergovernmental cities, despite its relatively poor performance on almost every other economic indicator. For the period 1960–1978, Newark's average housing value increased at a full 120.8 percent of the average intergovernmental city rate to $32,500 for the latter year.

The disparity between growth in median gross rent increases for the two sets of cities was not as pronounced as that for value. Non-intergovernmental city rent grew at a rate of only 15 percent greater than that for intergovernmental cities (Exhibit 3.24). Still, the average non-intergovernmental city's annual rent increase of nearly 10 percent since 1960, allowed it to surpass rents charged in the average intergovernmental city by 6.8 percent in 1978. Rental property in Newark follows the same general trend. Newark's median gross rent, while slightly higher than the average intergovernmental city in 1960, was 13.5 percent less by 1978. This drop in rents relative to the average intergovernmental city was the result of a net eighteen-year increase in rents of only 41.0 percent, a rate one-half of the average intergovernmental city increase.

Summary: Private Investments

New capital expenditures, housing value and median gross rent witnessed significant gains both in non-intergovernmental cities and for the nation as a whole. Intergovernmental cities also demonstrated increases in these indicators of private sector performance but lagged far behind non-intergovernmental cities and national averages.

In housing construction, both for new units authorized and for total units in place, intergovernmental cities showed net *losses* in contrast to considerable gains in non-intergovernmental cities and more modest gains in other locations nationally.

EXHIBIT 3.22. — *Housing: Total Units, 1960-1980 (Thousands)*

| | 1960 | 1970 | 1980 | CHANGE | | | | | |
				1960-1970 Absolute	1960-1970 Percent	1970-1980 Absolute	1970-1980 Percent	1960-1980 Absolute	1960-1980 Percent
INTERGOVERNMENTAL									
AKRON	94.3	95.8	96.7	+ 1.5	+ 1.6	+ 1.1	+ 1.1	+ 2.4	+ 2.5
BALTIMORE	290.2	305.5	302.7	+15.3	+ 5.3	- 2.8	- 0.9	+12.5	+ 4.3
BUFFALO	177.2	166.1	156.5	-11.1	- 6.3	- 9.6	- 5.8	-20.7	-11.7
CINCINNATI	171.7	172.8	172.7	+ 1.1	+ 0.6	- 0.1	- 0.1	+ 1.0	+ 0.6
CLEVELAND	282.9	264.1	239.6	-18.8	- 6.6	-24.5	- 9.3	-43.3	-15.3
LOUISVILLE	128.3	129.8	126.1	+ 1.5	+ 1.2	- 3.7	- 2.9	- 2.2	- 1.7
MILWAUKEE	241.6	246.1	253.1	+ 4.5	+ 1.9	+ 7.0	+ 2.8	+11.5	+ 4.8
MINNEAPOLIS	173.2	167.2	168.7	- 6.0	- 3.5	+ 1.5	+ 0.9	- 4.5	- 2.5
NEWARK	134.9	127.2	121.1	- 7.7	- 5.7	- 6.1	- 4.8	-13.8	-10.2
ROCHESTER	107.2	105.1	102.6	- 2.1	- 2.0	- 2.5	- 2.4	- 4.6	- 4.3
MEDIAN	172.5	166.7	162.6	- 5.8	- 3.4	- 4.1	- 2.5	- 9.9	- 5.7
NON-INTERGOVERNMENTAL									
ANAHEIM	32.7	56.1	83.6	+23.4	+71.6	+27.5	+49.0	+50.9	+155.7
AUSTIN	56.5	85.9	146.5	+29.4	+52.0	+60.6	+70.5	+90.5	+159.3
BATON ROUGE	45.8	56.4	84.1	+10.6	+23.1	+21.7	+49.1	+38.3	+83.6
COLUMBUS	152.0	182.5	236.7	+30.5	+20.1	+54.2	+29.7	+84.7	+55.7
NASHVILLE/DAVIDSON	53.6	147.3	179.1	+93.7	+174.8	+31.8	+21.6	+125.5	+234.1
OKLAHOMA CITY	115.1	139.0	177.1	+23.9	+20.8	+38.1	+27.4	+62.0	+53.9
SAN JOSE	68.9	139.8	219.0	+70.9	+102.9	+79.2	+56.7	+150.1	+217.9
TULSA	115.1	121.4	156.4	+ 6.3	+ 5.4	+35.0	+28.8	+41.3	+35.9
* VIRGINIA BEACH	NA	48.0	92.0	NA	NA	+44.0	+91.7	NA	NA
WICHITA	88.5	99.9	116.6	+11.4	+12.9	+16.7	+16.7	+28.1	+31.8
MEDIAN	68.9	121.4	177.1	+52.5	+76.2	+55.7	+45.9	+108.2	+157.0
U.S. TOTAL	56.6	67.7	82.8	+11.1	+19.7	+15.1	+22.4	+26.3	+46.5

* Preliminary Estimate.
Sources: U.S. Department of Commerce, Bureau of the Census, Census of Population and Housing, 1960 and 1970; U.S. Department of Commerce, Bureau of the Census, 1980 Census of Population and Housing, "Final Counts." Changes calculated by the Center for Urban Policy Research.

EXHIBIT 3.23. — *Housing: Owner Median Value, 1960-1978 (Thousands)*

				CHANGE					
	1960	1970	1978	1960-1970 Absolute	1960-1970 Percent	1970-1978 Absolute	1970-1978 Percent	1960-1978 Absolute	1960-1978 Percent
INTERGOVERNMENTAL									
AKRON	12.7	15.1	32.5	+ 2.4	+ 18.9	+ 17.4	+ 115.2	+ 19.8	+ 155.9
BALTIMORE	9.0	10.0	32.5	+ 1.0	+ 11.1	+ 12.5	+ 125.0	+ 13.5	+ 150.0
BUFFALO	11.7	12.8	18.8	+ 1.1	+ 9.4	+ 6.0	+ 46.9	+ 7.1	+ 60.7
CINCINNATI	15.1	16.4	32.5	+ 1.3	+ 8.6	+ 16.1	+ 98.2	+ 17.4	+ 115.2
CLEVELAND	13.9	16.7	27.5	+ 2.8	+ 20.1	+ 10.8	+ 64.7	+ 13.6	+ 97.8
LOUISVILLE	10.4	12.5	27.5	+ 2.1	+ 4.5	+ 15.0	+ 120.0	+ 17.1	+ 164.4
MILWAUKEE	15.1	18.2	40.5	+ 3.1	+ 20.5	+ 22.3	+ 122.5	+ 25.4	+ 168.2
MINNEAPOLIS	13.7	17.9	NA	+ 4.2	+ 30.6	NA	NA	NA	NA
NEWARK	13.5	17.3	32.5	+.3.8	+ 28.1	+ 15.2	+ 87.8	+ 19.0	+ 140.7
ROCHESTER	12.0	15.1	27.5	+ 3.1	+ 25.8	+ 12.4	+ 82.1	+ 15.5	+ 129.2
MEDIAN	12.7	15.1	27.5	+ 2.4	+ 18.9	+ 12.4	+ 82.1	+ 14.8	+ 116.5
NON-INTERGOVERNMENTAL									
ANAHEIM	16.4	24.8	NA	+ 8.4	+ 51.2	NA	NA	NA	NA
AUSTIN	10.8	15.9	NA	+ 5.1	+ 47.2	NA	NA	NA	NA
BATON ROUGE	12.9	17.4	NA	+ 4.5	+ 34.9	NA	NA	NA	NA
COLUMBUS	13.3	17.1	40.5	+ 3.8	+ 28.6	+ 23.4	+136.8	+ 27.2	+ 204.5
NASHVILLE/DAVIDSON	7.8	15.7	37.5	+ 7.9	+101.3	+ 21.8	+138.9	+ 29.7	+ 380.7
OKLAHOMA CITY	9.8	12.9	37.5	+ 3.1	+ 31.6	+ 24.6	+190.7	+ 27.7	+ 282.7
SAN JOSE	16.3	25.4	87.5	+ 9.1	+ 55.8	+ 62.1	+244.5	+ 71.2	+ 436.8
TULSA	9.8	14.4	NA	+ 4.6	+ 46.9	NA	NA	NA	NA
VIRGINIA BEACH	NA	21.4	NA	NA	NA	NA	NA	NA	NA
WICHITA	10.6	13.5	NA	+ 2.9	+ 27.4	NA	NA	NA	NA
MEDIAN	11.6	16.4	39.0	+ 4.8	+ 41.4	+ 22.6	+137.8	+ 27.4	+ 236.2

Sources: U.S. Department of Commerce, Bureau of the Census, Census of Housing, 1960; U.S. Department of Commerce, Bureau of the Census, Census of Housing Characteristics for States, Cities and Counties, 1970; U.S. Department of Commerce, Department of the Census, Annual Housing Survey, 1978. Changes calculated by the Center for Urban Policy Research.

EXHIBIT 3.24. — *Housing: Median Gross Rent, 1960-1978 (Absolute Dollars)*

				CHANGE					
	1960	*1970*	*1978*	*1960-1970 Absolute*	*1960-1970 Percent*	*1970-1978 Absolute*	*1970-1978 Percent*	*1960-1978 Absolute*	*1960-1978 Percent*
INTERGOVERNMENTAL									
AKRON	72	85	165	+ 13	+ 18.1	+ 80	+ 94.1	+ 93	+129.2
BALTIMORE	76	88	179	+ 12	+ 15.8	+ 91	+103.4	+103	+135.5
BUFFALO	70	70	163	-0-	-0-	+ 93	+132.9	+ 93	+132.9
CINCINNATI	66	80	176	+ 14	+ 21.2	+ 96	+120.0	+110	+166.7
CLEVELAND	79	79	145	-0-	-0-	+ 66	+ 83.5	+ 66	+ 83.5
LOUISVILLE	63	69	180	+ 6	+ 9.5	+111	+160.8	+117	+185.7
MILWAUKEE	87	95	205	+ 12	+ 13.8	+110	+115.8	+118	+135.6
MINNEAPOLIS	77	105	NA	+ 28	+ 36.4	NA	NA	NA	NA
NEWARK	77	104	155	+ 27	+ 35.1	+ 51	+ 49.0	+ 78	+101.3
ROCHESTER	78	100	190	+ 22	+ 28.2	+ 90	+ 90.0	+112	+143.6
MEDIAN	76	85	176	+ 9	+ 11.8	+ 91	+107.1	+100	+142.8
NON-INTERGOVERNMENTAL									
ANAHEIM	95	137	NA	+ 42	+ 44.2	NA	NA	NA	NA
AUSTIN	64	105	NA	+ 41	+ 64.1	NA	NA	NA	NA
BATON ROUGE	61	77	NA	+ 16	+ 26.2	NA	NA	NA	NA
COLUMBUS	81	87	195	+ 6	+ 7.4	+108	+124.1	+114	+140.7
NASHVILLE/DAVIDSON	53	81	180	+ 28	+ 52.8	+ 99	+122.2	+127	+239.6
OKLAHOMA CITY	61	72	173	+ 11	+ 18.0	+101	+140.3	+112	+183.6
SAN JOSE	90	132	256	+ 42	+ 46.7	+124	+ 93.9	+166	+184.4
TULSA	61	86	NA	+ 25	+ 41.0	NA	NA	NA	NA
VIRGINIA BEACH	NA	127	NA	NA	NA	NA	NA	NA	NA
WICHITA	72	82	NA	+ 10	+ 13.9	NA	NA	NA	NA
MEDIAN	71	84	188	+ 13	+ 18.3	+104	+123.8	+117	+164.8

Sources: U.S. Department of Commerce, Bureau of the Census, Census of Housing, 1960; U.S. Department of Commerce, Bureau of the Census, Census of Housing Characteristics for States, Cities and Counties, 1970; U.S. Department of Commerce, Bureau of the Census, Annual Housing Survey, 1978. Changes calculated by the Center for Urban Policy Research.

Private investment in the intergovernmental city, across a variety of indices, was either decreasing absolutely or lagging badly behind both national averages and averages for non-intergovernmental cities.

Conclusion

The distinguishing feature between healthy cities and those undergoing economic hardship is their ability to respond to changing market conditions. Factors such as regional, national and international competition, changing life-styles and patterns of demand, technological innovations and production processes, and aging capital facilities necessitate constant adjustments in a city's economic resource base in order for that economy to remain competitive. For some localities, business fluctuations will result in more competitive firms and employment opportunities, higher income levels, expanded markets and relatively stronger economies. Other communities will be unable to react to changing market conditions and will experience either slower economic growth rates or actual declines.

Although disaggregated industrial base characteristics (establishments, employment, sales and receipts and value added by SIC grouping) lend insight into specific problem areas for intergovernmental cities, the four primary indicators of economic activity, taken together, offer the clearest comparative measure of aggregate economic performance. From these indicators, it becomes obvious that the intergovernmental city represented the case of the city unable to favorably respond to changing market conditions.

According to population, employment, and per capita income performance indicators, the average intergovernmental city experienced either actual decline or at best, a relative decrease in levels compared with the non-intergovernmental city between 1960 and 1980. And, while relative intergovernmental city declines in per capita income were minor compared with net losses in population and employment, it is important to note that much of the intergovernmental city income is composed of transfer payments to individual residents which inflates the income of these cities.

When the four indicators of economic performance are aggregated, they produce a comparative index of urban stress. Taking a static measure of the absolute levels of economic activity for 1960–1963 and 1977–1980 reveals a significant shift in economic performance over the fourteen to twenty-year period (Exhibit 3.25). In 1960–1963, five intergovernmental cities ranked as the least distressed, while of the five most distressed cities, three were non-intergovernmental cities.

Level of Economic Activity—1960–1963

Most Distressed	*Least Distressed*
Baton Rouge	Milwaukee
Austin	Minneapolis
Louisville	Cincinnati
Newark	Baltimore
Anaheim	Cleveland

By 1977–1980, only two intergovernmental cities, Milwaukee and Minneapolis, maintained their status as least distressed, while Cleveland, Baltimore, and Cincin-

EXHIBIT 3.25.—*Comparative Index of Economic Performance:*
Level of Economic Activity, 1960–1963
(Ranked in Order of Least Distressed)[1]

	Rank	Score	Popu- lation	Employ- ment	Unemploy- ment	Per Capita Income
INTERGOVERNMENTAL						
AKRON	11	37	12	12	9	4
BALTIMORE	4	28	1	2	12	13
BUFFALO	10	36	4	6	15	11
CINCINNATI	3	27	5	5	8	9
CLEVELAND	5	30	2	1	13	14
LOUISVILLE	15	47	9	10	11	17
MILWAUKEE	1	16	3	3	5	5
MINNEAPOLIS	2	22	6	4	4	8
NEWARK	14	45	8	7	14	16
ROCHESTER	9	35	11	9	8	7
NON-INTERGOVERNMENTAL						
ANAHEIM	13	44	19	18	5	2
AUSTIN	16	51	16	16	1	18
BATON ROUGE	17	60	18	17	10	15
COLUMBUS	8	34	7	8	7	12
NASHVILLE-DAVIDSON	--	--	17	--	6	19
OKLAHOMA CITY	7	32	10	11	2	9
SAN JOSE	9	35	15	14	3	3
TULSA	6	31	13	13	4	1
VIRGINIA BEACH	--	--	--	--	--	--
WICHITA	12	40	14	15	6	5

[1]For example, 1 equals the highest population, employment and per capita income levels. Unemployment is ranked in reverse order, i.e., 1 equals the lowest unemployment figure.

Sources: Exhibits 3.1 through 3.4.

nati fell in the neutral, mid-city range. (See Exhibit 3.26 for the full twenty-city ranking.)

Level of Economic Activity—1977–1980

Most Distressed	Least Distressed
Newark	Milwaukee
Akron	Oklahoma City
Rochester	Louisville
Buffalo	Minneapolis
Columbus	Anaheim

Static levels of economic activity, however, do not indicate direction and are, therefore, insufficient gauges of economic performance. When change over time is considered, the ranking of cities further favored non-intergovernmental cities. The full city ranking is shown in Exhibit 3.27 and is summarized at the bottom of the next page.

EXHIBIT 3.26.—*Comparative Index of Economic Performance:*
Level of Economic Activity, 1977–1980
(Ranked in Order of Least Distressed)[1]

	Rank	Score	Population	Employ-ment	Unemploy-ment	Per Capita Income
INTERGOVERNMENTAL						
AKRON	15	61	18	16	13	14
BALTIMORE	6	35	1	2	15	17
BUFFALO	13	55	11	10	16	18
CINCINNATI	8	37	8	6	10	13
CLEVELAND	7	36	4	1	12	19
LOUISVILLE	9	39	14	8	8	9
MILWAUKEE	1	20	3	3	4	10
MINNEAPOLIS	4	25	9	7	6	3
NEWARK	16	63	13	13	17	20
ROCHESTER	14	57	17	11	14	15
NON-INTERGOVERNMENTAL						
ANAHEIM	10	43	19	15	7	2
AUSTIN	6	35	12	9	2	12
BATON ROUGE	--	--	20	--	9	11
COLUMBUS	12	52	5	4	7	16
NASHVILLE-DAVIDSON	--	--	6	--	5	8
OKLAHOMA CITY	2	21	7	5	3	6
SAN JOSE	5	29	2	12	11	4
TULSA	3	22	10	8	3	1
VIRGINIA BEACH	--	--	16	--	--	7
WICHITA	3	51	15	14	1	5

[1]For example, 1 equals the highest population, employment and per
capita income levels. Unemployment is ranked in reverse order, i.e.,
1 equals the lowest unemployment figure.

Sources: Exhibits 3.1 through 3.4.

Performance Based on Absolute Levels of Change
1960–1963 to 1977–1980

Most Distressed	Least Distressed
Buffalo	Austin
Newark	Tulsa
Rochester	Wichita
Cleveland	Oklahoma City
Akron	San Jose

Based on absolute change, not a single intergovernmental city ranked as least distressed, while all five most-distressed positions were held by intergovernmental cities. Although Milwaukee was ranked as the least-distressed city based on its static performance in 1977–1980, in terms of change, it rates in twelfth place. This situation arose because of Milwaukee's strong economic position prior to the 1960s. Although it has declined relative to the median non-intergovernmental city, its diverse economic base cushioned it from the immediate effects of manufacturing employment losses when measured in absolute terms.

EXHIBIT 3.27. — *Comparative Index of Economic Performance: Absolute Change,*
1960–1963 to 1977–1980 (Ranked in Order of Least Distressed)[1]

	Rank	Score	Population	Employ-ment	Unemploy-ment	Per Capita Income
INTERGOVERNMENTAL						
AKRON	12	52	12	11	14	15
BALTIMORE	10	48	11	13	11	13
BUFFALO	15	69	18	17	16	18
CINCINNATI	9	44	14	9	9	12
CLEVELAND	13	58	19	16	6	17
LOUISVILLE	7	32	16	8	5	3
MILWAUKEE	11	50	10	14	12	14
MINNEAPOLIS	8	35	15	12	4	4
NEWARK	14	64	13	15	17	19
ROCHESTER	13	58	17	10	15	16
NON-INTERGOVERNMENTAL						
ANAHEIM	5	26	3	1	13	9
AUSTIN	1	18	4	2	10	2
BATON ROUGE	--	--	5	--	--	6
COLUMBUS	6	28	8	7	8	11
NASHVILLE-DAVIDSON	--	--	2	--	2	1
OKLAHOMA CITY	4	24	7	5	7	5
SAN JOSE	7	32	1	3	18	10
TULSA	2	21	6	4	3	8
VIRGINIA BEACH	--	--	--	--	--	--
WICHITA	3	23	9	6	1	7

[1]For example, 1 equals the highest population, employment and per
capita income levels. Unemployment is ranked in reverse order, i.e.,
1 equals the lowest unemployment figure.

Sources: Exhibits 3.1 through 3.4.

On the basis of percent change in the basic economic indicators, an index which measures performance of a city over time, based on growth or decline relative to itself, these rankings do not differ significantly from those obtained in the former absolute change ordering. (See Exhibit 3.28 for the full twenty-city ranking.) Four out of five cities appear in each grouping.

Performance Based on Rates of Change
1960–1963 to 1977–1980

Most Distressed	Least Distressed
Cleveland	Tulsa
Buffalo	Wichita
Baltimore	Austin
Newark	Oklahoma City
Rochester	Anaheim

A final ranking is derived from a composite between actual level of economic activity for 1977–1980 and the rate of change between 1960–1963 and 1977–1980. This

EXHIBIT 3.28. — *Comparative Index of Economic Performance: Percentage Change, 1960–1963 to 1977–1980 (Ranked in Order of Least Distressed)*[1]

	Rank	Score	Population	Employ- ment	Unemploy- ment	Per Capita Income
INTERGOVERNMENTAL						
AKRON	9	46	10	9	14	13
BALTIMORE	13	57	16	14	11	16
BUFFALO	14	67	17	16	16	18
CINCINNATI	10	47	15	11	9	12
CLEVELAND	15	68	18	17	6	17
LOUISVILLE	7	34	12	8	5	9
MILWAUKEE	11	51	13	15	12	11
MINNEAPOLIS	6	33	14	12	4	3
NEWARK	12	55	11	13	17	14
ROCHESTER	11	51	11	10	15	15
NON-INTERGOVERNMENTAL						
ANAHEIM	4	24	4	3	13	4
AUSTIN	2	22	3	1	10	8
BATON ROUGE	--	--	8	--	--	10
COLUMBUS	8	42	6	6	8	14
NASHVILLE-DAVIDSON	--	--	2	--	2	2
OKLAHOMA CITY	3	23	7	2	7	7
SAN JOSE	5	30	1	5	18	6
TULSA	1	13	5	4	3	1
VIRGINIA BEACH	--	--	--	--	--	--
WICHITA	2	22	9	7	1	5

[1]For example, 1 equals the highest population, employment and per capita income levels. Unemployment is ranked in reverse order, i.e., 1 equals the lowest unemployment figures.

Sources: Exhibits 3.1 through 3.4.

ranking is detailed in Exhibit 3.29 and summarized below. This measurement brings one intergovernmental city, Minneapolis, into the top five performing cities category. Because of the regional government of which Minneapolis is a part, it has always been influenced heavily by other levels of government but has not had the dire economic consequences of most other intergovernmental cities. This is related to tax base sharing, growth controls and other land use experiments. As with all other categories reflecting change, all five most distressed cities are found within the intergovernmental city set.

Composite Between Actual Level of Economic Activity for 1977–1980 and Rate of Change Between 1960–1963 and 1977–1980

Most Distressed	*Least Distressed*
Buffalo	Tulsa
Newark	Oklahoma City
Rochester	Austin
Akron	Minneapolis
Cleveland	San Jose

EXHIBIT 3.29. — *Comparative Index of Economic Performance: Aggregate of 1977–1980 Level and Percentage Change, 1960–1963 to 1977–1980 (Ranked in Order of Least Distressed)*[1]

	Rank	Total Score
INTERGOVERNMENTAL		
AKRON	13	107
BALTIMORE	10	92
BUFFALO	16	122
CINCINNATI	9	84
CLEVELAND	12	104
LOUISVILLE	8	73
MILWAUKEE	7	71
MINNEAPOLIS	4	58
NEWARK	15	118
ROCHESTER	14	108
NON-INTERGOVERNMENTAL		
ANAHEIM	6	67
AUSTIN	3	57
BATON ROUGE	--	--
COLUMBUS	11	94
NASHVILLE-DAVIDSON	--	--
OKLAHOMA CITY	2	44
SAN JOSE	5	59
TULSA	1	35
VIRGINIA BEACH	--	--
WICHITA	8	73

[1]For example, 1 equals the highest population, employment and per capita income levels. Unemployment is ranked in reverse order, i.e., 1 equals the lowest unemployment figure.

Sources: Exhibits 3.1 through 3.4.

In terms of the most distressed city, four intergovernmental cities ranked most distressed in the 1977–1980 level of economic activity and in all indices of change. These cities are Buffalo, Cleveland, Newark and Rochester.

Our purpose in this chapter has been to verify the weak economic performance of intergovernmental cities. Across traditional economic indicators, employment base characteristics and private investment, the intergovernmental city performed poorly relative to both national averages and non-intergovernmental cities. In the face of continued fiscal retrenchment by upper levels of government, intergovernmental cities, locations of extraordinarily high levels of federal and state transfer payments, must work the hardest to maintain fiscal stability.

As the levels of economic activity in the intergovernmental city shifted downward, it experienced increasing social pressures and fiscal strains. Unemployment insurance and welfare benefits replaced payroll checks, while poverty, ill health and crime flourished. The anxiety of residents unable to find decent employment opportunities or to leave declining cities cannot accurately be measured. The level of need which they generated, however, can be ranked in comparison to other cities. This measurement is the subject of the next chapter.

NOTES

1. U.S. House of Representatives, Committee on Banking, Finance and Urban Affairs. "City Need and the Responsiveness of Federal Grant Programs" (Washington, DC: Government Printing Office, 1978), pp. 5–6.

2. Several studies ranking the economic performance of cities were reviewed including: J. Thomas Black, "The Changing Economic Role of Central Cities," in *The Prospective City: Economic, Population, Energy, and Environmental Development*, Arthur P. Solomon, ed. (Cambridge, MA: MIT Press, 1980); Robert W. Burchell, David Listokin, George Sternlieb, et al., "Measuring Urban Distress: A Summary of the Major Urban Hardship Indices and Resource Allocation Systems," in *Cities Under Stress* (New Brunswick, NJ: Center for Urban Policy Research, 1981); Harvey A. Garn and Larry Clinton Ledebur, "The Economic Performance and Prospects of Cities," in *The Prospective City: Economic, Population, Energy, and Environmental Development*, Arthur P. Solomon, ed. (Cambridge, MA: MIT Press, 1980); Franklin J. James, "Economic Distress in Central Cities," in *Cities Under Stress*, Robert W. Burchell and David Listokin, eds. (New Brunswick, NJ: Center for Urban Policy Research, 1981); Richard P. Nathan and Charles Adams, "Understanding Central City Hardship," *Political Science Quarterly*, Vol. 91, No. 1 (Spring 1976); Touche-Ross and The First National Bank, *Urban Fiscal Stress: A Comparative Analysis of 66 Cities* (New York: Touche-Ross & Company, 1979); U.S. House of Representatives, Committee on Banking, Finance & Urban Affairs, "City Need and the Responsiveness of Federal Grant Programs" (Washington, DC: Government Printing Office, 1978); U.S. Department of Housing and Urban Development, *The President's National Urban Policy Report* (Washington, DC: Government Printing Office, 1980). Urban Distress indices reviewed include those developed by The Brookings Institution, Congressional Budget Office, Institute of the Future, U.S. Department of Housing and Urban Development, and the Department of Treasury.

3. Harvey A. Garn and Larry Clinton Ledebur, "The Economic Performance and Prospects of Cities," in *The Prospective City: Economic, Population, Energy and Environmental Development*, Arthur P. Solomon, ed. (Cambridge, MA: MIT Press, 1980), p. 150.

4. "Effective Buying Income," *Sales and Marketing Management* (July 1981).

5. David L. Birch, *The Job Generation Process* (Cambridge, MA: MIT Press, 1979).

6. Thomas Muller, *Central City Business Retention: Jobs, Taxes and Investment Trends* (Washington, DC: U.S. Department of Commerce, June 1978).

4

Social Hardship in Intergovernmental and Non-Intergovernmental Cities

T HIS CHAPTER provides a comprehensive evaluation of social hardship in intergovernmental versus non-intergovernmental cities. The research outlined here sheds light on five fundamental aspects of socioeconomic distress: (1) income and poverty, (2) health conditions, (3) incidence of crime, (4) levels of public assistance, and (5) educational skills and performances. These data are then used to construct a hardship index or ranking system of key distress indicators analogous to those discussed in Chapters 2 and 3, which is quite useful for evaluating differentials in hardship by both city and city group. As in the previous chapter, the end-state time of analysis is the late 1970s—the height of intergovernmentalism.

Income

If changes in citywide employment opportunities and unemployment show how urban investment flows affect local economies, income levels reflect the impact of local economic performance upon the well-being of a city's residents. Moreover, income is the most commonly utilized, and perhaps the best, indicator of socioeconomic distress. All of the major urban distress indices—Brookings, Treasury, CBO and HUD—utilize income and income-related variables as determinants of local socioeconomic need. Many of the funding formulas for federal programs also have made use of income statistics.

Trends in Per Capita Income

Exhibit 4.1 presents overall trends in per capita income for the two classes of cities. While both groups of cities started out with nearly identical income levels in 1960, by 1977 considerable divergence had occurred. Over this two-decade period, income rose faster in non-intergovernmental cities. Between 1960 and 1970, the per capita income level in these cities increased, on average, by over 60 percent. Throughout the 1970s, the rate of income growth was even more dramatic. By 1977, the per capita income level in non-intergovernmental cities was $6,127, more than triple that of 1960. This constitutes a two-decade growth rate exceeding 213 percent. Overall, Nashville experienced, by far, the largest rate of income growth; here, incomes rose by over 350 percent. Additionally, by 1977, Tulsa and Anaheim had per capita income levels that exceeded $6,500. In the remaining non-intergovernmental cities, per capita incomes essentially doubled, and were in the range of $6,000 by 1977.

Intergovernmental cities witnessed much more sluggish income growth over the same period. In the 1960s and the 1970s, the rate of growth in per capita income was significantly outdistanced by that of non-intergovernmental cities. Throughout both of these decades, the absolute income level in intergovernmental cities lagged ten to fifteen percent behind that of the other class of cities; their two-decade growth rate was nearly forty percent slower. By 1977, the income level in these cities was just $5,415, a total of $700 less than that of the average of non-intergovernmental cities. Moreover, this total fell beneath the average national per capita income of $5,730 by over $300. In non-intergovernmental cities, incomes exceeded the national figure by $400.

Newark shows, by far, the lowest 1977 per capita income, and the slowest overall rate of income growth. In Cleveland and Baltimore incomes were also very low. While the rest of the intergovernmental cities had incomes that were somewhat higher than the depressed levels for these three cities, only in Minneapolis did per capita income approach the levels found in most non-intergovernmental cities.

Real Per Capita Income

Trends in the real rate of per capita income growth substantiate the widening disparity in income levels found for our two classes of cities. This data shows the change in real income expressed in 1977 constant dollars and was obtained by using the Consumer Price Index (CPI) to convert 1960 and 1970 per capita income amounts into 1977 constant dollars. As Exhibit 4.2 indicates, between 1960 and 1977, intergovernmental cities experienced a 34.4 percent rate of growth in real income compared to a real growth rate of nearly 53 percent for non-intergovernmental cities. On average in intergovernmental cities, real per capita income, expressed in 1977 constant dollars, increased from $4,028 in 1960 to $5,415 by 1977. Of these cities, Newark witnessed, by far, the slowest rate of growth in real per capita income. Between 1960 and 1977, real per capita income in Newark increased by only $365, a rate of less than 10 percent for the seventeen-year period. Cleveland and Baltimore also showed sluggish gains in real income. Indeed, each of the intergovernmental cities, with the exception of Louisville and, to a lesser extent, Minneapolis, experienced relatively slow growth in real per capita income between 1960 and 1977.

Non-intergovernmental cities, however, registered much larger gains in real income over the same period. Here, per capita income in constant dollars rose from a base of $4,008 in 1960, to $4,990 in 1970, and $6,127 in 1977. By 1977, real per capita income in these cities outdistanced those of the intergovernmental cities by more than $700 or 12 percent. And, throughout the 1960s and 1970s, rates of real income growth in these cities outpaced those of intergovernmental cities by approxi-

EXHIBIT 4.1. — *Trends in Unadjusted Per Capita Income: 1960, 1970, 1977*

| | 1960 | 1970 | 1977 | CHANGE | | | | | |
				1960-1970 Absolute	1960-1970 Percent	1970-1977 Absolute	1970-1977 Percent	1960-1977 Absolute	1960-1977 Percent
INTERGOVERNMENTAL									
AKRON	$2,142	$3,274	$5,760	+1132	+52.8	+2486	+75.9	+3618	+168.9
BALTIMORE	1,866	2,876	5,242	+1010	+54.1	+2366	+82.3	+3376	+180.9
BUFFALO	1,913	2,877	4,942	+964	+50.4	+2065	+71.8	+3029	+153.3
CINCINNATI	2,043	3,132	5,763	+1089	+53.3	+2631	+84.0	+3720	+182.1
CLEVELAND	1,856	2,821	4,914	+965	+52.0	+2093	+74.2	+3058	+164.8
LOUISVILLE	1,764	2,949	5,835	+1185	+67.2	+2886	+97.9	+4071	+230.8
MILWAUKEE	2,105	3,183	5,826	+1078	+51.2	+2643	+83.0	+3731	+177.2
MINNEAPOLIS	2,246	3,483	6,569	+1237	+55.1	+3086	+88.6	+4323	+192.5
NEWARK	1,792	2,492	4,038	+700	+39.1	+1546	+62.0	+2246	+125.3
ROCHESTER	2,072	3,239	5,533	+1167	+56.3	+2294	+70.8	+3461	+167.0
WEIGHTED MEAN	$1,965	$3,006	$5,415	+1041	+53.0	+2409	+80.1	+3450	+175.6
NON-INTERGOVERNMENTAL									
ANAHEIM	$2,255	$3,787	$6,633	+1532	+67.9	+2846	+75.2	+4378	+194.1
AUSTIN	1,688	2,998	5,766	+1310	+77.6	+2768	+92.3	+4078	+241.6
BATON ROUGE	1,855	2,846	5,813	+991	+53.4	+2967	+104.3	+3958	+213.4
COLUMBUS	1,885	3,025	5,441	+1140	+60.5	+2416	+79.9	+3556	+188.6
NASHVILLE	1,288	3,003	5,879	+1775	+133.2	+2876	+95.8	+4591	+356.4
OKLAHOMA CITY	1,981	3,236	6,217	+1255	+63.4	+2981	+92.1	+4236	+213.8
SAN JOSE	2,205	3,394	6,462	+1189	+53.9	+3068	+90.4	+4257	+193.1
TULSA	2,298	3,492	6,950	+1194	+52.0	+3458	+99.0	+4652	+202.4
VIRGINIA BEACH	NA	3,088	6,070	NA	NA	+2982	+96.5	NA	NA
WICHITA	2,082	3,259	6,344	+1177	+56.5	+3085	+94.7	+4262	+204.7
WEIGHTED MEAN	$1,955	$3,199	$6,127	+1244	+63.6	+2928	+91.5	+4172	+213.4

Source: U.S. Department of Housing and Urban Development, Urban Data Report, "Changing Conditions in Large Metropolitan Areas"; 1980 U.S. Census Bureau, Current Population Reports Series P-25, "1977 Per Capita Money Income Estimates 1980."

EXHIBIT 4.2. — *Trends in Real Per Capita Income: 1960, 1970, 1977*
(In 1977 Constant Dollars)

	1960	1970	1977	CHANGE 1960-1970 Absolute	1960-1970 Percent	1970-1977 Absolute	1970-1977 Percent	1960-1977 Absolute	1960-1977 Percent
INTERGOVERNMENTAL									
AKRON	$4,391	$5,107	$5,760	+716	+16.3	+653	+12.8	+1369	+31.2
BALTIMORE	3,825	4,487	5,242	+662	+17.3	+755	+16.8	+1417	+37.0
BUFFALO	3,923	4,488	4,942	+565	+14.4	+454	+10.1	+1019	+26.0
CINCINNATI	4,188	4,886	5,763	+698	+16.7	+877	+17.9	+1575	+37.6
CLEVELAND	3,805	4,401	4,914	+596	+15.7	+513	+11.7	+1109	+29.1
LOUISVILLE	3,616	4,600	5,835	+984	+27.2	+1235	+26.8	+2219	+61.4
MILWAUKEE	4,315	4,965	5,826	+650	+15.1	+861	+17.3	+1511	+35.0
MINNEAPOLIS	4,604	5,433	6,569	+829	+18.0	+1136	+20.9	+1965	+42.6
NEWARK	3,674	3,887	4,038	+213	+5.8	+151	+3.9	+364	+9.9
ROCHESTER	4,248	5,053	5,533	+805	+18.9	+480	+9.5	+1285	+30.2
WEIGHTED MEAN	$4,028	$4,689	$5,415	+661	+16.4	+726	+15.5	+1387	+34.4
NON-INTERGOVERNMENTAL									
ANAHEIM	$4,623	$5,908	$6,633	+1645	+35.6	+725	+12.3	+2010	+43.5
AUSTIN	3,460	4,677	5,766	+1217	+35.2	+1089	+23.3	+2306	+66.5
BATON ROUGE	3,803	4,440	5,813	+637	+16.7	+1373	+30.9	+2010	+52.9
COLUMBUS	3,864	4,719	5,441	+855	+22.1	+722	+15.3	+1577	+40.8
NASHVILLE	2,640	4,685	5,879	+2045	+77.5	+1194	+25.5	+3239	+122.7
OKLAHOMA CITY	4,061	5,048	6,217	+987	+24.3	+1169	+23.1	+2156	+53.1
SAN JOSE	4,520	5,295	6,462	+775	+17.1	+1167	+22.0	+1942	+43.0
TULSA	4,711	5,448	6,950	+637	+13.5	+1502	+27.6	+2239	+47.5
VIRGINIA BEACH	NA	4,817	6,070	NA	NA	+1253	+26.0	NA	NA
WICHITA	4,268	5,084	6,344	+816	+19.2	+1260	+24.8	+2076	+48.6
WEIGHTED MEAN	$4,008	$4,990	$6,127	+982	+24.5	+1137	+22.8	+2119	+52.9

Note : Conversions to constant dollars obtained through use of the Consumer Price Index for selected cities as documented in Statistical Abstract of the United States, 1980, p. 489.

Source: See Exhibit 4.1.

mately 10 percent. Over this two-decade period, real income in non-intergovernmental cities increased by more than $2,100, compared to an absolute increase of
$1,300 for the intergovernmental city group. Of all cities, Nashville-Davidson
registered the most extraordinary gains in real per capita income. Between 1960 and
1977, real income in Nashville more than doubled, increasing by over $3,200. Real
income also grew quite rapidly in the remaining non-intergovernmental cities. With
the exception of Columbus, each of these cities logged increases in real per capita income of $2,000 or more and rates of growth between 45 and 120 percent. In fact,
only two of the intergovernmental cities—Louisville and Minneapolis—came close
to matching these trends.

City–Suburban Per Capita Income Differentials

The city–suburban per capita income differentials presented in Exhibit 4.3 account, at least in part, for the widening disparity in incomes between the two classes
of cities. Basically, the well-documented city-to-suburban outmigration has taken its
toll on incomes in intergovernmental cities; yet, non-intergovernmental cities have
emerged virtually unscathed from the dynamic of suburbanization. The latter in part
reflects the dramatic annexations that have taken place in non-intergovernmental
cities which are discussed in a subsequent chapter. While incomes in intergovernmental cities were much lower than incomes in peripheral areas, incomes in non-
intergovernmental cities and their suburbs were quite comparable. Indeed, for intergovernmental cities this trend toward high-suburban, low-city incomes, already
evident in 1960, widened consistently since that time. In these cities, an original
city–suburban differential of $300 in 1960 expanded to nearly $1,000 (in constant
dollars) by the mid-1970s. In 1960, city per capita incomes were approximately 90
percent of suburban incomes, but by the 1970s city incomes were just 80 percent of
incomes in peripheral areas.

Newark, the city with the lowest per capita income, is surrounded by the highest
income suburbs. Newark, therefore, shows by far the worst city–suburban differential. In 1960, incomes in Newark's suburbs exceeded city incomes by nearly $1,000
and by the mid-1970s, this gap had widened to nearly $2,800. By 1980, the per capita
income differential was close to $3,500. Clearly, center-city Newark had barely one-
half the per capita income of its surrounding municipalities. Cleveland shows a nearly
identical pattern; here, suburban per capita income exceeds center-city income by
nearly $2,000. While the situations in Baltimore, Rochester, Milwaukee, Buffalo
and Louisville were not so serious in 1977, since 1970 these cities have witnessed
trends similar to those affecting Newark and Cleveland. Of the intergovernmental
cities, only Cincinnati, Akron and Minneapolis showed substantial parity in
city–suburban per capita incomes. Yet, in the first two cases, this was largely due to
relatively depressed incomes in the suburbs rather than any real strength in city incomes.

In non-intergovernmental cities, city–suburban income parity was more or less the
rule. Here, the per capita income differential was just $30 in 1960, and it increased
only slightly since then. Throughout this period, city incomes have made up a consistent 97 percent of incomes in outlying areas. Of these cities, only Columbus ex-

EXHIBIT 4.3. — *City-to-Suburban Per Capita Income Differentials: 1960, 1970, 1975*

	1960				1970				1975			
	City Income	Suburban Income	Difference	Ratio	City Income	Suburban Income	Difference	Ratio	City Income	Suburban Income	Difference	Ratio
INTERGOVERNMENTAL												
AKRON	$2,142	$2,012	+130	1.05	$3,274	$3,439	-165	0.95	$4,614	$4,923	-309	0.94
BALTIMORE	1,866	2,063	-197	0.90	2,876	3,678	-802	0.78	4,330	5,442	-1112	0.80
BUFFALO	1,913	2,113	-200	0.90	2,877	3,616	-739	0.80	3,928	4,712	-784	0.83
CINCINNATI	2,043	2,031	+12	1.00	3,132	3,244	-112	0.97	4,517	4,684	-167	0.96
CLEVELAND	1,856	2,693	-837	0.68	2,821	4,116	-1295	0.69	3,925	5,722	-1797	0.69
LOUISVILLE	1,764	1,946	-182	0.90	2,949	3,326	-377	0.89	4,302	4,926	-624	0.87
MILWAUKEE	2,105	2,305	-200	0.91	3,183	3,809	-626	0.84	4,680	5,628	-948	0.83
MINNEAPOLIS	2,246	2,178	+68	1.03	3,483	3,723	-240	0.94	5,161	5,400	-239	0.96
NEWARK	1,792	2,747	-955	0.65	2,492	4,314	-1822	0.57	3,348	6,128	-2780	0.55
ROCHESTER	2,072	2,259	-187	0.91	3,239	3,870	-631	0.84	4,335	5,423	-1088	0.80
WEIGHTED MEAN	$1,965	$2,235	-270	0.89	$3,006	$3,714	-708	0.82	$4,314	$5,299	-985	0.81
NON-INTERGOVERNMENTAL												
ANAHEIM	$2,255	$2,361	-106	0.96	$3,787	$4,067	-280	0.93	$5,191	$5,842	-651	0.89
AUSTIN	1,688	1,520	+168	1.11	2,998	3,060	-62	0.98	4,379	4,658	-249	0.94
BATON ROUGE	1,855	1,493	+362	1.24	2,846	2,892	-46	1.01	4,187	4,188	-1	1.00
COLUMBUS	1,885	2,310	-425	0.81	3,025	3,635	-610	0.83	4,333	5,169	-836	0.84
NASHVILLE-DAVIDSON	1,288	1,934	-646	0.66	3,033	3,282	-249	0.92	4,606	4,727	-121	0.97
OKLAHOMA CITY	1,981	1,850	+131	1.07	3,236	3,084	+152	1.05	4,731	4,531	+200	1.05
SAN JOSE	2,205	2,390	-185	0.92	3,394	4,166	-772	0.81	4,970	6,120	-1150	0.81
TULSA	2,298	1,560	+738	1.47	3,492	2,546	+946	1.37	5,173	4,007	+1166	1.29
VIRGINIA BEACH	NA	NA	NA	NA	NA	NA	NA	NA	NA	NA	NA	NA
WICHITA	2,082	$1,896	+186	1.09	3,259	2,861	+398	1.14	4,951	4,454	+497	1.11
WEIGHTED MEAN	$1,955	$1,924	-31	0.99	$3,199	$3,288	+89	0.98	$4,724	$4,855	-130	0.97

Source: U.S. Department of Housing and Urban Development, *Urban Data Report,* "Changing Conditions in Large Metropolitan Areas," Tables 13 and 14, 1980.

hibits trends comparable to those found in most of the intergovernmental cities. While Anaheim and San Jose also possess large disparities in city–suburban per capita incomes, this is primarily due to the fact that these high-income cities are surrounded by very high-income suburbs. The remaining non-intergovernmental cities showed consistently small city–suburban income differentials. Indeed, Nashville and Baton Rouge possessed per capita incomes that were virtually identical to the income levels of their suburbs. Tulsa, Wichita and Oklahoma City had per capita incomes which *exceed* suburban incomes.

Summary

Exhibit 4.4 helps to clarify the divergence in income levels for our two classes of cities by providing a ranking of these twenty cities in terms of 1977 per capita income and other income-related components. First, there are two striking anomalies in the otherwise general trends. Columbus, a non-intergovernmental city, ranked among the cities with the lowest per capita income, while Minneapolis, an intergovernmental city, was situated near the top of this income distribution. Part of the explanation lies in the fact that both of these cities exhibit city–suburban income differentials that cut sharply against the grain of trends for their respective groups. Minneapolis, along with its high per capita income level, showed, by far, the greatest convergence between city and suburban incomes of any intergovernmental city. Columbus combined its relatively depressed income level with the largest disparity in city–suburban incomes of any non-intergovernmental city. Moreover, Columbus showed rising trends for both real total income and real retail sales, while Minneapolis exhibited serious declines along both of these indicators. In these two cities per capita income may be a poor indicator of economic trends which are influenced by forces originating outside the city.

Most importantly, intergovernmental cities comprised the bulk of the lowest income cities. Five-of-six low income cities were intergovernmental cities. Newark, Cleveland, and Buffalo showed the most severely depressed income levels, with Baltimore, Rochester and Columbus next in line. On the other hand, six-of-seven highest income cities were non-intergovernmental cities: Tulsa, Anaheim, San Jose, Wichita, Oklahoma City and Virginia Beach. The middle of this income distribution is where the greatest overlap occurs. Here, seven cities — four intergovernmental cities and three non-intergovernmental cities — varied in per capita income by no more than $120. Even in these cities, however — where per capita incomes were nearly identical—trends in real total income and retail sales reflect group patterns. That is, Akron, Cincinnati, Milwaukee, and Louisville showed significant declines along both of these indicators, while Baton Rouge, Austin and Nashville-Davidson registered substantial improvements.

The data clearly show the widening disparity in incomes between intergovernmental and non-intergovernmental cities—a trend which, as it continues unabated, means that intergovernmental cities are increasingly becoming repositories for lower-income households and dependent populations.

EXHIBIT 4.4. — *Comparative Ranking of Income (From Low to High), By City, 1977*

City	City Type	1977 Per Capita Income	City Index of Per Capita Income	Δ Real Total Income 1970-1976 (Percent)	Δ Real Retail Sales 1970-1976 (Percent)
Newark	I	$4,038	-27.0	-11.2%	-27.9%
Cleveland	I	4,914	-16.0	-14.1	-16.6
Buffalo	I	4.942	-13.0	- 9.4	-20.8
Baltimore	I	5,242	- 7.0	+ 3.3	-18.0
Columbus	N-I	5,441	- 6.0	+ 6.6	+ 4.9
Rochester	I	5,533	- 3.0	- 5.9	-24.9
Akron	I	5,760	0.0	- 5.2	- 5.1
Cincinnati	I	5,763	0.0	- 7.1	- 4.9
Austin	N-I	5,766	0.0	+44.7	+34.6
Baton Rouge	N-I	5,813	+ 1.0	+31.6	+21.3
Milwaukee	I	5,826	+ 1.0	- 3.6	- 2.3
Louisville	I	5,835	+ 1.0	- 4.0	-11.8
Nashville	N-I	5,879	+ 2.0	+11.3	+ 7.5
Virginia Beach	N-I	6,070	+ 7.0	NA	NA
Oklahoma City	N-I	6,217	+ 8.0	+16.6	+14.9
Wichita	N-I	6,344	+10.0	+14.0	+18.7
San Jose	N-I	6,462	+11.0	+34.2	+26.7
Minneapolis	I	6,569	+13.0	- 3.5	-11.1
Anaheim	N-I	6,633	+14.0	+24.5	+28.1
Tulsa	N-I	6,950	+20.0	+19.9	+26.0

Note: Index of per capita income has been abstracted from Advisory Commission on Intergovernmental Relations, Table A-33. This index shows the deviation of incomes in a particular city from a 168-city sample mean. It has been adjusted slightly to more accurately reflect changes in per capita income for 1977.

Source: Exhibit 4.1. Advisory Commission on Intergovernmental Relations, "Central City-Suburban Fiscal Disparity and City Distress, 1977," Tables A-33, A-34.

Health Conditions

While indicators of urban health are important measures of socioeconomic distress, they often go unnoticed in the analyses of urban hardship. The best available health indicators are mortality data which, by definition, provide a comprehensive list of fatalities by specific cause. Although data on the frequency and concentration of specific illnesses—morbidity data—would provide an excellent complement to data by cause of death, these data are not collected in any uniform manner for specific cities. In any case, using the available mortality data to determine the frequency and geographic concentration of fatalities from particular causes tells much about comparative local health conditions.

Exhibits 4.5 through 4.10 present time-series data for a variety of mortality-based indicators. The overall death rate provides initial approximations of citywide health standards and minor and indirect measures of the quality of locally available medical care. Rates of infant mortality and deaths from tuberculosis afford the best indicators of local health conditions. Deaths that are caused by flu and pneumonia pinpoint locations where generally survivable illnesses are leading to fatalities. Deaths from cancer and from stress-related causes provide limited measures of how poor environmental conditions or inadequate living conditions influence local health. Taken together, these data establish the basis for constructing a comparative index of overall health conditions in the two classes of cities.

Deaths from All Causes

The overall death rate was substantially higher in intergovernmental cities than in non-intergovernmental cities (Exhibit 4.5). When looked at over a two-decade time

EXHIBIT 4.5. — Total Deaths By All Causes and Death Rate, 1960, 1970, 1977

	1960		1970		1977	
	Total	Per 100,000	Total	Per 100,000	Total	Per 100,000
INTERGOVERNMENTAL						
AKRON	2,757	951	2,922	1,063	2,760	1,131
BALTIMORE	11,534	1,228	11,425	1,261	9,501	1,131
BUFFALO	6,821	1,280	6,505	1,451	5,279	1,475
CINCINNATI	6,254	1,244	6,057	1,338	5,219	1,373
CLEVELAND	10,180	1,162	9,262	1,233	7,713	1,267
LOUISVILLE	4,948	1,267	4,894	1,354	4,212	1,411
MILWAUKEE	7,630	1,029	7,194	1,003	6,293	993
MINNEAPOLIS	5,887	1,221	5,500	1,267	4,568	1,269
NEWARK	5,031	1,241	4,442	1,162	3,123	948
ROCHESTER	4,127	1,295	3,715	1,254	3,134	1,296
WEIGHTED MEAN	6,516	1,192	6,192	1,239	5,180	1,237
NON-INTERGOVERNMENTAL						
ANAHEIM	596	573	1,030	620	1,307	647
AUSTIN	1,316	704	1,615	638	1,899	588
BATON ROUGE	1,251	821	1,538	927	1,792	816
COLUMBUS	4,623	981	5,121	949	4,759	842
NASHVILLE-DAVIDSON	2,232	1,305	4,112	922	3,968	925
OKLAHOMA CITY	3,089	953	3,648	995	3,654	906
SAN JOSE	4,597	782	5,319	813	3,210	504
TULSA	2,377	907	2,839	860	2,962	887
VIRGINIA BEACH	73	NA	737	428	1,017	431
WICHITA	2,067	810	2,321	838	2,368	884
WEIGHTED MEAN	2,222	870	2,828	799	2,694	743

Source: Department of Health and Human Services (Formerly Department of Health, Education and Welfare), Vital Statistics of the United States: Volume II, Part B, Mortality. Section 7, Geographic Detail (For Years Indicated).

series, the gap in death rates between the two groups of cities grew quite steadily. From 1960 to 1977, the death rate in non-intergovernmental cities fell consistently, while the death rate in intergovernmental cities stayed virtually constant. In intergovernmental cities, the death rate consistently hovered around 1,200 deaths per 100,000. In non-intergovernmental cities, the death rate dropped from nearly 900 deaths per 100,000 to 700 deaths per 100,000 by 1977. Thus, an original differential of 300 deaths per 100,000 in 1960 expanded to almost 500 deaths by 1977. By this latter year, the overall death rate in intergovernmental cities exceeded that of non-intergovernmental cities by more than 40 percent.

Of the intergovernmental cities, Buffalo and Louisville had the highest overall death rates, exceeding 1,400 per year, while Newark and Milwaukee had relatively low death rates, between 900 and 1,000 annual deaths. In the remaining intergovernmental cities, the death rate hovered in the range of 1,200 to 1,300 yearly deaths. Of the non-intergovernmental cities, even those cities with the highest death rates paled by comparison to intergovernmental cities. Although Nashville-Davidson and Oklahoma City had the highest overall death rates of the non-intergovernmental cities, their rates still fell beneath the lowest death rates for any intergovernmental city. Tulsa, Wichita, Baton Rouge and Columbus had very moderate overall death rates. Anaheim, Austin, San Jose and especially Virginia Beach, showed by far the lowest overall death rates. While much of this variance is explained by secular factors of age distribution, hospital location and the like, there remains a strong statistical difference between city groupings.

Infant Mortality

Infant mortality—to a greater extent than the overall death rate—is a key indicator of local health conditions. Despite the great strides that have been made in reducing infant mortality, its incidence remains quite high in intergovernmental cities. From 1960 to 1977, infant mortality decreased in both classes of cities; yet, both the absolute decreases and the rate of decline have been much swifter in non-intergovernmental cities (Exhibit 4.6). In 1977, an infant mortality rate of fourteen infants per 100,000 in intergovernmental cities compared to an infant mortality rate of twelve infants per 100,000 in non-intergovernmental cities. Moreover, the individual cities with the most serious incidences of infant mortality were all intergovernmental cities. In Baltimore and Newark the infant mortality rate was in the twenty-plus range while in Cleveland and Rochester this rate exceeded fifteen infant mortalities per year. Of the intergovernmental cities then, only Minneapolis, Akron and Milwaukee possessed relatively low rates of infant mortality. On the other hand, all of the non-intergovernmental cities exhibited rates of infant mortality of fifteen or under per 100,000 people. Baton Rouge, Wichita, and Columbus showed the highest totals, while Nashville, Oklahoma City, Tulsa and Anaheim were all in the moderate ten-to-thirteen infant mortality range. San Jose, Virginia Beach and Austin showed the lowest rates of infant mortality, eight and six per 100,000 respectively.

EXHIBIT 4.6. — *Total Infant Mortality and Infant Mortality Rate: 1960, 1970, 1977*

	1960		1970		1977	
	Total	Per 100,000	Total	Per 100,000	Total	Per 10,000
INTERGOVERNMENTAL						
AKRON	141	49	75	27	27	11
BALTIMORE	506	54	230	25	154	20
BUFFALO	195	37	132	35	47	13
CINCINNATI	230	46	114	25	40	10
CLEVELAND	452	52	235	31	97	16
LOUISVILLE	189	48	88	24	40	13
MILWAUKEE	332	45	140	17	59	9
MINNEAPOLIS	192	40	104	24	34	9
NEWARK	224	55	188	49	80	24
ROCHESTER	120	38	82	28	44	18
WEIGHTED MEAN	258	46	139	29	62	14
NON-INTERGOVERNMENTAL						
ANAHEIM	44	42	31	19	20	10
AUSTIN	90	48	38	15	19	6
BATON ROUGE	70	46	55	33	32	15
COLUMBUS	217	46	116	21	86	15
NASHVILLE-DAVIDSON	89	52	118	26	58	13
OKLAHOMA CITY	157	48	108	29	53	13
SAN JOSE	98	48	71	16	54	8
TULSA	98	37	75	23	44	13
VIRGINIA BEACH	8	NA	34	20	18	8
WICHITA	118	46	84	30	41	15
WEIGHTED MEAN	99	46	73	23	43	12

Source: Department of Health and Human Services (Formerly Department of Health, Education and Welfare), Vital Statistics of the United States: Volume II, Part B, Mortality. Section 7, Geographic Detail (For Years Indicated).

Tuberculosis

The rate of death from tuberculosis is another key indicator of local health conditions. As with infant mortality, despite significant improvements in controlling tuberculosis, its incidence remains highest in the intergovernmental cities. Indeed, in the non-intergovernmental cities the rate of death from tuberculosis was much lower originally, and it has dropped off more considerably over the past two decades (Exhibit 4.7). By 1977, the average rate of death from tuberculosis in these cities was one-half the rate of death from this disease in intergovernmental cities. However, two non-intergovernmental cities failed to conform to this overall trend. While Louisville, Newark, Baltimore and Buffalo experienced the highest rates of death from tuberculosis, Oklahoma City and Baton Rouge—both non-intergovernmental cities—along with Akron and Cleveland, also exhibited significant rates of tubercu-

EXHIBIT 4.7. — *Total Deaths and Death Rate Caused By Tuberculosis: 1960, 1970, 1977*

	1960		1970		1977	
	Total	Per 100,000	Total	Per 100,000	Total	Per 100,000
INTERGOVERNMENTAL						
AKRON	10	3.4	5	1.8	5	2.0
BALTIMORE	163	17.4	94	10.4	30	3.7
BUFFALO	78	14.7	22	4.8	12	3.1
CINCINNATI	46	9.2	22	4.8	7	1.7
CLEVELAND	102	11.6	33	4.4	13	2.1
LOUISVILLE	59	15.1	26	7.2	15	4.6
MILWAUKEE	46	6.2	16	2.2	11	1.7
MINNEAPOLIS	18	3.7	8	1.8	3	0.8
NEWARK	49	12.1	43	11.2	13	4.1
ROCHESTER	25	7.9	14	4.7	4	1.6
WEIGHTED MEAN	60	10.1	28	5.3	11	2.5
NON-INTERGOVERNMENTAL						
ANAHEIM	1	1.0	1	0.6	1	0.5
AUSTIN	11	5.9	3	1.2	4	1.2
BATON ROUGE	13	8.6	8	4.8	5	2.3
COLUMBUS	25	5.3	8	1.5	8	1.3
NASHVILLE-DAVIDSON	18	10.5	13	2.9	8	1.6
OKLAHOMA CITY	24	7.4	9	2.4	11	3.0
SAN JOSE	13	6.4	9	2.0	7	1.2
TULSA	15	5.7	5	1.5	2	0.6
VIRGINIA BEACH	1	NA	2	1.2	2	0.8
WICHITA	9	3.5	5	1.8	2	0.7
WEIGHTED MEAN	13	6.0	6	2.0	5	1.3

Source: Department of Health and Human Services (Formerly Department of Health, Education and Welfare), Vital Statistics of the United States: Volume II, Part B, Mortality. Section 7, Geographic Detail (For Years Indicated).

losis death. On the other hand, three non-intergovernmental cities—Tulsa, Wichita, and Virginia Beach—showed the lowest rates of death from tuberculosis. In all of the remaining cities, the rate of death from tuberculosis was relatively moderate.

Influenza and Pneumonia

The rate of death from influenza or pneumonia provides some indication of how poor health conditions, possibly in combination with inadequate medical services, can lead to death from otherwise survivable illnesses. Again, despite the fact that the rate of deaths caused by flu and pneumonia has generally decreased between 1960 and 1977, intergovernmental cities continued to show the worst incidence of death from these causes. As Exhibit 4.8 indicates, in 1960, 44 out of every 100,000 people died of flu or pneumonia in these cities; this total dropped off to an average of 40 deaths in 1970, and 34 deaths by 1977. In non-intergovernmental cities, however, only 17 people died from these illnesses in 1977, down from 24 deaths in 1970 and 29 deaths in 1960. Indeed, the death rate from influenza and pneumonia by 1977 was twice as high in intergovernmental cities as it was in non-intergovernmental cities.

The data presented in Exhibit 4.8 call into question arguments which pin this differential in deaths from these causes strictly on the colder climates of most intergovernmental cities. While Rochester and Minneapolis showed the highest rates of death from flu and pneumonia, the death rate from these illnesses was also significant in relatively warm locations, such as Louisville, Nashville, Oklahoma City and Tulsa. Of the intergovernmental cities, Rochester, Minneapolis and Louisville evidenced the highest death rates from flu and pneumonia, followed by Buffalo, Cleveland, and Cincinnati. Interestingly, Baltimore, Milwaukee, and Akron possessed extremely moderate death rates from these causes, while Newark experienced the lowest rate of death from flu and pneumonia. Again, the non-

EXHIBIT 4.8. — *Total Deaths and Death Rate Caused By Influenza and Pneumonia: 1960, 1970, 1977*

	1960		1970		1977	
	Total	Per 100,000	Total	Per 100,000	Total	Per 100,000
INTERGOVERNMENTAL						
AKRON	55	19	66	24	56	23
BALTIMORE	477	51	317	35	207	26
BUFFALO	267	50	276	60	138	39
CINCINNATI	226	45	236	52	145	38
CLEVELAND	323	37	265	35	187	31
LOUISVILLE	191	49	140	39	126	42
MILWAUKEE	348	47	184	26	154	24
MINNEAPOLIS	242	50	180	41	162	45
NEWARK	170	42	146	38	64	19
ROCHESTER	157	47	151	50	119	49
WEIGHTED MEAN	245	44	196	40	136	34
NON-INTERGOVERNMENTAL						
ANAHEIM	25	24	24	14	32	16
AUSTIN	55	29	65	26	55	17
BATON ROUGE	36	24	45	27	20	9
COLUMBUS	142	30	163	30	104	18
NASHVILLE-DAVIDSON	92	54	125	28	95	22
OKLAHOMA CITY	78	24	104	28	94	23
SAN JOSE	55	27	89	20	111	17
TULSA	85	32	81	24	70	21
VIRGINIA BEACH	0	NA	23	13	20	8
WICHITA	109	43	70	25	54	20
WEIGHTED MEAN	68	29	79	24	66	17

Source: Department of Health and Human Services (Formerly Department of Health, Education and Welfare), Vital Statistics of the United States: Volume II, Part B, Mortality. Section 7, Geographic Detail (For Years Indicated).

intergovernmental cities showed much lower death rates when compared to the intergovernmental cities. Nashville, Oklahoma City, Tulsa, and Wichita—the non-intergovernmental cities with the highest death rates from these causes—did not even approach the worst of the intergovernmental cities. The rate of death from flu and pneumonia was relatively moderate in the bulk of the non-intergovernmental cities. Moreover, San Jose, Anaheim, Austin, Columbus, and especially Virginia Beach and Baton Rouge exhibited by far the lowest rates of death from these illnesses.

Cancer

The incidence of death caused by cancer was also greatest in the intergovernmental cities. Indeed, while the rate of death from cancer had remained relatively constant in non-intergovernmental cities, the cancer death rate showed a very substantial two-decade increase in intergovernmental cities. As Exhibit 4.9 indicates, in 1960, 200 deaths per 100,000 people resulted from cancer in these cities. By 1977, however, this total had increased to over 250 cancer-related deaths per 100,000. In non-intergovernmental cities, a rate of 133 cancer deaths fell slightly to 127 deaths in 1970, and then increased somewhat to 154 deaths by 1977. By 1977, the cancer death rate in intergovernmental cities exceeded that of non-intergovernmental cities by more than forty percent or nearly one hundred deaths per year. Again, individual intergovernmental cities showed the highest rates of death from this cause. Buffalo and Cincinnati experienced the worst rates of death from cancer. Baltimore, Louisville, Minneapolis, and Rochester also showed high rates of cancer-related death. In contrast, highly industrialized places like Milwaukee and Akron experienced relatively moderate rates of death from cancer. Of all the cities, Virginia Beach, Austin and Anaheim showed the smallest rates of death from this cause. The remaining non-intergovernmental cities all exhibited moderate rates of death from cancer.

Stress-Related Deaths

Exhibit 4.10 presents data on deaths from various stress-related illnesses. Included in this category are deaths caused by cirrhosis of the liver, ulcers of any type, and suicides. These measures give some indication of the relationship between stress-producing environments and poor health. Once again, the rate of death from these causes in intergovernmental cities significantly outdistanced that of non-intergovernmental cities. Here, the stress-related death rate was twenty-five percent higher: forty-one deaths per 100,000 compared to thirty-one deaths per 100,000. Of all the sample cities, four intergovernmental cities — Louisville, Cleveland, Baltimore and Cincinnati — had the highest rates of death from stress-related causes, while five non-intergovernmental cities—Austin, Virginia Beach, Baton Rouge, and Columbus—showed the lowest rates of death from these causes. The remaining cities clustered very closely with relatively moderate rates of stress-related death.

EXHIBIT 4.9. — *Total Deaths and Death Rate Caused By All Cancers: 1960, 1970, 1977*

	1960		1970		1977	
	Total	Per 100,000	Total	Per 100,000	Total	Per 100,000
INTERGOVERNMENTAL						
AKRON	515	177	542	197	528	216
BALTIMORE	1,856	198	2,018	223	2,117	269
BUFFALO	1,085	204	1,146	248	1,093	305
CINCINNATI	1,110	221	1,136	251	1,165	302
CLEVELAND	1,751	199	1,641	219	1,509	247
LOUISVILLE	797	204	833	230	839	281
MILWAUKEE	1,309	177	1,355	189	1,361	215
MINNEAPOLIS	959	199	991	138	928	258
NEWARK	788	194	636	166	573	174
ROCHESTER	709	222	637	215	661	273
WEIGHTED MEAN	1,088	200	1,094	208	1,077	256
NON-INTERGOVERNMENTAL						
ANAHEIM	86	83	44	26	294	145
AUSTIN	215	115	286	113	387	120
BATON ROUGE	174	114	230	139	348	159
COLUMBUS	745	158	939	174	978	173
NASHVILLE-DAVIDSON	283	165	662	148	869	203
OKLAHOMA CITY	495	153	625	170	733	182
SAN JOSE	276	135	526	118	658	108
TULSA	390	149	526	160	590	177
VIRGINIA BEACH	8	100	124	72	215	91
WICHITA	319	125	402	145	494	184
WEIGHTED MEAN	299	130	436	127	557	154

Source: Department of Health and Human Services (Formerly Department of Health, Education and Welfare), Vital Statistics of the United States: Volume II, Part B, Mortality. Section 7.

Summary

Generally speaking, health conditions in intergovernmental cities are significantly worse than those in non-intergovernmental cities. The index presented in Exhibit 4.11 substantiates this contention by providing a detailed ranking of cities in terms of their relative performance across a variety of health indicators. This index synthesizes all of the health data previously outlined, giving extra weight to infant mortality and tuberculosis which are key indicators of local health.

Economically distressed intergovernmental cities comprised the bulk of cities with the poorest health conditions. Louisville, Baltimore, Buffalo and Cleveland experienced the worst local health conditions. These cities were followed by Rochester, Newark, and Cincinnati, where health conditions were also very poor. Overall, intergovernmental cities accounted for ten of the eleven cities with the worst health conditions.

Non-intergovernmental cities fared substantially better than intergovernmental cities. Oklahoma City was the only non-intergovernmental city to rank among the

EXHIBIT 4.10. — *Total Deaths and Death Rate Caused By Stress-Related**
Ailments: 1960, 1970, 1977

	1960 Total	1960 Per 100,000	1970 Total	1970 Per 100,000	1977 Total	1977 Per 100,000
INTERGOVERNMENTAL						
AKRON	74	25	95	36	84	34
BALTIMORE	336	36	507	56	331	42
BUFFALO	193	36	213	46	136	38
CINCINNATI	178	35	173	38	165	43
CLEVELAND	430	49	381	51	332	55
LOUISVILLE	144	37	182	50	137	46
MILWAUKEE	265	36	273	38	229	36
MINNEAPOLIS	178	37	178	41	186	52
NEWARK	168	41	152	40	109	33
ROCHESTER	114	36	109	37	80	33
WEIGHTED MEAN	208	37	226	43	179	41
NON-INTERGOVERNMENTAL						
ANAHEIM	37	36	42	25	69	34
AUSTIN	42	22	52	21	75	23
BATON ROUGE	34	22	55	33	55	25
COLUMBUS	164	35	173	32	139	25
NASHVILLE-DAVIDSON	44	26	142	32	134	31
OKLAHOMA CITY	89	27	133	36	162	40
SAN JOSE	82	40	160	36	211	33
TULSA	50	19	97	29	130	39
VIRGINIA BEACH	1	NA	37	22	54	23
WICHITA	70	27	67	24	85	32
WEIGHTED MEAN	61	28	96	29	111	31

Note: Stress-related* causes of death include deaths brought on by cirrhosis, ulcers and suicides.

Source: Department of Health and Human Services (Formerly Department of Health, Education and Welfare), Vital Statistics of the United States: Volume II, Part B, Mortality. Section 7, Geographic Detail (For Years Indicated).

poor-health intergovernmental cities. Moreover, non-intergovernmental cities—Anaheim, San Jose, Austin and Virginia Beach—comprised locations with the best local health conditions. The remaining non-intergovernmental cities exhibited moderate-to-good rankings along most indicators of urban health.

Health trends thus correlate significantly with previously documented trends in economic performance and income. By and large, non-intergovernmental cities matched economic prosperity and burgeoning resources with good local health. In older, declining intergovernmental cities, however, very poor and typically worsening health conditions were more the rule.

EXHIBIT 4.11. — *Comparative Index of Local Health Conditions
(From Worst to Least), By City, 1977*

Rank	Compo- site Score	City Type	Over- all Death	In- fant Mor- tality	Tuber- culosis	Flu and Pneu- monia	Cancer	Stress- Related
LOUISVILLE	139	I	2	8	1	3	3	3
BALTIMORE	134	I	7	2	3	7	5	5
BUFFALO	138	I	1	8	4	4	1	8
CLEVELAND	126	I	6	4	7	6	7	1
ROCHESTER	119	I	4	3	11	1	4	12
NEWARK	112	I	10	1	2	14	14	12
CINCINNATI	108	I	3	14	9	5	2	4
OKLAHOMA CITY	103	N-I	12	8	5	9	12	6
AKRON	91	I	8	13	8	9	8	10
MINNEAPOLIS	89	I	5	16	16	2	6	2
MILWAUKEE	83	I	9	16	9	8	9	9
NASHVILLE	82	N-I	11	8	11	11	10	16
BATON ROUGE	78	N-I	16	5	6	19	16	17
COLUMBUS	70	N-I	15	5	13	15	15	17
WICHITA	69	N-I	14	5	18	13	11	15
TULSA	69	N-I	13	8	19	12	13	7
ANAHEIM	39	N-I	17	14	20	16	17	10
SAN JOSE	38	N-I	19	18	14	16	19	12
AUSTIN	29	N-I	18	20	14	16	18	19
VIRGINIA BEACH	19	N-I	20	19	16	20	20	19

Note: Infant mortality and tuberculosis, which are key indicators of
health, are weighted double.

Component scores for individual cities were calculated using a
reversed ordinal scale -- 20 through 1. Thus, the worst cases
(i.e., ranks 1, 2, 3...) received scores of 20, 19, 18...respec-
tively. These individual scores were then summed to obtain the
total or composite score.

Source: Exhibits 4.5 through 4.10.

Crime and Public Safety

Crime is certainly the most worrisome of all urban social problems. Few urban
problems provoke so much anxiety or such tremendous public outcry as the extraordinary growth in criminal activity witnessed over the past two decades. Opinion
surveys indicate that lawlessness and fear of crime top the list of the most important
issues concerning the residents of large cities. Indeed, while the causes of crime go
unaddressed and the prescriptions remain hapless, the dangerous—almost terrify-
ing—state of affairs in our crime-prone urban centers is irrefutable. The statistics on
the rapid mounting of urban crime across the United States substantiate this charge.
Nationally, since 1960, crimes against persons have shown a threefold increase,

while incidents of property crime have shown an even more rapid, fivefold rate of increase. Moreover, crime is most fearsomely concentrated in central cities. As both the nightly news stories and the data indicate, rates of crime in urban centers far outdistance national averages.

Decades of social research have generated a considerable body of knowledge on the causes and consequences of urban crime. This literature boasts a host of empirically based propositions which link the incidence and the geographic concentration of crime to economic distress, and debilitated social structure. At the city or community level, crime has been related to indicators of economic dislocation. At the individual level, criminality has been repeatedly linked with poverty and lack of opportunity. Moreover, recent studies of urban crime indicate that the suburban and intra-metropolitan population shifts which have sorted population increasingly along race and class lines mean that high crime rates along with the poor and the underemployed are very likely to be concentrated in older intergovernmental cities. This research also indicates that younger cities, where the pace of suburbanization and metropolitan differentiation has been much slower and where regional migration has brought high income populations into the city, generally experience more moderate crime rates.

Trends in Crime

The data substantiate these findings. For the most part, intergovernmental cities showed greater absolute numbers of criminal incidents and higher crime rates than non-intergovernmental cities. In intergovernmental cities, total criminal incidents increased from 14,243 in 1960, to 36,468 in 1970, and 34,620 in 1977 (Exhibit 4.12). This represents an absolute increase exceeding 170 percent. Over the same period, in these cities, property crimes increased by 16,772 incidents, a 155 percent growth rate; while violent crimes showed an astounding threefold increase of 3,606 total incidents.

In non-intergovernmental cities total crimes numbered 24,340 incidents by 1977, up from 7,218 incidents in 1960 and 19,176 incidents in 1970. While total crimes in these cities make up only 70 percent of total crimes in intergovernmental cities, non-intergovernmental cities have experienced swifter rates of increase in criminal incidents. Between 1960 and 1977, total incidents of crime in these cities increased by 18,813 total crimes. This represents a two-decade rate of growth exceeding 250 percent, a rate of increase which exceeded that of the intergovernmental cities by 80 percent. Similarly, property crimes in non-intergovernmental cities increased by 15,762 total incidents, a growth rate of over 200 percent. Violent crimes in these cities showed an amazing two-decade growth of nearly 700 percent or 1,723 incidents*.

Again, while intergovernmental cities exhibited a higher number of incidents of criminal activity across all major categories, the rate of increase in crime is considerably higher in non-intergovernmental cities. This is largely due to those cities experi-

---

*Violent plus property crime incidents do not add to total incidents because of inclusion of Virginia Beach in some yearly totals and not in others. Data was unavailable for Virginia Beach for these other years.

EXHIBIT 4.12.—*Trends in Total Incidence of Crime: 1960, 1970, 1977*

	1960	1970	1977	CHANGE					
				1960-1970 Absolute	1960-1970 Percent	1970-1977 Absolute	1970-1977 Percent	1960-1977 Absolute	1960-1977 Percent
INTERGOVERNMENTAL									
AKRON	9,024	17,842	17,907	+8,818	+97.7	+65	+0.4	+8,883	+98.4
BALTIMORE	22,577	81,602	67,287	+59,025	+261.4	-14,315	-17.5	+44,710	+198.0
BUFFALO	7,594	37,423	31,841	+29,829	+392.8	-5,582	-14.9	+24,247	+319.3
CINCINNATI	9,216	25,794	30,012	+16,578	+179.9	+4,218	+16.4	+20,796	+225.7
CLEVELAND	22,980	57,176	54,995	+34,196	+148.8	-2,181	-3.8	+32,015	+139.3
LOUISVILLE	12,524	23,514	20,312	+10,990	+87.8	-3,202	-13.6	+7,788	+62.2
MILWAUKEE	13,817	29,236	34,547	+15,419	+111.6	+5,311	+18.2	+20,730	+150.0
MINNEAPOLIS	15,980	34,344	32,478	+18,364	+114.9	-1,866	-5.4	+16,498	+103.2
NEWARK	23,185	37,606	30,313	+14,421	+62.2	-7,293	-19.4	+7,128	+30.7
ROCHESTER	5,531	20,138	26,510	+14,607	+264.1	+6,372	+31.6	+20,979	+379.3
WEIGHTED MEAN	14,243	36,468	34,620	+22,224	+172.1	-1,847	+0.8	+20,377	+170.6
NON-INTERGOVERNMENTAL									
ANAHEIM	3,625	11,613	16,043	+7,988	+220.4	+4,430	+38.1	+12,418	+342.6
AUSTIN	5,808	15,266	23,536	+9,458	+162.8	+8,270	+54.2	+17,728	+305.2
BATON ROUGE	5,923	12,360	20,862	+6,437	+108.6	+8,502	+68.8	+14,939	+252.2
COLUMBUS	13,661	34,930	43,229	+21,269	+155.7	+8,299	+23.8	+29,568	+216.4
NASHVILLE	7,291	20,818	26,096	+13,527	+185.5	+5,278	+25.4	+18,805	+257.9
OKLAHOMA CITY	11,825	19,828	27,890	+8,003	+67.7	+8,608	+43.4	+16,065	+135.8
SAN JOSE	9,687	31,499	39,218	+21,812	+225.2	+7,719	+24.5	+29,531	+304.9
TULSA	8,476	16,893	24,391	+8,417	+99.3	+7,499	+44.4	+15,915	+187.7
VIRGINIA BEACH	NA	7,576	11,633	NA	NA	+4,057	+53.6	NA	NA
WICHITA	5,880	20,973	20,504	+15,093	+256.7	-469	-2.2	+14,624	+248.7
WEIGHTED MEAN	7,218	19,176	24,340	+12,445	+164.7	+6,220	+37.4	+18,813	+250.2

Source: Federal Bureau of Investigation, Uniform Crime Reports, "Number of Offenses Known to Police." (For Year Indicated).

encing very low levels of crime in 1960, and any increase over a small base number looms as a large percentage. It also indicates that these new areas, given their scale and wealth, are ripe for criminal activity. Indeed, the tremendous growth in all types of criminal activity, especially violent crime, in San Jose and Austin, are examples of this trend.

Exhibit 4.13 helps to define differences in crime for the two classes of cities by presenting crime rates as a function of the population of these cities. While overall rates of crime have been quite similar for both intergovernmental and non-intergovernmental cities, over the past two decades the crime rate has shown a greater increase in intergovernmental cities. In 1977, the overall crime rate in intergovernmental cities was 79.3 crimes per 1,000 population; here approximately one person out of every twelve was annually affected by a crime. In non-intergovernmental cities, the overall crime rate was ten percent lower, 72.9 crimes per 1,000 population, affecting approximately one person out of every fourteen.

Aggregate crime rates for the two classes of cities tend to blur differences in local public safety which are far from subtle. Further, group means often function to distort substantial variation in data presented by individual city. Here, Rochester and Baton Rouge have extraordinarily high overall crime rates, that skew up the means for their respective groups. Because property crimes occur with much greater frequency than violent crime, the cities with the highest property crime rates showed, by far, the worst overall crime rates. This also is very evident in the above two cases, where the cities with the highest property crime rates and the highest overall crime rates had rates of violent crime which were quite moderate. The violent crime rates in these two cities paled in comparison with those of Newark, Baltimore or Cleveland. Consequently, even though the overall crime rate was highest in Rochester and Baton Rouge, the types of crimes occurring in other cities, while less frequent, often were much more serious. The overall crime rate is an insufficient indicator of the seriousness of criminal activity across specific cities. Since this measure minimizes the impact of the most serious offenses, it is necessary to ferret out city-to-city differentials by type of crime.

Violent Crime

For intergovernmental cities, the rate of violent crime far outdistanced that of non-intergovernmental cities. The national average for violent crime—including murder, rape, robbery, and assault, in 1977 was 4.6 violent crimes per 1,000 population. In other words, across the United States approximately one person out of every 200 was annually victimized by a violent crime. In intergovernmental cities, the rate of violent crime was more than double this national figure (Exhibit 4.13). Here, the violent crime rate was 11.1 incidents per 1,000 people. Indeed, the worst rates of violent crime were all found in intergovernmental cities. Baltimore, Cleveland and Newark showed rates of violent crime triple the national average. Cincinnati, Minneapolis and Rochester had rates which were double the national figure. In fact, all of the intergovernmental cities, with the exception of Milwaukee, showed extraordinarily high rates of violent crime.

In non-intergovernmental cities, in 1977, the violent crime rate was substantially

EXHIBIT 4.13.—*Trends in Total Crime Rates: 1960, 1970, 1977*
(Per 100,000 Population)

	TOTAL CRIME				VIOLENT CRIME				PROPERTY CRIME			
	1960	1970	1977	Δ1960-1977	1960	1970	1977	Δ1960-1977	1960	1970	1977	Δ1960-1977
INTERGOVERNMENTAL												
AKRON	31.2	64.9	73.4	+42.2	1.3	4.8	5.6	+4.3	29.9	60.1	67.8	+37.9
BALTIMORE	24.1	90.1	83.7	+59.6	3.3	20.9	17.8	+14.5	20.8	69.2	65.9	+45.1
BUFFALO	14.3	80.8	81.6	+67.3	0.9	34.7	10.3	+9.4	13.4	46.1	71.3	+57.9
CINCINNATI	18.4	56.8	74.5	+56.1	1.3	5.0	8.5	+7.2	17.1	51.8	65.9	+83.0
CLEVELAND	26.2	76.1	90.3	+64.1	2.3	10.6	15.5	+12.2	24.0	65.5	74.8	+50.8
LOUISVILLE	32.1	65.0	62.9	+30.8	2.7	6.1	6.7	+4.0	29.4	58.9	56.1	+26.7
MILWAUKEE	18.6	40.8	52.9	+34.3	0.9	2.1	3.9	+3.0	17.7	38.7	49.0	+31.3
MINNEAPOLIS	33.2	79.1	90.2	+57.0	1.7	6.4	8.7	+7.0	31.5	72.8	81.5	+50.0
NEWARK	57.2	98.4	93.6	+36.4	7.9	18.9	19.1	+11.0	49.3	79.5	74.5	+25.2
ROCHESTER	17.4	68.3	103.6	+86.2	0.5	4.3	8.0	+7.5	16.9	64.0	95.5	+78.6
WEIGHTED MEAN	26.0	72.4	79.3	+46.4	2.2	9.5	11.1	+8.9	23.7	60.1	68.2	+44.5
NON-INTERGOVERNMENTAL												
ANAHEIM	34.9	70.0	79.4	+44.5	0.8	2.6	5.6	+4.8	34.1	67.4	73.8	+39.7
AUSTIN	31.1	60.5	72.8	+41.7	1.7	4.9	3.9	+2.2	29.3	55.6	68.9	+39.6
BATON ROUGE	38.9	74.5	102.3	+63.4	1.9	6.3	9.2	+7.3	37.0	68.2	93.1	+56.1
COLUMBUS	29.0	64.7	81.3	+52.3	2.8	5.4	6.1	+3.3	26.2	59.3	75.2	+49.0
NASHVILLE	42.6	46.7	60.8	+18.2	1.8	6.7	6.9	+5.1	40.9	40.0	53.9	+13.0
OKLAHOMA CITY	36.5	53.9	75.0	+38.5	1.4	3.7	7.2	+5.8	35.1	47.5	67.8	+32.7
SAN JOSE	47.5	71.6	67.3	+19.8	0.7	3.2	4.6	+3.9	46.8	68.4	62.7	+15.9
TULSA	32.4	51.2	73.0	+40.6	1.3	3.1	5.4	+4.1	31.1	48.1	67.6	+36.5
VIRGINIA BEACH	NA	44.0	49.3	NA	NA	1.6	2.0	NA	NA	42.4	47.3	NA
WICHITA	23.1	75.7	76.5	+53.4	1.1	3.5	5.2	+4.1	22.0	72.2	71.3	+49.3
WEIGHTED MEAN	30.5	60.7	72.9	+42.4	1.6	4.3	5.5	+3.9	32.2	56.4	67.2	+35.0

Source: Federal Bureau of Investigation, Uniform Crime Reports, "Number of Offenses Known to Police." (For Year Indicated).

EXHIBIT 4.14. — *Trends in Violent Crime Incidents: 1960, 1970, 1977*

| | 1960 | 1970 | 1977 | CHANGE | | | | | |
				1960-1970 Absolute	1960-1970 Percent	1970-1977 Absolute	1970-1977 Percent	1960-1977 Absolute	1960-1977 Percent
INTERGOVERNMENTAL									
AKRON	360	1,310	1,360	+950	+263.9	+50	+3.8	+1,000	+277.8
BALTIMORE	3,117	18,910	14,283	+15,793	+506.7	-4627	-24.5	+11,166	+358.2
BUFFALO	505	2,610	4,005	+2,096	+415.0	+1404	+54.0	+3,500	+693.1
CINCINNATI	635	2,255	3,439	+1,620	+255.1	+1184	+52.5	+2,804	+441.6
CLEVELAND	1,996	7,962	9,421	+5,966	+298.1	+1459	+18.3	+7,425	+372.0
LOUISVILLE	1,047	2,217	2,181	+1,177	+111.7	-36	-1.6	+1,134	+108.3
MILWAUKEE	684	1,512	2,535	+828	+121.0	+1023	+67.7	+1,851	+270.6
MINNEAPOLIS	811	2,766	3,130	+1,955	+241.1	+364	+13.2	+2,319	+285.9
NEWARK	3,209	7,232	6,175	+4,023	+125.4	-1057	-14.6	+2,966	+92.4
ROCHESTER	166	1,275	2,059	+1,109	+668.1	+784	+61.5	+1,893	+114.0
WEIGHTED MEAN	1,253	4,804	4,859	+3,552	+300.7	+55	+23.0	+3,606	+301.4
NON-INTERGOVERNMENTAL									
ANAHEIM	78	427	1,130	+349	+447.4	+703	+164.6	+1,052	+1,348.7
AUSTIN	326	1,244	1,260	+918	+281.6	+16	+1.2	+934	+286.5
BATON ROUGE	288	1,053	1,867	+765	+265.6	+814	+77.3	+1,579	+548.3
COLUMBUS	1,312	2,914	3,238	+1,602	+122.1	+324	+11.1	+1,926	+146.8
NASHVILLE	303	3,000	2,957	+2,697	+890.1	-43	-1.5	+2,654	+875.9
OKLAHOMA CITY	459	1,349	2,695	+890	+193.9	+1,346	+99.8	+2,236	+487.1
SAN JOSE	148	1,401	2,680	+1,253	+846.6	+1,279	+91.3	+2,532	+1,710.8
TULSA	331	1,035	1,805	+704	+212.7	+770	+74.4	+1,474	+445.3
VIRGINIA BEACH	NA	273	463	NA	NA	+190	+69.5	NA	NA
WICHITA	274	970	1,397	+696	+254.0	+427	+44.0	+1,123	+409.8
WEIGHTED MEAN	391	1,367	1,949	+1,097	+390.4	+583	+63.2	+1,723	+695.5

Source: Federal Bureau of Investigation, Uniform Crime Reports, "Number of Offenses Known to Police." (For Year Indicated).

lower than intergovernmental cities, and quite comparable to the national rate. In these cities, approximately 5.2 individuals per 1,000 population annually fell victim to a violent crime. Although Baton Rouge had the highest violent crime rate of the non-intergovernmental cities, this rate was much smaller than the equivalent rates of Newark, Baltimore or Cleveland. Of the remaining non-intergovernmental cities, only Nashville-Davidson and Oklahoma City had violent crime rates that were substantially higher than the national average. Austin, San Jose, and Virginia Beach possessed rates of violent crime that were at or below the national average.

Moreover, as Exhibit 4.15 indicates, intergovernmental cities in 1977, experienced very high rates for most types of violent crime. Here, rates of murder, rape, robbery and assault were more than double national averages. Of these cities, Cleveland had a murder rate more than five times the national rate, and the murder rate was double the national average in Newark, Louisville, Baltimore, Cincinnati and Rochester. Extremely serious rates of robbery and assault were found in all of these cities along

EXHIBIT 4.15. — *Detailed Crime Rates By Type of Crime, 1977*
(Per 100,000 Population)

	Murder	Rape	Robbery	Aggra-vated Assault	Burglary	All Larceny	Auto Theft
INTERGOVERNMENTAL							
AKRON	10	60	251	236	1,911	4,363	507
BALTIMORE	21	62	941	752	1,898	3,925	2,536
BUFFALO	12	61	483	472	2,381	3,337	1,419
CINCINNATI	18	72	403	360	2,081	4,036	477
CLEVELAND	41	98	1,062	346	2,584	2,715	2,185
LOUISVILLE	20	48	423	183	1,840	3,080	693
MILWAUKEE	8	33	213	135	1,084	3,272	547
MINNEAPOLIS	11	90	459	310	2,706	4,372	1,074
NEWARK	28	100	989	789	2,708	3,200	1,542
ROCHESTER	18	34	429	322	3,257	5,557	738
WEIGHTED MEAN	19	66	615	412	2,134	3,657	1,025
NON-INTERGOVERNMENTAL							
ANAHEIM	3	60	296	201	2,809	3,974	473
AUSTIN	10	58	158	163	2,242	4,271	383
BATON ROUGE	14	59	189	653	2,724	5,970	618
COLUMBUS	13	62	329	204	2,384	4,444	690
NASHVILLE-DAVIDSON	19	44	393	233	2,034	2,832	527
OKLAHOMA CITY	18	67	208	431	2,396	3,515	862
SAN JOSE	7	57	177	219	2,063	3,613	591
TULSA	8	51	146	334	2,180	3,992	589
VIRGINIA BEACH	7	34	64	91	943	3,597	193
WICHITA	13	45	266	197	1,821	4,805	503
WEIGHTED MEAN	12	54	232	261	2,160	3,980	576
NATIONAL AVERAGE	9	30	187	242	1,411	2,723	448

Source: Federal Bureau of Investigation, Uniform Crime Reports, "Number of Offenses Known to Police." (For Year Indicated)

with Minneapolis and Buffalo. Only Milwaukee, of the intergovernmental cities, managed to escape the pressing problem of excessive violent crime.

In non-intergovernmental cities, in 1977, rates for violent crimes were far less serious. Only Baton Rouge, Oklahoma City, and Nashville-Davidson experienced relatively serious rates of murder, rape, robbery or assault. In the remaining non-intergovernmental cities, rates for these violent crimes were much more moderate. San Jose, Tulsa, and Virginia Beach had murder rates beneath the national average, and Anaheim had a murder rate that was one-third the national figure. These cities, plus Tulsa and Wichita, experienced rates of robbery and assault that were, for the most part, beneath national averages. Virginia Beach exhibited rates of robbery and assault that were less than one-third national rates.

Property Crime

While property crimes were generally not as serious as violent crimes, they were much more common. In 1977, the national rate for property crime was forty-five incidents per 1,000 people. That is, about one person in twenty fell victim to a property crime, or about ten times as many people were affected by property crimes than were affected by violent crimes. Both intergovernmental and non-intergovernmental cities had very similar rates of property crime. In either type of city, approximately sixty-eight property crimes occurred per 1,000 population, meaning that one person in every fourteen annually fell victim to a property crime (Exhibit 4.13). In both classes of cities the frequency of property crime exceeded the national average by over 50 percent.

Rochester and Baton Rouge experienced the highest rates of property crime. As noted earlier, by virtue of their extraordinarily large property crime rates, these cities also exhibited the highest overall crime rates. In Baton Rouge and Rochester property crimes occurred at a rate exceeding ninety incidents per 1,000. Here, property crimes affected nearly one person in ten. These rates were unmatched in any of the other sample cities and are more than double the national average.

With the exception of Baton Rouge and to a lesser extent Wichita, in 1977, intergovernmental cities showed the highest rates of property crime. Overall, crimes against property were very frequent in Buffalo, Cleveland, Newark, and Minneapolis. Additionally, Akron, Baltimore and Cincinnati all exhibited relatively high rates of property crime. Once again, Milwaukee was the only intergovernmental city that experienced property crime at or around the national rate.

While motor vehicle theft was the least frequent type of property crime, it was perhaps the key indicator of the safety of personal property in any central city. As Exhibit 4.15 indicates, in 1977, in intergovernmental cities the rate of auto theft was almost double the rate for non-intergovernmental cities, and a similar multiple of the national average. Moreover, the highest rates of auto theft were found in Baltimore and Cleveland where rates were four-five times the national average. Auto theft was also very frequent in Newark, Buffalo and Minneapolis. Additionally, Rochester and Louisville exhibited rates of motor vehicle theft that were 1.5 times the national average. On the other hand, most of the non-intergovernmental cities had auto theft rates that were comparable to the national rate. Indeed, both Austin

EXHIBIT 4.16. — *Trends in Property Crime Incidents: 1960, 1970, 1977*

| | 1960 | 1970 | 1977 | CHANGE | | | | | |
				1960-1970 Absolute	1960-1970 Percent	1970-1977 Absolute	1970-1977 Percent	1960-1977 Absolute	1960-1977 Percent
INTERGOVERNMENTAL									
AKRON	8,664	16,532	16,547	+7,868	+90.8	+15	+0.1	+7,883	+91.0
BALTIMORE	19,460	62,692	53,004	+43,232	+222.2	-9,688	-15.5	+33,544	+172.4
BUFFALO	7,089	21,362	27,836	+14,273	+201.4	+6,474	+30.3	+20,747	+292.7
CINCINNATI	8,581	23,539	26,573	+14,958	+174.3	+3,034	+12.9	+17,992	+209.7
CLEVELAND	20,984	49,214	45,574	+28,230	+134.5	-3,640	-7.4	+24,590	+117.2
LOUISVILLE	11,477	21,297	18,131	+9,820	+85.6	-3,166	-14.9	+6,654	+58.0
MILWAUKEE	13,133	27,724	32,012	+14,591	+111.1	+4,288	+15.5	+18,879	+143.8
MINNEAPOLIS	15,169	31,578	29,348	+16,409	+108.2	-2,230	-7.1	+14,179	+93.5
NEWARK	19,976	30,374	24,138	+10,398	+52.1	-6,236	-20.5	+4,162	+20.8
ROCHESTER	5,365	18,863	24,451	+13,498	+251.5	+5,588	+29.6	+19,086	+355.8
WEIGHTED MEAN	9,858	30,318	29,761	+17,327	+143.2	-556	+2.3	+16,772	+155.4
NON-INTERGOVERNMENTAL									
ANAHEIM	3,547	11,186	14,913	+7,639	+215.4	+3,727	+33.3	+11,366	+320.4
AUSTIN	5,482	14,022	22,276	+8,540	+155.8	+8,254	+58.9	+16,794	+306.3
BATON ROUGE	5,635	11,307	18,995	+5,672	+100.7	+7,688	+68.0	+13,360	+237.1
COLUMBUS	12,349	32,016	39,991	+19,667	+159.3	+7,975	+24.9	+27,642	+223.8
NASHVILLE	6,988	17,818	23,139	+10,830	+155.0	+5,321	+29.9	+16,151	+231.1
OKLAHOMA CITY	11,366	18,479	25,195	+7,113	+62.6	+6,716	+36.3	+13,829	+121.7
SAN JOSE	9,539	30,098	36,538	+20,559	+215.5	+6,440	+21.4	+26,999	+283.0
TULSA	8,145	15,858	22,586	+7,713	+94.7	+6,728	+42.4	+14,441	+177.3
VIRGINIA BEACH	NA	7,303	11,170	NA	NA	+3,867	+52.9	NA	NA
WICHITA	5,606	20,003	19,107	+14,397	+256.8	-896	-4.5	+13,501	+240.8
WEIGHTED MEAN	7,629	17,809	23,391	+11,347	+168.3	+5,582	+36.4	+15,762	+206.6

Source: Federal Bureau of Investigation, Uniform Crime Reports, "Number of Offenses Known to Police." (For Year Indicated).

and Virginia Beach had rates that were significantly less than the national figure.

The final two types of property crime—burglary and larceny—are the most frequent criminal incidents. Nationally, one person in twenty-five falls victim to either of these crimes. Burglary and larceny are very serious problems for the two classes of cities. In 1977, the rates for these offenses were 1.5 times the national averages. In intergovernmental cities burglary and larceny combined affected approximately one person in seventeen. In non-intergovernmental cities, the combined rate for these crimes was only slightly different. Here, approximately one person in sixteen fell victim to burglary or larceny.

During the 1960s and 1970s *incidents* of property crime increased at a faster rate though lower absolute number in non-intergovernmental than intergovernmental cities. Both classes of cities exceeded the national rate of growth in property crime incidents for this period (Exhibit 4.16).

Summary

Exhibit 4.17 presents a comparative index of crime for the twenty cities in 1977. As previously stated, overall crime rates, taken by themselves, remain inadequate comparative indicators of criminal activity, primarily because they minimize the impact of high rates of violent crimes. The ranking system presented here considers both the differential frequencies of criminal incidents by city as well as the relative seriousness of various crimes. In doing so, this index shows, rather conclusively, that serious crimes were most heavily concentrated in intergovernmental cities. Cleveland and Newark had, by far, the most serious crime problems. They consistently showed the highest rates of violent crime and very high rates of property crime as well. Crime was an extremely serious problem in Baltimore, Rochester, Minneapolis and Buffalo. More disturbing yet, these cities also exhibited an extraordinarily high incidence of violent crime. Indeed, in terms of the index, the six highest crime cities were all intergovernmental cities; and of the eleven cities with the worst crime problems, eight were intergovernmental cities.

Of the non-intergovernmental cities, only Baton Rouge, Oklahoma City and Columbus experienced serious crime problems. Even in these cities, levels of crime were not comparable to those in most intergovernmental cities. More important was the very low rate of violent crime found in such non-intergovernmental locations as Columbus and Oklahoma City. The remaining non-intergovernmental cities were part of a large group of low-to-moderate crime cities. Wichita, Nashville and Anaheim experienced relatively moderate overall crime problems. Crime was far less serious in Tulsa, Austin and San Jose. These cities exhibited relatively low rates of property crime and violent crime alike; rates which were at or slightly below the national average. Virginia Beach had, by far, the smallest incidence of crime of all the cities. Here, the frequency of property crime was comparable to the national rate, while the frequencies for all types of violent crime were significantly below national rates.

Crime constitutes a serious urban problem. Although it is a key measure of urban socioeconomic variance, it is seldom evaluated for such purposes. According to this analysis, towards the end of the 1970s, property crime decreases occurred in both

EXHIBIT 4.17. — *Comparative Index of Local Crime By City*
(From Worst to Least), 1977

Rank	Score	City Type	Total Crime	Vio- lent Crime	Prop- erty Crime	Murder	Robbery	Auto Theft
CLEVELAND	110	I	4	3	5	1	2	1
NEWARK	109	I	3	1	6	2	3	2
BALTIMORE	97	I	6	2	14	3	1	3
ROCHESTER	96	I	1	8	1	6	7	7
MINNEAPOLIS	89	I	5	6	3	13	5	5
BUFFALO	86	I	7	4	9	12	4	4
BATON ROUGE	80	N-I	2	5	2	11	16	10
OKLAHOMA CITY	78	N-I	11	9	11	6	6	5
COLUMBUS	73	N-I	8	12	4	10	9	10
CINCINNATI	62	I	12	7	14	6	17	18
LOUISVILLE	53	I	17	11	17	4	18	6
WICHITA	53	N-I	10	17	8	10	16	12
NASHVILLE	52	N-I	18	10	18	5	9	14
ANAHEIM	48	N-I	9	13	7	20	18	11
AKRON	47	I	13	13	11	14	15	13
TULSA	37	N-I	14	15	13	16	12	19
AUSTIN	32	N-I	15	18	10	14	19	18
SAN JOSE	32	N-I	16	16	16	18	11	17
MILWAUKEE	25	I	19	18	19	16	13	14
VIRGINIA BEACH	8	N-I	20	20	20	18	20	20

Note: Component scores for individual cities were calculated using a reversed ordinal scale -- 20 through 1. Thus, the worst cases (i.e., ranks 1, 2, 3...) received scores of 20, 19, 18...respectively. These individual scores were then summed to obtain the total or composite score.

Source: Exhibits 4.12 through 4.16.

classes of cities, and appeared independent of characteristics of local economic performance or municipal fiscal capacity. Violent crime, however, which was probably a clearer indicator of the seriousness of urban crime, remained very highly concentrated in intergovernmental cities.

Public Assistance: Dependent Populations and Payment Patterns

The bulk of the findings thus far indicate that most of the intergovernmental cities were hardship cities. It is now necessary to look at differences in dependent populations of the two classes of cities.

Welfare Caseloads and Recipients

The findings presented in Exhibit 4.18 indicate intergovernmental cities typically possess much larger dependent populations than non-intergovernmental cities and

EXHIBIT 4.18. — *Public Assistance Caseloads, Total Payments, and
Average Monthly Benefits, By City, 1980*

	Total AFDC Recip- ients	Total AFDC Case- load	Annual AFDC Payments (in thousands (of dollars)	Average Monthly Benefit Per Receipient	Average Monthly Benefit Per Case
INTERGOVERNMENTAL					
AKRON	20,340	7,325	$ 21,552	$ 88.32	$245.24
BALTIMORE	132,308	46,855	123,648	77.88	219.91
BUFFALO	38,059	13,170	51,384	112.52	326.67
CINCINNATI	38,895	13,532	41,124	88.12	253.26
CLEVELAND	90,992	29,899	100,248	91.81	264.73
LOUISVILLE	34,198	12,598	26,844	65.42	177.59
MILWAUKEE	68,233	22,174	108,264	132.23	370.73
MINNEAPOLIS	38,869	14,384	54,504	116.85	320.41
NEWARK	80,312	36,176	93,552	97.07	312.13
ROCHESTER	26,005	8,169	35,928	115.12	367.06
TOTAL	568,211	204,282	$657,048	--	--
MEAN	56,821	20,428	$ 65,705	$ 98.47	$285.77
NON-INTERGOVERNMENTAL					
ANAHEIM	6,362	2,205	$ 9,468	$124.07	$364.19
AUSTIN	6,440	2,197	2,651	34.30	100.56
BATON ROUGE	13,829	4,495	7,680	46.29	142.39
COLUMBUS	41,353	14,185	44,568	89.81	261.82
NASHVILLE- DAVIDSON	16,998	6,219	8,628	42.29	115.61
OKLAHOMA CITY	15,552	5,113	14,936	85.36	259.65
SAN JOSE	37,114	12,674	54,240	121.78	359.53
TULSA	12,000	3,916	12,096	84.00	257.41
VIRGINIA BEACH	4,609	1,767	4,152	75.07	195.81
WICHITA	11,704	4,300	14,304	101.82	277.13
TOTAL	165,961	57,071	$173,723	--	--
MEAN	16,596	5,707	$ 17,372	$ 80.48	$233.41

Source: 1980, U. S. Department of Health and Human Services, Social Se-
curity Administration, Office of Policy, Office of Research and
Statistics, "Public Assistance Recipients and Cash Payments by
State and County, February 1980."

that these cities provide far greater total welfare outlays as well. In 1980, the overall welfare caseload* for intergovernmental cities was nearly four times that of non-intergovernmental cities—204,000 versus 57,000 cases. (The aggregate population of intergovernmental cities is only 12 percent greater than the aggregate population of non-intergovernmental cities.) Similarly, there were substantially more welfare recipients** in these cities. In intergovernmental cities, nearly 570,000 people were on the welfare rolls in 1980, while almost 400,000 fewer people, 170,000, were receiving welfare in non-intergovernmental cities.***

Moreover, all of the intergovernmental cities, in 1980, had extraordinarily large dependent populations, while only San Jose and Columbus of the non-intergovernmental cities had substantial numbers of people collecting welfare. Of all the sample cities, Baltimore had, by far, the largest welfare population with over 130,000 individuals receiving AFDC. In Cleveland, Newark and Milwaukee, in 1982, over 65,000 people collected welfare. In the rest of the intergovernmental cities, 35,000 or more people received AFDC benefits. In most of the remaining non-intergovernmental cities, however, less than 20,000 people were on welfare. Indeed, in Anaheim, Austin and Virginia Beach, less than 7,000 collected welfare.

Annual Aid to Families with Dependent Children Payments

It is also important to view differences in total payments expended for welfare in the two classes of cities. Total public assistance payments in intergovernmental cities significantly exceeded those made in non-intergovernmental cities. In 1980, total annual welfare payments of nearly $660 million in the intergovernmental cities outpaced total payments of approximately $170 million in non-intergovernmental cities by close to one-half billion dollars (Exhibit 4.18). Of course the same cities with the largest dependent populations showed the highest overall payment patterns. Baltimore, Milwaukee and Cleveland, in the early 1980s, had over $100 million each expended for welfare, while the Newark equivalent was about $90 million annually. In Minneapolis and Buffalo, AFDC expenditures were also very substantial, in the range of $50 million. Of the non-intergovernmental cities, once again, only Columbus and San Jose inhabitants as a group received total AFDC payments that were comparable to those observed for intergovernmental cities. Indeed, the bulk of the non-intergovernmental cities, including Nashville-Davidson, Tulsa, Oklahoma City, Wichita, Baton Rouge and Anaheim, each had $15 million or less in welfare payments. In Virginia Beach and Austin, total AFDC payments were considerably under $5 million annually, or one-twentieth of the payment levels of the high-need, intergovernmental cities.

---

*"Welfare case" refers to a single household of any size receiving payments. For example, if one household is receiving AFDC payments for three children, this equals one AFDC case.

**"Welfare recipient" refers to any person receiving AFDC payments. In the welfare case specified above, there are three welfare recipients.

***Data on citywide welfare recipient caseloads and total payments where not available from published documents was obtained directly from county welfare offices. Source: CUPR Survey, January 1982.

Average Monthly Benefits

Exhibit 4.19 indicates that average monthly AFDC benefits were, by and large, highest in intergovernmental cities. Here, in 1980, the average benefit per recipient was nearly $100, while the average benefit per case was almost $285. In intergovernmental cities AFDC benefit levels were, on average, 25 percent higher than those in non-intergovernmental cities. The residents of intergovernmental cities such as Buffalo, Milwaukee, Newark, Minneapolis and Rochester received relatively high monthly benefits, approximately $100 per recipient or $300 per case. The rest of these cities had moderate benefits in the range of $250 per case or $85 per individual. Of the intergovernmental cities, only Louisville and Baltimore—more or less southern cities—provided relatively small AFDC benefits. Yet, even these amounts significantly outstripped the very small benefit levels found in most of the non-intergovernmental cities. In Austin, Baton Rouge and Nashville, average monthly benefits appeared to be well below basic sustenance levels, and in the majority of the non-intergovernmental cities monthly public assistance payments were not much higher. Of these cities, only the California locations—San Jose and Anaheim, along with Columbus—provided benefits comparable to those found in most intergovernmental cities.

Public Assistance Benefits and Poverty Levels

Exhibit 4.20 contrasts average yearly public assistance incomes with established indicators of urban poverty. In 1979, in intergovernmental cities, average yearly public assistance incomes equaled $5,500, 77 percent of the poverty line, and 43 percent of the Bureau of Labor Statistics lower budget amount. In the non-intergovernmental cities, public assistance incomes were even lower. Here, welfare families averaged less than $5,000 in yearly income, 68 percent of the poverty level and just 38 percent of the BLS lower urban budget. Welfare families received the highest income in Minneapolis and Milwaukee—two intergovernmental cities with a low incidence of socioeconomic distress across all indicators—as well as Rochester and Buffalo, both highly distressed cities. Public assistance households received very little subsistence in Austin, Baton Rouge and Nashville-Davidson.

Welfare Dependence as a Function of Total Population

Exhibit 4.21 reports data on local welfare dependence as a function of citywide population. By showing welfare dependence both in terms of population and as a constant per capita payment distributed across population, these measures provide good comparative indicators both of the concentration of dependent populations in a city and the differential benefit patterns across cities.

These measures clearly highlight previously observed patterns of welfare dependence for the two classes of cities. As of 1980, intergovernmental cities possessed much greater dependent populations and showed much higher per capita

EXHIBIT 4.19.—*Trends in Public Assistance Caseloads, Total Payments, and Average Monthly Benefits, By County: 1964, 1973, 1980*

	1964	1973	1980	1964-1973 Absolute	1964-1973 Percent	1973-1980 Absolute	1973-1980 Percent	1964-1980 Absolute	1964-1980 Percent
TOTAL AFDC RECIPIENTS									
Intergovernmental	248,992	713,776	660,072	+464,784	+186.7	-53,704	-7.5	+411,080	+165.1
Non-Intergovernmental	91,690	276,836	246,719	+185,146	+201.9	-30,117	-10.5	+155,029	+169.1
TOTAL AFDC CASES									
Intergovernmental	60,186	206,989	227,164	+146,803	+243.9	+20,175	+9.7	+166,978	+277.4
Non-Intergovernmental	22,307	81,022	84,400	+58,715	+263.2	+3,378	+4.2	+62,093	+278.4
TOTAL AFDC PAYMENTS (in thousands of dollars)									
Intergovernmental	$118,392	$541,368	$764,124	+422,976	+357.3	+222,756	+41.1	+645,732	+545.4
Non-Intergovernmental	28,572	160,620	284,280	+132,048	+462.2	+123,660	+77.0	+255,708	+895.0
AVERAGE MONTHLY BENEFIT PER INDIVIDUAL									
Intergovernmental	$39.88	$65.23	$98.47	+$25.36	+63.6	+$33.24	+51.0	$+58.60	+146.9
Non-Intergovernmental	30.72	44.21	80.48	+13.49	+43.9	+36.27	+82.0	+49.76	+162.0
AVERAGE MONTHLY AFDC BENEFIT PER CASE									
Intergovernmental	$162.08	$221.62	$285.77	+$59.54	+36.7	+$64.15	+28.9	+$123.69	+76.3
Non-Intergovernmental	128.10	150.10	233.41	+22.18	+17.3	+83.13	+55.3	+105.31	+82.2

Source: See Exhibit 4.18.

Exhibit 4.20. — *Annual Public Assistance Benefit Levels Compared with Common Indicators of Income Poverty: 1979*

	AFDC	Food Stamps	Total	Rank Out of 50 States	Percent of Poverty Level Cut-off	As Percent of BLS Lower Budget	As Percent of BLS Intermediate Budget
INTERGOVERNMENTAL							
AKRON	$3,492	$1,488	$4,980	31	69.5%	39.1%	24.3%
BALTIMORE	3,204	1,572	4,776	36	66.7	37.5	23.3
BUFFALO	5,712	816	6,528	3	91.2	51.3	31.8
CINCINNATI	3,492	1,488	4,980	31	69.5	39.1	24.3
CLEVELAND	3,492	1,488	4,980	31	69.5	35.4	24.3
LOUISVILLE	2,820	1,680	4,500	39	62.8	35.4	21.9
MILWAUKEE	5,496	888	6,384	5	89.1	50.2	31.1
MINNEAPOLIS	5,088	1,008	6,096	8	85.1	47.9	29.7
NEWARK	4,488	1,188	5,676	14	79.3	47.0	27.7
ROCHESTER	5,712	816	6,528	3	91.2	51.3	31.8
WEIGHTED MEAN	$4,300	$1,243	$5,543	20	77.4%	43.8%	28.0%
NON-INTERGOVERNMENTAL							
ANAHEIM	$5,076	$1,008	$6,084	10	85.0%	47.8%	29.7%
AUSTIN	1,680	2,028	3,708	48	51.8	29.1	18.1
BATON ROUGE	2,064	1,908	3,972	45	55.5	31.2	19.4
COLUMBUS	3,492	1,488	4,980	31	69.5	39.1	24.3
NASHVILLE-DAVIDSON	1,776	2,004	3,780	47	52.8	29.7	18.4
OKLAHOMA CITY	3,708	1,416	5,124	27	71.6	40.3	25.0
SAN JOSE	5,076	1,008	6,084	10	85.0	47.8	29.7
TULSA	3,708	1,416	5,124	27	71.6	40.3	25.0
VIRGINIA BEACH	3,408	1,512	4,920	33	68.7	38.7	24.0
WICHITA	3,672	1,428	5,088	29	71.1	40.0	24.8
WEIGHTED MEAN	3,366	$1,521	$4,886	30	68.3%	38.4%	23.8%

Note : All annual benefit amounts pertain to a four-person family. Poverty level and Bureau of Labor Statistics income cut-off levels are as follows:

		BLS Budgets	
Poverty Level	Lower	Intermediate	Higher
$7,160	$12,277	$20,517	$31,187

Sources: Advisory Commission on Intergovernmental Relations, Public Assistance: The Growth of a Federal Function, 1980.
-- U.S. Department of Commerce, Statistical Abstract of the United States, 1980, Table No. 812, "Urban Budgets For a 4-Person Family, 1970 to 1979."

EXHIBIT 4.21. — *Percent of Total Population Receiving Public Assistance and Per Capita Monthly Benefit Amount, 1980*

	Percent Receiving AFDC	Per Capita Benefit Amount
INTERGOVERNMENTAL		
NEWARK	24.4%	$23.68
BALTIMORE	16.8	13.09
CLEVELAND	15.9	14.56
LOUISVILLE	11.5	7.49
MILWAUKEE	10.8	14.23
ROCHESTER	10.8	12.39
BUFFALO	10.6	11.96
MINNEAPOLIS	10.5	12.24
CINCINNATI	10.1	8.90
AKRON	8.6	7.57
WEIGHTED MEAN	13.5	12.99
NON-INTERGOVERNMENTAL		
COLUMBUS	7.3	6.57
BATON ROUGE	6.3	2.91
SAN JOSE	5.8	7.10
WICHITA	4.2	4.38
OKLAHOMA CITY	3.9	3.29
NASHVILLE-DAVIDSON	3.7	1.58
TULSA	3.3	2.79
ANAHEIM	3.0	3.56
AUSTIN	1.9	1.65
VIRGINIA BEACH	1.8	1.32
WEIGHTED MEAN	4.4	3.86

Source: 1980, U.S. Department of Health and Human Services, Social Security Administration, Office of Policy, Office of Research and Statistics, "Public Assistance Recipients and Cash Payments by State and County, February 1980."

payments.* In these cities, approximately 13.5 percent of the overall population received welfare, compared to just 4.4 percent of the population of non-intergovernmental cities. Newark, by far, had the largest AFDC population—comprising nearly 25 percent, or one-quarter, of its total population. In Cleveland and Baltimore over 15 percent of the total population received AFDC. In the rest of the intergovernmental cities over 10 percent of the total population collected public assistance.

None of the non-intergovernmental cities, on the other hand, possessed such wide patterns of welfare dependence. In most of these cities less than 5 percent of the total population received AFDC. Indeed, in Austin and Virginia Beach, less than 2 percent of the total population collected any form of welfare.

Summary

The analysis of data on public assistance shows quite clearly that both larger dependent populations and higher welfare benefits were found in intergovernmental cities. Most non-intergovernmental cities showed miniscule rates of welfare dependence and very small payments to complement their booming economies. Nashville-Davidson, Virginia Beach and Austin, as well as Oklahoma City, Tulsa and Wichita all had small dependent populations and provided low benefits to these populations. Especially in cities like Nashville and Austin, little in the way of public assistance was provided to residents.

Yet, the data also indicate that while the intergovernmental cities with highest degrees of distress and the lowest incomes—Newark, Cleveland, Baltimore, Buffalo, Louisville and Rochester—had the largest welfare populations, they did not necessarily provide high levels of benefits. For example, two high-need intergovernmental cities with large dependent populations—Louisville and Baltimore—gave relatively small per capita welfare benefits. To complicate the matter further: three fast-growing, low-need non-intergovernmental cities—Columbus, San Jose and Anaheim—gave high average benefits, and in the first two cases to significant numbers of recipients. On the one hand then, four relatively low-need cities—two non-intergovernmental cities plus Milwaukee and Minneapolis of the intergovernmental group—provided relatively high average monthly benefits to substantial numbers of people. On the other hand, two very high-need cities—Louisville and Baltimore—while serving significant populations, offered only limited AFDC benefits. These caveats notwithstanding, concentrations of dependent populations and high benefit amounts followed previously documented differentials in economic performance, fiscal viability and socioeconomic hardship.

Educational Performance and Achievement

Indicators of educational performance are difficult both to obtain and to analyze. Uniform educational data are unavailable on a city-to-city basis. Complicating this,

---

*AFDC payments represent 90 percent of aggregate welfare outlays.

available measures of performance present problems because test instruments differ by location as do local test emphases. Not only is this the case for achievement scores but for other school data as well. Enrollees in gifted or college preparatory programs may vary according to local priorities for such programs rather than local need or talent. Similarly, methods of sanction for disciplinary problems may vary markedly from the actual level of disciplinary problems or cases reported for any jurisdiction. These problems notwithstanding, using data obtained from the U.S. Department of Education, Office of Civil Rights and from the National Assessment of Educational Progress, some insight as to basic educational need in intergovernmental and non-intergovernmental cities is available.

Disciplinary Problems and Special Educational Needs

National surveys of school districts have been conducted biannually for the Department of Education by private contractors to assure that the anti-discriminatory requirements of Title VI of the Civil Rights Act (1964), Title IX of the Education Amendments (1972), and Section 504 of the Rehabilitation Act (1973) are being enforced to protect the rights of minorities, women and the handicapped, respectively. As part of these surveys data are collected on both suspensions and students classified as seriously emotionally disturbed.

Suspensions indicate school entry denial to a student for at least one school day. Suspensions, as a source of data, provide some index of local disciplinary problems or classroom unrest. In Exhibit 4.22, suspensions are presented per 1,000 students for each city classified as either intergovernmental or non-intergovernmental. In 1981, the simple mean of suspensions per 1,000 students showed significant differences between intergovernmental and non-intergovernmental cities. Suspensions in intergovernmental cities were 50 percent higher than in non-intergovernmental cities. In the first case, the number of suspensions represented 8.5 percent of the local school population; in the latter it represented 5.7 percent of the population.

Another measure of educational need is the number of students classified as "seriously" emotionally disturbed. This is a designation provided by the school district's psychologist and indicates a release of these students from most traditional course-work and activities and replacement of these activities with an educational program much more suited to their individual progress, ability to concentrate, and skill levels. It is a measure of the school district's special service burden. Exhibit 4.22 indicates the number of emotionally disturbed children per 1,000 students in each of the designated intergovernmental and non-intergovernmental cities. What is clear from this exhibit is the fivefold difference in designated emotionally disturbed school population between intergovernmental and non-intergovernmental cities in 1981. The rate of emotionally disturbed children in intergovernmental cities was six per 1,000; in non-intergovernmental cities, it was just below 1.2. While admittedly, criteria for this designation as well as its individual recognition vary considerably by location, the level of intergovernmental city impaction was clearly far above that observed for non-intergovernmental cities.

EXHIBIT 4.22. — *Suspensions and Emotionally Disturbed Per 1,000 Students in School Districts of Intergovernmental and Non-Intergovernmental Cities, 1981*

	Suspensions 1978-1979	(Per 1000 students)	Emotionally Disturbed 1978-1979	(Per 1000 students)
INTERGOVERNMENTAL				
AKRON	89.80		0.86	
BALTIMORE	93.90		1.94	
BUFFALO	41.00		8.72	
CINCINNATI	92.50		4.09	
CLEVELAND	109.10		0.12	
LOUISVILLE	95.50		3.10	
MILWAUKEE	164.70		10.49	
MINNEAPOLIS	64.80		12.94	
NEWARK	21.70		5.37	
ROCHESTER	74.10		12.42	
SIMPLE MEAN	84.70		6.01	
NON-INTERGOVERNMENTAL				
ANAHEIM	57.20		0.74	
AUSTIN	55.10		3.46	
BATON ROUGE	70.40		0.77	
COLUMBUS	32.80		1.90	
NASHVILLE	59.60		0.77	
OKLAHOMA CITY	80.80		1.57	
SAN JOSE	54.90		0.75	
TULSA	33.40		0.14	
VIRGINIA BEACH	78.80		1.31	
WICHITA	44.00		0.43	
SIMPLE MEAN	56.70		1.18	

Source: U.S. Department of Education, Office of Civil Rights, *Directory of Elementary and Secondary School Districts, School Year 1981-1982*, Volume 1. For school districts in cities indicated.

Reading and Mathematics Achievement

A test of student skills nationally is conducted annually by the National Assessment of Educational Progress, a non-profit research institute located in Denver, Colorado. The test is administered to 5,000 randomly sampled students in the fourth, eighth and twelfth grades—ages 9, 13 and 17 respectively. One means of data aggregation and comparison includes categorizing cities of over 200,000 population by "advantaged urban" and "disadvantaged urban," designations which reflect 1970 employment characteristics of residents of these cities. High per capita incomes, educational levels and white-collar employment locations were designated advantaged urban; locations of low income, high unemployment, and significant proportions of the population drawing public assistance were designated "disadvantaged" urban. Eight of ten of the non-intergovernmental cities as well as other cities fell within the advantaged set; nine of ten of the intergovernmental cities and other cities fell within the disadvantaged set.

As indicated by Exhibit 4.23, reading skills, measured by the average percent of correct responses to a standardized test, in disadvantaged urban locations were only 80 percent of those of advantaged urban locations. This is true for all three age groups tested. For mathematics skills the picture was even bleaker. Disadvantaged urban locations fell behind advantaged urban locations by 50 percent. While in both reading and mathematics there was some closing of the gap over the monitoring period (5 to 10 years) much of the parity that was being achieved was due to advantaged locations' scores *dropping* rather than disadvantaged locations' scores *rising*.

Summary

While admittedly Exhibits 4.22 and 4.23 represent only the beginnings of serious comparison across indicators of disciplinary sanction, special educational needs and educational skills attainment, as of the early 1980s, there were clear gaps between intergovernmental and non-intergovernmental cities. These point to differing needs, learning environments and basic skills in the two classes of cities.

Conclusion

Exhibit 4.24 presents a composite ranking of socioeconomic distress in the twenty sample cities. Just prior to the beginning of the 1980s, the most severe concentrations of social distress were found in older, economically declining, intergovernmental cities. The cities experiencing the most acute distress were all intergovernmental cities. Cleveland, Newark, Baltimore, and Buffalo exhibited very severe levels of hardship across all major social indicators. In these cities, incomes were extremely low, large sectors of the population were on unemployment or on welfare, crime and health problems were acute and educational achievement levels very low. To a lesser but nonetheless serious extent, Rochester, Louisville, Cincinnati and Akron also exhibited high degrees of socioeconomic hardship. Of the intergovernmental cities then, only Milwaukee and Minneapolis showed more moderate degrees of distress. Interestingly, both of these midwestern cities provided substantial public assistance benefits and served significantly large welfare clienteles. Here, public sector initiatives took the form of filling in the gaps and ameliorating the more onerous social consequences left in the wake of significant private disinvestment.

In non-intergovernmental cities, overall socioeconomic conditions were likely to be considerably better. None of these cities ranked among the high-need cities; rather, all evidenced low or, at worst, moderate degrees of social hardship. For example, the most distressed of the non-intergovernmental cities—Columbus and Baton Rouge—experienced levels of distress that were only slightly more serious than hardship in Milwaukee and Minneapolis. Those next in line, in Oklahoma City, Nashville-Davidson, and Wichita, experienced much more moderate levels of socioeconomic need. Indeed, five of seven moderate need cities were non-intergovernmental cities. Moreover, these younger, more economically vibrant cities

EXHIBIT 4.23. — *Reading and Mathematics Achievement Scores By Type of Urban Development, 1981*

AVERAGE PERCENT OF CORRECT RESPONSES* BY AGE

READING

	Age 17			Age 13			Age 9		
	1971	1975	1980	1970	1974	1979	1971	1975	1980
National Average	68.94	68.98	68.23	60.01	59.91	60.78	63.98	65.25	67.89
Advantaged Urban	75.75	76.01	73.53	67.14	66.67	67.93	71.57	71.29	73.14
Disadvantaged Urban	60.68	59.28	59.24	49.83	48.86	53.40	52.76	55.18	57.96
Disadvantaged as a Percent of Advantaged Scores	.80	.78	.80	.74	.73	.78	.74	.77	.79

MATHEMATICS

	Age 17		Age 13		Age 9	
	1973	1978	1972	1977	1973	1978
National Average	51.68	48.13	52.59	50.55	38.10	36.83
Advantaged Urban	59.52	57.28	63.60	59.37	46.65	45.97
Disadvantaged Urban	40.74	35.06	34.72	36.69	25.28	27.73
Disadvantaged as a Percent of Advantaged Scores	.68	.61	.55	.62	.54	.60

* Children in School.

Source: National Assessment of Educational Progress, 1981 Test Scores, Denver, Colorado.

EXHIBIT 4.24.—*Overall Comparative Ranking of Socioeconomic Distress, 1977, 1980, 1981*

RANK	Composite Score	City Type	Unemployment Rate, 1981 (worst to least)	Per Capita Income, 1977 (lowest to highest)	Health Conditions, 1977 (worst to least)	Crime 1977 (worst to least)	Public Assistance 1980, Percent Receiving AFDC (most to least)
High Need							
CLEVELAND	92	I	3	2	4	1	3
NEWARK	91	I	4	1	6	2	1
BALTIMORE	88	I	6	4	2	3	1
BUFFALO	85	I	1	3	3	6	7
ROCHESTER	74	I	11	6	5	4	5
LOUISVILLE	68	I	10	11	1	11	4
CINCINNATI	66	I	5	8	7	10	9
AKRON	62	I	2	7	9	15	10
Moderate Need							
COLUMBUS	58	N-I	8	5	14	9	11
BATON ROUGE	56	N-I	7	10	13	7	12
MILWAUKEE	49	I	9	12	11	19	5
MINNEAPOLIS	48	I	16	18	10	5	8
OKLAHOMA CITY	40	N-I	19	15	8	8	15
NASHVILLE-DAVIDSON	38	N-I	13	13	12	13	16
WICHITA	34	N-I	15	16	15	11	14
Low Need							
SAN JOSE	27	N-I	12	17	18	18	13
ANAHEIM	23	N-I	14	19	17	14	18
AUSTIN	23	N-I	18	9	19	17	19
TULSA	16	N-I	20	20	16	16	17
VIRGINIA BEACH	14	N-I	17	14	20	20	20

Note: Component scores for individual cities were calculated using a reversed ordinal scale—20 through 1. Thus, the worst cases (i.e., ranks 1, 2, 3 . . .) received scores of 20, 19, 18 . . . respectively. These individual scores were then summed to obtain the total or composite score.

Source: Prior substantive exhibits in text

comprised all of the low-need cities. While San Jose, Anaheim, and Austin experienced lower levels of social distress across most indicators, conditions were even better in Tulsa and Virginia Beach.

In short, older declining cities experienced very high degrees of distress, while in cities where the economic climate was more robust, socioeconomic hardship appeared far less serious. Put quite simply, incomes were lower, unemployment higher, educational achievement poorer, health and crime conditions worse, and welfare dependence more serious in intergovernmental than in non-intergovernmental cities.

5

Housing in the Intergovernmental City

THE PURPOSE of the chapter which follows is to detail the characteristics of the housing found in intergovernmental and non-intergovernmental cities. The nature of the housing stock (type, age, construction), its completeness and condition, as well as receptivity by occupants, are the major themes covered here. In addition, demographic profiles of the owners and tenants are included to provide insight into the differences in social structure which may exist in one class of cities versus another.

The chapter is divided by the two basic partitions discussed above: (1) characteristics of the housing stock, and (2) socioeconomic profiles of owners and tenants. Initially, a macro-view of differences by intergovernmental/non-intergovernmental city grouping is provided using data from the 1980 *Annual Housing Survey**. This is complemented by detailed insight garnered from sample data in one intergovernmental city, Newark, New Jersey. The chapter builds on the housing growth statistics discussed in the final sections of Chapter 3.

Housing in Intergovernmental Versus Non-Intergovernmental Cities: A Macro-View

The Structure

As of 1980, the housing of intergovernmental versus non-intergovernmental cities was primarily multifamily. Close to 60 percent of the housing of intergovernmental cities comprised structures of more than one unit; the equivalent for non-intergovernmental cities was about half the above percentage or thirty percent. Thus, in intergovernmental cities, structure condition, quality, etc., are influenced more heavily by characteristics of the multifamily stock. In non-intergovernmental cities qualities of single-family housing dominate the overall housing profile. The information which follows is presented by single and multifamily categories to adequately portray this significant difference in housing form in the two classes of cities.

*As of 1984 called the *American Housing Survey*.

Age and Size of Housing

In 1980, the median age of housing in the intergovernmental city was 50 years; the equivalent for non-intergovernmental cities was just over twenty years (Exhibit 5.1). The intergovernmental city experienced its building boom in the 1930s, whereas the non-intergovernmental city was largely a creature of the 1960s. Over 60 percent of the multifamily housing stock of intergovernmental cities was constructed before 1940; the figure for non-intergovernmental cities was barely 12 percent. On the other hand, 45 percent of the multifamily housing constructed in non-intergovernmental cities was built subsequent to 1970; the equivalent for non-intergovernmental cities was less than 10 percent. Even in the bygone era of generous mortgage subsidy programs, a building's actuarial life was seldom defined as more than 30 years. As of 1980 then, 75 percent of the multifamily housing stock of intergovernmental cities was past its actuarial life. By contrast, almost half of the multifamily housing of non-intergovernmental cities was barely into significant payments of mortgage principal.

The median age of single-family housing, while greater in both intergovernmental and non-intergovernmental cities, exhibited the same trends as multifamily housing; much more single-family housing was built in intergovernmental cities prior to 1940, much less was built post-1970. Intergovernmental cities had old single and multifamily housing; non-intergovernmental cities had very youthful multifamily housing and less so, but still relatively youthful, single-family housing. Newark's age distribution was even more pronounced than most intergovernmental cities. Seventy percent of its multifamily housing and all of its single-family housing was built prior to 1940.

Age of housing frequently reflects its size. In the earlier building periods structures and units were built larger. Also there was a greater distribution of units across size categories. Typically this meant significant unit representation at the extremes of size categories. More recent building periods have witnessed both a tendency to reduce the scale of housing units (particularly multifamily) and to build to the middle market of size category.

This trend is reflected in the size distribution of housing in intergovernmental versus non-intergovernmental cities. In 1980, close to 40 percent of the multifamily housing in intergovernmental cities was of a size of five rooms or more; 5 percent of the units had only one room (Exhibit 5.1). By contrast, in non-intergovernmental cities 8 out of 10 multifamily units had two to four rooms. Over time there was much more building to the center of the size market in non-intergovernmental cities. There was thus more homogenization of unit size in housing supply and potentially more capacity for the interchangeability of units.

Single-family house size exhibited less significant difference in intergovernmental versus non-intergovernmental cities. While houses were generally 20 percent larger in intergovernmental cities, the percentage of houses of seven rooms or more was only 10 percent greater. This obviously reflected a national housing market which had standardized its housing delivery to primarily sizes of three or four bedrooms.

As of 1980, multifamily units in the older intergovernmental cities were concentrated in structures of two-to-four units. Over forty percent of multifamily units in intergovernmental cities were found in this size category of structures; the figure for non-intergovernmental cities was barely one-third this rate. Approximately 10 per-

EXHIBIT 5.1. — *1980 Housing Age, Size, Completeness (Percent of Units with)*

AGE OF HOUSING	Multi-family Pre-1940	Post-1970	Single Family Pre-1940	Post-1970
Intergovernmental	61.2	9.7	66.9	2.7
Non-Intergovernmental	12.1	44.3	20.0	20.0
Newark	69.0	4.2	98.0	0.1

SIZE OF HOUSING	Multi-family 1 Room	5 Rooms or More	Single Family 7 Rooms or More
Intergovernmental	4.9	37.3	29.3
Non-Intergovernmental	1.9	14.3	26.1
Newark	14.6	33.8	66.0

SIZE OF STRUCTURE	Multi-Family 2-4 Units	20 Units or More
Intergovernmental	41.3	10.2
Non-Intergovernmental	13.4	11.0
Newark	16.5	16.8

SHARED OR NO KITCHEN	Multi-Family Shared Kitchen	No Kitchen	Single Family Shared Kitchen
Intergovernmental	.6	2.3	.4
Non-Intergovernmental	.8	1.1	.3
Newark	-	2.4	-

SHARED OR NO BATH	Multi-Family Shared Bath	No Bath	Single Family No Bath
Intergovernmental	2.7	-	.2
Non-Intergovernmental	.8	.4	-
Newark	-	-	-

Source: U.S. Department of Commerce, U.S. Department of Housing and Urban Development. Annual Housing Survey, 1980.

cent of the multifamily units in both categories of cities was found in structures of over 20 units (Exhibit 5.1). Thus, over 75 percent of the multifamily housing in non-intergovernmental cities was in structures from 5 to 19 units.

The City of Newark's housing was typified by both large single and multifamily structures. Two-thirds of its single-family housing consisted of structures containing more than seven rooms; 17 percent of multifamily housing was in buildings of twenty units or more.

Structural Completeness

Housing in the United States in terms of amenities and size is excellent overall, reasonably consistent throughout the country, and has few peers internationally. In fact, so standard is complete plumbing in most housing units that it no longer can be used as an index of housing quality. Further, housing unit density, another index of housing quality, has been generally decreasing for the previous two decades both as a function of increasing unit size and decreasing household size.

In 1980, approximately 2 percent of the multifamily households in intergovernmental cities had no kitchens; about one-quarter of this figure (0.5 percent) shared kitchens. While for the former this was double the rate for non-intergovernmental cities (1.1 percent), it was still a very low percentage of the aggregate for multifamily units (Exhibit 5.1). Recalling that non-intergovernmental cities are largely composed of single-family dwellings, and this form of housing usually has a kitchen, the lack of a kitchen is essentially nonexistent in non-intergovernmental cities. Further, the phenomenon of a shared kitchen was only half as frequent in the single-family, non-intergovernmental city as it was in the multifamily, intergovernmental city.

A somewhat similar scenario held true for the presence or shared use of a bath in intergovernmental and non-intergovernmental cities. While the rate of shared baths in intergovernmental cities was, on average, four times the rate of that of non-intergovernmental cities, overall it affected less than three percent of the housing units in the former category of cities. While housing in intergovernmental versus non-intergovernmental cities was older and larger, it was much more comparable in terms of the basic presence of kitchens and baths. Essentially all units in both city types had a bath/kitchen and seldom were they shared.

Structural Condition

Viewing the data in Exhibit 5.2 on housing condition, it is clear that as of 1980, both single and multifamily housing was superior in non-intergovernmental versus intergovernmental cities. It should be pointed out that in most cases fewer than 10 percent of the units in either intergovernmental or non-intergovernmental cities were characterized by specific indicators of housing condition deficiency. The condition of single-family housing was significantly better than multifamily housing in intergovernmental cities and very good, but roughly equivalent, in non-intergovernmental cities. Thus if one were to rank from best to worse the housing condition by type in the two locations it would appear as follows:

Best and Approximately Equivalent	Single and multifamily housing— non-intergovernmental city
Slightly Inferior Overall	Single-family housing—intergovernmental city
Significantly Inferior Overall	Multifamily housing—intergovernmental city

In structures employing the 1980 *Annual Housing Survey's* interviewee responses on unit characteristics as indicators of relative housing quality, those dealing with interior masonry, inoperative plumbing/heating, and signs of vermin were highly correlated with the true condition of a unit/building. The latter was verified through statistical correlation using a resample of a portion of the originally sampled units.

EXHIBIT 5.2. — *1980 Housing Condition (Percent of Units with)*

CRACKS OR HOLES IN WALL OR CEILING[1]	Multi-Family Cracks or Holes	Single Family Cracks or Holes
Intergovernmental	10.8	6.1
Non-Intergovernmental	6.7	5.0
Newark	14.5	23.4

BROKEN PLASTER – OVER ONE SQUARE FOOT[2]	Multi-Family Broken Plaster	Single Family Broken Plaster
Intergovernmental	7.7	4.1
Non-Intergovernmental	2.7	2.6
Newark	9.5	11.6

TOILET BREAK LAST THREE MONTHS[3]	Multi-Family Toilet Break	Single Family Toilet Break
Intergovernmental	6.3	4.5
Non-Intergovernmental	2.5	5.7
Newark	6.2	8.0

USE OF AUXILIARY HEATER	Multi-Family Auxiliary Heater	Single Family Auxiliary Heater
Intergovernmental	19.8	4.3
Non-Intergovernmental	5.4	0.8
Newark	30.3	6.7

SIGNS OF MICE OR RATS IN LAST THREE MONTHS[4]	Multi-Family Anywhere	In-Building	Single Family Anywhere	In-Building
Intergovernmental	13.6	6.0	13.0	6.8
Non-Intergovernmental	3.3	0.0	15.0	5.4
Newark	20.2	20.0	14.0	8.0

Source: U.S. Department of Commerce, U.S. Department of Housing and Urban Development. Annual Housing Survey, 1977[3,4], 1980[1,2].

Interior masonry variables were represented by interviewee reporting of: (1) cracks or holes in walls/ceilings, and (2) the presence of broken plaster of over one square foot in size. In both instances these conditions were found to exist in intergovernmental cities (multifamily housing) two to three times more often than non-intergovernmental cities (single-family housing). Ten percent of those responding in intergovernmental cities reported cracks or holes; the equivalent figure for non-intergovernmental cities was just over 5 percent. Similarly, 7.5 percent of the units in intergovernmental cities had instances of significant broken plaster; the figure for non-intergovernmental cities was about 2.5 percent (Exhibit 5.2).

Inoperative plumbing and heating were more prevalent in intergovernmental versus non-intergovernmental cities. Again, however, the basic functional condition of housing in most neighborhoods was evident. Fully 93 percent of the multifamily housing in intergovernmental cities had not had a toilet break in the last three months; the figure for non-intergovernmental cities was only 2 percent better at 95 percent. The use of an auxiliary heater to augment insufficient heat or as a primary heating replacement was significantly skewed to intergovernmental cities, however. The frequency of use in intergovernmental cities, in part reflecting their colder climates, was over four times as great. Still, only one-in-five households in intergovernmental cities found this to be necessary (Exhibit 5.2). In Newark the rate was one-half again as high (30 percent) as other intergovernmental cities. While statistically, the lack of primary heat did not appear to be an overwhelming problem, when it was present, the condition was usually severe. When asked in the Newark sample how often the primary heating system failed, 8 percent of the residents sampled stated that the *stove* had malfunctioned only four to six times over the previous winter. In other words, in several locations the kitchen stove was the source of primary heat during the winter and it too had malfunctioned.

Signs of mice and rats appeared more frequently in intergovernmental cities. Approximately 14 percent of the respondents in multifamily units in intergovernmental cities had seen mice or rats in proximity to the property; the percentage was approximately the same for those occupying single-family units in non-intergovernmental cities. The figure for mice or rats in the building was one-half to one-third the rate of exterior sightings in both classes of cities (Exhibit 5.2). Newark had double the exterior vermin sighting rate and triple the interior sightings.

Neighborhood Condition

To evaluate neighborhoods across cities, interviewees in the 1980 *Annual Housing Survey* were asked to report on abandonment on the street where their house was located and to rate, on a scale of 1 to 5, the quality of both their structure and neighborhood. Most research on the responses to these questions suggests that two of these variables (abandonment, neighborhood rating) are reasonable indicators of neighborhood quality. The literature further suggests that reports of proximate structure abandonment is a reasonably decent indicator of the most deteriorating neighborhoods. Here the difference between intergovernmental and non-intergovernmental cities was perhaps most striking. Close to 12 percent of the residents surveyed in intergovernmental cities reported abandoned housing on their street. For non-intergovernmental cities, the rate was less than 3 percent. (The fact that any abandoned housing was reported in non-intergovernmental cities was probably more of a tribute to the inclusion of boarded public buildings and/or fire-damaged housing within an individual respondent's definition of abandonment.)

Neighborhood and structure ratings tend to be slightly inflated as the socioeconomic characteristics of residents of an area decline. Thus, the poor generally are not as critical of the structures and neighborhoods that they occupy as those who are more affluent. Thus, while direction may be inferred from the responses of city residents extreme differences rarely present themselves. This holds true for both the neighborhood and the structure rating. In both cases there was an approximately 10 percent higher rating in non-intergovernmental cities. Ratings for both neighborhood and structure fell in the fair-to-good range—closer toward fair in intergovernmental cities; closer towards good in non-intergovernmental cities. Single-family neighborhoods and structures were rated higher in both categories of cities (Exhibit 5.3). In Newark, while structures were rated on a par with other intergovernmental cities, neighborhoods were rated significantly inferior.

The Landlords

Information on landlords of multifamily buildings is available only on those *resident* and interviewed in the sample of the 1980 *Annual Housing Survey*. While this limits somewhat the degree to which findings may be generalized, the comparison between the two city groupings is still able to be made. Further, the characteristics

EXHIBIT 5.3. — *1980 Proximity to Abandoned Housing, and Neighborhood and Structure Ratings (Percent of Units with; Raw Ratings)*

OBSERVED ABANDONED HOUSING ON STREET[1]	Multi-Family	Single Family
Intergovernmental	11.7%	9.1%
Non-Intergovernmental	2.7%	2.7%
Newark	29.1%	35.8%

NEIGHBORHOOD RATING[2] (1=Excellent, 4=Poor)	Multi-Family Neighborhood Rating	Percentile[4]	Single Family Neighborhood Rating	Percentile[4]
Intergovernmental	2.76	(74)	2.54	(77)
Non-Intergovernmental	2.59	(76)	2.29	(80)
Newark	3.10	(68)	2.84	(72)

STRUCTURE RATING[3] (1=Excellent, 4=Poor)	Multi-Family Structure Rating	Percentile[4]	Single Family Structure Rating	Percentile[4]
Intergovernmental	2.64	(75)	2.35	(79)
Non-Intergovernmental	2.52	(77)	2.25	(81)
Newark	2.72	(74)	2.55	(77)

[4]1=100, 2=85, 3=70, 4=55.

Source: U.S. Department of Housing and Urban Development. U.S. Department of Commerce. *Annual Housing Survey, 1978*[1], *1980*[2,3].

reported here for resident owners in intergovernmental cities follow closely those reported for all owners in the Newark sample which follows.

As of 1980, the landlords of multifamily housing in intergovernmental versus non-intergovernmental cities were: 1) younger; 2) more often of minority background; 3) married; and 4) better educated. Yet on average, they received considerably less aggregate household income.

Landlords in intergovernmental cities were ten times more likely to be black and triple the frequency to be married. Typically, they had three-to-four-person families composed of married adults in their twenties and one-to-two pre-school children. While only one-in-five had some exposure to college, almost all had completed high school (Exhibit 5.4).

In 1980, landlords in intergovernmental cities earned significantly less than their equivalents in non-intergovernmental cities. As a whole, their household incomes were only 75 percent of those of non-intergovernmental cities. As landlords in this first city grouping were more likely to be resident in the buildings they owned, and as such lived rent free, a portion of this income disparity could be explained as being compensated for by an indirect housing allowance.

What is apparent here is that many of the housing ideals encouraged by the subsidy programs of the 1960s and 1970s ultimately became realized. An increasing percentage of the housing that remained in intergovernmental cities was owner-occupied and owned by minorities of relatively stable family structure.

As will be indicated by the demographic and cash flow analyses of Newark properties, owners of properties performed most repairs and maintenance themselves. In addition, they frequently maintained "full-time jobs" in a non-real estate profession. The two incomes as well as income from immediate and extended families allow them to continue to operate. The ecology of inner-city rental management or ownership is frail and complex. If disturbed for a prolonged period (national recession, continued inter- or intra-metropolitan pressures, etc.) the results could be very damaging to the future viability of these properties.

The Tenants

Race, Marital Status, Age, and Education

In 1980, the households of intergovernmental versus non-intergovernmental cities were significantly more often black, single, female-headed, at the extremes of age, and inferiorly educated.

The percentage black population of intergovernmental cities, at close to 30 percent, was nearly three times the black percentage of non-intergovernmental cities (11 percent). The City of Newark contained four times the national average resident black population. The remaining white populations of intergovernmental cities evidenced decreasing Western European backgrounds and increasing Spanish origins (Exhibit 5.5).

In 1980, intergovernmental cities had larger proportions of their household heads at the extremes of age distribution. Over 15 percent of households in intergovernmental cities had heads over 25; the figure for non-intergovernmental cities was

EXHIBIT 5.4.—*1980 Demographic Characteristics of Landlords*
(Resident Landlords—Multi-Family Buildings)

RACE (% BLACK)	*Multi-Family* *Black*		
Intergovernmental	22.2		
Non-Intergovernmental	2.0		
Newark	48.6		
MARITAL STATUS (% MARRIED)	*Multi-Family* *Married*		
Intergovernmental	50.3		
Non-Intergovernmental	14.3		
Newark	50.4		
SEX OF FAMILY HEAD (% FEMALE)	*Multi-Family* *Female*		
Intergovernmental	36.6		
Non-Intergovernmental	43.3 (Primarily Widow)		
Newark	33.2		

AGE OF HEAD *(% OVER/UNDER AGE GROUP)*	*% Under 35*	*Multi-Family* *% Over 65*	*Median*
Intergovernmental	26.8	24.2	52.0
Non-Intergovernmental	3.0	42.9	57.0
Newark	3.0	4.0	49.2

EDUCATION OF HEAD *(% MORE THAN HIGH SCHOOL)*	*Multi-Family* *Some College*	*Median*
Intergovernmental	22.3	11.5
Non-Intergovernmental	28.5	10.9
Newark	5.0	10.5

FAMILY INCOME (MEDIAN)	*Multi-Family* *Income*
Intergovernmental	$12,927
Non-Intergovernmental	$16,613
Newark	$15,165

Source: U.S. Department of Commerce, U.S. Department of Housing and Urban
Development. Annual Housing Survey, 1980.

barely one-third that rate. Similarly, more than 20 percent of household heads in intergovernmental cities were over 65, a figure 15 percent above that for non-intergovernmental cities. Generally speaking, the type of age distribution found in intergovernmental cities signaled strong components of a dependent population — one whose prime residents were outside the most productive income years. In contrast, in 1980, 75–80 percent of the heads of households in non-intergovernmental cities fell within the age range of the active labor force (Exhibit 5.5).

EXHIBIT 5.5. — *1980 Demographic Characteristics of Residents*
(Percent of Units with)

RACE (% BLACK)

	Multi-Family Black	Single Family Black
Intergovernmental	29.9	28.7
Non-Intergovernmental	11.2	11.2
Newark	51.5	43.4

MARITAL STATUS (% MARRIED)

	Multi-Family Married	Single Family Married
Intergovernmental	30.3	61.6
Non-Intergovernmental	29.0	69.9
Newark	44.4	43.7

SEX OF FAMILY HEAD (% FEMALE)

	Multi-Family Female	Single Family Female
Intergovernmental	48.0	29.8
Non-Intergovernmental	40.2	21.4
Newark	44.3	45.7

AGE OF HEAD
(% OVER/UNDER AGE GROUP)

	Multi-Family Age		Single Family Age	
	Under 25	Over 65	Under 25	Over 65
Intergovernmental	15.3	21.6	0.7	24.4
Non-Intergovernmental	32.2	15.7	4.8	17.9
Newark	9.4	14.7	0.1	46.1

EDUCATION OF HEAD
(% MORE THAN HIGH SCHOOL)

	Multi-Family Some College	Single Family Some College
Intergovernmental	28.2	29.6
Non-Intergovernmental	42.9	45.2
Newark	9.7	21.8

Source: U.S. Department of Commerce, U.S. Department of Housing and Urban Development. Annual Housing Survey, 1980.

Over 40 percent of the households in intergovernmental cities were headed by females—almost double the rate of non-intergovernmental cities. When this was cross-tabulated by race and age, female-headed households in intergovernmental cities were formerly married, young minority or elderly white households. Female-headed households in non-intergovernmental cities were single, working-age and much more often white.

The education level of the head of household in non-intergovernmental cities was perhaps the most striking. The figure reporting some college (45 percent) was 50 percent more than in intergovernmental cities (Exhibit 5.5). These figures on educational attainment combined with those previously reported on aptitude and achievement bode poorly for the technological competitiveness of intergovernmental city residents.

Income and Sources of Income

Socioeconomic characteristics usually bear directly on household income as well as sources of income. In this case both aggregate income spread and sources of income evidenced significant differences between intergovernmental and non-intergovernmental cities. In 1980, non-intergovernmental cities at just under $18,000 per household had 50 percent more income per household than did intergovernmental cities ($13,000)(Exhibit 5.6). For the sample of ten intergovernmental versus non-intergovernmental cities this translated into one-half billion dollars of extra buying power (100,000 households x $5,000/household) for the average non-intergovernmental city. At $125 to support one square foot of retailing space, residents of non-intergovernmental cities could support an additional 4 million square feet of commercial uses. Link this with the rapidly rising income streams and labor force participation rates in non-intergovernmental cities and their individual and aggregate dominance becomes quite apparent.

Sources of income in intergovernmental and non-intergovernmental cities further demonstrate the contrasts between the two groupings. In 1980, over 80 percent of household income in non-intergovernmental cities was from salaries or dividends; the figure for intergovernmental cities was less than 70 percent. Social security, welfare, and unemployment percentages of income in intergovernmental cities were at one and one-half to two times the rate of non-intergovernmental cities. These percentages of "non-productive" income had further shortcomings to jurisdictions where they were high in that their rate of growth was cut due to changes in eligibility and escalator requirements.

Housing in an Intergovernmental City: A Longitudinal, Micro View of Newark, New Jersey, Properties

The section which follows focuses on a sample of rental structures in a single intergovernmental city — Newark, New Jersey. Its purpose is to provide insight into some of the structural changes taking place in an intergovernmental city over a near two-decade observation period. This is a more detailed look at a single site than has been the case in the first portion of this chapter. The vehicle for observation is multiple, recurring surveys of rental structures in Newark's core neighborhoods. The original 1964 sample focused on 569 rental structures which were both substantially occupied and largely generators of reasonable returns on the owners' investment. The buildings were located in the core twenty-five tracts of the city and were chosen so as to provide a structured probability sampling. (Original sample selection is discussed in the chapter on methodology.)

The structures, which in 1964 varied in condition from slight to moderate deterio-

EXHIBIT 5.6. — *1980 Resident Total Family Income and Income from Non-Salary Sources (Dollars and Percent of Income)*

TOTAL FAMILY INCOME	Multi-Family Total Income (Median)	Single Family Total Income (Median)
Intergovernmental	$10,275	$16,522
Non-Intergovernmental	$11,233	$18,951
Newark	$10,422	$16,229

NON-SALARY INCOME SOURCES		
SOCIAL SECURITY AS A PERCENT OF INCOME	Multi-Family Social Security	Single Family Social Security
Intergovernmental	19.2	18.3
Non-Intergovernmental	12.0	12.9
Newark	24.9	18.5
PENSION AS A PERCENT OF INCOME	Multi-Family Pension	Single Family Pension
Intergovernmental	2.7	4.4
Non-Intergovernmental	4.4	3.3
Newark	1.0	12.7
WELFARE AS A PERCENT OF INCOME	Multi-Family Welfare	Single Family Welfare
Intergovernmental	9.3	3.0
Non-Intergovernmental	4.4	1.5
Newark	8.4	5.2
UNEMPLOYMENT AS A PERCENT OF INCOME	Multi-Family Unemployment	Single Family Unemployment
Intergovernmental	0.5	0.4
Non-Intergovernmental	0.3	0.2
Newark	0.7	0.5
ALIMONY AS A PERCENT OF INCOME	Multi-Family Alimony	Single Family Alimony
Intergovernmental	0.5	0.9
Non-Intergovernmental	0.6	0.9
Newark	2.5	1.2

Source: U.S. Department of Commerce, U.S. Department of Housing and Urban Development. Annual Housing Survey, 1980.

ration, as of 1981 were mostly abandoned with the remainder barely hanging on. These were the buildings which had to be maintained in the interim period for the city to retain much of its original form and vitality. What will become obvious as this section unfolds is that these buildings did not maintain their viability nor did subsequent series of owners possess sufficient capacity and/or commitment to reverse the trends that began evolving almost two decades ago. The macro and micro reasons which have contributed to the failure to maintain the city's private housing stock attractive to occupants (white, black, immigrant, inmigrant) left the city with significant private structure attrition and with public ownership of large amounts of vacant land, as well as abandoned and occupied buildings.

Only 231 buildings of the original 569 remained in 1981. Of these, fifty were vacant and abandoned. Approximately the same number of properties as those standing (231) were vacant land, in which the structure was removed (234). Another ninety-four were redeveloped—the bulk for public institutions or publicly-assisted housing. Newark, in the early 1980s, was characterized by both significant private disinvestment and an abundance of multitiered public redevelopment. The chapter which follows details the changes which took place in the housing of the city as well as its owners and occupants. These changes are the ingredients of the social and economic deterioration that spawned the intergovernmental city.

The definition of a longitudinal study is that it provides perspective over time. In this section of the chapter characteristics of the properties, owners, and tenants of a sample of buildings in Newark will be viewed over a seventeen-year period, 1964–1981. The chapter will discuss socioeconomic characteristics of owners and tenants as well as the condition and operating characteristics of the buildings which they owned or occupied. Where appropriate, cash flow analyses of a group of properties and capsulized cases of individual properties will be presented to illustrate the qualitative and quantitative nature of the changes that have taken place in this city's housing.

The Structures

Clearly the most dominant trend which took place in the City of Newark was the virtual disappearance by 1981 of over two-thirds of the 569 structures which were originally sampled. Admittedly located in the worst areas of the city in 1964, only three-in-ten structures (181) remained viable by 1981. Close to 340 had been demolished, 241 due to abandonment and potential fire, health and safety reasons; the remaining 97 due to redevelopment, primarily in the form of public institutions or housing. In 1981, 8.8 percent or 50 structures were abandoned—either in a vacant secured or vacant-open status (Exhibits 5.7 and 5.8).

The buildings that were demolished, except for commercial occupancy and level of furnishing, represented a cross section of the structure stock as a whole. Subsequent to a loss of seven out of ten buildings, the distribution of structure size, construction material, building height and building condition (relative to others) remained approximately the same. In 1964, just over 70 percent of the sampled rental buildings in Newark were of frame construction; in 1981 the percentage of frame construction was almost the same. Similarly, 1964 and 1981 sample buildings, on average, were three to four stories, 4.5 units in size, with four rooms per unit. Over the period 1964 to 1981, the level of commercial occupancy in the sample building set was halved. In 1964, close to ninety buildings (16 percent) exhibited some form of commercial occupancy; by 1981 barely twenty buildings (8 percent) had commercial tenants.* Buildings with commercial occupants disappeared at almost twice the rate of all residential buildings over the seventeen-year period.

---

*90 of 569 structures = 16 percent; 20 of 241 structures = 8 percent.

EXHIBIT 5.7.—*Structural Characteristics:*
Landlord and Building Surveys, 1964, 1972, 1981

PROPERTY STATUS	1964	1972	1981
Occupied	100.0	62.4	31.9
Abandoned (Original Structure Standing)	0.0	7.0	8.8
Vacant Land (Original Structure Demolished)	0.0	30.8	42.2
Redeveloped (Original Structure Demolished and Land Reused)	0.0	1.8	17.1
Total	100.0	100.0	100.0
n =	569	569	569

NUMBER OF UNITS IN DWELLINGS	1964	1972	1981
Median	4.5	4.4	4.4
Total	100.0	100.0	100.0
n =	377	291	139

TYPE OF CONSTRUCTION (FRAME OR MASONRY)	1964	1972	1981
Frame	71.9	81.4	71.0
Masonry	28.1	18.6	29.0
n =	567	388	234

FURNISHED OR UNFURNISHED	1964	1972	1981
Structures With Any Furnished Units (Percent)	5.7	6.0	16.0
n =	388	300	131

DEGREE OF COMMERCIAL OCCUPANCY	1964	1972	1981
Structures With Any Commercial Occupancy (Percent)	16.4	8.1	8.7
n =	566	384	231

QUALITY OF PARCEL RELATIVE TO NEIGHBORING PROPERTIES	1964	1972	1981
Structures Rated Poorer Than Neighbors (Percent)	12.2	14.2	25.3
n =	567	387	233

QUALITY OF STREET VERSUS ENTIRE BLOCK	1964	1972	1981
Street Rated Poorer Than Block (Percent)	15.5	16.2	15.9
n =	388	298	131

Source: Rutgers University, Tenement Landlord Samples 1964, 1972, 1981

EXHIBIT 5.8.—*Structure Operational and Financial Characteristics:*
Landlord, Building, Tax and Title Surveys: 1964, 1972, 1981

TYPE OF OWNER	1964	1972	1981
Private Individuals	81.5	56.7	34.6
Corporations	18.5	4.6	7.8
Non-Profit	0.0	13.2	7.9
Public	0.0	25.5	49.7
Total	100.0	100.0	100.0
n =	569	569	569

PROFESSIONAL BUILDING MANAGEMENT	1964	1972	1981
Percent Non-resident Professional Manager	14.6	28.2	14.6
n =	388	299	137

WEEKLY RENT COLLECTION BY LANDLORDS	1964	1972	1981
Owners Collecting Weekly Rents (Percent)	6.0	4.5	2.1
n =	387	300	135

REPAIRS DONE BY SELF	1964	1972	1981
Repairs Done Primarily by Owner (Percent)	6.0	5.5	55.0
n =	388	301	137

AVERAGE RENT	1964	1972	1981
Median	$72	$100	$187
n =	320	270	121

PRESENCE OF MORTGAGE	1964	1972	1981
First Mortgage in Force (Percent)	59.8	14.2	55.7
n =	569	388	201

PRESENCE OF SECOND MORTGAGE	1964	1972	1981
Second Mortgage in Force (Percent)	14.4	6.0	6.7
n =	569	385	231

COST TO PUT BUILDING IN GOOD CONDITION	1964	1972	1981
Dollars	$95	$244	$696
n =	375	290	122

Source: Rutgers University, Tenement Landlord Samples 1964, 1972, 1981

Unit rent also shows interesting trends. In 1964, at $72 contract rent per month, Newark mirrored metropolitan rental averages. In 1981, at $187 per month, Newark trailed metropolitan averages ($237) by 30 percent. In less than two decades Newark's housing stock moved from average desirability to undesirable as reflected in precipitous local rent level decreases, relative to other portions of the metropolitan area.

Slightly over one-half of the buildings in 1981 were mortgaged—about the same percentage as was the case in 1964. Very few of the buildings (less than 7 percent) had second mortgages which usually indicates that large capital improvements were not being made. The frequency of second mortgages was one-half the rate of that during the mid-1960s period.

Cash Flow of Rental Buildings

The cash flow of multifamily buildings in one intergovernmental city provides insight into the realities of the inner-city housing market. Exhibit 5.9 shows the annual cash flow of 116 Newark multifamily buildings grouped according to number of units. Income is primarily the sum of monthly rents and, secondarily, miscellaneous income from vending or laundry machines and irregularly provided, special tenant services. Expenses are divided among the reasonably standard array of operating service categories: payroll, heating, maintenance and repair, debt retirement, taxes, water and sewer charges, insurance, legal fees, and vacancy or bad debt losses.

Income

Annual income per unit for the three groupings of multifamily structures varied from approximately $1,500 to just over $2,050. It was least in three-to-six-unit structures and greatest in structures of seven-to-twenty-four units. Monthly income (mostly rent) varied from $128 to $171; it was less than the average per apartment rental level of $150 to $225 by the amount lost to unproductive occupied units—principally, those occupied by the owner or owner's family (Exhibit 5.9).

Expenses

Annual expenses per unit for the three size category groupings were dominated by heating costs which ran from 38 to 47 percent of total expenses. Heating costs were two and one-half to three times the next most severe expense—property taxes.

In 1972, prior to a decade of oil price increases which brought the cost of crude from $5 to $25 a barrel, the local cost of fuel oil in Newark was 30 cents per gallon; in 1982, the cost during an oil glut was $1.05 per gallon. The local public utility charged 20 cents per million BTU for natural gas in 1972; by 1982 the cost was $1.00. These increases were five times the percentage increase in monthly rentals taking place in this rent-controlled city over the same time period (Exhibit 5.9).

Taxes and water and sewer charges are relatively fixed expenses and significant in

EXHIBIT 5.9. — *Average Annual Cash Flow of Newark Rental Properties: By Size Grouping, 1981*

	Two Units (n=18)		3-6 Units (n=83)		7-24 Units (n=14)	
ANNUAL INCOME (Per Unit)						
	$1,832		$1,542		$2,058	
Monthly Income	($153)		($128)		($171)	
Monthly Rent	($226)		($150)		($175)	
	Dollars	*(Percent)*	*Dollars*	*(Percent)*	*Dollars*	*(Percent)*
ANNUAL EXPENSES (Per Unit)						
Payroll	$ 0	(0)	$ 14	(0)	$ 64	(3)
Heating	1,233	(47)	590	(39)	755	(38)
Maintenance & Repair	233	(9)	195	(13)	187	(9)
Debt Retirement	316	(12)	151	(10)	159	(8)
Taxes	453	(17)	264	(17)	331	(16)
Water & Sewer	210	(8)	148	(10)	163	(8)
Insurance	176	(7)	96	(6)	155	(8)
Legal Fees	0	(0)	3	(0)	8	(0)
Vacancy/Bad Debt	0	(0)	80	(5)	165	(8)
TOTAL	$2,621	(100)	$1,541	(100)	$1,987	(100)
UNADJUSTED PROFIT/LOSS	$-789		$ +1		$ +71	
OWNER OCCUPANCY CREDIT	$+882		$ +254		$ +35	
ADJUSTED PROFIT/LOSS	$+ 93		$ +255		$ +106	

Source: Rutgers University, Center for Urban Policy Research, 1981.

the aggregate. Together, in 1981, they represented approximately 25 percent of monthly expenses. Taxes in the City of Newark were relatively stable over the last decade. On the other hand, water and sewer charges increased fourfold. In the case of the latter, what formerly was a relatively trivial expense turned into a regular outlay equal to one-half the tax bill. The tax situation will also change in the near future. In 1982, for the first time in fifteen years, the community's tax base underwent revaluation. This meant a doubling of the assessed value of the average residential property. While the current aggregate tax rate (municipal, school and county shares) will probably drop by close to 20 percent, the average residential property will experience an increase in its annual property tax payments of close to 80 percent. The average three-to-four family structure in 1981 paid approximately $1,200 in property taxes annually; this would increase to close to $2,200 as the results of the property revaluation are gradually instituted.

Maintenance and repair bore the brunt of the heating and water cost increases experienced by Newark properties. In 1981, in the smallest (two units) and largest (seven to twenty-four units) size groupings, less than 10 percent of total expenses was allocated to maintenance and repair; in the other category it was 13 percent. There were whole categories of repairs in Newark rental properties that were not made. These included plastering, locks and fixtures, window weights, tiling and flooring, etc. According to one Newark landlord, "the necessities (plumbing, heating, electricity, window or door replacement) were done and done quickly; the rest were a waste of money and not even considered."

In 1981, payroll and legal fees on Newark's rental properties were almost nonexistent (Exhibit 5.9). The former reflected the high proportion of resident ownership in the remaining Newark residential properties; the latter suggested the nature of the relationship between landlord and tenants—the most significant determinant of structure-related legal fees. In Newark, "good tenants" were sought out and encouraged to stay; troublesome or deadbeat tenants were evicted and rarely formally opposed this action. The nature of the expenditures detailed here are further related to the growing proportion of owner occupancy in the buildings that remain. The resident landlord acts as a building superintendent and general handyman, thus limiting most out-of-pocket payroll expenses. In addition, the presence of this individual on-site allowed problems with tenants which might have required a legal settlement to be avoided or to be settled without initiating litigation.

Debt retirement was a relatively small component (10–13 percent) of the operational outlays of the three size ranges of Newark rental structures. Approximately 50 percent of the buildings had remaining first mortgage obligations and an almost negligible percentage had incurred second mortgages. Further, the interest rates of most remaining first mortgages were below 12 percent, thus the impact on regular cash flow was much less than what it would be if the buildings were of much more recent vintage.

Fire insurance, for Newark properties which have this coverage, is issued under the New Jersey FAIR Plan. This is a high-risk pool shared by insurers doing business in the State of New Jersey. Homeowners are guaranteed access to insurance albeit at higher rates than the standard risk case. In 1981, fire insurance coverage was maintained by 90 percent of the occupied buildings. Virtually all of the mortgaged buildings and approximately 70 percent of the buildings which had fire insurance were inadequately covered, however. Since there was a limited market for most

Newark properties, the bulk of the properties were covered for less than one-half the current public buyout price. The public buyout price was approximately equivalent to the property reassessments which were yet to be invoked and 25 percent more than the private market resale price.

In 1981, vacancy or bad debt losses (5–8 percent) were relatively low for this class of inner-city properties. As the neighborhood worsened and abandonment claimed other properties, those that remained were highly sought after. Although their modest rents were unequalled in the metropolitan area, they were not able to increase appreciably, due to both regulatory restriction and the inability of current occupants to meet any increase.

Net Cash Flow

In 1981, the net cash flow (unadjusted profit) was essentially break-even in the larger categories of buildings and a significant loss in the smaller, two-unit structures. Owner profit varied from a high of 3 percent annually to a low of 40 percent loss (Exhibit 5.9). When unrefined income is credited by the rental income lost due to owner-occupancy the profit margin improves somewhat. Profit moved to the plus side of the ledger in all cases and varied from 5 to 17 percent. It was lowest in the largest (seven to twenty-four units) and smallest (two units) size categories of buildings and highest in the middle-size category (three to six units). The owner-occupancy credit was determined by adding to the income stream the rent that the unit in the structure would command were it not occupied by the owner.

From the data presented here owning residential rental property in at least one intergovernmental city, in 1981, was a losing proposition. The only way any profit could be realized was to credit the occupancy costs of the owner as income and adjust the cash flow stream. Even then, profits were very modest and the payroll costs if realistically viewed* could take away from any positive side ledger bulge.

Rental housing in the City of Newark was inexpensive in part due to demand (what the market would bear) and in part due to supply (what the rent control would allow). There has been no concurrent abatement of expenses. This left net cash flows small and existent only if credits were taken for owner-occupancy—an increasing phenomenon for those who must or choose to live in or around the city.

The Landlords

The crux of the findings of the original *Tenement Landlord* study was that Newark's landlords, for the most part, were not large-scale property owners who made a majority of their income from real estate. Neither did they employ professionals to maintain their properties nor did they occupy offices/residences at great distances from their holdings. Rather these landlords were small operators with minor real estate income sources, often living in the parcels and performing a large

---

*An argument can realistically be made that if the owner did not live in the building, payroll costs reflecting his maintenance, repair and general security inputs, would be significantly higher.

share of repair work themselves. For the parcels that remained in 1981, these findings were more true than they were seventeen years prior (Exhibits 5.8 and 5.10).

In 1964, 30 percent of the landlords were black; by 1981, over half the owners (54.6 percent) were black. In the early (1964) and interim (1972) surveys, Newark landlord incomes exceeded national median incomes by over 10 percent; by 1981, landlord incomes actually lagged national medians by approximately the same percentage. In essence Newark landlords, typically not much different in socioeconomic characteristics than the city of which they were a part, currently reflected racial and income level changes generic to the city.

Newark landlords in the mid-1960s classified their primary occupations as proprietor–craftsman, white collar professionals or some aspect of the real estate construction industry (20 percent each). Properties owned by non-labor force participants (retirees–housewives–disabled) were almost nonexistent. By the 1980s, proprietor–craftsmen and housewives–retirees–disabled represented close to one-third of the owners each and the real estate construction industry accounted for another 20 percent. Housewives–retirees–disabled not only replaced white collar professionals as significant property owners in the city, they became one of its leading ownership components.

In 1981, over 80 percent of the remaining private owners of rental property in Newark lived within the city's bounds; 70 percent of these lived in the structure itself. All of the increase in city residency, a 25 percent growth over the period 1964–1981, could be attributed to an increase in the percentage of resident landlords. This increase in resident landlords did not reflect an increase in the number of buildings with resident landlords but rather a significant loss from the structure stock of buildings in which no landlord resided. The finding in the 1972 study of a strong linkage between abandonment and absentee landlords was clearly reflected in 1981 resident landlord percentages.

By 1981, Newark property holders, on average, owned property for seventeen years, a 30 percent increase in average length of tenure since the mid-1960 period. Even though over one-half of the property owners were in possession of more than one property (a 10 percent decrease since 1964) only 10 percent of the landlords made more than one-third of their income from these properties—a threefold decrease since the sample during the 1960s. Newark landlords, for lack of sellout opportunities, were holding on with very little in the form of financial return for their efforts.

For occupied buildings, the sixteen-year period witnessed significant increases in public and some non-profit ownership and reciprocal decreases in private and corporate holdings. For privately owned buildings, weekly rent collections, never a large factor, virtually went out of existence while the rate of owner-initiated repairs increased tenfold from 6 to 55 percent.

The Tenants

As in 1964, 80 to 85 percent of the tenants in the rental structures of Newark were black. The white tenantry, although maintaining a relatively constant percentage, changed considerably in their composition. Where at one time they were second-generation European immigrants (Russian, Italian, Irish, Polish, German), more

EXHIBIT 5.10.—*Ownership Characteristics: Landlord Survey, 1964, 1972, 1981*

RACE OF LANDLORD	1964	1972	1981
White (Percent)	70.0	60.0	44.6
n =	386	281	172

LANDLORD INCOME	1964	1972	1981
Dollars	$7167	$12,515	$16,037
n =	306	270	144

LANDLORD OCCUPATION	1964	1972	1981
Proprietor-Craftsman (Percent)	21.1	37.9	31.5
White Collar-Professional	22.6	19.4	13.0
Real Estate/Construction	21.1	21.7	22.0
Housewife	4.4	6.5	10.5
Retired/Disabled	12.6	14.5	23.0
Total	100.0	100.0	100.0
n =	389	243	144

LENGTH OF PROPERTY OWNERSHIP	1964	1972	1981
Median (Years)	13.1	14.5	16.9
n =	380	287	172

RESIDENCY OF OWNER (OCCUPIED BUILDINGS)	1964	1972	1981
In Parcel (Percent)	36.6	27.2	56.5
In City (Percent)	24.8	30.2	25.5
n =	383	265	135

MULTIPLE PROPERTY OWNERSHIP	1964	1972	1981
Percent Owning More Than One Property	57.4	52.4	50.8
n =	387	288	179

MAKE LIVING FROM REAL ESTATE	1964	1972	1981
Percent More Than 1/3 of Income	36.6	27.0	10.3
n =	385	287	174

Source: Rutgers University, Tenement Landlord Samples 1964, 1972, 1981

recently they were first generation Spanish and Portuguese. The Spanish (mainly Puerto Rican) were dispersed throughout the city; the Portuguese were located in one or two tightly compacted neighborhoods. The same trend did not hold true for blacks. In 1964, black households were composed of second-generation northern industrial workers. In 1981, although there had been some replacement by southern black inmigrants, there were very few West Indian, African, Haitian or Cuban blacks. The northern industrial worker, typically unemployed, remained as the dominant population segment of the local black population (Exhibit 5.11).

In 1964, very few of the tenants (less than 5 percent) in the sample were on welfare; in 1981 more than one-third received regular public assistance. Fifty percent of the black tenants were on welfare. Ten percent of the white tenants received some form of public assistance, 20 percent within the Spanish subsector, less than 1 percent within the Portuguese component. At the time of the original survey, tenants were considered to have a minimal impact on the maintenance of a structure; by 1981 they were believed to significantly influence both structure life and quality.

Despite (1) the increasing percentage of blacks, (2) the change in remaining whites to Iberian origins, and (3) the growing welfare dependency and behavioral impact of the new resident population, the remaining landlords (although significantly decreased in number) appeared at least as optimistic about the future as the original set of landlords. In 1981, over 60 percent felt that their building would be worth more five years into the future. This figure was approximately the same as 1964. Another index of the landlords' view was whether they felt that they could get their home improvement money back. Although only three in ten indicated that they could, the percentage was again the same as was observed eighteen years earlier.

The Owners, The Tenants, and Their Properties

The following five case studies of property attrition typified the housing market in the City of Newark in the late-1970s, early-1980s. They reflect in large part the socioeconomic characteristics of owners, the relationship between owners and tenants including the latter's rent-paying capacity, and finally, what happened to the structures that this mix of owners, tenants and their characteristics influence.

The brief descriptions included here are history—the structures and their inhabitants are now gone. The always painful lesson of history is that it has significant repetitive components. What has happened over the period described here is continuing to occur daily and rendering structures surplus at an alarming rate.

The Disabled War Veteran

In 1947, a returning war veteran of Greek extraction bought a three-story frame structure for $11,000 on one of the major commercial streets of Newark. He wanted to establish a small fish market to be operated by himself and his wife and rent out two apartments above the store for additional income. The loan to acquire money for the down payment would be paid down by his disability pension. The business was a moderately successful one and when interviewed in 1964, the owner proudly displayed both the condition of the building and the fixturing which he had installed there. By 1971 the store was vacant; the owner, forced to move his business by the changing condition of the neighborhood, had as his only hope that the state would take the parcel for

EXHIBIT 5.11.—*Tenant Characteristics and Landlords' Views of Future: Landlord Survey, 1964, 1972, 1981*

PRESENCE OF WHITE TENANTS	1964	1972	1981
Structures With Predominantly White Tenants (Percent)	18.7 (No Spanish, No Portuguese)	12.7 (One-Half Spanish, No Portuguese)	13.6 (All Hispanic or Portuguese)
n =	385	284	127

FAMILIES IN A STRUCTURE ON PUBLIC ASSISTANCE	1964	1972	1981
Median (Percent)	0.0	33.8	36.3
n =	387	234	109

LANDLORDS' VIEW OF TENANTS' EFFECT ON MAINTENANCE (RATING 1-5: 1 = HIGH IMPACT, 5 = LOW IMPACT)	1964	1972	1981
Scale	4.2	3.1	1.8
n =	274	210	131

LANDLORDS' VIEW OF TAXES' EFFECT ON MAINTENANCE (RATING 1-5: 1 = HIGH IMPACT, 5 = LOW IMPACT)	1964	1972	1981
Scale	4.5	4.3	1.0
n =	323	268	140

LANDLORDS' VIEW OF FUTURE WORTH OF BUILDING	1964	1972	1981
Percent Responding Worth More in 5 Years	68	42	62
n =	353	264	120

LANDLORDS' VIEW OF POTENTIAL FOR INVESTMENT RETURN	1964	1972	1981
Yes, Definitely or Probably Get Money Back (Percent)	30.4	24.7	28.3
n =	383	267	126

Source: Rutgers University, Tenement Landlord Samples 1964, 1972, 1981.

a new highway which was being discussed at the time. Community groups could not agree on the road's location and ultimately the project was cancelled. In September of 1977, final judgment on the parcel through tax sale was given over to the City of Newark. The building is completely abandoned.

The Inheritor of "Free" Property

Large-scale property owners, as detailed in earlier studies, were moving out of Newark as early as 1964–65 and certainly there was a very strong thrust by 1972. Not uncommonly, a method of getting out was to take the structure's superintendent and make him a "present" of a troubled building. Parcel #450 is a twenty-four-family, four-story, walk-up, masonry structure which was turned over to the resident handyman via a no-cash transaction but with a very large mortgage.

The earlier owner simply felt that he could not handle the parcel any longer. The tenants were changing and they couldn't afford to pay the rent increases necessary to keep the building going. Very little rent was being collected. In addition there was a large number of outstanding housing code violations and continuous "hassling" of the original owner by city building inspectors. By turning the parcel over to a local black, he felt that there would be less in the way of operating friction between the owner, tenants and inspectors and, besides, there was no bona fide purchaser in the wings. If the transaction worked out the previous owners were no worse off than before—and might even have a large tax loss based upon the mortgage.

Penniless owners, no matter how enthusiastic, cannot run troubled buildings. In the seventeen-year record of this building, it went from a run-down but solid facility into a worn-out wreck, vacant to all occupants but squatters.

The Lottery Winner

When the owner of parcel #544 was interviewed in 1964 he was very excited. He and his wife, each in their early twenties, had won the lottery in Puerto Rico and had invested their returns ($10,000) in a local four-family house. He was in the process of putting in central heat and was planning on buying another property as soon as he could afford it, to further ensure his family's future. At the time, both were employed in a small factory in Newark. Seventeen years later, he was a much embittered individual. He bought his second property only to have it vandalized by welfare tenants and ultimately it had to be abandoned. And while his original property is in good condition, the area in which it is sited is a wasteland. He is firmly convinced that he will never be able to get his money out of the property even though he now owns the building free and clear after paying off the mortgage. In 1980, no matter how he discriminated, his rental market was increasingly composed of partial families on public assistance.

The Insurance Settlement Beneficiary

A Puerto Rican factory worker was hit by a car in Newark and after a number of months in the hospital, took his insurance settlement and bought a three-family house, Parcel #582 in Newark, in 1964. As he put it, it was the first thing he had ever owned. By 1971, the owner remarked that he had paid on his mortgage for seven years—and the building was worth less then than when he had originally purchased it; i.e., his equity if anything, had been reduced despite amortization payments. By 1977, the parcel had moved into the hands of the city on a tax lien and foreclosure. The former owner by now is close to sixty years old. To the degree that his old age depended upon built-up equity in his building, it turned out to be a very feeble crutch indeed.

The Fledgling Black Entrepreneur

Mr._____ bought Parcel #263 in 1969 for $18,500. It was a six-family frame house just outside the Central Ward. The parcel had a land assessment of $3,500 and a building assessment of $15,000. While it did not have central heat, the building was in excellent condition at the time of purchase. This was part of a group purchase which he had made as a member of a syndicate of small-scale black entreprenuers who hoped to put together sufficient properties to warrant full-time operation. They were performing repairs and building operations primarily by themselves. By 1979, the parcel was foreclosed by the city. The real estate aspirants of the holding suffered the same fate—the fledgling enterprise was at an end.

Summary

The housing of intergovernmental versus non-intergovernmental cities was older, larger and much more often multifamily. It was usually of inferior condition, although the overall quality of housing in both intergovernmental and non-intergovernmental cities has been remarkably high.

The owners in intergovernmental cities were much more often resident in one of the parcels that they owned. Resident owners in intergovernmental cities were more apt to be minority households, younger, married, slightly better educated and have lower incomes than those of non-intergovernmental cities.

Using Newark as a case study it was found that the major current landlord was the public sector—an increasing number of properties were being defaulted upon by private owners with no subsequent private sector purchaser. This is true because the cash flow of rental structures was barely profitable and of insufficient magnitude to allow real estate to be a prime source of an owner's income.

Tenement landlords in inner cities largely reflected the characteristics of the resident populations. The population they served was heavily minority, often poor and one whose income frequently came from non-salary sources.

In intergovernmental cities, the market was characterized by structure attrition with only modest replacement. What replacement did take place had been initiated through public or quasi-public efforts. Little, if any, private redevelopment took place or was currently underway.

In Newark, there has been only modest, if any, spin-off effect of the public institutional or housing redevelopment that has taken place. Commercial strips have not, by and large, been uplifted by the purchases of employees of proximate medical or educational facilities nor has "housing in a clump" saved neighborhood housing shells that were teetering on the edge of abandonment. If anything, private neighborhoods appeared unable to stabilize in spite of the level of public redevelopment. In this case, the publicly regenerated city was almost entirely public.

6
The Rise of Intergovernmentalism

OVER THE PAST SEVERAL DECADES, the United States experienced a dramatic change in both the method in which federal dollars were allocated to address national concerns and in the funding priority of functions deemed to be of national interest. From the late 1940s to the beginning of the 1980s, federal expenditure patterns shifted markedly from an emphasis on national defense to a concentration on human resources and community and economic development. At the same time, intergovernmental transfer payments to state and local governments grew at rates disproportionate to rates of increase in total federal spending.

The net result of these federal budget trends was a rapid growth of programs to aid states and their localities, as well as a massive expansion of payments to, and services for, variously defined, dependent populations. In 1980 alone, payments to individuals consumed over 47 percent of total federal budget outlays at a cost of more than $226 billion. States and local governments were also well represented in the 1980 budget; they accounted for $91.5 billion, or 15.8 percent of all federal expenditures.

Reflecting national budget trends, state and local governments also increased substantially their levels of funding for human resource programs, both through direct payments and by way of intergovernmental transfers to local communities. The combined federal and state aid to local governments, in 1980, equaled 77.2 percent of all local own-source income, and nearly 40 percent of all local general revenues.

Plagued with severe economic and social difficulties, intergovernmental cities increasingly relied on federal and state treasuries to supplement revenues derived from their steadily declining local tax bases. Moreover, as those cities' populations were more often comprised of the low-skilled working poor and hard-core unemployed, intergovernmental cities also benefitted substantially, albeit indirectly, from social programs which directly provided income, goods, and services to the poverty or near-poverty population.

Having documented the dependence of intergovernmental cities on transfer payments from the federal and state governments in previous chapters, this chapter disaggregates outside income into broad functional areas and highlights some of the most popular intergovernmental aid programs of the late 1960s and 1970s. Since a significant portion of state allocations to cities originated at the federal level, and because independent state aid to local governments by city is not readily available, this chapter concentrates solely on programs which were federally supported. Also presented here is the high level of dependency of individuals in intergovernmental cities on direct aid programs, thus offering yet another dimension to the intergovernmental cities' reliance on state and federal financial assistance. The intent is to show that federal aid to intergovernmental cities was not concentrated in any single functional area; rather, that transfer payments from the federal and state governments played an intricate role in the overall operations of these cities. Moreover, this chapter illustrates how direct payments to individuals have been substantial in intergovernmental cities, and that those funds have served an important part in the intergovernmental cities' overall economy.

To the extent that the increasing dependence of intergovernmental cities on outside funding sources occurred in a much larger context, i.e., the shift in federal spending priorities away from defense outlays to a concentration on social welfare programs and intergovernmental aid, this chapter begins with a review of these macro trends.

Changing Priorities in Federal Spending

As late as 1960, national defense consumed, by far, the largest portion of federal budget outlays. As indicated in Exhibit 6.1, defense spending totaled $45.9 billion of a total national budget of $97.8 billion. During that same year, all human resources and community development programs combined, accounted for only $28.4 billion, or less than one-third of federal expenditures. During the decade of the Sixties,

EXHIBIT 6.1.—*Changing Priorities of Defense and Human Resources/Community Development Spending, 1960–1980*

	1960	1970	1977	1980
(Total Expenditures in $ Billions)				
Total Budget Outlays	97.8	196.6	402.7	579.6
National Defense	45.9	80.3	95.7	135.9
Human Resources & Community Development	28.4	75.8	222.0	313.4
Education, Training & Social Services	NA	7.3	21.0	30.8
Health	NA	13.0	38.8	58.2
Income Security	NA	43.8	137.9	193.1
Veterans Benefits	NA	8.7	18.0	21.2
Community Development	NA	3.0	6.3	10.1
(As a Percent of Total Federal Outlays)				
Total Budget Outlays	100.0	100.0	100.0	100.0
National Defense	46.9	40.8	23.7	23.4
Human Resources & Community Development	29.0	38.6	55.1	54.1
Education, Training & Social Services	NA	3.7	5.2	5.3
Health	NA	6.6	9.6	10.0
Income Security	NA	22.3	34.2	33.3
Veterans Benefits	NA	4.4	4.5	3.7
Community Development	NA	1.5	1.6	1.7

Note: NA=Not Available.
Source: U.S. Office of Management and Budget, The Budget of the United States, 1982.

however, human resources grew annually at better than twice the rate of defense spending, for an average of $4.7 billion, or 16.7 percent per year. The net result was that by 1970, human resources and community development expenditures had increased to almost 95 percent of defense outlays. Also, by 1970, the defense budget had fallen to account for only 40.8 percent of total federal spending, while human resource programs had grown to 38.6 percent.

During the first half of the 1970s, outlays for human resource programs grew at their fastest pace. Between 1970 and 1977, this category of funding grew by $21 billion yearly or 200 percent. Defense outlays, on the other hand, actually declined in real terms, as that component of the budget expanded by less than nineteen percent, or $2.2 billion per year. By 1977, human resources, including community development programs, were 55 percent of all federal outlays.

For the following three years, until 1980, defense spending slightly outpaced human resource spending in percentage terms. In 1980, defense outlays were a mere 43.4 percent of human resource and community development expenditures, and they constituted less than one-quarter of all federal disbursements.

Within the human resource category, income security was the largest program area; income security benefits increased by $149.3 billion during the 1970 decade alone. Income security programs grew as a percentage of total federal outlays between 1970 and 1980 from 22.3 percent to 33.3 percent. Health expenditures were the second largest human resources program. Health-related benefits expanded from a 1970 level of $13 billion to a 1980 figure of $58.2 billion. As a proportion of total federal spending, health programs registered a modest gain from 6.6 percent to 10 percent during that ten-year period.

Payments to individuals are also a reflection of the shift in priority from military outlays to social program expenditures of the 1970s (Exhibit 6.2). In 1960, individuals received $23.6 billion in payments which, as a proportion of total outlays, was 25.6 percent. By 1980, payments to individuals had increased by a factor of 9.6, and accounted for almost one-half of all federal spending.

Exhibit 6.3 indicates that grants to states and local governments, which served to deflate the overall importance of military expenditures, have also grown at rates far exceeding both the growth in the military budget and total federal spending. In 1950, federal expenditures for states and local governments was only $2.3 billion, or 5.3

EXHIBIT 6.2—*Federal Payments to Individuals, 1960–1980*

	1960	1965	1970	1978	1980
Total aid to individuals ($ Billions)	23.6	32.3	63.2	206.5	226.9
As a percent of total federal outlays	25.6	27.3	32.1	45.8	47.3

Source: U.S. Department of Commerce, Bureau of the Census, 1980 *Statistical Abstract of the United States.*

EXHIBIT 6.3.—*Federal Grant-in-Aid Outlays, 1950–1980*

	1950	*1960*	*1965*	*1970*	*1978*	*1980*
Total Grants-in-Aid ($ Millions)	2,253	7,020	10,904	24,014	77,889	91,472
As a percent of total budget	5.3	7.6	9.2	12.2	17.3	15.8
As a percent of domestic spending	8.8	15.9	16.5	21.1	22.9	21.1

Source: U.S. Office of Management and Budget, *The United States Budget: Special Analysis H*, 1982.

percent of total federal outlays. By 1980, those grants had grown by just under $3 billion per year for the entire thirty-year period.

Federal Assistance to State and Local Governments

Many federal activities and policies affect, in a significant way, the finances of state and local governments. For example, federal procurement policies, particularly in the area of defense, are responsible for billions of dollars in contracts each year which strengthen defense industries and thus add to the resource base of their respective economies. The location of federal installations is also an important revenue source to local governments and to states at large. Tax policies, such as those regarding allowances for depreciation on new construction as opposed to rehabilitation, are often cited as a principal federal aid favoring and supporting new growth areas over older declining regions.

The most significant direct federal assistance to states and local governments, however, is the grant-in-aid. In 1980, grants-in-aid provided more than 98 percent of all intergovernmental aid. By comparison, loans, which are the second principal source of direct federal assistance, were estimated to be only $1.1 billion, or slightly more than one percent of all grants-in-aid. Moreover, loans, unlike grants, must be repaid.

The Growth of Federal Grants

Historical Overview

Although federal grants to state and local governments did not consume a significant portion of the national budget until after World War II, the birth of federal aid programs pre-dates the Constitution. In 1785, under the Articles of Confederation, Congress provided federally owned land in the form of grants to encourage and support education in the Northwest Territory.[1] This land-grant policy was reaffirmed in the Northwest Ordinance of 1787, and land continued to serve as the predominant form of federal grant for the next century.

A major turning point in the federal-grant system was the Morrill Act of 1862, which offered federal assistance to establish and maintain land-grant colleges. Although *land* continued to serve as the major form of aid, this Act established the basic pattern for the operation of the categorical grant system in existence today.[2] The Morrill Act established a set of minimum requirements which were to be met in order to participate in the grant program. Briefly stated, the principal requirements were (1) restricted use of the grant to the program's stated objectives, (2) a state-matching element, and (3) a report on the use of the grant.

By the early 1920s, Congress had enacted several federal assistance programs in the form of annual *monetary* grants, principally for agriculture and highways. However, the first important growth period for federal grants did not occur until the 1930s. During those Depression years, the government launched a broad array of welfare, income-security, health and low-rent housing programs. Direct grants from the federal government to local governments also emerged during this extremely difficult economic period.

Recent Trends

Although grants-in-aid to state and local governments have increased continuously since the late 1940s, the most significant growth in federal assistance occurred during the mid-1960s and throughout most of the 1970s. In 1950, federal grants-in-aid totalled a mere $2.2 billion and accounted for little more than 5 percent of total federal expenditures (Exhibit 6.3). Increasing at an average annual rate of $577 million, grant-in-aid assistance grew by only $8.7 billion during that entire fifteen-year period. From 1965 to 1978, however, grant-in-aid outlays to state and local units of government mushroomed. Exhibit 6.4 reveals that for the first five years alone, 1965 to 1970, grants increased by $13 billion, or better than $2.6 billion per year. That annual growth increment was 4.5 times the average yearly expansion in grants for the previous 1950–1965 period. By 1978, federal intergovernmental grants had increased by an additional $53.8 billion, or $6.7 billion per year. Totaling $77.9 billion, grants-in-aid represented 17 percent of total federal outlays and 23 percent of all federal domestic spending.

After 1978, the rate of growth in grants-in-aid declined significantly. By 1980, federal spending had increased by just 8.7 percent per year, down substantially from the 28 percent annual growth rate which it had maintained prior to 1978. Moreover, federal assistance to governmental units declined as a percentage of total federal expenditures and domestic outlays, to 15.8 percent and 21.1 percent, respectively.

On the receiving end of federal grant payments, state and local governments have become increasingly dependent on federal assistance. In 1980, grant-in-aid payments accounted for 26.3 percent of all state and local government expenditures, up from 10.4 percent in 1950 (Exhibit 6.5). Furthermore, states have been the principal recipients of federal intergovernmental aid; the states' share of grant-in-aid payments in 1980 was nearly 75 percent (Exhibit 6.6). It is interesting to note, however, that although states received three-quarters of all grants-in-aid, their share has declined

EXHIBIT 6.4. — *Growth of Federal Grant-in-Aid Outlays, 1950–1980 ($ millions)*

	1950–1960		1960–1965		1965–1970	
	Absolute	Percent	Absolute	Percent	Absolute	Percent
Total	4767	211.6	3884	55.3	13110	120.2
Annual	476.7	21.2	776.8	11.1	2622	24.0

	1970–1978		1978–1980	
	Absolute	Percent	Absolute	Percent
Total	53875	224.3	13583	17.4
Annual	6734.4	28.0	6791.5	8.7

Source: See Exhibit 6.3. Calculations by the Center for Urban Policy Research.

greatly since 1960, when states received more than 90 percent of this source of federal assistance. Local governments, on the other hand, have increased their share of transfer payments from 8.6 percent in 1960 to a 1980 figure of 25.4 percent.

Individuals, in similar fashion to states, received a significant, though dwindling share of federal intergovernmental payments (Exhibit 6.7). Although individuals captured 37.4 percent of all grants-in-aid in 1980, this share represented a 33 percent decline since 1950, when individuals received more than one-half of all grant-in-aid outlays.

Types of Grants-in-Aid

Prior to 1970, most federal aid was in the form of categorical grants. Categorical grants were fairly rigid with regard to future possible uses. Each grant was accompanied by specific requirements dictating the use of the grant. Initially, categorical grants were considered to be a highly efficient way to ensure that federal monies

EXHIBIT 6.5.—*Federal Grant-in-Aid Outlays as a Percentage of Total State and Local Expenditures, 1950–1980*

	1950	*1960*	*1965*	*1970*	*1978*	*1980*
	10.4	14.7	15.3	19.4	26.4	26.3

Source: U.S. Office of Management and Budget, *The United States Budget: Special Analysis H*, 1982.

EXHIBIT 6.6.—*Percentage Distribution of Federal Grant-in-Aid Outlays Between State and Local Governments, 1960–1980*

	1960	1970	1977	1980
Percent distribution of inter-governmental aid				
To states	91.4	88.1	73.5	74.6
To local governments	8.6	11.9	26.5	25.4

Source: U.S. Department of Commerce, Bureau of the Census, *Governmental Finances* (for years indicated).

were being used for what Congress considered to be national priorities. However, as the grant system expanded and became increasingly complex, state and local governments balked at the numerous administrative requirements and growing inflexibility imparted by the ever-enlarging categorical grant system. The result was that starting in the early 1970s, broad-based and general purpose grants, which comprised only 8.3 percent and 1.5 percent of all grants-in-aid, respectively, in 1972, accounted for nearly 21 percent of the total federal grant outlays in 1980 (Exhibit 6.8).

Briefly stated, broad-based grants offer considerable discretion with regard to their use, since they merely require that the aid be used within a broadly defined functional area, such as employment and training. General purpose grants, of which revenue sharing is the largest, offer almost complete flexibility in their use. Rather than program requirements which outline acceptable uses for funds, such as those requirements found in both categorical and broad-based grants, general purpose grants are encumbered by only a few minor restrictions regarding what the grant may *not* be used for.

Functional Distribution of Grants-in-Aid

Over the years, federal distribution of grants-in-aid has changed dramatically. As indicated by Exhibit 6.9, in 1960, 80 percent of all grant-in-aid monies were con-

EXHIBIT 6.7.—*Grants to Individuals, 1950–1980*

	1950	1960	1965	1970	1978	1980
Total payments to individuals ($ Millions)	1,257	2,479	3,931	9,023	25,981	34,174
As a percentage of total grants	55.8	35.3	36.1	37.6	33.4	37.4

Source: U.S. Office of Management and Budget, *The United States Budget: Special Analysis H*, 1982.

EXHIBIT 6.8.—*Distribution of Federal Grant-in-Aid Outlays
by Type of Grant, 1972–1980*

	1972	1976	1977	1978	1979	1980
General Purpose Grants Total ($ Millions)	516	907	2,748	2,780	1,485	1,765
Percent of all Grants	1.5	12.1	13.9	12.3	10.1	9.4
Broad-based Grants Total ($ Millions)	2,855	6,292	8,259	11,533	11,680	10,281
Percent of all Grants	8.3	10.6	12.1	14.8	14.1	11.2
Other Grants Total ($ Millions)	31,001	45,651	50,649	56,753	62,845	72,597
Percent of all grants	90.2	77.3	74.0	72.9	75.8	79.4

Source: U.S. Office of Management and Budget, *The United States Budget: Special Analysis H*, 1982.

centrated in two areas: transportation and income security. By 1980, those same functional categories accounted for only 34 percent of federal transfers, while education, training, employment and social services consumed 24 percent, and health payments were 17 percent of the total allocation.

These shifts in expenditure emphases were largely the result of severe cutbacks in highway expenditures in recent years due to the near completion of the interstate highway system; income security reductions because of removal of supplementary income and food stamps from grants-in-aid to direct federal expenditures; and the explosive growth in medical care costs. The latter was principally attributable to Medicaid, which ballooned at a rate of more than 47 percent per year since 1969. In fact, of the total health assistance level of $15.8 billion, Medicaid, at $14.4 billion accounted for more than 90 percent of all health funding, with the eleven remaining health programs sharing $1.4 billion.

In 1980, education, training, employment and social services totalled in excess of $21.8 billion. Those funds were divided among 28 programs, of which the largest recipients were employment and training assistance, elementary and secondary education, grants to states for social services and human development services.

Income security outlays were $18.5 billion in 1980, of which subsidized housing programs, public assistance and child nutrition were the principal beneficiaries. Transportation, with outlays of $13.1 billion, was the fourth largest functional area. Of those funds, highway construction totalled $8.8 billion, while urban mass transit constituted $2.3 billion.

General purpose fiscal assistance was also significant at $8.5 billion, and, although the natural resources and environment function is relatively small, wastewater treatment and plant construction grants alone were slightly more than $4.8 billion.

EXHIBIT 6.9.—*Distribution of Federal Grant-in-Aid
Outlays by Function, 1960–1980*

| | Percentage Distribution | | | | | Actual ($ Millions) |
	1960	1965	1970	1975	1980	1980
Natural resources and environment	1	2	2	5	6	5,362
Agriculture	5	6	4	1	1	569
Transportation	41	37	22	12	14	13,087
Community and regional development	1	5	5	6	7	6,486
Education, training, employment, and social services	7	8	25	22	24	21,862
Health	3	5	16	17	17	15,758
Income security	39	34	24	20	20	18,495
General purpose fiscal assistance	2	2	2	16	9	8,478
Other	*	1	1	2	2	1,375
TOTAL	100	100	100	100	100	91,472

*0.5 percent or less.

Source: U.S. Office of Management and Budget, *The United States Budget: Special Analysis H*, 1982.

It is interesting to note that although grant-in-aid expenditures were more evenly spread across functions than they were in 1960, seven of fourteen functions consumed 98 percent of all federal aid to state and local governments. Moreover, of 125 programs listed by the Office of Management and Budget, twenty-five programs received 80 percent of all grant-in-aid outlays.

Dependency of Municipal Governments on Intergovernmental Transfers

In addition to direct intergovernmental payments from the federal government, local governments receive federal aid which is passed through states, as well as direct state financial assistance. In 1965, intergovernmental transfer payments were already a sizable part of municipal government expenditures: they constituted 22 percent of the total (Exhibit 6.10). By 1970, with general revenues growing at an annual rate of 13.5 percent and intergovernmental transfers increasing yearly by 25 percent, intergovernmental revenues grew to 30 percent of total municipal general revenues. By 1980, with general revenues of $76.1 billion and intergovernmental payments at $28.3 billion, transfer payments from federal and state sources comprised 37 percent of all general revenues of municipal governments. For cities over 50,000 population that share was slightly greater at 40 percent. During the full 1965 to 1980 period, locally raised revenues decreased as a proportion of general revenues from 78 percent to 63 percent for all cities, while for larger cities, that decline was only slightly greater.

From 1965 to 1980, federal aid to cities grew more than threefold, from 4 percent to 14 percent. State aid during the same period rose only 23 percent. The largest period of direct federal aid growth to cities occurred between 1970 and 1978, when it increased by 27 percent annually. Federal aid to cities, as a proportion of total general revenues, peaked in 1978 just prior to the elimination of temporary eco-

EXHIBIT 6.10. — *Federal and State Aid to City Governments,
1965–1980 ($ Billions)*

	1965	1970	1978	1980
All Municipalities				
Total General Revenue	15.9	26.6	65.5	76.1
Total Intergovernmental Aid	3.5	7.9	25.8	28.3
From Federal Government	0.6	1.3	10.2	10.9
From State Governments	2.7	6.2	14.5	15.9
Total Own-Source Revenue	12.4	18.7	39.7	47.8
Cities With Greater Than 50,000 Population				
Total General Revenue	11.8	20.4	48.3	55.6
Total Intergovernmental Aid	2.7	6.6	19.9	22.0
From Federal Government	0.4	1.2	8.1	8.6
From State Governments	2.1	5.1	11.1	12.5
Total Own-Source Revenue	9.1	13.8	28.5	33.6
Intergovernmental Aid as Percent of Total General Revenue				
All Municipalities	22.0	29.7	39.4	37.2
Cities of Greater Than 50,000	22.9	32.4	41.2	40.0
Federal Aid as Percent of Total General Revenue				
All Municipalities	3.8	4.9	15.6	14.3
Cities of Greater Than 50,000	3.4	5.9	16.8	15.5
State Aid as Percent of Total General Revenue				
All Municipalities	17.0	23.3	22.1	20.9
Cities of Greater Than 50,000	17.8	25.0	23.0	22.5
Own-Source Revenue as Percent of Total General Revenue				
All Municipalities	78.0	70.3	60.6	62.8
Cities of Greater Than 50,000	77.1	67.6	59.0	60.4

Source: U.S. Department of Commerce, Bureau of the Census, City Government Finances (for years indicated).

nomic stimulus programs. In that year, large cities were dependent upon the federal government for almost 17 percent of their general revenues.

Principal Intergovernmental and Direct Aid Programs

Since the early 1960s, the intergovernmental city experienced a substantial reduction in its employment base across multiple industrial sectors. Once financially powerful and independent industrial urban complexes, most intergovernmental cities found themselves unable to generate new businesses or to encourage firms to move within their borders. As their revenue bases dwindled, and their economies became even more fragile, intergovernmental cities increasingly relied upon outside sources of revenue to maintain basic thresholds of municipal service.

During the 1970 decade, sources of intergovernmental funding grew and diversified. As of 1980, intergovernmental cities relied on federal and state expenditures for programs ranging from secondary education to economic development. Indeed, while grants-in-aid were greater in some functional areas than others, on balance, intergovernmental cities were dependent on outside revenues for almost every functional area of their operations. Broad categories, such as income security, housing, health, employment, job training, and economic development were all aided by federal and state subsidies.

At the same time that intergovernmental cities experienced a massive exodus of their industrial base, the residents most financially able to aid these cities also left at record rates. The net result of these trends was the gradual formation of a city of dual dependency. The low-skilled working poor and structurally unemployed increasingly dominated the local population. As their incomes neared the poverty line, they entered various stages of dependency. While many intergovernmental transfers are passed through to cities, the federal government funds numerous direct-aid programs to individuals. Direct-aid programs to individuals replicate the same basic functional areas as grants-in-aid. Income security, housing assistance, and economic development aid are all directly provided to individuals whose incomes are not enough to lift them to some minimally defined living standard.

This section will document the dependence of intergovernmental cities across multiple functions. The intent will be to illustrate how these localities became dependent upon federal and state transfer payments, not in an aggregate sense, but rather to support a broad array of local activities. It will, in short, illustrate the intricacy of their dependency. Once this has been established, the implications of sustained budget cuts on cities may have greater meaning. By and large, the emphasis here will be on intergovernmental aid. However, some major direct-aid programs have been included to illustrate, where appropriate, the dual-dependency phenomenon of intergovernmental cities.

The individual program analysis is organized by the following broad areas of public subsidy:

Income Security
Income Maintenance and
Insurance

Education, Training, Employment
and Social Services
Education

Food and Nutrition
Community and Regional
  Development
  Housing and Community Development
  Economic Development
    Business Development
    Municipal Assistance

Employment & Training
Social Services
Health
Transportation
State and Local Fiscal Assistance
Antirecession Fiscal Assistance

After briefly reviewing a number of the most popular intergovernmental aid programs, as well as direct grants and loans to individuals, this section compares program participation between intergovernmental and non-intergovernmental cities. This examination illustrates first, the differential between intergovernmental and non-intergovernmental cities across program areas and second, how the dependency is even more pronounced when population figures are considered.

Two references are principally relied upon throughout the program analysis section. Data regarding program participation rates and ranges in grant amounts were abstracted from the *Catalog of Federal Domestic Assistance*. Aggregate national figures for programs, however, were found in the *Geographic Distribution of Federal Funds*. While these two references report similar funding levels in most instances, there are occasional discrepencies between the two documents. Thus, while the figures which follow represent the best available estimates for individual program funding by city, one must be consistent in the source of these estimates.

Finally, it is important to remember that intergovernmental cities may not necessarily receive more federal aid than non-intergovernmental cities in all federal programs. Rather, intergovernmental cities receive the bulk of aid from many of the largest and most visible grant-in-aid initiatives. Further, the magnitude and visibility of these programs make them the most likely to be cut as cities are continuously asked to fend for themselves in the mid- and late-1980s.

Income Security

Income Maintenance and Insurance

Each year, the federal government has provided a broad range of individuals and families with billions of dollars in cash assistance. Income support programs can be divided into two broad categories: (1) earned income assistance and (2) unearned payments. The latter form of transfer payment encompasses those issued strictly on the basis of financial need. Aid to Families with Dependent Children (AFDC) is the largest cash-assistance program of this category. Social Security Insurance programs typify the former type of cash assistance. A chief distinction between the two types of income security is that with the latter, eligibility must be established based on financial need and must be continuously reestablished to remain a beneficiary of the program.

AFDC has been the cornerstone program of cash assistance to needy individuals. This program served 10.1 million persons monthly at a cost of $7.1 billion in 1980. Allocated from the federal government to states in the form of formula grants, AFDC payments can be used by eligible recipients to cover the cost of food, shelter and clothing, as well as other necessities as recognized by each state's program. AFDC payments can also be applied to the care of specified children in foster homes. The federal contribution to state AFDC programs pays more than half the total benefits received. Eligibility standards, as well as benefit levels, are determined by each individual state. Payments from the federal government to different states varied widely, from $1.3 million to $1.0 billion in 1980. The average state received $121.5 million to support its AFDC program.

Unemployment insurance is the direct responsibility of state governments. An unemployment insurance tax is the means by which states raise money to cover the cost of their programs. The federal government, however, supports state programs by providing grants to cover the cost of administration of unemployment programs and also to subsidize the cost of extended benefits. Federal, military, and civilian employees as well as CETA workers are eligible for unemployment benefits derived from federal unemployment tax collections. Eligible recipients of state unemployment payments include employees whose employers made contributions to state unemployment funds. In 1980, approximately $11.9 billion in unemployment insurance taxes were collected, while $16.9 billion in benefits were paid. Federal grants totalled $1.1 billion, with the average state receiving $21.2 million. The range in distribution among states was enormous; states received from $1.1 million to $151.2 million. Federal benefits in 1980 were estimated at an additional $2.5 billion.

The core of Social Security Insurance benefits is comprised of three programs: Retirement, Disability, and Survivor's Insurance. Combined, these programs alone, which provide benefits directly to individuals, total more than the cost of all grants-in-aid to states and local governments.

Retirement benefits are for persons 65 years of age and over who have worked the required number of years to establish eligibility. While persons age 62 years are also eligible, participation prior to the 65th birthday results in permanently reduced benefits. In 1980, retired persons age 65 years and over received from $158.60 to a maximum of $1,000.60 monthly in benefits. For those who retired at 62 years of age, monthly benefits ranged significantly lower, from $97.60 to $572.00. The estimated enrollment during that year was 22.8 million persons. The total federal expenditure for Social Security retirement benefits was $7.4 billion.

Disability Insurance is meant to compensate for earnings which are lost due to a physical or mental impairment. Payments are made throughout the period of disability to impaired individuals and eligible dependents. In some instances, vocational rehabilitation costs are paid for disabled persons receiving disability insurance. Nearly 4.8 million disabled individuals and their dependents received $16.1 billion in Disability Insurance, in 1980. Payments ranged from $134.10 to $989.30 monthly.

The final insurance, Survivor's Insurance, is payable to dependents of a deceased worker if that worker contributed to and was therefore eligible for Survivor's Insurance. Survivor's Insurance costs taxpayers some $27.7 billion in 1980 for benefits ranging from a minimum of $122.00 per month to a maximum monthly payment of $1,000.60. There were approximately 7.6 million Survivor's recipients in 1980.

Income Maintenance Transfers in Intergovernmental Versus Non-Intergovernmental Cities

Aid to Families with Dependent Children (AFDC) has been a popular federal aid program in both intergovernmental and non-intergovernmental cities. As illustrated in Exhibit 6.11, the AFDC program expanded nationally by $599 million or 35 percent each year between 1969 and 1977, for an eight-year gain of $4.8 billion. During the following three years, AFDC increased by only $619.2 million or 3 percent annually.

Between 1969 and 1977, intergovernmental city residents increased their dependency on AFDC by fully 82 percent annually or $3 million each year. Although

EXHIBIT 6.11. — *Maintenance Assistance: Aid to Families with Dependent Children, 1969–1980 (Dollars)*

	Per Capita			Absolute (000)		
	1969	1977	1980	1969	1977	1980
INTERGOVERNMENTAL						
Akron	4.03	45.34	62.89	1,115	11,368	14,906
Baltimore	12.16	63.61	82.18	11,054	52,353	64,677
Buffalo	13.19	105.00	85.88	6,201	40,989	30,744
Cincinnati	5.62	49.43	68.34	2,581	20,067	26,311
Cleveland	10.25	73.01	107.04	7,832	45,780	61,440
Louisville	6.17	70.64	68.73	2,252	22,204	20,482
Milwaukee	2.64	75.32	NA	1,896	49,710	NA
Minneapolis	6.80	54.89	106.99	2,985	21,354	39,586
Newark	16.38	174.42	149.58	7,944	60,174	49,211
Rochester	12.94	108.97	64.61	3,713	28,113	22,895
MEDIAN (All Cities)	10.25	70.04	82.18	3,713	28,113	30,744
MEDIAN (Recipient Cities Only)	10.25	70.04	82.18	3,713	28,113	30,744
NON-INTERGOVERNMENTAL						
Anaheim	0.66	17.05	23.38	111	3,495	5,191
Austin	1.12	5.80	5.68	275	1,845	1,966
Baton Rouge	2.36	NA	29.47	389	NA	6,454
Columbus	5.90	41.42	53.63	3,147	23,114	30,302
Nashville-Davidson	1.98	17.73	13.69	794	7,925	6,242
Oklahoma City	5.69	24.73	30.41	2,072	9,717	12,255
San Jose	8.21	53.96	54.32	3,563	31,510	34,604
Tulsa	4.66	20.46	25.16	1,506	7,203	9,084
Virginia Beach	0.53	9.95	9.31	86	2,339	2,440
Wichita	5.22	29.53	33.84	1,435	8,208	9,440
MEDIAN (All Cities)	4.66	20.46	25.16	1,506	7,925	9,084
MEDIAN (Recipient Cities Only)	4.66	20.46	25.16	1,506	7,925	9,084
					(million)	
U.S. TOTAL	8.45	29.50	31.39	1,697	6,490	7,109

Note: NA = Not Available.

Source: Executive Office of the President, Community Services Administration, <u>Geographic Distribution of Federal Funds</u> (1981).

AFDC aid continued to rise between 1977 and 1980, it did so at a significantly lower rate of increase per year. For those three years, AFDC payments increased by only 3 percent annually. For the initial inter-period, non-intergovernmental cities expanded AFDC benefits by 53 percent per year and during the latter three years by 4.9 percent. The net result of these growth patterns was that by 1980, intergovernmental cities received, on average, 3.4 times the level of AFDC aid as non-intergovernmental cities and 2.6 times the level of aid as the nation as a whole. Non-intergovernmental cities were awarded only 80 percent of the national per capita average.

Although Newark's population decline during the 1970s was not as great as that of the average intergovernmental city, its dependency on AFDC payments far outranked that of any other city examined. Newark's AFDC funding in 1980 was $150 per capita, almost six times the level of aid in non-intergovernmental cities. Additionally, Newark's 1980 aid level was down 14.3 percent from 1977, when each Newark resident represented $175 in AFDC payments.

Unemployment Insurance benefits are noted in Exhibit 6.12. From 1969 to 1977, non-intergovernmental cities were the principal beneficiaries of Unemployment Insurance. For example, in 1969, intergovernmental city unemployment aid was 31 percent of that for non-intergovernmental cities, and in 1977, that ratio remained unchanged. In 1980, however, the intergovernmental–non-intergovernmental city relationship was reversed as non-intergovernmental cities then received only 45 percent of the amount of unemployment aid distributed in intergovernmental cities.

Intergovernmental city populations, for all Social Security Insurance programs, received the greatest level of benefits compared with those in non-intergovernmental cities. For example, in 1980, per capita non-intergovernmental city benefits for Retirement Insurance were 40 percent of those for persons in intergovernmental cities (Exhibit 6.13); Disability Insurance payments for non-intergovernmental city residents were 47 percent of those for intergovernmental city residents (Exhibit 6.14); and Survivor's Insurance assistance in non-intergovernmental cities was 46 percent of the level received by the average intergovernmental city (Exhibit 6.15).

Although the intergovernmental city population has steadily declined throughout the 1970s, Social Security payments have risen unabated. This is a function of an expanding elderly population in this category of cities as well as increasing benefit levels per recipient. From 1974 to 1977, the average intergovernmental city received an additional $65 million to its local economy through Social Security Retirement Aid. For the three years 1977 to 1980, intergovernmental city Retirement assistance expanded by another $45 million. Viewing the 1974 to 1980 period as a whole, the intergovernmental city population increased its dependency on Retirement Insurance by fully 73 percent per year.

Non-intergovernmental cities also received substantial and growing aid from Retirement funds. In fact, the rate of aggregate dollar growth in non-intergovernmental cities exceeded that for intergovernmental cities between 1974 and 1980. However, increasing populations throughout that period held the per capita growth down relative to intergovernmental cities.

A similar pattern of program expansion occurred in both Disability Insurance and Survivor's Insurance. In these programs, expansion was greater during the early Seventies. The period from 1977 to 1980 reflects sharp declines in the rate of growth from the preceding period. For all three programs, intergovernmental cities received

EXHIBIT 6.12. — *Unemployment Insurance, 1969–1980 (Dollars)*

	Per Capita			Absolute (000)		
	1969	1977	1980	1969	1977	1980
INTERGOVERNMENTAL						
Akron	0.33	1.22	2.61	92	303	618
Baltimore	2.23	13.53	9.22	2,031	11,131	7,252
Buffalo	0.90	4.61	9.39	421	1,798	3,360
Cincinnati	0.68	3.67	NA	312	1,489	NA
Cleveland	0.50	2.46	9.59	378	1,540	5,506
Louisville	1.00	3.22	9.08	365	1,019	2,707
Milwaukee	0.54	2.19	NA	386	1,445	NA
Minneapolis	0.79	3.94	5.72	345	1,531	2,118
Newark	1.05	0.89	NA	511	3,027	NA
Rochester	0.65	2.19	14.19	185	564	3,433
MEDIAN (All Cities)	0.65	3.22	9.22	365	1,531	3,360
MEDIAN (Recipient Cities Only)	0.65	3.22	9.22	365	1,531	3,360
NON-INTERGOVERNMENTAL						
Anaheim	NA	NA	NA	NA	NA	NA
Austin	12.35	61.69	40.68	3,037	19,618	1,383
Baton Rouge	6.66	40.89	6.95	1,099	8,301	1,521
Columbus	6.33	37.45	6.46	3,372	20,897	3,652
Nashville-Davidson	2.91	15.87	3.03	1,167	7,093	1,380
Oklahoma City	3.32	13.06	4.13	1,210	5,131	1,664
San Jose	0.73	2.42	4.79	318	1,413	3,052
Tulsa	0.81	0.80	3.90	262	283	1,408
Virginia Beach	0.23	0.45	1.28	37	105	335
Wichita	0.51	1.46	0.73	139	405	2,043
MEDIAN (All Cities)	3.32	13.06	4.13	1,167	5,131	1,521
MEDIAN (Recipient Cities Only)	3.32	13.06	4.13	1,167	5,131	1,521
					(million)	
U.S. TOTAL	2.05	4.07	4.89	411	896	1,108

Note: NA = Not Available.

Source: Executive Office of the President, Community Services Administration, Geographic Distribution of Federal Funds (1981).

more than the national per capita average while non-intergovernmental cities benefited considerably less than the general population. Across all three insurance programs, as of 1980, Virginia Beach residents were the least dependent, while Louisville, Buffalo, Rochester and Cincinnati all ranked as principal recipients. Interestingly, in all cases, Newark, reflecting the infrequent labor force participation of
many residents, ranked below the average intergovernmental city in per capita Social
Security benefits.

Food and Nutrition

The provision of food subsidies to low-income households in the United States
has been provided principally through the direct federal aid, Food Stamp program.
Households receive coupons redeemable for food at retail stores in a quantity reflec-

EXHIBIT 6.13. — *Social Security Retirement Insurance, 1974–1980 (Dollars)*

	Per Capita			Absolute (000)		
	1974	1977	1980	1974	1977	1980
INTERGOVERNMENTAL						
Akron	269.9	385.4	520.9	70,180	95,586	123,458
Baltimore	186.8	280.9	388.7	160,295	231,199	305,898
Buffalo	367.8	564.6	593.7	154,837	220,213	292,535
Cincinnati	355.0	533.1	736.9	151,233	216,441	283,689
Cleveland	308.9	84.0	727.6	210,050	303,460	417,668
Louisville	332.8	504.1	731.6	108,452	159,802	218,013
Milwaukee	262.4	387.0	NA	180,415	255,423	NA
Minneapolis	339.2	502.2	706.9	138,377	195,351	261,559
Newark	123.9	176.6	232.4	44,740	60,926	76,459
Rochester	429.4	642.6	909.9	117,651	165,784	220,197
MEDIAN (All Cities)	308.9	502.2	706.9	151,233	216,441	261,559
MEDIAN (Recipient Cities Only)	308.9	502.2	706.9	151,233	216,441	261,559
NON-INTERGOVERNMENTAL						
Anaheim	107.9	155.3	203.9	20,277	31,841	45,263
Austin	116.8	172.2	236.6	33,879	54,749	81,852
Baton Rouge	138.4	193.0	262.5	25,875	39,177	57,479
Columbus	149.5	211.2	278.9	82,230	117,877	157,581
Nashville-Davidson	123.6	180.5	246.1	54,115	80,664	112,231
Oklahoma City	185.0	265.1	353.0	70,672	104,179	142,264
San Jose	133.8	157.7	207.9	60,419	92,086	132,459
Tulsa	170.8	244.2	328.5	58,409	85,959	118,602
Virginia Beach	53.7	80.5	126.9	11,179	18,912	33,258
Wichita	179.4	260.9	363.7	49,864	72,526	101,481
MEDIAN (All Cities)	143.9	186.7	254.3	51,990	83,312	106,856
MEDIAN (Recipient Cities Only)	143.9	186.7	254.3	51,990	83,312	106,856
					(million)	
U.S. TOTAL	167.40	239.58	327.93	35,624	52,708	74,273

Note: NA = Not Available.

Source: Executive Office of the President, Community Services Administration, Geographic Distribution of Federal Funds (1981).

tive of family size and income level. Food coupons are used the same as cash and, with very few exceptions, can be used to buy any food for human consumption. At a cost of $8.7 billion, the Food Stamp program served an average of 21.1 million persons per month throughout 1980. The Food Stamp program is administered jointly by states and the federal government: the federal government pays the total cost of the food coupons, and assists the states in financing administrative costs of the program. As of 1980, every state was participating in this program.

Concern for the nutritional intake of children is a dominant theme of other food programs for lower-income families. This fact is evidenced by the variety of programs which have been enacted to provide food aid directly to children. Two of the most important programs which are reviewed here are the National School Lunch program, the largest child nutrition program, and the School Breakfast program.

Essentially, both the School Lunch and School Breakfast programs have provided

EXHIBIT 6.14. — *Social Security Disability Insurance,*
1974–1980 (Dollars)

	Per Capita			Absolute (000)		
	1974	1977	1980	1974	1977	1980
INTERGOVERNMENTAL						
Akron	49.27	80.14	98.97	11,511	19,874	23,455
Baltimore	31.19	55.89	77.00	26,758	45,995	60,958
Buffalo	82.87	119.10	161.82	46,466	46,450	57,930
Cincinnati	54.59	104.91	134.85	23,257	42,592	51,919
Cleveland	52.71	103.28	134.60	35,845	64,758	77,308
Louisville	63.32	119.44	176.26	21,277	37,861	52,526
Milwaukee	35.53	62.20	NA	24,335	41,053	NA
Minneapolis	39.66	72.55	90.62	16,180	28,223	33,530
Newark	33.62	62.93	78.89	12,138	21,711	25,958
Rochester	58.64	118.91	165.53	16,067	30,679	40,059
MEDIAN (All Cities)	48.49	91.71	116.82	21,277	37,861	51,918
MEDIAN (Recipient Cities Only)	48.49	91.71	116.82	21,277	37,861	51,918
NON-INTERGOVERNMENTAL						
Anaheim	25.65	47.31	54.76	4,822	9,698	12,156
Austin	18.64	32.89	41.53	5,406	10,459	14,368
Baton Rouge	41.63	69.23	77.16	7,785	14,054	16,897
Columbus	31.35	58.83	73.38	17,240	32,820	41,448
Nashville-Davidson	23.90	38.43	48.18	10,469	17,178	21,969
Oklahoma City	29.33	54.24	61.47	11,202	21,315	24,773
San Jose	27.80	48.65	51.25	14,764	28,413	32,649
Tulsa	27.91	47.14	54.20	9,546	16,593	19,565
Virginia Beach	13.54	23.40	34.14	2,816	5,498	8,944
Wichita	27.01	43.92	55.55	7,510	12,210	15,497
MEDIAN (All Cities)	27.41	47.22	54.48	8,666	15,324	20,767
MEDIAN (Recipient Cities Only)	27.41	47.22	54.48	8,666	15,324	20,767
					(million)	
U.S. TOTAL	29.53	51.20	70.93	6,283	11,265	16,066

Note: NA = Not Available.
Source: Executive Office of the President, Community Services Administration, Geographic Distribution of Federal Funds (1981).

free or reduced-price meals to eligible students. The programs are available to public, non-profit and private schools of high-school grade or under, for reimbursement of meals meeting minimum nutritional requirements established by the Department of Agriculture. Participation in the programs requires sizable state matching funds. For example, with the National School Lunch program, all states whose average per capita income is equal to or greater than the national average must spend $3 for every $1 of federal outlay. States with lower per capita incomes must match the federal grants at a lower rate. In 1980, the average assistance per meal in the National School Lunch program was 17.6 cents cash and 15.7 cents in food. Special assistance to needy children was approximately 77 cents per meal. An estimated 4.4 million meals were served, of which 45.5 percent or 2 million were served to poor or near-poor children. While a considerably smaller program, the School Breakfast program, also reached millions of children in 1980; that year the program

EXHIBIT 6.15.—*Social Security Survivor's Insurance,*
1974–1980 (Dollars)

	Per Capita			Absolute (000)		
	1974	1977	1980	1974	1977	1980
INTERGOVERNMENTAL						
Akron	96.0	150.2	212.3	24,950	37,246	50,322
Baltimore	73.2	111.8	156.3	62,586	92,050	122,976
Buffalo	133.3	211.3	310.7	56,103	82,415	112,218
Cincinnati	135.7	208.2	302.2	57,802	84,533	116,328
Cleveland	120.7	193.2	285.5	82,065	121,131	163,852
Louisville	130.0	208.4	309.5	43,680	66,077	92,255
Milwaukee[1]	85.0	128.9	NA	58,200	85,086	NA
Minneapolis	102.9	158.2	226.0	41,998	61,521	83,633
Newark	49.4	72.6	95.8	17,847	25,057	31,514
Rochester	109.0	171.2	245.5	29,866	44,166	59,403
MEDIAN (All Cities)	109.0	193.2	245.5	43,680	84,533	92,255
MEDIAN (Recipient Cities Only)	109.0	193.2	245.5	43,680	84,533	92,255
NON-INTERGOVERNMENTAL						
Anaheim	41.9	57.1	72.3	7,869	11,706	16,041
Austin	49.2	71.3	104.2	14,258	22,687	36,066
Baton Rouge	79.6	114.4	158.7	14,894	23,232	34,749
Columbus	60.8	90.1	121.6	33,417	50,276	68,711
Nashville-Davidson	47.9	70.0	95.7	20,983	31,303	43,633
Oklahoma City	62.2	93.4	129.6	23,756	36,699	52,226
San Jose	43.0	62.7	81.8	22,827	36,588	52,123
Tulsa	59.9	89.4	124.2	20,494	31,453	44,849
Virginia Beach	35.5	52.3	75.0	7,384	12,282	19,653
Wichita	56.6	85.0	119.5	15,724	23,630	33,348
MEDIAN (All Cities)	52.9	78.2	111.9	18,109	27,467	39,850
MEDIAN (Recipient Cities Only)	52.9	78.2	111.9	18,109	27,467	39,850
					(million)	
U.S. TOTAL	59.18	87.40	122.09	12,595	19,229	27,653

Note: NA=Not Available.
[1]City not included in median calculation due to incomplete data.
Source: Executive Office of the President, Community Services Administration,
Geographic Distribution of Federal Funds (1981).

subsidized 611 million breakfasts. Federal cash assistance was estimated at 45.2 cents per meal. Over $2 billion was expended on the School Lunch program in 1980.

Food and Nutrition Programs in Intergovernmental
Versus Non-Intergovernmental Cities

Exhibit 6.16 shows that between 1969 and 1977, the Food Stamp program expanded annually by $606 million or 224 percent. By 1980, that program had grown by an additional $3.6 billion for an average annual growth rate of 70.6 percent. In-

EXHIBIT 6.16. — *Food Stamps, 1969–1980 (Dollars)*

	Per Capita			Absolute (000)		
	1969	1977	1980	1969	1977	1980
INTERGOVERNMENTAL						
Akron	2.92	30.28	38.68	808	7,510	9,166
Baltimore	0.70	65.43	108.70	640	53,892	86,658
Buffalo	2.65	46.06	35.53	1,247	17,964	12,719
Cincinnati	3.82	25.23	33.38	1,752	10,244	12,850
Cleveland	6.63	39.56	51.88	5,068	24,805	29,777
Louisville	0.18	38.11	55.67	67	12,081	16,590
Milwaukee	0.54	10.72	NA	388	7,707	NA
Minneapolis	1.06	13.04	17.75	466	5,072	6,569
Newark	-	48.35	66.64	-	16,673	21,925
Rochester	-	11.35	23.34	-	2,927	5,649
MEDIAN (All Cities)	1.06	38.11	38.68	640	12,081	12,850
MEDIAN (Recipient Cities Only)	1.86	38.11	38.68	724	12,081	12,850
NON-INTERGOVERNMENTAL						
Anaheim	0.09	6.71	10.64	15	1,375	2,362
Austin	-	14.39	30.10	-	4,575	10,415
Baton Rouge	6.27	30,80	70.26	94	6,252	15,387
Columbus	2.43	35.30	40.49	1,293	19,695	22,874
Nashville-Davidson	0.67	157.00	53.36	269	70,180	24,334
Oklahoma City	-	13.43	23.89	-	5,277	9,628
San Jose	0.24	12.93	14.14	105	7,551	9,004
Tulsa	-	12.82	23.19	-	4,513	8,372
Virginia Beach	0.29	4.97	14.50	47	1,168	3,798
Wichita	-	8.16	19.03	-	2,268	5,308
MEDIAN (All Cities)	0.17	13.18	23.54	31	4,926	9,710
MEDIAN (Recipient Cities Only)	0.75	13.18	23.54	100	4,926	9,710
					(million)	
U.S. TOTAL	1.15	23.10	38.30	231	5,083	8,674

Note: NA=Not Available.

Source: Executive Office of the President, Community Services Administration, Geographic Distribution of Federal Funds (1981).

tergovernmental cities were major recipients in the Food Stamp expansion during the first inter-period; intergovernmental Food Stamp participation grew by 223.4 percent each year from 1969 to 1977. For the final three years, until 1980, intergovernmental cities experienced a sharp drop in the rate of growth in Food Stamp use by their residents. On average, participation increased by a mere 2 percent per year.

On a per capita basis, nevertheless, intergovernmental cities were strongly overrepresented in Food Stamp participation when compared to non-intergovernmental cities. In 1980, the average intergovernmental city resident received $39 in Food Stamp Bonus Coupons compared with $24 worth of Stamps by non-intergovernmental city residents.

The School Breakfast program did not enjoy participation by all intergovernmental or non-intergovernmental cities for any year recorded. However, as indicated by Exhibit 6.17, program participation did grow significantly between 1969 and 1980. In 1969, six intergovernmental and two non-intergovernmental cities received School Breakfast program grants. By 1980, nine non-intergovernmental and eight intergovernmental cities received this category of federal money. In the aggregate, intergovernmental cities in 1980 received only eight percent more school breakfast federal aid than non-intergovernmental cities. On a per capita basis, however, the dependency of intergovernmental cities was more pronounced: intergovernmental cities received fully 47 percent more breakfast aid per person. Cleveland, which received 181 percent more Food Stamp aid per capita than the average intergovernmental city, also had the highest 1980 per capita School Breakfast program participation level. At nearly $4 per capita, Cleveland's per person participation was more than two times the rate of the average intergovernmental city. Newark, which was the second largest per capita recipient of Food Stamp allocations, held the same position with regard to the School Breakfast program; Newark also received more than twice the average per capita benefit.

In 1969, the School Lunch program was funded at $189.6 million or $0.94 per person nationally (Exhibit 6.18). By 1980, that per capita figure had increased to $10.38. Only intergovernmental cities, on average, received per capita benefits of this magnitude. Non-intergovernmental cities received 13 percent less than intergovernmental cities and the same percentage less than the nation as a whole. As noted, several intergovernmental cities received large amounts of per capita aid. Newark, for example, was granted $22.54 for each resident. Buffalo and Baltimore were also above the national average at $13.20 and $14.18 per capita respectively. Although most non-intergovernmental cities received substantially less than the national average, one city, Austin, had a higher per capita level than any city studied except Newark. Austin received more than $19 per capita to subsidize school lunches.

Community and Regional Development

Housing and Community Development

The adverse conditions of densely-populated, low-income, central city neighborhoods have received attention since the turn of the century. Interest in and awareness of urban slums and blighted districts culminated in the late 1930s with the first public housing program specifically for low-income persons. Since that time, several housing programs have been promulgated to uplift deteriorating urban communities.

Until the 1960s, urban development programs concentrated on the physical aspects of cities. Programs such as Urban Renewal were more concerned with the physical environment than with the economic and social deprivation suffered by slum inhabitants. The Demonstration Cities and Model Development Act of 1966 marked a major change in this orientation. The Model Cities program authorized by this Act emphasized the broad spectrum of economic and social problems which ex-

EXHIBIT 6.17. — *School Breakfast Program, 1969–1980 (Dollars)*

	Per Capita			Absolute (000)		
	1969	1977	1980	1969	1977	1980
INTERGOVERNMENTAL						
Akron	-	0.03	1.07	-	6	254
Baltimore	-	0.41	1.20	-	334	941
Buffalo	-	0.66	3.24	-	259	1,161
Cincinnati	*	1.19	1.75	0.1	484	674
Cleveland	0.08	2.45	3.98	64	1,538	2,287
Louisville	0.04	-	-	14	-	-
Milwaukee	*	0.05	NA	2	35	NA
Minneapolis	0.03	0.45	0.64	11	176	238
Newark	0.01	0.94	3.65	4	325	1,201
Rochester	-	1.27	2.77	-	328	670
MEDIAN (All Cities)	0.01	0.66	1.75	0.1	325	674
MEDIAN (Recipient Cities Only)	0.03	0.80	2.26	11	327	808
NON-INTERGOVERNMENTAL						
Anaheim	-	0.05	0.17	-	10	37
Austin	-	1.62	8.15	-	514	2,821
Baton Rouge	-	3.41	3.28	-	693	719
Columbus	0.01	0.52	3.08	3	289	1,177
Nashville-Davidson	-	0.54	1.16	-	241	531
Oklahoma City	0.01	0.45	1.22	2	175	493
San Jose	-	0.39	1.98	-	520	1,261
Tulsa	-	0.46	0.61	-	161	221
Virginia Beach	-	-	-	-	-	-
Wichita	-	0.09	0.18	-	25	51
MEDIAN (All Cities)	-	0.49	1.19	0	208	625
MEDIAN (Recipient Cities Only)	0.01	0.52	1.22	3	241	719
					(million)	
U.S. TOTAL	0.02	0.64	1.45	3	142	327

Note: NA=Not Available.
*Less than $0.01 per capita.

Source: Executive Office of the President, Community Services Administration, Geographic Distribution of Federal Funds (1981).

isted in most inner-city communities. Model Cities activities included not only physical rehabilitation of deteriorating structures but also job training, employment opportunities, and a wide range of social services. Although Model Cities was a relatively short-lived program, many elements of that effort were continued into urban program initiatives throughout the Seventies.

The three programs reviewed below represent some of the largest housing and community development programs, and reflect the diversity in community development initiatives which developed over the past twenty years.

The Community Development Block Grant (CDBG) program in 1974 consolidated several former community development categorical programs which formerly

EXHIBIT 6.18. — *National School Lunch Program, 1969–1980 (Dollars)*

	Per Capita			Absolute (000)		
	1969	1977	1980	1969	1977	1980
INTERGOVERNMENTAL						
Akron	0.02	7.17	7.12	5	1,177	1,688
Baltimore	0.08	12.26	13.20	74	10,093	10,390
Buffalo	0.10	8,02	14.18	49	3,126	5,075
Cincinnati	0.10	8.81	6.58	46	3,576	2,533
Cleveland	0.06	12.98	10.68	44	8,139	6,130
Louisville	0.06	-	-	21	-	-
Milwaukee	0.15	6.91	NA	110	4,561	NA
Minneapolis	0.10	5.28	6.29	44	2,052	2,327
Newark	0.08	17.04	22.54	40	5,878	7,415
Rochester	0.05	8.42	10.14	15	2,172	2,453
MEDIAN (All Cities)	0.08	8.42	10.14	44	3,126	2,533
MEDIAN (Recipient Cities Only)	0.08	8.61	10.91	44	3,351	3,804
NON-INTERGOVERNMENTAL						
Anaheim	0.08	2.70	3.16	12	553	701
Austin	0.44	7.88	19.10	108	2,575	6,610
Baton Rouge	0.48	15.13	13.39	77	3,072	2,933
Columbus	0.06	5.82	7.35	25	3,248	4,152
Nashville-Davidson	0.18	7.37	9.19	39	3,292	4,192
Oklahoma City	0.24	6.13	8.61	86	2,410	3,471
San Jose	0.06	7.01	9.55	24	4,096	6,083
Tulsa	0.15	6.24	8.25	48	2,196	2,979
Virginia Beach	0.25	5.00	7.00	41	1,175	1,834
Wichita	0.06	5.00	6.70	16	1,389	1,870
MEDIAN (All Cities)	0.16	6.19	8.93	40	2,493	3,225
MEDIAN (Recipient Cities Only)	0.16	6.19	8.93	40	2,493	3,225
					(million)	
U.S. TOTAL	0.94	7.07	10.38	190	1,630	2,351

Note: NA=Not Available.

Source: Executive Office of the President, Community Services Administration, Geographic Distribution of Federal Funds (1981).

supported a wide array of neighborhood redevelopment activities. Focused principally on low- and moderate-income persons, Block Grant funds from this point on could be used for the acquisition, development and redevelopment of real property, provision and improvement of public facilities, and relocation and demolition activities. Block Grant entitlements were awarded on the basis of a dual formula which employed factors such as population, age of housing, extent of poverty, growth lag, and housing overcrowding. There was no local matching requirement for Community Development Block Grants. Outlays from the federal government in 1980 totalled $2.7 billion for Block Grant entitlements.

Low-Income Housing Assistance (public housing) was authorized in 1937. It is the oldest housing program for low-income persons. The objective of the program has been to provide low-income families with acceptable and affordable housing. Public housing has been operated by local public housing agencies which provide housing to those qualified by: (1) acquiring existing housing units, (2) letting contracts to private developers, and assuming control upon completion, and (3) engaging in construction through competitive bidding. In addition to grants for construction or acquisition of public housing units, federal assistance also has been available for the maintenance and operation of these properties. Initially, federal funding of public housing was to cover only the capital cost of the program while operating costs were to be borne by tenants. However, since 1964, payment ceilings have been placed on rent contributions of public housing residents, not to exceed 25 percent, and more recently, 30 percent of their incomes. Since 1980, skyrocketing energy, construction costs, and finance charges have resulted in relatively little public housing construction despite fairly high funding levels; a full $1.2 billion was expended on the public housing program in 1980.

The Section 8 program has also provided housing assistance payments to participating private owners, as well as to public housing agencies in return for the provision of standard housing to lower-income persons. The Section 8 program was developed to offer lower-income families more flexibility in the selection of the housing units which they occupy. The program was premised on the belief that by allowing lower-income families and individuals more freedom of movement than was allowed by traditional public housing programs, greater income and racial integration would occur. Moreover, it was thought that with increased mobility of lower-income tenants, new construction and rehabilitation would be stimulated in the private market due to the increased purchasing power of these low-income households.

By the end of 1980, 1.2 million units were receiving Section 8 subsidies at a cost of $965.8 million to the federal government. Tenants contributed no less than 15 percent and no more than 25 percent of their incomes toward rent.

Housing and Community Development Transfers in
Intergovernmental Versus Non-Intergovernmental Cities

The fact that the CDBG program has not expanded in the same manner as most grant-in-aid programs is evident in Exhibit 6.19. In fact, Block Grants have declined each year, both relatively and absolutely. Moreover, for the four years prior to 1980 there was no significant shift in program funding between the two sets of cities. To the extent that there have been minor national funding increases, these funds largely have been channeled to intergovernmental cities. Coupled with their declining populations, per capita intergovernmental city gains indicate a slight upward trend in Block Grant assistance. Those figures, therefore, mask the irregular, fluctuating patterns which actually occurred in the Block Grant program's funding between 1977 and 1980.

Since 1977, intergovernmental cities have received financial aid through the CDBG far in excess of that obtained by non-intergovernmental cities. In 1980, for example, intergovernmental cities, on average, received three-to-four times the Block Grant aid awarded to non-intergovernmental cities. From 1977 to 1980, the average intergovernmental city received $43.2 million more than the equivalent non-

EXHIBIT 6.19. — *Community Development Block Grants, 1977-1980 (Dollars)*

	Per Capita				Absolute (000)			
	1977	1978	1979	1980	1977	1978	1979	1980
INTERGOVERNMENTAL								
Akron	39.59	-	36.35	37.93	9,819	-	8,760	8,989
Baltimore	35.29	34.82	39.03	42.96	29,042	28,240	31,185	33,808
Buffalo	26.53	56.12	63.07	67.73	10,346	21,269	22,768	24,249
Cincinnati	45.43	42.86	46.31	50.13	18,448	17,101	18,155	19,299
Cleveland	-	83.14	62.47	68.36	-	50,633	36,979	39,239
Louisville	27.25	38.37	42.48	46.44	8,639	11,933	12,914	13,838
Milwaukee	19.12	30.72	33.30	35.84	12,621	20,030	21,446	22,794
Minneapolis	38.80	45.46	49.48	53.97	15,093	17,365	18,606	19,968
Newark	56.55	49.79	48.81	51.74	19,508	16,930	16,302	17,024
Rochester	54.04	49.38	49.36	53.60	13,943	12,493	12,193	12,972
MEDIAN (All Cities)	37.05	44.16	47.56	49.09	13,282	18,698	18,381	19,634
MEDIAN (Recipient Cities Only)	38.80	45.46	47.56	49.09	15,093	20,030	18,381	19,634
NON-INTERGOVERNMENTAL								
Anaheim	9.55	9.30	9.81	10.20	1,957	1,963	2,119	2,264
Austin	23.08	18.47	16.70	16.97	7,338	6,039	5,627	5,870
Baton Rouge	27.42	27.56	28.84	29.83	5,567	5,732	6,172	6,533
Columbus	15.23	15.52	16.50	17.47	8,498	8,691	9,289	9,868
Nashville-Davidson	21.50	18.60	17.70	18.55	9,609	8,369	8,020	8,457
Oklahoma City	20.82	18.73	17.87	17.78	8,183	7,418	7,149	7,167
San Jose	10.63	10.53	11.07	11.48	6,209	6,341	6,854	7,314
Tulsa	22.82	17.85	15.47	15.45	8,033	6,338	5,537	5,579
Virginia Beach	9.40	9.65	10.12	10.55	2,208	2,354	2,560	2,764
Wichita	39.10	28.10	20.71	16.57	10,870	7,841	5,777	4,623
MEDIAN (All Cities)	21.16	18.53	16.60	16.77	7,761	6,880	5,916	6,202
MEDIAN (Recipient Cities Only)	21.16	18.53	16.60	16.77	7,761	6,880	5,916	6,202
U.S. TOTAL	12.08	12.49	12.14	12.01	2,695	2,777	2,729	2,720 (million)

Note: NA = Not Available.
Source: Executive Office of the President, Community Services Administration, Geographic Distribution of Federal Funds (1981).

intergovernmental city. For essentially similarly sized, intergovernmental cities, Block Grants, in 1980, ranged from a high of $39.2 million in Cleveland to a low in Akron of $8.7 million. For similar non-intergovernmental cities, the range was significantly smaller; block grants ranged from $2.2 million in Anaheim to $9.8 million in Columbus.

Exhibit 6.20 outlines Low-Income Housing Assistance (public housing) between intergovernmental and non-intergovernmental cities. Between 1974 and 1977, low-income public housing grants increased by 52 percent, from $539.7 million to $821.8 million. For the following three years, until 1980, Low-Income Housing Assistance grew by an additional $333.8 million or 41 percent. This growth pattern, however, was not reflected in the intergovernmental or non-intergovernmental cities which received grants during that six-year period. To the contrary, for intergovernmental cities already receiving public housing grants, these grants tended to be significantly higher during the early 1970s than they were in 1980. From the data presented here, it appears that the national increase in public housing funding was not channeled in the form of larger aid packages to currently funded cities but, rather, to cities which had no existing subsidy. For example, in 1974, only two non-intergovernmental cities were reported to have received low-income housing assistance payments; by 1980, seven-of-ten non-intergovernmental cities were availing themselves of these grants.

On balance, however, intergovernmental cities throughout the 1970s received a much greater share of public housing assistance than non-intergovernmental cities. In 1974, the average non-intergovernmental city did not participate in housing funding, while the average intergovernmental city received $12.3 million from that program. Further, even if only those cities that did receive benefits from the public housing program were considered, their average grant award was only 28 percent of the average aid to intergovernmental cities. Finally, in 1980, the average non-intergovernmental city received only 36 percent of the level of the average intergovernmental city funding.

Three intergovernmental cities consistently have received significant grants from public housing, ranging from two, to more than three times the average intergovernmental city public housing subsidy. These cities include Baltimore, with a 1980 award of $17.4 million, Newark at $15 million, and Cleveland, which received $10.9 million. Finally, one intergovernmental city, Minneapolis, and three non-intergovernmental cities, including Anaheim, San Jose and Virginia Beach, were listed as not having secured any public housing assistance funds for 1980. Anaheim and Virginia Beach, moreover, did not participate in the public housing program in any year reported.

For both intergovernmental and non-intergovernmental cities, reliance (on a per capita basis) on Section 8 assistance has declined since 1977. Housing allowances peaked in intergovernmental cities in 1979 when each intergovernmental city resident accounted for close to $8 in Section 8 grants (Exhibit 6.21). Non-intergovernmental cities, on the other hand, relied most heavily on housing assistance payments in the first year reported, 1977, with per capita aid of just under $7. By 1980, non-intergovernmental city dependence on the Section 8 program decreased by one-half, while the average intergovernmental city lost 23.5 percent of its peak 1979 per capita housing assistance funding.

EXHIBIT 6.20. — *Low-Income Housing Assistance, 1974–1980 (Dollars)*

	Per Capita			Absolute (000)		
	1974	1977	1980	1974	1977	1980
INTERGOVERNMENTAL						
Akron	–	13.88	19.99	–	3,443	4,738
Baltimore	14.33	2.97	22.14	12,298	2,448	17,427
Buffalo	–	5.72	10.55	–	2,230	3,778
Cincinnati	–	10.00	13.91	–	4,058	5,354
Cleveland	33.35	13.54	19.07	22,680	8,488	10,946
Louisville	31.98	11.16	18.88	10,744	3,538	5,625
Milwaukee	9.59	4.95	NA	6,572	3,266	NA
Minneapolis	35.31	14.77	–	14,406	5,747	–
Newark	78.47	30.23	45.69	28,326	10,430	15,023
Rochester	–	27.15	10.48	–	2,005	2,354
MEDIAN (All Cities)	14.33	13.54	18.88	12,298	3,538	5,354
MEDIAN (Recipient Cities Only)	33.35	13.54	18.97	14,406	3,538	5,490
NON-INTERGOVERNMENTAL						
Anaheim	–	–	–	–	–	–
Austin	–	4.44	6.96	–	1,413	2,407
Baton Rouge	–	5.33	6.64	–	1,082	1,454
Columbus	–	8.31	10.80	–	4,637	6,103
Nashville-Davidson	–	7.24	9.80	–	3,236	4,468
Oklahoma City	6.61	6.61	10.63	2,524	2,596	4,283
San Jose	–	53	–	–	31	–
Tulsa	–	4.50	7.34	–	1,583	2,648
Virginia Beach	–	–	–	–	–	–
Wichita	19.63	1.64	2.01	5,456	457	560
MEDIAN (All Cities)	–	4.97	6.80	0	1,248	1,931
MEDIAN (Recipient Cities Only)	13.12	4.91	7.34	3,990	1,498	2,648
					(million)	
U.S. TOTAL	2.54	3.74	5.10	540	822	1,156

Note: NA=Not Available.

Source: Executive Office of the President, Community Services Administration, Geographic Distribution of Federal Funds (1981).

Newark is noteworthy both in absolute dollars and per capita terms with regard to the Section 8 program. Housing assistance payments were over $30 per capita, more than five times the level of funding for the average intergovernmental city and more than ten times the level in the average non-intergovernmental city. Finally, it is worth noting that, since 1977, non-intergovernmental cities have received less per capita aid than the nation as a whole.

EXHIBIT 6.21. — Rent Supplements: Section 8, 1977-1980 (Dollars)

	Per Capita				Absolute (000)			
	1977	1978	1979	1980	1977	1978	1979	1980
INTERGOVERNMENTAL								
Akron	3.87	8.92	11.50	4.33	959	2,185	2,771	1,025
Baltimore	9.50	8.33	13.02	4.82	7,819	6,754	10,403	3,791
Buffalo	4.17	6.80	5.53	6.64	1,626	2,576	1,997	2,378
Cincinnati	10.95	4.69	18.21	5.78	4,446	1,870	7,140	2,226
Cleveland	2.57	4.43	6.26	5.70	1,614	2,697	3,707	3,270
Louisville	5.72	7.31	8.98	6.59	1,813	2,273	2,730	1,965
Milwaukee	15.61	7.66	4.77	3.06	10,301	4,994	3,071	1,947
Minneapolis	7.36	2.48	5.23	5.88	2,861	949	1,967	2,174
Newark	24.06	23.62	23.02	30.22	8,300	8,029	7,688	9,941
Rochester	2.52	3.30	4.41	6.63	651	835	1,089	1,604
MEDIAN (All Cities)	6.54	7.05	7.62	5.83	2,337	2,425	2,921	2,200
MEDIAN (Recipient Cities Only)	6.54	7.05	7.62	5.83	2,337	2,425	2,921	2,200
NON-INTERGOVERNMENTAL								
Anaheim	8.92	6.52	1.89	6.01	1,829	1,376	408	1,335
Austin	1.74	2.10	2.27	3.01	552	687	766	1,042
Baton Rouge	1.45	-	3.50	11.14	294	-	748	234
Columbus	6.14	4.39	11.03	8.49	3,424	2,456	6,209	4,798
Nashville-Davidson	14.92	5.49	1.38	1.94	6,667	2,472	623	885
Oklahoma City	2.67	1.02	6.74	5.94	1,051	404	2,696	2,393
San Jose	2.89	4.87	6.62	0.55	1,690	2,929	4,100	350
Tulsa	7.76	3.72	-	1.82	2,733	1,322	-	657
Virginia Beach	11.35	2.89	3.51	3.01	2,667	705	888	789
Wichita	7.78	2.70	0.64	2.69	2,051	754	179	751
MEDIAN (All Cities)	6.76	3.31	2.89	3.01	1,940	1,038	757	837
MEDIAN (Recipient Cities Only)	6.76	3.72	3.50	3.01	1,940	1,322	766	837
							(million)	
U.S. TOTAL	5.87	4.07	5.59	4.26	1,291	905	1,256	966

Note: NA = Not Available.
Source: Executive Office of the President, Community Services Administration, Geographic Distribution of Federal Funds (1981).

Economic Development

Federal initiatives to stimulate economic activity have been of two principal types: (1) programs to assist directly private businesses, and (2) grants to local and state units of government. The former set of programs offered direct loans and loan guarantees to assist businesses which faced difficulties in securing capital from private sources. Municipal assistance was largely composed of grants for the construction and improvement of highways and mass-transit systems. Since 1980, cities have also received fiscal assistance in the form of shared revenues, which can be utilized in a variety of ways to improve local economic conditions.

It is important to note that the two types of economic aid outlined above, while separate and distinct, were viewed to be mutually reinforcing. Financial support for local businesses has a direct impact on the local economy. Businesses create jobs, pay taxes, and attract other firms. On the other hand, grants to local governments which enable them to improve municipal facilities and services, enhance the overall business environment. In some instances, the provision of capital infrastructure, such as roads or sewer lines, creates business opportunities which previously did not exist.

A third category of economic development program is one in which the federal government provides municipalities with funds to be used as seed money to stimulate private redevelopment activities. Under this arrangement, municipal governments and private developers must work together in a public/private collaborative effort. The Urban Development Action Grant (UDAG) is an example of such a program.

Because economic stimulus programs are so widely diversified, they all are not reviewed in this subsection. Transportation and wastewater treatment assistance, for example, are broken down below as independent categories, similar to Revenue Sharing and Anti-Recessionary Fiscal Assistance. This organization is useful for viewing future budget reductions in the chapters which follow.

Business Development Assistance

In large part, the private market has been an efficient vehicle for the provision of capital needs generated by new and expanding businesses, as well as firm relocations and renovations. Small and particularly minority businesses, however, were often unable to fulfill their equity and working capital needs through private financial markets, especially during periods of tight money. As a result, they were either squeezed out of the market altogether or were forced to pay excessively high interest rates.

Further, private sources of capital were often lacking in geographic areas considered to be at high risk due to their underdeveloped or deteriorating status. But, paradoxically, these high-risk areas were often the very locations where business development was most urgently needed. In response to these unmet capital needs, the federal government developed an extensive set of business development programs to provide short, medium and long-range financial assistance through direct *loans* and *loan-guarantees* to qualifying businesses. To a much lesser extent, business development *grants* were also available. Grants, however, were not so much offered to firms to assist the business entity itself, but rather as incentives to attract and encourage firms to locate or remain in specific geographic areas. The programs below illustrate what has been the broad federal response to business development capital needs and will demonstrate how business grants were used to influence business activity. It will be obvious from the program descriptions which follow that Congress sought to combine both objectives previously mentioned in almost all programs, i.e., to provide needed business assistance loans, loan guarantees and grants in designated distressed geographical locations.

Though today almost totally out of business, the Economic Development Administration (EDA) in the past administered economic development programs to both private parties and municipal governments. For the promotion of private businesses, EDA offered direct and guaranteed/insured loans which could be used for new industrial and commercial development, as well as existing firm expansions in areas where financial assistance was not otherwise available. Long-term loans covered up to 65 percent of the cost of acquisition of fixed assets such as land, building, and equipment. Working capital was limited to short-term borrowing. EDA guaranteed up to 90 percent of the unpaid balance for both types of loans. Many other sources of financial assistance could be used with the EDA loan including local development corporations, state and local agencies, private banks, and the applicants themselves. In fact, at a minimum, applicants had to make a 10 to 15 percent equity commitment to the project. Fixed-asset loans could be extended up to a maximum of twenty-five years while working capital loans were offered only for a period of up to five years. Loan guarantees, on the other hand, were available for the life of the loan or lease.

Although EDA business development loans have been available since 1966, 13.7 percent of EDA's cumulative 1966–1980 projects occurred in 1980. Those projects accounted for fully 14.5 percent of total EDA loans offered. Loan guarantees were also high in 1980; they totalled 4 percent of all projects undertaken since 1966. The range of financial assistance in 1980 was from $260,000 to $5.2 million, with an average project size of $1.5 million. EDA offered fifty loans and 160 loan guarantees in 1980.

Unlike EDA loans and loan guarantees which were available to any individual or corporation regardless of firm size or present net worth, small business loans administered by the Small Business Administration (SBA) were restricted to individuals or corporations who met predetermined size standards. For example, eligible manufacturers generally could not employ more than 250 workers. The use of small business loans was also more restricted than those of EDA; gambling, publishing media and financing real property held for investment were all excluded activities. Small business loans were further considerably smaller than their EDA counterparts; the average direct SBA loan in 1980 was $54,782, while the typical loan guarantee was $113,589. SBA's smallest loan was a mere $1,000, while its greatest single expense was $350,000. Total direct loans for 1980 were $197.8 million, with $2.4 billion in loan guarantees. The SBA also offered more restrictive loans than its general Small Business Loan. Economic Opportunity Loans provided a maximum of $100,000 in loans to low-income or socially or economically disadvantaged individuals. The principal objective of this loan program was to strengthen and preserve business opportunities for socially and economically disenfranchised persons. Restrictions on the use of funds were basically the same as those imposed on the standard Small Business Loans described above. In 1980, a total of $62.5 million in loans was approved, with the average loan equaling $20,425.

Urban Development Action Grants (UDAG) are the final form of assistance outlined here. Unlike other financial assistance programs for businesses previously discussed, UDAG was a grant, and thus not subject to repayment. Additionally, UDAG funds were awarded to cities, where it could be demonstrated that city officials and private businesses could work in close cooperation on development ventures. The objective of UDAG also differed from other business incentive programs previously reviewed. UDAGs were specifically created to aid severely distressed cities and urban counties by providing neighborhood revitalization and economic development. Grants were also available to cities and counties which contained "pockets of poverty." Lagging per capita incomes, stagnating tax bases, high rates of poverty, high rates of unemployment, deteriorating housing and population, and business out-migration were all characteristics of prime sites for UDAG expenditures.

A principal feature of the UDAG program was its requirement for private financial commitment to a project before UDAG funds were awarded. The program was designed to achieve a high degree of leveraging of private funds. With a funding level of $613.3 million in 1980, the UDAG program was one of the most active economic stimulus programs during that year. Further, during 1978 and 1979, slightly less than $900 million of UDAG money supposedly leveraged more than $6 billion from the private sector. UDAGs were directed to both large and small cities. The average small city grant in 1980 was $976,000, while large cities averaged more than $2.6 million.

Business Development Transfers in Intergovernmental
Versus Non-Intergovernmental Cities

Both small business and economic opportunity loans have been funded at relatively low levels over the past decade. Nevertheless, given the nature of the loan program, i.e., relatively low levels of financial assistance to small enterprises, it is conceivable that relatively low funding levels could produce seed-type benefits for businesses in the cities in which they were located. For example, loans to small businesses which were failing due to extremely harsh, but temporary economic conditions, could shore up those enterprises and thus, retain jobs and add to the stability of the neighborhood in which they were located. Massive infusions of aid may not have been necessary or even appropriate. Exhibits 6.22 and 6.23 indicate that for both SBA programs, 1980 absolute funding levels are similar, with non-intergovernmental cities receiving only slightly more aid than intergovernmental cities. On a per capita basis, the scenario is also true. In 1980, intergovernmental city residents received $130,000 for economic opportunity loans compared with an average of $136,000 for persons in non-intergovernmental cities. For small business loans, intergovernmental city recipients borrowed $0.91 for every $1 borrowed by non-intergovernmental city residents.

It is clear from Exhibit 6.24 that there is virtually no comparison to be made be-

EXHIBIT 6.22. — *Small Business Loans, 1969–1980 (Dollars)*

	Per Capita			Absolute (000)		
	1969	1977	1980	1969	1977	1980
INTERGOVERNMENTAL						
Akron	0.20	0.36	1.02	54	90	241
Baltimore	-	2.86	1.54	-	2,352	1,213
Buffalo	0.27	1.19	-	129	462	-
Cincinnati	0.29	3.34	3.25	134	1,354	1,250
Cleveland	0.92	1.83	1.58	701	1,145	908
Louisville	1.13	1.28	2.39	411	406	712
Milwaukee	0.31	0.34	NA	225	225	NA
Minneapolis	NA	0.80	0.34	NA	311	127
Newark	0.53	1.07	1.06	256	370	348
Rochester	1.78	2.15	0.60	510	555	145
MEDIAN (All Cities)	0.41	1.55	1.30	195	509	530
MEDIAN (Recipient Cities Only)	0.53	1.55	1.54	256	509	712
NON-INTERGOVERNMENTAL						
Anaheim	NA	0.58	0.95	NA	118	210
Austin	0.20	2.09	3.00	48	664	1,037
Baton Rouge	NA	0.82	1.40	NA	167	307
Columbus	0.94	3.28	0.22	500	1,830	124
Nashville-Davidson	1.15	1.15	1.75	463	516	799
Oklahoma City	0.29	0.29	3.94	106	115	1,586
San Jose	0.13	1.01	0.50	55	588	316
Tulsa	2.03	0.26	0.74	655	92	266
Virginia Beach	0.68	0.19	1.39	110	45	365
Wichita	4.29	2.26	4.07	1,180	628	1,135
MEDIAN (All Cities)	0.92	1.08	1.57	282	552	582
MEDIAN (Recipient Cities Only)	0.92	1.08	1.57	282	552	582
U.S. TOTAL	-	0.84	0.90	90	(million) 185	204

Note: NA=Not Available.

Source: Executive Office of the President, Community Services Administration, Geographic Distribution of Federal Funds (1981).

tween intergovernmental and non-intergovernmental cities with regard to Urban Development Action Grant (UDAG) program participation. For the first three years of funding, 1978 through 1980, only one non-intergovernmental city received UDAG funding compared to all ten intergovernmental cities which had UDAG aid for at least two of the three funding years. This skew towards distressed cities was the essence of the UDAG program. In fact, several hardship indices were created by HUD to implement this targeting. Similar to other project grants, UDAG assistance fluctuated from year to year and, thus, does not offer a clear pattern of growing dependency on such aid. Nevertheless, intergovernmental cities received a significant amount of aid through the UDAG program; in 1980, intergovernmental city Action

EXHIBIT 6.23. — *Economic Opportunity Loans, 1969–1980 (Dollars)*

	Dollars Per Thousand Population			Absolute (000)		
	1969	1977	1980	1969	1977	1980
INTERGOVERNMENTAL						
Akron	54	48	443	15	12	105
Baltimore	NA	1,707	1,076	NA	1,552	847
Buffalo	98	779	39	46	304	14*
Cincinnati	-	510	982	-	207	378
Cleveland	79	169	869	60	106	499
Louisville	63	243	436	23	77	130
Milwaukee	42	42	NA	30	28	NA
Minneapolis	NA	134	22	NA	52	8
Newark	62	533	565	30	184	186
Rochester	213	12	124	61	3	30
MEDIAN (All Cities)	63	243	443	30	92	130
MEDIAN (Recipient Cities Only)	71	243	443	30	92	130
NON-INTERGOVERNMENTAL						
Anaheim	NA	-	270	NA	-	60
Austin	-	563	431	-	179	149
Baton Rouge	NA	847	151	NA	172	33
Columbus	317	747	97	73	417	55
Nashville-Davidson	19	255	283	17	114	129
Oklahoma City	14	92	352	5	36	142
San Jose	74	62	386	32	36	246
Tulsa	-	-	-	-	-	-
Virginia Beach	129	277	668	21	65	175
Wichita	327	730	108	90	203	30
MEDIAN (All Cities)	76	266	318	19	90	136
MEDIAN (Recipient Cities Only)	103	277	352	27	114	149
					(million)	
U.S. TOTAL	0.25	0.27	0.28	49	59	63

Note: NA=Not Available.
*Indirect Federal support.

Source: Executive Office of the President, Community Services Administration, Geographic Distribution of Federal Funds (1981).

Grants ranged from a low in Akron of $1 million to a high in Baltimore of $13.2 million. Newark was the second highest recipient of aggregate Action Grant assistance, receiving a total of $12.9 million; Newark was the highest per capita recipient as it secured $40 per person compared to the average intergovernmental city's per capita aid of $8.

Further, as outlined earlier, a second dimension of the UDAG program was its ability to leverage private capital (Exhibit 6.25). During UDAG's first two years, intergovernmental cities raised $6 for every dollar of federal UDAG assistance awarded. An additional $99 million was generated from other public funds.

Economic Development Administration, Business Development projects favored

EXHIBIT 6.24. — *Urban Development Action Grants, 1978–1980 (Dollars)*

	Per Capita			Absolute (000)		
	1978	1979	1980	1978	1979	1980
INTERGOVERNMENTAL						
Akron	-	51.93	4.22	-	12,515	1,000
Baltimore	12.33	9.84	16.80	10,000	7,860	13,225
Buffalo	-	5.72	3.14	-	2,064	1,125
Cincinnati	16.70	26.76	5.00	6,773	10,489	1,925
Cleveland	12.32	2.74	5.48	7,500	1,620	3,143
Louisville	6.4	26.32	-	2,000	8,000	-
Milwaukee	-	19.72	9.93	-	12,700	6,314
Minneapolis	-	21.01	17.89	-	7,899	6,619
Newark	2.94	6.29	39.16	1,000	2,102	12,855
Rochester	-	24.90	10.33	-	6,150	2,500
MEDIAN (All Cities)	1.47	20.36	7.70	500	7,880	2,822
MEDIAN (Recipient Cities Only)	12.32	20.36	9.93	6,773	7,880	3,143
NON-INTERGOVERNMENTAL						
Anaheim	-	-	-	-	-	-
Austin	-	-	-	-	-	-
Baton Rouge	-	-	-	-	-	-
Columbus	-	-	-	-	-	-
Nashville-Davidson	-	-	-	-	-	-
Oklahoma City	-	-	-	-	-	-
San Jose	-	-	-	-	-	-
Tulsa	-	-	-	-	-	-
Virginia Beach	-	-	-	-	-	-
Wichita	-	-	1.14	-	-	319
MEDIAN (All Cities)	-	-	-	0	0	0
MEDIAN (Recipient Cities Only)	-	-	.57	0	0	319
U.S. TOTAL	0 .18	1.78	2.71	400	(million) 400	613

Note: NA=Not Available.

Source: Executive Office of the President, Community Services Administration, Geographic Distribution of Federal Funds (1981).

intergovernmental cities and in particular, Newark (Exhibit 6.26). With a total of twelve projects valued at $19.5 million or $57 per capita, Newark led all cities in terms of total projects, total aid and total per capita assistance. In fact, Newark received six times more projects than the average intergovernmental city from 1966 to 1980; in per capita terms, this amounts to 19 times the aid of other intergovernmental cities. Even if only cities which received business assistance grants were considered, Newark still captured $7.50 per capita for every dollar sent to other intergovernmental cities. Since 1966, only four-of-ten non-intergovernmental cities have obtained EDA business development grants compared to seven-of-ten intergovernmental cities.

EXHIBIT 6.25. — *Urban Development Action Grant Projects: Analysis of the First Two Years, 1978–1979*

	Total Projects	Total UDAG Grants ($ Million)	UDAG Per Capita ($ Absolute)	Total Private Investment ($ Million)	Other Public Funds ($ Million)	Types of Projects		
						Neighborhood	Commercial	Industrial
INTERGOVERNMENTAL								
AKRON	4	18.5	73	93.5	8.5	1	1	2
BALTIMORE	5	22.1	26	139.9	53.5	4	1	–
BUFFALO	4	6.4	16	19.4	–	2	1	1
CINCINNATI	3	17.3	42	113.2	8.4	2	–	1
CLEVELAND	4	9.2	14	70.2	1.8	2	1	1
LOUISVILLE	2	10.0	30	86.2	12.0	–	2	–
MILWAUKEE	2	12.7	19	64.2	13.2	1	1	1
MINNEAPOLIS	4	8.7	23	37.1	1.9	2	1	1
NEWARK	11	16.3	48	61.4	.3	4	3	4
ROCHESTER	3	7.2	27	37.1	–	2	–	1
TOTAL	42	128.4	318	722.2	99.6	20	11	11
MEDIAN (*All Cities*)	4	11.4	27	67.2	5.2	2	1	1
MEDIAN (*Recipient Cities Only*)	4	11.4	27	67.2	8.5	2	1	1
NON-INTERGOVERNMENTAL								
ANAHEIM	–	–	–	–	–			
AUSTIN	–	–	–	–	–			
BATON ROUGE	–	–	–	–	–			
COLUMBUS	–	–	–	–	–			
NASHVILLE	–	–	–	–	–			
OKLAHOMA CITY	–	–	–	–	–			
SAN JOSE	–	–	–	–	–			
TULSA	–	–	–	–	–			
VIRGINIA BEACH	–	–	–	–	–			
WICHITA	–	–	–	–	–			

Source: U.S. Department of Housing and Urban Development, Urban Development Action Grant Annual Report (For Years Indicated).

EXHIBIT 6.26. — *Business Development Projects: Economic Development Administration, Cumulative, 1966–1980*

	Total Projects	Loans ($ Millions)	Guarantees ($ Millions)	Total (Per Capita)
INTERGOVERNMENTAL				
Akron	-	-	-	-
Baltimore	3	3.0	3.2	7.53
Buffalo	3	3.4	-	8.72
Cincinnati	-	-	-	-
Cleveland	3	2.2	-	3.51
Louisville	3	0.4	3.6	12.62
Milwaukee	1	-	1.4	2.12
Minneapolis	1	-	1.0	2.57
Newark	12	18.0	1.5	56.52
Rochester	-	-	-	-
MEDIAN (All Cities)	2	0.2	0.5	3.04
MEDIAN (Recipient Cities Only)	3	3.4	1.5	7.53
NON-INTERGOVERNMENTAL				
Anaheim	-	-	-	-
Austin	-	-	-	-
Baton Rouge	2	-	1.4	6.90
Columbus	3	5.5	-	9.86
Nashville-Davidson	-	-	-	-
Oklahoma City	2	-	0.6	1.53
San Jose	-	-	-	-
Tulsa	-	-	-	-
Virginia Beach	1	0.3	-	1.28
Wichita	-	-	-	-
MEDIAN (All Cities)	-	-	-	-
MEDIAN (Recipient Cities Only)	2.5	2.9	1.0	4.21

Source: U.S. Department of Commerce, Economic Development Administration, Annual Report (1966-1980).

Municipal Aid Programs

With the exception of certain utilities or other types of quasi-public services, cities do not own and operate profit-making enterprises. Therefore, economic development assistance to municipalities differs significantly from incentives to private businesses. Grants to stimulate activities which were channeled to cities largely supported the construction or maintenance of essential capital facilities such as sewer lines, mass transit facilities, highways, and others. Open-ended grants, those with little or no restrictions on their use, were also a popular form of economic aid. The latter form of assistance was meant to provide a flexible pool of money for localities to use to address what they considered to be their most important economic needs. The former type sought to enhance the business environment by improving the quality of local public services.

Other grants which fall outside of these two general areas included those for planning/technical assistance, and those to counteract specified cyclical or long-term market failures. A sampling of these types of programs to aid municipal governments is reviewed below.

Unlike grants for mass transit, highway or waste-water treatment facilities, public works grants awarded by the Economic Development Administration (EDA) were used for the improvement of almost any public facility provided such use supported and encouraged commercial and industrial development and expansion, created new long-term employment opportunities, and benefitted primarily economically deprived and structurally unemployed individuals.

At maximum, grants would pay for 50 percent of total project cost. In severely depressed areas, an additional 30 percent of project costs could be obtained from supplementary federal sources. EDA also extended low-interest loans of up to forty years in instances where funds could not be borrowed through private sources or federal agencies at reasonable rates. As there were no minimum or maximum grant sizes, the range of projects varied widely, from $50,000 to $7.1 million in 1980. During that year, $243.5 million was used to assist a total of 315 projects.

Administered by the EDA, planning grants have been available to be used in designated redevelopment areas (as determined by the Department of Commerce) and adjoining counties and labor market areas. The basic objective of planning grants was to foster economic development planning at state, multi-county, and local levels. Rather than pay for land, plant and equipment, and high construction labor costs, planning grants covered only planning and administrative expenses. Consequently, planning grants were considerably smaller than the capital improvement grants listed above. In 1980, total planning grants amounted to $33.7 million for 377 projects.

Municipal Assistance Programs in Intergovernmental
Versus Non-Intergovernmental Cities

On average, intergovernmental cities between 1966 and 1980 received four public works grants for every two such projects in non-intergovernmental cities. Funding between intergovernmental and non-intergovernmental cities was 4.7 times greater in the average intergovernmental city (Exhibit 6.27). For that entire fourteen-year period, the average intergovernmental city received $5.2 million in public works grants; the figure for non-intergovernmental cities was $1.1 million.

By far, the principal recipient of public works project grants has been Newark, New Jersey. At $15.1 million, Newark received $2.90 for every $1 of assistance to the average intergovernmental city and better than $13 for every dollar of public works aid to non-intergovernmental cities. On a per capita basis, Newark received almost four times the aid awarded to other intergovernmental cities. For non-intergovernmental cities, Wichita received the greatest number of grants (seven) valued at

EXHIBIT 6.27. — *Public Works Projects: Economic Development Administration, Cumulative, 1966–1980*

	Total Projects	Amount ($ Millions)	Amount (Per Capita)
INTERGOVERNMENTAL			
Akron	2	2.9	11.69
Baltimore	8	9.7	11.79
Buffalo	9	6.2	15.90
Cincinnati	1	1.4	3.45
Cleveland	7	4.6	7.74
Louisville	3	3.4	10.73
Milwaukee	4	5.7	8.64
Minneapolis	1	0.3	0.77
Newark	9	15.1	43.77
Rochester	1	3.0	11.63
MEDIAN (All Cities)	4	5.2	11.18
MEDIAN (Recipient Cities Only)	4	5.2	11.18
NON-INTERGOVERNMENTAL			
Anaheim	-	-	-
Austin	2	1.2	3.77
Baton Rouge	3	1.0	4.93
Columbus	2	5.4	9.82
Nashville-Davidson	1	0.1	0.22
Oklahoma City	4	2.0	5.09
San Jose	1	0.4	0.69
Tulsa	2	2.1	6.14
Virginia Beach	-	-	-
Wichita	7	7.7	27.70
MEDIAN (All Cities)	2	1.1	4.35
MEDIAN (Recipient Cities Only)	2	1.6	5.01

Source: U.S. Department of Commerce, Economic Development Administration, Annual Report (1966-1980).

an average of $1.1 million per grant. Wichita, at approximately $28 per resident, was second only to Newark in the receipt of public works grants.

On the whole, non-intergovernmental cities have received twice as many economic development planning grants as intergovernmental cities, and three times the level of funding. Exhibit 6.28 shows that even when population is considered, per capita aid to intergovernmental cities was a mere 44 percent of that for non-intergovernmental cities. Nevertheless, fully nine of ten intergovernmental cities have participated in the planning grant program. Although these grants are relatively small when combined with other EDA and general federal aid programs, they have been highly sought by intergovernmental cities.

EXHIBIT 6.28. — *Planning Grants: Economic Development
Administration, Cumulative, 1966–1980*

	Total Grants	Amount ($ Millions)	Amount (Per Capita)
INTERGOVERNMENTAL			
Akron	3	0.2	.81
Baltimore	7	0.7	0.85
Buffalo	4	0.4	1.03
Cincinnati	2	0.2	0.49
Cleveland	5	0.4	0.64
Louisville	3	0.3	0.95
Milwaukee	5	0.6	0.91
Minneapolis	-	-	-
Newark	2	0.2	0.58
Rochester	1	0.1	0.39
MEDIAN (All Cities)	3	0.25	0.72
MEDIAN (Recipient Cities Only)	3	0.3	0.81
NON-INTERGOVERNMENTAL			
Anaheim	-	-	-
Austin	4	1.4	4.40
Baton Rouge	23	1.9	9.36
Columbus	12	1.2	2.15
Nashville-Davidson	19	1.2	2.69
Oklahoma City	14	1.2	3.05
San Jose	1	0.1	0.17
Tulsa	2	0.2	0.59
Virginia Beach	-	-	-
Wichita	9	0.3	1.08
MEDIAN (All Cities)	6.5	0.75	1.62
MEDIAN (Recipient Cities Only)	10.5	1.2	2.42

Source: U.S. Department of Commerce, Economic Development Administration, Annual Report (1966-1980).

Education, Training, Employment, and Social Services

The problems experienced in urban public school systems, particularly in cities
with high levels of unemployment and public assistance participation, require no
elaboration here. While children from poor families have special educational needs,
the schools they attend are, by and large, the least able to afford such programs.

Schools located in essentially poor communities cannot support the more extensive facilities and personnel required by educationally deprived or special-need, low-
income children. In an effort to offer children equal opportunity to the benefits of
education, the federal government has promulgated numerous education programs
over the past twenty years. Federal education grants have assisted public, private

and non-private schools, as well as day care centers. Although the largest portion of federal education expenditures, 41 percent in 1980, was directed to elementary and secondary education, federal aid spans from early childhood to higher education, and includes vocational training and special education grants for the gifted and talented.

Title I of the Elementary and Secondary Education Act of 1965 has been the principal financial vehicle through which the federal government has aided educationally disadvantaged students. With 1980 outlays of $2.5 billion, Title I aid for the educationally deprived reached an estimated 5.6 million school children at a cost of about $446 per child. In addition to deprived children, Title I aid also has been channeled through a state-administered program to handicapped, migrant, neglected and delinquent children.

Programs which spanned the educational spectrum included Head Start for children from 3 years of age until school-age, and Basic Education Opportunity Grants (BEOG) for post-secondary education. BEOG's were applied to undergraduate studies at colleges, universities and vocational-technical schools, as well as hospital schools of nursing. The BEOG program was the principal federal effort to financially aid low-income students in post-secondary, public or non-private institutions of higher learning. Approximately 2.7 million students received BEOG's during the 1979–1980 academic year with outlays of $2.1 billion. The maximum amount of the grant per individual was $1,800 per year for a period of up to four years (or five years in some instances). Related higher education aid programs included supplemental education opportunity grants, college work study programs, national defense/direct student loans, and veterans' educational assistance.

At the opposite extreme of the educational spectrum were Head Start grants which provided comprehensive educational, nutritional, social and other services to pre-school children, principally of low-income families. A full 90 percent of the Head Start enrollees came from families of incomes below the poverty level or from families receiving AFDC. Ten percent of aggregate allocations were also set aside for handicapped children.

The goal of Head Start was to assist poor children to overcome background deficiencies before they entered primary school. Up until this time, the largest public pre-school program, Head Start served approximately 7.4 million children for low-income families since 1965. Reaching 378,500 children in 1980, it was funded at a level of $725,000,000.

Education Transfers in Intergovernmental
Versus Non-Intergovernmental Cities

Chapter 5 has reviewed, in detail, educational expenditures by city with a view toward own-source revenues and state and federal assistance. This section will not replicate the efforts of that chapter. Suffice it to say, that both intergovernmental and non-intergovernmental cities were highly dependent upon federal and state education assistance and that greater social and economic need in intergovernmental cities generated substantially higher per capita federal financial support. Since Basic Education Opportunity Grants, Child Development Assistance and Job Corps aid were not included in the previous education expenditure analysis, this section examines these three programs.

Nationally, the Head Start program expanded on a per capita basis by only 15 percent from 1974 to 1980 (Exhibit 6.29). Intergovernmental city participation during that period increased by a full 33 percent per year or by 200 percent over the entire six-year time span. Although slightly lower than the average per capita benefit of the nation in 1974, intergovernmental cities were receiving twice the average national assistance by 1980. Non-intergovernmental cities received per capita Head Start grants on par with the general population.

EXHIBIT 6.29. — *Child Development: Head Start, 1974–1980 (Dollars)*

	Per Capita			Absolute (000)		
	1974	1977	1980	1974	1977	1980
INTERGOVERNMENTAL						
Akron	2.25	3.44	5.92	585	854	1,404
Baltimore	2.37	3.84	4.21	2,029	3,158	3,314
Buffalo	-	2.95	6.18	-	1,152	2,213
Cincinnati	2.06	2.96	6.58	878	1,201	2,534
Cleveland	3.35	3.55	8.37	2,279	2,223	4,802
Louisville	2.83	5.04	6.31	951	1,599	1,881
Milwaukee	2.45	2.59	NA	1,676	1,645	NA
Minneapolis	1.20	1.52	1.88	488	593	694
Newark	0.52	10.87	18.19	189	3,695	5,983
Rochester	-	1.77	3.60	-	456	871
MEDIAN (All Cities)	2.06	3.44	6.18	585	1,201	2,213
MEDIAN (Recipient Cities Only)	2.25	2.96	6.18	585	1,201	2,213
NON-INTERGOVERNMENTAL						
Anaheim	-	-	-	-	-	-
Austin	5.50	3.78	4.40	1,595	1,202	1,521
Baton Rouge	6.80	6.33	6.47	1,271	1,284	1,417
Columbus	1.30	1.78	3.86	712	995	2,179
Nashville-Davidson	1.40	1.56	2.75	614	696	1,253
Oklahoma City	3.21	3.64	3.60	1,227	1,432	1,449
San Jose	0.98	0.02	2.70	519	10	1,722
Tulsa	1.25	1.28	1.51	426	449	545
Virginia Beach	-	-	-	-	-	-
Wichita	2.16	3.28	4.27	600	913	1,192
MEDIAN (All Cities)	1.35	1.67	3.17	608	846	1,335
MEDIAN (Recipient Cities Only)	2.69	2.53	3.73	663	1,099	1,433
					(million)	
U.S. TOTAL	2.78	2.09	3.20	593	460	724

Note: NA=Not Available.

Source: Executive Office of the President, Community Services Administration, Geographic Distribution of Federal Funds (1981).

Basic Education Opportunity Grants grew by only 9 percent between 1977 and 1980 in intergovernmental cities; the rate of increase for non-intergovernmental cities was 14 percent (Exhibit 6.30). Nevertheless, intergovernmental cities, on average, received much more in the form of Basic Education Opportunity Grants than their non-intergovernmental counterparts. In 1977, total funding for intergovernmental cities was more than 90 percent greater than that for non-intergovernmental cities. By 1980, non-intergovernmental cities still received only 55 percent of the Basic Education Opportunity Grants awarded to intergovernmental cities. Although Newark received per capita Head Start aid at three times the intergovernmental city level, it was not the principal recipient of Basic Grants in 1980. In fact, Newark's $16 per capita funding was considerably less than the average support for intergovernmental cities at $20 per person. Rochester, at $34, was by far the largest recipient of Basic Education Opportunity Grant monies. That figure was $22 greater than the average aid to non-intergovernmental city residents and almost $25 more than the national per capita average. In absolute dollars, Baltimore received the greatest funding at $10.3 million.

Employment and Training

Employment and training activities, along with educational initiatives, differed greatly from other social need programs. Unlike Food Stamps or medical care or housing subsidies which addressed an immediate need but did not equip the recipient to obtain these goods or services independently at some future date, employment and training grants were geared toward assisting their participants to become self-sufficient.

Almost all training assistance in the United States, in recent years, has been provided under various titles of the Comprehensive Employment and Training Act (CETA) of 1974. The objective of CETA was to establish a unified system of federal, state and local employment training programs, principally for economically disadvantaged, under-employed and unemployed persons.

The principal CETA titles have been: Title I-B—Comprehensive Employment and Training Services; Title II-C—Upgrading and Retraining; Title II-D—Transitional Public Service Employment; Title IV—Youth Employment Programs; Title VI—Counter-Cyclical Public Employment Program; and Title VII—the Private Sector Initiative Program. Titles VI and VII were not part of the original CETA legislation. Title VI was promulgated in response to the severe national economic downturn of the mid-1970s, as a counter-cyclical economic stimulus. It provided temporary public service jobs to terminated workers during periods of high unemployment. The Private Sector Initiative Program, Title VII, has also been a relatively recent addition to CETA legislation. It was initially enacted in 1979 as a demonstration program to encourage private employers to train and hire economically disadvantaged individuals. Title IV programs were for youths between the ages of 14 and 21 years. Programs included employment on community-planned projects, year-round work and training projects, and part-time summer training activities. Title II programs included classroom instruction, on-the-job training, work experience, counseling and placement, upgrading and retraining, and traditional public service employment. Title II grants were restricted to economically disadvantaged persons.

EXHIBIT 6.30. — *Basic Education Opportunity Grants, 1977-1980 (Dollars)*

	Per Capita				Absolute (000)			
	1977	1978	1979	1980	1977	1978	1979	1980
INTERGOVERNMENTAL								
Akron	11.76	12.45	10.43	12.79	2,916	3,049	2,513	3,031
Baltimore	17.88	18.11	13.37	13.04	14,712	14,689	10,679	10,266
Buffalo	10.06	8.50	16.0	19.54	3,923	3,220	5,904	6,994
Cincinnati	16.29	13.12	18.70	18.78	6,612	5,236	7,329	7,230
Cleveland	12.54	19.76	16.36	12.39	7,864	8,990	9,685	7,109
Louisville	12.78	12.82	13.55	23.50	4,051	3,988	4,119	7,004
Milwaukee	10.31	10.22	13.87	NA	6,801	6,664	8,933	NA
Minneapolis	24.06	20.14	27.81	35.41	9,360	7,835	10,457	13,100
Newark	19.28	17.28	17.88	15.88	6,650	5,874	5,973	5,224
Rochester	19.59	21.08	25.48	34.10	5,053	5,332	6,294	8,251
MEDIAN (All Cities)	17.88	14.76	16.36	19.59	6,631	5,814	6,294	7,230
MEDIAN (Recipient Cities Only)	17.88	14.76	16.36	19.59	6,631	5,814	6,294	7,230
NON-INTERGOVERNMENTAL								
Anaheim	1.83	1.69	2.99	2.41	375	356	646	535
Austin	18.39	14.09	18.32	18.50	5,848	4,608	6,172	6,402
Baton Rouge	46.58	45.29	40.86	41.23	9,455	9,418	8,744	9,029
Columbus	17.44	14.71	18.58	22.57	9,730	8,236	10,463	12,753
Nashville-Davidson	17.13	14.64	17.38	18.77	7,655	6,588	7,871	8,560
Oklahoma City	7.06	10.29	10.42	11.48	2,774	4,074	4,166	4,628
San Jose	7.18	6.00	6.27	4.83	4,194	3,611	3,878	3,074
Tulsa	6.05	5.59	6.86	7.74	2,128	1,983	2,456	2,794
Virginia Beach	0.08	0.05	0.13	0.32	18	13	34	83
Wichita	8.85	7.68	10.54	11.94	2,459	2,143	2,940	3,332
MEDIAN (All Cities)	12.99	8.98	10.48	11.71	3,484	3,843	4,022	3,980
MEDIAN (Recipient Cities Only)	12.99	8.98	10.48	11.71	3,484	3,843	4,022	3,980
U.S. TOTAL	7.89	7.44	8.81	9.06	1,736	1,654 (million)	1,980	2,053

Note: NA=Not Available.
Source: Executive Office of the President, Community Services Administration, Geographic Distribution of Federal Funds (1981).

CETA grants have been awarded to "prime sponsors," that is, to local units of government with 100,000 or more population. Although the CETA program peaked in 1978 with 750,000 enrollees, in 1980 enrollments remained high. During that year, there were a total of 696,532 participants in Titles II, VI and VII, with an additional 966,292 youth enrollees under Title IV.

Initially authorized by the 1964 Equal Opportunity Act, the Job Corps was yet another attempt to open employment opportunities for economically disadvantaged individuals. Largely a residential program, the Job Corps served disadvantaged youths, aged 16 to 21, who stood to gain from intensive educational and vocational training. Job Corps enrollees were given room, board, medical and dental care, recreation and monthly allowances.

Reauthorized under Title IV, CETA, the program was greatly expanded as of 1977. By 1979, Job Corps program slots had increased by almost 40 percent. Between 1979 and 1980 the program grew by an additional 23.5 percent, from 85,000 to 105,000 participants. The average cost per participant in 1980 was $3,955.

Employment and Training Transfers in Intergovernmental Versus Non-Intergovernmental Cities

Although the Comprehensive Employment and Training Act was geared to economic distress, non-intergovernmental cities in 1980 received more CETA grant money in both absolute and per capita terms than did intergovernmental cities (Exhibit 6.31). As early as 1974, non-intergovernmental cities received $2 more per capita than intergovernmental cities. By 1980, that gap had increased by over $21. In absolute aid, in 1974, intergovernmental cities led non-intergovernmental cities in CETA receipts by less than one percent. By 1980, non-intergovernmental cities received 28 percent more CETA dollars than the average intergovernmental city.

All intergovernmental cities participated in CETA funding in 1980; nine non-intergovernmental cities also handled CETA programs. Counting only those non-intergovernmental cities which chose to participate significantly increases the funding variation between intergovernmental and non-intergovernmental cities. When only these cities are examined, non-intergovernmental cities received almost 58 percent more aid than their intergovernmental counterparts.

Job Corps assistance increased markedly in the average intergovernmental city, from a 1969 level of $8,000 to a 1980 figure of $1.5 million (Exhibit 6.32). This trend parallels the average non-intergovernmental city's participation during the same period which expanded from $1,000 to only $409,000. Yet, comparing the two sets of cities on a per capita basis in 1980, reveals that non-intergovernmental cities received Job Corps assistance at a level of only 38 percent that of intergovernmental cities. When comparing only those cities which received grants, the discrepancy between the two city sets narrows slightly: non-intergovernmental city aid increases to 50 percent of the intergovernmental cities' funding level. Finally, although not all intergovernmental cities participated in the Job Corps program, when they did, their funding was almost four times the national per capita average. When non-intergovernmental cities received Job Corps monies, they tended to be funded at twice the national per capita average.

EXHIBIT 6.31. — *Comprehensive Employment and Training,*
1974–1980 (Dollars)

	Per Capita			Absolute (000)		
	1974	1977	1980	1974	1977	1980
INTERGOVERNMENTAL						
Akron	9.40	112.41	50.47	2,443	27,878	11,962
Baltimore	10.68	145.09	111.63	9,166	119,405	87,849
Buffalo	14.08	108.25	96.34	5,928	42,218	34,488
Cincinnati	15.49	84.53	59.01	6,600	34,318	22,717
Cleveland	17.79	125.64	40.00	12,095	78,778	22,960
Louisville	13.65	90.65	40.47	4,588	28,735	12,060
Milwaukee	8.68	73.39	NA	5,944	48,437	NA
Minneapolis	11.75	112.84	23.82	4,796	43,895	8,812
Newark	28.83	139.63	130.68	10,407	48,173	42,993
Rochester	14.31	40.33	33.12	3,922	10,404	8,014
MEDIAN (All Cities)	14.08	112.41	50.47	5,928	42,218	22,717
MEDIAN (Recipient Cities Only)	14.08	112.41	50.47	5,928	42,218	22,717
NON-INTERGOVERNMENTAL						
Anaheim	18,03	NA	NA	3,390	NA	NA
Austin	48.03	238.13	123.14	13,929	75,725	42,606
Baton Rouge	44.01	390.00	336.58	8,229	79,170	73,711
Columbus	23.89	282.88	168.80	13,140	157,846	95,374
Nashville-Davidson	20.96	266.47	156.88	9,180	119,118	71,537
Oklahoma City	10.55	162.43	72.0	4,031	63,835	29,015
San Jose	11.09	61.15	39.85	5,887	35,713	25,381
Tulsa	9.01	35.78	14.35	3,081	12,595	5,179
Virginia Beach	-	-	-	-	-	-
Wichita	6.32	13.46	8.95	1,757	3,743	2,497
MEDIAN (All Cities)	11.09	162.43	72.0	5,887	63,835	29,015
MEDIAN (Recipient Cities Only)	16.03	200.28	97.57	7,058	69,780	35,811
					(million)	
U.S. TOTAL	7.44	38.85	25.46	1,584	8,546	5,768

Note: NA=Not Available.

Source: Executive Office of the President, Community Services Administration, Geographic Distribution of Federal Funds (1981).

Social Services

During the 1960s, numerous anti-poverty efforts were launched which addressed not the physical deterioration of neighborhoods, but rather, the social well-being of financially deprived people. Unfortunately, there was little coordination between federally supported anti-poverty efforts. Moreover, there were virtually no opportunities for low-income residents to participate in the planning, implementation or evaluation of programs which directly impacted their lives.

EXHIBIT 6.32.—*Job Corps, 1969–1980 (Dollars)*

	Per Capita			Absolute (000)		
	1969	*1977*	*1980*	*1969*	*1977*	*1980*
INTERGOVERNMENTAL						
Akron	0.03	-	-	8	-	-
Baltimore	NA	3.93	4.26	NA	2,231	3,351
Buffalo	0.02	-	0.08	8	-	29
Cincinnati	-	3.73	10.17	-	1,514	3,914
Cleveland	3.55	5.09	2.55	2,714	3,191	1,466
Louisville	0.03	0.06	9.21	10	19	2,743
Milwaukee	0.01	0.04	NA	9	25	NA
Minneapolis	NA	-	3.56	NA	-	1,317
Newark	(2)	-	0.05	1	-	17
Rochester	0.02	5.61	18.46	6	1,448	4,467
MEDIAN (All Cities)	0.02	0.06	2.55	8	19	1,466
MEDIAN (Recipient Cities Only)	0.02	3.93	5.88	8	1,481	2,690
NON-INTERGOVERNMENTAL						
Anaheim	NA	-	-	NA	-	-
Austin	0.94	3.22	4.63	230	1,024	1,603
Baton Rouge	NA	3.24	2.66	NA	658	582
Columbus	-	0.38	0.50	-	206	283
Nashville-Davidson	(2)	0.38	0.70	0.1	171	319
Oklahoma City	(2)	0.62	1.24	1	244	498
San Jose	-	3.27	8.87	-	1,910	5,651
Tulsa	-	3.39	5.40	-	1,192	1,949
Virginia Beach	-	-	-	-	-	-
Wichita	-	-	-	-	-	-
MEDIAN (All Cities)	-	0.50	0.97	1	225	409
MEDIAN (Recipient Cities Only)	0.47	1.92	2.94	115	634	1,776
					(million)	
U.S. TOTAL	0.96	0.74	1.49	192	162	337

Note: NA=Not Available.

Source: Executive Office of the President, Community Services Administration, Geographic Distribution of Federal Funds (1981).

With the authorization of Community Action Programs under the Economic Opportunity Act of 1964, Congress attempted to remedy the lack of communication between program administrators and eligible recipients, encourage citizen participation in anti-poverty efforts, and foster coordination between various federal anti-poverty initiatives.

Community Action Programs, as of 1980, were relatively minor financially, compared with physically-oriented community development programs. Although there were 893 community action agencies serving counties which contained 75 percent of the nation's population and 86 percent of its poor, funding for that year was little more than $411 million.

Social Service Transfers in Intergovernmental
Versus Non-Intergovernmental Cities

The Community Action Program experienced a slow, but steadily increasing popularity, in both sets of cities since 1969. This program has not had strong support at the federal level. Thus, Community Action funding reflects an inconsistent pattern from year to year. For example, Exhibit 6.33 reveals that in 1969, the program made available $500.7 million in grants. In 1977, only $334.8 million was available through the Community Action Program and in 1980, funding had risen

EXHIBIT 6.33. — *Community Action, 1969–1980 (Dollars)*

	Per Capita			Absolute (000)		
	1969	1977	1980	1969	1977	1980
INTERGOVERNMENTAL						
Akron	–	3.34	3.71	–	827	879
Baltimore	NA	3.98	3.81	NA	3,274	2,997
Buffalo	*	3.29	3.66	.1	1,283	1,300
Cincinnati	–	3.28	3.78	–	1,333	1,454
Cleveland	–	3.14	2.88	–	1,969	1,655
Louisville	*	4.15	3.98	.1	1,316	1,185
Milwaukee	–	2.67	NA	–	1,760	NA
Minneapolis	NA	0.77	0.81	NA	300	300
Newark	2.08	5.79	5.31	101	1,999	2,075
Rochester	–	4.21	4.47	–	1,086	1,082
MEDIAN (All Cities)	0.0	3.34	3.78	0	1,325	1,377
MEDIAN (Recipient Cities Only)	2.08	3.34	3.78	51	1,325	1,377
NON-INTERGOVERNMENTAL						
Anaheim	NA	–	–	NA	–	–
Austin	2.83	1.35	2.21	696	430	766
Baton Rouge	NA	4.60	5.80	NA	933	1,269
Columbus	–	1.88	3.20	–	1,046	1,805
Nashville-Davidson	–	0.58	4.75	–	261	2,168
Oklahoma City	–	4.16	3.89	–	1,634	1,566
San Jose	–	2.61	2.59	–	1,524	1,650
Tulsa	–	1.36	1.47	–	479	532
Virginia Beach	–	–	–	–	–	–
Wichita	–	4.28	2.50	–	1,190	969
MEDIAN (All Cities)	–	1.62	2.54	0	763	1,268
MEDIAN (Recipient Cities Only)	2.83	1.88	2.59	696	1,046	1,566
					(million)	
U.S. TOTAL	2.49	1.52	1.82	501	335	41

Note: NA=Not Available.
        *Less than $0.01 per capita.

Source: Executive Office of the President, Community Services Administration, Geographic Distribution of Federal Funds (1981).

slightly to $411.7 million. In 1980, the average intergovernmental city resident received $1.24 more for Community Action activities than individuals in non-intergovernmental cities. In absolute dollars, in 1980, the average intergovernmental city received $1.4 million in Community Action assistance. That figure was 9 percent greater than the average Community Action award to non-intergovernmental cities in that same year.

Health

The correlation between poor health and poverty has long been recognized. Improper diets, inadequate shelter and clothing, unsanitary and unsafe living environments, insufficient preventative health care, inaccessibility to health facilities and insufficient financial resources to afford proper medical treatment, all contribute to a disproportionate level of poor health among lower income households. In Chapter 4, a comparative index of health conditions revealed that nine of the ten cities with the worst cumulative health conditions were also the poorest economically. Moreover, while intergovernmental cities displayed the worst overall health conditions, they contained, on average, over three times the number of public assistance recipients.

In response to the inadequate health care suffered by low-income individuals, Congress, in 1965, enacted the medical assistance program better known as Medicaid. This program was designed to provide financial assistance to the state for payment of medical assistance on behalf of the cash assistance recipient. Medicaid, which by 1980 was funded at $14.4 billion, has been the principal medical assistance program for the poor. It is estimated to have been used by 22.9 million people during that year.

A second obstacle to the provision of adequate health care services to underserved populations was the health care delivery system itself. Realizing the system was in need of improvement, Congress established Community Health Centers to provide low-income residents with improved access to health care services. This program, although significantly smaller than Medicaid, provided a wide range of ambulatory care services to 5 million individuals throughout 872 centers nationally. In 1980, the cost to support this program was $317.6 million.

Health Transfers in Intergovernmental
Versus Non-Intergovernmental Cities

In both Medicaid and Community Health Center programs, intergovernmental cities were, by far, the principal beneficiaries in absolute dollars, as well as in per capita terms. Exhibit 6.34 shows that in 1969, non-intergovernmental cities received, on average, $49.1 million dollars for Medicaid benefits. This figure was equivalent to $4 per capita. Intergovernmental cities, however, received over $3 million in Medicaid allocations in 1969, or 38 percent more per capita than non-intergovernmental cities. Although total population in intergovernmental cities declined precipitously during the 1970s, the dependency of their populations on Medicaid grew by

EXHIBIT 6.34.—*Medical Assistance Program:*
Medicaid, 1969–1980 (Dollars)

	Per Capita			Absolute (000)		
	1969	1977	1980	1969	1977	1980
INTERGOVERNMENTAL						
Akron	2.67	47.69	77.53	739	11,827	18,375
Baltimore	10.82	95.00	152.04	9,834	78,184	119,652
Buffalo	17.57	124.03	208.27	8,257	48,373	74,562
Cincinnati	0.45	62.45	102.26	2,047	25,356	39,369
Cleveland	4.08	70.06	114.28	3,115	43,930	65,596
Louisville	4.58	56.32	102.18	1,671	17,852	30,443
Milwaukee	3.88	122.58	NA	2,790	80,906	NA
Minneapolis	7.60	54.52	123.37	3,338	21,208	45,647
Newark	NA	125.46	213.05	NA	43,283	70,094
Rochester	13.97	112.83	217.55	4,008	29,109	52,646
MEDIAN (All Cities)	6.09	66.3	118.80	3,227	27,233	49,147
MEDIAN (Recipient Cities Only)	6.09	66.3	118.80	3,227	27,233	49,147
NON-INTERGOVERNMENTAL						
Anaheim	4.77	34.92	40.43	763	7,158	8,976
Austin	4.12	27.80	35.56	1,613	8,840	12,304
Baton Rouge	2.85	NA	NA	470	NA	NA
Columbus	2.47	42.49	65.20	1,317	23,710	36,839
Nashville-Davidson	0.27	28.23	45.65	108	12,618	20,818
Oklahoma City	5.45	35.09	55.51	1,984	13,786	22,369
San Jose	8.20	56.37	69.71	3,557	32,918	44,408
Tulsa	5.99	35.60	49.80	1,935	12,532	17,979
Virginia Beach	0.07	10.52	15.06	11	2,472	3,945
Wichita	2.99	46.01	58.41	822	12,790	16,297
MEDIAN (All Cities)	4.12	35.09	49.80	1,013	12,790	20,818
MEDIAN (Recipient Cities Only)	4.12	35.09	49.80	1,013	12,790	20,818
					(million)	
U.S. TOTAL	11.59	45.19	63.60	2,328	9,943	14,406

Note: NA=Not Available.

Source: Executive Office of the President, Community Services Administration, Geographic Distribution of Federal Funds (1981).

$4.2 million per year, reaching a 1980 level of $49 million per average intergovernmental city or $119 per capita. Meanwhile, non-intergovernmental cities, which experienced major growth in total population throughout the 1970s, increased their Medicaid dependency by only $1.8 million per year. That rate of growth established a 1980 average Medicaid benefit of only $50 per capita, less than half the per capita benefit of intergovernmental cities. Like most grant-in-aid programs, Medicaid's greatest growth occurred during the first half of the 1970s. Reflecting this overall trend, Medicaid benefits in the average intergovernmental city between 1969 and

1977 climbed, on a per capita basis, by 124 percent each year. From 1977 to 1980, that rate of growth dropped dramatically to only 26.4 percent annually. The range of transfers varied widely both among intergovernmental cities and between intergovernmental and non-intergovernmental cities. While in 1980, Akron received $177 per capita, residents in Rochester, Newark and Buffalo received an average of $217, $213 and $209 respectively. Non-intergovernmental cities ranged from a low in Anaheim of $15 per person to a high of $70 in San Jose.

From 1974 to 1980, funding for Community Health Centers increased by $118.2 million or slightly more than 59 percent (Exhibit 6.35). During that same period, in-

EXHIBIT 6.35. — *Community Health Centers, 1974–1980 (Dollars)*

	Per Capita			Absolute (000)		
	1974	1977	1980	1974	1977	1980
INTERGOVERNMENTAL						
Akron	-	-	-	-	-	-
Baltimore	3.41	3.65	8.25	2,929	3,001	6,495
Buffalo	0.13	-	0.67	56	-	240
Cincinnati	2.90	5.42	11.14	1,236	2,200	4,290
Cleveland	8.99	11.32	8.30	5,432	7,099	4,764
Louisville	6.43	6.15	7.67	2,161	1,949	2,285
Milwaukee	-	-	NA	-	-	NA
Minneapolis	1.24	-	0.78	506	-	288
Newark	-	2.17	7.17	-	750	2,360
Rochester	-	13.34	16.67	-	3,442	4,035
MEDIAN (All Cities)	1.24	3.65	7.67	506	1,949	2,360
MEDIAN (Recipient Cities Only)	3.16	5.78	7.96	1,699	2,601	3,198
NON-INTERGOVERNMENTAL						
Anaheim	-	-	-	-	-	-
Austin	-	-	-	-	-	-
Baton Rouge	-	-	-	-	-	-
Columbus	2.00	-	-	1,100	-	-
Nashville-Davidson	10.68	6.37	6.24	4,678	2,847	2,844
Oklahoma City	0.57	3.01	3.04	216	1,182	1,225
San Jose	-	-	-	-	-	-
Tulsa	5.13	4.66	5.25	1,755	1,639	1,896
Virginia Beach	-	*	*	-	173	153
Wichita	-	-	-	-	-	-
MEDIAN (All Cities)	-	-	-	0	0	0
MEDIAN (Recipient Cities Only)	3.57	4.66	5.25	1,378	1,411	1,561
					(million)	
U.S. TOTAL	0.94	0.97	1.40	199	214	318

Note: NA=Not Available.
*Less than $0.01 per capita.

Source: Executive Office of the President, Community Services Administration, Geographic Distribution of Federal Funds (1981).

tergovernmental cities increased their reliance on Community Health Center grants by 25 percent per year. Most non-intergovernmental cities did not participate in the Community Health Center program. However, for those that did receive grants, they expanded their level of funding by 47 percent during that six-year period.

Considering only cities which received funds, non-intergovernmental cities attracted $0.50 per person more than intergovernmental cities in 1974. By 1980, this pattern was sharply reversed as intergovernmental cities received fully $3 more per capita aid than non-intergovernmental cities.

Rochester, in addition to receiving the highest per capita Medicaid benefits, was also the greatest recipient of Community Health Center grants; at $17 per person, its per capita funding was more than twice that of the average intergovernmental city.

Environment and Natural Resources

Construction grants for wastewater treatment funds have been applied to both public and private systems and have included projects which provide for industrial as well as residential waste treatment. Wastewater treatment grants cover up to 75 percent of total project costs. Innovative, alternative technological or demonstration projects could receive up to 85 percent of the financial support from federal wastewater treatment grants. In 1980, projects ranged in size from $675 to $290.8 million for a total expenditure of $4.6 billion. As of mid-1980, a total of 19,545 projects were aided by EPA's wastewater treatment grants at a combined cost of $25.9 billion.

Environmental Transfers in Intergovernmental
Versus Non-Intergovernmental Cities

Due to the fact that individual grants were the primary mechanism for wastewater treatment, there exists no consistent financial pattern over time. Rather, federal subsidies by city fluctuated sharply on an almost yearly basis. For example, as noted in Exhibit 6.36, in 1977 the average intergovernmental city received $37.8 million in wastewater treatment grants. In 1976, one year later, these same cities received $4.5 million, down ninefold from the previous year. Nevertheless, over time, intergovernmental cities have received more federal aid for construction of wastewater treatment facilities than have non-intergovernmental cities. For the four individual years, 1977 to 1980, intergovernmental city assistance was greater than that of non-intergovernmental cities by ratios of 8 to 1, 6 to 1, 5 to 1, and 18 to 1, respectively.

Transportation

Similar to wastewater treatment grants, urban mass transit capital improvement funds were narrowly defined to assist a single public infrastructure system. While mass transit funds could be used in a variety of ways, e.g., to purchase buses or subway cars, real property or other equipment, such purchases had to be geared toward

EXHIBIT 6.36.—*Construction Grants for Wastewater Treatment, 1977-1980 (Dollars)*

	Per Capita				Absolute (000)			
	1977	1978	1979	1980	1977	1978	1979	1980
INTERGOVERNMENTAL								
Akron	73.21	24.84	10.77	248.78	18,156	6,088	2,595	58,961
Baltimore	46.02	5.56	32.82	16.03	37,874	4,509	26,223	12,616
Buffalo	274.38	5.21	85.80	4.35	107,008	1,975	30,974	1,557
Cincinnati	755.80	13.57	24.13	7.90	30,685	5,414	9,459	3,042
Cleveland	281.43	15.93	73.88	38.12	176,456	9,701	43,739	21,881
Louisville	64.04	5.62	14.95	1.58	20,301	1,748	4,545	471
Milwaukee	32.64	32.71	18.82	NA	21,542	21,326	12,120	NA
Minneapolis	1.22	–	–	–	475	–	–	–
Newark	440.90	15.72	28.37	218.83	152,110	5,345	10,667	71,995
Rochester	321.65	4.38	115.70	73.33	82,986	1,108	38,644	17,745
MEDIAN (All Cities)	274.38	5.62	28.37	16.03	37,874	4,509	10,667	12,616
MEDIAN (Recipient Cities Only)	274.38	9.60	30.60	27.08	37,874	4,927	18,445	15,181
NON-INTERGOVERNMENTAL								
Anaheim	–	–	–	–	–	–	–	–
Austin	0.59	12.22	–	0.04	188	3,996	–	14
Baton Rouge	5.60	1.59	18.14	0.08	1,137	331	3,882	18
Columbus	36.92	4.89	6.60	16.41	20,601	2,738	3,716	9,272
Nashville-Davidson	79.27	40.64	11.64	9.82	35,433	18,288	5,273	4,478
Oklahoma City	66.78	2.38	33.04	23.10	26,245	942	13,216	9,309
San Jose	0.85	0.04	0.56	0.14	496	24	347	89
Tulsa	0.49	1.22	0.51	0.04	172	433	183	14
Virginia Beach	52.52	11.21	168.27	109.77	12,342	2,735	42,572	28,760
Wichita	30.03	1.73	1.72	4.65	8,348	483	480	1,297
MEDIAN (All Cities)	17.81	3.31	4.16	2.39	4,743	713	2,098	693
MEDIAN (Recipient Cities Only)	17.81	3.31	4.16	2.39	8,348	942	3,799	1,297
U.S. TOTAL	30.03	4.89	9.12	4.65	7,501 (million)	2,853	4,192	4,640

Note: NA = Not Available.
Source: Executive Office of the President, Community Services Administration, Geographic Distribution of Federal Funds (1981).

the improvement of the mass transportation network. In 1980, a total of $2.3 billion in grants was awarded, with the average grant totaling $5 million.

Transportation Transfers in Intergovernmental
Versus Non-Intergovernmental Cities

By a three-to-one margin, urban mass transit grants favored intergovernmental versus non-intergovernmental cities in 1980 (Exhibit 6.37). In 1974, only four non-intergovernmental cities received mass transit capital improvement grants ranging

EXHIBIT 6.37. — *Urban Mass Transit Fund, 1974–1980 (Dollars)*

	Per Capita			Absolute (000)		
	1974	1977	1980	1974	1977	1980
INTERGOVERNMENTAL						
Akron	5.21	22.17	-	1,355	5,498	-
Baltimore	0.71	234.98	86.66	607	193,387	68,204
Buffalo	-	27.04	343.86	-	11,382	123,100
Cincinnati	0.77	35.04	-	326	14,226	-
Cleveland	12.56	91.38	81.11	8,541	57,293	46,557
Louisville	26.18	12.64	4.93	8,796	4,006	1,473
Milwaukee	0.18	7.55	NA	120	4,983	NA
Minneapolis	-	0.02	14.18	-	6	5,247
Newark	-	-	91.79	-	-	30,000
Rochester	10.92	17.62	14.17	2,991	4,546	3,429
MEDIAN (All Cities)	0.74	22.17	14.18	607	5,490	3,429
MEDIAN (Recipient Cities Only)	8.06	24.60	81.11	2,173	8,436	30,000
NON-INTERGOVERNMENTAL						
Anaheim	-	-	-	-	-	-
Austin	-	5.98	6.41	-	1,901	2,218
Baton Rouge	-	5.06	1.92	-	946	421
Columbus	10.02	7.44	4.43	5,511	4,153	2,500
Nashville-Davidson	10.18	5.99	5.70	4,459	2,679	2,601
Oklahoma City	*	2.32	0.01	1	912	4
San Jose	-	7.98	5.91	-	9,239	6,060
Tulsa	*	6.97	5.48	3	2,453	1,978
Virginia Beach	-	-	-	-	-	-
Wichita	0.32	1.62	3.61	90	449	1,008
MEDIAN (All Cities)	*	5.52	4.02	0	1,424	1,493
MEDIAN (Recipient Cities Only)	0.32	5.99	4.95	90	2,177	2,098
					(millions)	
U.S. TOTAL	3.06	11.28	10.31	172	2,481	2,336

Note: NA = Not Available.
*Less than $0.01 per capita.

Source: Executive Office of the President, Community Services Administration, Geographic Distribution of Federal Funds (1981).

from $3,000 in Tulsa to $5.5 million in Columbus. Assistance to intergovernmental cities during that same period ran from a low of $120,000 in Milwaukee to a high of $8.8 million in Louisville. In 1977, Baltimore alone received more than $193.4 million in grants to improve its mass transit facilities, while the largest single allocation to a non-intergovernmental city was $9.2 million in San Jose. Because intergovernmental cities received more absolute mass transit aid with fewer total residents, a per capita examination does not alter the basic relationship of the two city groupings. However, it is interesting to note that in 1980, for each Buffalo resident, there was a total of $345 received for urban mass transit construction, compared with $15 for the average intergovernmental city and $4 for non-intergovernmental cities.

General Revenue Sharing

Title I of the State and Local Fiscal Assistance Act of 1972 distributed $55.8 billion to state and local units of government between January, 1972 and September, 1980, for an average of more than $6 billion annually. In 1980 alone, almost 40,000 state and general purpose local governments shared $6.8 billion in Revenue Sharing allocations.

Revenue Sharing funds have been the most flexible form of federal financial assistance offered to states and localities. Revenue Sharing grants were restricted by minimal conditions and could be used to finance almost any governmental objective.

Funds were distributed on the basis of two formulas. The first, currently employed by twenty states, took into account five factors, including population, tax effort, relative per capita income, urbanized population, and personal income tax collections. The remaining thirty states, as well as local units of government, received funding based on three variables: population, tax effort, and relative per capita income. Because of the consistently high funding levels and widespread participation, Revenue Sharing assistance became an almost predictable local revenue.

Revenue Sharing Transfers in Intergovernmental
Versus Non-Intergovernmental Cities

Exhibit 6.38 indicates that between 1972 and 1980, Revenue Sharing allocations nationally maintained their 1972 level. Funded at approximately $6 billion per year between 1972 and 1977, and just over $6.8 billion from 1978 to 1980, the Revenue Sharing program was not cut back until 1981 when states were eliminated from eligibility. Until 1980, states had received approximately one-third of all General Revenue Sharing allocations.

For the entire period, 1972 to 1981, the average non-intergovernmental city Revenue Sharing allocation was 69 percent of that received by intergovernmental cities. On a per capita basis, higher population by intergovernmental cities during the early 1970s narrowed the margin between the two city sets; intergovernmental cities received only 13 percent more Revenue Sharing dollars than did non-intergovernmental cities (Exhibit 6.39).

EXHIBIT 6.38.—*General Revenue Sharing Allocations: Periods 1-12,*
January 1972 to September 1980 (Dollars)

	1 (6 mo.)	2 (6 mo.)	3 (6 mo.)	4 (1 yr.)	5 (1 yr.)	6 (1 yr.)
($ Millions)						
Total Allocation	2,650	2,650	2,988	6,050	6,200	6,350
Per Capita	12.75	12.75	14.22	28.78	29.18	29.55
To State Governments						
To Local Governments						

	7 (6 mo.)	8 (9 mo.)	9 (1 yr.)	10 (1 yr.)	11 (1 yr.)	12* (1 yr.)	TOTAL
($ Millions)							
Total Allocation	3,325	4,988	6,850	6,850	6,850	4,567	60,318
Per Capita	15.31	22.72	30.88	30.55	30.24	19.98	276.91
To State Governments							18,766
To Local Governments							41,552

*Payments to state governments not authorized.

Source: U.S. Department of the Treasury, Office of Revenue Sharing, General Revenue Sharing Quarterly Payment (January, 1981).

While the range in assistance between intergovernmental cities was fairly narrow in aggregate absolute dollar terms, per capita aid ranged from a low of $346 per capita in Cleveland to $928 per resident in Louisville. Baton Rouge, however, had the single largest aggregate per capita stipend of any city: each resident in Baton Rouge represented over $1,750 in Revenue Sharing payments. Baton Rouge was also the largest absolute dollar recipient; totalling $356.1 million, Baton Rouge Revenue Sharing aid was 64 percent greater than that of the average intergovernmental city and more than twice the level of assistance to other non-intergovernmental cities.

Anti-Recessionary Fiscal Assistance

The final grant program to be reviewed is the Anti-Recessionary Fiscal Assistance program, established by Title II of the 1976 Public Works Employment Act. Anti-Recessionary grants were made available, on a temporary basis, to state and local governments to counteract recessionary pressures and to stimulate national economic growth and expansion. High unemployment rates and the size of general

EXHIBIT 6.39. — *State and Local Fiscal Assistance: Revenue Sharing,*
January 1972 to January 1981 (Dollars)

	Total ($ Million)	Per Capita
INTERGOVERNMENTAL		
Akron	156.2	629.8
Baltimore	286.9	348.6
Buffalo	169.8	435.4
Cincinnati	218.5	438.2
Cleveland	217.0	346.1
Louisville	294.1	927.8
Milwaukee	175.6	266.1
Minneapolis	168.5	433.2
Newark	242.7	703.5
Rochester	127.8	495.3
MEDIAN (All Cities)	217.0	436.8
NON-INTERGOVERNMENTAL		
Anaheim	78.7	383.9
Austin	115.5	363.2
Baton Rouge	356.1	1,754.2
Columbus	140.2	251.3
Nashville-Davidson	173.5	388.1
Oklahoma City	161.0	409.7
San Jose	88.2	151.0
Tulsa	208.1	591.2
Virginia Beach	161.6	687.7
Wichita	97.7	351.4
MEDIAN (All Cities)	150.6	386.0

Source: U.S. Department of the Treasury, Office of Revenue Sharing,
<u>General Revenue Sharing Quarterly Payment</u> (January, 1981).

Revenue Sharing entitlements determined individual funding eligibility. From July 1976 to July 1978, more than $3 billion was dispersed to state and local governments in the form of Anti-Recessionary Fiscal Assistance payments.

Anti-Recessionary Fiscal Assistance Payments in Intergovernmental Versus Non-Intergovernmental Cities

Similar to Revenue Sharing assistance, approximately two-thirds of the available Anti-Recessionary Fiscal Assistance aid went to local governments with one-third reserved for states (Exhibit 6.40). Unlike Revenue Sharing assistance, however, aid to intergovernmental and non-intergovernmental cities varied sharply. In the aggregate, the average intergovernmental city received 8.4 times the level of Anti-Recessionary funding of the average non-intergovernmental city ($6.5 billion versus $776 million). Newark, with the second highest total payments, had by far the greatest per

EXHIBIT 6.40. — *Anti-Recessionary Fiscal Assistance, 1976–1978 ($ Millions)*

| | 1976 | | 1977 | | | |
	July–Sept.	Oct.–Dec.	Jan.–March	April–June	July–Sept.	Oct.–Dec.
Payments	312.5	250.0	312.5	312.5	520.2	429.3
Per Capita	1.44	1.15	1.42	1.42	2.37	1.96
To State Governments						
To Local Governments						

| | 1978 | | | |
	Jan.–March	April–June	July–Sept.	TOTAL
Payments	399.0	308.1	186.9	3028.2
Per Capita	1.80	1.39	0.84	13.79
To State Governments				1021.7
To Local Governments				2006.6

Source: U.S. Department of the Treasury, Office of Revenue Sharing, Antirecession Payment Summary 9 (July 1978).

EXHIBIT 6.41.—*Anti-Recessionary Fiscal Assistance, by City, 1976–1978 (Dollars)*

	PER CAPITA								ABSOLUTE (000)							
	1-3	4	5	6	7	8	9	Total	1-3	4	5	6	7	8	9	Total
INTERGOVERNMENTAL																
Akron	3.20	1.13	1.71	1.32	1.15	0.63	0.56	9.65	792.6	279.0	423.2	326.8	281.0	154.3	137.5	2,394.4
Baltimore	5.30	2.80	4.52	3.69	4.09	2.38	2.38	24.28	4,362.9	2,308.1	3,719.8	3,037.2	3,319.0	1,930.0	1,272.3	19,985.2
Buffalo	6.96	2.45	3.68	3.03	3.39	2.56	1.44	23.29	2,713.2	953.4	1,434.9	1,183.4	1,284.7	968.4	546.0	9,084.0
Cincinnati	4.70	2.08	3.31	2.89	3.18	0.85	0.66	17.60	1,909.0	844.0	1,345.3	1,174.0	1,268.6	340.3	262.7	7,43.8
Cleveland	5.11	1.65	2.50	2.16	2.01	1.52	0.71	15.54	3,205.8	1,032.9	1,567.6	1,353.3	1,224.2	922.8	434.9	9,741.4
Louisville	5.43	0.76	1.71	0.26	0.30	0.47	0.44	9.35	1,722.6	239.6	543.3	83.5	92.3	146.1	137.0	2,964.5
Milwaukee	2.73	1.06	1.80	1.48	1.65	0.09	0.11	8.90	1,800.4	700.4	1,189.6	975.2	1,078.2	56.2	71.0	5,871.0
Minneapolis	1.73	0.68	1.04	0.76	0.59	-	-	4.78	671.0	265.6	404.7	295.0	224.3	-	-	1,860.5
Newark	11.95	5.01	6.99	7.47	7.39	4.75	2.19	45.55	4,121.4	1,729.8	2,411.8	2,583.0	2,512.2	1,614.5	742.8	15,715.5
Rochester	0.91	1.09	1.75	1.69	1.62	1.04	0.56	10.35	235.6	280.0	452.4	436.3	410.0	261.8	140.5	2,670.5
MEDIAN (All Cities)	5.21	1.39	2.15	1.18	1.83	0.94	0.61	12.94	1,854.7	772.2	1,267.5	1,074.6	1,246.4	301.1	201.6	6,507.4
MEDIAN (Recipient Cities Only)	5.21	1.39	2.15	1.18	1.83	10.35	0.66	12.94	1,854.7	772.2	1,267.5	1,074.6	1,246.4	301.1	201.6	6,507.4
NON-INTERGOVERNMENTAL																
Anaheim	0.93	0.14	0.16	0.07	-	0.19	0.11	1.60	190.5	27.9	31.9	14.7	-	40.4	22.7	327.6
Austin	-	0.04	-	-	0.07	-	-	0.12	-	13.3	-	-	23.7	-	-	37.0
Baton Rouge	1.88	0.79	1.36	2.35	3.12	1.33	0.83	11.52	382.2	106.0	275.2	477.6	648.1	276.8	172.6	2,338.6
Columbus	1.76	0.55	1.08	0.62	0.69	-	0.20	4.91	984.5	306.1	604.8	347.0	383.7	-	112.7	2,738.8
Nashville-Davidson	1.54	-	-	-	-	-	-	1.54	689.7	-	-	-	-	-	-	689.7
Oklahoma City	2.32	0.24	0.29	0.18	0.44	-	0.27	3.03	912.2	94.8	112.6	69.2	265.3	-	164.6	1,188.9
San Jose	1.86	0.50	0.69	0.77	-	0.41	-	4.98	1,085.0	290.6	402.4	449.8	-	247.4	-	2,905.3
Tulsa	2.15	-	0.20	0.10	0.31	-	-	2.45	756.7	-	70.5	34.7	72.4	-	-	861.8
Virginia Beach	0.46	0.28	0.53	0.37	-	-	0.30	2.26	108.9	66.7	125.1	87.3	-	-	70.3	530.6
Wichita	0.42	0.49	0.27	0.09	-	-	-	0.85	115.5	136.3	75.0	25.1	-	-	-	236.4
MEDIAN (All Cities)	1.65	0.26	0.28	0.14	6.04	-	0.05	2.35	536.0	80.8	93.8	52.0	12.0	-	11.4	775.8
MEDIAN (Recipient Cities Only)	1.76	0.39	0.41	0.27	0.38	0.41	0.27	2.35	536.0	80.8	93.8	52.0	12.0	-	11.4	775.8

Source: U.S. Department of the Treasury, Office of Revenue Sharing, *Antirecession Payment Summary 9* (July 1978).

capita amounts. Newark's total Anti-Recessionary Fiscal Assistance payments of $15.7 million were second only to Baltimore's $20 million. Baltimore, with a much larger population than Newark, received only $25 in Anti-Recessionary aid per capita compared to a Newark figure of $45 (see Exhibit 6.41).

Conclusion

Throughout the past twenty years, federal and state governments increasingly have become involved in local fiscal, economic and social problems through the enactment of literally hundreds of grant-in-aid and other forms of subsidy programs. Moreover, these governments' initiatives have provided individuals with billions of dollars of financial assistance each year to address a broad array of personal hardships.

The programs reviewed in this chapter have been federal programs. State transfers come largely in the form of educational grants and are discussed in a previous chapter. The programs covered here do not represent all federal aid provided either to cities or to individuals. They do, however, constitute by far, the bulk of major federal urban assistance initiatives, as well as payments for direct aid to individuals.

This chapter has shown that intergovernmental cities received a substantially greater share of aid from principal federal grants than did non-intergovernmental cities. For example, of the twenty-eight programs reviewed here, seventeen were funded at $1.0 billion or more in 1980.* Exhibit 6.42 shows that of those seventeen

EXHIBIT 6.42.—*Non-Intergovernmental City Aid Revenues as a Percent of Intergovernmental City Receipts (Per Capita), 1980*

Programs	Percent
Aid to Families with Dependent Children	30.6
Social Security Retirement Insurance	36.0
Social Security Disability Insurance	46.6
Social Security Survivor's Insurance	45.6
Unemployment Insurance	44.8
Food Stamps	60.9
School Lunch Program	88.1
Community Development Block Grants	34.2
Low-Income Housing (Public Housing)	36.0
Housing Assistance (Section 8)	51.6
Basic Education Opportunity Grants	59.8
Comprehensive Employment and Training Act	142.7
Medicaid	41.9
Urban Mass Transit Grants	28.3
Wastewater Treatment Grants	14.9
Revenue Sharing Payments	88.4
Anti-Recessionary Fiscal Assistance	18.2

*Includes Anti-Recessionary Fiscal Assistance grants which averaged $1.0 billion during its three years of operation.

grants, non-intergovernmental cities received less than 50 percent of the aid granted to intergovernmental cities in eleven programs. Moreover, non-intergovernmental cities received greater funding than the average intergovernmental city in only one program. Combining all seventeen grants, non-intergovernmental cities received, on average, only 51.1 percent of the aid which flowed to intergovernmental cities. Finally, beyond these major assistance initiatives, intergovernmental cities on a per capita basis, have received by far the greatest proportion of the smaller economic assistance and social program funding as well.

Having now identified the specific programs upon which intergovernmental cities are most dependent, Chapter 8 will outline program budget reductions for the next several years. The two chapters may be used together to obtain an appreciation for the scale of federal involvement, as well as, the impact of budget cuts on intergovernmental cities.

NOTES

1. U.S. Office of Management and Budget, *The United States Budget: Special Analysis K* (1969) (Washington, D.C.: U.S. Government Printing Office, 1970), p. 156.

2. Advisory Commission on Intergovernmental Relations, *Fiscal Balance in the American Federal System* (Washington, D.C.: ACIR, 1967), Vol. 1, p. 138.

7

Revenue and Expenditure Emphases in the Intergovernmental City

T HIS CHAPTER summarizes budgetary trends in intergovernmental cities. It takes the view that both components of the city fisc—revenue and expenditure—are inextricably interrelated. The demands placed on the expenditure side of the municipal budget, to meliorate complex social problems or to induce economic reinvestment, significantly shape the parameters of the city's revenue-raising effort. External constraints on revenue, stemming from declining tax bases or from dwindling intergovernmental receipts, in turn, shape the amount of outlay the city can afford.

Prior to proceeding, a few summary points are required to frame the details which follow. Generally speaking, both municipal budgeting and local fiscal performance reflect local socioeconomic conditions.[1] As cities decline, pressures are placed on both the revenue and expenditure sides of the municipal fisc. Private disinvestment —in industry, retail trade, and housing—simultaneously erodes the revenue-generating capacity of the locality. As affluent residents leave and dependent populations within the city increase, demands for social services and associated public employment rise. These pressures on municipal outlays are further compounded by the need to encourage private reinvestment through enhanced municipal services and public facilities. With expenditures mounting concurrently with shrinkages in locally raised revenues, acute fiscal strains emerge, and bond ratings deteriorate.

According to this general picture of fiscal stress, declining cities turn to federal and state transfers in response to insufficient local revenues. Since increased demands for services cannot be met, intergovernmental revenues are called upon to fill the gap.[2] Growing cities, although they also provide a large array of services, are able to avoid such far-flung reliance on intergovernmental transfers precisely because their local revenue-generating capacities are much more buoyant.

This chapter begins with a discussion of local expenditures in intergovernmental and non-intergovernmental cities. The expenditure patterns for these classes of cities are then evaluated in light of indicators of local service needs. The next section turns to a discussion of the revenue side of the local fisc. This section begins with an analysis of the changing tax base of intergovernmental versus non-intergovernmental cities, presenting a short case study of Newark, New Jersey. It concludes with a detailed evaluation of the composition of own-source versus intergovernmental revenues for both intergovernmental and non-intergovernmental cities.

We will begin by viewing the variation in municipal spending levels for the two classes of cities. Again, the late 1970s forms the terminal point of the empirical analysis.

Expenditure Patterns in Intergovernmental Versus Non-Intergovernmental Cities

Exhibit 7.1 presents seventeen-year trends in municipal expenditures for intergovernmental versus non-intergovernmental cities. Over this period, total general expenditures have been consistently higher and have shown more significant rates of increase in intergovernmental cities. From 1962 to 1979, general expenditures in these cities rose from $213 to $1,109 per capita, an increase of nearly $900 or over 420 percent. In non-intergovernmental cities, despite a substantial rate of increase over the same period, general expenditures remained below the amounts expended in intergovernmental cities for any given year. In this category of cities, general expenditures increased by about 330 percent over the same period, from $196 per capita in 1962 to $842 by 1979. In 1979, general expenditures in non-intergovernmental cities were approximately $270 per capita or 25 percent lower than municipal outlays in intergovernmental cities.

Education Expenditures

Educational spending is the most costly single function performed at the local level. It accounts for about 40 percent of total local outlays in both intergovernmental and non-intergovernmental cities. Approaching 1980, intergovernmental cities spent more for education than non-intergovernmental cities—$437 compared to $343 per capita. Educational spending also grew much more rapidly in intergovernmental cities. Over the past two decades, educational spending rose by nearly 500 percent as opposed to one-half this growth rate in non-intergovernmental cities.

Expenditures for Municipal Functions

Intergovernmental cities also spend more for municipal functions (all expenditures aside from education). In 1979, these cities spent $672 per capita for municipal services, up from $177 in 1962. This is about $200 more per capita than was spent for similar services in non-intergovernmental cities (Exhibit 7.1).

In terms of specific municipal expenditure categories, intergovernmental cities showed the greatest percentage increases in non-discretionary outlays such as public safety (403 percent), housing (506 percent) and government administration (559 percent). Non-intergovernmental cities showed much more moderate increases in public safety (333 percent) and housing (307 percent), but significantly greater increases in spending for capital-intensive areas such as transportation (529 percent), public works (405 percent) and hospitals (545 percent). This trend was also evident in the differential growth in interest payments for these two classes of cities. Interest payments increased by over 570 percent in non-intergovernmental cities, compared with a more sluggish 375 percent rate of increase for their intergovernmental counterparts. Fast-growing, non-intergovernmental cities have thus tended to expand their capital outlays for roads, utilities, and other facilities necessary to accommodate rapidly increasing populations. Intergovernmental cities, faced with declining populations, job losses, and high socioeconomic dependency have been forced to use the local budget to meliorate pressing socioeconomic problems. These cities typically channeled greater proportions of municipal resources into operating costs for essential services like police, fire or education while defraying long-term capital improvements (Exhibit 7.1). Ultimately, intergovernmental cities have not had as wide discretion in setting local spending priorities.

Detailed Expenditure Contrasts

Exhibits 7.2 and 7.3 provide detail on expenditure patterns for each of the twenty sample cities. Here, the trends observed for individual cities clearly reflect the aggregate patterns. As of the beginning of the 1980s, most of the intergovernmental cities spent more than non-intergovernmental cities. Of the intergovernmental cities, the most highly distressed communities possessed the highest levels of aggregate (municipal and school) expenditure, from $1,100 to $1,300 per capita. Most of these cities also devoted very large percentages of expenditure to non-discretionary municipal functions such as government administration, public safety, or health and welfare. Three additional intergovernmental cities—Akron, Minneapolis, and Milwaukee—spent between $950 and $1,000 per capita, while only Louisville of the intergovernmental cities spent less than this amount (approximately $800 per capita) (Exhibit 7.1).

In 1979, individual non-intergovernmental cities spent considerably (35 percent) less than intergovernmental cities. Of the former, only Baton Rouge and Wichita spent more than $1,000 per capita. Each represents a special case. On the one hand, Baton Rouge is the capital of Louisiana and spent significant amounts of money in the areas of public safety and government administration for what amounted to be "state" functions. On the other hand, Wichita took a substantial loan to refinance previously bonded debt and to initially finance a variety of capital improvements. In both cases this swelled operational outlays. The remaining non-intergovernmental cities each spent between $750 and $800 per capita. All of these cities devoted a very large share of total outlays to capital improvements in the service categories of public works and transportation.

Expenditures for Wages and Salaries

Expenditures for wages and salaries comprised a greater percentage share of outlays in high-growth, non-intergovernmental cities. As Exhibit 7.4 indicates, in 1979,

EXHIBIT 7.1. — *Trends in Expenditures, Intergovernmental Versus Non-Intergovernmental Cities, 1962-1979 (in Per Capita Dollars)*

Expenditure Category	1962	1967	1972	1979	1962-1967		1967-1972		1972-1979		1962-1979	
					Absolute	Percent	Absolute	Percent	Absolute	Percent	Absolute	Percent
Total General Expenditures												
Intergovernmental	213.23	323.70	591.98	1109.59	109.97	51.82	268.78	83.16	517.61	87.44	896.36	420.37
Non-intergovernmental	195.79	283.48	389.76	842.46	87.69	44.79	106.28	37.49	452.70	116.15	646.67	330.29
All Municipal												
Intergovernmental	171.81	252.45	468.77	672.24	80.64	46.94	216.32	85.69	203.47	43.41	500.43	291.27
Non-intergovernmental	117.18	146.84	212.38	499.08	29.66	25.31	65.54	44.63	286.70	134.99	381.90	325.91
All School Districts*												
Intergovernmental	71.28	118.74	209.66	437.35	47.46	66.58	90.92	76.57	227.69	108.60	366.07	513.56
Non-intergovernmental	102.57	145.80	204.11	343.40	43.23	42.15	58.31	39.99	139.29	68.24	240.83	234.80
Education												
Intergovernmental	75.23	131.84	239.24	437.35	56.61	75.25	107.4	81.46	198.11	82.81	362.12	481.35
Non-intergovernmental	98.98	138.76	195.45	343.40	39.78	40.19	56.61	40.85	147.95	75.70	244.42	246.94
Public Safety												
Intergovernmental	30.45	41.31	77.99	153.27	10.86	35.67	36.68	88.79	75.28	96.53	122.82	403.35
Non-intergovernmental	21.18	23.21	37.70	91.69	2.03	9.58	14.49	62.43	53.99	143.21	70.51	332.91
Public Works												
Intergovernmental	25.16	34.36	71.67	124.39	9.20	36.57	37.31	108.59	52.72	73.56	99.23	394.40
Non-intergovernmental	22.17	32.56	38.52	107.89	10.39	46.87	5.96	18.30	69.37	180.09	85.72	386.65

Source: See bottom of next page.

EXHIBIT 7.1 (Continued)

Transportation												
Intergovernmental	17.45	18.53	27.96	66.30	1.08	6.19	9.43	58.89	38.34	137.12	48.85	279.94
Non-intergovernmental	18.57	16.95	22.54	79.71	-1.62	- 8.72	5.59	32.98	57.17	253.64	61.14	329.24
Housing												
Intergovernmental	11.23	16.96	31.77	68.06	5.73	51.02	14.81	87.32	36.29	114.23	56.83	506.06
Non-intergovernmental	2.69	3.93	6.10	10.96	1.24	46.10	2.17	55.22	4.86	79.67	8.27	307.43
Health & Hospitals												
Intergovernmental	9.27	13.30	24.59	33.26	4.03	43.47	11.29	84.89	8.67	35.26	23.99	258.79
Non-intergovernmental	4.78	5.99	9.25	30.84	1.21	25.31	3.26	54.42	21.59	233.41	26.06	545.19
Public Welfare												
Intergovernmental	8.27	13.46	31.65	8.48	5.19	62.76	18.19	135.14	-23.17	- 73.21	0.21	2.54
Non-intergovernmental	0.28	0.72	1.84	2.75	0.44	157.14	1.12	155.56	0.91	49.46	2.47	882.14
Libraries												
Intergovernmental	2.40	3.50	5.31	9.92	1.10	45.83	1.81	51.71	4.61	-86.23	7.52	313.33
Non-intergovernmental	2.37	2.41	3.25	6.15	0.04	1.69	0.84	34.85	2.90	89.23	3.78	159.49
Government Administration												
Intergovernmental	7.15	9.49	19.08	47.13	2.34	32.73	9.59	101.05	28.05	147.01	39.98	559.16
Non-intergovernmental	5.68	7.67	12.89	34.81	1.99	35.04	5.22	68.06	21.92	170.05	29.13	512.85
Interest on Debt												
Intergovernmental	6.19	8.15	17.13	29.45	1.96	31.66	8.98	110.18	12.32	71.92	23.26	375.77
Non-intergovernmental	5.64	7.45	15.60	37.84	1.81	32.09	8.15	109.40	22.24	142.56	32.20	570.92
Other												
Intergovernmental	20.42	41.72	57.10	129.67	21.30	104.31	15.38	36.86	72.57	127.09	109.25	535.01
Non-intergovernmental	17.57	17.95	32.28	97.82	0.38	2.16	14.33	79.83	65.54	203.04	80.25	456.74

Note: *School District expenditures for 1962, 1967, and 1972 based on a sample of six intergovernmental cities (N=6), and seven non-intergovernmental cities (N=7). For 1979, sample equals ten cities for each group (N=10). See Appendix.

Source: U.S. Department of Commerce, Bureau of Census, Census of Governments, 1962, 1967, 1972. *Government Finances* (annual report), 1979.

EXHIBIT 7.2. — *Detailed Dollar Per Capita Distribution of Expenditures, 1979*

	Education	Transportation	Welfare	Health and Hospitals	Public Safety	Public Works	Housing	Libraries	Government Administration	Interest on General Debt	Other and Unallocable	Total Municipal	Total School District	TOTAL
INTERGOVERNMENTAL														
AKRON	425.53	53.76	–	10.48	98.49	125.11	95.64	–	29.35	26.89	85.42	525.14	425.53	950.67
BALTIMORE	387.71	102.32	6.27	105.22	176.94	119.58	52.75	11.28	67.37	31.34	241.74	927.72	387.72	1315.44
BUFFALO	441.08	28.67	0.15	2.71	135.53	156.11	91.28	–	40.12	41.54	203.38	695.54	438.84	1134.38
CINCINNATI	366.08	71.51	–	53.13	214.60	214.60	71.82	–	30.38	20.90	126.68	768.33	366.08	1134.41
CLEVELAND	567.96	60.47	3.13	15.03	173.47	139.97	52.63	–	40.46	35.74	87.20	608.17	567.90	1176.07
LOUISVILLE	241.53	26.91	–	17.67	126.48	74.93	103.41	16.71	31.95	17.12	113.53	528.70	241.53	770.23
MILWAUKEE	473.22	72.28	–	15.71	135.63	109.71	65.11	14.94	33.46	18.19	27.14	492.69	472.69	965.38
MINNEAPOLIS	349.79	85.60	–	15.86	117.42	124.11	101.81	22.25	35.18	38.37	90.86	631.48	349.79	981.27
NEWARK	521.26	12.66	88.11	11.37	188.25	124.71	2.54	13.77	68.17	22.74	157.84	643.72	521.26	1164.98
ROCHESTER	576.76	98.93	–	–	157.58	98.14	88.79	23.56	95.86	40.02	111.13	699.86	576.51	1276.37
WEIGHTED MEAN	437.43	66.30	8.48	33.26	153.27	124.39	68.06	9.92	47.13	29.45	129.67	672.24	437.15	1109.39
NON-INTERGOVERNMENTAL														
ANAHEIM	360.50	29.80	–	–	102.57	107.67	7.18	10.40	78.51	19.11	36.83	392.03	360.50	752.54
AUSTIN	372.76	41.14	0.86	122.01	80.32	83.20	17.13	16.94	30.44	22.45	40.92	455.88	372.27	828.16
BATON ROUGE	438.58	71.05	0.49	101.76	139.42	98.00	6.90	10.23	70.95	65.92	184.71	749.44	438.58	1188.02
COLUMBUS	308.92	72.56	–	14.29	115.16	133.38	17.33	–	30.22	33.09	62.73	478.78	308.92	787.70
NASHVILLE-DAVIDSON	303.69	38.96	10.14	69.18	98.49	116.67	3.54	7.71	36.96	39.74	60.50	474.93	303.69	778.62
OKLAHOMA CITY	252.25	96.28	–	0.24	95.89	184.78	18.35	–	28.01	37.37	56.47	518.11	96.28	770.35
SAN JOSE	437.43	99.86	–	1.74	79.16	6.45	6.12	8.46	16.63	14.24	21.41	312.15	437.43	749.58
TULSA	292.45	122.87	–	9.27	77.75	107.41	17.81	0.92	23.61	59.75	55.27	475.48	292.45	767.99
VIRGINIA BEACH	322.27	58.56	20.19	12.74	71.72	90.49	2.48	5.85	67.56	36.18	80.18	436.05	322.27	758.32
WICHITA	356.73	148.60	–	12.98	60.31	85.39	8.27	6.72	17.96	84.10	586.63	1010.97	356.73	1367.71
WEIGHTED MEAN	343.40	79.67	2.75	30.84	91.69	110.62	10.96	6.13	34.81	37.84	97.82	499.08	343.40	842.48

Source: U.S. Department of Commerce, Bureau of Census, Census of Governments, *Government Finances* (annual report), 1979.

EXHIBIT 7.3. — *Detailed Percent Distribution of Expenditures, 1979*

	Education	Transportation	Welfare	Health and Hospitals	Public Safety	Public Works	Housing	Libraries	Government Administration	Interest on General Debt	Other and Unallocable	Total Municipal	Total School District	TOTAL
INTERGOVERNMENTAL														
AKRON	44.76	5.66	-	1.10	10.40	13.16	10.06	-	3.09	2.83	8.99	55.24	44.76	100.0
BALTIMORE	29.47	7.78	4.77	8.88	13.45	9.09	4.01	8.58	5.12	2.38	18.37	70.53	29.47	100.0
BUFFALO	38.88	2.53	0.01	0.24	11.95	13.76	8.05	-	3.54	3.66	17.93	61.31	38.69	100.0
CINCINNATI	32.27	6.26	-	4.68	15.58	18.92	6.33	-	2.68	1.84	11.40	67.73	32.27	100.0
CLEVELAND	48.29	5.14	0.27	1.28	14.75	11.90	4.47	-	3.44	3.04	7.41	51.71	48.29	100.0
LOUISVILLE	31.36	3.49	-	2.29	11.64	16.42	13.43	2.17	4.15	2.22	14.74	68.64	31.36	100.0
MILWAUKEE	49.02	7.49	-	1.63	14.05	11.36	6.74	1.55	3.47	1.84	2.81	51.04	48.96	100.0
MINNEAPOLIS	35.65	8.72	-	1.62	11.97	12.65	10.37	2.27	3.59	3.91	9.26	64.35	35.65	100.0
NEWARK	44.74	1.09	7.56	0.98	16.16	5.22	2.18	1.18	5.85	2.38	13.55	55.26	44.74	100.0
ROCHESTER	45.19	7.75	-	-	12.35	7.69	6.96	1.85	7.51	3.14	8.71	54.83	45.17	100.0
WEIGHTED MEAN	39.42	5.97	0.76	3.00	13.81	11.21	6.13	0.89	4.25	2.65	11.69	60.58	39.40	100.0
NON-INTERGOVERNMENTAL														
ANAHEIM	47.91	3.96	-	-	13.63	14.30	0.95	1.38	10.43	2.54	4.89	52.09	47.91	100.0
AUSTIN	45.01	4.97	0.10	14.73	10.00	10.05	2.07	2.05	3.68	2.71	4.94	55.05	44.95	100.0
BATON ROUGE	36.92	5.98	0.04	8.57	11.74	8.25	0.58	0.86	5.97	5.55	15.55	63.08	36.92	100.0
COLUMBUS	39.22	9.21	-	1.81	14.62	16.93	2.20	-	3.84	4.20	7.96	60.78	39.22	100.0
NASHVILLE-DAVIDSON	39.00	5.00	1.30	8.83	12.65	14.98	0.45	0.99	4.75	5.10	7.77	61.00	39.00	100.0
OKLAHOMA CITY	32.75	12.50	-	-	12.45	23.99	2.38	-	3.64	4.85	7.33	67.26	32.75	100.0
SAN JOSE	58.36	13.32	-	0.23	10.56	8.61	0.81	1.13	2.22	1.90	2.86	41.64	58.36	100.0
TULSA	38.08	16.00	-	1.21	10.12	13.99	2.32	0.12	3.07	7.78	7.20	61.91	38.08	100.0
VIRGINIA BEACH	42.50	7.72	2.66	1.68	9.46	11.93	3.24	0.77	8.91	4.77	10.57	57.50	42.50	100.0
WICHITA	26.08	10.87	-	0.95	4.41	6.24	0.60	0.49	1.31	6.15	42.89	73.92	26.08	100.0
WEIGHTED MEAN	40.76	9.46	0.33	3.66	10.88	13.12	1.30	0.73	4.13	4.49	11.61	59.24	40.76	100.0

Source: U.S. Department of Commerce, Bureau of Census, Census of Governments, *Government Finances* (annual report), 1979.

these cities deployed approximately 54 percent of local expenditures to cover the costs of employee wages. When Wichita, which had extraordinarily low municipal wage costs, is excluded from the sample, employee wage costs rise to 57 percent of total outlays. This is approximately one-fifth more than the share allocated to wages and salaries in intergovernmental cities. However, declining intergovernmental cities spent for municipal wages nearly 20 percent more in absolute dollar terms—$540.68 versus $457.26 per capita. Given the fact that wage rates in non-intergovernmental cities across most categories of public service were not significantly different from intergovernmental cities, it is clearly the number of personnel per service category that contributed to the higher costs in intergovernmental cities.

EXHIBIT 7.4. — *Expenditures for Wages and Salaries, 1979*
(in Dollars Per Capita)

	Per Capita Wages and Salaries	As Percent of Total Expenditures
INTERGOVERNMENTAL		
AKRON	434.81	45.7
BALTIMORE	639.46	48.6
BUFFALO	496.15	43.7
CINCINNATI	530.79	46.8
CLEVELAND	519.68	44.2
LOUISVILLE	385.19	50.0
MILWAUKEE	551.70	57.1
MINNEAPOLIS	514.17	62.4
NEWARK	600.00	51.5
ROCHESTER	576.86	45.2
WEIGHTED MEAN	540.68	48.8
NON-INTERGOVERNMENTAL		
ANAHEIM	487.08	64.7
AUSTIN	509.97	61.6
BATON ROUGE	599.92	50.5
COLUMBUS	395.14	50.2
NASHVILLE-DAVIDSON	508.26	65.3
OKLAHOMA CITY	424.71	55.1
SAN JOSE	403.55	53.8
TULSA	364.21	47.4
VIRGINIA BEACH	590.21	77.8
WICHITA	383.15	28.0
WEIGHTED MEAN	457.26	53.6

Source: U.S. Department of Commerce, Bureau of Census, Census of Governments, <u>Government Finances</u> (annual report), 1979.

Summary

Generally speaking, intergovernmental cities spent significantly more both overall and for municipal functions and slightly more for education than non-intergovernmental cities. Intergovernmental cities devoted proportionally larger shares of local resources for essential operating services such as police and fire protection, but significantly less for capital infrastructure improvement. Non-intergovernmental cities, on the other hand, were likely to funnel large shares of outlays toward debt service for forthcoming capital improvement projects.

Service Needs and Local Expenditures

The precise fit between a community's service "needs" and actual expenditure commitments is difficult to measure. To date, realistic forecasts of the level of outlays needed to address the array of socioeconomic problems of declining cities have not even been attempted. Measurements of investments needed to upgrade obsolete capital plants, when done, have been very imprecise. Probably, the best indicator of the seriousness of decline in social services lies in the extraordinarily high levels of distress found in older, intergovernmental cities. As a consequence, these communities are faced with the unenviable task of using municipal revenues to address a wide range of serious social and economic problems. As Chapter 3 has shown, declining intergovernmental cities were characterized by substantial job loss, consistent erosion of their economic base, high unemployment, and deteriorating citywide incomes. Since businesses virtually abandoned many of these older cities, local government had to devote significant outlays for economic or housing redevelopment just to compensate for losses encountered through the flight of private capital. Intergovernmental cities were further beset by a host of social problems including extraordinarily high crime rates, inadequate health conditions, and faltering educational standards (Chapter 4). Because personnel levels to staff essential agencies such as police and fire departments or local schools had to be maintained, spending was defrayed from the maintenance and replacement of the city's capital stock—including schools, roads, mass transit, water systems and sewer plants. The increasingly obvious demise in service quality of older intergovernmental cities was thus found in their rapidly eroding and dilapidated capital plants. These are facilities which did not have regular replacement or repair and whose actuarial if not actual life was long past.

Capital Obsolescence in Declining Cities

George Peterson and staff at The Urban Institute have compiled useful estimates of capital stock conditions and capital spending needs for a large sample of cities.[3] While their classification scheme for cities—declining versus growing—differs somewhat from the one employed here, there is enough overlap to warrant a review of their findings. Basically, the results of their work imply that older declining (intergovernmental) cities not only possessed sorely inadequate capital facilities, but were incapable of devoting the level of resources needed to upgrade them to an acceptable state. This is a significantly different situation than was found in growing (non-intergovernmental) cities.

Roads and Highways

Exhibit 7.5 presents data on street and highway conditions in a wide range of cities, as compiled by the U.S. Department of Transportation (DOT). In 1975, declining cities possessed the smallest percentage of roads in good condition and the largest proportion in disrepair. In these cities, only 36 percent of the roads surveyed were sound, another 50 percent were in fair shape, while 14 percent were evaluated as poor. In growing cities, on the other hand, 63 percent of all roads were in good shape, 31 percent were fair and only 6 percent were in poor condition. Close to double the percentage of roads were in good shape in growing versus declining cities.

Bridges

Exhibit 7.6 presents data on the quality of bridges in urban areas, also obtained from DOT surveys. Basically, the pattern observed for roads repeats itself. As of 1978, in declining cities, 2.3 percent of all bridges were structurally deficient, while

EXHIBIT 7.5. — *Condition of Roads and Highways, 1975*

Category of Urbanized Area	Percent of Highway Mileage on Federal Aid System by Condition Rating		
	Good	Fair	Poor
Declining Cities[a]	36%	50%	14%
Growing Cities[b]	63%	31%	6%

[a]Baltimore, Chicago, Cincinnati, Cleveland, Detroit, Louisville, Milwaukee, Minneapolis, New Orleans, Philadelphia, Pittsburgh, St. Louis, San Francisco, Seattle, Washington, D.C.

[b]Atlanta, Columbus, Denver, Indianapolis, Kansas City, Los Angeles, Nashville, Norfolk, Oklahoma City, Portland, Toledo, Tulsa, Baton Rouge, Charlotte, Jacksonville, Memphis, Miami, Omaha, Phoenix, San Diego, San Jose, Tucson.

Source: U.S. Department of Transportation, Federal Highway Administration, Computer Print-Out on Urban Mileage and Travel by Pavement Condition and Pavement Type from the 1976 National Highway Inventory and Performance Study, in George E. Peterson, "Transmitting the Municipal Fiscal Squeeze to a New Generation of Taxpayers: Pension Obligations and Capital Investment Needs," in Robert Burchell and David Listokin (eds.), *Cities Under Stress: The Fiscal Crises of Urban America*, New Brunswick, New Jersey: Center for Urban Policy Research, 1981.

an additional 13.5 percent were functionally obsolete. In contrast, only 0.6 percent of all bridges in growing cities were structurally deficient, and just 5 percent more were functionally obsolete. Triple the percentage of bridges in intergovernmental (declining) versus non-intergovernmental (growing) cities needed major refurbishing or replacement.

Sewer Plants

Exhibit 7.7 summarizes data compiled by the Environmental Protection Agency (EPA) on the sewer investment needs for growing versus declining cities as of 1976. Again, declining cities faced the greatest need to upgrade. On average, these cities required an investment commitment of close to $400 per capita to bring their sewer systems to adequate quality standards. Of this amount, $67 per capita was needed

EXHIBIT 7.6. — *Structural Condition of Bridges, 1978*

Category of City	Total Bridge Count	Count of Structurally Deficient Bridges[1] (percent of total)	Count of Functionally Obsolete Bridges[2] (percent of total)
Declining City Average[a]	170	4 (2.3%)	23 (13.5%)
Growing City Average[b]	494	3 (0.6%)	25 (5.0%)

[a]Baltimore, Chicago, Cincinnati, Cleveland, Detroit, Louisville, Minneapolis, Oakland, St. Louis, San Francisco, Seattle.

[b]Atlanta, Columbus, Dallas, Denver, Fort Worth, Indianapolis, Kansas City, Long Beach, Los Angeles, Nashville, Norfolk, Oklahoma City, Portland, Toledo, Tulsa, Austin, Baton Rouge, Charlotte, El Paso, Jacksonville, Memphis, Miami, Omaha, Phoenix, San Antonio, San Diego, San Jose, Tucson.

[1]A structurally deficient bridge is one that has been restricted to light vehicles only or closed.

[2]A functionally obsolete bridge is one whose deck geometry, load carrying capacity, clearance or approach roadway alignment can no longer safely service the system of which it is an integral part.

Source: U.S. Department of Transportation, Federal Highway Administration, Bridge Inventory File print-out by city, data as of October 4, 1978, in George E. Peterson, "Transmitting the Municipal Fiscal Squeeze to a New Generation of Taxpayers: Pension Obligations and Capital Investment Needs," in Robert Burchell and David Listokin (eds.), *Cities Under Stress: The Fiscal Crises of Urban America*, New Brunswick, New Jersey: Center for Urban Policy Research, 1981.

EXHIBIT 7.7. — *Sewer Investment Needs Per Capita, 1976*

Classification and City	Repair and Rehabilitation of Sewer Lines, Correction of Infiltration and Inflow	Secondary Treatment Plant Upgrading to Meet Discharge Standards	Total*
Declining City[a] Average	$67	$63	$399
Growing City[b] Average	$13	$44	$284
Intergovernmental Cities			
Baltimore	$ 13	$ 0	$150
Buffalo	46	5	262
Cincinnati	13	1	455
Cleveland	345	0	723
Milwaukee	96	3	533
Newark	29	239	503

Notes: *Includes construction of new sewer lines, further investment in treatment plants to meet ambient water quality standards, excludes investment to eliminate overflow and separate sanitary sewers from storm-water systems.

[a]Baltimore, Boston, Buffalo, Chicago, Cincinnati, Cleveland, Detroit, Milwaukee, Newark, New Orleans, New York, Philadelphia, Pittsburgh, St. Louis, San Francisco, Seattle, Washington.

[b]Albuquerque, Houston, Jacksonville, Memphis, Phoenix, San Antonio, San Diego.

Source: U.S. Environmental Protection Agency, compiled for 1976 Need Study in George E. Peterson, "Transmitting the Municipal Fiscal Squeeze to a New Generation of Taxpayers: Pension Obligations and Capital Investment Needs," in Robert Burchell and David Listokin (eds.), *Cities Under Stress: The Fiscal Crises of Urban America*, New Brunswick, New Jersey: Center for Urban Policy Research, 1981.

just to repair existing lines and connections, and another $63 was required to upgrade treatment facilities. This compared to an average per capita investment commitment need of $285 in growing cities. Of the intergovernmental cities, Baltimore and Buffalo required the least amount of upgrading. Newark, Cincinnati, Milwaukee, and Cleveland needed an enormous commitment of funds to improve outdated sewer systems. Moreover, each of these cities required extensive upgrading of treatment facilities as well as basic repairs in existing sewer lines and storm water systems.

Summary

Overall, as of the late 1970s, declining intergovernmental cities faced a tremendous need for current and future improvements in their capital plants. Of these,

Newark, Buffalo, and Cleveland needed very significant across-the-board spending commitments to bring their infrastructure up to par. Yet, these highly distressed cities were least likely to be able to undertake such improvements given necessary revenue channeling to basic operating functions. Today, the backlog of urgent projects in these cities is already vast and staggeringly expensive. For example, in 1978, Newark was placed under court order to bring its wastewater treatment facilities to current standards. At that time, it was estimated that such extensive improvement required local debt issuance almost four times as large as the entire debt limitation for the city as set down by the State of New Jersey. As of 1984, this upgrading has not been achieved. With large dependent populations, high unemployment, high crime rates and low incomes, declining intergovernmental cities have consistently denied resources to capital projects in order to shore up operational services. As intergovernmental resources become even more scarce, worsening infrastructure and more deteriorated capital plants can be expected for these cities.

Revenue Patterns in Intergovernmental Versus Non-Intergovernmental Cities

On the other side of the municipal budget is revenues. Briefly, the following discussion evaluates the changing revenue bases of intergovernmental versus non-intergovernmental cities by proceeding through analyses in three areas. First, changes in the tax base for the two classes of cities are delimited. Second, the impact of the municipal bond market on local finance is explored. Third, variations in the actual composition of the revenue base for intergovernmental and non-intergovernmental cities are examined.

Changes in the Assessed Value of the Tax Base

Changes in the local property tax base are central to the fiscal performance of any city. The value of taxable property reflects the vibrance of the local economy and provides a good indicator of fiscal health. In declining intergovernmental cities, private disinvestment has combined with municipal political fragmentation to usher in a prolonged period of rapidly diminishing taxable assets beginning in the 1960s. Since suburban jurisdictions are usually fiscally independent from older core communities, these cities must attempt to squeeze considerable amounts of revenue out of faltering local economies. The attendant inability of declining intergovernmental cities to generate adequate local revenue has, in turn, engendered increasing budgetary pressures and potential fiscal shortfalls.

Exhibits 7.8 and 7.9 detail changes in the assessed value of property for the twenty sample cities. These measures have been standardized for differences in assessment ratios and have been rendered in 1980 constant dollars to show actual changes in the value of assessments.

The trends observed for the tax bases of intergovernmental versus non-intergovernmental cities are striking. Over the past twenty years, older intergovernmental cities witnessed consistent attrition and staggering depreciation in the value of tax-

EXHIBIT 7.8.—*Changes in Property Tax Base: Market Value of Assessed Properties, 1960 to 1980 (in Millions of 1980 Constant Dollars)*

	1960	1970	1980	1960 to 1970 Absolute	1960 to 1970 Percent	1970 to 1980 Absolute	1970 to 1980 Percent	1960 to 1980 Absolute	1960 to 1980 Percent
INTERGOVERNMENTAL									
AKRON	3,631	3,877	2,768	+ 246	+ 6.8	- 1,109	- 28.6	- 863	- 23.8
BALTIMORE	7,743	7,681	7,529	+ 62	+ 0.7	- 152	- 1.9	- 214	- 2.7
BUFFALO	9,653	6,605	4,144	- 3,048	- 31.5	- 2,461	- 37.2	- 5,509	- 57.1
CINCINNATI	6,270	5,804	5,341	- 466	- 7.4	- 463	- 7.9	- 929	- 14.8
CLEVELAND	12,225	9,500	5,342	- 2,725	- 22.3	- 4,158	- 43.7	- 6,883	- 56.3
LOUISVILLE	3,378	3,690	2,695	- 188	- 4.8	- 995	- 27.0	- 1,183	- 30.4
MILWAUKEE	7,929	9,816	9,342	+ 1,887	+ 23.8	- 474	- 4.8	+ 1,413	+ 17.8
MINNEAPOLIS	8,997	7,636	7,309	- 1,361	- 15.1	- 327	- 4.3	- 1,688	- 18.8
NEWARK	3,288	3,421	1,064	+ 133	+ 4.0	- 2,357	- 68.9	- 2,224	- 67.6
ROCHESTER	3,587	4,693	3,507	+ 1,106	+ 30.8	- 1,186	- 25.3	- 80	- 2.2
TOTAL	67,200	62,723	49,042	- 4,477	- 6.7	- 13,681	- 21.8	- 18,158	- 27.0
MEAN N=10 cities	6,720	6,272	4,904	- 448	- 6.7	- 1,368	- 21.8	- 1,816	- 27.0
NON-INTERGOVERNMENTAL									
ANAHEIM	295	1,353	NA	+ 1,058	+359.0	NA	NA	NA	NA
AUSTIN	NA	NA	NA	NA	NA	NA	NA	NA	NA
BATON ROUGE	NA	NA	NA	NA	NA	NA	NA	NA	NA
COLUMBUS	5,146	6,936	8,456	+ 1,790	+ 34.8	+ 1,520	+ 21.9	+ 3,310	+ 64.3
NASHVILLE-DAVIDSON	1,519	7,133	8,464	+ 5,614	+369.6	+ 1,331	+ 18.6	+ 6,945	+457.1
OKLAHOMA CITY	3,106	3,781	4,672	+ 675	+ 21.7	+ 891	+ 23.6	+ 1,566	+ 50.4
SAN JOSE	NA	NA	12,034	NA	NA	NA	NA	NA	NA
TULSA	2,938	4,949	5,459	+ 2,011	+ 68.4	+ 510	+ 10.3	+ 2,521	+ 85.8
VIRGINIA BEACH	NA	2,346	7,318	NA	NA	+ 4,972	+212.0	NA	NA
WICHITA	2,539	2,815	4,009	+ 276	+ 10.9	+ 1,194	+ 42.4	+ 1,470	+ 57.9
TOTAL	15,249	27,960	38,378	+12,711	+ 83.4	+10,418	+ 37.3	+23,129	+151.7
MEAN N=6 cities	2,541	4,640	6,396	+ 2,099	+ 83.4	+ 1,756	+ 37.3	+ 3,855	+151.7

Note: These measures have been adjusted to reflect standardized market values of assessments. Assessment ratios were taken from U.S. Department of Commerce, Bureau of Census, Governments Division. Assessment (sales-price) ratios were adapted from U.S. Department of Commerce, Bureau of Census, Census of Governments, Volume 2, "Taxable Property Values and Assessment Sales Price Ratios." 1967, 1972, 1975. Constant dollar adjustments were made by using the Consumer Price Index (CPI) for all urban areas, as cited in U.S. Department of Commerce, Statistical Abstract of the United States 1980, Table No. 81, "Consumer Price Indexes -- Selected Cities of SMSA's:1960-1979.Bureau of Census, Moody's Municipal and Governmental Manual, 1960, 1970, 1980.

Source: Moody's Investor Service: <u>Moody's Municipal and Governmental Manual</u>, 1960, 1970, 1980.

EXHIBIT 7.9.—*Changes in Property Tax Base: Market Value of Assessed Properties, 1960 to 1980 (Per Capita, in 1980 Constant Dollars)*

	1960	1970	1980	1960 to 1970 Absolute	1960 to 1970 Percent	1970 to 1980 Absolute	1970 to 1980 Percent	1960 to 1980 Absolute	1960 to 1980 Percent
INTERGOVERNMENTAL									
AKRON	12,520.16	14,098.60	11,679.82	+1578.44	+ 12.6	-2418.78	-17.2	- 840.34	- 6.7
BALTIMORE	8,245.64	8,477.76	9,566.49	+ 232.12	+ 2.8	+1088.73	+12.8	+1320.85	+16.0
BUFFALO	18,145.06	14,465.57	11,575.78	-3679.49	- 20.3	-2889.79	-20.0	-6569.28	-36.2
CINCINNATI	12,489.90	12,784.64	13,873.31	+ 294.74	+ 2.4	+1088.67	+ 8.5	+1383.41	+11.0
CLEVELAND	13,955.93	12,649.91	9,306.82	-1306.02	- 9.4	-3343.09	-26.4	-4649.11	-33.3
LOUISVILLE	9,943.51	10,194.60	9,044.41	+ 251.09	+ 2.5	-1150.19	-11.3	- 899.10	- 9.0
MILWAUKEE	10,699.91	13,690.51	14,688.39	+2990.60	+ 27.9	+ 997.88	+ 7.2	+3988.48	+37.3
MINNEAPOLIS	18,666.45	17,595.03	19,754.09	-1071.42	- 5.7	+2169.06	+12.3	+1087.64	+ 5.8
NEWARK	8,118.01	8,953.14	3,233.85	+ 835.13	+ 10.3	-5719.29	- 6.3	-4884.16	-60.1
ROCHESTER	11,279.42	15,906.80	14,511.42	+4627.38	+ 41.0	-1395.38	- 8.8	+3232.00	+28.7
WEIGHTED MEAN N=10 cities	12,274.06	12,477.45	11,632.33	+ 203.39	+ 1.7	- 815.12	- 6.5	- 641.73	- 5.2
NON-INTERGOVERNMENTAL									
ANAHEIM	2,835.45	8,153.27	NA	+5317.82	+187.5	NA	NA	NA	NA
AUSTIN	NA	NA	NA	NA	NA	NA	NA	NA	NA
BATON ROUGE	NA	NA	NA	NA	NA	NA	NA	NA	NA
COLUMBUS	10,926.51	12,843.66	14,966.73	+1917.15	+ 17.5	+2123.07	+ 16.5	+4040.22	+ 37.0
NASHVILLE-DAVIDSON	8,884.19	15,994.35	18,560.42	+7110.16	+ 80.0	+2566.07	+ 16.0	+9676.23	+108.9
OKLAHOMA CITY	9,587.40	10,273.13	11,592.68	+ 685.73	+ 7.1	+1319.55	+ 12.8	+2005.28	+ 20.9
SAN JOSE	NA	NA	18,891.16	NA	NA	NA	NA	NA	NA
TULSA	11,215.06	14,996.87	15,121.46	+3781.81	+ 33.7	+ 124.59	+ 0.8	+3906.40	+ 34.8
VIRGINIA BEACH	NA	13,637.74	27,931.18	NA	NA	+14293.44	+104.8	NA	NA
WICHITA	9,955.06	10,164.25	14,369.65	+ 209.19	+ 2.1	+4205.4	+ 41.4	+4414.59	+ 44.3
WEIGHTED MEAN N=6 cities	10,227.22	13,108.17	16,499.38	+2280.95	+ 28.2	+3391.21	+25.9	+6272.16	+ 61.3

Note: These measures have been adjusted to reflect standardized market values of assessed properties. Assessment ratios were taken from U.S. Department of Commerce, Bureau of Census, Census of Governments, Volume 2, "Taxable Property Values and Assessment Sales Price Ratios." 1961, 1972, 1977.

Source: Moody's Investor Service: Moody's Municipal and Governmental Manual 1960, 1970, 1980.

able properties. At the same time, growing non-intergovernmental cities saw unrelenting expansion of their tax roles. In 1960, the assessed value of all residential property in aging intergovernmental cities was, on average, much higher than that for non-intergovernmental cities ($6.7 versus $2.5 billion). This differential was narrowed over the course of the 1970s: by 1980, the average assessed value of all property in growing non-intergovernmental cities substantially outdistanced the average valuation of intergovernmental cities ($4.7 versus $6.3 billion).

On average then, in real dollars, declining cities lost $1.8 billion in assessed property value since 1960, fully 27 percent of their assessed valuation. By far, the most dramatic losses occurred in Cleveland and Buffalo. These cities each lost more than 55 percent of their assessed value in 1960 ($6.9 billion and $5.5 billion respectively). Additionally, Newark lost over $2.2 billion in assessments, nearly 70 percent of the assessed value of its tax base in 1960. Akron, Cincinnati, Louisville, and Milwaukee have also lost substantial amounts of assessed property. Of the intergovernmental cities, Baltimore and Rochester retained basically stable assessment totals; only Milwaukee witnessed sizeable increases in the total value of its assessments.

The situation, as of 1980, for vibrant non-intergovernmental cities was striking by comparison. These cities, on average, added $3.9 billion in assessed property value. This represents a twenty-year growth rate in excess of 150 percent. Here, the two cities which annexed most extensively since the 1960s, Nashville and Virginia Beach, showed by far the greatest gains in assessed valuations. Assessed valuations also rose substantially in all of the remaining non-intergovernmental cities.

The Shrinking Tax Base of an Intergovernmental
City: The Case of Newark, New Jersey

Changes in the property tax base for Newark, New Jersey, are detailed in Exhibit 7.10. While Newark may not be the prototype of the declining intergovernmental city, it certainly represents the type of change taking place in this class of cities.

Newark's property tax base was severely impacted over the last two decades. Since 1968, almost 10,000 pieces of property were lost from the city's tax roles. For the most part, this drop represented residential properties which fell into tax delinquency and were abandoned by private owners. These properties, including cleared vacant land, were transferred to local government and granted tax-exempt status. As the bulk of property ownership in Newark became public, the number of properties on the city's exempt list shot upward.

In 1982, 8,387 properties fell under non-taxable status, an increase of 300 percent (6,464 parcels) since the late 1960s. Today, 1984, a full 20 percent of all real estate in Newark is exempt from taxation.

With thousands of formerly improved parcels off the tax roles, Newark lost much in the way of assessed valuation. In 1968, there were 48,487 real estate parcels in the city assessed at $4.4 billion dollars. By 1980, only 38,939 properties remained, valued at $1.7 billion. Not including inflation, since 1968—through property attrition and depreciation of value—Newark lost nearly $2.7 billion in assessments, a full 60 percent of its total valuation.

In 1984, tax-exempt property comprises over 20 percent of the city's real estate parcels, up from just 6.5 percent in 1970. In terms of assessments, this shift is even

EXHIBIT 7.10. — *Trends in Newark, New Jersey's Property Tax Base, 1970-1980*

TAXABLE REAL ESTATE

	1968	1970	1975	1980	Change	Percent
- Number of Properties	48,487	46,334	42,155	38,939	-9,548	-19.7
- Assessed Valuation* (millions of dollars)	4,426	3,640	2,512	1,737	-2,689	-60.8

NON-TAXABLE REAL ESTATE

	1965	1970	1975	1980	Change	Percent
- Number of Properties	1,923	3,234	6,429	8,387	+6,464	+336.1
- Assessed Valuation* (millions of dollars)	1,705	1,911	1,913	2,385	+ 680	+ 39.8

TOTAL REAL ESTATE

	1970	1975	1980	Change	Percent
- Number of Properties	49,568	48,584	27,326	-2,242	- 4.5
- Assessed Valuation* (millions of dollars)	5,551	4,425	4,122	-1,429	- 25.8

PERCENT NON-TAXABLE

	1970	1975	1980	Percent Change
- Of Total Properties	6.5	15.2	21.5	+15.0
- Of Total Assessed Valuation	34.4	43.2	57.9	+23.5

RATIO: NON-TAXABLE TO TAXABLE (based on assessed valuation)

	1970	1975	1980	Change
	.525	.761	1.373	+.848

Note: *Assessed valuation of property has been adjusted to reflect real market value of property and to show change in constant dollars. Equalization ratios were adapted from U.S. Department of Commerce, Bureau of Census, Census of Governments Volume 2, "Taxable Property Values and Assessment Sales-Price Ratios," 1967, 1972, 1977. Constant dollar adjustments were made by using the Consumer Price Index for all urban areas, as cited in U.S. Department of Commerce, Bureau of Census, Statistical Abstract of the United States, 1980, Table No. 811, "Consumer Price Indexes -- Selected Cities of SMSA's: 1960-1979."

Source: City of Newark, *Special Reports*, 1981.

more dramatic. Today, nearly 60 percent of the assessed value of property in Newark is nontaxable. This represents a 24 percent increase since 1970. The assessed value of Newark's tax-exempt property currently exceeds the value of its taxable property by a considerable margin.

Summary

Differentials in economic performance have framed trends in the value of taxable property for the two classes of cities. Growing non-intergovernmental cities—distinguished by vibrance in all sectors of their economies—witnessed dramatic expansions in the value of taxable assets. In aging intergovernmental cities, however, private disinvestment left property values reeling. As the property tax levy ceased to function, these cities were left to the insurmountable task of meeting rapidly escalating expenditures with sorely depleted revenues.

The Municipal Bond Market and the Cost of Credit

The loss of economic function in declining intergovernmental cities and the pressing fiscal problems that accompanied it not only weakened their property tax bases, but held onerous consequences for their participation in the municipal bond market as well. By the mid-1970s, as John Petersen demonstrated, several factors converged to cause major borrowing difficulties for older declining cities.[4] Institutional investors became increasingly alarmed over the credit conditions of these cities, and, in particular, about their ability and willingness to repay privately financed loans in the face of chronic economic and fiscal deterioration. Such doubts among lenders were compounded by uncertainties regarding the legal responsibilities for disclosure of a city's fiscal status. Related fears also surfaced over the enforceability of bond holder repayment against competing claims in the case of default (i.e., employee wages, outstanding bills, pensions, etc.). While the position of older cities in the municipal bond market was declining for years, the steep recession of 1974–75, and New York City's "fiscal crisis" abruptly brought this deteriorating situation to a head.

By 1976, the credit ratings of many declining cities started to plummet. At this time, several major big-city borrowers were either entirely excluded from the tax-exempt market or forced to pay very high rates of interest to borrow. A sharp division between stronger and weaker borrowers, analogous to growing and declining cities, emerged. The municipal bond market was effectively split into two mutually exclusive tiers: one characterized by low credit costs and high degrees of liquidity; the other distinguished by hard-to-get and expensive credit.

Exhibit 7.11 presents a summary of the distribution of Moody's bond ratings for our twenty sample cities between 1960 and 1980. Over the entire period and especially during the 1970–1980 subcomponent, two general trends stood out. On the one hand, the bond ratings for declining intergovernmental cities, in a number of cases, moved consistently downward, or in the remaining cases, remained constant. This produced lower levels of liquidity and higher costs of credit for these cities. On the other hand, the position of growing non-intergovernmental cities in the municipal

EXHIBIT 7.11. — *Moody's Municipal Bond Ratings: General Obligation Bonds, 1960–1980*

	1960	1970	1976	1980	Rating Change: 1970-80
INTERGOVERNMENTAL					
AKRON	Aa	A	Aa	Aa	Upgraded
BALTIMORE	Aa	A	A1	A1	Slightly Upgraded
BUFFALO	Aaa	Aa	Ba	Baa	Downgraded
CINCINNATI	Aaa	Aa	Aa	Aa	Unchanged
CLEVELAND	Aa	A	A	Caa	Downgraded
LOUISVILLE	Aa	Aa	Aa	Aa	Unchanged
MILWAUKEE	Aaa	Aaa	Aaa	Aaa	Unchanged
MINNEAPOLIS	A	Aaa	Aa	Aaa	Unchanged
NEWARK	A	Baa	Baa	Baa	Unchanged
ROCHESTER	Aaa	Aaa	Aaa	Aa	Downgraded

MEDIAN RATING: Aa - Unchanged

	1960	1970	1976	1980	Rating Change: 1970-80
NON-INTERGOVERNMENTAL					
ANAHEIM	A	Baa	A1	A1	Upgraded
AUSTIN	A	Aa	Aaa	Aaa	Upgraded
BATON ROUGE	Baa	Baa	Baa	Baa1	Slightly Upgraded
COLUMBUS	Aa	Aa	Aa	Aa	Unchanged
NASHVILLE-DAVIDSON	Aa	Aa	Aa	Aa	Upgraded
OKLAHOMA CITY	A	A	Aa	Aa	Upgraded
SAN JOSE	Aa	A1	Aa	Aa	Upgraded
TULSA	A	A	A1	Aa	Upgraded
VIRGINIA BEACH	Baa	A	Aa	Aa	Upgraded
WICHITA	A	A1	Aa	Aa	Upgraded

MEDIAN RATING: Aa - Upgraded

Source: Moody's Investor Service, Moody's Municipal and Governmental Manual, 1960, 1970, 1976, 1980.

bond market consistently moved upward. As of 1980, these cities possessed better access to credit and reduced credit costs.

More importantly, at the same time that the position of older cities in the bond market slipped, conditions peculiar to the market itself caused the point spread separating the major rating categories to widen. Consequently, the cost of credit separating low level (Baa) from high level (Aaa) bonds increased substantially. By early 1976, the point spread between these two rating categories rose to an astronomical 374 points (Exhibit 7.12). Since each 100 points corresponds to 1 percent of interest, a spread of 374 points means that cities with bond ratings of Baa pay approximately 3.7 percent more in interest than cities with Aaa ratings. For example, if the prevailing interest is 15 percent, cities with Baa ratings pay approximately 18.7 percent interest on loans; if the prevailing interest rate happens to be 18 percent, cities with Baa ratings pay 21.7 percent. Simply put, as credit markets tighten, typically in response to recession or restrictive monetary policy, cities whose bond ratings fall, even if only slightly, suffer disproportionately in terms of escalating

EXHIBIT 7.12. — *Fluctuations in Point Spreads for Municipal Bonds,
1976–1978**

	MOODY RATING				Cumulative Point Spread Baa- Aaa
	Aaa	Aa	A	Baa	
1976					
First quarter	-94	-20	NA	270	374
Second quarter	-72	-31	22	231	303
Third quarter	-82	-51	32	130	202
Fourth quarter	-89	-42	-25	NA	NA
1977					
First quarter	-52	-34	10	121	173
Second quarter	-43	-24	3	128	171
Third quarter	-19	-29	-17	NA	NA
Fourth quarter	-46	-29	-7	95	141
1978					
First half	-56	-32	-6	27	83
Second half	-62	-37	-38	56	118

*Spread between 20-year reoffering yield and bond buyer index.

Note: Based on 148 general obligation bond sales among the largest 100 cities
in the United States. Point spreads represent first quarterly averages
for 1976 and 1977, and semiannual averages for 1978.

Source: John E. Petersen, "Big City Borrowing Costs and Credit Quality," in
Robert W. Burchell and David Listokin, Cities Under Stress: The
Fiscal Crises of Urban America, New Brunswick, New Jersey: Center
for Urban Policy Research, 1981.

credit costs. (See Exhibit 7.13 for fluctuations in average bond yields between 1960
and 1980.)

Higher credit costs not only impair a city's access to credit, but slipping bond
ratings send signals to a host of actors outside the bond market. Consistent reductions in bond ratings indicate loss of confidence in the city's credit worthiness and
overall fiscal situation. This conjures up visions of imminent bankruptcy, setting off
creditors and municipal employees to demand immediate payments. Such increased
pressure to pay bills can further erode the city's fiscal balance and lead to even
greater slippage in bond ratings.

Lastly, the prevailing Moody's bond ratings for declining cities are, in effect,
premised on constant flows of intergovernmental transfers to these communities.
Since intergovernmental aid is a recognized source of revenue for cities, their
Moody's ratings are propped up by their reliance on intergovernmental transfers.
Thus, an abrupt halt in the flow of federal or state aid to declining cities would fur-

EXHIBIT 7.13. — *Fluctuations in Average Bond Yields, 1960–1980*

	Average Yield	AAA	AA	A	BAA	Cumulative Spread	Point Spread
1960	3.92	3.49	3.73	4.02	4.43	0.94	94
1970	6.74	6.38	6.60	6.88	7.13	0.75	75
1976	7.04	6.16	6.60	7.59	7.78	1.62	162
1980	9.88	9.44	9.64	9.80	10.64	1.20	120

Source: Moody's Investor Service: Moody's Municipal and Government Manual, 1960, 1970, 1976, 1980.

ther erode their position in the bond market. This could easily trigger a series of substantial defaults, and cause severe disruption in the market itself.

The Composition of the Revenue Base

It is now necessary to turn to the actual composition of the revenue base for intergovernmental and non-intergovernmental cities. Exhibit 7.14 presents a broad overview of trends in the composition of local revenues for both classes of cities. These trends are then discussed in detail in the sections which follow. Here, general revenues are broken down into basic sub-categories: intergovernmental (federal and state) versus own-source (taxes, miscellaneous revenues and user charges); and also as revenues flowing directly to municipal government versus revenues directed to school districts. This line of analysis is helpful in clarifying long-run variations in the distribution of intergovernmental revenue; it is also useful for isolating more subtle differences in revenue emphases.

Trends in General Revenue

As of 1979, despite rapidly deteriorating tax bases and an increasingly expensive market for municipal credit, aging intergovernmental cities continued to raise considerably more general revenue than economically robust non-intergovernmental cities. This stemmed both from the higher expenditure and service requirements faced by these declining communities, and from the differential flow of intergovernmental transfers. As Exhibit 7.14 shows, eight of ten intergovernmental cities raised in excess of $1000 per capita in general revenues, while only one non-intergovernmental city—Baton Rouge—generated this level of revenue. Overall, intergovernmental cities raised nearly 30 percent more in general revenue than non-intergovernmental cities.

EXHIBIT 7.14.—*Detailed Dollar Distribution of Per Capita Revenues by Source, 1979*
(Includes Both Municipal and School District Revenue)

	Total General Revenue	INTERGOVERNMENTAL REVENUES			OWN-SOURCE REVENUES					
		All	From Federal	From State	All	Taxes	Property Tax	Sales Tax	Income Tax	Charges and Miscellaneous
INTERGOVERNMENTAL										
AKRON	939.71	430.79	157.65	264.79	508.92	373.99	223.78	0.46	136.24	134.93
BALTIMORE	1382.87	817.03	264.97	544.58	565.84	423.72	269.67	41.02	96.96	142.12
BUFFALO	1186.12	788.26	240.34	451.67	397.85	276.27	245.98	24.16	-	121.58
CINCINNATI	1246.70	527.68	183.97	256.28	719.02	448.45	202.54	3.66	226.60	270.57
CLEVELAND	1254.99	592.69	141.72	449.43	662.30	470.55	304.17	2.56	158.42	191.75
LOUISVILLE	832.26	409.25	220.98	162.55	423.01	326.73	126.01	12.10	149.29	96.28
MILWAUKEE	1003.21	529.77	68.00	455.27	473.44	332.12	325.94	1.93	135.69	141.34
MINNEAPOLIS	1057.55	525.52	145.68	366.89	532.03	366.25	330.97	20.60	-	165.78
NEWARK	1189.14	808.01	77.01	725.19	381.13	320.32	211.00	83.82	-	60.81
ROCHESTER	1177.42	660.93	206.58	279.20	516.49	387.28	362.73	19.70	-	129.21
WEIGHTED MEAN N=10	1159.80	628.55	171.41	424.47	531.25	381.16	268.13	21.03	98.15	150.09
NON-INTERGOVERNMENTAL										
ANAHEIM	746.60	361.25	43.63	294.91	385.35	234.88	136.73	87.75	-	150.47
AUSTIN	795.49	256.95	74.35	177.54	538.53	315.73	253.52	56.58	-	222.80
BATON ROUGE	1188.08	532.87	203.07	328.20	655.21	490.47	152.36	228.82	-	163.84
COLUMBUS	796.76	330.00	99.82	221.93	466.76	302.46	156.51	2.18	138.08	164.30
NASHVILLE-DAVIDSON	909.04	318.20	138.12	176.62	590.84	381.76	230.69	120.25	-	209.08
OKLAHOMA CITY	798.42	320.23	171.41	141.10	478.19	306.54	147.19	153.03	-	171.65
SAN JOSE	850.50	412.66	31.21	364.26	437.84	285.55	162.70	49.57	-	152.29
TULSA	802.11	253.03	92.47	149.74	549.08	310.03	155.53	146.97	-	239.07
VIRGINIA BEACH	711.49	293.28	61.55	228.41	418.21	304.00	172.36	96.08	-	114.21
WICHITA	914.21	349.89	119.42	217.35	564.32	307.66	277.15	24.01	-	256.66
WEIGHTED MEAN N=10	842.74	340.22	98.96	228.84	502.79	319.10	183.09	86.25	20.01	183.62

Note: For a discussion of compilation of revenue data, especially for school districts, see Appendix.

Source: U.S. Department of Commerce, Bureau of Census, Census of Governments, <u>Government Finances</u> (annual report), 1979.

Total general revenues also rose at a slightly faster pace in intergovernmental than in non-intergovernmental cities. From 1962 to 1979, general revenues in these older cities increased by more than 455 percent from $210 to $1,150 per capita. In contrast, total general revenues in younger non-intergovernmental cities rose by 373 percent, from $78 to $843 per capita. For both classes of cities, the largest component increases occurred during the 1970s, a period of time of significant growth in municipal local taxes and charges.

Own-Source Revenue

Non-intergovernmental cities, characterized by vibrant local economies and expanding tax bases, increased locally raised revenues at a slightly faster pace than intergovernmental cities. However, despite the fact that the latter group benefitted from much greater amounts of federal and state aid, declining intergovernmental cities continued to raise larger per capita amounts of own-source revenue. Between 1962 and 1979, both classes of cities increased locally raised revenues by approximately the same amount, $378 dollars per capita. However, own-source collections in non-intergovernmental cities increased by 305 percent compared to 246 percent in intergovernmental cities. Indeed, own-source collections in non-intergovernmental cities gained most dramatically during the 1970s. During this decade, these revenues caught up with own-source revenues raised in declining cities. As of 1979, intergovernmental cities raised slightly more revenue locally ($531 versus $502 per capita) than non-intergovernmental cities. This should be viewed in the context that, on average, their expenditures were 50 percent more.

It is now important to look briefly at the basic subcomponents of own-source revenue: tax collections and revenues from user charges and miscellaneous sources. While total tax collections for both classes of cities increased by approximately the same amount and at nearly the same rate, non-intergovernmental cities increased revenues raised from user charges and other miscellaneous sources at a much faster pace than intergovernmental cities. Between 1962 and 1979, per capita tax collections in intergovernmental cities rose by 214 percent ($259) compared to a similar increase of 255 percent ($229) for non-intergovernmental cities. In percentage terms, non-intergovernmental cities raised approximately 38 percent of total revenues from taxes compared to 33 percent for intergovernmental cities. In dollar terms, intergovernmental cities raised considerably more revenue from taxes than non-intergovernmental cities, $381 versus $319 per capita.

Taxes

The tax base structures of the two classes of cities differ quite substantially. Intergovernmental cities are generally more dependent on revenue from taxes than non-intergovernmental cities. As Exhibits 7.14 and 7.15 show, in 1979, these cities generated an average of $268 per capita or over half of locally raised revenue from the property tax (Exhibit 7.16). Non-intergovernmental cities generated significantly less revenue and a smaller proportion of own-source revenue from the property tax. Many intergovernmental cities—Akron, Baltimore, Cincinnati, Cleveland,

EXHIBIT 7.15. — *Detailed Percent Distribution of Revenues, by Source, 1979*
(Includes Both Municipal and School District Data)

	Total General Revenue	INTERGOVERNMENTAL REVENUES			OWN-SOURCE REVENUES					
		All	From Federal	From State	All	Taxes	Property Tax	Sales Tax	Income Tax	Charges and Miscellaneous
INTERGOVERNMENTAL										
AKRON	100.00	45.84	16.78	28.18	54.16	39.80	23.81	0.05	14.50	14.36
BALTIMORE	100.00	59.08	19.16	39.38	40.92	30.64	19.51	2.97	6.66	10.28
BUFFALO	100.00	66.46	20.26	38.08	33.54	23.29	20.74	1.19	-	10.25
CINCINNATI	100.00	42.33	14.76	20.56	57.67	35.97	16.25	0.29	18.18	21.70
CLEVELAND	100.00	47.23	11.29	35.81	52.77	37.49	24.24	0.20	12.62	15.28
LOUISVILLE	100.00	49.17	26.55	19.53	50.83	39.26	15.14	14.55	17.94	11.57
MILWAUKEE	100.00	52.81	6.78	45.38	47.19	33.11	32.49	1.43	13.53	14.09
MINNEAPOLIS	100.00	49.69	13.78	34.69	50.13	34.63	31.30	1.95	-	15.68
NEWARK	100.00	67.95	6.53	60.98	32.05	26.94	17.74	7.05	-	5.11
ROCHESTER	100.00	56.13	17.55	23.71	43.87	32.89	30.81	1.67	-	10.97
WEIGHTED MEAN N=10	100.00	54.19 (100.00)	14.80 (32.50)	36.60 (67.50)	45.81 (100.00)	32.86 (71.75)	23.12 (50.47)	1.81 (3.95)	8.46 (18.45)	12.94 (28.25)
NON-INTERGOVERNMENTAL										
ANAHEIM	100.00	48.39	5.84	39.50	51.61	31.46	18.31	11.75	-	20.15
AUSTIN	100.00	32.30	9.35	22.32	67.70	39.69	31.87	7.11	-	28.00
BATON ROUGE	100.00	44.85	17.09	27.62	55.15	41.28	12.82	19.26	-	13.79
COLUMBUS	100.00	41.42	12.53	27.85	58.58	37.96	19.64	0.27	17.33	20.62
NASHVILLE-DAVIDSON	100.00	35.00	15.20	19.43	65.00	42.00	25.36	13.23	-	23.00
OKLAHOMA CITY	100.00	40.11	21.47	17.67	59.89	38.40	18.44	19.17	-	21.50
SAN JOSE	100.00	48.52	3.67	42.83	51.48	33.59	19.13	5.83	-	17.91
TULSA	100.00	31.55	11.53	18.67	68.45	38.65	19.39	18.32	-	29.80
VIRGINIA BEACH	100.00	41.22	8.65	32.10	58.78	42.73	24.23	13.51	-	16.05
WICHITA	100.00	38.27	13.06	23.77	61.73	33.65	30.32	2.63	-	28.07
WEIGHTED MEAN N=10	100.00	40.35 (100.00)	11.74 (32.50)	27.15 (67.50)	59.65 (100.00)	37.86 (63.42)	21.73 (36.43)	10.23 (17.10)	2.47 (3.97)	21.79 (36.38)

Note: For a discussion of compilation of revenue data, especially for school districts, see Appendix.

Source: U.S. Department of Commerce, Bureau of Census, Census of Governments, Government Finances (annual report), 1979.

Louisville, and Milwaukee—also raised considerable revenues through local income tax levies. On average, income taxes represented close to 20 percent of locally raised revenues. Of the non-intergovernmental cities, only Columbus employed a similar levy. However, non-intergovernmental cities generated about four times as much local revenue via local sales taxes, $86 versus $21 per capita. Here, the percentage share contrasts are very striking. Non-intergovernmental cities raised over 17 percent of local revenue from the sales tax while intergovernmental cities raised less than 4 percent from such levies. In intergovernmental cities property and income taxes represented 70 percent of own-source revenues; in non-intergovernmental cities, the figure was barely 40 percent. Obviously, a tax on retail sales in declining cities cannot support local public services whereas in growth locations it can. Where it cannot be counted on for support it must be augmented with an income tax, user charges or other miscellaneous revenues.

User Charges and Miscellaneous Revenues

The last category of own-source revenues comprises all local resources raised from user charges and miscellaneous revenues. As of 1979, non-intergovernmental cities earned more local revenue from these sources. These cities raised $183 per capita from user charges and miscellaneous revenues, while intergovernmental cities raised slightly over $150. User charges and miscellaneous revenues accounted for nearly 22 percent of all revenues raised in non-intergovernmental cities and only half that rate in intergovernmental cities (Exhibit 7.16). Over the past two decades, revenues from these sources increased by 435 percent in non-intergovernmental cities, and at a much more sluggish rate in intergovernmental cities.

Trends in Intergovernmental Revenue

Although both classes of cities have increased their reliance on intergovernmental transfers, declining intergovernmental cities have done so to a much greater extent. In 1962, both groups of cities received comparable amounts of per capita federal and state aid. By 1979, however, intergovernmental cities increased their reliance on intergovernmental transfers by over tenfold compared to an increase of approximately one-half that rate for non-intergovernmental cities. During the 1960s, per capita transfers flowing to these declining cities doubled, increasing from just $55 per capita in 1962 to $104 per capita in 1967. By 1972, the flow of intergovernmental resources doubled again, increasing to $245 per capita. Over the course of the 1970s, the flow of transfers to intergovernmental cities nearly quadrupled the 1967 rate, rising to $628 per capita by 1979 (Exhibit 7.16). This represented a cumulative increase of $573 in intergovernmental cities compared to an increase of just $286 in non-intergovernmental cities. As of the beginning of the 1980s, intergovernmental cities received more than double the amount of combined federal and state transfers than those flowing to non-intergovernmental cities.[5]

Exhibit 7.17 details trends in intergovernmental transfers for each of the twenty sample cities. From 1962 to 1979, the flow of intergovernmental transfers to Newark increased most dramatically. Here, intergovernmental transfers rose from just $25

EXHIBIT 7.16.—*Trends in Revenues, Intergovernmental Versus Non-Intergovernmental Cities, 1962-1979 (in Dollars Per Capita)*

	1962	1967	1972	1979	1962-1967 Absolute	Percent	1967-1972 Absolute	Percent	1972-1979 Absolute	Percent	1962-1979 Absolute	Percent
ALL GENERAL REVENUE												
- Intergovernmental	208.95	318.94	584.85	1159.80	+109.99	+ 52.6	+265.91	+ 83.4	+ 574.95	+ 98.3	+950.85	+455.1
- Non-intergovernmental	177.96	236.84	387.86	842.74	+ 58.88	+ 33.1	+151.02	+ 63.7	+ 454.88	+117.3	+644.78	+373.6
ALL INTERGOVERNMENTAL REVENUE												
- Intergovernmental	55.50	103.95	244.44	628.55	+ 48.45	+ 87.3	+140.49	+135.2	+ 384.11	+157.2	+573.05	+1032.6
- Non-intergovernmental	53.96	74.97	130.64	340.22	+ 21.01	+ 38.9	+ 55.67	+ 74.3	+ 209.58	+160.4	+286.26	+ 530.5
FROM FEDERAL SOURCES												
- Intergovernmental	11.37	22.20	50.32	171.41	+ 10.83	+ 95.3	+ 28.12	+126.7	+121.09	+240.6	+160.04	+1407.6
- Non-intergovernmental	9.59	10.95	32.58	98.96	+ 1.36	+ 14.2	+ 21.63	+197.5	+ 66.38	+203.7	+ 89.37	+ 931.9
FROM STATE SOURCES												
- Intergovernmental	44.13	78.68	193.05	424.74	+ 34.55	+ 78.3	+114.37	+145.4	+231.69	+120.0	+380.61	+ 862.5
- Non-intergovernmental	40.82	60.01	92.46	228.84	+ 19.19	+ 47.0	+ 32.45	+ 54.1	+136.38	+147.5	+188.02	+ 460.1
OWN-SOURCE REVENUES												
- Intergovernmental	153.45	214.99	340.41	531.25	+ 61.54	+ 40.1	+125.42	+ 58.3	+190.84	+ 56.1	+377.80	+ 246.2
- Non-intergovernmental	124.00	161.87	256.38	502.79	+ 37.87	+ 30.5	+ 94.51	+ 58.4	+246.41	+ 96.1	+378.79	+ 305.5
ALL TAX REVENUES												
- Intergovernmental	121.47	164.71	222.90	381.16	+ 43.24	+ 35.6	+ 58.19	+ 35.4	+158.26	+ 71.0	+259.69	+ 213.8
- Non-intergovernmental	89.69	118.73	194.43	319.10	+ 29.04	+ 32.4	+ 75.70	+ 63.8	+124.67	+ 64.1	+229.41	+ 255.8

Source: See bottom of next page.

Exhibit 7.16 (Continued)

ALL CHARGES												
- Intergovernmental	31.98	50.28	80.93	150.09	+ 18.30	+ 57.2	+ 30.65	+61.0	+ 69.16	+85.5	+118.02	+ 369.0
- Non-intergovernmental	34.30	42.74	61.95	183.67	+ 8.44	+ 24.6	+ 19.21	+44.9	+121.72	+196.5	+149.37	+ 435.5
MUNICIPAL REVENUE												
- Intergovernmental	168.19	252.08	465.86	694.95	+83.89	+49.9	+213.78	+84.8	+229.09	+ 49.2	+526.76	+ 313.2
- Non-intergovernmental	81.27	107.38	191.69	481.75	+26.11	+32.1	+ 84.31	+78.5	+290.06	+151.3	+400.48	+ 492.8
SCHOOL DISTRICT REVENUE*												
- Intergovernmental	69.70	112.21	118.93	464.64	+42.51	+61.0	+ 6.72	+ 6.0	+345.71	+290.7	+394.94	+ 566.6
- Non-intergovernmental	99.23	142.85	208.67	280.47	+43.62	+44.0	+ 65.82	+46.1	+ 71.80	+ 34.4	+181.24	+ 182.6
MUNICIPAL INTERGOVERNMENTAL												
- Intergovernmental	48.49	86.08	208.04	350.65	+37.57	+77.5	+121.98	+141.7	+142.61	+ 68.5	+302.16	+ 623.1
- Non-intergovernmental	19.08	25.37	54.16	136.27	+ 6.29	+33.0	+ 28.79	+113.5	+ 82.11	+151.6	+117.19	+ 614.2
SCHOOL INTERGOVERNMENTAL*												
- Intergovernmental	13.53	30.00	36.39	301.57	+16.47	+121.7	+ 6.39	+ 21.3	+265.18	+728.7	+288.04	+2128.9
- Non-intergovernmental	36.85	57.85	86.33	218.13	+21.00	+ 57.0	+ 28.48	+ 49.2	+131.80	+152.7	+181.28	+ 491.9

*School District totals for 1962, 1967 and 1972 based on a sample of six intergovernmental cities (N=6) and seven non-intergovernmental cities (N=7). For 1979 sample equals ten cities (N=10); for each group, see Appendix.

Source: U.S. Department of Commerce, Bureau of Census, Census of Governments, 1962, 1967, 1972. Government Finances (annual report), 1979.

EXHIBIT 7.17. — *The Growth in Intergovernmental Revenues, 1962-1979*
(in Dollars Per Capita)

	Intergovernmental Revenue				1962-1967		1967-1972		1972-1979		1962-1979	
	1962	1967	1972	1979	Absolute	Percent	Absolute	Percent	Absolute	Percent	Absolute	Percent
INTERGOVERNMENTAL												
AKRON	48.28	46.04	95.08	430.29	- 2.24	- 4.6	+ 49.04	+106.5	+335.21	+352.6	+382.01	+791.2
BALTIMORE	118.47	177.29	482.47	817.03	+ 58.82	+ 49.6	+305.18	+172.1	+334.56	+ 69.3	+698.56	+ 589.7
BUFFALO	51.99	119.92	313.16	788.26	+ 67.93	+130.7	+193.24	+161.1	+475.10	+151.7	+736.27	+1416.2
CINCINNATI	49.38	94.94	226.35	527.68	+ 45.56	+ 92.3	+131.41	+138.4	+301.33	+133.1	+478.30	+ 968.6
CLEVELAND	27.57	52.76	113.86	592.69	+ 25.19	+ 91.4	+ 61.10	+115.8	+478.83	+420.5	+565.12	+2049.8
LOUISVILLE	33.40	80.21	118.75	409.25	+ 46.81	+140.1	+ 38.54	+ 48.0	+290.50	+244.6	+375.85	+1125.9
MILWAUKEE	62.78	110.41	162.91	529.77	+ 47.63	+ 75.9	+ 52.50	+ 47.6	+366.86	+225.2	+466.99	+ 743.9
MINNEAPOLIS	35.68	56.07	176.24	525.52	+ 20.39	+ 57.1	+120.17	+214.3	+349.28	+198.2	+489.57	+1372.1
NEWARK	25.42	91.59	259.31	808.01	+ 66.17	+260.3	+167.72	+183.1	+548.70	+211.6	+782.59	+3078.6
ROCHESTER	66.04	71.95	290.65	660.93	+ 5.91	+ 8.9	+219.00	+304.4	+370.28	+127.4	+594.89	+ 900.8
WEIGHTED MEAN	55.50	103.95	244.44	628.55	+ 46.18	+ 91.9	+125.79	+149.8	+384.11	+ 157.1	+573.05	+1032.5
NON-INTERGOVERNMENTAL												
ANAHEIM	140.60	135.18	156.31	361.25	- 5.42	- 3.9	+ 21.13	+ 15.6	+204.94	+131.1	+220.65	+ 156.9
AUSTIN	41.25	60.49	101.60	256.95	+ 19.24	+ 46.6	+ 41.11	+ 68.0	+155.35	+152.9	+215.70	+ 522.9
BATON ROUGE	95.04	156.56	277.60	532.87	+ 61.52	+ 64.7	+121.04	+ 77.3	+255.27	+ 92.0	+437.83	+ 460.7
COLUMBUS	41.18	45.18	92.21	330.00	+ 4.00	+ 9.7	+ 47.03	+104.1	+237.79	+257.9	+288.82	+ 701.4
NASHVILLE-DAVIDSON	79.52	79.83	116.73	318.20	+ 0.31	+ 0.04	+ 36.90	+ 46.2	+201.47	+172.6	+238.68	+ 300.2
OKLAHOMA CITY	42.37	67.93	109.88	320.23	+ 25.56	+ 60.3	+ 41.95	+ 61.8	+210.35	+191.4	+277.86	+ 655.8
SAN JOSE	40.91	19.08	51.12	412.66	- 21.83	- 53.4	+ 32.04	+167.9	+361.54	+707.2	+371.75	+ 908.7
TULSA	36.38	54.02	102.79	253.03	+ 17.64	+ 48.5	+ 48.77	+ 90.3	+150.24	+146.2	+216.65	+ 595.5
VIRGINIA BEACH	NA	74.67	141.13	293.28	NA	NA	+ 66.46	+ 89.0	+152.15	+107.8	NA	NA
WICHITA	47.35	95.17	208.77	349.89	+ 47.82	+101.0	+163.60	+171.9	+141.12	+ 67.6	+302.54	+ 638.9
WEIGHTED MEAN	53.96	74.97	130.64	340.02	+ 21.01	+ 38.9	+ 55.67	+ 74.3	+209.38	+160.3	+286.06	+ 530.1

Note: For 1962, 1967 and 1972, San Jose is excluded from weighted means, see Appendix.

Source: U.S. Department of Commerce, Bureau of Census, *Census of Governments*, 1962, 1967, 1972. *Government Finances* (annual report), 1979.

to over $800 per capita, a phenomenal 3,000 percent rate of growth. Over the same period, federal and state transfers expanded by over 2,000 percent in Cleveland, and in excess of 1,000 percent in Buffalo, Louisville, and in non-intergovernmental cities.

In 1979, individual intergovernmental cities received much greater amounts of federal, state and local aid per capita than individual non-intergovernmental cities. As Exhibit 7.17 indicates, three intergovernmental cities—Baltimore, Newark and Buffalo—received aid in the range of $800 per capita. Five other intergovernmental cities—Cincinnati, Cleveland, Milwaukee, Minneapolis and Rochester—were the beneficiaries of more than $500 per capita in intergovernmental assistance. Only two of these cities, Louisville and Akron, received combined federal, state, and local transfers in the range of $400 to $500 per capita.

By contrast, each of the ten non-intergovernmental cities received significantly less intergovernmental aid per capita. As a group, these cities garnered an average of $340 in intergovernmental aid, just 45 percent of the average received by the ten declining cities. In three non-intergovernmental cities, federal, state, and local revenue transfers accounted for less than $300 per capita. In five others, intergovernmental transfers ranged between $300 and $400. Of the non-intergovernmental cities, only Baton Rouge and San Jose received intergovernmental transfers in excess of $400 per capita.

Federal Transfers

Federal transfers rose at a faster pace in intergovernmental cities, and in 1979, represented twice the amount of federal aid flowing to the high growth non-intergovernmental cities. Between 1962 and 1979, federal aid to intergovernmental cities increased by over 1,400 percent from $11 to $170 per capita (Exhibit 7.16). This compares to a ninefold rate of increase for non-intergovernmental cities, where federal transfers rose from $10 to just under $100 per capita. Interestingly, federal and state transfers accounted for similar shares of intergovernmental revenues in both classes of cities. State aid represented two-thirds of the transfers; federal aid the remaining one-third.

Absolutely, as of 1979, federal aid comprised approximately 15 percent of general revenues in intergovernmental cities, and nearly 20 percent less (12 percent) in non-intergovernmental cities. Overall, intergovernmental cities received about $100 per capita more in federal assistance—about double the amount of non-intergovernmental cities.

Flows of federal transfers varied substantially by city, however (Exhibits 7.16 and 7.17). For example, Newark—which received the highest overall amount of intergovernmental resources—received an extraordinarily small amount of federal aid, $77 per capita or barely 6 percent of general revenues. The same pattern was evident for Milwaukee. This is due to two factors. First, in these two cities many indirect federal transfers flow through the state and are treated as direct state transfers. This has the effect of lowering actual federal transfer statistics and increasing the apparent level of state transfers. Second, these cities have benefitted heavily from recurring grants which flow from the federal level; yet because they must be repeatedly qualified for, they are not allowed to enter the general fund for revenue purposes. This has the effect of causing federal revenues not to be counted as part of general revenues.

These two situations notwithstanding, some basic trends can be outlined. In 1979, a host of intergovernmental cities stood at the top of the ledger for per capita reliance on federal transfers. Baltimore, Buffalo and Louisville received over $200 per capita—about 20 percent—of local revenues from federal transfers. Only Baton Rouge of the non-intergovernmental city group benefitted from a comparable amount of federal aid.

Moreover, Louisville received the largest share of federal transfers; approximately 27 percent of its local revenue came from federal aid. At the other end of the spectrum Anaheim and San Jose of the non-intergovernmental cities garnered less than $50 per capita or just 5 percent of local revenue from federal transfers. Virginia Beach and Austin also derived less than 10 percent of all revenues from federal aid. Overall, six of ten non-intergovernmental cities received less than $100 per capita in federal aid while six of ten intergovernmental cities benefitted from more than $200 in per capita federal transfers.

State Transfers

As of 1979, state versus federal aid accounted for a 211 percent share of intergovernmental revenues in both classes of cities. Consequently, intergovernmental cities received far greater dollar amounts of state aid than did non-intergovernmental cities. Indeed, this substantial variation in flows of state aid accounted for much of the difference in overall flows of intergovernmental revenues for the two classes of cities.

Between 1962 and 1979, state transfers to declining intergovernmental cities increased by 860 percent from $44 per capita to $425 per capita. In contrast, state aid to younger non-intergovernmental cities rose much more sluggishly from a similar base of $41 per capita in 1962 to $229 in 1979, a rate nearly one-half the intergovernmental city rate. As of this date, state aid to intergovernmental cities was almost double state aid to non-intergovernmental cities. State aid also accounted for a far greater absolute share of general revenues in declining intergovernmental cities, 37 percent versus just 27 percent for non-intergovernmental cities (Exhibit 7.16).

At the beginning of the 1980s, Newark received, by far, the greatest amount of state aid—$725 per capita, over 60 percent of its total general revenues. Baltimore, Buffalo, Cleveland, and Milwaukee also received over $400 in state aid; between 35 and 45 percent of all local revenues. On the other hand, state aid accounted for the smallest proportion of local revenue, less than 20 percent or $180 per capita, in Austin, Nashville, Oklahoma City, Tulsa and Louisville for intergovernmental cities.

In the aggregate, intergovernmental transfers were twice the per capita dollar level in intergovernmental ($600) versus non-intergovernmental ($300) cities. Within each city grouping state transfers represented two-thirds of all transfers, although reasonable variation existed on a city-by-city basis (Exhibit 7.17).

School District Transfers

While the rise in both federal and state transfers to the school systems of intergovernmental cities was quite dramatic, both intergovernmental and non-intergovernmental cities benefitted from substantial percentage shares of intergovernmental transfers to their school systems. Levels of intergovernmentalism were much higher here than was the case for municipally provided public services. From 1962 to 1979, transfers to the school systems of intergovernmental cities increased by more than 2,000 percent from $13 to over $300 per capita. This was more than quadruple the rate of increase for non-intergovernmental cities.

Combined transfers to the school systems of intergovernmental cities accounted for nearly 63 percent of all educational revenues. The bulk of these transfers—about 90 percent—were derived from the state government. In non-intergovernmental cities, transfers also made up a substantial 61 percent share of all educational revenues. Here, federal transfers comprised nearly four times the share of intergovernmental resources than was found for intergovernmental cities (Exhibit 7.18).

In 1979, every city—except Nashville—received more than 40 percent of its educational revenues from intergovernmental sources. At the top of the scale, Newark derived 84 percent of its educational revenues, $479 per capita, from other than local sources. Buffalo received $320 per capita, or 70 percent of its educational revenue from these same non-local sources. Cleveland also received a substantial amount of intergovernmental aid for education—nearly $400 per capita. These cities plus Louisville and Cleveland garnered more than 60 percent of their educational revenues from federal and state sources. The remaining intergovernmental cities received between 45 and 55 percent from transfer payments (Exhibit 7.18).

However, while most of the non-intergovernmental cities got approximately 25 percent smaller dollar amounts of intergovernmental transfers, they derived similar percentage shares of educational revenues from intergovernmental sources. San Jose received $326 per capita or nearly 69 percent of its educational revenues from intergovernmental transfers. Anaheim and Baton Rouge benefitted from more than $250 per capita in federal and state aid—over 60 percent of local educational revenues. The remaining non-intergovernmental cities—with the exception of Nashville—received in the range of 50 to 55 percent of their educational revenues from transfers (approximately $150 per capita).

Overall, federal and state aid to school systems comprised similar shares of local revenues in both intergovernmental and non-intergovernmental cities. Just over 60 percent of all transfers to these cities flowed to their school districts. The federal role in education in non-intergovernmental cities was three times the percentage share and twice the per capita dollar allocation. Continued cutbacks in federal aid could also have an impact on non-intergovernmental cities in the area of public services.

Transfers to Municipal Government

Intergovernmental cities benefitted to a far greater extent from transfers flowing directly to their local governments, excluding school systems. Indeed, this particular component may be the key to understanding the intergovernmental–non-intergov-

EXHIBIT 7.18. — *School District Revenues, 1979 (in Dollars Per Capita)*

	Total General Revenue	INTERGOVERNMENTAL REVENUE		OWN-SOURCE REVENUE		
		All	From State	All	Taxes	Charges and Miscellaneous
INTERGOVERNMENTAL						
AKRON	424.57	227.65	226.83	196.93	179.91	59.21
BALTIMORE	401.84	243.85	239.81	157.99	154.66	3.33
BUFFALO	460.08	320.54	287.94	139.53	135.93	3.60
CINCINNATI	438.90	199.57	195.99	239.33	133.19	106.14
CLEVELAND	637.06	392.52	389.88	244.07	227.75	16.79
LOUISVILLE	247.69	148.63	141.21	101.25	90.29	10.96
MILWAUKEE	469.06	266.89	251.91	202.17	190.25	11.93
MINNEAPOLIS	405.31	207.01	195.78	198.30	162.98	8.29
NEWARK	568.99	478.91	475.66	90.11	79.45	10.65
ROCHESTER	551.29	249.83	244.68	301.45	218.67	82.79
WEIGHTED MEAN N=10	484.64	301.57 (63%)	269.27	186.96	161.83	32.09
NON-INTERGOVERNMENTAL						
ANAHEIM	394.79	274.46	250.21	120.30	99.59	20.71
AUSTIN	357.23	175.47	169.53	181.76	158.07	23.69
BATON ROUGE	424.53	258.49	256.68	166.04	150.88	15.16
COLUMBUS	347.04	193.70	182.75	153.34	138.30	15.04
NASHVILLE-DAVIDSON	316.39	120.68	111.80	195.71	180.79	14.93
OKLAHOMA CITY	256.12	141.77	131.48	114.72	88.24	26.48
SAN JOSE	473.72	325.70	320.86	148.02	119.11	28.92
TULSA	299.74	149.42	137.81	150.27	130.38	19.89
VIRGINIA BEACH	347.25	193.89	170.34	153.36	138.05	13.40
WICHITA	375.67	186.32	183.23	189.36	158.62	30.74
WEIGHTED MEAN N=10	350.47	218.13 (61%)	139.52	132.09	115.73	16.26

Note: For a discussion of data compilation, see Appendix.

Source: U.S. Department of Commerce, Bureau of Census, Census of Governments, Government Finances (annual report), 1979.

EXHIBIT 7.19.—*Transfers to Municipal Governments Versus Transfers to School Districts (Percent of General Revenues), 1979*

	For all Purposes	For Municipal Purposes Only	For School District Purposes Only	Municipal as Percent of all Transfers
INTERGOVERNMENTAL				
AKRON	45.84	39.44	53.62	47.16
BALTIMORE	59.08	58.43	60.68	70.15
BUFFALO	66.46	64.42	69.67	59.34
CINCINNATI	42.33	40.62	45.47	62.18
CLEVELAND	47.23	32.39	61.61	29.61
LOUISVILLE	49.17	44.75	60.01	61.61
MILWAUKEE	52.81	49.21	56.90	49.62
MINNEAPOLIS	49.69	48.83	51.07	60.61
NEWARK	67.95	53.07	84.18	40.73
ROCHESTER	56.13	65.66	45.32	62.20
WEIGHTED MEAN	54.19	50.46	64.90	55.79
NON-INTERGOVERNMENTAL				
ANAHEIM	48.39	24.66	69.52	24.01
AUSTIN	32.30	18.60	49.12	31.71
BATON ROUGE	44.85	35.99	60.89	51.49
COLUMBUS	41.42	30.31	55.82	41.30
NASHVILLE-DAVIDSON	35.00	33.33	38.15	62.08
OKLAHOMA CITY	40.11	32.93	55.35	55.73
SAN JOSE	48.52	23.08	68.75	21.07
TULSA	31.55	20.62	49.85	40.95
VIRGINIA BEACH	41.22	27.29	55.83	33.89
WICHITA	38.27	30.38	49.59	46.75
WEIGHTED MEAN	40.35	28.29	49.75	40.08

Source: U.S. Department of Commerce, Bureau of Census, Census of Governments, *Government Finances* (annual report), 1979.

ernmental distinction. Over the past two decades, transfers to municipal governments increased at approximately the same rate (620 percent) in both classes of cities. Yet, declining intergovernmental cities, at the beginning of the 1980s, benefitted from much greater per capita amounts of federal and state aid. This was largely due to the initial difference in the intergovernmental support base which favored heavily intergovernmental cities even in this early period. By 1979, dollar per capita revenue transfers to intergovernmental cities nearly doubled transfers to non-intergovernmental cities ($350 versus $136 per capita) (Exhibit 7.20).

Transfers to municipal government also comprised a larger proportion of municipal revenues in older intergovernmental cities than was the case for non-intergovernmental cities. Approximately 50 percent of all municipal revenue for these cities stemmed from intergovernmental sources; this compared to 28 percent for non-intergovernmental cities (Exhibit 7.19).

EXHIBIT 7.20. — *Municipal Revenues, 1979*
(Excluding School Districts, in Dollars Per Capita)

	Total General Revenue	INTERGOVERNMENTAL REVENUES			OWN-SOURCE REVENUES					
		All	From Federal	From State	All	Taxes Total	Property Tax	Sales Tax	Income Tax	Charges and Miscellaneous
INTERGOVERNMENTAL										
AKRON	515.13	203.14	157.29	37.96	311.99	194.08	43.87	0.46	136.24	117.91
BALTIMORE	981.03	573.18	260.94	304.76	407.85	269.00	114.96	41.01	92.15	138.84
BUFFALO	726.05	467.72	235.51	163.72	258.33	140.34	110.03	24.18	-	117.99
CINCINNATI	807.81	328.11	180.41	60.30	479.90	315.26	69.36	3.66	226.61	164.44
CLEVELAND	617.92	200.16	139.45	57.11	417.76	242.80	76.42	2.46	158.43	174.96
LOUISVILLE	582.38	260.62	215.82	21.34	321.76	237.05	70.65	12.11	149.31	85.31
MILWAUKEE	534.24	262.88	53.37	203.36	271.36	141.94	135.90	1.94	-	129.42
MINNEAPOLIS	652.25	318.51	137.37	171.11	333.74	203.28	168.48	20.61	-	130.46
NEWARK	620.13	329.10	75.67	249.54	291.03	240.87	131.55	83.82	-	50.16
ROCHESTER	626.13	411.09	204.82	34.52	215.04	161.62	141.09	19.70	-	46.42
WEIGHTED MEAN N=10	694.95	350.65	166.09	154.87	344.30	219.33	108.62	21.03	98.15	124.97
NON-INTERGOVERNMENTAL										
ANAHEIM	351.80	86.75	38.67	44.70	129.91	135.24	37.14	87.76	-	129.77
AUSTIN	438.17	81.49	69.22	8.02	356.69	157.66	95.55	56.58	-	199.11
BATON ROUGE	762.46	274.38	202.86	71.52	488.08	339.40	87.10	228.83	-	148.68
COLUMBUS	482.60	173.67	128.40	45.27	309.19	214.82	55.13	144.84	-	94.11
NASHVILLE-DAVIDSON	592.65	197.53	129.25	64.82	395.12	204.68	53.44	120.25	-	190.44
OKLAHOMA CITY	541.94	178.46	168.40	9.62	363.48	218.31	60.31	15.52	-	145.17
SAN JOSE	376.78	86.97	29.74	43.40	289.82	166.45	43.59	79.81	-	123.37
TULSA	502.43	103.61	91.39	11.94	398.82	179.65	26.51	146.97	-	219.17
VIRGINIA BEACH	364.25	99.40	38.01	58.08	264.85	163.78	32.14	96.09	-	101.07
WICHITA	538.54	114.65	111.51	8.41	263.83	104.87	83.41	16.89	-	158.96
WEIGHTED MEAN N=10	481.75	136.27	93.15	37.51	345.48	183.56	52.89	86.25	20.01	161.92

Note: For a discussion of data compilation, see Appendix.

Source: U.S. Department of Commerce, Bureau of Census, Census of Governments, Government Finances (annual report), 1979.

In intergovernmental cities in 1979, federal and state aid accounted for approximately similar amounts of municipal revenues ($166 per capita federal versus $155 state). Non-intergovernmental cities—although they benefitted from much smaller amounts of total aid—received a much greater percentage share of aid from the federal government. Federal aid at $93 per capita comprised 70 percent of all aid for municipal functions of non-intergovernmental cities (Exhibit 7.20).

The highest levels of aggregate intergovernmental transfers (federal and state) to municipal government at the beginning of the 1980s, were found in Baltimore, Rochester, and Buffalo. Here, total transfers to city hall exceeded $400 per capita and more than 60 percent of all municipal revenues. Cincinnati, Minneapolis and Newark also received large amounts of transfers or over $300 per capita. This constituted between 40 and 50 percent of total municipal revenues. The remaining intergovernmental cities, for the most part, received in excess of 40 percent of their municipal revenues from intergovernmental sources.

The ten non-intergovernmental cities had transferred much less aggregate dollar amounts as well as smaller percentage shares of intergovernmental aid to their local governments. In 1979, only Baton Rouge received municipal transfers on par with intergovernmental cities. Anaheim, Austin, San Jose, Virginia Beach and Tulsa received municipal transfers in the range of $100 per capita or 20 percent of all revenues. The remaining non-intergovernmental cities got less than $200 per capita in municipal transfers, about 30 percent of all revenues from these sources. To reiterate: in 1979, federal and state aid to municipalities in dollars per capita was two and one-half times as high in intergovernmental than in non-intergovernmental cities. Further, declining intergovernmental cities received over 50 percent of all municipal revenue from transfers. Non-intergovernmental cities received just 28 percent of their municipal revenue from federal and state sources.

Intergovernmental Transfers and the Local Budget

Overall, intergovernmental cities witnessed an accelerated increase in their reliance on intergovernmental transfers as a share of all local resources. Indeed, Exhibit 7.21 suggests a bold trendline. Between 1962 and 1979, aging intergovernmental cities increased their reliance on intergovernmental transfers twofold. In these cities, aid from all levels of government comprised just 27 percent of general revenues in 1962, expanding rapidly to nearly 55 percent by 1979. Over the same period, reliance on transfers in non-intergovernmental cities also increased, but much more sluggishly. In 1962, non-intergovernmental cities received approximately 30 percent of all local revenue from transfers. By 1979, these cities were receiving 40 percent of their total revenues from transfers.

Looking back over time, an interesting trend is apparent. In 1962, growing cities received a greater proportion of general revenues from intergovernmental transfers. This differential was equalized by 1967; transfer dependence in declining cities shot past growing cities over the course of the 1970s. Thus, intergovernmentalism—as we have defined it—emerged during the previous decade. By 1979, aging intergovernmental cities were getting over half of all revenues from transfers. This compared to a 40 percent share in non-intergovernmental cities.

EXHIBIT 7.21. — *The Growth in Intergovernmental Transfers, 1962–1979*
(as Percent of All General Revenue from Municipal and School District Sources)

	1962	1967	1972	1979	1962–1967	1967–1972	1972–1979	1962–1979
INTERGOVERNMENTAL								
AKRON	26.58	17.52	24.11	45.84	- 9.06	+ 6.59	+21.73	+19.26
BALTIMORE	43.74	42.82	60.19	59.08	- 0.92	+17.37	- 1.11	+15.34
BUFFALO	30.44	43.15	55.13	66.46	+12.71	+11.98	+11.33	+36.02
CINCINNATI	18.16	22.52	27.46	42.33	+ 4.36	+ 4.94	+14.87	+24.17
CLEVELAND	16.27	20.19	24.15	47.23	+ 3.92	+ 3.96	+23.08	+30.96
LOUISVILLE	19.05	26.94	31.49	49.17	+ 7.89	+ 4.55	+17.68	+30.12
MILWAUKEE	30.19	37.01	34.60	52.81	+ 6.82	- 2.41	+18.21	+22.62
MINNEAPOLIS	18.59	23.12	34.20	49.69	+ 4.53	+11.08	+15.49	+31.10
NEWARK	11.58	28.50	43.22	67.95	+16.92	+14.72	+24.73	+56.37
ROCHESTER	33.48	46.62	48.84	56.13	+13.14	+ 2.22	+ 7.29	+22.65
WEIGHTED MEAN	26.96	32.59	41.80	54.19	+ 5.63	+ 9.21	+12.39	+27.23
NON-INTERGOVERNMENTAL								
ANAHEIM	46.45	41.71	34.62	48.39	- 4.74	- 7.09	+13.77	+ 1.94
AUSTIN	27.47	33.31	32.46	32.30	+ 5.84	- 0.85	- 0.16	+ 4.83
BATON ROUGE	37.89	37.14	39.99	44.85	- 0.75	+ 2.85	+ 4.86	+ 6.96
COLUMBUS	24.93	22.58	26.15	41.42	- 2.35	+ 3.57	+15.27	+16.49
NASHVILLE-DAVIDSON	43.80	31.30	29.76	35.00	-12.50	- 1.54	+ 5.24	- 8.80
OKLAHOMA CITY	28.19	28.80	32.14	40.11	+ 0.61	+ 3.34	+ 7.97	+11.92
SAN JOSE	30.80	20.55	29.56	48.52	-10.25	+ 9.01	+18.96	+17.72
TULSA	22.81	25.43	29.25	31.55	+ 2.62	- 3.82	+ 2.30	+ 8.74
VIRGINIA BEACH	NA	49.36	45.64	41.22	NA	- 3.72	- 4.42	+ NA
WICHITA	23.82	35.56	45.06	38.27	+11.74	+ 9.50	- 6.79	+14.45
WEIGHTED MEAN	30.02	31.56	33.68	40.35	+ 1.54	+ 2.12	+ 6.67	+10.33

Note: For 1962, 1967 and 1972, San Jose is excluded from weighted means, see Appendix.

Source: U.S. Department of Commerce, Census of Governments, 1962, 1967, 1972. *Government Finances* (annual report), 1979.

Newark evidenced by far the most accelerated reliance on transfers as a proportion of general revenues. Here, reliance on transfers as a share of the local budget increased sixfold from 12 to 68 percent since 1962. Newark went from the least dependent of any city (including intergovernmental as well as non-intergovernmental cities) to most dependent. Buffalo, Cleveland, Louisville and Milwaukee also showed substantially increasing reliance on intergovernmental transfers. Transfers in these cities doubled or tripled over the same time period. The remaining intergovernmental cities upped the share of transfers comprising overall local revenues by about 20 percent.

While most of the non-intergovernmental cities also became more reliant on revenue transfers since 1962, these cities exhibited a much more sluggish rate of increase. Here, the most severe cases of intergovernmentalism—Columbus, San Jose, and Wichita—paled by comparison to the declining intergovernmental cities. In these cities, dependence on intergovernmental transfers increased by 50–75 percent over the past two decades. Anaheim, Austin, Baton Rouge and Tulsa increased their reliance on transfers by less than 30 percent. In Nashville and Virginia Beach the share of the local budget supported by intergovernmental transfers actually declined. While there was intergovernmentalism in non-intergovernmental cities, it was to support infrastructure development, not to buoy up declining operational services.

At the beginning of the 1980s, there was a good deal of variation in transfer dependence among the twenty cities in the sample. Overall, intergovernmental cities derived 54.2 percent of all revenues from transfers, versus 40.4 percent for non-intergovernmental cities. Again, Newark and Buffalo showed the greatest reliance on federal, state and local aid. These cities received significant amounts of per capita revenues from transfers; in the range of 65 to 70 percent of all local revenues came from intergovernmental sources. Transfers accounted for more than 50 percent of general revenues in Baltimore, Milwaukee, and Rochester, and just slightly less than this amount in Louisville and Minneapolis. Cleveland received approximately 45 percent of all revenues from intergovernmental transfers.

In several non-intergovernmental cities transfers also comprised a significant share of local revenues, though not nearly at the levels found in any of the worst-case intergovernmental cities. Transfers constituted 45 to 50 percent of total revenues in both the California cities of Anaheim and San Jose. Here the primary component of intergovernmental assistance was state aid to education. Baton Rouge—probably the most fiscally pressed of the non-intergovernmental cities—also derived around 45 percent of total revenues from transfers. Anaheim City and Virginia Beach received almost 40 percent of their general revenues from transfers. Austin, Nashville and Tulsa received the smallest shares of intergovernmental revenue of any of the sample cities. In these cities approximately 30 to 35 percent of total resources came from combined intergovernmental sources.

In sum, transfers constituted a noticeable share of local revenues in both classes of cities, though the highest levels of reliance on transfers were concentrated in high distress, intergovernmental cities. Aging intergovernmental cities witnessed much more rapid rates of growth in transfer dependence. Finally, even though cities in both groups got a share of local resources from transfers, declining intergovernmental cities exhibited a far greater dependence on prevailing flows of aid. This is true because intergovernmental transfers to these cities were high, and alternative means for generating local revenue were very restricted.[6]

Conclusions

There are a number of basic findings which are central to understanding municipal budgeting in intergovernmental versus non-intergovernmental cities. On the expenditure side, several trends are apparent.

- Aging intergovernmental cities spent more overall than younger non-intergovernmental cities ($1,110 versus $842 per capita).
- Intergovernmental cities spent more for education than non-intergovernmental cities ($437 versus $343 per capita). Additionally, over the past two decades, educational spending rose at a much faster pace in declining cities.
- Intergovernmental cities devoted proportionally larger shares of local resources for essential services such as police and fire protection but significantly less for capital infrastructure development. Non-intergovernmental cities spent less than intergovernmental cities across most categories, although they were likely to funnel proportionally larger shares of outlays toward long-term capital improvements.
- Declining intergovernmental cities exhibited a tremendous need for upgrading current services, especially in the area of capital facilities. Much of this stemmed from conscious deferrals of capital improvements as part of a strategy to overcome sharp fiscal constraints. Today, retrenchment, cutbacks, and declines in service quality define the terrain of municipal budgeting for these cities.

Turning to the revenue side, a series of interrelated trends have been identified.

- Faced with higher levels of expenditure and greater service needs, older intergovernmental cities were forced to generate substantially more general revenue than growing non-intergovernmental cities. This differential was indeed striking—$1,160 versus $843 per capita. Since tax collections and own-source revenue efforts accounted for similar dollar amounts of resources in both groups of cities, most of this variation in total revenues stemmed from the differential flows of federal and state transfers.
- Even though the tax bases of declining intergovernmental cities were much more constrained, both classes of cities generated very similar amounts of own-source revenue. However, the structure of own-source revenue differed substantially by city. Simply put, intergovernmental cities were more dependent on revenues raised through the property tax and, in some cases, via local income taxes. Non-intergovernmental cities, on the other hand, raised more revenue through local sales taxes and user charges.
- Although transfers comprised a significant share of local revenues in both classes of cities, the highest levels of reliance on transfers were found in high-distress intergovernmental cities. Indeed, Newark and Buffalo, along with Baltimore, Milwaukee and Rochester, were significantly dependent on aid from federal and state sources. These aging intergovernmental cities also witnessed the most rapid rates of growth in transfer dependence. As of 1979, intergovernmental cities benefitted from twice the amount of per capita transfers that flowed to non-intergovernmental cities ($628 versus $340 per capita).
- While both classes of cities benefitted from substantial flows of transfers to their school systems, intergovernmental cities, in 1979, received significantly greater per capita amounts of transfers for education, $302 versus $218 per capita.
- Intergovernmental cities were much more reliant on transfers flowing solely to their municipal governments. Indeed, this was the key area of intergovernmental dependence. In 1979, direct transfers to local government accounted for 2½ times as much revenue as

they did in non-intergovernmental cities ($351 versus $136 per capita). Intergovernmental cities also derived a much larger proportion of municipal revenues from transfers. Here, transfers to municipal governments comprised approximately 50 percent of all municipal revenue, compared to 28 percent of all revenue in non-intergovernmental cities.

- State transfers (both municipal and school) accounted for a greater proportion of aid in both classes of cities. Moreover, intergovernmental cities received far greater amounts of state aid than non-intergovernmental cities. In 1979, state aid to these cities was approximately double state aid to younger non-intergovernmental cities ($425 versus $229). State aid also accounted for a greater proportion of general revenues in declining intergovernmental cities (37 percent versus 27 percent).

- Federal aid, while it comprised a smaller proportion of all revenues in both classes of cities, was about double the amount in intergovernmental versus non-intergovernmental cities ($171 versus $99 per capita).

NOTES

1. The literature on municipal finance is extensive. Representative studies include: Thomas Muller, "The Declining and Growing Metropolis: A Fiscal Comparison," in George Sternlieb and James W. Hughes (eds.), *Post-Industrial America: Metropolitan Decline and Inter-Regional Job Shifts*, New Brunswick, N.J.: Center for Urban Policy Research, 1975; Thomas Muller, "Changing Expenditure and Service Demand Patterns of Stressed Cities," in Robert W. Burchell and David Listokin (eds.), *Cities Under Stress: The Fiscal Crises of Urban America*, New Brunswick, N.J.: Center for Urban Policy Research, 1981; Roy Bahl, Bernard Jump, and Larry Schroeder, "The Outlook for City Fiscal Performance in Declining Regions," in Bahl (ed.), *The Fiscal Outlook for the Cities: Implications of a National Policy*, Syracuse, N.Y.: Syracuse University Press, 1978; Roy Bahl and Larry Schroeder, "Fiscal Adjustments in Declining Cities," in Burchell and Listokin (eds.), *Cities Under Stress*, op. cit.; Roy Bahl (ed.), *Urban Government Finance: Emerging Trends*, New York: Sage Publications, 1981; Astrid E. Merget, "Disparity and Diversity: Profiles of City Finances," *Urban Data Service Reports*, Vol. 13, No. 8, August 1981; John E. Petersen, "City Finances 1978–1980: The JEC/MFOA Survey Results," *Governmental Finances*, Vol. 9, No. 2, June 1980; George Sternlieb and James W. Hughes, "New Dimensions of the Urban Crisis," in Burchell and Listokin (eds.), *Cities Under Stress*, op. cit.

The U.S. Congress, Joint Economic Committee has also done surveys and commissioned work in this area: See Congress of the United States, Joint Economic Committee, *Trends in the Fiscal Condition of Cities 1979–81*, U.S. Government Printing Office, 1981; *State and Local Finance: Adjustments in a Changing Economy*, U.S. Government Printing Office, 1980.

2. Numerous attempts have been made to develop specific models and indicators of urban fiscal strain. Representative examples of this growing literature include: Terry Clark et al., "How Many New Yorks?" (unpublished paper), University of Chicago, 1976; Terry Clark and Lorna C. Ferguson, *Political Processes and Urban Fiscal Strain* (1982); Philip Dearborn, "Urban Fiscal Studies," in John E. Petersen and Catherine L. Spain (eds.), *Essays in Public Finance and Financial Management: State and Local Examples*, Chatham, N.J.: Chatham House, 1980; David Stanley, "Cities in Trouble," in Charles Levine (ed.), *Managing Fiscal Stress* (Chatham, N.J.: Chatham House, 1980); Touche-Ross, Inc., "Urban Fiscal Stress: A Comparative Analysis," in Burchell and Listokin (eds.), *Cities Under Stress*, op. cit. For two excellent reviews see: Jeff Stonecash and Patrick McAfee, "The Ambiguities and Limits of Fiscal Strain Indicators," *Policy Studies Journal*, Vol. 10, No. 2, December 1981; Roger Friedland, "Central City Fiscal Strains: The Public Costs of Private Growth," *International Journal of Urban and Regional Research*, Vol. 5, No. 3, September 1981.

3. See George E. Peterson, "Capital Spending and Capital Obsolescence: The Outlook for Cities," in Roy Bahl (ed.), *The Fiscal Outlook for the Cities*, op. cit.; and George E. Peterson, "Transmitting the Municipal Fiscal Squeeze to a New Generation of Taxpayers: Pension Obligations and Capital Investment Needs," in Burchell and Listokin (eds.), *Cities Under Stress*, op. cit. See also David A. Grossman, "The Infrastructure Blues: A Tale of New York and Other Cities," *Governmental Finances*, Vol. 9, No. 2, June 1980; Margaret A. Corwin and Judith Getzels, "Capital Expenditures: Causes and Controls," in Burchell and Listokin (eds.), *Cities Under Stress*, op. cit.

4. John E. Petersen, "Big City Borrowing Costs and Credit Quality," in Burchell and Listokin (eds.), *Cities Under Stress*, op. cit.

5. See Thomas Dye and James H. Ammons, "Frostbelt and Sunbelt Cities: What Difference it Makes," *The Urban Interest*, Vol. 2, No. 1, Spring 1980; Fred Teitelbaum, "The Relative Responsiveness of State and Federal Aid to Distressed Cities," *Policy Studies Review*, Vol. 1, No. 2, November 1981.

6. This section draws upon the work of Wolman and Peterson at the Urban Institute. For a statement of their work, see Harold Wolman and George Peterson, "Policy Consequences of Local Expenditure Constraint," *The Urban Interest*, Vol. 2, No. 2, Fall 1980.

8

The Dismantling of Intergovernmentalism

FACED WITH SPIRALING INFLATION, high interest rates and rapid growth in federal expenditures, the Reagan Administration embarked on a program of sustained fiscal austerity. The object of this initiative was to cut the rate of increase in federal spending and to stimulate and encourage sustained industrial productivity and private sector investment. Consisting of both a budget component and a tax element, the Administration's economic initiative coupled a sharp decrease in the rate of growth of the federal budget with the largest income tax cut in the nation's history. While the latter continues to lag predicted effects, the deep recession and high inflation of the early 1980s, at mid-decade, seem now past.

The Omnibus Budget Reconciliation Act of 1981, which established the FY 1982 budget, trimmed the projected rise in federal budget authority by $53.2 billion or 6.7 percent. By far, the most severely affected segment of the budget was federal grants to state and local governments (including indirect payments for individuals) which accounted for fully $28.4 billion or 53 percent of total cuts. In fact, budget authority reductions in three grant-in-aid programs constituted $20.7 billion or nearly 40 percent of all 1982 budget authority cutbacks.

In FY 1983, the Reagan Administration was able to secure budget savings similar to those planned for in the 1981 Reconciliation Act. Grant-in-aid outlays, excluding payments to individuals, are projected to fall steadily through 1987; payments to individuals, while remaining generally stable through 1987, will fall sharply in real terms assuming a projected annual inflation rate of 6 percent.

To the extent that the Administration's economic initiatives have been successful, all of the nation's cities and especially declining intergovernmental cities benefit significantly. Indeed, today's distressed cities are, in part, the result of a national downturn in economic activity, stagnant industrial output and recurrent recessions. This obviously erodes their ability to raise revenues and pay for public services.

Although cities experiencing the greatest levels of economic, fiscal and social difficulties stand to benefit in the long run from a national upturn in economic activity, preliminary investigations revealed that the immediate impacts of sustained budget reductions were felt most severely by distressed cities. And, if only in the short run, not only did declining urban areas bear a disproportionate burden of rollbacks in federal aid, needy cities also lost substantial amounts of indirect revenues as entitlement programs for the poor and near-poor were also curtailed.

As of now, cities have only begun to feel the repercussions from the historic contraction in the federal budget. Because of this, data are just now becoming available to analyze the specifics of intergovernmental versus non-intergovernmental city impact. Short of such an analysis, this chapter will concentrate on an examination of the projected reductions in outlays in program areas in which intergovernmental cities participate heavily. The link between cutbacks and dependence will serve as a preliminary indication of sustained impact.

After an overview of proposed spending for the next several years, specific attention will be given to principal urban aid programs, as well as to entitlement payments to individuals. It should be noted that tax revisions incorporated in the Economic Recovery Tax Act of 1981 will also affect state and, to a lesser extent, local revenues. Inasmuch as this review is restricted to grants-in-aid and entitlement programs, however, the numbers presented here will represent essentially primary impacts. It is also important to remember that the analysis which follows concentrates heavily on the Reagan Administration initiatives and proposals. This, as opposed to the estimates of Democratic counterparts or oversight agencies, presents the most severe picture of overall proposed budget reductions as well as social versus defense program priorities.

Notwithstanding the above, it is probably true that the *general* direction of change discussed here is largely independent of one administration or another. In fact, most of what has been acted on during the first term of the Reagan Administration were ''issues'' of the Carter years. While the magnitude and specific concentration of the cuts are subject to debate, there is little argument that cuts, somewhere, were inevitable. The federal deficit, as a percent of GNP, is the highest in history.

1981 Omnibus Budget Reconciliation Act

As shown in Exhibits 8.1 and 8.2, the Congressional Budget Office's estimates for FY 1982 spending anticipated outlays to total $738.7 billion and budget authority to reach $795.6 billion.* The 1981 Omnibus Budget Reconciliation Act reduced sharply the rate of increase in federal spending, cutting fully $53.2 billion from budget authority and reducing expected outlays by $35.2 billion. As a proportion of total federal spending, those cutbacks represented 6.7 percent of all budget authority and 4.8 percent of FY 1982 outlays.

Rollbacks in the national budget did not affect all budget functions equally. Rather, cuts in federal expenditures were concentrated in a few functional areas. For example, over 36 percent of budget authority and fully 30 percent of all outlay reductions were achieved from cuts in income security. An additional 18 percent of budget authority and a similar percentage of budget outlay savings were attained at

---

Budget authority is the maximum obligation the government may incur in the immediate year or over a period of years. Since authority is the upper limit of new spending commitments that can be made by an agency or department, it represents long-term spending implications. *Outlays*, on the other hand, are the actual amount of dollars spent or projected to be expended on a particular budget account for a given year. Generally speaking, outlays are the most important number to determine immediate and short-term program impacts of budget

EXHIBIT 8.1. — *Changes in 1982 Budget Authority Based on 1981 Omnibus Budget Reconciliation Act by Function ($ Millions)*

	FY1982 CBO Current Policy Baseline	Dollar Reduction From Base In Function	Percent Function Reduced From Base	Percent Reductions Made in Function
National Defense	$198,073	$ -2,580	-1.0%	-4.8%
International Affairs	17,143	-1,001	-5.8	-1.9
General Science, Space and Technology	7,191	-54	-0.8	-0.1
Energy	9,418	-5,540	-58.8	-10.4
Natural Resources and Environment	14,006	-5,042	-36.0	-9.5
Agriculture	5,567	-194	-3.5	-0.4
Commerce and Housing Credit	8,068	-1,617	-20.0	-3.0
Transportation	23,671	-2,962	-12.5	-5.6
Community and Regional Development	9,510	-2,062	-21.7	-3.9
Education, Training, Employment, and Social Services	36,937	-9,377	-25.4	-17.6
Health	85,719	-2,320	-2.7	-4.4
Income Security	283,671	-19,430	-6.8	-36.5
Veterans Benefits and Services	25,546	-456	-1.8	-0.8
Administration of Justice	4,916	-267	-5.4	-0.5
General Government	5,486	-242	-4.4	-0.5
General Purpose Fiscal Assistance	6,436	-39	-0.6	-0.1
TOTAL BUDGET AUTHORITY	$795,649	$-53,208	-6.7	100.0

Source: Princeton University Urban and Regional Research Center, Background Material on Fiscal Year 1982 Federal Budget Reductions (December 1981).

changes. The analysis period will encompass the years 1982–1987: 1982, to obtain a firm hand-hold on where we have been; 1987, to provide a short-run view of the future in a rapidly changing world.

EXHIBIT 8.2. — *Changes in 1982 Budget Outlays Based on 1981 Omnibus Budget Reconciliation Act by Function ($ Millions)*

	FY1982 CBO Current Policy Baseline	Dollar Reduction From Base In Function	Percent Function Reduced From Base	Percent Reductions Made in Function
National Defense	$183,756	$ -2,583	-1.4%	-7.3%
International Affairs	11,355	-369	-3.2	-1.0
General Science, Space and Technology	6,992	-52	-0.7	-0.1
Energy	11,422	-4,671	-40.9	-13.3
Natural Resources and Environment	14,291	-1,156	-8.1	-3.3
Agriculture	6,542	-1,308	-20.0	-3.7
Commerce and Housing Credit	6,404	-1,321	-20.6	-3.7
Transportation	22,572	-1,920	-8.5	-5.4
Community and Regional Development	11,056	-1,059	-9.6	-3.0
Education, Training, Employment, and Social Services	35,870	-6,417	-17.9	-18.2
Health	76,581	-2,791	-3.6	-7.9
Income Security	255,736	-10,647	-4.2	-30.2
Veterans Benefits and Services	25,054	-448	-1.8	-1.3
Administration of Justice	4,961	-223	-4.5	-0.6
General Government	5,340	-218	-4.1	-0.6
General Purpose Fiscal Assistance	6,439	-40	-0.6	-0.1
TOTAL BUDGET OUTLAYS	$738,677	$-35,249	-4.8	100.0

Source: Princeton University Urban and Regional Research Center, Background Material on Fiscal Year 1982 Federal Budget Reductions (December 1981).

the expense of education, training, employment and social services. In fact, of sixteen functions listed in Exhibit 8.1, five absorbed 80 percent of all reductions in budget authority. Exhibit 8.2 indicates that more than 62 percent of all projected outlays savings could be accounted for in only three functions of public spending.

If the impact of the Administration's scaling down of federal spending is measured in terms of reductions as a percentage of total monies allocated, energy was the principal loser in both budget authority and budget outlay categories. From FY 1982, the energy function was cut by close to 60 percent in budget authority and over 40 percent in outlays. Interestingly, absolute dollar cutbacks in energy were only 28 percent of the dollar loss suffered by income security, as measured in budget authority. Yet, due to the previous large dollar commitment to income security programs, that function was deflated by only 7 percent in total authority. And, in terms of outlays, it was scaled down by just over 4 percent.

Looking at *budget authority*, other functions which were sharply cut back as a percentage of total size include: natural resources and environment (-36 percent); community and regional development (-22 percent); and commerce and housing credit (-20 percent). In addition to energy, four other functions which experienced heavy financial losses in 1982 *outlays* were commerce and housing credit (-21 percent); agriculture (-20 percent); education, training, employment and social services (-18 percent); and community and regional development (-10 percent).

As previously mentioned, the 1981 Omnibus Budget Reconciliation Act, in terms of budget authority reductions, was most severe on grants to state and local governments. That portion of the budget absorbed 53 percent of the total budget authority savings for FY 1982. In terms of outlays, however, grants-in-aid accounted for only 28 percent of all FY 1982 expenditure rollbacks. The big loser in immediate outlays was social service departmental operations. A more detailed analysis of grant-in-aid expenditures follows.

Projected Budget Trends

Exhibits 8.3 and 8.4 reflect proposed budget authority and outlay estimates through FY 1987, as set forth in the Administration's FY 1983 budget. Exhibit 8.3 shows that in terms of *budget authority*, agriculture funding is scheduled to decline by more than half through 1987; natural resources and environment expenditures will fall by 36 percent; and education, training, employment and social services authority will contract by 29 percent. In contrast, national defense is projected to increase substantially during the five-year period.

Although the income security function received the largest dollar reduction in FY 1982 budget authority, it is expected to rise between 1982 and 1987 by 38 percent or $95.7 billion. Almost all of this increase can be attributed to the tremendous scale of the Social Security obligation which, even under modified guidelines, will expand by $95 billion over the next several years. Budget authority for general retirement will decline by $5.2 billion or 70 percent, and housing assistance payments will drop by $3.8 billion or nearly 58 percent. Other income security programs include federal employee retirement, which is projected to rise by 24 percent, and unemployment compensation and food or nutrition assistance, both of which will remain relatively stable through 1987. It should be noted that in actuality, assuming a 6 percent an-

EXHIBIT 8.3. — *Budget Authority by Function, 1982-1987 ($ Billions)*

	Administration Estimates						Average Annual Change 1982-1987		Net Change 1982-1987	
	1982	1983	1984	1985	1986	1987	Absolute	Percent	Absolute	Percent
National Defense	218.9	263.0	291.0	338.0	374.9	408.4	+37.9	+17.3	+189.5	+86.6
International Affairs	18.5	18.1	17.4	16.4	15.9	15.6	- 0.6	- 3.1	- 2.9	-15.7
General Science, Space and Technology	7.0	7.8	7.7	7.3	6.7	6.7	- 0.1	- 0.9	- 0.3	- 4.3
Energy	4.8	4.3	4.5	4.1	4.5	4.5	- 0.1	- 1.3	- 0.3	- 6.3
National Resources and Environment	10.0	8.4	7.7	7.3	7.0	6.4	- 0.7	- 7.2	- 3.6	-36.0
Agriculture	9.6	6.9	7.3	4.5	4.5	4.5	- 1.0	-10.6	- 5.1	-53.1
Commerce and Housing Credit	6.3	3.4	4.2	4.6	5.4	5.8	- 0.1	- 1.6	- 0.5	- 7.9
Transportation	21.0	19.1	19.2	19.5	19.8	20.1	- 0.2	- 0.9	- 0.9	- 4.3
Community and Regional Development	6.6	6.7	6.9	7.0	7.0	7.0	+ 0.1	+ 1.2	+ 0.4	+ 6.1
Education, Training, Employment and Social Services	23.5	18.8	17.7	17.8	17.3	16.8	- 1.3	- 5.7	- 6.7	-28.5
Health	79.2	77.8	81.4	93.6	115.7	128.3	+ 9.8	+12.4	+49.1	+62.0
Income Security	252.3	257.6	281.9	310.2	323.6	348.8	+19.1	+ 7.6	+95.7	+37.9
Veterans Benefits and Services	24.8	25.7	26.3	27.0	27.9	28.8	+ 0.8	+ 3.2	+ 4.0	+16.1
Administration of Justice	4.3	4.5	4.6	4.5	4.6	4.6	+ 0.1	+ 1.4	+ 0.3	+ 7.0
General Government	5.2	5.3	5.4	5.2	5.1	5.1	*	- 0.4	- 0.1	- 1.9
General Purpose Fiscal Assistance	6.4	6.7	6.9	7.2	7.5	7.7	+ 0.3	+ 4.1	+ 1.3	+20.3
Total Budget Authority	765.5	801.9	858.0	943.5	1014.1	1078.2	+62.5	+ 8.2	+312.7	+40.8

*less than $1.0 million

Source: U.S. Office of Management and Budget, The United States Budget, 1983 (February 1982).

EXHIBIT 8.4.—*Budget Outlays by Function, 1982-1987 ($ Billions)*

	Administration Estimates						Average Annual Change 1982-1987		Net Change 1982-1987	
	1982	1983	1984	1985	1986	1987	Absolute	Percent	Absolute	Percent
National Defense	187.5	222.1	253.0	292.1	331.7	364.2	+35.3	+18.8	+176.7	+94.2
International Affairs	11.1	12.0	12.3	13.0	12.5	11.9	+0.2	+1.4	+0.8	+7.2
General Science, Space and Technology	6.9	7.6	7.8	7.4	6.9	6.7	*	-0.6	-0.2	-2.9
Energy	6.4	4.2	3.8	3.8	4.0	4.1	-0.5	-7.2	-2.3	-35.9
National Resources and Environment	12.6	9.9	8.4	7.7	6.9	6.3	-1.3	-10.0	-6.3	-50.0
Agriculture	8.6	4.5	5.1	4.6	2.8	2.8	-1.2	-13.5	-5.8	-67.4
Commerce and Housing Credit	3.3	1.6	1.3	-.5	-.8	-.7	NA	NA	NA	NA
Transportation	21.2	19.6	18.8	19.4	19.7	19.7	-0.3	-1.4	-1.5	-7.1
Community and Regional Development	8.4	7.3	6.7	6.9	6.7	6.7	-0.3	-4.0	-1.7	-20.2
Education, Training, Employment and Social Services	27.8	21.6	19.3	17.8	17.3	16.8	-2.2	-7.9	-11.0	-39.6
Health	73.4	78.1	84.9	93.5	102.4	111.9	+7.7	+10.5	+38.5	+52.5
Income Security	250.9	261.7	274.8	290.1	305.7	323.1	+14.4	+5.8	+72.2	+28.8
Veterans Benefits and Services	24.2	24.4	25.6	26.9	27.9	28.7	+0.9	+3.7	+4.5	+18.6
Administration of Justice	4.5	4.6	4.6	4.5	4.5	4.6	*	+0.4	+0.1	+2.2
General Government	5.1	5.0	5.2	4.9	4.8	4.6	-0.1	-2.0	-0.5	-9.8
General Purpose Fiscal Assistance	6.4	6.7	6.8	7.1	7.3	7.6	+0.2	+3.8	+1.2	+18.8
Total Budget Outlays	725.3	757.6	805.9	868.5	927.0	978.9	+50.7	+7.0	+253.6	+40.0

*Less than $1.0 Million
NA - Not Applicable

Source: U.S. Office of Management and Budget, The United States Budget, 1983 (February 1982).

nual rate of inflation, programs remaining stable in funding will experience real dollar declines.

Finally, with regard to budget authority through 1987, health expenditures are expected to rise at a rate second only to defense. Growing by about $10 billion each year, the health function expands from $79.2 billion in FY 1982 to $128.3 billion by FY 1987. As with income security, this increase takes place almost exclusively in a single, broad-based entitlement program. Medicare benefits will grow by 78 percent, and will account for 82 percent of the increase in health spending. While Medicare adds $40.4 billion to its budget during that five-year period, Medicaid expenditures will grow by a mere $6.4 billion.

Exhibit 8.4 reflects proposed *outlay* estimates for FY 1982 through FY 1987. In terms of absolute dollars, national defense is projected to increase, by far, the greatest of any function. During that five-year time span, defense outlays are expected to rise by $176.7 billion. Indeed, expansion of the defense budget accounts for 70 percent of the total increase in federal spending through 1987. Income security, growing by $72.2 billion, is second only to national defense in terms of its net dollar increase by 1987. Finally, health expenditures also expand significantly through the next five years. This function will have added $38.5 billion to its budget as of 1987. Again, the expansion of single-purpose, broad-base entitlements, i.e. Social Security and Medicare, within these latter two areas accounts for almost all of their growth.

In terms of outlay cutbacks, education, training, employment and social services will experience the sharpest reduction in total dollar expenditures. This function is projected to drop by $2.2 billion per year for a total of $11 billion by 1987. Fully 64 percent of the total expenditure cut in this area is to come from education programs; they are expected to fall by $7.1 billion through 1987.

Composition of Total Budget Outlays

Exhibit 8.5 shows that between 1981 and 1985, outlays for defense will grow by $132.8 billion and its share of total budget outlays will increase from 24 percent to 34 percent. This will begin to reverse a trend of income security dominance which emerged during the last decade. Social Security benefits, reflecting their impact on any budget proposal, will nonetheless increase their share of total outlays from 21 percent in 1981 to 23 percent in 1985. Finally, net interest will expand as a percent of all federal outlays from 11 to 12 percent of all total outlays.

Although other-payments-to-individuals, a function which includes means-tested (personal hardship–oriented) entitlements, increases by $29 billion between 1981 and 1985, its share of total outlays will fall from 27 percent to 24 percent. Other non-defense spending, including direct grants to state and local governments, will experience the greatest dollar loss between 1981 and 1985. As a share of total outlays, this category of spending will drop from 17 percent to 8 percent. Exhibit 8.6 indicates that the rapid expansion of the defense budget will not be achieved at the sole expense of human resource and community development programs. Although many individual human resource and community development grants are to be reduced substantially, human resources and community development as a whole are projected to shift from 53 percent of all budget outlays in 1982 to 50 percent by 1987.

EXHIBIT 8.5. — *Composition of Total Budget Outlays, 1981–1985*

(*$ Billions*)	*Actual* 1981	*Administration Estimates*			
		1982	*1983*	*1984*	*1985*
National Defense	159.8	187.5	221.1	253.0	292.1
Social Security	138.0	154.6	173.5	188.5	202.3
Other Payments to Individuals	178.6	196.9	192.3	196.8	207.6
Net Interest	68.7	83.0	96.4	98.7	100.8
Other Nondefense	112.1	103.3	74.3	69.0	65.8
Total Budget Outlays	657.2	725.3	757.6	805.9	868.5
Percent Change					
National Defense	17.6	17.4	17.9	14.4	15.4
Social Security	17.8	12.0	12.2	8.6	7.3
Other Payments to Individuals	15.9	10.2	-2.3	2.3	5.5
Net Interest	31.0	20.8	16.1	2.4	2.1
Other Nondefense	-4.4	- 7.9	-28.1	-7.1	-4.6
Total Budget Outlays	14.0	10.4	4.5	6.4	7.8
Percent Share of Budget Outlays					
National Defense	24.3	25.9	29.2	31.4	33.6
Social Security	21.0	21.3	22.9	23.4	23.3
Other Payments to Individuals	27.2	27.1	25.4	24.4	23.9
Net Interest	10.5	11.4	12.7	12.2	11.6
Other Nondefense	17.1	14.2	9.8	8.6	7.6
Total Budget Outlays	100.0	100.0	100.0	100.0	100.0

Source: U.S. Congressional Budget Office, An Analysis of the President's Budgetary Proposal to Fiscal Year 1983 (February 1982).

Growth of defense outlays, with relatively stable human resource funding, will result in significant cutbacks in all other categories of federal spending. Indeed, "other" outlays will decline from 21 percent in 1982 to 13 percent in 1987.

Finally, Exhibit 8.7 shows that federal spending for payments to individuals will continue to grow through 1985. During that time period, outlays for payments to individuals will expand by $93.1 billion or nearly 30 percent, while other non-defense outlays will decline by $46.3 billion or 41 percent. However, as indicated in Exhibit 8.7, 67 percent of the increase in payments to individuals can be attributed to Social Security. Means-tested programs such as Medicaid, Food Stamps and AFDC payments are scheduled to remain relatively stable. In real terms (taking into account inflation), these programs can expect to fall by 34 percent over the five-year projection period.

Federal Aid to State and Local Governments

The 1981 Omnibus Budget Reconciliation Act dramatically cut the expected growth in budget authority for grants to state and local governments based on 1981

EXHIBIT 8.6.—*Human Resources and Community Development as a*
Percent of Total Budget Outlays, 1982–1987

| | Administration Estimates | | | | | |
	1982	1983	1984	1985	1986	1987
National Defense	25.9	29.2	31.4	33.6	35.8	37.2
Human Resources	53.0	51.9	51.0	50.1	49.6	49.8

Education, Training,
    Employment and
    Social Services
	3.8	2.9	2.4	2.0	1.9	1.7

Health	10.1	10.3	10.5	10.8	11.0	11.4
Income Security	34.6	34.5	34.1	33.4	33.0	33.0
Veterans Benefits	3.3	3.2	3.2	3.1	3.2	2.9
Community Development	1.2	1.0	0.8	0.8	0.7	0.7
Total Budget Outlays	100.0	100.0	100.0	100.0	100.0	100.0

Source: U.S. Office of Management and Budget, The United States Budget, 1983
(February 1982).

CBO baseline budget estimates. Grants-in-aid, including payments to individuals, accounted for more than one-half of the total 1982 federal budget savings. In response to this reduction in budget authority, outlays for FY 1981 fell by 23 percent and represented fully 20 percent of the total national budget outlay reductions for that year. Compared with 1981 outlays, 1982 expenditures dropped by $3.6 billion or 4 percent.

The bulk of budget reductions in the area of federal aid to state and local governments was achieved through a dramatic alteration of the grant-in-aid system. Premised on an assumption that less federal interference and red tape would translate into greater flexibility and cost savings at state and local levels, the Omnibus Budget Reconciliation Act consolidated seventy-seven categorical and two existing block grants into nine new functional block grants. The new grants were then funded at a level considerably less than their predecessor programs. The nine block grants were for maternal and child care health; primary health care; preventative health and health services; alcohol, drug abuse and mental health; low-income energy assistance; social services and community services; state education block grants; and community development for small cities.

Although consolidation of categorical grants was used to achieve the greatest budget savings, the Reagan Administration also was successful in reducing federal intergovernmental aid by sharply decreasing funding for some programs while eliminating other grants completely. In October 1981, for example, OMB reported that sixty-two categorical grants that had been funded in FY 1981 would not be funded in the following fiscal years.[1]

In FY 1983, the Administration proposed additional measures which reduced the size and complexity of the grant-in-aid system through seven new consolidated grants and additions to three existing block grants. Exhibit 8.8 shows both the consolidated grants established in the 1981 Omnibus Budget Act and those of the Administration's 1983 budget.

Exhibit 8.7. — *Outlays for Payments to Individuals, 1981–1985 ($ Billions)*

	Actual	Administration Estimates			
	1981	1982	1983	1984	1985
Social Insurance Programs					
Social Security (OASDI)	139.6	156.6	173.5	188.5	202.3
Railroad retirement	5.3	5.3	---	---	---
Medicare	42.5	49.5	55.3	61.2	68.3
Unemployment compensation	19.7	25.2	22.6	19.8	18.0
Civil Service retirement and disability	17.7	19.4	21.1	22.4	23.9
Veterans' compensation and readjustment benefits	10.8	11.5	11.9	12.0	12.3
Other	11.8	12.6	15.1	15.4	15.8
Subtotal	247.4	280.1	299.5	319.3	340.7
Means-Tested Programs					
Guaranteeed student loans and other education	6.2	6.3	5.7	4.3	3.9
Medicaid	16.8	17.8	17.0	18.6	20.4
Food stamps	11.3	11.2	9.6	9.7	10.0
Other food and nutrition programs	4.9	4.2	4.1	4.2	4.3
Housing	6.8	8.1	8.5	8.9	9.4
Supplemental security income	7.2	7.9	8.9	7.8	8.6
Assistance payments (AFDC)	8.5	8.1	5.5	5.5	5.5
Veterans' pensions	3.8	3.9	4.0	4.1	4.2
Other	3.8	4.0	3.1	2.9	2.8
Subtotal	69.3	71.5	66.4	66.0	69.1
Total	316.7	351.6	365.9	385.3	409.8

Source: U.S. Congressional Budget Office, An Analysis of the President's Budgetary Proposal for Fiscal Year 1983 (February 1982).

Exhibit 8.9 indicates the growing importance of general-purpose as well as broad-based grants between 1972 and 1985. In 1972, broad-based grants constituted only eight percent of all federal grants-in-aid; by 1981, they had grown to 11 percent. By 1985, broad-based grants will expand to 19 percent of all grant-in-aid outlays. General-purpose grants, which in 1972 were only 2 percent of all outlays, had grown to 7 percent by 1981. Under the Reagan Administration's proposals that category of grants-in-aid will expand slightly, to 9 percent of all grant-in-aid outlays by 1985. Finally, categorical grants which accounted for 90 percent of all grant-in-aid outlays in 1972 are projected to fall to only 73 percent in 1985.

A principal target of both the FY 1982 budget savings and spending reductions for FY 1983 was federal assistance to state and local governments. As shown in Exhibits 8.10 and 8.11, FY 1982 outlays declined from $94.8 billion in 1981 to $91.2 billion in 1982. Between 1982 and 1983, grants-in-aid fell more sharply, dropping by $9.8

EXHIBIT 8.8. — *Broad-Based Aid Enacted in 1981 or Proposed for
1983 and Outlays, 1982–1985 ($ Millions)*

	1982	1983	1984	1985
Enacted in 1981:				
State community development block grant				
for small cities[1]	(10)	(200)	(500)	(650)
State education block grant	666	578	441	335
Community services	348	100	100	100
Social services	2,400	1,974	1,974	1,974
Preventive health and health services	95*	83*	81	81
Alcohol, drug abuse, and mental health	376	409	432	432
Subtotal	3,862	3,141	3,028	2,922
Block grants enacted in 1981 and proposed				
for change in 1983:				
Services for women, infants, and children[2]	313	900	1,000	1,000
Primary health care	413	313	417	417
Energy and emergency assistance[3]	1,574	1,168	1,168	1,168
Subtotal	1,887	2,381	2,585	2,585
Proposed consolidations:				
Vocational and adult education		162	392	441
Education for the handicapped		37	643	836
Training and employment		900	2,250	1,800
Rehabilitation services		516	603	633
Child welfare grant		380	380	380
Rental rehabilitation grants			75	150
Combined welfare administration		2,181	2,181	2,181
Subtotal		4,176	6,524	6,421
TOTAL	5,749	9,698	12,137	11,928

[1]Outlays are based on estimated state participation.
[2]Formerly maternal and child health block grant.
[3]Formerly low-income energy assistance program.
*Budget Authority.

Source: Executive Office of the President, Office of Management and Budget:
The Budget of the United States Government, Special Analysis H, 1983
(February 1982).

billion or almost 11 percent in a single year. From 1983 to 1985, federal aid will rise slowly. However, by 1985, grants to state and local governments will have fallen by $11.3 billion from their 1981 level.

When grants-in-aid are broken down into direct aid for state and local governments and payments for individuals, the situation for cities and states is even more severe. Exhibit 8.10 shows that since 1980, payments for individuals have consumed a growing percentage of all grant-in-aid outlays. From 1980 to 1985, payments to individuals will expand by $9.1 billion or 27 percent, while direct assistance to state and local governments will decline $17.1 billion or 30 percent. As a percent of total grant-in-aid outlays, payments to individuals will increase from 37 percent in 1980

EXHIBIT 8.9. — *Outlays for General-Purpose, Broad-Based, and Other Grants, 1972–1985 (Percent)*

	ACTUAL					ESTIMATE		
	1972	1976	1980	1981	1982	1982	1984	1985
Percentage Distribution								
General-purpose grants	1.5	12.1	9.4	7.2	7.1	8.3	8.3	8.5
Broad-based grants	8.3	10.6	11.3	10.6	13.5	17.1	19.2	18.8
Other grants	90.2	77.3	79.3	82.2	79.4	74.6	72.5	72.7
Total	100.0	100.0	100.0	100.0	100.0	100.0	100.0	100.0

Source: Executive Office of the President, Office of Management and Budget: The Budget of the United States Government, Special Analysis H, 1983 (February 1982).

EXHIBIT 8.10. — *Trends in Grant-in-Aid Outlays, 1960–1985*

($ Millions)	Actual				Administration Estimates				
	1960	1970	1980	1981	1982	1983	1984	1985
Total Grants-in-Aid	7.0	24.0	91.5	94.8	91.2	81.4	81.9	83.5
Grants for Payment to Individuals	2.5	9.0	34.2	39.9	41.5	37.6	40.0	43.3
Other	4.5	15.0	57.3	54.8	49.7	43.9	41.9	40.2
Grants as a Percent of:								
Total Budget Outlays	7.6	12.3	15.9	14.4	12.6	10.7	10.2	9.6
Domestic Expenditures	15.9	21.3	21.2	19.5	17.3	15.5	15.1	14.8
State and Local Expenditures	14.7	19.2	26.3	25.3	NA	NA	NA	NA

Source: U.S. Office of Management and Budget, The United States Budget: Special Analysis H, 1983 (February 1982).

EXHIBIT 8.11. — *Annual Changes in Grant-in-Aid Outlays, 1978-1985 ($ Billions)*

	Actual				Administration Estimates			
	1978[1]	1979	1980	1981	1982	1983	1984	1985
Total Grants-in-Aid								
Absolute	+ 9.5	+ 5.0	+ 8.6	+ 3.3	- 3.6	- 9.8	+ 0.5	+ 1.6
Percent	+13.9	+ 6.4	+10.4	+ 3.6	- 3.8	-10.7	+ 0.6	+ 2.0
Grants for Payment to Individuals								
Absolute	+ 2.1	+ 2.8	+ 5.4	+ 5.7	+ 1.6	- 3.9	+ 2.4	- 2.3
Percent	+ 8.8	+10.8	+18.8	+16.6	+ 4.0	- 9.4	+ 6.4	- 5.8
Other								
Absolute	+ 7.3	+ 2.2	+ 3.2	- 2.5	- 5.1	- 5.8	- 2.0	- 1.7
Percent	+16.4	+ 4.2	+ 5.9	- 4.4	- 9.3	-11.7	- 4.5	- 4.1

[1]Percent change from 1977.

Source: U.S. Office of Management and Budget, The United States Budget: Special Analysis H, 1983 (February 1982).

to more than 50 percent in 1985. Direct assistance to state and local governments during that same period will fall from 63 percent to 48 percent.

Much of the increase in grant-in-aid outlays for individuals can be attributed to a rapidly growing Medicaid program. This shift in emphasis on grants for payment to individuals means that capital improvement projects such as waste and water treatment and urban mass transit construction will be significantly curtailed. Exhibit 8.12 shows outlays for direct grants to state and local governments by major category and illustrates, by activity, the projected declining role of these direct grants between 1981 and 1985.

Including payments to individuals, federal assistance to state and local governments peaked in 1978 as a percentage of total federal outlays (17 percent), federal domestic spending (23 percent), and state and local expenditures (27 percent)*. Exhibit 8.10 indicates that grants-in-aid will decline steadily as a percentage of the total budget and as a proportion of the domestic outlays over the period 1983–84. By 1985, federal aid to state and local governments will constitute less than 10 percent of all federal outlays. As a proportion of total domestic spending, grants-in-aid will account for under 15 percent.

Exhibit 8.13 shows the percentage distribution of federal grant-in-aid funding by function, while Exhibit 8.14 reflects actual dollar funding levels. From Exhibit 8.13, it is clear that there have been extreme fluctuations in the functional distribution of federal grant-in-aid monies over the past twenty years. In FY 1981, income security was funded at $21.3 billion and accounted for 23 percent of all grant-in-aid outlays. By 1985, income security expenditures are projected to increase slightly to $22 billion, but as a percentage of all grants-in-aid, the income security function will expand to 26 percent. Education, training, employment and social services was the second largest function in 1981 with outlays of $21.1 billion. Unlike health expenditures, however, education and training programs have been slated for severe cutbacks and by 1985, are expected to decrease by one-half, to $10.7 billion. As a percentage of all grant-in-aid outlays, education, training, employment and social service programs will decline to 13 percent.

Although health outlays were the third principally funded function in 1981, at $19 billion, they are expected to experience the greatest growth by 1985. Health expenditures in that year should total $22.5 billion and account for fully 27 percent of all federal assistance to state and local governments. All other functions are projected to remain relatively stable with regard to their percentage of total outlays.[2]

Having now briefly reviewed the functional changes in the FY 1982–1983 budgets, relative to 1981 and prior years, the remainder of this chapter will analyze principal grant-in-aid programs, as well as entitlements to individuals, for the next several years. The analysis will proceed in the following manner:

Income Security	Health
Income Maintenance and Insurance	General Health Care
Food and Nutrition	Environment and Natural Resources
Community and Regional Development	Environment
Housing and Community Development	Transportation
Economic Development	Highways

*Not shown in tabular format.

EXHIBIT 8.12. — *Outlays for Direct Grants to State and Local Governments, 1981–1985 ($ Billions)*

	ACTUAL 1981	ADMINISTRATION ESTIMATE				CHANGE 1981–1985	
		1982	1983	1984	1985	Absolute	Percent
Energy Conservation Grants	0.5	0.5	0.2	0.1	-	NA	NA
Environmental Protection Agency Construction Grants	3.9	4.0	3.4	2.8	2.7	- 1.2	- 30.8
Other Natural Resources and Environment	1.1	1.1	0.8	0.7	0.7	- 0.4	- 36.7
Agriculture	0.8	0.9	0.9	0.9	0.9	+ 0.1	+ 12.5
Highway Grants	9.1	8.2	8.2	8.2	8.3	- 0.8	- 8.8
Urban Mass Transportation Fund	3.8	3.7	3.1	2.9	2.9	- 0.9	- 23.7
Airport Grants	0.5	0.5	0.4	0.5	0.6	+ 0.1	+ 20.0
Community Development Grants	4.0	4.0	3.4	3.2	3.5	- 0.5	- 12.5
Urban Development Action Grants	0.4	0.5	0.6	0.5	0.5	+ 0.1	+ 25.0
Rental Rehabilitation Grants	-	-	-	0.1	0.1	NA	NA
Area and Regional Development	1.2	1.0	0.8	0.5	0.3	- 0.9	- 75.0
Elementary, Secondary, and Vocational Education	6.6	6.7	5.1	4.2	3.6	- 3.0	- 45.5
Training and Employment	8.0	4.2	2.0	2.7	2.3	- 5.7	- 71.3
Social Services	6.2	6.1	4.8	4.8	4.8	- 1.4	- 22.6
Combined Welfare Administration	-	-	1.7	1.7	1.7	NA	NA
General Revenue Sharing	5.1	4.6	4.6	4.6	4.6	- 0.5	- 9.8
Other General Purpose Fiscal Assistance	1.6	1.7	2.0	2.2	2.5	+ 0.9	+ 56.3
Other	2.0	1.9	1.7	1.2	1.1	- 0.9	- 45.0
TOTAL	54.8	49.6	43.7	41.8	41.1	-13.7	- 25.0

Note: NA=Not applicable.

Source: U.S. Congressional Budget Office, *An Analysis of the President's Budgetary Proposals for Fiscal Year 1983* (February 1982).

EXHIBIT 8.13. — *Percentage Distribution of Federal Grant-in-Aid Outlays by Function, 1960–1985*

	Actual				Estimates			
	1960	1970	1980	1981	1982	1983	1984	1985
Energy	*	*	1	1	1	1	*	*
Natural resources and environment	2	2	6	5	6	5	4	4
Agriculture	3	3	1	1	1	1	1	1
Transportation	43	19	14	14	14	15	14	14
Community and regional development	2	7	7	6	7	6	5	5
Education, training, employment, and social service	7	27	24	22	19	15	14	13
Health	3	16	17	20	22	24	25	27
Income security	39	24	20	23	24	25	26	26
General purpose fiscal assistance	2	2	9	7	7	8	8	9
Other	*	1	1	1	1	1	*	*
TOTAL	100	100	100	100	100	100	100	100

*0.5% or less

Source: Executive Office of the President, Office of Management and Budget: The Budget of the United States Government: Special Analysis H, 1983 (February 1982).

EXHIBIT 8.14. — *Federal Grant-in-Aid Outlays by Function, 1981–1985 ($ Millions)*

Function	Actual 1981	Estimate 1982	Estimate 1983	Estimate 1984	Estimate 1985
National defense	75	82	106	72	72
Energy	617	679	409	100	–
Natural resources	4,944	5,110	4,166	3,554	3,389
Agriculture	829	896	859	860	876
Commerce and housing credit	4	5	2	2	2
Transportation	13,462	12,534	11,889	11,654	11,899
Community and regional development	6,124	5,933	5,010	4,441	4,551
Education, training, employment, and social services	21,146	17,310	12,281	11,853	10,737
Health	18,895	20,122	19,469	20,799	22,544
Income security	21,341	21,718	20,331	21,411	22,076
Veterans benefits and services	74	66	65	70	72
Administration of justice	333	257	118	55	33
General government	208	190	163	182	160
General purpose fiscal assistance	6,710	6,319	6,549	6,798	7,104
Total Outlays	94,762	91,220	81,418	81,853	83,517

Source: Executive Office of the President, Office of Management and Budget: The Budget of the United States Government: Special Analysis H, 1983 (February 1982).

Education, Training, Employment, and
  Social Services
  Education
  Training and Employment
  Social Services

Urban Mass Transit
General Fiscal Assistance
  Revenue Transfers

Income Security

Income security benefits are paid to the aged, the disabled, the unemployed and low-income families. Income security is divided into two component substantive areas: (1) income maintenance and insurance, and (2) food and nutrition. With the exception of Social Security benefits and Unemployment Compensation, all income security programs suffer significant cuts as evidenced in the 1983 Budget and projections for the future.

Income Maintenance and Insurance

Social Security payments* (Old Age Survivor's and Disability Insurance) continue to increase at the rate of 10 percent per year due to: (1) an increasing number of applicants, (2) higher benefits due to cost of living and adjustments, and (3) higher wages upon which benefits are based. The report of the National Committee on

*As required by the Social Security Amendments of 1983, Social Security and Medicare will be shown in future budgets as one function.

Social Security Reform in January 1983 has increased the retirement age to 66 (to take effect after the year 2000) and has frozen the cost of living increment for six months. These changes have been combined with the extension of coverage to new federal workers and a tax on a portion of benefits paid to higher income beneficiaries. In the short run, this has eliminated the projected deficit and in the long run will reduce slightly the year-to-year increase.

Unemployment Compensation

The level of Unemployment Compensation reflects estimates of average annual labor force participation. The Reagan Administration based its 1982 estimates of outlays on an unemployment rate of 8.9 percent and 1983 estimates of 8.1 percent. By 1985–1987 the Administration projects an unemployment rate of 6.5 percent. This would allow a 9–10 percent annual reduction in unemployment compensation. The Congressional Budget Office (CBO) baseline projects a much more modest 3–4 percent reduction in unemployment compensation based on higher rates of anticipated unemployment. Current (1984) unemployment rates of approximately 7 percent indicate the Reagan Administration projections to be more accurate.

Aid to Families with Dependent Children

Fourteen program changes in AFDC have eliminated approximately $1.2 billion from the FY 1982 program level. These include job search requirements, unrelated adult income counted in household income, benefits keyed to workfare, and so on. Administration costs to state and local governments would be provided to states in a block grant and capped at 95 percent of current levels. This and other measures would reduce program levels by another $.9 billion. This combined reduction of $2.1 billion for FY 1982 will be maintained in the future. With erosion for inflation, at 6 percent annually, AFDC by 1987 will be at 40 percent of its 1982 level (Exhibit 8.15).

Supplemental Security Income

Supplemental Security Income, cash assistance to low-income individuals who are aged, blind or disabled, would increase at a rate of 3 percent per year over the next five years. The program's outlays of $8 billion in 1982 would increase to over $9 billion by 1987. In real terms, this would be an actual decrease of approximately 15 percent.

EXHIBIT 8.15. — *Income Security Outlays, Reagan Administration (R) Projections[1] and Congressional Budget Office (CBO) Baselines[2], 1982-1987 ($ Billions)*

		1982	1983	1984	1985	1986	1987	Simple Average Annual Percent Change
I. INCOME SECURITY								
A. Income Maintenance and Insurance								
1. Social Security (OASDI)	R	156	173	188	202[3]	-	-	10.0
	CBO	156	171	186	202	218	235	10.1
2. AFDC	R	7.6	5.4	5.5	5.5	5.6	5.6	-5.2
	CBO	8	8	8	9	9	10	6.3
3. Unemployment Compensation	R	25.2	22.6	19.8	18.0[3]	-	-	-9.5
	CBO	24	21	20	20	20	20	-3.3
4. Supplemental Security Income	R	7.9	8.9	7.8	8.6	8.9	9.2	3.3
	CBO	8	9	8	9	10	11	7.5
B. Food and Nutrition								
1. Food Stamps	R	10.3	9.6	9.7	10.0	10.2	10.4	0.2
	CBO	11	12	12	13	14	15	7.2
2. Nutrition Assistance	R	3.7	3.5	3.7	3.9	4.1	4.3	3.2
	CBO	4	5	6	6	7	7	15.0

Note: CBO figures are rounded; Base Year 1982 is usually the same for both estimates.

Source: [1]Office of Management and Budget, Major Themes and Additional Budget Details, FY-1983, February 1982. [2]Congressional Budget Office, Baseline Budget Projections for Fiscal Years 1983-1987 – Part II, February 1982. [3]Office of Management and Budget, Budget of the United States Government, FY1983, February 1982.

Food and Nutrition

Food Stamps

Under the Reagan Administration, the Food Stamp program outlays will remain approximately the same through 1987. This contrasts sharply with a 40 percent increase in outlays estimated by the Congressional Budget Office for this same time period. The program currently serves 20 million individuals. A number of changes will be incorporated to redirect the program specifically to the dependent poor. These include the incorporation of energy assistance payments in household income; eliminating applicants whose monthly benefits are less than $10; less-than-whole-dollar benefit rounding; $.05 increase in benefit–work reduction; job search requirements, etc.

Child Nutrition

The child nutrition program (school lunches or breakfasts, child care meals, summer meals, snacks, nutrition education, WIC, special milk, assistance for Puerto Rico, etc.) will experience an overall 3 percent increase through 1987.

The special milk program was all but discontinued in FY 1983; summer feeding and nutritional educational and training programs have also been scheduled for near-termination. Supplemental Food for Women, Infants and Children (WIC) has been reduced by 34 percent from FY 1982 to FY 1983. The school breakfast and child care feeding programs will be reduced and provided in the form of a non-school food program grant to states. The school lunch program will be reduced slightly in 1983 following the more severe reductions of 1982 (Exhibit 8.15).

Income security programs are characterized by slight reductions in growth of entitlement (across-the-board) programs and reasonably severe cuts in means-tested (hardship) programs.

Community and Regional Development

Housing and Community Development

Community Development Block Grant

The Community Development Block Grant (CDBG) funding levels will be extended into the future at $3.5 billion, approximately 20 percent less in outlays than their 1981 and 1982 levels. In FY 1981, approximately $2.8 billion went to 669 large cities and urban counties; $1.2 billion to 1,830 smaller communities. In 1981, the split of funds between entitlement and non-entitlement cities was reduced from 75/25 to 70/30. Further, by 1982 there were 732 entitlement cities, i.e., more needy cities competing and less money to compete for.

While the current Administration has made statements that it is committed to continuing this program and several tragic infrastructure failures in 1983 would seem to sustain this position, even under estimates of inflation at 6 percent for the next several years, by 1987 this program will be 50 percent beneath its 1981 level. Community Development loan guarantees of $300 million in FY 1982, used as seed money for economic development ventures, were discontinued in FY 1983 (Exhibit 8.16).

Housing Subsidies

The key to understanding future housing subsidies is acknowledgment that there will be little increase in the total number of households or housing units assisted through federal housing subsidies. This will be bitterly opposed, as housing availability to all income groups has always been the essence of the American dream. Nonetheless, the subsidy focus will be almost exclusively on tenants in existing housing and the shift of subsidies from one program to another to upgrade and maintain the current subsidized stock.[3]

Section 8, for instance, originally conceived to provide assistance for the development of new, rehabilitated and existing housing, will be directed primarily to existing housing. FY 1983 contained approximately $10 billion for new construction or substantial rehabilitation, down sevenfold from 1981 and fifteenfold from 1979. This new construction is reserved primarily for housing the elderly and handicapped. There are no proposed FY 1983 outlays for moderate rehabilitation, a decrease of $25 billion from 1981 and $35 billion from 1979 (Exhibit 8.16).

A small number of Section 8 Existing Housing Certificates have been used to convert Section 23 commitments to Section 8. Most of the Administration housing effort is currently directed at the employment of "Modified" Section 8 Housing Certificates. This is by no means a replacement of programs at existing levels, but rather both a change of substance and of magnitude. Modified Section 8 Housing Certificates are based upon tenants paying 30 percent of income for rent or a threshold minimum rent (Community Development Amendments of 1981). HUD's contribution is based entirely on 30 percent of income or minimum rents. If a tenant finds an apartment cheaper than 30 percent of income, he may use the difference for other purposes. If it is more costly, the difference may be paid out-of-pocket. The HUD commitment is a flat contribution for five years with a potential for tenant reapplication after five years, if still qualified. In FY 1983, HUD obligated 106,000 commitments:

(1) 60,000 Certificates to convert Section 8 Existing Housing commitments to Modified Certificates;
(2) 30,000 Certificates for the Rental Rehabilitation initiative;
(3) 10,000 Certificates for use with sale of HUD-owned properties;
(4) 5,000 Certificates to tenants of abandoned, demolished, or old public housing; and
(5) 1,000 Certificates to Section 8 New Construction units of prior years whose owners do not renew five-year Section 8 contracts.

Current budgets have no additional authority for public housing development; local authorities are given the option of using new construction commitments for modernization. Urban Homesteading got $12 million in FY 1983 primarily for the

EXHIBIT 8.16. — *Community and Regional Development Outlays, Reagan Administration (R) Projections[1] and Congressional Budget Office (CBO) Baselines[2], 1982–1987 ($ Billions)*

		1982	1983	1984	1985	1986	1987	Simple Average Annual Percent Change
II. COMMUNITY AND REGIONAL DEVELOPMENT								
A. Housing & Community Development								
1. CDBG	R	4.0	3.3	3.2	3.5	3.5	3.5	- 2.5
	CBO	.4	.4	.4	.4	.4	.4	0.0
2. Rent Supplement/Assistance	R	.2	1.2	2.1	2.4	1.9	1.2	0.0 ('83-'87)
3. Section 8 New Const/ Sub Rehab Mod Rehab Existing Housing	R	17.3	10.0	-	-	-	-	-20.0
4. Subsidized Housing New Production	R	.01	.03	.3	.7	1.3	2.0	20.0
5. Modified Section 8 Certificates	R	0	6.1	4.4	5.4	8.1	5.2	20.0
6. Elderly/Handicapped Housing	R	.7	.3	.1	.2	.0	- .2	-20.0
7. Public Housing Operating Subsidies	R	1.3	1.1	1.0	1.0	1.0	0.9	- 6.2
8. Section 312	R	.1	0	.1	.2	.2	-	-20.0
9. Rental Rehab Grants	R	0	0	.1	.2	.2	.2	20.0

Source: See bottom of next page.

EXHIBIT 8.16. (continued)

		1982	1983	1984	1985	1986	1987	*Simple Average Annual Percent Change*
II. COMMUNITY AND REGIONAL DEVELOPMENT								
B. Economic Development								
1. Economic Development Admin. & Trade Adjust. Asst. Prog.	*R*	.5	.3	.2	.1	.01	0.0	-20.0
	CBO							
2. UDAG	*R*	.5	.6	.5	.5	.5	.4	- 4.0
	CBO	.5	.6	.6	.5	-	-.3	0.0
3. SBA Loans	*R*	.2	.1	0	0	0	0	-20.0
	CBO							
4. SBA Guarantees	*R*	3.1	2.9	2.9	2.3	1.8	1.2	-11.6
	CBO							

Note: CBO figures are rounded; Base Year 1982 is usually the same for both estimates.
Source: 1Office of Management and Budget, Major Themes and Additional Budget Details, FY-1983, February 1982.
2Congressional Budget Office, Baseline Budget Projections for Fiscal Years 1983-1987 - Part II, February 1982.
3Office of Management and Budget, Budget of the United States Government, FY1983, February 1982.

transfer of HUD, FMHA and VA properties to local governments for homesteading. This is a 10 percent decrease over 1981 operating subsidies, although there was a one-shot $3.0 billion demonstration grant during that year. Section 312 Rehabilitation Loans funded at $232 million in FY 1981 have been replaced by a new Rehabilitation Grant program funded at $150 million in FY 1983 (Exhibit 8.16).

The FY 1983 budget included $121 billion for housing programs. This was down $100 billion from 1981 and $200 billion from 1979. FY 1983 was only 60 percent of FY 1981's appropriations. Continuing at current levels, in five years inflation would erode housing subsidies by an additional 30 percent.

Economic Development Programs

Economic Development Administration

The Administration has consistently tried to eliminate a main public sponsor of economic development, the Economic Development Administration (EDA). No funds were requested for EDA in FY 1983 although a $200 million phaseout budget for 1982 was extended into 1983. The Community Development Block Grant (CDBG) and the Urban Development Action Grant (UDAG) are programs which are supposed to carry out similar purposes as EDA. Increased funding is *not* proposed, however, for either of these two programs given the demise of EDA. This represents a decrease of over $500 million from FY 1979 and $400 million from FY 1981. Trade Adjustment Assistance ($15 million annually) under the International Trade Administration (Commerce) was also eliminated subsequent to 1983 (Exhibit 8.16).

Urban Development Action Grants

Urban Development Action Grants (UDAG) will be continued at approximately the $450 million level in FY 1983 and into the future. This is a 10 percent smaller outlay than in FY 1982, but a 35 percent reduction from FY 1981.

The Administration's emphasis on private initiatives for economic development is reflected in the retention of this program due to its private-sector leveraging capacity. Again, even though there is no direct cut planned for the future, inflation coupled with the 1981 reductions will render this program in 1987 at about 50 percent of its 1981 strength.

Small Business Administration

The Small Business Administration (SBA) Direct Loan Program which had outlays of $219 million in 1981 has been largely discontinued by FY 1983. This reflects the Administration's desire not to provide direct subsidy to the private business sector. An indirect subsidy, the Loan Guarantee program, will have its commitments reduced from $3.6 billion in FY 1981 to $1.2 billion in FY 1987. This is a 67 percent reduction over this six-year period (Exhibit 8.16). The Minority Business Development Agency has received a slight increase from $47 to $60 billion from FY 1981 to FY 1983 for the purposes of management and technical assistance, and will be maintained at this level into the future.

Overall, economic development programs have been, and will continue to be, cut significantly as the Administration continues to opt for budget cuts and regulatory reform rather than subsidy as a means for achieving economic and business development.

Education, Training, Employment and Social Services

Education

Central to the Reagan Administration's education policy is the dismantling of the Department of Education as a Cabinet-level agency and replacing it with a Foundation for Education Assistance. Program reduction is also a major thrust, with the new Foundation to administer thirty-eight programs rather than the current Department's 149. Thirty programs would be consolidated into six broader authorities and twenty-three would be eliminated. FY 1983 budget for the Foundation was just under $9 billion, plus approximately $2 billion for transferred programs. This is a decrease of $3 billion, or 23 percent from the FY 1982 Continuing Resolution level of $13 billion for the Education Department. It is a decrease of $4.8 billion, or 32 percent below FY 1981 outlays. After a blue-ribbon commission report on the inferior quality of education in the United States, future Administration program thrusts will reward efficiency both in the classroom and in overall education management. While such things as merit pay for skilled teachers will be opposed by the National Education Association, this is the type of Reagan Administration thinking for the future.

Elementary, Secondary, and Vocational Education

Education grant programs, including Chapter 1 of the Education Consolidation and Improvement Act of 1981 (ECIA), provide funds to state and local education services for the educationally disadvantaged. They are planned to undergo a 45 percent reduction from FY 1982 to FY 1987 (Exhibit 8.17). Given inflation at a 6 percent rate during this period, by 1987 these programs would be operating at one-fourth their currently budgeted strength.

Training and Employment

Comprehensive Training and Employment Act

The Administration has sought to eliminate all of the programs currently funded under the Comprehensive Employment and Training Act (CETA) and to replace

EXHIBIT 8.17. — *Education, Training, Employment, and Social Service Outlays Reagan Administration (R) Projections[1] and Congressional Budget Office (CBO) Baselines,[2] 1982–1987 ($ Billions)*

		1982	1983	1984	1985	1986	1987	Simple Average Annual Percent Change
III. EDUCATION, TRAINING, EMPLOYMENT AND SOCIAL SERVICES								
A. Education								
1. Elementary, Secondary, Vocational Education (also Indian, Adult, Handicapped, Rehabilitated)	R	6.2	4.8	4.1	3.6	3.5	3.5	-8.4
	CBO	6	6	6	7	7	8	6.7
B. Training and Employment								
1. CETA	R[4]	4.2	2.1	2.8	2.4	2.4	2.4	-8.6
	CBO	3	3	3	4	4	4	6.7
C. Human Services								
1. Social Services and Community Action	R	6.4	5.1	5.0	5.0[3]	-	-	-7.3
	CBO	6	6	6	7	7	8	6.7

Notes: CBO Figures are rounded; Base Year 1982 is usually the same for both estimates.
[4]Includes CETA, TAA, CSEA.

Source: [1]Office of Management and Budget, Major Themes and Additional Budget Details, FY-1983, February 1982.
[2]Congressional Budget Office, *Baseline Budget Projections for Fiscal Years 1983-1987 – Part II,* February 1982.
[3]Office of Management and Budget, *Budget of the United States Government,* FY1983, February 1982.

them with a three-part program: a block grant to states, the Job Corps, and a national program for special target groups who are unable to find jobs. The proposed outlays for the new program are 50 percent less than they were in FY 1982 and 77 percent less than in FY 1979. Future outlays show a moderate increase from 1983 to 1984 and a leveling off from 1985 to 1987 (Exhibit 8.17). In current dollars, training and employment programs by 1987 are only 55 percent of their 1982 levels; in constant dollars, they are only one-quarter of their 1982 levels.

Social Services

Community Action and Social Services

Human services includes five programs under the Community Action grouping, as well as eight programs under Social Services. The Reagan Administration's budget crunching has included cutbacks and changes as well as the elimination of several major programs. Legal services, VISTA and the Work Incentive Program were cut severely. Community Action Programs would drop to $205 million in FY 1983, down from $1.1 billion in 1979. Head Start and the Aging Programs will be continued at FY 1982 levels. Overall, Human Service programs will decrease by close to 25 percent by FY 1985, over 40 percent if inflation is considered (Exhibit 8.17).

Health

General Health Care

Medicaid

Large cuts are planned for domestic health programs. These cuts currently, and will in the future, face significant congressional reaction. FY 1983 and subsequent budgets will evidence continued reductions in Medicaid and shifts to block grants for current categorical programs such as Family Planning, Black Lung and Migrant Health.

Although not shown due to inflation and participant increases, Medicaid outlays would be reduced by close to $1 million in FY 1983 through Reagan Administration regulatory and legislative changes (Exhibit 8.18).

Medicare

Medicare costs increased sharply in FY 1983, reflecting inflation and participant growth. Under current law and policy, this program will grow about 12 percent, or $6 billion in FY 1983. A number of changes are proposed by the Administration — these could limit the growth of the program by $15 billion by 1987 (Exhibit 8.18).

EXHIBIT 8.18. — *Health and Environment and Natural Resource Outlays*
Reagan Administration (R) Projections[1] and Congressional Budget Office (CBO)
Baselines,[2] 1982–1987 ($ Billions)

		1982	1983	1984	1985	1986	1987	Simple Average Annual Percent Change
IV.	**HEALTH**							
	A. General Health							
	1. Medicare	R	49.5	55.3	61.2	68.4	75.6	83.0	13.5
		CBO	50	58	68	78	90	103	21.2
	2. Medicaid	R	17.8	17.0	18.6	20.4	22.1	24.3	7.3
		CBO	18	20	22	25	28	30	13.3
	3. Health Planning	R	.12	.06	.02	.01	0	0[3]	-20.0
		CBO							
V.	**ENVIRONMENT AND NATURAL RESOURCES**							
	A. Public Facilities							
	1. Wastewater Treatment Grants	R	4.1	3.4	2.8	2.9[3]	–	–	-9.8
		CBO	4	4	4	3	3	3	-5.0

Note: CBO figures are rounded; Base Year 1982 is usually the same for both estimates.

Source: [1]Office of Management and Budget, Major Themes and Additional Budget Details, FY-1983, February 1982. [2]Congressional Budget Office, Baseline Budget Projections for Fiscal Years 1983-1987 - Part II, February 1982. [3]Office of Management and Budget, Budget of the United States Government, FY1983, February 1982.

There include establishment of a prospective payment system for hospital insurance, increasing supplementary medical insurance premiums and deductibles, and temporarily freezing physician reimbursements. The likelihood is that changes in this program's structure will come although they will be hard fought.

Health Planning Grants

Health planning grants to health systems agencies and state health planning and development agencies will have only a $3 million phaseout budget by FY 1987 (Exhibit 8.18). In 1981, outlays for these services were $160 million; in 1983 they were approximately $70 million. The intent in removing funding for this program is to reduce its regulatory impact and hopefully to encourage private market growth of similar services.

Environment and Natural Resources

The Administration's FY 1983 budget for environmental programs proposes cutbacks of locally directed EPA and Department of the Interior activities. EPA's operating budget is cut back by 12 percent from FY 1982 to FY 1983. Department of the Interior programs for cities are to be substantially eliminated. Urban Parks, Land and Water Conservation and Historic Preservation programs had minimal funding in FY 1983. This is a reduction of $320 million from FY 1979, $180 million from FY 1981. New areas of growth in this function are proposed outlays for cleaning up hazardous waste sites/chemical spills and budget authority for acid-rain research.

Environment

Wastewater Treatment Grants

Wastewater Treatment Grant outlays were projected at $2.9 billion for FY 1985. This was down $1.4 billion from FY 1982 and about one-half the originally proposed 1977 program outlays of $5 billion annually (Exhibit 8.18). This is considerable shrinkage in the program at a time when many cities are under court-ordered mandates to complete their wastewater treatment facilities.

Transportation

The Reagan Administration in its FY 1983 budget undertook significant cuts in urban transportation programs. Public transportation subsidies were down close to 40 percent from 1982, urban highway programs were 44 percent under 1982 outlays, and subsidies to Amtrak were 18 percent below 1982 levels and 33 percent below 1981.

Highways

The Administration plans a complete phaseout of local urban transportation programs by FY 1985 to concentrate on interstate and primary highway programs — programs of a "national" nature. The backbone of this policy change is the Surface Transportation Assistance Act of 1982 which relies on user charges for revenues. Deteriorating interstates will receive funds for rehabilitation or expansion whereas projects that benefit particular states or localities will receive lower priority. Special interest highway categories (billboard removal, grade crossing upgrading, etc.) will be eliminated.

Federal Aid Urban Systems

Although highway programs of national interest will continue, the Federal Aid Urban Systems (FAUS) will be down 44 percent from FY 1982. This is one of the few highway programs that cities can use to improve local roads. It was scheduled for complete phaseout by FY 1984.

Urban Mass Transit

FY 1983 experienced $640 million in transit operating subsidies, an 88 percent decrease from FY 1982. The program will be phased out by 1985. The decrease in authorizations will soon be followed by significant decreases in outlays (Exhibit 8.19). The Reagan Administration's position is that operating subsidies are not a federal responsibility and must be borne by increases in the fare box. Capital assistance grants will continue for existing and for some new facilities, supported by one cent per gallon of the existing motor fuels tax. Planning and research will be more narrowly focused on short-term, practical projects. By FY 1987, outlays will be only 80 percent of their 1981 levels; barely 50 percent in constant dollars.

General Fiscal Assistance

General Revenue Sharing was continued in FY 1983 at its 1982 level (Exhibit 8.19). The program will continue through FY 1987. Since the revenue-raising ability of the federal government is reduced as a result of tax cuts, and state governments appear more fiscally solvent, much of the original purpose of the Revenue-Sharing program has been lost. The Administration hopes to turn this program over to the state at a point in time near the program's expiration date.

Summary

Exhibit 8.20 presents a listing of the programs that emerged and were directed to cities over the previous two decades. The first column of this exhibit lists the incidence of these programs in intergovernmental versus non-intergovernmental cities;

EXHIBIT 8.19.—*Transportation and General Fiscal Assistance Outlays,*
Reagan Administration (R) Projections[1] and Congressional Budget Office (CBO)
Baselines,[2] 1982–1987 ($ Billions)

		1982	1983	1984	1985	1986	1987	Simple Average Annual Percent Change
VI. TRANSPORTATION								
A. Capital Construction								
1. Highways	R	8.3	8.3	8.3	8.4	8.5	8.5	0.5
	CBO	8	8	9	9	10	10	4.3
2. Urban Mass Transit	R	3.7	3.1	3.0	3.0	3.0	3.0	-3.8
	CBO	4	4	4	4	4	5	7.0
VII. GENERAL FISCAL ASSISTANCE								
A. Federal Assistance								
1. General Revenue Sharing	R	4.6	4.6	4.6	4.6[3]	-	-	0.0
	CBO	5	5	5	5	5	6	4.0

Note: CBO figures are rounded; Base Year 1982 is usually the same for both estimates.

Source: [1]Office of Management and Budget, Major Themes and Additional Budget Details, FY-1983, February 1982.
[2]Congressional Budget Office, Baseline Budget Projections for Fiscal Years 1983-1987 - Part II, February 1982.
[3]Office of Management and Budget, Budget of the United States Government, FY1983, February 1982.

EXHIBIT 8.20. — *Percent and Dollar Changes in Major Grant-in-Aid and Entitlement Programs, 1982–1987*

	1981 Ratio of IGC to N-IGC Federal Assistance	$ BILLIONS			CHANGE			
		1982	1987	1987	Actual 1982–1987		Percent 1982–1987	
		Current	Current	Constant	Current	Constant	Current	Constant
AFDC	3.4	7.6	5.6	3.7	− 2.0	− 3.9	−26	−51.3
Social Security	2.3	156	233 ¹	154	+77	− 2	+49.4	− 1.3
Unemployment	2.2	25.2	13.2¹	8.7	−12.0	−16.5	−47.6	−65.5
Food Stamps	1.3	10.3	10.4	6.9	+ 0.1	− 3.4	+ 1.0	−33.0
Nutrition Assistance*	-0.8	3.7	4.3	2.8	+ 0.6	− 0.9	+16.2	−24.3
CDBG	3.2	4.0	3.5	2.3	− 0.5	− 1.7	−12.5	−42.5
Public Housing	2.8	1.3	0.9	0.3	− 0.4	− 1.0	−30.8	−76.9
Section 8²	2.6							
UDAG	NA	0.5	0.4	0.3	0.1	0.2	−20.0	−40.0
CETA	-0.8	4.2	2.4	1.6	− 1.8	− 2.6	−42.9	−61.9
Medicaid	2.4	17.8	24.3	16.0	+ 6.5	− 1.8	+36.5	−10.1
UMTA	2.3	3.7	3.0	2.0	− 0.7	− 1.7	−18.9	−45.9
Wastewater Treatment	18.5	4.1	2.1¹	1.4	− 2.0	− 2.7	−48.8	−65.9
Revenue Sharing	1.1	4.6	4.6	3.0	0.0	− 1.6	0.0	−34.8

*Includes school breakfast and lunch programs only.

NA = Not applicable. The average non-intergovernmental city did not receive UDAG assistance.

¹Assumes 1982–1985 rate of increase to continue unchanged through 1987.

²See Exhibit 8.16 for details on changes in the Section 8 housing programs.

Source: Exhibits 8.15–8.19.

the second two columns show the reduction of these programs due to proposed budget cuts in current and constant dollars. Reductions reflect the 1983 Reagan Administration budget, and the conversion from current to constant dollars is a compounded inflation rate of six percent annually.

Discussion certainly can surround both choice of estimate as well as the inflation rate employed. Yet, given the above choices, over the next several years, cities will experience an average of 20 to 30 percent cutbacks in most programs in current dollars and 50 to 60 percent in constant dollars. Further, a large share of the most severe cuts is found in programs which have in the past favored intergovernmental cities. Cities, and intergovernmental cities in particular, are bearing the brunt of economic recovery. In addition, once recovery has been sustained, there will not be a rebirth of intergovernmental transfers. The intergovernmental city and the spending necessary to sustain it are a thing of the past. A strategy of city maintenance became too expensive in terms of competing national priorities.

The overt curtailment of public subsidy to cities, in the form of reduction and elimination of grant-in-aid and entitlement programs, is unparalleled in the history of modern municipal finance. The Reagan Administration, faced with the prospect of "public" cities in 1980, has significantly decreased their subsidy dependence by mid-decade. Further, this across-the-board, unyielding policy of mandatory municipal self-sufficiency has not been challenged at the second term by the Democrats. Future fiscal relationships for cities will be among municipal peers or in the short run, between states and cities. For much of the foreseeable future the federal government is retreating rapidly from municipal finance.

The reaction by cities to permanent cuts in subsidies has involved a number of strategies and will be covered in the following chapter.

NOTES

1. U.S. Advisory Commission on Intergovernmental Relations, "The First Ten Months: Grants-in-Aid, Regulatory and Other Changes," *Intergovernmental Perspective*, Vol. 8, No. 1, Winter 1982.

2. Executive Office of the President, Office of Management and Budget, *The Budget of the United States Government, FY 1985*. OMB, February 1, 1984.

3. Raymond J. Struyk, Neil Mayer and John A. Tuccillo, *Federal Housing Policy at President Reagan's Midterm*. Washington, D.C.: The Urban Institute, 1983.

9
Streamlining and Restructuring
the Intergovernmental City

Introduction: The Local Impact of
Domestic Spending Reductions

CUTBACKS ACCOMPLISHED UNDER the FY 1982 Budget, together with FY 1983–1985 spending reduction proposals, pose harshly uneven impacts for the two classes of cities. According to a number of analyses performed under the auspices of the Joint Economic Committee of the Congress, the current round of domestic spending reductions hits hardest at the least-advantaged, most-distressed cities. A two-year old staff report by the Joint Economic Committee spelled out the differential impact of the FY 1982 Budget cuts.

> It is not only that declining cities receive more aid and therefore are losing greater absolute amounts of aid. Rather the percentage of aid that these high unemployment declining cities are losing is almost double the proportion of lost aid suffered in low unemployment growing cities.[1]

For example, in 1981 local officials in Boston anticipated losing over $50 million in federal funds. Baltimore faced an enormous loss of over $330 million in federal outlays. Detroit stood to lose even more, up to $500 million in federal assistance.[2] The differential impact of the budget cuts is perhaps best summarized by the chief official of a fast-growing Sunbelt city, Mayor Rusk of Albuquerque.

> If I were the mayor of Newark, I would be worried, but it's different being the mayor of Albuquerque. In the short term, the lack of [federal] money is going to be painful. But our community has the capacity to replace federal intervention with local funds.[3]

Recent reports by the Joint Economic Committee document these trends.[4] The reports conclude that declining cities have had to reduce expenditures, increase taxes and postpone capital projects, in order to balance their annual budgets. Further the most drastic reductions in service levels have taken place in those declining cities where the rate of unemployment exceeded 6 percent. These high-distress cities have been forced to cut back services across the board, budgeting for real decreases in expenditures in every service (i.e. police, fire, sanitation, health, and recreation).

Cutbacks in services were only one side of the story. According to the Joint Economic Committee, most declining cities have also been forced to drastically increase

295

tax collections. As Exhibit 9.1 shows, these cities have upped revenues from a variety of taxes. More than 60 percent have increased their property tax rates. An additional 12 percent have raised their sales taxes. Nineteen percent have raised income taxes. Nearly 40 percent have called for increases in a variety of other levies.

Most importantly, the Joint Committee report directly addresses the issue of the local impact of domestic spending cuts. In their survey, local officials were called upon to estimate the size of FY 1982 federal aid rollbacks, based upon FY 1981 levels of assistance. The results of this survey, reported in Exhibit 9.2, were quite dramatic. All of the declining cities reported real reductions in federal aid. Of these, 27 percent indicated that reductions took away more than 36 percent of FY 1981 assistance. In contrast, none of the growing cities anticipated losing that much federal revenue. Further, the bulk of the declining cities—over 45 percent—anticipated losing between 10 and 35 percent of the previous year's federal assistance. The remaining declining cities predicted decreases in federal aid in the range of 5 to 10 percent. None of these cities expected higher funding levels; yet, nearly 7 percent of the growing cities expected increases in federal assistance. The overall thrust of the data can be put quite simply: the neediest, most distressed cities lost the largest and most disproportionate share of federal funds.

Last, there is the issue of the "delayed effect" of the domestic spending cuts.[5] For many cities facing FY 1982, federal grant accounts often had unspent balances that could be carried forward to offset cuts in federal funds. For example, the effects of cuts in federal education aid were delayed because those grants are forward funded, i.e., appropriated in one year for use in the following year. Hence, the effects of the FY 1982 cuts were postponed until the 1983 school year. Little adjustment was required at the local level. The impact of cuts was less than their potential reality.

Cuts in federal welfare aid actually created savings for some localities. As federal eligibility criteria were tightened, many households were removed from the AFDC and Medicaid rolls. This meant that local governments could actually spend less in matching funds for welfare. These savings were often used to replace lost funds in other service areas.

The full effects of reductions in capital gains (i.e., highways and sewers) were also delayed. Because of the tremendous front-end costs involved in sunk capital projects, a large chunk of committed funds already in the federal aid pipeline were unaffected by FY 1982 spending rollbacks. These funds again could be used to offset reductions in other areas.

The delayed effects of the FY 1982 domestic spending reductions have enabled many local governments to escape serious fiscal destabilization. These cities have responded over the short term in a hurried, piecemeal fashion, moving funds into and out of service areas in order to balance their subsequent budgets. These stopgap measures thus far have worked to offset the more onerous effects of federal retrenchment. Further, a very strong national economy has provided local and state surpluses based on unpredicted own-source revenue growth. Short-term measures and a healthy economy potentially mask a very difficult situation.

EXHIBIT 9.1. — *Changing Revenue-Raising Strategies in an Era of Fiscal Constraint: Types of Tax Increases, 1981–1982*

	Property Tax Increase	Sales Tax Increase	Income Tax Increase	Other Tax Increase	Total Revenue Raised (In Millions of Dollars)
Total City Respondents n=20	60.0% (12)	25.0% (5)	15.0% (3)	30.0% (6)	$455
Declining Cities n=16	62.5% (10)	12.5% (2)	18.8% (3)	37.5% (6)	$415
Growing Cities n=4	50.0% (2)	75.0% (3)	0.0% (0)	0.0% (0)	$40
High Unemployment Cities n=10	60.0% (6)	20.0% (2)	10.0% (1)	20.0% (2)	$316
Moderate Unemployment n=6	66.6% (4)	16.6% (1)	33.3% (2)	66.6% (4)	$100
Low Unemployment Cities n=4	50.0% (2)	50.0% (2)	0.0% (0)	0.0% (0)	$39

Source: U.S. Congress, Joint Economic Committee, <u>Emergency Interim Survey: Fiscal Condition of 48 Large Cities</u>, January, 1982.

Resource Constraint at the State Level

The states, despite general national prosperity, cannot make up the difference in reduced federal aid. As they enter new budget years, many states are confronting severe financial problems.[6] Several states are experiencing acute budget shortfalls. Many have cut programs, some have laid off workers, most have raised taxes. Again, there is a regional taxonomy to state financial problems. Acute fiscal stress among state governments is concentrated in the Mid-Atlantic region, the Midwest and the Far West. States in the Sunbelt and the New England states (i.e., Massachusetts, Maine, Vermont) appear to be fiscally sound. Here, some examples are illustrative.

By the end of FY 1982, three states were experiencing tremendous deficits—in excess of $2 billion. California faced a budget shortfall of $2.5 billion. In Minnesota, the projected deficit was $1.3 billion. In Michigan, the deficit was also expected to exceed $1 billion. Other states expecting acute budgetary shortfalls included Ohio ($500 million), Oregon ($250 million), Wisconsin ($350 million), and Washington ($250 million). In addition, Connecticut, Idaho, Indiana, Rhode Island, and West Virginia all faced smaller but nonetheless substantial deficits.

Most of these states, along with many others, responded to fiscal stress by cutting

EXHIBIT 9.2.—*Impact of Budget Cuts on Declining Versus Growing Cities*

	Estimated Size of Federal Cutbacks As Percent of 1981 Aid Levels			
	More Than 36	*9 To 36*	*0 To 9*	*Increase*
Declining Cities	27.3%	45.4%	27.3%	0%
n=22	(6)	(10)	(6)	(0)
Growing Cities	0%	44.4%	38.9%	16.7%
n=18	(0)	(8)	(7)	(3)
High Unemployment Cities	23.6%	52.9%	17.6%	5.9%
n=17	(4)	(9)	(3)	(1)
Moderate Unemployment Cities	7.7%	38.5%	46.1%	7.7%
n=13	(1)	(5)	(6)	(1)
Low Unemployment Cities	10.0%	40.0%	40.0%	10.0%
n=10	(1)	(4)	(4)	(1)
TOTAL n = 40 cities	15.0%	45.0%	32.5%	7.5%
	(6)	(18)	(13)	(3)

Source: U.S. Congress, Joint Economic Committee, Emergency Interim Survey: Fiscal Condition of 48 Large Cities, January 1982.

back programs and laying off employees. For example, Kentucky trimmed $400 million from its FY 1982 budget, cut its work force by 2,500 workers, and instituted a hiring freeze. Michigan trimmed its budget by $350 million and laid off nearly 10,000 workers. In Idaho, one-third of the state's work force (4,700 employees) were put on a four-day work week. Ohio, West Virginia, and New Jersey placed a hiring freeze on state jobs. Pennsylvania, Iowa, and Nebraska reduced their work forces by more than 1,000 employees. Indiana and Wisconsin froze employee compensation. Rhode Island laid off 480 state workers. Illinois laid off nearly 2,000 over the course of FY 1983. Finally, twenty states raised taxes or imposed new ones. Of these, three states—Connecticut, Rhode Island, and Minnesota—have drastically accelerated their tax collections.

These are just some examples of the financial difficulties and management problems confronting states—largely states in declining regions. Overall eighteen states have cut spending, lapsed into deficits, or raised taxes. Twenty states have laid off workers or have stopped replacing those who leave. Others have instituted pay freezes and shortened work weeks.

In sum, potential fiscal problems at the state level complicate an already dire financial picture for declining cities. Other than social insurance (pension) funds, the growth in state government revenues has been flat. As sharp resource constraints hit the local level, state government is forced to solve its own financial problems. This, in turn, leaves declining, fiscally stressed, intergovernmental cities no place to turn for fiscal support.

Summary

An earlier chapter examined the impact of a series of Reagan Administration budget cuts on intergovernmental versus non-intergovernmental cities. It also looked briefly at the capacity for state assistance to fill the gaps left by substantial reductions in federal aid. Using this information as well as the descriptive information summarized here, some general conclusions can be offered.

- Reductions in federal spending have hit most harshly on older, declining intergovernmental cities. This is not only because aid levels have traditionally been highest in these cities, but because actual reductions have been highest there.
- State governments have also been adversely impacted by domestic spending cuts and also by more general resource constraints. At the same time that states in declining regions are being called upon to provide assistance to fiscally distressed municipalities, they are experiencing financial traumas of their own. The states clearly cannot fill in the gaps left by tremendous reductions in intergovernmental federal aid.
- As a consequence, both state and local governments have responded to fiscal stress simply by retrenching, that is, by cutting programs and laying off workers. This, in turn, has meant drastic declines in both the quality and quantity of public services. In this way, the costs of domestic spending reductions have been passed on to their ultimate beneficiaries. Simply put, state and local governments have not replaced lost federal dollars with their own funds. The poor and the residents of older declining cities have been affected much more than the treasuries of state or local governments.
- Federal budget cuts and more general resource constraints have produced an atmosphere of confusion and uncertainty in public finance. At the state and local levels, only short-term, very hurried ameliorative measures have been used to cope with sharp revenue shortfalls. This is further complicated by the fact that reductions in a host of programs have been deferred and will begin to take effect only in 1985–1986.

In sum, the long-term effects of the Reagan Administration cuts on state and local finance are, at this juncture, finally becoming clear. Out of this confusion and uncertainty some form of financial planning is emerging. This is the topic of the remainder of this chapter.

Institute Retrenchment Management

The response to decreased revenues in intergovernmental and non-intergovernmental cities alike has been to cut back services, and while doing so, attempt to provide reasonably adequate public services. This type of activity has been labeled as "retrenchment management" and consists of a series of steps which: (1) reduce the scope of basic services; (2) move towards the examination of non-basic services; (3)

seek to enhance the revenue base; and (4) attempt to employ various strategies of control and management to enhance efficiency.

Carol W. Lewis and Anthony T. Logalbo suggest a checklist of "Cutback Principals and Practices" for city managers. An abbreviated form of this list is included in Exhibit 9.3.[7] The remainder of this section focuses on strategies that may be employed by intergovernmental cities for retrenchment. These recommendations should not be thought to be exclusive to this group of communities, however. Budgetary constraints brought about by fiscal conservancy in all categories of cities allow the following procedures to have broad-base application.

EXHIBIT 9.3. — *Cutback Principles and Practices for City Managers*

I. *In cutting back and withdrawing from services, the local manager may wish to:*

1. Institute a review of municipal services by preparing a comprehensive schedule of services by output and cost (not by department) and a scheduled, periodic review of all programs and activities (to eliminate those no longer needed).

2. Identify alternative service levels and establish a process for setting priorities among activities and levels.

3. Subject to detailed scrutiny labor intensive services (since service cuts here mean layoffs); those services subject to steep current and prospective cost increases; and those available from other governments and from the private sector in the community.

4. Measure the cost of services in a way the taxpayer can understand (e.g., for garbage collection, calculate the cost per collection point, either household or business, rather than just the number of tons collected).

5. Identify mandated services and service levels, federal and state, statutory, administrative, and judicial, that cannot be cut back; explore possibilities for reimbursement and/or for transferring service responsibilities to other local units or the state.

6. Consider the effects of cuts on equity, in addition to the effects on efficiency, personnel levels, and legal compliance. The burden of service changes may fall disproportionately on those least able to pay for alternatives.

7. Identify and analyze the trade-offs among current and future savings, past expenditures, and revenue impact.

8. Examine current and prospective changes in the target population, and changing patterns in the use of services that may suggest terminating the service or shifting resources (e.g., alternative use of public buildings). . . .

II. *In reducing expenditures, the local manager may wish to:*

1. Establish enterprise funds for services that can be supported by charges and fees (e.g., utilities, parking and recreational facilities). This moves the service or facility off the tax rate and should increase its responsiveness to changes in public demand for particular services. Appropriate administrative and overhead costs can be allocated to enterprise activities.

2. Consider regional service and utility agreements, resource recovery systems, and purchasing consortiums. Interlocal management development agreements (e.g., circuit rider grantsman) have the advantage of holding down the investment in expertise for a single, small locality.

3. Selectively postpone hiring, procurement, and disbursements in accordance with a systematic policy.

4. Centralize purchasing and procurement for major and bulk items and institute a competitive bidding policy for certain purchases. Bidding can be limited to periodic occasions to ensure that the main supplier, under a negotiated contract, is still offering competitive prices. . . .

III. *To improve the resource base through planning and development, the local manager may wish to:*

1. Maximize net collections by sending bills out on time, evaluating delinquencies, and using in-house or other collection agencies.

2. Increase licenses, permits, fines, and fees to statutory limits.

3. Link locally set fees to price increases in the particular service or to the Consumer Price Index and publicize unit costs of service.

4. Institute service charges for services that are inappropriately subsidized by the property tax where unit costing is relatively feasible. Sliding-scale fees can be based on income and use (e.g., recreational facilities).

5. Earn revenues from use of money (investment earnings) and from use of property through leasing and rentals. Overall cash and debt management policies can be instituted. . . .

6. Approach tax-exempt institutions for payments in lieu of property taxes.

IV. *To improve personnel management, the local manager may wish to:*

1. Publicize that because of the current burden of personnel services on local budgets, there can be no significant reduction in the operating budget without personnel cutbacks. To maintain service levels, this requires increased productivity and a firm management position in labor negotiations.

2. Tie collective bargaining proposals to current and prospective constraints (ability-to-pay). The long-term costing of contracts, including provisions for pension and fringe benefits, can be undertaken. Miminum manning and similar provisions that are not linked to productivity or that reduce management flexibility should be resisted.

3. Explore the use of professional negotiating services. Approach collective bargaining with fully developed management proposals. Tie increases in benefits and salaries to the merit principle and to productivity increases. . . .

Source: Carol W. Lewis and Anthony T. Logalbo, "Cutback Principles and Practices: A Checklist for Managers." *Public Administration Review*, March–April 1980, pp. 184–188.

Prepare an Expenditure–Revenue–Service Status Report

In order to better manage reductions in intergovernmental aid, communities should conduct a status report of their expenditures and revenues as well as the quality and quantity of public services offered. This compilation can provide a sense of current status and future direction by channeling inquiry into the following three areas.

The status report should first pinpoint functional areas of *expenditure* emphasis by type of service (e.g., police, public works, and recreation) and category of outlay (e.g., operating versus capital or direct compensation versus fringe). This breakdown, highlighting the major categories of governmental expenditure outflows, can suggest those significant budgetary items which should be carefully scrutinized if substantial cutbacks are to be realized.

Secondly, the status report should note how services are currently funded. This review should include a detailed breakdown of intergovernmental *revenue* accounts, both past and pending, so as to pinpoint the degree of vulnerability to reductions in particular sources of revenue. The revenue analysis should also list the full array of local revenue items, a cataloging which could suggest future heightened use of currently underutilized income sources such as user charges or permit levies.

Thirdly, the status overview should sketch the *type and range of services* offered by municipal, school, and special district units of government. The sanitation department may provide pickup twice a week from residential properties, once a week from commercial establishments, and offer once-a-month pickup of bulk items (e.g., discarded appliances, furniture, shrubs, etc.). The fire department may provide inspection services and emergency medical care in addition to primary fire fighting services.

A full specification of services provides important baseline data to local policy-makers, enabling them to review the significance of these offerings and ultimately decide whether the services should be retained or rescinded under conditions of fiscal austerity. The service review should also note existing utilization of nonpublic delivery strategies such as volunteers in schools, contracting with private vendors, etc. Such listing provides important input for reviewing the current, and possibly future, expanded application of nontraditional service delivery approaches—a topic discussed in depth in a subsequent section of this chapter.

The government expenditure–revenue–service report would be enhanced if conducted on a comparative basis whereby one community's profile is matched against that of comparable jurisdictions. This approach can point to relative "excesses" in a community's costs, revenue reliance, and service luxuries at least to the extent that the behavior of similar communities stands as a valid benchmark. Cross-jurisdictional comparisons are also useful for pointing to possibilities of innovative service delivery strategies.

The expenditure–revenue–service status report is a management aid for coping with fiscal austerity. It may be repeatedly referred to as a valuable tool for the restructuring of both revenues and expenditures.

Reconsider and Restructure Local Revenues

Before delving into details it is important to realize that *not much can be done in the short run to brighten the revenue picture confronted by intergovernmental cities.* Their major income source, intergovernmental aid, has been reduced, and this level of assistance cannot be replaced by equivalent increases in local resources. First, and most apparent, the socially and economically distressed population of the intergovernmental city may not be able to bear much additional tax load. Second, increasing the local tax burden might serve to drive out the remaining pockets of affluent residents and local businesses in the intergovernmental city—occupants whose continued presence is vital if such cities are to have a base of sustenance in the future.

While the revenue crunch confronted by the intergovernmental city is not easily rectified, slight improvements to the revenue ledger are possible. Alternative modifications include (1) increasing traditional local revenue; (2) turning to new local revenues; and (3) considering extralocal revenue sources.

Increase Traditional Local Revenues

As indicated in Chapter 6, significant dependence on intergovernmental aid is a relatively new phenomenon dating from the mid-to-late 1960s. The curtailment of intergovernmentalism initially fosters a return to renewed emphasis on *local* revenue sources. This approach has already been taken (see Exhibit 9.1). As reported by the U.S. Conference of Mayors: "Despite restrictions on city revenues, many cities are responding to federal budget cuts by raising local taxes. Of the ninety-six cities responding, forty (41 percent) have raised or will raise taxes, and one (1 percent) tried, but failed."[8]

As previously discussed, increasing local taxes may have negative long-term effects on the city. It must therefore be done very carefully, taking into account the magnitude of revenue improvement versus the impact on local businesses and residents.

One position the city may take is to try to increase revenues by focusing on those groups which may not be paying their "fair-share" of taxes. The tax-exempt sector—concert halls, hospitals, museums, etc.—is a leading example. In many intergovernmental cities, about one-third to one-half of the tax base is exempt. In an era of fiscal austerity, these cities cannot continue to bear fully the costs of servicing their tax-exempt sector.

One approach to the tax-exempt embroglio is redefining the statutory definitions and administrative interpretations of those organizations eligible for preferred tax treatment. New York City's action in this regard is illustrative.[9] For many years, religious, educational, charitable, hospital, cemetery, and "moral–mental health" organizations as well as bar and medical associations were all exempt from local property taxation. In 1971, a New York State law was enacted (Section 420) establishing two categories—"A" and "B"—for property tax purposes. The "A"

EXHIBIT 9.4. — *Types of Tax Increases Reported by Cities Affected by Federal Aid Cutbacks*

Tax Increase Categories	Number of Cities	Percentage
Property	18	51
User fees	11	31
City income	3	9
Utility	2	6
Sales	1	3
TOTAL	35	100

Source: United States Conference of Mayors, <u>The FY82 Budget and the Cities</u> (Washington, D.C., November 1981).

category consisted of religious, educational, charitable, hospital, cemetery, and "moral–mental health" entities, which continued to be tax exempt. The "B" category included other groups, such as bar and medical associations. Section 420 gave localities the discretion of taxing or exempting the "B" groups. In 1971, New York City enacted an ordinance obligating Section 420 "B" organizations to *pay* property taxes. About a decade later, attempts were made at further closure whereby certain categories of charitable and "moral–mental health" entities would be taxed; New York even questioned the scope of exemption to be accorded certain religious organizations/activities.[10]

Some narrowing of the types of entities eligible for property tax absolvement is surely in order. It is clearly not an easy step. New York is again illustrative. After it disallowed exemptions to bar and medical associations in 1971, the city was subject to legal suits for the better part of a decade. There is also the question of the role that cultural and educational facilities in intergovernmental cities should play. These communities have lost many of their traditional private sector participants. What is left are the educational, cultural, and eleemosynary activities which draw people to the city and give city residents an added reason to remain. Tampering with the tax-exempt status of museums, hospitals and so on might cause these often financially hard-pressed entities to fold or to leave to another jurisdiction. While a potential source of "windfall" revenue, the tax-exempt sector must be dealt with very carefully.

A less drastic means of addressing the tax-exempt issue is for the city to retain its current tax-exempt coverage but to elicit voluntary contributions from exempt organizations. Such an approach was attempted successfully by New York City at the height of its fiscal crunch. Added relief could also be afforded by the municipality receiving in-lieu payments from federal/state bodies of government owning tax-exempt buildings in intergovernmental communities. Newark, for example, is now receiving in-lieu payments from the State of New Jersey from such state properties located within its boundaries as the Rutgers-Newark campus and state offices.

Turn to New Local Revenues

Chapter 7 of this study examined the revenue emphases of intergovernmental cities. Outside aid from federal and state governments was important as was the real property tax. Other types of local resources were relatively underutilized in these types of communities. These included: commuter taxes, sales taxes, and user charges. Given the intergovernmental aid cutbacks they are facing, it may well pay intergovernmental cities to consider turning to these underutilized local revenues. Such a move is especially suggested if the municipal expenditure–revenue–service status report indicates that a community has overlooked such accounts relative to its neighbors.

Turning to currently underutilized local income avenues is a move which must be conducted with caution. Additional tax levies are particularly problematical. As is the case with increasing traditional local tax levies, imposition of many "non-traditional" local levies might be counterproductive to the economic long-term interests of the intergovernmental city. A sales tax hike could cause remaining retailers to leave, a wage tax could similarly affect major service and other employers. There is also the question of state restriction on the imposition of certain local revenues such as the commuter tax.

Other now-underutilized local revenues pose less dangerous long-term risk to the intergovernmental city and do not need state enabling legislation for their imposition. User charges are a prime example. They are defined by the Census as "amounts received from the public for performance of specific services benefitting from the person charged."[11] User charges have long been in place in cities nationally although their incidence varies. Shore communities have a long history of employing them in the form of beach, gaming and other fees. Smaller, as opposed to larger, communities have disproportionately turned to this source. Geographic location is another differentiating characteristic: local governments in the Pacific and Mountain regions rely most on user charges; their counterparts in the New England and Middle Atlantic areas exhibit the least dependence; Southern and Midwestern jurisdictions lie between these extremes.

Recent financial upheavals have led traditional users (e.g., smaller localities in the Pacific region) to increase their dependence on user charges and have induced new converts to this revenue source (e.g., larger New England municipalities). In the wake of Proposition 13, California communities raised approximately $125 million in new or increased fees—about one-fifth the amount they lost in property taxes. Federal aid cutbacks have also encouraged local user charges.[12] A recent United States Conference of Mayors survey examined the type of tax increases inspired by cities affected by federal budget cuts.[13] As seen in Exhibit 9.4, the imposition of user fees was the second most popular local tax response.

Growing popularity of user fees is viewed as more than simply a reaction to post-intergovernmentalism.[14] A charging approach to paying for services is deemed as offering not only a new *revenue* flow but also an advantage as far as governmental expenditures are concerned. The alleged cost edge goes to the heart of the user charge system. Under this approach there is a direct and strong incentive to provide market-demanded services at a fair price since doing otherwise may be met by consumer resistance. In short, business acumen has been instituted to guide municipal agencies; no such feedback/restraints exist under the current taxation method of financing municipal services. As summarized by Selma Mushkin of the Urban Institute:[15]

> Under present resource allocation practices within the public sector itself, the wrong product is sometimes produced, in the wrong quantity, and with no (or inappropriate) quality differentiation. If it is feasible to determine benefit values and to identify the beneficiaries of a public program, pricing (i.e., user charges) becomes a viable means of ensuring that the allocation of public resources becomes more efficient.

Since user fees offer expenditure as well as revenue advantages, we shall defer further discussion until the final section of this chapter, which focuses on several expenditure reduction strategies. Many of these latter approaches, such as privatization and contracting out, are conceptually very close to user fees in the sense that they all inject market discipline, and hopefully efficiency, into the municipal service delivery system.

Turn to Extralocal Revenues

An underlying difficulty facing the intergovernmental city attempting to enlarge its local revenues is the relative scarcity and vulnerability of wealth within its borders. An obvious solution would be to expand the intergovernmental city's boundaries so as to allow it to garner revenues from economically viable suburbs. Such an extralocal approach could be accomplished via: annexation, whereby an intergovernmental city would incorporate its neighbors; or, less drastically, by tax-base sharing, whereby the intergovernmental jurisdiction would retain its political borders yet would share in the economic growth of the entire region's tax base.

Not surprisingly, such an extralocal strategy is politically very problematical as the residents and units of government beyond the boundaries of the intergovernmental city do not wish to share their revenues. There are further hurdles, such as legal requirements. Most state statutes governing annexation permit such action only if a specified set of conditions are met. For example, the annexing entity must be "financially sound and possess the ability to maintain the annexed area's municipal services."[16] Do these preconditions describe the intergovernmental city looking to expand beyond its boundaries? Finally, the conceptual basis for an extralocal solution may be inapplicable. This strategy, personified by annexation, is envisioned as a means for a central community to reap the benefits of economic vitality in jurisdictions just outside its borders. This scenario may describe a Houston but it is the antithesis of stagnant, if not distressed conditions prevailing around the periphery of intergovernmental cities. To illustrate, one of Newark's immediate suburbs, East Orange, New Jersey, is perhaps more impacted than Newark itself. The only way an extralocal approach could work is for the intergovernmental city to reach beyond its immediate distressed ring to the more flourishing outer suburbs. Such a long reach, however, would compound the legal and political problems mentioned above. In summary, an extralocal revenue strategy offers intergovernmental cities reasonable conceptual, yet minimal practical relief. In this respect it joins the other revenue-raising strategies discussed already.

Reconsider and Restructure Local Expenditures

Intergovernmental cities can attain the greatest fiscal respite by rethinking the scope, nature, and means of delivering municipal services. Possible courses of action include the following: (1) shift service responsibilities; (2) reduce service provision costs; (3) modify service expenditure commitments and standards; and (4) modify service delivery and strategies.

Shift Service Responsibilities

One approach is for the intergovernmental city to transfer some of its current service area duties to state, county, or other units of government. Cincinnati reacted to acute fiscal pressure in the mid-1970s by persuading the State of Ohio to take over responsibility for the University of Cincinnati.[17] Similarly, in response to New York

City's fiscal crunch in the 1970s, New York State began to pay for the city's college system (CUNY). Buffalo and Rochester have both transferred police functions to the county. Buffalo has also given its zoo to a private non-profit organization. Trenton, New Jersey, has convinced parent Mercer County to take over maintenance of the two main roads that bisect the city.[18]

Many such changes have taken place in Newark. This city historically paid the expenses of its major municipal health facility—Martland Hospital—from its own resources. Today, the lion's share of Martland's costs is picked up by the county (Essex) and state. Newark once cared for and paid for its own parks; Essex County has recently assumed both roles. Similar shifts to county aegis have occurred with respect to Newark's vocational and other specialized schools.

Transfer of a once-local service responsibility to an upper level of government surely works to reduce the expenditure pressures confronting intergovernmental cities. This strategy will be effective, however, only to the extent that the state, county or regional entity is willing to take on added service obligations and commensurate expenditures — expansionism that is very unlikely in an era when all governmental bodies are seeking to contract their financial obligations. Realistically, shifting service responsibilities off the shoulders of the intergovernmental city is likely to be a rare phenomenon prompted only by exceptional distress situations to the shedding jurisdiction or commensurate benefit to the receiving jurisdiction (e.g., transferred services such as zoos or museums clearly offer benefits to citizens of the region as long as these activities can be participated in safely).

If intergovernmental cities cannot readily shed their service load, they can at least try to provide services at a lower cost. Frills such as non-critical travel and reproduction costs can be cut. Improved inventory controls can reduce warehouse and interest costs while improving product availability. Inexpensive energy conservation measures such as adjusting thermostats and caulking windows can lower heating and air conditioning bills. Self-insurance may offer relief to spiralling insurance premiums. Purchasing telephones as opposed to renting them can often provide both cost and operating benefits. Rental of city offices from private owners should also be scrutinized: are the rents fair; is free space available in underutilized or surplus city-owned properties?

The above shopping list offers some financial relief in non-personnel costs; many of these strategies have already been effected by hard-pressed municipalities. For true service delivery savings, however, attention must be focused on employee expenses. These latter outlays dominate total service expenditures. Reductions in payroll costs can be accomplished either by decreasing the total *number* of municipal employees or by scaling down in actual dollars the *compensation package* offered to each worker.

Work-force cuts have become commonplace in financially hard-pressed communities. Detroit and New York both experienced large-scale layoffs in their uniformed forces, although the latter city has recently been able to augment its police-fire department staffing as its fiscal posture has improved. In the wake of Proposition 13, many California cities reduced their public staffing, especially in service areas considered non-essential.[19] (The issue of service priority is discussed shortly). Exhibit 9.5 indicates the changes occurring in California's largest libraries. One response to reduced library funding (from $7.86 per capita in 1975–76 to $6.83 per person in 1979–80) was a 10 percent staff cut, from 4,200 to 3,700 workers.[20]

EXHIBIT 9.5. — *Characteristics of California's Largest Public
Library Systems After Adoption of Proposition 13*

Library System Characteristics	Fiscal Year		
	1975-76	1977-78	1979-80
Operating expenses, FY 1978 dollars per capita	7.86	7.58	6.38
Paid staff, full-time employees	4,713	3,962	3,863
Volunteers, hours weekly	918	1,249	1,726
Capital spending as percent of total	14.6	7.3	2.2
Books added per thousand persons	101	90	80
Non-book circulation per thousand persons	162	147	107
Interlibrary loan transactions	77,147	78,163	60,668
Hours open weekly	NA	16,690	15,088
Number of service outlets	NA	1,037	1,152

Note: NA = Not available

Source: Mark David Menchik et. al., How Fiscal Restraint Affects Spending and Services in Cities (Santa Monica, California: Rand, 1982).

In certain instances, staff reductions have been far more severe. Such slashing is especially noticeable in soft money-funded programs in intergovernmental cities facing severe state and federal aid cutbacks. In Newark, for example:

All departments reported a trimming of staff. The city's personnel roster has been pared from 5,832 in 1970 to 4,004 in 1982. That reduction represents a job reduction in excess of 30 percent. Moreover, this trend has been unidirectional since 1976. The city's business administrator estimates that in 1983 the basic work force will be trimmed to below 4,000 people, while the people working for the city on "soft" federal money, which was as many as 3,000 in 1975, will be down to 500.[21]

How can the municipal work force be pruned? A common, relatively painless and efficient approach is to let attrition take its toll—freeze or severely restrict new hiring and do not replace those who leave, retire, etc. Prince Georges County (Maryland) followed this staff policy in the wake of TRIM—a 1979 charter amendment freezing county property tax revenues.

Department heads must send written memos to the county executive's office explaining why they need to fill vacancies before they are allowed to do so. And very few have gotten approval to hire. . . . More than 300 positions in county government [have been] eliminated.[22]

A more painful and less efficient approach than natural attrition is to directly terminate a portion of the public payroll. Non–civil service workers (e.g., CETA employees) are often let go first. Next to go are civil service staff affected by reductions in force—layoffs following the elimination of whole departments or service areas. Examples include: reading teachers rendered surplus by elimination of a supplemental instruction program; municipal lifeguards let go when a city decides to limit the number of protected beaches; and sanitation workers terminated when a municipality drops its paid garbage collection force and solicits a private scavenger to charge residents directly.

In addition to reducing the size of the public payroll, intergovernmental cities must scrutinize the *remuneration* offered to its workers — both direct salaries and fringe benefits. The compensation package review is most meaningful if conducted on a comparative basis—what do city workers receive versus the salary and fringes accorded to employees in other jurisdictions or the private sector? Such side-by-side review was one of the components of the municipal expenditure–revenue–service status report described earlier.

An example of a comparative compensation analysis is shown in Exhibit 9.6, which lists the cost of a police patrolman in Newark and other New Jersey cities and older suburbs. Newark's salaries are roughly in line with those in the other localities. Its fringe benefits, however, are somewhat higher. Patrolmen receive twenty-one vacation days. Police vacation allotments in most of the other jurisdictions are shorter, especially for entry-level staff. Another fringe benefit concerns longevity bonuses. Newark offers its uniformed services a handsome bonus of 4 to 14 percent of base salary. The comparative communities provide lesser bonuses.

EXHIBIT 9.6. — *Contract Terms for Unionized Municipal Police Departments: Newark and Selected New Jersey Municipalities, 1982*

MUNICIPALITY	HIGHEST PATROLMAN SALARY	WORK HOURS PER WEEK	LONGEVITY BONUS	VACATION DAYS	PERSONAL LEAVE DAYS
NEWARK	$22,000	37	4% to 14%	21	3
CAMDEN	$21,000	40	3% to 7%	12-25	2
EAST ORANGE	$23,000	32	2% to 15%	15-20	varies
JERSEY CITY	$24,000	40	2% to 10%	12-30	10
LONG BRANCH	$23,000	40	1% to 6%	15-20	3
MORRISTOWN	$24,000	40	1% to 3%	7-28	2
PATERSON	$21,000	40	2% to 10%	10-28	4
PLAINFIELD	$20,000	40	2% to 8%	12-28	3

Source: Rutgers University, Center for Urban Policy Research survey of indicated local police departments, 1982.

Comparative public employee compensation reviews have become commonplace in many intergovernmental cities. Since its fiscal crunch of the mid-1970s, New York annually conducts such an analysis. These studies are often a first step to freezes, if not actual cutbacks, in city worker salaries and benefits. New York City's investigation, for instance, indicated that municipal clerical workers received salaries in excess of the private sector scale, and the city work force in general was accorded better fringe benefits relative to other cities. Both of these excesses have since scaled down.

Following the service cost reduction steps outlined above—eliminating unnecessary non-personnel outlays, reducing the city work force and bringing staff compensation costs in line with new fiscal realities—the municipality will be left with fewer people and equipment with which to service its population. Given this contraction, it behooves cities to explore how they can increase their service delivery efficiency—"getting more bang from each buck being spent." The detailed means for achieving this goal could be the subject of an entirely separate monograph; some critical steps are outlined below, however.

As a first step towards achieving heightened productivity, communities must establish something akin to a management data base. Few localities measure the output of their services—what activities and assistance are being made available or goods produced—as opposed to simply accounting for what is being spent. The expenditure–revenue–service status report previously described, was in part, a rough attempt to define delivered service output. More sophisticated gauges are possible.[23] Exhibit 9.7 gives examples of possible output measures for a municipal public works department including "road miles sealed" for the pavement repairing division and "cubic yards of snow removed" for the highway division. With output measures in place, it is then possible to create productivity measures (i.e., "cost per road mile sealed or cubic yard of snow removed"—see Exhibit 9.7). The productivity measures in turn allow municipal program administrators to chart the progress with which efficiency is being improved. It can also inspire them to think how greater gains in productivity might be achieved. Interestingly, the gathering of such management information was one of the first responses undertaken by New York City in the height of its fiscal crunch. City officials benefitted immensely by translating the line-item dollar budget into an aggregation of service output and efficiency measures. It is not suggested here that PPBS (Planning, Programming, Budgeting System) be resurrected; a mere listing of services by function, and a provision of first-generation output measures will suffice. All that is needed is a vehicle to show what is provided and in what quantity.

Such data management will hopefully spur municipal officials to seek and implement more productive means of providing services. Robert W. Poole, author of *Cutting Back City Hall*, terms such changes "thinking smarter" and cites numerous examples of their application.[24] A selected group of approaches, organized by service function, is shown below:

Fire Protection
- Unless otherwise indicated, respond with a mini-pumper as opposed to a full-size fire truck. The mini-pumper is less costly to purchase and requires fewer firemen to operate.
- Since most fires are reported by telephone, eliminate all but essential fire boxes. This change will allow significant capital and routine maintenance savings.

EXHIBIT 9.7. — *Work Output and Productivity Measures:*
A Public Works Department Example

Program	Cost Center	Work Load Measures	Productivity Measures
Pavement Repairing	Pothole Filling	Tons Asphalt Applied	Cost/Ton Applied
	Crack Sealing	Lane Miles Sealed	Cost/Lane Mile Sealed
Street Resurfacing	Asphalt Overlay	Lane Miles Overlayed	Cost/Lane Mile Overlayed
	Chip Seal Coating	Lane Miles Coated	Cost/Lane Mile Coated
Concrete Repair	Sidewalk Repair	Lineal Ft. Repaired	Cost/Lineal Foot Repaired
	Curb/Gutter Repair	Lineal Ft. Repaired	Cost/Lineal Feet Repaired
	Crosspan Repair	Crosspans Repaired	Cost/Crosspan Repaired
	Radii Repair	Radii Repaired	Cost/Radii Repaired
Snow Removal	Snow Plowing	Lane Miles Plowed	Cost/Lane Mile Plowed
	Snow Removal	Cu. Yds. Snow Removed	Cost/Cu. Yd. Snow Removed
Street Cleaning	Street Sweeping	Lane Miles Swept	Cost /Lane Mile Swept
Street Grading	Gravel Streets	Lane Miles Graded	Cost/Lane Mile Graded
	Shoulders	Miles of Shoulders Graded	Cost/Mile Shoulder Graded
Vegetation Control	Right-of-Way Mowed	Miles Mowed	Cost/Mile Mowed
	Mowing City Lots	Acres Mowed	Cost/Acre Mowed
	Weed Control	Acres Mowed	Cost/Acre Mowed
Drainage Maint.	Ditch Mowing	Miles of Ditch Mowed	Cost/Mile Ditch Mowed
	Debris Clearanc	Miles of Ditch Cleared	Cost/Mile Ditch Cleared

Source: Donald Oatman, "It's Time for Productivity Accounting in Government," Governmental Finance, Vol. 8, November 1979, p. 11.

Police and Criminal Justice

- In areas which permit, assign one as opposed to two officers per patrol vehicle; replace full size sedans with compacts.
- Wherever possible, allow lower-cost civilians to perform tasks which do not require a uniformed officer (i.e., dispatching, record keeping).
- Improve scheduling of police officer courtroom appearances so as to reduce wasted time.
- Hire professional court administrators.

Garbage and Solid Waste

- Replace old rear-loading garbage trucks with side-loading vehicles. The latter can be operated with a smaller crew.
- Provide garbage transfer stations so as to reduce lengthy trips to incinerator or land-fill sites.
- Assign more efficient garbage pickup routes.
- Encourage recycling of solid waste by private firms—a strategy reducing the public sector difficulty and cost of disposal.

Other Public Works

- Modify work crew scheduling so as to better correspond to need; decentralize the city yard to reduce time spent traveling to work sites; limit overtime expenses (night or weekend work) to emergencies only.

Other Service Areas

- Transit—where warranted, replace larger buses with smaller jitneys.

One intended benefit of effecting these and other service efficiencies is to retain service *quality* standards, despite the fact that fewer dollars are available to pay for services. As expressed by Poole:

> Your city's police force can nearly double its strength during high-crime hours without increasing the police budget. A few police departments are doing just that, because they've thought up a smarter way to schedule their patrol officers. Analyzing the records of calls for service by hour of the day, they saw that in most cases demand for police response was three or four times higher in the evening hours than in the early hours of the morning and twice as high as in the morning and afternoon hours. In cooperation with their officers, they devised a new shift schedule based on a ten-hour day, four days a week. Using ten-hour shifts they could arrange things so that six of the twenty-four hours in a day were covered by overlapping shifts—putting twice as many officers on duty during the overlap. This overlap, of course, was programmed to occur during the high-crime peak hours. Although most existing "ten plans" were adopted as a means of raising service levels without increasing the budget, they could also be used as a *means of preserving an existing level of service while permitting a budget cut*. (emphasis added)[25]

It is unlikely, given the magnitude of state and federal aid cutbacks, that management changes will suffice for retaining the range and quality of services now offered by intergovernmental cities. These communities therefore face the continued task of contracting their municipal service offerings.

Reduce Service Expenditure Commitments and Standards

Fiscal austerity has forced many communities to scale back the range and quality of the services, equipment and capital plant they provide their citizens. One of the first items to go are *new capital facilities*. Financially hard-pressed cities have had to replace the dream of the new infrastructure with the reality of making do with older highways, bridges, mass transit, police and fire stations, libraries, schools, and so on. Even *maintenance* of the existing capital plant has been severely curtailed.

There are many such examples. Following Proposition 13, California's library system almost eliminated capital spending; this expense item fell from about 15 percent of total library outlays in 1975–76 to 2 percent just two years later (see Exhibit 9.5).[26] A survey by the United States Conference of Mayors of local responses to federal aid cutbacks revealed:

> Sixty-three percent of the cities have deferred capital spending as a result of federal budget cuts or plan to do so. . . .Denver stated that it had "almost totally" deferred capital spending, particularly affecting expansion of libraries, bridges, and waste-water drainage. . . .Allentown. . . has deferred a sewer run-off system; Buffalo, street resurfacing, street lighting, and an updating of city water lines; Des Moines, halted a major sewer project, which had been in planning for several years; in Omaha, two fire stations, three senior citizen centers, and water and sewer projects have been deferred. . . and Youngstown has noted that bridges and streets that need repair are not being repaired.[27]

Reflecting recent deaths from bridge and tunnel failures, it is clear that capital facilities must be maintained or not used. A clear prioritizing of capital facilities retention and improvement should be undertaken.

Fiscal austerity has also forced cuts affecting *operating* services. To return to the California library example, in the aftermath of Proposition 13, libraries reduced non-book lending (records, films, art) and interlibrary transactions—two "luxury" activities requiring relatively more staff time (see Exhibit 9.5). Library hours were also curtailed.[28] Intergovernmental cities, confronted with state and federal aid diminishment, have already undertaken multiple service curtailments. Newark has slashed a range of public health service programs including: rat and pest control, diabetes and hypertension screening, venereal disease and alcohol–drug abuse centers, and lead paint poisoning prevention.[29] Toledo, Ohio has halved its special pickup garbage collection cycle from weekly to bimonthly, cut its park and recreation activities, and eliminated the Consumer Protection Department.[30]

Given the wide range of possible service retrenchments, what should be cut? There are no firm criteria but cities, in making hard-and-fast cuts, appear to have considered the following:

1. *Service Need.* Services are ranked as to their essential nature and those considered most critical are curtailed least. Police and fire protection often fall into this relatively protected category; recreation and cultural services, in contrast, are deemed less essential and hence are more vulnerable to cuts.

2. *Public Profile.* To the maximum extent possible, services most in the public eye are spared while more "invisible" offerings are pruned. It is partially for this reason that maintenance of capital facilities, and research planning activities are usually the first to go under conditions of budgetary constraint.

3. *Service Cost.* Searching for maximum immediate savings, those charged with municipal budget cuts will first seek out the most expensive service items.
4. *"Across-the-Board."* All services are reduced equally. In many respects, a non-criterion based decision.
5. *Other Factors.* Political and bureaucratic clout clearly are influential.

Given the magnitude of revenue curtailment brought about by a reduction in intergovernmentalism, cities will continue to reduce the range and quality of the services, equipment, and capital facilities offered to citizens. As this process continues, greater attention will be paid to defining the criteria appropriate for guiding retrenchment. More citizen-public official interchange will enter the process. In this regard, the Interpretive Structural Modeling (ISM) approach developed at the Academy for Contemporary Problems can be especially useful.[31] ISM is designed to facilitate group prioritizing of a complex set of alternatives into "desirable" and "undesirable" categories. Its application to ordering service/expenditure cuts is shown in Exhibit 9.8.

Modify Service Delivery Strategies

The approaches considered thus far while entailing some tinkering with municipal service cost influences, retain the traditional approach of local service provision—delivery by public agencies and financing by public tax dollars. This response is perhaps too mild. The revenue revolution heralded by the dismantling of intergovernmentalism must be met by an equally radical change in service strategies. One such shift is to inject *private market* discipline into, if not private sector implementation of, service provision.[32] A range of possible options is listed in Exhibit 9.9.

One modification—relying on *user charges*—was introduced earlier in this chapter. The difference between user fees and traditional service provision bears repeating. While in both cases service implementation is by a public body, in the user charge case, the public agency acts as a near-private entity since it is dependent on satisfying the consumers of its services. The agency must determine what services are demanded by the public and must then act to satisfy this need at a reasonable charge. It is hoped that these market pressures will force savings in the costs of delivering services.

In a sense, user fees retain public implementation, employing the structures of the private sector. The next two approaches presented in Exhibit 9.9 turn to the private sector even more strongly. *Contracting out* refers to the "purchase of certain services by government from private sources . . . and financed by tax collections."[33] *Privatization* similarly entails service implementation by a private entity; however, this entity is paid directly by the party receiving the service—there is no transfer of public tax dollars, rather a fee is paid from one private individual to another. To illustrate, if a municipality hires a private scavenger to collect garbage and then pays for such work with public tax dollars, this arrangement is an example of contracting out. If the private scavenger picks up a homeowner's garbage and is paid directly by the homeowner, this approach is termed privatization.

While there is a distinction between contracting out and privatization, this difference should not obscure a close conceptual kinship—service provision has left the

EXHIBIT 9.8. — *Example of Interpretive Structural Modeling (ISM) Ranking of Expenditure Cuts by Priority*

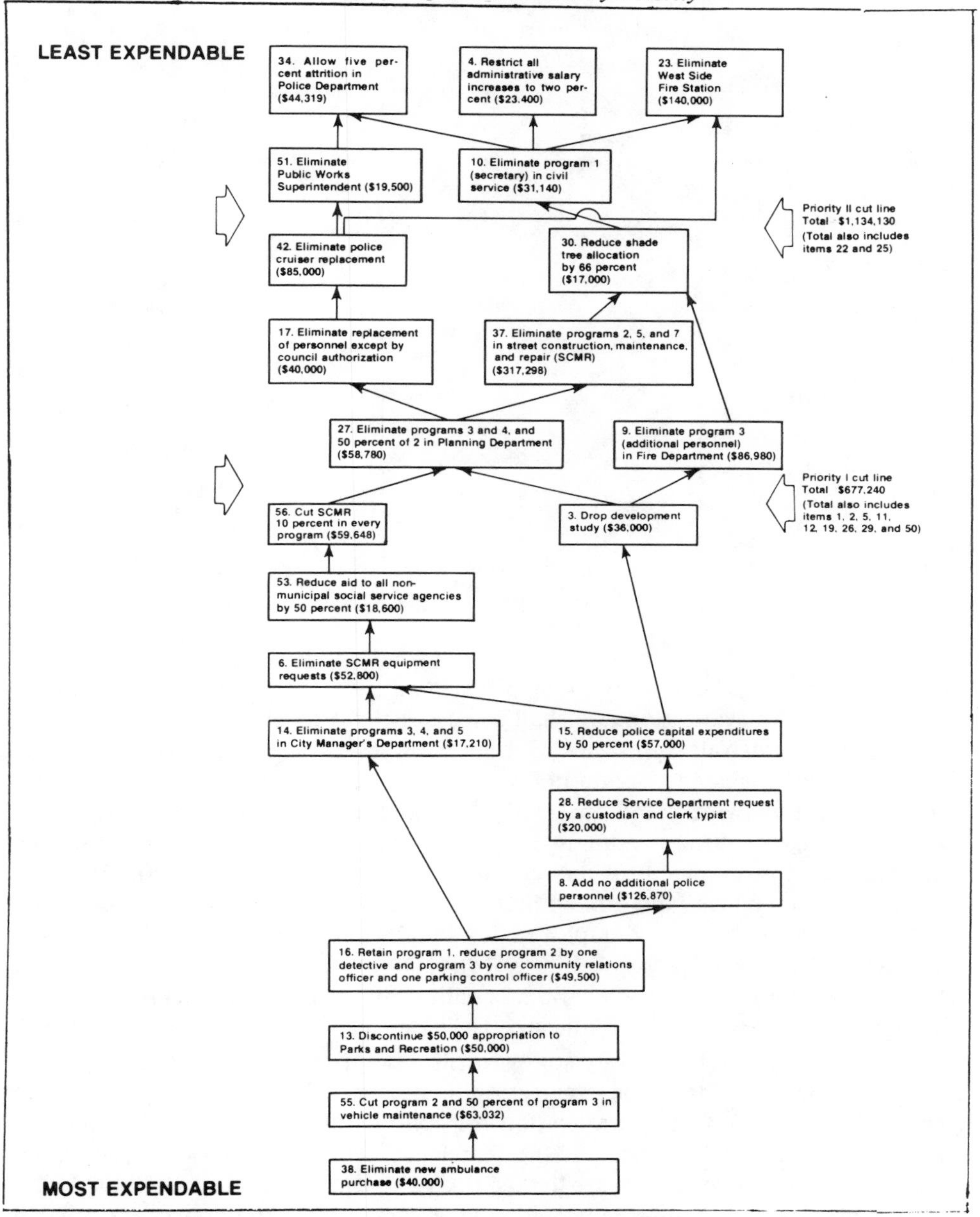

Note: Ranking is based on focused group evaluations.

Source: Bryce, Herrington J. (Ed.), Managing Fiscal Retrenchment in Cities (Academy for Contemporary Problems, 1980), Columbus, Ohio.

EXHIBIT 9.9. — *Alternative Service Delivery Approaches*

STRATEGY	SERVICE	
	IMPLEMENTATION	FINANCING
Traditional	Public (municipal agency)	Public (tax dollars)
User Fee or Public Utility	Public (acting as private sector entity)	Public (paid by service beneficiary)
Contract Out	Private	Public (tax dollars)
Privatization	Private	Private (paid by service beneficiary)
Voluntarism	Private	Private (paid by donor)

Source: See text.

public domain and is being satisfied by private entities. Given the similarities of contracting out and privatization, we shall discuss the two together.

There are numerous instances of both of these service approaches on the American municipal scene. A late 1970s survey of over 200 municipalities and counties indicated how widespread contracting out had become.[34] About 80 percent of the city managers/business administrators responding for the municipalities used this approach for architectural services, about 70 percent for engineering services and street maintenance, and almost half for solid waste collection.[35] Outside contracting was also frequently employed for building maintenance, ambulance services, and other activities (see Exhibit 9.10).

There are several reasons why a municipality will turn to private entities for service support or delivery. Most frequently, the municipal corporation will lack specialized skills and turn to the private sector to fill this gap. It is for this reason that so much of the contracting is for engineering, planning and related technical services (see Exhibit 9.10). A further motivation for contracting out, and the one that has provoked recent strong interest, is the search for economy in service costs. Contracting out (and privatization) are looked to as efficient service distribution vehicles because they draw on firms competing in the private market. In this arena, price and product win the jobs.[36] This situation is diametrically opposed to the traditional arrangement of public service delivery with no direct competition and theoretically no incentive to economize or deliver a superior product.

EXHIBIT 9.10. — *Type and Frequency of Contracted-out Services by Level of Government*

	COUNTY (N=55)		MUNICIPALITY (N=170)		TOTAL (N=225)	
	Number	Percent	Number	Percent	Number	Percent
Architectural services	47	85	134	79	181	80
Engineering services	37	67	112	66	151	67
Street construction	31	56	126	74	149	66
Building repair	29	53	85	50	114	51
Solid waste collection	31	56	64	38	95	42
Equipment maintenance	20	36	67	39	87	39
Legal counsel	13	24	64	38	81	36
Building maintenance	21	38	50	29	77	34
Ambulance services	20	36	61	36	71	32
Vehicle maintenance	15	27	55	32	70	31
Administrative support	14	25	49	29	63	28
Children's day care	6	11	52	30	58	26
Food service, employees	20	36	29	17	54	24
Elderly, nursing	13	24	41	24	51	23
Land use/planning	6	11	45	26	49	22
Halfway houses	11	2	30	17	41	18
Street maintenance	12	22	27	16	39	17
Snow removal	12	22	25	15	37	16
Grounds maintenance	13	24	19	11	32	14
First aid employees	4	7	27	16	31	14
Elderly, recreation	4	7	23	14	27	12
Leaf collection	8	14	8	5	16	7
Public recreation	3	5	12	7	15	7
Misc. police services	4	7	5	3	15	7
Police communications	2	3	13	8	10	4
Building inspection	4	7	6	4	9	4
Janitorial services	3	5	4	2	9	4
Transportation related[1]	2	3	5	3	7	3
Park maintenance	2	3	7	4	7	3
Consulting, miscellaneous	0	0	3	2	7	3
Sewer/water/sanitation[2]	6	11	1	5	7	3
Uniforms - laundry/rental	5	9	2	1	3	1
Escalator/elevator repair	0	0	1	5	1	4

[1]Includes towing, hauling, buses, toll bridges, etc.
[2]Includes treatment, testing, recycling, landfills, meters.

Source: Patricia S. Florestano and Stephen B. Gordon, "A Survey of City and County Use of Private Contracting," The Urban Interest (Spring 1981).

Is anticipated cost advantage of contracting out and privatization realized in practice? Many studies answer in the affirmative. In the early 1970s, municipally provided sanitation in Queens (New York) cost over $200 per household annually while privately contracted sanitation services in a nearby suburb cost approximately $70 per year.[37] Investigations conducted by Richard Ahlbrandt[38] and E. S. Savas[39] in the mid-1970s documented significant cost savings, on the order of about 2:1, arising from private as opposed to public sector service delivery. More recent studies have reached similar conclusions. Eileen Berenyi examined sanitation costs in ten cities which shifted from municipal sanitation provision to a contracted-out arrangement.[40] After controlling for inflation, quality of service and other variations,

Berenyi found that in all cases, service cost savings were realized, with the savings ranging from 7 to 30 percent (see Exhibit 9.11). The private sanitation companies were able to achieve the cost advantage by being more innovative and efficient. As compared to the city provision, the private scavengers used fewer men per truck, followed a more efficient pickup route, and utilized relatively larger and efficient trucks.

The frequency of savings achieved by private sector approaches discussed in this section does not mean that this competitive advantage is exclusive. Present fiscal pressures have prompted municipal agencies themselves to adopt many of the time-cost saving approaches which have given private purveyors of services their cost edge. New York City's recent shift to technologically advanced garbage trucks, requiring a smaller crew to man, is illustrative. Wage differentials between municipal employees and workers in private firms have similarly been narrowed as the latter, fearful for their jobs, have consented to fringe and other givebacks.

While there are complex interceding forces affecting the comparative costs of traditional versus more free-market service delivery options, the evidence at hand favors the latter. Consequently, fiscally hard-pressed municipalities should seriously explore the benefits of employing user fees, contracting out, and/or privatization as methods of service delivery. In making such an evaluation, city officials must all look beyond the singular objective of economy to the many variables on which the different strategies vary. These include (see Exhibit 9.12):

1. *Market feedback*—How fast and to what extent are the strategies affected by market (i.e., consumer) preferences?

2. *Competition*—How many purveyors will likely offer the service?

3. *Public control*—What is the degree of public control over the service?

4. *Consumer freedom*—To what extent can an individual consumer pick and choose the type/cost services consumed?

5. *Service universalism*—To what degree are the services available to everyone, even the poor?

6. *Federal-state tax interface*—To what extent are the service costs paid by the consumer deductible from federal or state income taxes (in the form of lowering taxable income)?

7. *State revenue-expenditure interface*—To what extent are service expenditures-revenues affected by state revenue or expenditure caps?

The service delivery options differ on many of the above-mentioned variables (see Exhibit 9.12). Market feedback is a case in point. Traditional service delivery has little feedback. Relatively few citizens contact the public department providing services as most feel this is futile ("Can't fight City Hall"). Through their votes, citizens provide a type of feedback of their satisfaction with public service delivery but elections are infrequent and then are only a very limited barometer of public service satisfaction. There is also the problem that citizens' complaints or suggestions regarding services, however communicated, are often largely ignored by public offices. Market feedback is improved with contracting out. Here, the private purveyor of services will pay more attention to citizen complaints and suggestions, for failure to do so may endanger continuation of their contract with the city. Stronger market feedback is provided by user fees and privatization. In these cases, consumers di-

EXHIBIT 9.11. — *Cost Comparisons of Residential Refuse
Collection Before and After Privatization*

City	Year of Change	Number of Households	Annual Municipal Cost In Year Prior to Change (per HH)	Projected Municipal Cost In Year After Change (per HH)	Annual Contract Cost (per HH)	Net Transition Gain (per HH)	% Change in Cost
Berwyn, Illinois	1976	15,800	$41.67[2]	$43.31	$40.06[2]	NA[3]	- 7.5
Pekin, Illinois	1976	10,334	$76.18	$81.32	$70.21	NA	-13.6
Covington, Kentucky	1975	17,569	$30.28	$30.28	$26.11	$ 7.22	-13.7
Middletown, Ohio	1972	16,200	$27.34	$29.83	$21.00	$ 4.58	-29.6
Gainesville, Florida	1977	14,921	$59.17	$62.79	$48.12	$18.60	-23.4
Camden, New Jersey	1974	25,000[1]	$62.81[2]	$67.67[2]	$54.01[2]	$ 4.73	-20.2

[1]Camden's 25,000 figure is the total number of refuse collection customers and includes some commercial stops.
[2]Cost includes disposal.
[3]NA=Not Available.

Source: Eileen Brettler Berenyi, "Contracting Out Refuse Collection: The Nature and Impact of Change," The Urban Interest (Spring 1981).

EXHIBIT 9.12. — *Performance of Alternative Service
Delivery Approaches on Selected Criteria*

EVALUATION CRITERIA[1]

STRATEGY	Market Feedback	Competition	Public Control	Consumer Freedom	Service Universalism	Federal Tax Interface	State Expenditure/ Revenue Interface
Traditional	Decreasing	Decreasing	Increasing	Decreasing	Increasing	Increasing	Increasing
Contract Out							
User Fee							
Privatization	Increasing	Increasing	Decreasing	Increasing	Decreasing	Decreasing	Decreasing

[1]See text.

Source: Rutgers University, Center for Urban Policy Research, 1982.

rectly "vote" support through their willingness to continue to pay for the services offered.

The service strategies also differ in their level of purveyor competition. The traditional approach is monopolistic—there is only *one* service entity, the designated public agency. In contrast, privatization is characterized by a high level of competition as many firms compete for the consumers' choice. The other strategies are somewhat in between. For example, contracting out is more "competitive" than the traditional service strategy, yet is less so than privatization because only a few firms may desire such work—the learning, paper work, and other costs of responding to a municipal request for services are likely to reduce the number of interested entrants.

Other variations are indicated in Exhibit 9.12. For instance, user fees are not deductible for federal or state income tax purposes, nor do they usually count in the enumeration for state expenditure and revenue limitations. In contrast, the tax dollars which pay for contracted services usually *are* deductible for income tax purposes and usually *are* included in state cap computations.

These service strategy rankings can help guide municipal officials in their determination of when and where different service delivery strategies should be opted for. For example, in instances where consumer freedom seems to be most appropriate, such as recreation, consideration should be given to those service approaches maximizing this flexibility (e.g., user fees or privatization). Other service areas will have different priorities. Basic health protection such as rodent extermination and infant inoculations may require service universalism—available to everyone including the poor. Full-service coverage, in turn, is usually best achieved by traditional and contract-out service strategies as opposed to user fees and privatization, for the latter strategies may preclude the participation of those of modest income. This affordability issue is an important concern in evaluating the effects of turning to nontraditional service approaches.

> The employment of user charges, contracting out, and privatization will have serious implications for equity in the financing and distribution of public goods. Use of them will result in lower-income groups paying a larger share of the cost of public services. The subsidies to the poor that exist when governments are financed by progressive forms of taxation—particularly property and individual income taxes—will disappear when each consumer begins to pay the full costs of the services he or she uses. Those with lower incomes will spend a larger proportion of their income on services that were formerly free than will the more affluent.[41]

These equity concerns can be addressed. Privatization-user fees will not penalize the poor if the latter are given vouchers or other financial assistance to satisfy the charges levied by the company providing services. Such support could be keyed to the importance of the service, i.e., support might be forthcoming to pay for police and fire protection and reduced or withheld for certain types of recreation. The modification would povide a safety net for the poor yet would still realize the service cost savings associated with user fees and privatization.

In summary, municipal officials in intergovernmental and non-intergovernmental cities as well, must continue to analyze whether their current means of service provision should be replaced by alternatives. In conducting this review, they should consider the differing characteristics of the various strategies and also give thought to how the alternative strategies themselves might be adjusted to best satisfy local needs. The mixed voucher–privatization program mentioned above is illustrative of a conceptually blended approach to service delivery. Other items must also be scrutinized. There may be possible legal restrictions in state constitutions and local charters to certain means of providing public services. Further, the interest, expertise and capacity of local firms to perform once-public functions must also be checked.

It is likely that city governments will select a *variety* of service delivery strategies. As an example, financial accounting may be contracted out, recreation services paid for by user charges, garbage collection shed from the public sector to privatization, and police protection made more efficient.

Pushing the Conceptual Boundaries—Voluntarism

The enormity of change brought about by the retrenchment of intergovernmentalism calls for further pushing of the boundaries of service delivery mechanisms. Voluntary assistance by business, civic groups, block associations, and so on could provide limited assistance. Examples of voluntarism include: counseling provided by seasoned executives to fledgling small businesses or even to the municipal corporation itself; crime watch and other security duties performed by citizen police auxiliary forces; and reading instruction or foster care provided by retirees.

Voluntarism represents an even further shift in the service delivery spectrum. The traditional concept saw services as a public monopoly. The trio of user fees, contracting out, and privatization conceptually took services to the private sector. Voluntarism takes the privatization concept one step further. There are no contractual guides—assistance is delivered by a private donor to a private recipient.

Voluntarism is not simply a matter of fiscal necessity, born of a shrunken public purse, but offers numerous advantages to the providers. Businesses, neighborhood groups and so on all benefit from improving the appearance, economic vigor, and security of the area where they live or work. Tax loads are another consideration; it may be less costly for a business to provide certain nominally "public" services out of its own pocket than to have the same made available by a costly municipal department supported by public tax dollars.

Most cities are characterized by at least some examples of voluntarism. Selected past efforts by businesses, civic, and other groups in Newark, include the following:

- Prudential and other insurance companies provide financing for new construction and housing rehabilitation.
- The Seton Hall University Law Center, located in downtown Newark, offers consumer and juvenile aid, and other legal assistance.
- A citizen crime watch patrol has been formed for Newark neighborhoods.
- The Salvation Army constructed two major capital facilities. The first provides recreational, cultural, and vocational activities; the second offers drug and alcohol counseling.[42]

Emerging voluntarism in intergovernmental cities such as Newark represents a beginning which must be nurtured to further encourage such efforts. In part, this will require support from by local municipal officials—they should not view voluntarism as competition. Espousal of voluntarism should also stress private sector self-interest—"We all rise and fall together." Voluntarism could also be abetted by the federal government. Changes in federal tax treatment, for instance, are one possibility. To illustrate, under current law, mothers volunteering their services to civic, neighborhood, and similar groups are considered to be "non-working" and hence are not permitted child-care deductions; changing their status would reduce considerably out-of-pocket costs for volunteer activities. Voluntarism, while by no means an encompassing answer to financial austerity, is nonetheless a growing approach to at least peripheral public service delivery.

Conclusion

The purpose of this chapter was to illustrate the types of changes already underway in cities facing financial stress. For cities in this condition, on the one hand, it means a search to heighten existing revenues and to search for alternatives. On the other hand, it also means a significant reduction in the quality and quantity of public services as well as redefinition of what services are to be provided by the public sector.

On the revenue side, there must be movement to diversify components of the income stream, i.e., more reliance on sales taxes and fees/permits and other user charges, less reliance on property and income taxation. States will, in all probability, lead the way with enabling legislation. This is apparent in Tennessee, which for the first time since 1957, has raised the gasoline tax in part to supplement municipal revenues. In Arkansas, a revision to local sales taxes brought additional monies to local governments. In Idaho, locals were allowed to raise the annual permit fees for beer and wine licenses also for the purpose of revenue augmentation.

On the expenditure side, contracting-out and privatization must replace direct public provision. This will affect both the cost of public services per capita as well as aggregate units of demand. Numerous examples of contracting out and privatization exist and need not be elaborated here.

The point which must be emphasized is that cities must limit their services to meet projected costs. And while state governments may authorize changes in enabling legislation to enable cities to help themselves, states, for the most part, are not giving any more money away. In a recent ICMA survey, forty-one of fifty states reported some legislative change affecting cities—the bulk of which was devoted to taking money from, rather than providing money to, them.

Another point which must be kept in mind is that private service provision has a threshold of public participants. The poor may not be able to afford the services society deems necessary to promote public health, safety and welfare. Public sanitation, after all, came to cities because the more affluent owners of neighborhood businesses complained about the vermin and odors from the discarded garbage of the residences of the poor. While it is absolutely essential for fiscal stability to pare services, we must also be cognizant of a threshold level of public sector commitment to those whom the private market is unable to serve.

Other consequences of this chapter's strategies also deserve close scrutiny. Increasing local taxes in intergovernmental cities runs the risk of inducing the cities' remaining businesses and affluent households to leave for less costly jurisdictions.

Reducing local operating service levels can have a similarly adverse effect. Slashing capital maintenance outlays lowers immediate expenditures but forces the municipality to pay an inevitably higher price for these activities in the future. Pruning the size of the municipal payroll may ultimately increase local economic hardship, as the intergovernmental city has served as the employer of last resort for many of its marginally trained residents. These and other trade-offs add to the difficulty of deciding on the appropriate responses to fiscal austerity.

NOTES

1. U.S. Congress, Joint Economic Committee, *Emergency Interim Survey: Fiscal Condition of 48 Large Cities*, U.S. Government Printing Office, January 14, 1982.

2. U.S. Congress, Joint Economic Committee, *The Regional and Urban Impacts of the Administration's Budget and Tax Proposals*. A Study prepared by Marshall Kaplan, Robyn S. Phillips, and Franklin James, U.S. Government Printing Office, July 31, 1981.

3. Ibid., p. 25.

4. Although the cities included in the Joint Economic Committee report do not correspond exactly to our twenty cities, there is enough overlap to warrant a close look at their findings. Eight of ten intergovernmental cities are listed under their declining city classification. Seven of the non-intergovernmental cities are included in the growing city classification. Their groupings are as follows:

Declining Cities	*Growing Cities*
*Baltimore	Albuquerque
Birmingham	*Austin
Boston	*Baton Rouge
*Buffalo	Charlotte
Chicago	*Columbus
*Cincinnati	Dallas
*Cleveland	El Paso
Denver	Honolulu
Detroit	Jacksonville
Ft. Worth	Long Beach
Indianapolis	Los Angeles
Kansas City	Memphis
*Louisville	Miami
*Minneapolis	*Nashville
*Newark	*Oklahoma City
New Orleans	Phoenix
New York	San Antonio
Oakland	San Diego
Omaha	*San Jose
Philadelphia	Tucson
Pittsburgh	*Tulsa
Portland	
St. Louis	
San Francisco	
Seattle	
Toledo	

5. Much of this section is based upon the work of Richard Nathan and associates in field network study of the Reagan budget cuts. See Richard P. Nathan, Philip Dearborn, Clifford Goldman and

*Indicates correspondence to sample city.

Associates, "Initial Effects of the Fiscal Year 1982 Reductions in Federal Spending." *National Tax Journal*, 35:3, 1982.

6. Much of the data which follows is taken from Council of State Governments, "The Economic Health of the States: The Current Prognosis." *CSG Backgrounder*, August 1982.

7. Carol W. Lewis, and Anthony T. Logalbo, "Cutback Principles and Practices: A Checklist for Managers," *Public Administration Reivew*, March/April 1980, pp. 184–188.

8. United States Conference of Mayors, *The FY 82 Budget and the Cities* (Washington, D.C.: Conference of Mayors, 1981).

9. See David Listokin, *Landmarks Preservation and the Property Tax* (New Brunswick: Rutgers University, Center for Urban Policy Research, 1981).

10. Ibid.

11. See Anthony Pascal, "User Charges, Contracting Out, and Privatization in an Era of Fiscal Retrenchment." *The Urban Interest* (Spring 1981), p. 7.

12. Robert W. Poole, Jr., *Cutting Back City Hall* (New York: Universe Books, 1980).

13. United States Conference of Mayors, *The FY 82 Budget and the Cities.*

14. See Advisory Commission on Intergovernmental Relations, *Local Revenue Diversification* (Washington: ACIR, 1974); F. D. Stocker, "Diversification of the Local Revenue System," *National Tax Journal*, Vol. 29, September 1976, pp. 312–321.

15. S. J. Mushkin and R. M. Bird, "Public Prices — an Overview," in S. J. Mushkin, *Public Prices for Public Products* (Washington, D.C.: Urban Institute, 1972).

16. See National League of Cities, *Adjusting Municipal Boundaries: Law and Practices* (Washington, D.C.: League, 1980); See also Chester W. Bain, *Annexation in Virginia* (Charlottesville, NC: University Press of Virginia, 1970); Andrew Reschovsky and Eugene Knaff, "Tax Base Sharing," *Jounal of the American Institute of Planners*, Vol. 43 (1977), pp. 361–70; William A. Fishel, "An Evaluation of Proposals for Metropolitan Sharing of Commercial and Industrial Ratables," *Journal of the American Planning Association*, July 1980, pp. 315–22.

17. Harold Wolman and George Peterson, "Policy Consequences of Local Expenditure Constraint," draft manuscript (no date).

18. Ibid.

19. Mark David Menchik, et al., *How Fiscal Restraints Affect Spending and Services in Cities* (Santa Monica: RAND, 1982).

20. Ibid.

21. Martin A. Bierbaum, "The Impact of the Reagan Domestic Program on Newark, New Jersey" (Photocopy, April 10, 1982).

22. Michael Eastman, "Experiences of a County with Budget Trimming," in Herrington J. Bryce (editor), *Managing Fiscal Retrenchment* (Columbus: Academy for Contemporary Problems, 1980).

23. Donald Oatman, "It's Time for Productivity Accounting in Government." *Government Finance*, Vol. 8, No. 3, November 1978, p. 9.

24. Poole, *Cutting Back City Hall.*

25. Ibid., p. 35.

26. Menchik, et al., *How Fiscal Restraints Affect Spending and Services in Cities.*

27. Conference of Mayors, *The FY 82 Budget and the Cities.*

28. Menchik, et al., *How Fiscal Restraints Affect Spending and Services in Cities.*

29. Martin A. Bierbaum, "The Impact of the Reagan Domestic Program in Newark, New Jersey" (Photocopy, April 10, 1982).

30. United States Conference of Mayors, *The FY 82 Budget and the Cities.*

31. James G. Coke and Carl M. Moore, "Group Processes for Making Public Expenditure Reduction Decisions," in Bryce, *Managing Fiscal Retrenchment in Cities.*

32. Poole, *Cutting Back City Hall*; Jeffrey D. Straussman, "Quasi-Market Alternatives to Local Government Service Provision," *The Urban Interest* (Spring 1981), p. 3; R. S. Ahlbrandt, "Implications of Contracting for a Public Service," *Urban Affairs Quarterly* (March 1974), pp. 337–359; "When the Government Lets Somebody Else Do its Job," *National Journal* (October 1977), pp. 1410–1414; D. D. Fisk, et al., *Private Provision of Public Services: An Overview* (Washington, D.C.: *Urban Interests*, 1978); P. S. Florestano, "The Municipal Connection: Contracting for Public Services with the Private Sector," *Municipal Management*, Vol. 1 (Fall 1978), p. 61; P. S. Florestano and S. B. Gordon, "Public Versus Private: Small Government Contracting with the Private Sector," *Public Administration Review*, Vol. 40 (January-February 1980), p. 29.

33. James Alexander, "Contracting Out and the Municipal Budget," *New Jersey Municipalities* (March 1981), p. 6.

34. Patricia S. Florestano and Stephen B. Gordon, "A Survey of City and County Use of Private Contracting," *The Urban Interest* (Spring 1981), pp. 22.

35. Ibid.

36. See note 25.

37. "Ways Private Firms Can Save Money for Burdened Cities," *U.S. News & World Report*, November 17, 1975, pp. 79–82.

38. Ahlbrandt, "Implications for Contracting for a Public Service."

39. E. S. Savas, "Municipal Monopolies vs. Competition in Delivering Urban Services," *Urban Analysis*, Vol. 2 (1974), pp. 93–106.

40. Eileen Brettler Berenyi, "Contracting Out Refuse Collection: The Nature and Impact of Change," *The Urban Interest* (Spring 1981), p. 30.

41. Pascal, "User Charges, Contracting Out, and Privatization in an Era of Fiscal Retrenchment," p. 10.

42. Examples taken from *Newark*, a monthly publication of the Greater Newark Chamber of Commerce.

10

The Future of the Intergovernmental City

HAVING DETAILED the forces of economic decline impacting intergovernmental cities, the subsequent growth of the federal transfers targeted to these distressed communities, and finally, the dismantling of the vast array of federal domestic programs for both state and local governments, this chapter summarizes and presents the principal research findings of the study. Additionally, this section offers preliminary insight into the future of both intergovernmental and non-intergovernmental cities.

Part I of this chapter summarizes the conceptual frame, empirical validation of economic/social/physical hardship, rise and fall in intergovernmental dependence, and restructurings/adjustments of intergovernmental cities. It emphasizes the general trend towards federal/state dependence which took place over the past two decades as well as the conditions in distressed cities which seemed to justify this high level of public reliance.

Part II discusses the future of intergovernmental and non-intergovernmental cities in light of the changes taking place in the fabric of the United States economy. It views intergovernmental cities as past manufacturing-based locations which have lost much of their industrial employment, yet which have not been able to replace this loss with a share of the new high technology industries. This latter form of employment is an increasingly significant factor in the United States economy.

Summary

Conceptual Underpinnings: The Rise of Intergovernmentalism

The conceptual frame of the intergovernmental city consists of (1) the role of the city, (2) the causes of urban disinvestment, (3) the demographic effects of capital flight, and (4) the rise and fall of the publicly supported economy.

National and international economies, technological innovation, transportation shifts, obsolescent capital plants, and the unresponsiveness of city hall have rendered all but a few nodal concentrations or large cities non-competitive. The loss of investments in the central core depleted the city's revenue-generating base. Further, the socioeconomic shifts engendered by disinvestment as well as sustained demand for municipal services, placed greater pressure on expenditures. The result of the growing mismatch between revenues and expenditures was acute budgetary strain. Unable to obtain increased resources from the private sector or to favorably compete in the public bond market, the city was forced to procure resources from the only sources left—the state and federal governments. An intergovernmental city was born.

During the 1960s state and federal governments began to actively engage in transfers to local governments. States opted to provide the enabling statutes for property tax relief measures aimed at generating increased revenues, i.e., city income taxes, regional tax base sharing, etc. Many states also created direct urban aid packages to those cities that were most depressed.

Likewise, the federal approach focused on resource distribution. An entire array of direct revenue transfers to people supplemented the revenue flows to cities. While state programs provided the larger share of transfers to cities, especially for education, federal aid quadrupled from 1968 to 1975. And it was during this period that, faced with potential collapse, many municipal governments willingly opened their coffers to intergovernmental support.

Private disinvestment remained a fact of life for many central cities throughout the 1970s. Assistance from both state and federal sources was viewed by most municipalities as the only route towards financial security. Intergovernmental transfers became not a supplement, but rather, the primary support for local public services. At the end of the 1970s, trends toward fiscal conservatism at both state and federal levels emerged, significantly curtailing the flow of transfer funds. By the second term of the Reagan Administration in the mid-1980s cities were leaner and meaner. Governments had to work to increase locally provided revenues and to limit locally initiated expenditures. Cities had to learn to build private-public partnerships as never before.

Yet, clearly intergovernmental versus non-intergovernmental is not an "either-or" situation. There exist varying degrees of intergovernmental transfer in all cities; thus the experience of intergovernmental cities could easily be applicable to those locations less dependent upon revenue transfers from other levels of government. Further, resource depletions synonymous with intergovernmental cities could easily be present in the growth belt if, as indicated in recurring reports, the economies of these cities do not keep growing.

The Intergovernmental City—Empirical Verification

How do you empirically define an intergovernmental city? Once defined, which cities fall within this range of definition? Are there other cities where intergovernmentalism is not a fact of life? How do these city sets differ and compare? In order to view more closely the social, physical and economic structure of cities characterized by intergovernmentalism, two groups of cities were isolated: one representing fiscal dependence (intergovernmental), the other fiscal independence (non-intergovernmental). These groups served as the observation points for most subsequent data comparisons.

Cities were selected from a 1980 population size range of 220,000 to 1,000,000. The lower level of this population threshold was used to isolate for study cities which possessed a broad and sophisticated public service system. Approximately sixty-four cities fell within this range. The upper threshold was utilized to eliminate from this total the seven largest cities (New York, Chicago, Philadelphia, Los Angeles, Houston, Dallas, and Detroit), as well as Honolulu and Washington, D.C. These cities were not included because of their unique servicing patterns, in part reflecting international roles or diseconomies of scale and resultant overly high expenditure levels.

The remaining fifty-five cities were categorized as either declining, stable, or growing. Declining communities were defined as those that lost both population and households. Stable communities were defined as those that lost population but not households, i.e., experienced total population losses at about the local rate of household shrinkage. Finally, growing communities were those that had gained both population and households. These city sets were then viewed for their association with intergovernmentalism. Intergovernmentalism was defined as large aggregate (municipal and school) per capita expenditures, a majority of which were paid for by intergovernmental transfers. Highly correlated were intergovernmentalism and cities of declining population on the one hand and an absence of intergovernmentalism and cities of stable or expanding population on the other.

Ten cities were then chosen from each of the declining and growing population categories. The ten "intergovernmental" cities drawn from the declining city category were those that required the greatest amounts of revenue per capita to cover the cost of public services, and those most dependent upon state and federal assistance to meet this need. Conversely, the ten "non-intergovernmental" cities drawn from the growth city category were those that raised the smallest amount of revenue per capita and those least dependent on fiscal transfers from state and federal governments.

The remaining sections of this summary use this distinction to compare the physical, economic, and social structures of these two groups of cities as well as the rise and fall of intergovernmentalism over their most recent history.

Economic Hardship in the Intergovernmental City

A much different economic picture was present in intergovernmental than in non-intergovernmental cities. This difference was vividly apparent by viewing classic measures of economic performance. The economic performance criteria used to exhibit these differences were: (1) primary economic indicators, (2) industrial base characteristics, and (3) private investment. The variables employed here were culled from multiple studies on the measurement of economic performance. They included population, employment, unemployment, and income trends. Industrial base characteristics consisted of establishments, employment, sales, and value of production. Private investments comprised new capital expenditures in manufacturing as well as new housing units authorized.

The results of the analyses pointed to weak economic performance of the intergovernmental cities. According to population, employment, and per capita income performance indicators, intergovernmental cities experienced either actual decline or at best, an extremely slow rate of growth relative to both non-intergovernmental cities and the nation as a whole. Job growth, firm expansions, sales figures, and capital construction in intergovernmental cities all were down. Further, private residential and non-residential capital investment was off significantly. While there were relatively small differences in household income levels in the two categories of cities, it should be noted that not only was income in intergovernmental cities historically high (a difficult position to retrench from even in hard times) but a share of the aggregate income of intergovernmental cities was composed of non-salary assistance payments to individuals which contributed to a further unnatural inflation of the income profile of these cities. Economic inferiority was quick to be recognized by national thrift institutions. Bond ratings in most intergovernmental cities fell over the last twenty years. This reduced the possibility of and made more costly future debt extensions. Given increasing fiscal conservatism on the part of state and federal governments, intergovernmental cities must come to grips with very severe economic problems with only very limited, and largely unaugmented, local resources.

When levels of economic activity declined, and fiscal assistance was limited, the intergovernmental city experienced increasing internal strain and external pressure. Poverty and crime flourished as welfare and unemployment payments replaced payroll checks. The level of social need generated by residents further increased.

Social Hardship in the Intergovernmental City

The social structure of a city was defined largely through the performance of its residents across basic social indicators. These indicators included: (1) income and poverty, (2) health statistics, (3) public safety, (4) levels of public assistance, and (5) educational skills and performance.

A composite ranking of social distress derived from these individual indicators showed that social hardship was significantly concentrated in large, old Northeastern and North Central cities. The highest levels of social distress were found in the economically stagnant, intergovernmental cities. Newark, Cleveland, Baltimore, and Buffalo were the types of cities which exhibited severe levels of social hardship across most specifically chosen, social indicators.

In these locations: (1) incomes were declining; (2) mortality data (fatalities by specific cause) showing deaths from cancer, influenza, pneumonia, and tuberculosis were twice as high as elsewhere; (3) incidents of total crime were 1.5 times as frequent; (4) welfare caseloads were at three times the level (the welfare payment per case was also 25 percent higher); and (5) educational achievement and performance were significantly lower.

Social conditions tended to be much better in the high growth, non-intergovernmental cities. None of these cities ranked among those cities of high social distress. At worst, a few non-intergovernmental cities showed moderate levels of distress, while well over half of the non-intergovernmental cities delineated fit into the category of low need. The most distressed non-intergovernmental cities—Baton Rouge and Columbus—exhibited distress levels only slightly higher than Minneapolis and Milwaukee, the best of the intergovernmental cities. The next group—Oklahoma City, Nashville-Davidson, and Wichita—exhibited much lower levels of distress. Finally, low social need characterized the younger, economically vibrant non-intergovernmental cities of San Jose, Anaheim, Austin, Tulsa and Virginia Beach.

Housing in the Intergovernmental City

The housing of intergovernmental versus non-intergovernmental cities was older, much more often multifamily, and considerably larger. The median age of housing in intergovernmental cities was fifty years—two and one-half times the median age of housing in non-intergovernmental cities. Sixty percent of the housing in intergovernmental cities was multifamily, approximately double the proportion of multifamily housing in non-intergovernmental cities. Thirty-five percent of multifamily housing in intergovernmental cities contained five rooms or more; the equivalent for non-intergovernmental cities was less than 15 percent. The size of single-family housing units, especially in terms of number of rooms, was approximately equivalent.

Although housing in intergovernmental cities was more frequently lacking basic amenities (kitchens, baths) or in a worse state of repair (presence of cracks or holes, more frequent sightings of vermin), it was generally of reasonably high quality. Fewer than 3 percent of the units in intergovernmental cities lacked complete plumbing, and no more than 10 to 15 percent were severely deteriorated by most definitions of this condition.

The owners of housing in intergovernmental cities were increasingly resident, minority families, inadequately educated and inferiorly paid. The cash flow from real estate holdings was sufficiently low to necessitate full-time occupations in other professions.

The residents of housing in intergovernmental cities were often minority with significant shares of the remaining white population of Spanish origin. Residents were poor, households were often female-headed, very old or very young in age, with a significant share of household income coming from non-salary sources. Residents of intergovernmental cities were often forced to remain in these cities because housing was not available elsewhere. Often these residents encouraged their offspring to leave the city before they too had no choice. While for the most part these were gritty people, they had growing complaints about local public services, particularly police, sanitation, and mass transit facilities.

The Rise of Intergovernmentalism

As a reaction to these conditions, there was explosive growth in federal grants-in-aid to states and cities over the past two decades along with a concurrent increase in state transfer payments to cities. At the federal level, this was part of a general trend which witnessed a relative decrease in defense spending from 1960 to 1980, and an upsurge in human resource and community and economic development spending. Allocations for the latter categories of expenditures grew tenfold over a decade —twice as fast as the national budget as a whole. From 1960 to 1980 human resources and community and economic development allocations went from one-half to twice the level of defense outlays.

The major functional areas within which grants-in-aid are structured consist of: (1) income security; (2) community and regional development; (3) education, training, employment and social services; (4) health; (5) transportation; and (6) general state and local fiscal assistance. Within these structural areas, there was massive growth of: (1) AFDC and School Lunch and Breakfast programs; (2) CDBG, Public Housing, Section 8, UDAG, EDA/SBA Business Loans, and EDA Public Works and Planning Grants; (3) Job Corps, Head Start, BEOG and CETA grants; (4) Medicaid and Community Health Centers Grants; (5) UMTA; and (6) Revenue Sharing assistance. These grants typically favored intergovernmental cities by margins of two-to-three to one.

In addition to direct federal aid to cities and their inhabitants, state aid, through 1980, also increased significantly. On average, states increased aid to local governments by factors of three-to-five to one. In almost all cases they were targeted to "high need" cities or school districts. Further, the likelihood that these "high need" locations were also repositories of additional federal funding was also very high.

Revenue and Expenditure Emphases in the Intergovernmental City

Revenue and expenditure emphases varied considerably in intergovernmental and non-intergovernmental cities. Where differences existed, the least healthy position was almost always found in the intergovernmental city.

On the expenditure side, the data showed that the intergovernmental city was at a definite disadvantage. It spent significantly more than the non-intergovernmental city across most areas of public service. Intergovernmental cities spent a proportionally higher amount of local resources for essential services (police, fire, general government, health and welfare), though employee wages per job category tended to be lower. Furthermore, declining intergovernmental cities showed lower "other expenses" and debt service costs. The former indicated that money not spent on services, equipment and supplies meant that repairs usually were not being made; the latter suggested that, in addition, few public works projects are being initiated.

On the revenue side, intergovernmental cities again appeared at a distinct disadvantage. Having higher levels of expenditure, older intergovernmental cities generated substantially greater revenue than non-intergovernmental cities. This was complicated by their shrinking tax bases which reflected significant private disinvestment. Further, intergovernmental cities raised revenues primarily through property tax and increasingly through local income taxes—revenues where the ability to secure more was extremely limited. Thus, intergovernmental cities recurringly faced revenue shortfalls, even though their remaining residents and businesses were being taxed at extraordinary levels.

Non-intergovernmental cities, on the other hand, had expanding property tax bases and an array of revenue resources. The sales tax, user charges and fees and permits were significant revenue contributors in non-intergovernmental cities. As for capital expenditures, the vast majority of roads and highways, bridges, and sewer plants and lines were rated good to excellent in growing (non-intergovernmental) cities; the same percentage were rated fair or poor in declining (intergovernmental) cities.

Intergovernmental cities, by definition, were significantly more reliant on revenue transfers than were non-intergovernmental cities. Overall, on average, intergovernmental cities received twice the dollar amount of federal and state aid than did non-intergovernmental cities. Two-thirds of overall revenue transfers were from the state and were largely concentrated in educational (school district) support. The federal government, typically spending less money overall than state governments, was however, a large supporter of municipal service activities.

The Dismantling of Intergovernmentalism

Those cities defined as intergovernmental, as well as others which may or may not meet the criteria, had been receiving a variety of federal funds in significant amounts for over a decade. Cities in their recent histories were dependent on these sources of funds as stabilizing influences. Many of the programs from which these funds flow have now been dismantled.

Direct federal aid, in the form of grants to cities, was reduced and restructured as block grants to states. Grant-administering agencies now have the authority, within broad federal guidelines, to allocate funds according to their own formulas. These new "super grants" were constructed from a host of categorical grants, many of them appearing small, but with an underlying endemic nature to them. Significantly reduced funding is another characteristic of these new grants. The impact is thus felt in both the level of funds to cities, as well as the method of allocation, necessitating a complete restructuring of past political realities.

Where grants were not consolidated with reduced funding, they have been phased out, forcing cities to drop programs outright or attempt to maintain them with their own locally raised funds. Demands for some services, meanwhile, have increased as economic conditions have deteriorated and income maintenance programs were reduced.

The majority of the budget reductions have taken place in funding categories which were inextricably and fundamentally related to older, declining cities. Also, while these programs have a disproportionate effect on declining localities, they also have an impact on cities generally.

The Future of the Intergovernmental City

The past two decades have witnessed major changes in the regional and intra-metropolitan economic structure of the United States; the 1980s represent the watershed. Simply put, fundamental shifts in industry and population have shaped the decline of aging manufacturing cities, and the rise of a host of younger cities whose growth has been rooted in high-tech industries. There has been a simultaneous deconcentration of people and jobs nationally. This development has impacted most seriously on the older, declining cities which we have here termed "intergovernmental." Younger, growing, "non-intergovernmental cities" have been able to sidestep the onerous consequences of deconcentration because of their ability to continuously spawn growth industries and also due to their active annexation efforts.

This portion of the chapter examines some of the macroeconomic trends and political processes underlying this pattern of uneven regional development. It emphasizes that the prevailing pattern of regional differentiation is not merely the result of intermetropolitan shifts of people and jobs. Rather, it has resulted from the gradual decline of old-line industries located primarily in intergovernmental cities in the Northeast and the North Central region, and the concomitant rise of a group of high-growth industries in non-intergovernmental cities. Put another way: aging cities have declined because their economies have been composed of shrinking manufacturing sectors, and because they have proven incapable of generating or attracting new growth industries. In contrast, the rapid economic expansion of younger cities found its roots in a host of regionally specific, high-tech and service industries. The critical dimension was thus not the shift of firms but rather the death of some and the birth of others each taking place in different geographic areas.

In closing, this chapter will draw upon past trends and current conditions to present a cautious forecast of the future of these two classes of cities.

Decline of Older Core Industries

At least since the 1970s, older core manufacturing industries have declined in national importance. Many of the giant corporations involved in steel production, automobiles, non-electrical machinery, appliances, and textiles have closed plants in the United States or moved production facilities overseas.[1] A broad overview of the changing picture of manufacturing in the American economy is presented in Exhibit 10.1.

The outmigration or closing of large manufacturing plants has devastating ripple effects on local and regional economies. As unemployment rises and pressures on local labor markets increase, incomes drop, retail trade and services fall off, supplier firms close, and a recessionary cycle sets in.

The aging cities of the Manufacturing Belt, particularly those in the Middle Atlantic states and the North Central region, have declined precisely because their economies remain inextricably linked to these older core industries. For example, in

EXHIBIT 10.1.—*The Changing Shape of the American Economy: Changes in Employment, 1976–1981*

Sector	Growth Rate Percent Change in Employment
SLOW-GROWTH SECTORS	
Old-line Industry	9.5%
Government	7.1
FAST-GROWTH SECTORS	
High Technology	32.6
Energy	43.2
Services	26.3

Note: Excludes wholesale and retail trade; includes Hawaii and Alaska.

Source: George Sternlieb and James W. Hughes, *Demographic Trends and Economic Reality: Planning and Markets in the 1980s* (New Brunswick, New Jersey: Rutgers University Center for Urban Policy Research, 1982).

1980, the largest employers in Pittsburgh and Buffalo were iron and steel firms. In New York, the major production units are still apparel and printing. In Cleveland, fabricated metal production and non-electronic machinery continue to dominate the local economy.[2] These aging cities, tied to older forms of manufacturing, resemble the New England of several generations ago, when it was losing textiles, boot and shoe, and other labor-intensive industries to the South and other areas both inside and outside of the United States.[3]

The data presented in Chapter 3 on employment patterns for the twenty sample cities bear this out. Over the entire post-war period, declining intergovernmental cities have witnessed staggering and unrelenting losses in manufacturing employment and particularly in production workers (Exhibit 10.2). Research on regional labor markets also suggests that aging cities have lost enormous amounts of manufacturing employment, particularly high-wage production jobs.[4] As Exhibit 10.3 shows, job loss in declining cities has been concentrated in high-wage, blue-collar or "union" jobs. In these cities, there has also been significant losses in low-wage, non-unionized production employment. Interestingly, growing cities have witnessed the bulk of employment growth in non-union, non-manufacturing sectors, although they have also added substantial numbers of manufacturing jobs.

Growth of Technology-Intensive Manufacturing

Over the past two decades, virtually all significant gains in manufacturing employment have been concentrated in the Sunbelt, the home of most non-intergovernmental cities.[5] Together, the South and West have accounted for a 90 percent share of net national expansion in manufacturing employment over the period 1960 to 1975 (Exhibit 10.4). Further, rates of expansion in manufacturing employment in those two regions have been consistently in the range of thirty percent, more than triple the overall national rate of manufacturing growth.[6]

This has not been caused by simple regional relocations of existing plant or production facilities. Rather, the growth of a new class of high-tech and service cities has been premised upon the rise of new high-growth manufacturing industries. Exhibit 10.5 bears this out. Clearly the data show that the growth in manufacturing in the Southern tier has been fueled by the birth of new industries and firms. Here, the rate of start-ups was almost one and one-half times the rate of start-ups in the North. Interestingly, the rate of manufacturing plant closures was quite similar in the two regions.

Since 1950, a series of technology-intensive industries have witnessed the most rapid rates of growth in manufacture. These include aerospace, electronic equipment, computers, scientific instruments, defense-related equipment, and synthetic chemicals.[7] Indeed, of these industries, electronics has become the leading growth sector in the American economy, akin to the machine tool sector of the early twentieth century. Electronics is, in fact, assuming many of the key functions of the machine tool industry. Today, it provides some of the most necessary equipment for other industrial sectors, including food processing, apparel manufacture, transportation equipment, telecommunications, and data processing.

EXHIBIT 10.2.—*Changes in Manufacturing Employment Type, by Region, 1947–1976 (in Thousands)*

	1947–1963			1963–1976		
	Change in Total Employment	Change in Production Workers	Change in Non-production Workers	Change in Total Employment	Change in Production Workers	Change in Non-production Workers
New England	-50.2	-205.7	155.5	-85.7	-141.9	56.2
Mid-Atlantic	121.3	-399.1	520.4	-573.9	-568.6	-5.3
East North Central	160.9	-333.8	494.7	301.9	90.0	211.9
Manufacturing Belt	232.0	-938.6	1,170.6	-357.7	-620.5	262.8
West North Central	228.3	78.9	149.4	237.9	161.2	76.7
South Atlantic	600.9	320.3	280.6	609.7	397.3	212.4
East South Central	252.3	153.8	98.5	407.8	291.2	116.6
West South Central	313.8	169.3	144.4	488.2	327.4	160.8
Mountain	143.2	80.6	62.6	154.4	98.4	56.0
Pacific	884.4	444.8	439.6	266.0	182.4	83.6
Periphery	2,422.9	1,247.7	1,175.2	2,164.0	1,457.9	706.1

Source: John Rees, "Government Policy and Industrial Location in the United States," in U.S. Congress, Joint Economic Committee, Special Study on Economic Change, Volume 7, State and Local Finance: Adjustments in a Changing Economy, U.S. Government Printing Office, 1980.

EXHIBIT 10.3. — *Detailed Changes in Local Labor Markets,
Declining Versus Growing Cities, 1967–1974*

	Net Job Change	Absolute Change (Loss or Gain)	High Wage Mfg.	High Wage Non-Mfg.*	Low Wage* Mfg.	Low Wage* Non-Mfg.**
DECLINING CITIES						
Baltimore	-36,290 -	-33,867 (100.0)	-13,988 (41.3)	-9,349 (27.6)	-10,530 (31.1)	+466 (0.0)
Boston	-14,671 -	-31,875 (100.0)	-21,007 (65.9)	+35 (0.0)	-10,850 (34.1)	+8,002 (0.0)
New York	-222,181 -	-236,144 (100.0)	-117,675 (49.8)	-13,888 (5.9)	-97,230 (41.2)	-7,351 (3.1)
Philadelphia	-69,327 -	-66,338 (100.0)	-62,253 (93.8)	-1,877 (2.9)	-2,208 (3.3)	+10,142 (0.0)
TOTAL	-342,469 -	-368,206 (100.0)	-214,923 (58.4)	-25,114 (6.8)	-120,818 (32.8)	-7,351 (2.0)
GROWING CITIES						
Albuquerque	+35,056 -	+29,026 (100.0)	+4,756 (16.4)	+6,461 (22.3)	+1,855 (6.4)	+15,954 (54.9)
Denver	+53,814 -	+49,703 (100.0)	+8,030 (16.1)	+19,808 (39.9)	+112 (0.2)	+21,753 (43.8)
San Antonio	+68,518 -	+53,970 (100.0)	+6,906 (12.8)	+13,086 (24.2)	+1,460 (2.7)	+32,518 (60.3)
TOTAL	+157,388 -	+132,699 (100.0)	+19,692 (14.8)	+39,355 (29.7)	+3,427 (2.6)	+70,255 (52.9)

Notes: *Includes textile (SIC 22), apparel (SIC 23), lumber (SIC 24), furniture (SIC 25), and leather (SIC 31); retail trade, business services, health services, private educational services (SIC 73, 80, 82), and other services except legal and professional.

**Does not include government or construction employment

Source: Data adapted from Ben Harrison and Edward Hill, "The Changing Structure of Jobs in Older and Younger Cities," MIT-Harvard Joint Center for Urban Studies, Working Paper No. 58, 1979.

With the exception of New England, and the high-tech circumferential around Boston, the intergovernmental cities of the older manufacturing belt have proven incapable of generating or attracting these kinds of industries. Younger cities, in contrast, are the centers for high-tech industrial production. For example, the largest industries in Dallas–Fort Worth, Los Angeles, and San Diego are aircraft instrumentation and other forms of sophisticated electronics. The biggest employers in San Jose and Tucson are computer equipment and electronics. In sum, the rapid growth and fiscal independence of a new cluster of cities, predominantly in the South and West, have been virtually premised on the expansion of an essentially new and very specialized group of industrial employers.

EXHIBIT 10.4—*Change in Employment, by Region, 1960-1981 (in Thousands)*

	1960-1975			1975-1981		
	Number	Rate	Share	Number	Rate	Share
TOTAL EMPLOYMENT						
Northeast	3,305.9	21.7	13.8	1,819.4	9.8	12.8
North Central	5,534.9	36.2	23.2	2,548.5	12.2	17.9
South	9,662.3	69.9	40.5	5,973.5	25.4	41.9
West	5,376.1	69.5	22.5	3,914.8	29.9	27.4
U.S. TOTAL	23,879.2	46.6	100.0	14,256.2	18.8	100.0
MANUFACTURING EMPLOYMENT						
Northeast	-781.4	-13.9	0.0	177.0	3.7	9.1
North Central	234.4	4.2	10.5	177.5	3.1	9.2
South	1,469.0	29.9	66.1	935.9	18.2	48.3
West	520.3	27.8	23.4	648.1	27.1	33.4
U.S. TOTAL	1,469.3	8.8	100.0	1,938.5	10.7	100.0
PRIVATE NON-MANUFACTURING EMPLOYMENT						
Northeast	2,798.1	36.5	17.6	1,447.2	13.8	14.0
North Central	3,799.1	50.6	23.8	1,999.2	17.7	19.3
South	5,868.3	77.8	36.8	4,015.1	29.9	38.8
West	3,466.5	80.1	21.8	2,892.0	37.1	27.9
U.S. TOTAL	15,932.0	58.9	100.0	10,353.5	24.1	100.0
GOVERNMENT EMPLOYMENT						
Northeast	1,289.2	66.6	19.9	195.2	6.1	9.9
North Central	1,501.4	68.3	23.2	371.8	10.0	18.9
South	2,298.0	87.7	35.5	1,022.5	20.8	52.1
West	1,389.6	90.6	21.4	374.7	12.8	19.1
U.S. TOTAL	6,477.9	78.1	100.0	1,964.2	13.3	100.0

Source: George Sternlieb and James Hughes, "The National Economy and the Northeast: A Context for Discussion," paper presented for Economic Prospects of the Northeast Conference, State University of New York at Albany, April 1982.

EXHIBIT 10.5.—*Rates of Firm Closure and Birth, by Industry, for the North and South, 1969–1974 (Percent)*

Industry	North	South
	Closure Rate[a]	
Average	33	35
Agriculture	25	28
Mining	33	39
Construction	29	33
Manufacturing	30	33
Transportation, Communications, and Public Utilities	28	31
Wholesale/Retail Trade	36	37
Finance, Insurance, and Real Estate	28	29
Services	26	29
Public Administration	26	18
Unclassified	32	41
	Birth Rate[b]	
Average	20	29
Agriculture	14	21
Mining	14	25
Construction	19	38
Manufacturing	15	26
Transportation, Communications, and Public Utilities	18	24
Wholesale/Retail Trade	21	27
Finance, Insurance, and Real Estate	47	69
Services	24	29
Public Administration	20	29
Unclassified	01	01

Note: [a] When the Wholesale/Retail Trade industry is excluded, the average closure rate for the North is 29 percent, and for the South, 32 percent.

[b] When the Wholesale/Retail Trade industry is excluded, the average birth rate for the North is 19 percent, and for the South, 31 percent.

Source: Carol L. Jusenius and Larry C. Ledebur, "Documenting the 'Decline' of the North," Economic Development Research Report for U.S. Department of Commerce, Economic Development Administration, Office of Economic Research, 1978.

The Expansion of the Service Sector

Over the past two decades, the most rapid growth in the American economy has taken place in the service sector, including trade, finance, service, and government.[8] Traditionally, the downtown business districts of older central cities were the location of service industries. These areas were easily accessible by rail transportation and were the central locations for important services such as legal offices or accounting firms.

By the 1960s, a variety of factors combined to stall the growth of service-related industries in these aging cities. On the one hand, improved transportation and communication technologies made it possible for service-related firms to move to the suburbs. On the other, important support firms also began to relocate away from smaller cities to larger regional centers. Yet, a handful of older cities continued to attract service industries along with some high-tech manufacturing. For example, Boston, Cincinnati, and Minneapolis still provide a relatively broad range of office-related services for their respective metropolitan economies.

In the new high-tech cities and regions, however, the bulge in service-related industries has been astounding. High-tech industries have spawned fast-growing service firms in software, data processing, consultant engineering, and defense-related services. Other support firms—such as investment banks, insurance companies, law firms, management consultants, and information processing companies—have also come to play important economic roles. Non-profit organizations in education, research, and health and hospitals are also large employers. Surging populations have triggered enormous expansion in a host of services and also in government employment. Cultural entertainment and leisure-related business round out the picture. Basically, again as Chapter 3 has suggested, a cluster of youthful cities has been able to generate large amounts of employment in these new, rapidly growing sectors of the economy.

Summary

The central theme presented so far is quite simple: basic changes in the structure of the American political economy underscore a prevailing pattern of uneven regional development. Put at its most basic level, the older cities of aging regions have faltered as component sectors of their local economies and have declined in national importance. The younger cities of vibrant regions have simultaneously ridden the crest of a host of spatially concentrated high-growth industries.

Exhibits 10.5 and 10.6 portray the basic trends even clearer. Between 1969 and 1975, a new class of cities gained relatively larger shares of total employment, while older cities in other regions witnessed significant declines. As Exhibit 10.6 shows, only a small amount of this differential can be pinned to interregional relocations. These shifts occurred because rates of expansion of existing businesses were very substantial in the South. Looking across industries, new business start-ups were also greatest in the South. Again, rates of plant closure were very similar between regions.[9]

In sum, the data imply that the rise of this new class of cities is rooted in a particular cluster of rapidly expanding high-tech and service-related industries. Interestingly, the data appear to contradict the hypotheses of interregional shifts of prevailing industries. The emergence of new industries in new cities and regions has taken place at the same time that older manufacturing sectors have lost much of their importance to the American economy. Taken together, these developments have modified existing regional patterns by bringing a new group of service cities into the urban system, while undermining the status of the manufacturing cities of the past.

EXHIBIT 10.6.—*Components of Employment Growth in Selected Central Counties of Major Metropolitan Areas, 1969–1975*

Region	Percent Employment Change	Employment in New Businesses Minus Employment in Dying Businesses	Net Expansion of Employment in Existing Businesses	Net Resulting from Relocation
New England	-18.0	-18.5	-1.1	-0.5
Middle Atlantic	-22.1	-18.9	-0.4	-2.8
East North Central	-5.4	-13.8	9.7	-1.3
West North Central	8.1	-12.6	22.0	-1.2
South Atlantic	4.0	-12.4	12.0	4.4
Southeast	NA	NA	NA	NA
Southwest	12.1	-3.3	18.1	-2.7
Mountain	-9.3	-11.1	3.7	-1.9
Pacific	-2.3	-5.7	3.3	0.1

NA = Not Available

Source: Franklin W. James, "Economic Distress in Central Cities," in Robert W. Burchell and David Listokin (eds.), *Cities Under Stress: The Fiscal Crises of Urban America.* New Brunswick, New Jersey: Center for Urban Policy Research, 1981.

The Future of Intergovernmental Cities

Numerous older intergovernmental cities have become outmoded and inefficient in America's domestic economy. They may actually be physical and spatial relics of a bygone era. Most have been left virtually without significant function in the face of a new engine of economic expansion.

These aging cities are, for the most part, totally built-up. Except where abandonment has been rampant, few possess large tracts of open land. When sites in these cities are available, they are seldom attractive for industrial development because of their prevailing problems of crime, inadequately trained work force, transportation access difficulties, and so on. Unable to annex, they have expanded to their ultimate borders. Their infrastructure is old and dilapidated. Much of their housing stock is also old and actuarily and realistically unsuitable for rehabilitation. There thus remains only modest hope that market forces can significantly rejuvenate many intergovernmental cities.

The distressed situation of most of these aging cities is likely to worsen over the course of the mid- and late-1980s. Only a few older cities, due to unique characteristics related to college populations or regional location, e.g., Boston and Minneapolis, have attracted the newer industries and services. Even in these selected cases, the new jobs that have been created are not nearly sufficient to replace the tremendous losses in manufacturing employment that have occurred there. What has developed here parallels the city-within-a-city phenomenon, of which Manhattan's relationship to New York City is exemplary: an inner borough of tall office buildings involved in service activities ringed by luxurious hotels, gentrified neighborhoods, and cultural amenities, surrounded by vast stretches of outer-borough (Bronx, Brooklyn, Queens) unemployment, poverty and physical–social deterioration.

Thus, cities which have lost their former roles as regional manufacturing centers will, in the short run, probably continue to decline. Residential and nonresidential deconcentration will continue, as a share of the remaining ethnic and middle-income minority households also leave the city for surrounding suburban enclaves. The resultant unemployment problem facing the older cities of the Manufacturing Belt will also continue. Eastern cities like Newark, Baltimore, and Buffalo have already lost a significant share of their high-wage blue-collar jobs; others in the Midwest and elsewhere—like Cincinnati, Cleveland and Louisville—may soon follow. In these cities jobs may continue to disappear, even if plants and industries remain. Basic manufacturing industries are becoming more technologically intensive in the face of escalating international competition. Increasingly automated factories will produce goods more cheaply, utilizing less labor.

In the immediate future, the most pressing problem confronting declining inter-governmental cities will be budget shortfalls. Most of these cities have lost a sub-stantial portion of their ratable bases over the past two decades. As such, they are currently pushing their taxing capacities to the maximum. These cities have depended on federal and state aid just to remain solvent. The impact of continued deficit re-duction and tax increases on intergovernmental cities will surely be felt.

In these cities, the combination of national austerity and local fiscal stress de-pendency translate into lean public services over the next several years.[10] Con-tinuously faced with fiscal insolvency, these cities are forced to drastically curtail both the quality and quantity of local public services. This type of retrenchment is already at hand in many intergovernmental cities. Inevitably, such harsh austerity measures will have serious short-term inputs on the quality of life in these older cities.

The Future of Non-Intergovernmental Cities

Non-intergovernmental cities may also encounter a few of the socioeconomic problems faced by aging intergovernmental cities. There is growing sophistication in the interpretation of the economy of the Sunbelt. The Sunbelt, and non-inter-governmental cities within it, are being viewed as heterogeneous and diverse. Re-flecting these differences, the South Atlantic region and Southern California, due to concentrations of manufacturing and high technology industries, are more suscep-tible to recession than originally imagined. The "Oil Patch" region and the Moun-tain States (coal producers) have experienced a slowing of growth related to lagging oil prices. In Fall 1982, the unemployment rate in Texas reached 8.7 percent and showed some sign of catching up to the national average. The growth of Florida and Arizona is limited by existing public service infrastructure and inadequate water supply.

Yet, most non-intergovernmental cities in these subregions possess robust local economies which contain more than adequate amounts of young, high-growth industries.[11] While social problems may be present, they are surely not on the scale of the problems facing older cities. Budgetary conditions in these cities will remain stable, at least for the short-to-medium term period.

On the other hand, some municipal fiscal problems may loom on the horizon for these growing cities. A number of analysts have predicted that, over the next five years, public employee compensation rates will increase substantially in the South, where average rates of compensation are currently quite low.[12] In fact, AFSCME— the largest public employee union—has already targeted Houston and Dallas for major organizing drives in the mid-1980s. Thus, over the next five-to-ten years, there is the distinct possibility that public employee wages and benefits in southern cities will start to catch up to those in older northern cities. If this is the case, expenditures will rise much more rapidly than public service levels. This, in turn, will force local governments to raise more revenues and may put some pressure on the local budget.

The vibrance witnessed in younger non-intergovernmental cities over the past decade may diminish in intensity but basically continue. The industrial base of these cities is rooted in the fastest growing sectors of the U.S. economy. Economic indicators show an unusually consistent trendline across cyclical downswings. The effect of recessions on these cities is simply a shift from fast to slower rates of expansion. Upswings, even when they are slight, also disproportionately benefit the cities of these regions.

Further, non-intergovernmental cities possess large, unencumbered tracts of open land for continued industrial and residential development. Their modern built environments make them more amenable to new forms of high-tech and post-industrial development. They possess few of the pressing social or economic problems which confront declining Northeast and North Central cities. Finally, even though these younger cities will no doubt feel the pinch of federal cutbacks, they are in a good position to replace lost intergovernmental revenues with locally raised funds.

Conclusion

Part I of this chapter summarized the general findings of this study. Part II sought to use these findings for future scenarios for both intergovernmental and non-intergovernmental cities. The chapter's findings can be listed as follows:

- The decline of older manufacturing industries and the recently-depressed level of the domestic economy have impacted quite seriously on the aging cities of older regions. A large number of high-wage blue-collar jobs have been eliminated in these cities. Growing concentrations of unemployment and poverty as well as sharp fiscal strains have resulted. Inevitably, it has been the case that when national economic growth stalls, these locations bear a larger share of the slowdown.

- The expansion of new high-tech industries has fueled the growth of a new cluster of cities located primarily in the South and West. These are communities which have annexed substantial amounts of peripheral territory and support public services from local taxes and revenues rather than from intergovernmental transfers. The rise of these cities has been premised primarily upon emergence of new indigenous growth industries, and not upon interregional relocations. Indeed, in periods of rapid economic expansion, these cities have benefitted disproportionately. Further, downswings have only lessened the pace of positive growth. The service sector has grown most rapidly in these younger, non-intergovernmental cities. In aging Northeastern and North Central regions, characteristic of intergovernmental city locations, service industries have tended to decentralize to the suburbs.

In light of these general trends a number of specific forecasts can be offered concerning the future of intergovernmental versus non-intergovernmental cities.

- Economic expansion in robust non-intergovernmental cities may slow over the course of the mid- to late-1980s, but growth will still take place. These cities possess a critical mass of industries which comprise the cornerstone of a changing U.S. economy. In the past, they have proven resilient to recessionary cycles and have benefited disproportionately from upswings. They should continue to perform throughout the decade.

- Federal cutbacks will not seriously disrupt business-as-usual in non-intergovernmental cities. Although a catch-up in public employee compensation (benefits as well as salaries) will bring about substantial increases in expenditures, the revenues are available to meet these expenditure requirements. With balanced budgets, good bond ratings, and a large pool of untapped ratables, these cities will continue to prosper throughout the decade.

- Older declining intergovernmental cities will see little growth in the 1980s. The local economies of these cities are rooted in increasingly non-competitive industrial sectors.

- Despite the widespread acknowledgment of capital obsolescence in older cities, the quality of infrastructure in these cities will continue to deteriorate. Slow economic growth, interregional economic shifts, inflation, reduced aid, and fiscal stress will force both state and local governments to defer capital construction, maintenance and renovation.

- Some local governments will either default or be unable to meet expenditure commitments. First large, then medium-sized cities will be affected. Municipal government will be streamlined. Continuing rounds of public employee layoffs—similar to those of 1975 and 1982—will take place.

- Cuts at the federal level pose very difficult, yet hopefully solvable, short-term futures for aging intergovernmental cities. These cities are already reaching their maximum taxing capacities; there are little own-source revenues left to garner. Faced with faltering intergovernmental revenues and sustained costs to deliver services, they will be forced to pare back substantially.

- Adjustments are already being made. Cities are reevaluating the public–private mix of services as well as the array and level of services they are offering to their citizenry. Today's intergovernmentally dependent city will surely become less intergovernmental. Tomorrow's intergovernmental city will provide less services, less often, while it brings its service structure into line with its ratable base.

Rarely in municipal finance has there been a magic bullet. For the intergovernmental city this is no exception. This type of city has a history of problems and a history of throwing upper-level public resources at these problems.

But the future seems much different from the past. Domestic cutbacks were talked about and dismissed as unachievable or politically naive; yet, they were made. Local governments were portrayed as federal funding addicts unable to go "cold turkey." Yet, they responded with a resiliency and determination heretofore unimaginable.

Five years ago, the most inconceivable thought was that the federal government would say "We have no more money" and that local governments would say "O.k., I guess we'll have to do without." This is exactly what happened. And it happened in full presence of a basic unevenness in city class—the haves (non-intergovernmental cities) and the have-nots (intergovernmental cities). Further, each of these types of cities has adjusted in its own characteristic way: the non-intergovernmental city by slower service growth; the intergovernmental city by service retrenchment.

The city of the future will always be a public corporation. Yet, it will not be intergovernmental as defined in this study. Its public nature will reflect its own destiny as opposed to significant determination by upper levels of government. The city in 1980 came to a turning point in American history. At that point public policymakers could conceive of certain cities as permanent wards of the state and federal governments. Five years later there is no ward system, and after much pain, there is a basic realization that if cities have to go it alone, they indeed can. Further, in the long run, this might be the better way.

This is a difficult concept for urbanists to swallow, for it has always been easier to placate rather than to discipline. But it has taught us all a very important lesson. Social engineering is a difficult and expensive undertaking. Where it is unavoidable, it must be attempted; where it is avoidable, this too is an equally prudent avenue of social policy.

NOTES

1. For a discussion of the causes of overseas migration of manufacturing industries, see Robert Gilpin, *U.S. Power and the Multinational Corporation*, New York: Basic Books, 1975; Raymond Vernon, *Sovereignty at Bay*, New York: Basic Books, 1972.

2. See Franklin James, "Economic Distress in Central Cities," in Robert Burchell and David Listokin (eds.), *Cities under Stress: The Fiscal Crises of Urban America*, New Brunswick, N.J.: Center for Urban Policy Research, 1981.

3. As a case example, see Bennett Harrison, "Rationalization, Restructuring, and Industrial Reorganization in Older Regions: The Transformation of New England Since World War II," *Working Paper No. 72*. MIT-Harvard Joint Center for Urban Studies, 1982.

4. See Bennett Harrison and Edward Hill, "The Changing Structure of Jobs in Older and Younger Cities," *Working Paper No. 58*. MIT-Harvard Joint Center for Urban Studies, 1979.

5. For the most recent data on regional trends, see George Sternlieb and James Hughes, "The National Economy and the Northeast: A Context for Discussion." Paper presented at *Economic Prospects for the Northeast Conference*, April 1982.

6. See John Rees, "Government Policy and Industrial Location in the United States," in U.S. Congress, Joint Economic Committee, *Special Study on Economic Change*, Volume 7; "State and Local Finance: Adjustments in a Changing Economy," USGPO, 1980; John Mollenkopf, "Paths Toward the Post-Industrial Service City: The Northeast and the Southwest," in Burchell and Listokin (1981), *op. cit.*

7. See Rees (1980), *op. cit.*

8. See Sternlieb and Hughes (1982); also Franklin James (1981).

9. Most of this data was originally collected from Dun and Bradstreet files by David Birch of MIT. See David Birch, *The Job Generation Process*, MIT Program on Neighborhood Change, 1979. Also, Carol L. Jusenius and Larry C. Ledebur, "Documenting the 'Decline' of the North," *Economic Development Research Report*, Department of Commerce, Economic Development Administration, Office of Economic Research, 1978.

10. U.S. Congress, Joint Economic Commitee, *Emergency Interim Survey: Fiscal Condition of 48 Large Cities.* USGPO, 1982, 1983.

11. See Marshall Kaplan, Robyn Phillips, and Franklin James, *The Regional and Urban Impacts of the Administration's Budget and Tax Proposals.* Prepared for U.S. Congress, Joint Economic Committee, USGPO, 1981.

12. See Roy Bahl, "The Next Decade in Local Government Finance: A Period of Adjustment"; and Shawna Grosskopf, "Public Employment's Impact on the Future of Urban Economies"; both in Roy Bahl (ed.), *Urban Government Finance, Sage Urban Affairs Annual Review Volume 20*, Sage Publications: Beverly Hills, California, 1981.

Appendix
Methodology and Data Sources

Introduction

This appendix details the methodological approach and primary/secondary data sources used to develop each of the inclusive chapters of this monograph. It also summarizes the field work that was undertaken in the course of the study and presents the information probes used to obtain the bulk of the primary data. The appendix is divided into three parts: Part I — Methodological and Data Summaries by Chapter; Part II — Field Work by Source of Information; and Part III — Survey Instruments and Coding Guides. The information presented in this appendix follows the below-listed sequence:

Part I—Methodological and Data Summaries

Chapter 1 Literature Search and Conceptual Overview
Chapter 2 Empirical Isolation of the Intergovernmental City
Chapter 3 Economic Hardship in the Intergovernmental City
Chapter 4 Social Hardship in the Intergovernmental and Non-Intergovernmental Cities
Chapter 5 Housing in the Intergovernmental City
Chapter 6 The Rise of Intergovernmentalism
Chapter 7 Revenue and Expenditure Emphases in the Intergovernmental City
Chapter 8 The Dismantling of Intergovernmentalism
Chapter 9 Streamlining and Restructuring the Intergovernmental City
Chapter 10 The Future of the Intergovernmental City

Part II—Fieldwork by Source of Information

1. The Property Maintenance Check
2. The Landlord Interview
3. The Tenant Interview
4. Tax and Title Searches

Part III—Survey Instruments and Coding Guides

1. The Property Maintenance Check and Vacant Lot Survey
2. 1981 Landlord Interview
3. 1981 Tenant Interview and Non-Profit Sponsor Interview
4. 1981 Property Tax Record Search
5. 1981 Title Search

Part I—Methodological and Data Summaries

Literature Search and Conceptual Overview

This portion of the study concentrated on the presentation of the conceptual frame of the intergovernmental city: (1) the role of the city, (2) causes of urban disinvestment by sector of the economy, (3) the demographic impacts of capital flight, and (4) the rise of the public economy. The Chapter seeks to establish theories of urban adjustment as well as to trace the roots and rationales for public (federal and state) intervention into the fiscal affairs of municipal governments. Bibliographic information was obtained from both computerized and manual literature searches and integrated into a chapter-length discussion of the evolvement of this category of publicly influenced cities. Representative resource material included: Banfield, *The Unheavenly City Revisited* (1977); Bluestone and Harrison, The Deindustrialization of America (1982) ; Burchell and Listokin (eds.), *Cities Under Stress* (1981); Solomon (ed.), *The Prospective City* (1980); Levine, *Managing Fiscal Stress*; Birch, *The Job Generation Process*; Drucker, "New Markets and the New Capitalism"; Kemp, *An American Renaissance*; Sternlieb and Hughes (eds.), *Post-Industrial America*; Thurow, *The Zero-Sum Society*; and Reich and Magaziner, *Minding America's Business* (1982). (See bibliography for more extensive references.)

Empirical Isolation of the Intergovernmental City

In this chapter data were obtained from the U.S. Census of Governments' tape (City Government Finances—1979–1980, School District Finances—1979–1980) to profile for cities of 1980 population size 220,000 to 1,000,000, both aggregate per capita general revenues and the proportion of revenues from intergovernmental sources. Cities were limited to this population size category at the lower threshold, to isolate for study approximately sixty-four locations of considerable magnitude and complexity. The upper threshold was employed to eliminate from this total the seven largest cities (New York, Chicago, Los Angeles, Philadelphia, Houston, Detroit, Dallas, etc.) and Washington, D.C. and Honolulu, because of unique servicing patterns and expenditure levels related to their national and international importance, and the pure scale of their public service operations.

The remaining fifty-five cities were grouped by population change categories: declining, stable, and growing. Stable communities (10) were defined as those who lost population but not households; i.e., they experienced population losses at the local rate of household size shrinkage. Declining communities (22) lost both population and households, i.e., 22 experienced a net loss in demand for local housing. Growing communities (23) gained both population and households; i.e., had total population and household gains in excess of the loss attributed to household size shrinkage.

Ten cities were selected from each of the declining and growing population change groupings. The ten "intergovernmental" cities were those that had to raise the largest amounts of revenue per capita to cover public service expenses and relied most heavily on federal and state assistance as a source of this revenue. The ten non-intergovernmental cities raised the smallest amount of revenue per capita and were the least fiscally dependent on other levels of government (see Exhibit A.1).

Once the cities were separated and grouped, data were assembled for each city in the respective sets across a variety of social and economic variables. Weighted means or medians were used to express group averages for intergovernmental/non-intergovernmental city comparisons.

Economic Hardship in the Intergovernmental City

Once city groups were established, this chapter sought to profile the basic economic differences which existed in intergovernmental versus non-intergovernmental cities. To show these differences: (1) primary economic indicators, (2) industrial base characteristics, and (3) private investment criteria were used as basic descriptors of economic performance. Primary economic indicators, culled from numerous studies on urban hardship, were population, employment, unemployment and income patterns. Industrial base characteristics included establishments, employment, sales and receipts and value of production. Private investment criteria included new capital expenditures in manufacturing and new units authorized in housing.

EXHIBIT A.1. — *Example of Data Presentation and Sources for Chapter 2: Intergovernmental and Non-Intergovernmental Cities, The Two City-Set Groupings*

Intergovernmental Cities	*Mean Intergovernmental City Fiscal Indices*	Non-Intergovernmental Cities	*Mean Non-Intergovernmental City Fiscal Indices*
AKRON		ANAHEIM	
BALTIMORE	Per Capita General Revenues*	AUSTIN	Per Capita General Revenues
BUFFALO	$1160	BATON ROUGE	$843
CINCINNATI		COLUMBUS	
CLEVELAND	Per Capita Intergovernmental	NASHVILLE-DAVIDSON	Per Capita Intergovernmental
LOUISVILLE	Transfers	OKLAHOMA CITY	Transfers
MILWAUKEE	$630	SAN JOSE	$340
MINNEAPOLIS		TULSA	
NEWARK	Percent Intergovernmental	VIRGINIA BEACH	Percent Intergovernmental
ROCHESTER	Transfers	WICHITA	Transfers
	55%		39%

*Includes Municipal and School

Source: U.S. Census of Governments, City Government Finances 1979-1980; School District Finances, 1979-1980.

Basic sources of information were the *Census of Population and Housing* (1960–1980), *Statistical Abstract of the United States* (1980), *County and City Data Book* (1977), *Sales and Marketing Management Magazine* (1964, 1968, 1974, 1981), *Census of Manufactures* (1963, 1967, 1972, 1977), *Census of Selected Service Industries* (1963, 1967, 1972, 1977), *Census of Wholesale Trade* (1963, 1967, 1972, 1977), and the *Annual Housing Survey* (1978–1980).

Data were calculated for each city and percent and absolute changes were calculated for population and housing from 1960 to 1980 and for all other economic variables from 1963 to 1977 (see Exhibit A.2).

Social Hardship in the Intergovernmental City

In similar fashion to the previous chapter, this chapter sought to focus on a comparison of the relative plight of intergovernmental cities—this time across social hardship indicators for the two city groupings. Again, variables were selected which have been established through repeated use and analysis as indicative of social dependency. These included measures of: (1) income and poverty, (2) health conditions, (3) incidence of crime, (4) levels of public assistance, and (5) educational skills and performance. As for the previous chapter, data were gathered at several time intervals between 1960 and 1980. Absolute and percentage growth were shown for intervening periods as well as for the aggregate twenty-year period. Weighted means were used to compare city group averages for the two classes of cities.

Basic data resources for this chapter were the *Urban Data Report: Mortality* (1960, 1970, 1977), *Uniform Crime Reports* (1960, 1970, 1977), *Public Assistance Recipients and Cash Payments by State and County* (1964, 1973, 1980), *Directory of Elementary and Secondary School Districts, School Year 1978–1979, Volume 1*, and *National Assessment of Educational Progress—1981 Test Scores* (see Exhibit A.3).

Housing in the Intergovernmental City

This chapter establishes the housing profiles of cities. It discusses the general distribution of the housing stock in intergovernmental and non-intergovernmental cities (single family–multi-family, tenure, age, size, interior–exterior condition) as well as tenant views of quality of structure and neighborhood. The purpose of the chapter is to show similarities and differences in the housing stock as well as the general satisfaction of the cities' residents with their housing and neighborhoods.

Basic data for this chapter emerged from the *Census of Housing* 1960 and 1970, *Census of Population and Housing 1980* and the *Annual Housing Survey 1978–1980* (see Exhibit A.4). In addition, data were garnered from a "1981 Property Maintenance Check" and "1981 Landlord-Tenant Surveys," specifically for the City of Newark.

The Rise of Intergovernmentalism

This chapter describes the rise of intergovernmentalism in the economy of a certain class of cities. It traces the growth of both federal and state assistance to local governments in the form of key economic and social programs. Its substantive thrust parallels that of the previous two chapters in that it shows federal and state contributions to shore up key areas of economic and social need: unemployment, firm failures and shifts, private tax base diminishment, public works deterioration, poverty, crime, ill-health and educational disadvantages.

Data for this chapter included: CBO, *City Need and the Responsiveness of Federal Grants Programs*; EDA, *Annual Reports 1966–1978, 1979, 1980*; HUD, *UDAG Annual Report 1978–1980*; HUD, *Annual CDBG Reports 1–5, 1976–1981*; Treasury, *General Revenue Sharing*

EXHIBIT A.2. — *Example of Data Presentation and Sources for Chapter 3: Manufactures, All Employees, 1963-1977 (Thousands)*

	1963	1967	1972	1977	CHANGE 1963-1967 Absolute	1963-1967 Percent	1967-1972 Absolute	1967-1972 Percent	1972-1977 Absolute	1972-1977 Percent	1963-1977 Absolute	1963-1977 Percent
INTERGOVERNMENTAL												
AKRON	58.7	62.0	50.5	44.4	+ 3.3	+ 5.6	- 11.5	- 18.5	- 6.1	- 12.1	- 14.3	- 24.4
BALTIMORE	103.9	106.7	91.2	72.9	+ 2.8	+ 2.7	- 15.5	- 14.5	-18.3	- 20.1	- 31.0	- 29.8
BUFFALO	57.0	66.7	53.2	46.4	+ 9.7	+ 17.0	- 13.5	- 20.2	- 6.8	- 12.8	- 10.6	- 18.6
CINCINNATI	76.6	84.5	68.2	64.4	+ 7.9	+10.3	- 16.3	- 19.3	- 3.8	- 5.6	- 12.2	- 15.9
CLEVELAND	168.9	171.3	131.0	120.8	+ 2.4	+ 1.4	- 40.3	- 23.5	-10.2	- 7.8	- 48.1	- 28.5
LOUISVILLE	58.0	64.0	60.2	61.0	+ 6.0	+10.3	- 3.8	- 5.9	+ 0.8	+ 1.3	+ 3.0	+ 5.2
MILWAUKEE	119.3	118.6	106.3	91.4	- 0.7	- 0.6	- 12.3	- 10.4	-14.9	- 14.0	- 27.9	- 23.4
MINNEAPOLIS	67.0	69.2	57.9	52.0	+ 2.2	+ 3.3	- 11.3	- 16.3	- 5.9	- 10.2	- 15.0	- 22.4
NEWARK	73.7	68.5	47.3	38.6	- 5.2	- 7.1	- 21.2	- 30.9	- 8.7	- 18.4	- 35.1	- 47.6
ROCHESTER	97.3	114.2	89.9	86.5	+16.9	+17.4	- 24.3	- 21.3	- 3.4	- 3.8	- 10.8	- 11.1
MEDIAN	75.2	76.9	64.2	62.7	+ 1.7	+ 2.3	- 12.7	- 16.5	- 1.5	- 2.3	- 12.5	- 16.7
NON-INTERGOVERNMENTAL												
ANAHEIM	45.8	18.9	30.4	39.5	-26.9	-58.7	+ 11.5	+ 60.8	+ 9.1	+ 29.9	- 6.3	- 13.8
AUSTIN	5.1	5.2	7.7	11.5	+ 0.1	+ 2.0	+ 2.5	+ 48.1	+ 3.8	+ 49.4	+ 6.4	+125.5
BATON ROUGE	6.2	11.0	13.0	11.4	+ 4.8	+77.4	+ 2.0	+ 18.2	- 1.6	- 12.3	+ 5.2	+ 83.9
COLUMBUS	65.9	65.4	62.1	55.5	- 0.5	- 0.8	- 3.3	- 5.0	- 6.6	- 10.6	- 10.4	- 15.3
NASHVILLE/DAVIDSON	34.0	46.8	45.9	48.4	+12.8	+37.6	- 0.9	- 1.9	+ 2.5	+ 5.4	+ 14.4	+ 42.4
OKLAHOMA CITY	24.4	26.3	33.8	35.1	+ 1.9	+ 7.8	+ 7.5	+ 28.5	+ 1.3	+ 3.3	+ 10.7	+ 43.9
SAN JOSE	24.2	31.1	30.6	38.4	+ 6.9	+28.5	- 0.5	- 1.6	+ 7.8	+ 25.5	+ 14.2	+ 58.7
TULSA	18.1	22.2	34.8	43.3	+ 4.1	+22.6	+ 12.6	+ 56.8	+ 8.5	+ 24.4	+ 25.2	+139.2
*VIRGINIA BEACH	0.2	0.5	1.1	NA	+ 0.3	+150.0	+ 0.6	+120.0	NA	NA	NA	NA
*WICHITA	16.2	NA	23.3	28.9	NA	NA	NA	NA	+ 5.6	+ 24.0	+ 12.7	+ 78.4
MEDIAN	24.3	24.3	32.2	39.0	-0-	-0-	+ 7.9	+ 32.5	+ 6.8	+ 21.1	+ 14.7	+ 60.5
U.S. TOTAL (*Mil*)	17.0	19.3	19.0	19.6	+ 2.4	+13.9	- 0.3	- 1.5	+ 0.6	+ 3.0	+ 2.6	+ 15.5

Sources: U.S. Department of Commerce, Bureau of the Census, *Census of Manufactures*, "Geographic Area Series" (For Years Indicated). Changes calculated by the Center for Urban Policy Research.

EXHIBIT A.3. — *Example of Data Presentation and Sources for Chapter 4: Reading and Mathematics Achievement Scores by Type of Urban Development, 1981*

AVERAGE PERCENT OF CORRECT RESPONSES* BY AGE

READING

	Age 17			Age 13			Age 9		
	1971	1975	1980	1970	1974	1979	1971	1975	1980
National Average	68.94	68.98	68.23	60.01	59.91	60.78	63.98	65.25	67.89
Advantaged Urban	75.75	76.01	73.53	67.14	66.67	67.93	71.57	71.29	73.14
Disadvantaged Urban	60.68	59.28	59.24	49.83	48.86	53.40	52.76	55.18	57.96
Disadvantaged as a Percent of Advantaged Scores	.80	.78	.80	.74	.73	.78	.74	.77	.79

MATHEMATICS

	Age 17		Age 13		Age 9	
	1973	1978	1972	1977	1973	1978
National Average	51.68	48.13	52.59	50.55	38.10	36.83
Advantaged Urban	59.52	57.28	63.60	59.37	46.65	45.97
Disadvantaged Urban	40.74	35.06	34.72	36.69	25.28	27.73
Disadvantaged as a Percent of Advantaged Scores	.68	.61	.55	.62	.54	.60

* Children in School.

Source: National Assessment of Educational Progress, 1981 Test Scores, Denver, Colorado.

EXHIBIT A.4. — *Example of Data Presentation and Sources for Chapter 5:*
Total Housing Units by City, 1960 and 1980

	1960	1980	Percent Change 1960-1980
INTERGOVERNMENTAL			
AKRON	94.3	96.7	+ 2.5
BALTIMORE	290.2	302.7	+ 4.3
BUFFALO	177.2	156.5	- 11.7
CINCINNATI	171.7	172.7	+ 0.6
CLEVELAND	282.9	239.6	- 15.3
LOUISVILLE	128.3	126.1	- 1.7
MILWAUKEE	241.6	253.1	+ 4.8
MINNEAPOLIS	173.2	168.7	+ 2.5
NEWARK	134.9	121.1	- 10.2
ROCHESTER	107.2	102.6	- 4.3
MEDIAN	172.5	162.6	- 5.7
NON-INTERGOVERNMENTAL			
ANAHEIM	32.7	83.6	+155.7
AUSTIN	56.5	146.5	+159.3
BATON ROUGE	45.8	84.1	+ 83.6
COLUMBUS	152.0	236.7	+ 55.7
NASHVILLE	53.6	179.1	+234.1
OKLAHOMA CITY	115.1	177.1	+ 53.9
SAN JOSE	68.9	219.0	+217.9
TULSA	115.1	156.4	+ 35.9
VIRGINIA BEACH	NA	92.0	NA
WICHITA	88.5	116.6	+ 31.8
MEDIAN	68.9	177.1	+157.0

Sources: U.S. Department of Commerce, Bureau of the Census, Census of
Population and Housing, 1960 and 1970; U.S. Department of Commerce,
Bureau of the Census, 1980 Census of Population and Housing,
"Final Counts." Changes calculated by the Center for Urban Policy
Research.

Quarterly Payments, 22nd-34th Payments 1978-1981; Treasury, *Antirecession Payment Summaries 1-9, 1975-1978*; ACIR, *Countercyclical Aid and Economic Stabilization 1978*; Rand, *Federal Activities in Urban Economic Development* (1980); HHS, *Urban Impacts of Federal Policies* (1979); ACIR, *Significant Features of Fiscal Federalism* (1972, 1976, 1980); Government Information Services, *Federal Funding Guide* (1982); Levitan, *Programs in Aid of the Poor for the 1980s* (1980); Steiner, *The State of Welfare* (1979); OMB, *Federal Aid to States and Local Governments*; HHS, *Medical Annual Reports* (1970-1980); HHS, *Food Stamps—Annual Reports* (1970-1980); and HHS, *Educational Impact Aid—Report* (1970-1980) (see Exhibit A.5).

EXHIBIT A.5.—*Example of Data Presentation and Sources for Chapter 6: Total Economic Development Administration Projects by City, 1966–1980*

	Total Public Works Projects	Amount ($ Millions)	Total Business Development Projects	Loans ($ Millions)	Guarantees ($ Millions)	Total Technical Assistance & Economic Adj. Projects	Amount ($ Millions)	Total Planning Grants	Amount ($ Millions)	Total Projects	Total Amount ($ Millions)
INTERGOVERNMENTAL											
AKRON	2	2.9	-0-	-0-	-0-	5	0.2	3	0.2	35	35.8
BALTIMORE	8	9.7	3	3.0	3.2	16	19.2	7	0.7	25	10.5
BUFFALO	9	6.2	3	3.4	-0-	9	.5	4	0.4	10	2.4
CINCINNATI	1	1.4	-0-	-0-	-0-	7	0.8	2	0.4		
CLEVELAND	7	4.6	3	2.2	3.6	36	4.3	5	0.3	15	8.7
LOUISVILLE	3	3.4	1	0.4	1.4	6	1.0	3	0.6	20	8.3
MILWAUKEE	4	5.7		-0-	1.0	10	0.6	-0-	-0-		
MINNEAPOLIS	1	0.3		-0-	1.5	3	0.1	2	0.2		
NEWARK	9	15.1	12	18.0	1.5	17	0.8	2	0.1	40	35.6
ROCHESTER	1	3.0	-0-	-0-	-0-	4	0.1	1		6	3.2
· TOTAL	45	52.3	26	27	10.7	113	27.6	32	3.1	151	104.5
· MEAN	4.5	5.2	2.6	2.7	1.1	11.3	2.8	3.2	0.3	15.1	10.5
NON-INTERGOVERNMENTAL											
ANAHEIM	-0-	-0-	-0-	-0-	-0-	-0-	-0-	-0-	-0-	-0-	-0-
AUSTIN	2	1.2	-0-	-0-	-0-	4	0.1	4	1.4	32	4.5
BATON ROUGE	3	1.0	2	-0-	1.4	4	0.2	23	1.9	26	13.0
COLUMBUS	2	5.4	3	5.5	-0-	9	0.9	12	1.2		
NASHVILLE-DAVIDSON	1	0.1	-0-	-0-	-0-	3	0.2	19	1.2		
OKLAHOMA CITY	4	2.0	2	-0-	0.6	17	0.6	14	1.2	37	4.4
SAN JOSE	1	0.4	-0-	-0-	-0-	15	1.4	1	0.1	17	1.9
TULSA	2	2.1	-0-	-0-	-0-	2	1.2	2	0.2		
VIRGINIA BEACH	-0-	-0-	1	0.3	-0-	-0-	-0-	-0-	-0-	-0-	-0-
WICHITA	7	7.7	-0-	-0-	-0-	-0-	-0-	9	0.3		
· TOTAL	22	19.9	8	5.8	2.0	54	4.6	84	7.5	112	23.8
· MEAN[1]	2.2	2.0	0.8	0.6	0.2	5.4	0.5	8.4	0.8	11.2	2.4
· MEAN[2]	2.8	2.5	1.0	0.7	0.3	6.8	0.6	10.5	0.9	14	3.0

Notes: [1]Mean = average of all cities (Total non-intergovernmental city projects ÷ 10).
[2]Mean = average of cities with grants only (Total non-intergovernmental city projects ÷ 8).

Source: U.S. Department of Commerce, Economic Development Administration, *EDA Directory of Approved Projects as of March 31, 1978.* U.S. Department of Commerce, Economic Development Administration, *EDA Directory of Approved Projects: April 1–September 30, 1978.* U.S. Department of Commerce, Economic Development Administration, *Annual Reports* (1979–1980).

Revenue and Expenditure Emphases
in the Intergovernmental City

This chapter draws primarily on the *Census of Governments*—"City Finances" and "Finances of School Districts"—for the budget years 1968, 1972, 1976, 1980. Its purpose is to show the differing levels of expenditure and expenditure allocation among the various categories of public service and to isolate revenue flows from sources of intergovernmental transfer as well as from the revenue-raising mechanisms which exist locally.

Data were presented for expenditures in the aggregate as well as by common municipal function: general government, public safety, public works, health and welfare, and recreation and culture. For comparability, expenditures on public education in dependent school systems were removed from the municipal budget and treated as independent school district expenditures (see Chapter 6 for more details). Revenues were presented in the aggregate as well as by major component and sub-component. For instance, for municipal revenues, recurring general revenues were divided into:

A. Intergovernmental
    1. State
    2. Federal

B. Own-Source
    1. Taxes
    2. Charges and miscellaneous revenues

In addition to information on expenditure and revenue orientations, data on tax base growth and municipal bond ratings over time were discussed for the two city sets. The bulk of information on bond rating and tax base variation was obtained from Moody's *Municipal and Governmental Manual* (1960, 1970, 1980) (see Exhibit A.6). Data were presented in the form of general obligation bond ratings and their directions of change and real property equalized valuations per capita and their rates of growth. Data on tax base change for the City of Newark and changes in the tax status within the sample of real properties were obtained from title and tax searches of the Newark sample properties.

Finally, data on major capital facilities were analyzed for both intergovernmental and non-intergovernmental cities. The bulk of the information presented here came from (1) DOT–Federal Highway Administration, *Urban Mileage and Travel by Pavement Condition and Pavement Type* (1976); (2) DOT, *National Bridge Inventory Survey* (1978); and (3) EPA, *Sewer Investment Needs by SMSA* (1976).

The Dismantling of Intergovernmentalism

This chapter focuses on the changes taking place in intergovernmental fiscal relations as a result of budget emphases and cutbacks at the national level. The same programs that have established the city as intergovernmentally funded are viewed for their future impact in light of projected federal cutbacks. In addition, state assistance, particularly in the form of educational funding, is also scrutinized for its long-term continuity.

The purpose of this chapter is to discuss the sweeping changes in fiscal assistance taking place at national and state levels as a prelude to the next chapter on restructuring the intergovernmental city. Major sources of data included: CBO, *Analysis of FY 1983 Reagan Budget*; CBO, *Baseline Budget Projections for FY 1983* (unpublished); Conference of Mayors, *Analysis of FY 83 Budget and Its Effects on Cities of Reagan Budget Cuts*; OMB, *Federal Aid to State and Local Governments* (Budget of the United States Government, 1983); OMB, *The United States Budget FY 1980–1983*; Princeton University, "Background Material on Fiscal Year 1982 Federal Budget Reductions" (1982); and U.S. Congress, "Omnibus Budget Reconciliation Act of 1981" (see Exhibit A.7).

EXHIBIT A.6.—*Example of Data Presentation and Sources for Chapter 7:*
Moody's Municipal Bond Ratings, General Obligation Bonds, 1960–1980

	1960	1970	1980	Rating Change: 1970-80
INTERGOVERNMENTAL				
AKRON	A	A	Aa	Upgraded
BALTIMORE	Aa	A	A1	Slightly Upgraded
BUFFALO	Aaa	Aa	Baa	Downgraded
CINCINNATI	Aaa	Aa	Aa	Unchanged
CLEVELAND	Aa	A	Caa	Downgraded
LOUISVILLE	Aa	Aa	Aa	Unchanged
MILWAUKEE	Aaa	Aaa	Aaa	Unchanged
MINNEAPOLIS	A	Aaa	Aaa	Unchanged
NEWARK	A	Baa	Baa	Unchanged
ROCHESTER	Aaa	Aaa	Aa	Downgraded

MEDIAN RATING: Aa - Unchanged

	1960	1970	1980	Rating Change: 1970-80
NON-INTERGOVERNMENTAL				
ANAHEIM	A	Baa	A1	Upgraded
AUSTIN	A	Aa	Aaa	Upgraded
BATON ROUGE	Baa	Baa	Baa1	Slightly Upgraded
COLUMBUS	Aa	Aa	Aa	Unchanged
NASHVILLE-DAVIDSON	Aa	Aa	Aaa	Upgraded
OKLAHOMA CITY	A	A	Aa	Upgraded
SAN JOSE	Aa	A1	Aa	Upgraded
TULSA	A	A	Aa	Upgraded
VIRGINIA BEACH	Baa	A	Aa	Upgraded
WICHITA	A	A1	Aa	Upgraded

MEDIAN RATING: Aa - Upgraded

Source: Moody's Municipal and Governmental Manual, Moody's Investor
Service: 1960, 1970, 1980.

Streamlining and Restructuring
the Intergovernmental City

This chapter summarizes the various efforts and progress to date of large urban areas that have been on the edge of fiscal bankruptcy. It begins with a discussion of the bankruptcy phenomenon in urban areas and tabulates the intergovernmental cities which are approaching this condition. In addition, it looks at the non-intergovernmental city set for reasons, other than improved socioeconomic environments, as to why this fiscal situation has been avoided. Further, urban finance and housing experts are polled for their views on the future of the intergovernmental city.

Data for this chapter comprised summaries of the fiscal restructuring which have taken place in New York City, Cleveland, Detroit, Buffalo, Newark, etc. They include Academy for Contemporary Problems, *Managing Fiscal Retrenchment in Cities*; GAO, *New York City's Fiscal Problems: A Long Road Still Lies Ahead* (1979); Peterson and Wolman, "Policy Consequences of Local Expenditure Constraint" (1981); and Kerlin and Chapman, "Active Approaches to Local Government Revenue Generation" (1980) (see Exhibit A.8).

EXHIBIT A.7.—*Example of Data Presentation and Sources for Chapter 8: Per Capita Expenditure Contrasts, 1962-1978 (Dollars)*

	Intergovernmental Cities			Non-Intergovernmental Cities		
	1962	1972	1978	1962	1972	1978
Total General Expenditures	$240.10	$623.33	$1,098.10	$167.55	$328.82	$606.26
Education	79.62	269.62	404.31	71.61	116.30	227.43
Welfare	21.52	57.80	30.34	1.98	0.40	0.92
Public Safety	34.78	81.79	145.87	23.27	45.25	90.13
Health	15.20	42.07	54.16	3.22	3.23	9.67
Housing	11.54	35.42	34.20	7.14	3.45	20.05
Public Works	31.91	63.31	100.89	33.36	46.64	95.27

Note : Expenditure items will not add to totals as not all expenditures are included.

Source : U.S. Department of Commerce, Bureau of Census, Census of Governments, Vol. 4, No. 1, "Finances of School Districts," and Vol. 4, No. 4., "Finances of Municipalities and Township Governments" (For years indicated).

Part II—Fieldwork by Source of Information

The Property Maintenance Check

Throughout the study, Newark, New Jersey is documented as an advanced case of the intergovernmental city. For the third time in sixteen years a group of 569 buildings were visited to secure information about their status and operations (see Property Maintenance Check in the next section).

In the original sample, buildings were picked according to condition, tenure status, and location within the city. Census tracts were chosen which had respectively 25 percent, 50 percent and 66.7 percent sound housing according to the 1960 Census definitions of sound, deteriorating, and dilapidated housing.* Within these groupings, Census blocks were picked which had at least twenty rental units per block. A random number table was used to select approximately ten to fifty blocks per set. Interviewers then went to each block; isolated structures of three or more rental units and a random number table were again employed to limit this selection to no more than five structures per block. The resulting sample was composed of 569 structures divided approximately equally between locations representing the three condition categories. In both subsequent resamples, the remaining structures of those originally selected were revisited. In 1972, slightly less than 400 structures remained standing; in 1981, the figure was just over 230.

In each of the two previous periods, a limited amount of data was obtained on structure configuration and condition. This consisted primarily of structure status, structure and unit

*A controversial classification found to be reasonably sound within a city but an unacceptable standard across cities.

EXHIBIT A.8.—*Example of Data Presentation and Sources for Chapter 9:*
Broad-Based Aid Enacted in 1981 or Proposed for 1983
(Outlays in Millions of Dollars)

	1982	1983	1984	1985
Enacted in 1981:				
State community development block grant for small cities[1]	(10)	(200)	(500)	(650)
State education block grant	666	578	441	335
Community services	348	100	100	100
Social services	2,400	1,974	1,974	1,974
Preventive health and health services	72	80	81	81
Alcohol, drug abuse, and mental health	376	409	432	432
SUBTOTAL	3,862	3,141	3,028	2,922
Block grants enacted in 1981 and proposed for change in 1983:				
Services for women, infants, and children[2]	313	900	1,000	1,000
Primary health care	–	313	417	417
Energy and emergency assistance[3]	1,574	1,168	1,168	1,168
SUBTOTAL	1,887	2,381	2,585	2,585
Proposed consolidations:				
Vocational and adult education	–	162	392	441
Education for the handicapped	–	37	643	836
Training and employment	–	900	2,250	1,800
Rehabilitation services	–	516	603	633
Child welfare grant	–	380	380	380
Rental rehabilitation grants	–	–	75	150
Combined welfare administration	–	2,181	2,181	2,181
SUBTOTAL	–	4,176	6,524	6,421
TOTAL	5,749	9,698	12,137	11,928

Notes : [1]Outlays are based on estimated state participation.
[2]Formerly maternal and child health block grant.
[3]Formerly low-income energy assistance program.

Source: Executive Office of the President, Office of Management and Budget: The Budget of the United States Government, 1983 (February 1982).

size, exterior construction, and two estimates of the quality of the structure and its surrounding environment. In the most recent survey, over eighty variables were used to summarize both exterior and interior structure condition. These included type of structure; condition of exterior roof, siding, foundation and attached porches; site cleanliness; presence and condition of major systems, etc.; frequency of repairs, and site visits by landlords. For unoccupied buildings a shorter version of the property maintenance check was used. For demolished buildings, a vacant lot survey provided information on the status and cleanliness of the improved or unimproved lot (see Vacant Lot Survey in the next section).

Interviewers in groups were taken to sample properties to test the maintenance check and to provide standardization within the group in terms of evaluation of property condition. Each standing structure in the sample was given a complete interior and exterior check and, for occupied structures, questions dealing with system performance/failure were asked of multiple tenants per building.

The information from this survey is found in the chapter on "Housing in the Intergovernmental City." It parallels *Annual Housing Survey* categories and is more detailed than the 1980 *Census of Population and Housing*.

The Landlord Interview

The landlord survey is a retrospective analysis that has obtained similar information from and about landlords for the third time in seventeen years. The survey instrument sought information about their demographic characteristics, experience and management practices in real estate, and view of future real estate operations. Approximately sixty out of 100 questions dealt with the above areas and in most cases were comparable to the information obtained in either 1964, 1972, or both years. About twenty-five comparable questions were asked about housing programs of the early 1960s which are no longer applicable today (see Landlord Interview in the next section).

The remaining forty questions were additions in the 1981 survey and dealt with landlords' views on (1) the effects on the local housing market of illegal aliens and gentrification on the one hand, and rent control and energy costs on the other; (2) the future of cities like Newark, and within it the role of local government; and (3) aspects of current and future housing operations in a declining city.

Resident landlords were surveyed via personal interview during the day and evening of the workweek or on the weekend. In-city and out-of-city in-metropolitan area (New Jersey, New York, Connecticut) non-resident landlords were contacted in the same manner as resident landlords; out-of-city out-of-metropolitan area landlords were contacted by telephone.

The tabulation below indicates the landlord interview completion rate:

Landlord Interview Completions

	Attempts	Refusals	No Contacts	Completions
Overall (1981)	244	18	42	184

	1964	1972	1981
By Year (1964–1981)	68.9% (392/569)	68.8% (216/314)	76.7% (184/244)

Refusals were called by telephone to confirm their non-participation. "No contacts" received three interview attempts at place of residence or business before being categorized as permanently unavailable. For non-English speaking Spanish and Portuguese households, the interview was conducted in the native tongue. As is indicated by the lower half of the above tabulations, the 1981 survey had the highest rates of completion of all prior landlord surveys. Landlord surveys by a geographic area of the city had approximately the same levels of completion.

For properties that were razed and became part of a subsequent private non-profit or limited profit housing venture, the director of the housing-sponsoring agency was interviewed. Five housing sponsors were interviewed that currently control twenty-two land parcels of the original survey. (See Nonprofit Interview in the next section.)

The Tenant Interview

For the first time in the history of the *Tenant Landlord* series, personal interviews were undertaken with the tenants of the buildings owned by the landlords in the sample. This was deemed necessary to obtain resident reaction to building conditions, landlords' management practices, and overall quality of the building, neighborhood, and city. In the tenant interviews, questions were asked about the age, configuration, rent, condition and presence or status of interior systems in the housing unit. In addition, information was sought on: tenant demographic characteristics, satisfaction with structure and neighborhood, future residency plans, and views of the effectiveness of public housing and economic development activities undertaken by the federal, state, and local governments (see Tenant Interview in the next section.)

Tenant Interview Completions

	Attempts	*Refusals*	*No Contacts*	*Completions*
Overall (1981)	536	90	43	403

An attempt was made to obtain complete coverage of all occupied buildings (181) as well as a 50 percent sample of all households within each building. For the most part, this was accomplished: only four buildings had no tenant interviews; approximately ten buildings had less than 50 percent sample representation. The overall completion rate was approximately 75 percent: 403 completions of 536 attempts. Refusals constituted 16 percent of the attempts; "no contacts" (after three callbacks) were about one-half (9 percent) the refusal rate. Interviews were conducted both during the day and evening of the workweek and on weekends, to assure the working population was not undersampled.

Tax and Title Searches

Tax and title searches were undertaken for each of the original 569 properties in the Newark sample. These were completed to obtain current tax status and ownership information for each property as well as to generate accurate lists of where property owners could be contacted. (See Tax and Title Search in the next section.)

Tax searches were completed in the City of Newark's Office of Tax Collection. Tax information on a particular property was obtained from historic collection data maintained on microfiche and accessed by block and lot. Status was determined as of February 1, 1981. Information obtained for each parcel included: (1) current real estate tax by half years; (2) real estate tax aggregate in total number of periods (half years) and dollars; (3) number and dollar amount of tax liens; (4) number and dollar amount of foreclosures; and (5) owner type, property class, and status.

Title searches were completed in the Essex County, New Jersey Hall of Records, using the *County Real Estate Directory* and judgment files. Title searches were run from the initial time of survey (1964) to the most recent survey period (1981).

Information sought via title search included (1) type of owner, (2) date of title, (3) mortgage source and amount (if any), (4) bona fide sales or transfers, and (5) transfer scenarios and patterns. Tax and title information for the City of Newark were used primarily in the chapter on "Housing in the Intergovernmental City" in the section dealing with the case example, Newark, over time. Both tax and title information were stored on computer tape and merged with other landlord, tenant and maintenance data compiled for each property.

Part III—Survey Instruments and Coding Guides

**The Property Maintenance Check and
Vacant Lot Survey**

1–3 I.D. Number

4–7. Skip

I. Exterior Maintenance Evaluation

8. Status of Structure
    (1) Occupied
    (2) Partially occupied (capable of being occupied)
    (3) Vacant (capable of being occupied)
    (4) Partially abandoned
    (5) Abandoned
    (6) Converted use
    (7) Owner-occupied, no tenants
    (8) Mixed-use commercial/residential
    (9) NA/DK

9. Quality of external appearance
    (1) Poorer than neighbors
    (2) Same as neighbors
    (3) Better than neighbors
    (9) NA/DK

10. Quality of street versus block
    (1) Same as
    (2) Better than
    (3) Poorer than
    (9) NA/DK

11. Type of structure
    (1) Single-family residential
    (2) Multi-family apartment
    (3) Rooming house
    (4) Commercial
    (5) Mixed residential and nonresidential
    (9) NA/DK

12. Exterior Wall Surface
    (1) Needs replacement; badly weathered, worn and unprotected surfaces, various missing sections, excessive cracks or holes
    (2) Moderate loose material or missing surface parts; several areas needing repair
    (3) Some loose surface material or parts/minor cracks; otherwise adequate weather protection
    (4) Surface material tight and intact—few or no cracks
    (9) NA/DK

13. Roof Structure
    (1) Sagging, buckling roof
    (2) Apparently firm structure
    (3) Not observable
    (4) No roof
    (9) NA/DK

14. Roof Surface
    (1) Needs replacement—missing sections (visible holes)
    (2) Missing some shingles, makeshift repairs—evidence of leaks
    (3) Intact; but worn
    (4) Like-new roof
    (5) Not observable
    (6) No roof
    (9) NA/DK

15. Condition of gutters and downspouts
    (1) Severely deteriorated
    (2) Moderate deterioration
    (3) Good condition
    (4) No gutters/downspouts
    (5) Not observable
    (9) NA/DK

16. Exterior stairs/rails (stairs and balconies; not masonry stoop)
    (1) Unsafe
    (2) Safe
    (3) None
    (9) NA/DK

17. Garage and/or parking facilities
    (1) No off-street parking
    (2) Uncovered off-street parking
    (3) Covered off-street parking
    (4) Garage—detached or attached and used for automobile storage
    (5) Garage—detached or attached and not used for automobile storage
    (9) NA/DK

18. Site Cleanliness
    (1) Not applicable
    (2) Major accumulations of litter/trash
    (3) Moderate accumulations of litter/trash
    (4) Minor accumulations of litter/trash
    (5) Very clean
    (9) NA/DK

19. Overall Condition of Dwelling
    (1) *Immediately hazardous*—requires major structural renovation
    (2) *Potentially hazardous*—requires minor structural or surface renovations or repairs
    (3) *Sound*—but requires some structural or surface repairs
    (9) NA/DK

20. Size of Structure—Number of Apartments
    (1) 1 unit
    (2) 2–3 units
    (3) 4–6 units
    (4) 7–12 units
    (5) 13–24 units
    (6) 25+ units
    (9) NA/DK

21. Number of Stories
    (1) 1–3
    (2) 4–6
    (3) 7–12
    (4) 13+
    (9) NA/DK

22. Does the building have a passenger elevator?
    (1) Yes
    (2) No
    (9) NA/DK

23. Primary Exterior Surface Material
    (1) Wood, shake, shingle or clapboard
    (2) Stone or brick
    (3) Aluminium or vinyl siding
    (4) Asbestos or asphalt siding
    (5) Concrete or stucco
    (9) NA/DK

24. Foundation Condition
    (1) Unsound, immediately hazardous
    (2) Potentially unsound
    (3) Apparently sound
    (4) Condition not observable
    (9) NA/DK

25. Exterior Wall Structure
    (1) Needs immediate replacement; severe leaning, buckling or sagging, apparent damage, loose structural members, holes or missing sections—*Hazardous to occupant*
    (2) Visible leaning, buckling or sagging of walls; columns or vertical support members needing repair—*Potentially hazardous*
    (3) Minor unevenness of wall surface, otherwise tight and secure; shows deferred maintenance
    (4) Apparently plumb, firm, solid structure
    (5) *Overall good condition*—requires only minor surface refinishing
    (6) *New, like new* or *superior* condition
    (9) NA/DK

26. Street Condition (Maintenance)
    (1) Unpaved street or paved street with severe chuckholes indicating needed repair
    (2) Paved street—minor chuckholes, cracks or surface deterioration indicating needed maintenance
    (3) Well-paved, well-maintained street
    (9) NA/DK

27. Pedestrian Walkway/Stoop Condition
    (1) Walkway appropriate but not present
    (2) Pedestrian walkways deteriorated severely
    (3) Pedestrian walkways moderately deteriorated; little maintenance evident
    (4) Pedestrian walkways show moderate maintenance
    (5) Pedestrian walkways show excellent maintenance
    (6) None present and inappropriate
    (9) NA/DK

_____ /	_____ /	_____ /	_____ /	_____ /	_____
28	29	30	31	32	33
Vacant Habitable	Ongoing Demolition	Abandoned Open	Abandoned Boarded Up	Vacant Lots	

_____ /	_____ /	_____ /	_____ /	_____ /	_____
34	35	36	37	38	39
Total # of Structures		Junkyard/ Dump/Truck Depot/Air- port	Industrial	RR Stop/ Bus Ter- minal	Commercial

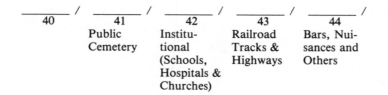

	/		/		/		/		/
40		41		42		43		44	

40	41	42	43	44
	Public Cemetery	Institutional (Schools, Hospitals & Churches)	Railroad Tracks & Highways	Bars, Nuisances and Others

II. Interior Maintenance Evaluation

45. Portion of building vacant
    (1) 1 unit
    (2) 2 units
    (3) 3 units
    (4) 4 units or more
    (5) Single commercial space
    (6) Multiple commercial spaces
    (7) All
    (8) None
    (9) NA/DK

46. Portion of the building abandoned (uninhabitable)
    (1) 1 unit
    (2) 2 units
    (3) 3 units
    (4) 4 units or more
    (5) Single commercial space
    (6) Multiple commercial spaces
    (7) All
    (8) None
    (9) NA/DK

Public Hall Check

	(1) Yes	(2) No		(9) NA/DK
47.	____	____ absence of or missing light		_____
48.	____	____ broken stairs		_____
49.	____	____ stair railings loose		_____

50. Can unauthorized entry be gained to vacant units from public hall?
    (1) Yes
    (2) No
    (9) NA/DK

51. Quality of overall structure
    (1) Uninhabitable
    (2) Barely habitable
    (3) Low quality but adequate
    (4) Moderate quality
    (5) High quality
    (6) Superior quality/luxury
    (9) NA/DK

III. Questions to Tenant

52. Does the owner or manager live on the property?
    (1) Yes, owner
    (2) Yes, manager
    (3) Yes, both live on property
    (4) No, neither lives on property
    (9) NA/DK

53. Does the landlord or his representative visit the building other than to collect rent?
    (1) Yes
    (2) No
    (9) NA/DK

54. If yes—for what purpose?
    (1) Makes repairs
    (2) Inspects building
    (9) NA/DK

55. Has the owner made repairs on building this year?
    (1) Yes
    (2) No
    (9) NA/DK

56. Skip

57. If yes, what type?
    (1) Plumbing
    (2) Electrical
    (3) External-Structural
    (4) Internal-Structural
    (5) Heating system
    (6) Paint
    (7) General maintenance

58. Skip

59. During this winter was there a breakdown in the heating system that lasted 6 hours or more?
    (1) Yes
    (2) No
    (9) NA/DK

60. How many times?
    (1) Once
    (2) Twice
    (3) Three times
    (4) Four to five times
    (5) More than five times
    (9) NA/DK

61. Has water been shut off for more than 6 hours in past three months?
    (1) Yes
    (2) No
    (9) NA/DK

62. How many times?
    (1) Once
    (2) Twice
    (3) Three times
    (4) Four to five times
    (5) More than five times
    (9) NA/DK

63. Is the building serviced by an exterminator regularly, only when needed, or not at all?
    (1) Regularly
    (2) Only when needed
    (3) Irregularly
    (4) Not at all
    (9) NA/DK

64. Do you pay for electricity separately?
    (1) Yes
    (2) No
    (9) NA/DK

65. What type of heating system is employed in your building?
    (1) Oil
    (2) Electric
    (3) Natural gas
    (4) Other _____
    (5) No heat
    (9) NA/DK

66. Do you pay for heating or cooking gas separately?
    (1) Yes
    (2) No
    (9) NA/DK

67. Do you have a thermostat?
    (1) Yes
    (2) No
    (9) NA/DK

68. If yes, can you control it?
    (1) Yes
    (2) No
    (9) NA/DK

69. Have you had enough heat this winter?
    (1) Yes
    (2) No
    (9) NA/DK

70. How often does your landlord or his representative visit the building?
    (1) Daily
    (2) Weekly
    (3) Monthly
    (4) Bimonthly
    (5) Semiannually
    (6) Annually
    (7) Never
    (8) Resident landlord manages
    (9) NA/DK
    (0) Irregularly

71-78. Skip

79 = 4

80 = *1*

Vacant Lot Survey (Formerly Occupied by Buildings) †

1-3 I.D. Number   _____

4. Condition of lot:
    (1) Unimproved—clean   _____
    (2) Unimproved—rubble-strewn   _____
    (3) Unimproved—abandoned cars and/or appliances   _____
    (4) Improved—paved for parking   _____
    (5) Improved—park or tot lot   _____

5. Condition of pavement:
    (1) Well-kept   _____
    (2) In need of repair   _____
    (3) Badly damaged or nonexistent   _____

7-20. Address of property   _____

21-69. Skip

70-79. Vacant — Lot (Spelled out)   _____

80. Card 9   _____

1981 Landlord Interview

Variable   Question
Number   Number
I.D. Number

*5   1. When did you or your immediate family first become an owner of rental
               real estate?
               (1) Pre-1930
               (2) 1931-1950
               (3) 1951-1960
               (4) 1961-1970
               (5) 1971-1975
               (6) 1976-1981
               (7)
               (8) DK
               (9) NA

*6   1a. When did you or your family first become the owner of the rental prop-
               erty at: _____
               (1) Pre-1930
               (2) 1931-1950
               (3) 1951-1960
               (4) 1961-1970
               (5) 1971-1975
               (6) 1976-1981
               (7)
               (8) DK
               (9) NA

      NOTE: The following questions specifically refer to the rental property at the above-
           cited address.

---

†Questions used for landlords with totally vacant or abandoned buildings or cleared vacant lots.
*Question numbers used for reference on computer.

Variable *Number*	*Question* *Number*

*7

2. How did you acquire the property?
  (1) Purchase
  (2) Inheritance
  (3) Debt repayment
  (4) Mortgage foreclosure
  (5) Tax foreclosure
  (6) Other_____
  (7)
  (8) DK
  (9) NA

*8

2a. If you purchased the property, what was your reason?
  (1) Home
  (2) Residential rental return
  (3) Speculation
  (4) Commercial rental return
  (5) Both (2) and (4)
  (6) Both (1) and (2)
  (7)
  (8) DK
  (9) NA

*9

3. Why do you retain the property?
  (1) Home
  (2) Residential rental return (and/or capital appreciation)
  (3) Speculation
  (4) Commercial rental return
  (5) Both (2) and (4)
  (6) Both (1) and (2)
  (7) Want to sell—not listed w/broker
  (8) Want to sell—listed w/broker
  (9) Want to sell—financing or buyers unavailable.

Blank—if no answer

10.

3a. What is the financial status of your property at
  _____

  (1) Profitable (positive cash flow)
  (2) Break even
  (3) Losing proposition (negative cash flow)
  (4) Other
  (5)
  (6)
  (7)
  (8) DK
  (9) NA

11

4. How is the building managed?
  (1) Non-resident manager
  (2) Resident manager/superintendent
  (3) No formal designated management system
  (4) Tenant part-time
  (5) Other—describe _____
  (8) DK
  (9) NA

Variable *Number*	*Question* *Number*

12   4a. Who manages the building?
        (1) Owner manages
        (2) Someone in family of owner manages
        (3) Employee or agent of owner manages
        (4) No one really manages
        (5) Other _____
        (8) DK
        (9) NA

13   4b. How are rents collected?
        (1) Non-resident manager collects
        (2) Resident manager/superintendent collects
        (3) Professional rent collector collects
        (4) Owner collects
        (5) Employee or rental agent collects
        (6) Rents mailed to owner or manager
        (7) No rent collected
        (8) DK
        (9) NA

14   5. How often are rents collected?
        (1) Weekly
        (2) Monthly
        (3) Irregularly
        (4) Not collected
        (5) Other_____
        (8) DK
        (9) NA

15   6. Are the bulk of the units furnished or unfurnished?
        (1) Furnished
        (2) Unfurnished
        (3) Some partially furnished, others not
        (4) All have minimal furniture
        (8) DK
        (9) NA

16   7. How many properties do you own?
        (1) No other
        (2) One or two additional parcels
        (3) Three-to-six additional
        (4) Seven-to-twelve additional
        (5) Thirteen to seventy-five additional
        (6) Seventy-six or more
        (7) Used to own others but not currently
        (8) DK
        (9) NA

17   8. Where are your properties?
        (1) No other
        (2) Newark solely
        (3) Newark plus other major, older New Jersey cities
        (4) Adjacent Newark suburbs
        (5) Other New Jersey suburbs
        (6) Out of state—New York Metropolitan Area

Variable Number	*Question Number*

        (7) Out of state—Elsewhere in the United States
        (8) DK
        (9) NA

18

9. Relative to this property what is the condition of the other properties that you own in Newark, other older New Jersey cities or Newark-proximate suburbs?
    (1) No other
    (2) All about the same
    (3) Most worse
    (4) Some better, some worse
    (5) Most better
    (6) Most are either heavily vacant or abandoned
    (7) Other _____
    (8) DK
    (9) NA

19

10. Do you make your living from real estate?
    (1) Full-time real estate involvement (three-fourths or more income from)
    (2) Substantial real estate involvement (one-third to three-fourths income from)
    (3) Minor real estate involvement (negligible supplement to income)
    (4) Holdings provide no supplement to income
    (8) DK
    (9) NA

20

11. How many apartments exist in this building?
    (1) One
    (2) Two
    (3) Three to six
    (4) Seven to twelve
    (5) Thirteen to twenty-four
    (6) Twenty-five to forty-nine
    (7) Fifty or more
    (8) Rooming house, _____rooms
    (9) NA/DK

21

12. What is the racial make-up of the tenantry?
    (1) mainly black
    (2) mainly Hispanic
    (3) mainly white
    (4) mixed black/white
    (5) mixed black/Hispanic
    (6) mixed white/Hispanic
    (7) mixed white/Hispanic/black
    (8) DK
    (9) NA

22

12a. What proportion of the households are Spanish-speaking?
    (1) 1–10%
    (2) 11–25%
    (3) 26–50%
    (4) 51–75%
    (5) 76–99%
    (6) All

Variable Number	*Question Number*

(7) None
(8) DK
(9) NA

23

13. What proportion of the households are on public assistance? (provide best estimate)
    (1) 1–10%
    (2) 11–25%
    (3) 26–50%
    (4) 51–75%
    (5) 76–99%
    (6) All
    (7) None
    (8) DK
    (9) NA

24

14. How do you think welfare tenants affect a property?
    A. Care and maintenance
        (1) Very positive effect
        (2) Moderately positive effect
        (3) Slightly positive effect
        (4) No effect
        (5) Slightly negative effect
        (6) Moderately negative effect
        (7) Very negative effect
        (8) DK
        (9) NA

25

    B. Rent Level
        (1) Lower it very much
        (2) Lower it moderately
        (3) Lower it slightly
        (4) No effect
        (5) Raise it slightly
        (6) Raise it moderately
        (7) Raise it considerably
        (8) DK
        (9) NA

*26

15. Has the vacancy rate changed in the general area?
    (1) Yes—increased considerably
    (2) Yes—increased slightly
    (3) Yes—decreased
    (4) No
    (8) DK
    (9) NA

*27

16. Has vacancy rate changed in your property?
    (1) Yes—increased considerably
    (2) Yes—increased slightly
    (3) Yes—decreased
    (4) No
    (8) DK
    (9) NA

28

17. Do you perform the maintenance repairs yourself?
    (1) Practically all repairs self-done
    (2) Approximately 50% self-done

Variable Number	Question Number

Variable Number | *Question Number*

(3) Less than one-third done by self
(4) Almost none done by self
(8) DK
(9) NA

*29   18. How much of your time does operating rental properties take?
(1) Full-time or nearly full-time
(2) Approximately one-half time
(3) One-fourth time (one day a week with or without evenings)
(4) One-eighth time (one-half day a week with or without evenings)
(5) Less—only a few hours a week
(6) Negligible amount
(7) Other
(8) DK
(9) NA

19. Rate each of the below-listed items as to its effect on maintaining the building. (1 = least effect; 5 = most effect)

30   19a. (1–5) Tenant's ability to afford repair-related rent increases
31   19b. (1–5) Tenant vandalism
32   19c. (1–5) Nonresident vandalism
33   19d. (1–5) Mortgage costs
34   19e. (1–5) Effects of surrounding neighborhood
35   19f. (1–5) Property tax costs
36   19g. (1–5) Permit or code improvement
37   19h. (1–5) Material costs
38   19i. (1–5) Labor costs
39   19j. (1–5) Insurance costs
40   19k.   (9) No answer

41   20. Have you thought about selling the property since you owned it?
(1) Yes, regularly
(2) Yes, occasionally
(3) No
(8) DK
(9) NA

42   21. How would the next potential owner finance the building?
(1) Loan from a commercial bank
(2) Loan from a savings and loan or mutual savings bank
(3) Loan through VA/FHA
(4) Loan through a mortgage company
(5) Previous owner would have to take back mortgage
(6) Buyer would have to pay cash
(8) DK
(9) NA

*43   22. If you were to buy another property outside the city, do you think you could get mortgage from a lending institution?
(1) Yes, private mortgage easy to get
(2) Yes, private mortgage; buy with difficulty
(3) Yes, insured mortgage from traditional lender
(4) Yes, insured mortgage from mortgage company
(5) No, owner would have to take back a mortgage
(6) No, I would have to use mostly cash

Variable Number	Question Number

Variable Number

Question Number

(7) No, there is no way I could move from here and buy elsewhere
(8) DK
(9) NA

44

23. Do you feel your building is in good operating condition?
(1) Yes, very good
(2) Yes, moderately good
(3) Yes, barely acceptable
(4) No, poor condition
(5) No, very poor condition
(6) No, building is unlivable
(8) DK
(9) NA

45

24. What do you think it would cost to put the building in good condition?
(1) Less than $500
(2) $501 to $2,000
(3) $2,001 to $5,000
(4) $5,001 to $10,000
(5) $10,001 to $20,000
(6) Over $20,000
(7) Building is beyond any sensible investment
(8) No expenditures are necessary
(9) NA

46

25. How much of a rent increase would be necessary to accomplish repairs necessary to put the building in good condition?
(1) Satisfied with present level
(2) Up to $10 per tenant per month
(3) $11–$20 per tenant per month
(4) $21–$30 per tenant per month
(5) $31–$50 per tenant per month
(6) $51–$75 per tenant per month
(7) $76–$100 per tenant per month
(8) Over $100 per tenant per month
(9) NA

47

26. Do you feel that you could get this rent increase and keep the building fully occupied?
(1) Yes, easily
(2) Yes, grudgingly
(3) Could go either way
(4) Not likely
(5) Definitely not
(8) DK
(9) NA

48

27. What is your current average monthly rent?
(1) Under $90
(2) $91–$125
(3) $126–$175
(4) $176–$225
(5) $226–$300
(6) $301–$400
(7) $401–$500
(8) Over $500
(9) NA

Variable Number	Question Number

49

28a. What types of repairs would you make if you felt that you could pass the costs along in the form of rent?
(1) More efficient or better heating system
(2) Insulation of walls or attic
(3) Combination storms and screens
(4) Exterior siding, gutters/leaders, roof
(5) Foundation, stoop or sidewalk repairs
(6) Interior wiring or plumbing
(7) Interior appliances or lighting
(8) Interior plastering, painting, hall, door, floor repairs, stairs
(9) NA

Indicate any additional:

(50) _____
(51) _____
(52) _____

53

29. Is the property resale market sufficiently strong that you feel you would be able to get your home improvement money back?
(1) Yes—definitely
(2) Yes—maybe
(3) Toss up
(4) Probably not
(5) Definitely not
(8) DK
(9) NA

54

30. Would you improve this property if given a low-interest, long-term mortgage?
(1) Yes
(2) Yes, if payments did not exceed current payments
(3) Yes, if payments did not exceed current payments by 25%
(4) Yes, if payments did not exceed current payments by 50%
(5) No, property isn't worth improving
(6) No, property doesn't need improvement
(7) Will not borrow, other
(8) DK
(9) NA

*55

31. Do you know of any of the current, government financial programs for older properties?
(1) Yes, FHA/VA home improvement loans
(2) Yes, NJHFA home improvement loans
(3) Yes, CDBG property maintenance grants and loans
(4) Yes, Section 312 rehabilitation loans
(5) Yes, most of the above, in detail
(6) Yes, most of the above, but not in detail
(7) No, I don't know of any
(8) No, I don't care—wouldn't use them.
Why? _____
_____
(9) NA

*56

32 A. Interest Payments
(1) 7 percent or less
(2) 8–10 percent

        (3) 11–13 percent
        (4) 14–15 percent
        (5) 16–18 percent
        (6) Over 18 percent
        (8) DK
        (9) NA

*57

32 B. Terms
        (1) Under three years
        (2) Three to five years
        (3) Six to ten years
        (4) Ten years
        (5) Eleven to fifteen years
        (6) More than fifteen years
        (8) DK
        (9) NA

*58

33. What source would you turn to for home improvement money?
        (1) Second mortgage—savings bank
        (2) Second mortgage—commercial bank
        (3) Second mortgage—mortgage company
        (4) Second mortgage—finance company
        (5) Personal loan from relative or friends
        (6) Personal resources—savings or sell assets
        (7) Rollover first mortgage
        (8) DK
        (9) NA

59

34. Are you in an area scheduled for targeted Community Development Block Grant assistance?
        (1) Yes
        (2) No
        (3) Not sure
        (8) DK
        (9) NA

60

35. Do you think that this designation will enhance the value of your property?
        (1) Yes
        (2) No
        (3) Not sure
        (8) DK
        (9) NA

61

36. Do you think your property will be worth more or less five years from now?
        (1) Much more
        (2) More
        (3) The same
        (4) Less
        (5) Much less
        (8) DK
        (9) NA

62

36a. Why do you think this is so?
        (1) Present tenants affect or landlord's efforts affect
        (2) Neighborhood affects

Variable Number	Question Number
	(3) Part of municipal situation (going under or coming back)
	(4) Part of regional situation
	(5) Local government affects
	(6) State and federal government affects
	(7) All or most of 1–4
	(8) All or most of 1–6
	(9) NA/DK

*63

37. Is the inmigration of legal or illegal aliens having any effect on the demand for housing in the city of Newark?
(1) Yes
(2) No
(8) DK
(9) NA

Comment: _____

_____

*64–75

37a. If yes, what ethnic groups and where?

Ethnic Group (E1–E4)	Location (AL1–AL4)	Positive or Negative (PN1–PN2)
(64)_____	(65)_____	(66)_____
(67)_____	(68)_____	(69)_____
(70)_____	(71)_____	(72)_____
(73)_____	(74)_____	(75)_____

E1–E4 Could Have	AL1–AL4 Could Have	PN1–PN2 Could Have
1. Puerto Ricans	1. Newark	1. Positive
2. Cubans	2. Central Ward	2. Negative
3. Haitians	3. Downtown	
4. Indian	4. Ironbound	
5. Other	5. North Newark	
6. Hispanic Caribbeans	6. South Newark	
7. Portuguese	9. NA/DK	
8. Other		
9. NA/DK		

76–77

38. What do you think is the biggest problem facing the City of Newark in its quest to return as a safe and pleasing place to live or conduct business in?

38a. Biggest problem	COMMON CODE (a & b)
	1. Public safety
38b. Second biggest problem	2. Housing
	3. Discipline and motivation of
	residents
	4. Taxes
	5. 1 & 2
	6. 1 & 3
	7. 1 to 4
	8. Other
	9. NA/DK

78–79

39. How has the energy crisis affected housing operations in the city?

*Variable
Number*

*Question
Number*

*39a. (78) Positive effect_____
                                            (why)

   (1) Jobs and residences close

*39b. (79) Negative   effect_____
                                            (why)

   (1) Heating costs

(80) Card 1

1–4 I.D. Number

*5

40. What do you think that city government should do to assist housing operations locally that is not already being done?
   (1) Lower taxes
   (2) Provide government financial assistance
   (3) Remove governmental regulations
   (4) Increase public safety
   (5) 1 & 3
   (6) 1 & 4
   (7) 1 to 4
   (8) Other_____

*6

41. Do you think there is any market to co-op or condominize your Newark properties?
   (1) Yes
   (2) No
   (7) DK
   (9) NA

*7

41a. If yes, why?
   (1) Only if backed by government guarantees
   (2) There is already evidence of this movement
   (3) Critical mass of urban infrastructure must influence choice
   (4) Other_____

   If no, why?
   (5) People too poor
   (6) Buildings too old
   (7) No real estate market
   (8) Other_____

*8

42. Do you think there is potential for an integrated middle-class population in the City of Newark?
   (1) Yes
   (2) No
   (7) DK
   (9) NA

*9

42a. If yes, why?
   (1) Newark has good location
   (2) Redevelopment is attracting whites
   (3) Changes must continue to take place in city's environment
   (4) Other_____

   If no, why?
   (5) City economically and physically unattractive
   (6) Whites won't live with blacks

Variable	*Question*
Number	*Number*

*10

43. Would you invest in abandoned property in the City of Newark?
    (1) Yes
    (2) No
    (8) DK
    (9) NA

*11

43a. If no, why?
    (1) Risks too high in abandoned property
    (2) All Newark properties are poor investments
    (3) Too old
    (4) No money
    (5) Just not interested in property anywhere

*12

43b. If yes, where and why?
    (1) All over the city—Newark is coming back
    (2) Any near-profitable property
    (3) Worth the risk
    (4) Risk must be diminished by government participation
    (5) Must have heavy individual input
    (6) Must have history of successful investment
    (7) Can't afford

*13

44. What are the real economics of average building operations—rents minus costs equal what kind of return? (Cite examples—try to get actual owner cash flow statements.)

*14

45. Describe the operations of a good (profitable) building.
    (1) Must have good tenants
    (2) Must have conscientious landlord
    (3) Rent must be high
    (4) Buildings must be reasonably taxed
    (5) 1 & 2
    (6) 1 & 3
    (7) 1–4
    (8) Other_____
    (9) NA/DK

*15

46. Describe the operations of a poor (unprofitable) building.
    (1) Poor tenants—tenant vandalism
    (2) Rent levels too low
    (3) Maintenance not being done
    (5) 1 & 2
    (6) 1 & 4
    (7) 1–4
    (8) Other_____
    (9) NA/DK

16

47. Summarize how the two situations differ.

    _____

    _____

    _____

*17

48. Has rent control had either a positive or negative effect on your rental property? Please explain.
    (1) No effect
    (2) Negative—building cash flow restricted

Variable Number	*Question Number*

(3) Negative—building has no market
(4) Negative—too much government participation in private market
(5) Negative—low rent ensures poor tenantry

*18

49. What is the biggest reason for abandoning buildings?
(1) Adverse cash flow
(2) Crime, vandalism, poor tenants
(3) Lack of concern by city government
(4) Built-in neglect of building (to cash flow)
(5) 1 & 2
(6) 1 & 3
(7) 1–4
(8) Other_____
(9) NA/DK

*19

50. What are examples of wasted repairs? (repairs that it doesn't pay to make given the nature and condition of the building)
(1) No repair is a waste
(2) Painting, plastering walls or paneling
(3) Cosmetic repairs
(4) Windows, doors, locks
(5) Major repairs (system replacement)
(6) External repairs (roof, siding, facade, yard)
(7) Minor repairs

*20

51. What type of repair requests do you perform right away?
(1) All repairs
(2) Plumbing
(3) Heating
(4) Electrical
(5) 2–4
(6) Windows, doors, locks
(7) Major repairs
(8) Minor repairs

*21

52. What type of repairs do you attempt to avoid or just don't make?
(1) Do not avoid
(2) Cosmetic
(3) Painting, wall, window repairs
(4) New heating system
(5) Roofing and external
(6) Hallways, exterior flooring
(7) Major repairs

*22

53. Would you or have you considered not paying the mortgage or property taxes on the building?
(1) Yes
(2) No
(8) DK
(9) NA

*23

53a. If yes, how do you do this and maintain control of the building?
(1) Just do it, don't maintain control
(2) Make payments just before city action
(3) You can do anything for a short time
(4) Intent is to lose control

Variable *Number*	*Question* *Number*
*24	53b. If yes, are there points in time when you must again make partial tax or mortgage payments to retain control? (1) No (2) Just before city acts (3) Do not pay anything
25	53c. If yes, do you think that by doing so, you have made an unconscious decision to abandon the building in the future? (1) Yes (2) Maybe (3) No
26	54. Is your building part of a corporation or held in a third party's name? (1) Yes (2) No (8) DK (9) NA
27	54a. If yes, describe the exact advantages of such a holding mechanism. (1) Legal protection (2) Tax advantage (8) Other
*28–29	55. Blacks and Hispanics are increasingly becoming owners of these types of properties. Do you think that they have any advantage or disadvantage that would render them better or worse owners? (1) Advantage(s) (2) Disadvantage(s) (3) Advantage(s) and disadvantage(s) (8) DK (9) NA Please explain each:
30	Advantage(s) (1) Minority owners are more responsible (2) Better relationship with tenants (3) City doesn't bother minority owners
31	Disadvantage(s) (1) Too little capital (2) Not familiar with building management (3) Do not maintain properties
*32	56. Do you think the racial or ethnic composition of a building has anything to do with the building becoming abandoned? (1) Yes (2) No (8) DK (9) NA
33–34	56a. If yes, Race or ethnic composition enhancing abandonment (1) Whites—don't care (2) Minorities on welfare (3) Minorities in general (8) Other_____ 56b. Race or ethnic composition retarding abandonment (8) Other_____

Variable Number	*Question Number*

35   57. Who will be better off ten years from now, a single family owner who, for example, sells his property in Newark for $30,000 and buys in an area such as South Jersey for $50,000, or an owner who puts $10,000 into his building in Newark and holds onto it?
(1) South Jersey
(2) Newark
(3) Other_____
(8) DK
(9) NA

36   57a. Please explain.
(1) South Jersey—better equity position
(2) South Jersey—better living environment
(3) South Jersey—better educational opportunities
(4) South Jersey—other _____
(5) Newark—city coming back
(6) Newark—home to residents
(7) Newark—other costs too high in suburbs

*37   58. Do you have fire insurance on the building?
(1) Yes
(2) No
(8) DK
(9) NA

*38   59. How many fires have you had over the past year?
(1) None
(2) 1–2
(3) 3–5
(4) 6–10
(5) More than 10
(8) DK
(9) NA

*39   59a. How often have the police visited the building this year to answer a complaint?
(1) Never
(2) 1–2 times
(3) 3–5 times
(4) 6–10 times
(5) More than 10
(7) NA
(8) DK

40   59b. How many fires have you reported to the insurance company?
(1) None
(2) 10%
(3) 11–30%
(4) 31–50%
(5) 51–75%
(6) 76–99%
(7) All
(8) DK
(9) NA

41   59c. If not all—why not?
(1) Do not want to risk losing insurance

Variable Number	*Question Number*
	(2) Too minor to report
	(3) Did not directly affect living structure
42	60. How often is your building vandalized?
	(1) Daily
	(2) Weekly
	(3) Monthly
	(4) Semiannually
	(5) Yearly
	(6) Never
	(7) Rarely
	(8) DK
	(9) NA
43	61. Who does most of the damage—outsiders or tenants?
	(1) Outsiders
	(2) Tenants
	(8) DK
	(9) NA
44	61a: What can be done to control this?
	(1) Better police protection
	(2) Better screening of tenants
	(3) More rules restricting tenants
	(4) Parental control of children
	(5) Involve tenants in building
	(6) Nothing can be done
	(7) Evict tenants
	(8) Other_____
	(9) NA/DK
45	62. Sex of owner
	(1) Male
	(2) Female
	(3) Co-ownership
	(8) DK
	(9) NA
46	62a. Place of residence of owner
	(1) Resident in parcel
	(2) Within a block of parcel
	(3) Within general neighborhood of parcel
	(4) Elsewhere in Newark
	(5) New Jersey—within twenty-mile radius of Newark
	(6) Balance of New Jersey
	(7) New York
	(8) Other_____
	(9) NA
47	62b. Race—ethnicity of owner
	(1) Black (American)
	(2) Black (West Indian)
	(3) Black (Spanish)
	(4) White (Jewish)
	(5) White (Italian/Irish)
	(6) White (Spanish)
	(7) White (Portuguese)
	(8) Oriental
	(9) White (Other)

Variable *Number*	*Question* *Number*
48	63. Income of owner (1) $10,000 or less (2) $10,001–$20,000 (3) $20,001–$30,000 (4) $30,001–$50,000 (5) $50,001–$75,000 (6) $75,001–$100,000 (7) Over $100,000 (8) DK (9) NA
49	64. Portion of income from Newark properties (1) <10% (2) 10–19% (3) 20–29% (4) 30–49% (5) 50–74% (6) 75% + (7) Loss or none (8) DK (9) NA

50–75 - Skip

76   Do you have a mortgage or loan on the building?
         (1) Yes   (2) No   (8) DK   (9) NA

         If yes, where did you get it from?

         _____

         (Use code from question 21)

80 - Card 2

Variable Number *Card #3*		*Variable* *Name*
1–4 I.D. Number	_____	ID3
5–9 Gross Rental Income (Annual)	_____	GRI

Expenses Annualized

10–13	Payroll	_____	PAY
14–18	Heating	_____	HEAT
19–22	Maintenance & Repair	_____	MAINT
23–26	Taxes	_____	TAXES
27–30	Vacancy & Bad Debt	_____	VACANCY
31–35	Mortgage	_____	MORTG
36–39	Water & Sewer	_____	WATER
40–43	Insurance	_____	INSUR
44–47	Legal Fees	_____	LEGAL
48–52	Total Unadjusted Costs Unadjusted Profit_____ Unadjusted Loss_____	_____	TUC
53–56	Credit 33⅓% of expenses to reflect owner occupancy		OWNOCC

Variable
Number

57–61	Adjusted Costs	_____	ADJCST
62–66	Adjusted Profit	_____	ADJPRO
67–71	Adjusted Loss	_____	ADJLOSS
72–76	SPECIAL CODES	_____	SC1 to SC5
77–79	Skip		
80	Card 3	_____	CD3

**1981 Tenant Interview and
Non-Profit Sponsor Interview**

Race (Recorded by Interviewer)

1. Black (American)
2. Black (W.I.)
3. Black (Spanish)
4. White (Jewish)
5. White (Italian-Irish)
6. White (Spanish)
7. White (Portuguese)
8. Oriental
9. White (Other)

Variable Number
Card #1
1–4 I.D. Number_____

5. How long have you been living in this apartment?
    (1) Less than one month
    (2) One to five months
    (3) Six to eleven months
    (4) One to two years
    (5) Three to five years
    (6) More than five years
    (9) NA/DK

6. Could you tell me how many rooms you have in your apartment (not counting bathrooms, entryways or closets)?
    (1) One
    (2) Two
    (3) Three to four
    (4) Five to six
    (5) More than six
    (9) NA/DK

7. How many bedrooms (rooms used exclusively for sleeping)?
    (1) One
    (2) Two
    (3) Three
    (4) Four
    (5) Five
    (6) Six or more
    (9) NA/DK

8. And how many bathrooms?
    (1) One

(2) One and one-half
(3) Two
(4) Two and one-half
(5) Three or more
(9) NA/DK

9. Are your bathroom facilities shared by another family not in your household?
   (1) Yes (____) indicate number of households that share
   (2) No
   (3) Yes, 2 share
   (4) Yes, 3 share
   (5) Yes, 4 plus share
   (9) NA/DK

10. Does your bathroom have a washbasin, toilet and tub/shower?
    (1) Yes
    (2) No
    (3) Washbasin
    (4) Toilet
    (5) Tub-shower
    (6) Washbasin-toilet
    (7) Washbasin-tub/shower
    (8) Toilet-tub/shower
    (9) NA/DK
    (0) All

11. Do they all work?
    (1) Yes
    (2) No
    (9) NA/DK

12. Are your kitchen facilities shared by another household that does not live with you?
    (1) Yes (____) indicate number of households that share
    (2) No
    (3) Yes, 2 share
    (4) Yes, 3 share
    (5) Yes, 4+ share
    (9) NA/DK

13. Does your kitchen have a stove, refrigerator and sink?
    (1) Yes
    (2) No
    (3) No stove
    (4) No refrigerator
    (5) No sink
    (6) No stove-refrigerator
    (7) No stove-sink
    (8) No refrigerator-sink
    (9) NA/DK
    (0) No stove-sink-refrigerator

14. Do they all work?
    (1) Yes
    (2) No (_____) doesn't work.
    (9) NA/DK

About your electrical system:

	(1)	(2)	(9)
15. (1) Do all outlets work?	Yes____	No____	NA/DK____
16. (2) Is any wiring exposed?	Yes____	No____	NA/DK____

17. (3) Have fuses blown once
    in past 90 days?

	(1) Yes	(2) No	(9) NA/DK
	_____	_____	_____

18. Has your toilet broken down in the last 90 days for more than 6 hours?
- (1) Yes
- (2) No
- (3) Never works
- (9) NA/DK

19. How many times?_____

20. When the heating system is working do auxiliary heaters have to be used to keep the house warm?
- (1) Yes
- (2) No
- (9) NA/DK

21. Have you seen mice or rats over past three months?
- (1) Yes
- (2) No
- (9) NA/DK

22. Do you have a private telephone in your unit/house?
- (1) Yes
- (2) No
- (9) NA/DK

23–25. Skip

26. Does the unit have:

	(1) Yes	(2) No	(9) NA/DK
27. (1) Storm doors	_____	_____	_____
28. (2) Storm windows	_____	_____	_____
29. (3) Insulated attic/roof or walls	_____	_____	_____

30. Do you know who your landlord is?
- (1) Yes
- (2) No
- (9) NA/DK

31. Have you personally ever met your landlord or his/her representative?
- (1) Yes, landlord
- (2) Yes, only representative
- (3) No
- (9) NA/DK

32. Are there repairs that you have asked for which have not been made?
- (1) Yes
- (2) No
- (9) NA/DK

33–35. If yes, what are they? (maximum 3 repairs)
- (1) Plumbing
- (2) Electrical
- (3) Windows, doors, locks
- (4) Extermination
- (5) Internal structural
- (6) External structural
- (7) Heating system
- (9) NA/DK

36. In general terms, how would you rate your apartment unit?
    (1) Excellent
    (2) Very good
    (3) Fair
    (4) Poor
    (5) Very poor
    (9) NA/DK

37. How would you rate your building?
    (1) Excellent
    (2) Very good
    (3) Fair
    (4) Poor
    (5) Very poor
    (9) NA/DK

38. Do you feel one or the other of the below-listed conditions is excessively bothersome?

	(1) Yes	(2) No	(9) NA/DK
39. Street or highway noise			
40. Heavy traffic			
41. Streets or roads continuously in need of repair			
42. Roads impassable due to snow or water			
43. Poor street lighting			
44. Neighborhood crime including vandalism			
45. Trash, junk, litter on streets, sidewalks and empty lots			
46. Boarded-up buildings on same block			
47. Traffic and noise from local industries, businesses or stores			
48. Odors, smoke, gas			
49. Airplane noise			

50. Where did you live before you moved into this apartment?

ENTER   HERE_____
                (address)   (state)

    (1) Same building
    (2) Same neighborhood (different building)
    (3) Same city (different neighborhood)
    (4) Same state (different city)
    (5) Out of state
    (6) Out of the country (continental United States)
    (7) Other_____
    (9) NA/DK

51–52. Why did you move away from your previous residence?
    (1) Job related (better accessibility)
    (2) Job related (change in employment)
    (3) Unit too small
    (4) Unit too large
    (5) Unit inadequate in terms of quality
    (6) Rent increase
    (7) Eviction (private displacement)
    (8) Urban renewal (public displacement)

(9) Other housing unit reasons
(10) Newly married—to start own home
(11) Widowed, separated, divorced
(12) Dissatisfied with neighborhood
(13) Dissatisfied with schools
(14) Other _____
(19) NA/DK

53. Not counting bathrooms, how many rooms did you have in your previous residence?
(1) One
(2) Two
(3) Three
(4) Four to six
(5) More than six
(9) NA/DK

54. Did you own or rent your previous residence?
(1) Own
(2) Rent
(3) Other_____
(4) Resident in apartment owned or rented by relative
(9) NA/DK

55. If rent, approximately how much did you pay in rent per month?

(1) Less than $75	56	57	58
(2) $75 to $99			
(3) $100 to $124	(Enter Exact Rent)		
(4) $125 to $149	59	60	61
(5) $150 to $199			
(6) $200 to $249	(Additional for Heat)		
(7) $250 to $299	62	63	64
(8) $300 to $400			
(0) More than $400	(Additional for Electricity & Gas)		
(9) NA/DK			

65. Approximately how much is your rent for *this apartment*?

(1) Less than $75	66	67	68
(2) $75 to $99			
(3) $100 to $124	(Enter Exact Rent)		
(4) $125 to $149	69	70	71
(5) $150 to $199			
(6) $200 to $249	(Additional for Heat)		
(7) $250 to $299	72	73	74
(8) $300 to $400			
(0) More than $400	(Additional for Electric & Gas)		
(9) NA/DK			

75. How does your present *apartment* compare with your previous residence?
(1) Substantial improvement
(2) Slight improvement
(3) About the same
(4) Previous better
(9) NA/DK

76. How would you compare this *neighborhood* with where you lived before?
(1) Substantial improvement
(2) Slight improvement
(3) About the same
(4) Previous better
(9) NA/DK

77–78. (Skip)

79. = 2

80. = 1

Variable Number
Card #2
1–4 I.D. Number_____

5. What method did you use to find the apartment you now are renting?
    (1) Personal recommendation
    (2) Newspaper listing
    (3) "For rent" sign
    (4) Phone book listing
    (5) Rental agency listing
    (6) Other_____
    (9) NA/DK

6. Given a choice, what kind of area would you *most prefer* to live in?
    (1) Large city
    (2) Small city
    (3) Suburb
    (4) Small town
    (5) Rural area
    (6) Other_____
    (9) NA/DK

7. What would you prefer the racial or ethnic composition of that locality to be?
    (1) Mainly black
    (2) Mainly Hispanic
    (3) Mainly white
    (4) Mixed—black/white
    (5) Mixed—black/Hispanic
    (6) Mixed—white/Hispanic
    (7) Mixed—white/Hispanic/black
    (8) No preference
    (9) NA/DK

8. Do you presently have plans to move from this apartment within the next year or two?
    (1) Yes, definitely
    (2) Would like to but plans not definite
    (3) No
    (4) Other_____
    (9) NA/DK

9. If you would like to move, but as of the present time have no definite plans, what is the main reason you have not finalized your plans?
    (1) Lack of financial resources (funds to move)
    (2) Have not identified appropriate job opportunities elsewhere
    (3) Financial reasons related to some form of public assistance
    (4) Unable to locate suitable housing elsewhere
    (5) Have children in local school(s) and prefer to have them continue their education where they are currently attending
    (6) Other_____
    (9) NA/DK

10. If you have considered relocating or have made definite plans to move, where do you intend to go?
    (1) Same building (different unit)
    (2) Same neighborhood (different building)
    (3) Same city (different neighborhood)

(4) Same state (different city)
(5) Different state
(6) Out of the country (continental United States)
(7) Other_____
(9) NA/DK

11. Would you prefer to remain in your present neighborhood if municipal services and the general housing stock were improved?
    (1) Yes (no qualifications)
    (2) Yes—but only if employment opportunities were also improved
    (3) Yes—other _____
    (4) No
    (9) NA/DK

12. Given the condition of this building and its neighborhood, do you think this building is worth renovating?
    (1) Yes—minor renovations and improved maintenance
    (2) Yes—major renovation
    (3) No—the building does not need repairs other than standard maintenance
    (4) No—the building is not worth any further investment
    (9) NA/DK

13. If given appropriate assistance, are you capable and willing to help repair your own apartment unit?
    (1) Yes
    (2) No
    (9) NA/DK

14. If given the opportunity, would you and/or other tenants like to take over the ownership and operation of this building?
    (1) Yes—(no restrictions)
    (2) Yes—I would like to but do not feel capable
    (3) Yes—but only in cooperation with other tenants
    (4) No
    (9) NA/DK

15. Have you, individually or in conjunction with others, attempted to acquire money to renovate your apartment building from some public agency or private concern?
    (1) Yes
    (2) No
    (9) NA/DK

16. Have you, individually or in conjunction with others, attempted to take over ownership of your building?
    (1) Yes
    (2) No
    (9) NA/DK

17. Has your neighborhood changed since you've been a resident here?
    (1) Has improved greatly
    (2) Has improved slightly
    (3) Has remained stable
    (4) Has declined slightly
    (5) Has declined greatly
    (6) Have not noticed
    (7) Other_____
    (9) NA/DK

18. Given the condition of your neighborhood and building, what do you think of the current rent levels?
    (1) Too high

(2) Slightly high
(3) Are appropriate
(4) Slightly low
(5) Very low
(6) Other_____
(9) NA/DK

19. If maintenance in your building were improved and/or certain repairs were made, would you be willing to pay more rent?
    (1) Yes—but not more than $20 to $40 additional
    (2) Yes—but not more than $41 to $80 additional
    (3) Yes—but not more than $81 to $150 additional
    (5) No—cannot afford any rent increase
    (6) No—present apartment is satisfactory without an increase
    (7) No—neighborhood is not worth more rent
    (8) Other_____
    (9) NA/DK

Please rate the following improvements in terms of need, as they would apply to your neighborhood. (1 = most needed; 2 = strongly needed; 3 = needed; 4 = slightly needed; 5 = not needed)

20–33 (1–5) Increased personal and property safety (crime and vandalism) _____
   (1–5) Increased fire protection _____
   (1–5) Improved municipal services such as street cleaning
    and garbage disposal _____
   (1–5) Improved transportation service _____
   (1–5) Improved housing conditions _____
   (1–5) Improved schools _____
   (1–5) Increased private services such as grocery stores,
    fast food, drug stores, laundromats, etc. _____
   (1–5) Improved local employment _____
   (1–5) Improved accessibility to distant employment _____
   (1–5) More parks and open spaces _____
   (1–5) Increased public social services such as day care
    services, health facilities, etc. _____
   (1–5) Improved cultural facilities _____
   (1–5) Improved entertainment facilities _____
   (1–5) Improved accessibility to religious institutions _____

34. Do you feel that your neighborhood receives adequate attention from City Hall?
    (1) Yes
    (2) No
    (3) Other_____
    (9) NA/DK

35. Are you aware of any public or publicly assisted redevelopment projects planned for or under construction in your neighborhood at the present time?
    (1) Yes
    (2) No
    (9) NA/DK

36. If yes, please list_____
_____

37–39. If you feel that your neighborhood is either (37) declining, (38) stable or (39) improving, please list briefly those things which serve as your indicators.
    (1) Crime rate/truant delinquency
    (2) Housing abandonment or bad conditions
    (3) Lack of commercial facilities

(4) Unemployment—lack of jobs
(5) Drug abuse
(6) Bad schools
(7) Lack of recreational facilities
(8) Loss of middle class
(9) NA/DK
(0) Lack of personal commitment to property or neighborhood

40. Would you leave Newark to seek housing elsewhere in New Jersey if given a chance?
(1) Yes
(2) No
(9) NA/DK

41. If yes, where would you go? (Have interviewee specify place; interviewer code below.)
(1) Neighboring inner-ring integrated suburb
(2) Neighboring inner-ring predominantly white suburb
(3) Outer-ring suburb
(4) Rural area/non-metro area
(5) Large New Jersey city   Place:_____
(8) Unspecified
(9) NA/DK

42–44. Why would you choose this location?
(1) Employment opportunities
(2) Family ties/friends
(3) Safe location—less crime
(4) Better housing
(5) Better neighborhood
(6) Better schools
(9) NA/DK

45–47. What is stopping you from making this move?
(1) Financial resources
(2) Family ties
(3) Children in school
(4) Age
(5) Indifferent, unspecified
(9) NA/DK

48. Would you leave this section of the country if given a chance?
(1) Yes
(2) No
(9) NA/DK

49. Where would you go?   Place:_____
(1) Northeast
(2) North Central
(3) South
(4) West
(5) Puerto Rico
(8) Unspecified
(9) NA/DK

50–52. If yes, why would you choose this location?
(1) Employment opportunities
(2) Family ties/friends
(3) Safer location—less crime
(4) Better housing
(5) Better neighborhood
(6) Better schools
(9) NA/DK

53–55. What is stopping you from moving there?
  (1) Financial resources
  (2) Family ties
  (3) Children in school
  (4) Age
  (5) Indifferent, unspecified
  (9) NA/DK

56. If conditions get worse will you attempt to leave the city regardless of attachments?
  (1) Yes
  (2) No
  (9) NA/DK

57. What do you think is really going to happen to Newark in the future? Can the city come back?
  (1) Yes
  (2) No
  (3) Indifferent
  (9) NA/DK

58. If you had the money would you invest in abandoned property in Newark?
  (1) Yes
  (2) No
  (9) NA/DK

59. Why?
  (1) House
  (2) Investment
  (3) Home investment
  (9) NA/DK

60. Would you like your children to reside in Newark permanently and raise their families here?
  (1) Yes
  (2) No
  (3) Indifferent
  (9) NA/DK

61. Why?
  (1) City looks better
  (2) More jobs
  (3) Better educational facilities
  (9) NA/DK

62. Do you think all of the new public housing and institutional construction (colleges, medical school, county buildings, state and federal offices) have been good for Newark?
  (1) Yes
  (2) No
  (9) NA/DK

63. How many people live in your household?
  (1) One
  (2) Two
  (3) Three
  (4) Four
  (5) Five to six
  (6) Six to eight
  (7) More than eight
  (9) NA/DK

64. Are any bedrooms used by three or more persons for sleeping?

(1) Yes
(2) No
(9) NA/DK

65. If yes, how many?_____

66-78. (Skip)
79. = 2
80. = 2

Variable Number
Card #3

1-4 I.D. Number_____

5. In what general category was your total income last year? (INCO)
    (1) Less than $5,000
    (2) $5,000 to $9,999
    (3) $10,000 to $14,999
    (4) $15,000 to $19,999
    (5) $20,000 to $24,999
    (6) $25,000 to $29,999
    (7) $30,000 or more
    (9) NA/DK

6. How many members of the household contribute income to the household? (CONTRI)
    (1) One
    (2) Two
    (3) Three
    (4) Four
    (5) Five
    (6) More than 5
    (9) NA/DK

IMPR1/   IMPR2/   IMPR3/   If you had your say, what would you recommend to im-
_____   _____   _____   prove the quality of life in this city?
   7   8   9

    (1) Reduced crime/more police protection
    (2) More, better jobs
    (3) Better public facilities (schools, recreation)
    (4) Better housing
    (5) Better, more responsive local government
    (6) Better social service in general
    (7) Increased public assistance (i.e. welfare)
    (8) Increased commitment of local residents to the community
    (9) NA/DK

INCOME SOURCES:

TYPE	YES	NO	PERCENT	
		(10)		(11–13)
Social Security	1	2	____/____/____/	____/
		(14)		(15–17)
Welfare	1	2	____/____/____/	____/
		(18)		(19–21)
Alimony or child support	1	2	____/____/____/	____/
		(22)		(23–25)
Unemployment	1	2	____/____/____/	____/
		(26)		(27–29)

Pension	1	2 (30)	____/____/____/____ (31-33)	
Inheritance	1	2	____/____/____/____	

34–78. (Skip)
79. = 2
80. = 3

Variable Number
Card #4

1–4 I.D. Number_____

Family Status	Age	M	F	DK	Occupation	Full	Part	DK	Education
___ 5	___/___ 6 7	1	2 8	9	___/___ 9 10	1	2 11	9	___/___ 12 13
___ 14	___/___ 15 16	1	2 17	9	___/___ 18 19	1	2 20	9	___/___ 21 22
___ 23	___/___ 24 25	1	2 26	9	___/___ 27 28	1	2 29	9	___/___ 30 31
___ 32	___/___ 33 34	1	2 35	9	___/___ 36 37	1	2 38	9	___/___ 39 40
___ 41	___/___ 42 43	1	2 44	9	___/___ 45 46	1	2 47	9	___/___ 48 49
___ 50	___/___ 51 52	1	2 53	9	___/___ 54 55	1	2 56	9	___/___ 57 58
___ 59	___/___ 60 61	1	2 62	9	___/___ 63 64	1	2 65	9	___/___ 66 67
___ 68	___/___ 69 70	1	2 71	9	___/___ 72 73	1	2 74	9	___/___ 75 76

77–78. (Skip)
79. = 2
80. = 4

Coding Notes

A. *Family Status:*

1 = Head
2 = Spouse
3 = Son/Daughter
4 = Other Relative
5 = Non-relative
6 = Status unknown

B. *Age:*

98 = Child under 16 age unknown
99 = Age unknown

C. *Occupation:*

01 Professional
02 Managers, Administrators
03 Clerical

E. *Outer Ring*

Roselle

04 Craftsmen
05 Operatives Except Transport
06 Transport Operatives
07 Laborers
08 Service workers
09 Household workers
10 Sales
11 Retired
12 Student
13 Housewife
14 Unemployed
15 Other
16 Welfare families
99 NA/DK

Cedar Grove
Nutley

F. *Large New Jersey Cities*

Jersey City
Trenton
Passaic
Camden
New Brunswick
Hoboken
Union City
Hackensack

D. *City*

Integrated suburbs

Hillside	Elizabeth
Irvington	Orange
Montclair	

Non-integrated white inner-ring suburbs

Belleville	Glen Ridge	Upper Montclair
Kearny	Union	South Orange
Bloomfield	North Arlington	Maplewood
Harrison	East Newark	

1981 Property Tax Record Search

Variable Number
Card #1

1–3 I.D. Number

4–7 Block Number

8–9 Lot Number

Real Estate Tax: for current fiscal year

10–13. First Half

                Amount_____

14–17. Second Half

                Amount_____

   18. Property Tax Arrears: [1]   [2]
                           Yes_____   No_____

19–32. Address of Property (Spelled out)

33–34. Period of arrears
       (Number—Fraction) $_____

35–38. Dollars of Arrearage: $_____

39–42. Year of first tax lien   _____

43–49. Private or public holding (spelled out)   _____

50–53. Year of last tax lien   _____

    54. Number of tax title liens   _____

55–58. Total amount of tax title liens $_____

59–62. Year of first foreclosure   _____

63–66. Year of second foreclosure   _____

    67. Number of foreclosures   _____

68–71. Dollar amount of foreclosures $_____

72. Type of Owner
    1. Private individuals
    2. Private corporation
    3. Non-profit/public corporation
    4. Public agency (tax listed) (City, County, State)
    5. Other

73. Was owner (either present or current) put on partial payments?

    1. Yes_____   2. No_____

74. If yes, did it make parcel viable?

    1. Yes_____   2. No_____

75. Property Class
    1. Vacant land   4. Commercial (4a)
    2. Residential   5. Institution (4b)
    3. Farm   6. Apartments (4c)

76. 1972 Structure Status
    1. Vacant
    2. Occupied
    3. Demolished

77. 1981 Structure Status
    1. Occupied
    2. Standing—vacant abandoned
    3. Demolished
    4. Demolished—improved
    5. Consolidated—unimproved
    6. Public housing—redeveloped
    7. Public institution—redeveloped
    8. Private residential—redeveloped
    9. Private non-residential—redeveloped

78. Area
    1. 1
    2. 2
    3. 3

79. On/Off Tax Role

    1. On_____   2. Off_____

80. *Card Number*
    1

1981 Title Search

Variable Number
Card #1
1–4 I.D. Number

5–17. Address of Property

18. Type of owner
    (1) Individual (including joint ownership by husband and wife)
    (2) Two or more individuals
    (3) Corporation (realty or other)
    (4) Financial institutions
    (5) Church
    (6) Redevelopment company
    (7) VA/FHA
    (8) Public ownership (city)
    (9) Public ownership (state or federal)

19. Address of owner
    (1) Same address
    (2) Same general neighborhood of Newark (i.e., within one mile)
    (3) Elsewhere in the city of Newark
    (4) New Jersey other than Newark
    (5) Outside New Jersey, inside NY metropolitan area
    (6) Outside New Jersey, outside NY metropolitan area

20. Date of title_____
                                                    (Year
    (1) Zero–one year old
    (2) Two–four years old
    (3) Five–six years old
    (4) Seven–ten years old
    (5) Eleven–fifteen years old
    (6) Sixteen–twenty years old
    (7) Over twenty years old
    (8) Not recorded

21. Property class_____
                                            (Describe property
    (1) 1 Vacant land
    (2) 2 Residential (1–3 family)
    (3) 4A Commercial
    (4) 4B Industrial
    (5) 4C Apartments (4 family or more)
    (6) Other

    Lot size (to nearest foot)_____

22–24. Frontage_____

25. Skip

26–28. _____ Depth

29. Skip

30. Lot configuration
    (1) regular
    (2) irregular

31–35. $_____ Land assessment

36–37. Skip

38–42. $_____ Building assessment

43–44. Skip

45. Mortgage source by name_____
    (1) No mortgage shown
    (2) Commercial bank
    (3) Savings and loan/savings bank
    (4) Individual grantor
    (5) Prior owner
    (6) Mortgage company
    (7) Government agency
    (8) Realty and construction company
    (9) Not given
    (0) Not applicable—public

46–50. $_____ First mortgage amount (at time of purchase)

51–52. Skip

53. First mortgage interest
    (1) Not listed
    (2) 4–6 percent
    (3) 7–8 percent
    (4) 9–10 percent
    (5) 11–12 percent
    (6) 13–14 percent
    (7) 15+ percent
    (8) Bond
    (9) Other
    (0) Not applicable

54. Mortgage term
    (1) 3 years and refinance
    (2) 5 years and refinance
    (3) 10 years
    (4) 20 years
    (5) 25 years
    (6) 30 years

55–59. $_____ total amount paid for property (be careful to note method for determining this item.)

            00009—Actual transfer price unknown
            00001—Nominal transfer

60. Classified for case study
    (1) No
    (2) Yes, interesting ownership pattern
    (3) Yes, involved foreclosure or public turnover
    (4) Yes, significant changes in value of worth
    (5) Yes, significant dedication to property
    (6) Yes, redevelopment company holding

61–62. Skip

63. Second mortgage
    (1) Yes
    (2) No
    (3) Not applicable

64. Third mortgage
    (1) Yes
    (2) No
    (3) Not applicable

65. Second mortgagor by name_____
    (1) No mortgage shown
    (2) Savings bank
    (3) Commercial bank
    (4) Savings and loan
    (5) Individual grantee
    (6) Mortgage company
    (7) Construction or home improvements
    (8) Not applicable

66–72. Skip

73. Number of mortgage foreclosures_____

74. Total sales since 1964
    (1) None
    (2) One
    (3) Two
    (4) Three
    (5) Four
    (6) Five
    (7) More than five

75. Total transfers since 1964
    (1) None
    (2) One
    (3) Two
    (4) Three
    (5) Four
    (6) Five
    (7) More than five

76–77. Private transfer scenario
    01. Private individuals retain
    02. Private individuals to private individuals
    03. Private individuals to corporation
    04. Private individuals to bank & mortgage companies
    05. Private individuals to city via donation
    06. Private individuals to city via foreclosure
    07. Private individuals to Housing Authority
    08. Private individuals to county/state/federal
    09. Private individuals to VA/HUD
    10. Private individuals to redevelopment corporation/churches
    11. Other
    12. NA/DK

78. Corporate transfer scenario
    (1) Corporation retains
    (2) Corporation to private individuals
    (3) Corporation to corporation
    (4) Corporation to city via foreclosure
    (5) Corporation to city via donation
    (6) Corporation to Housing Authority
    (7) Corporation to county/state/federal
    (8) Corporation to redevelopment corporation/churches
    (9) NA/DK

79. Transfer patterns
    (1) Single private (corporation or individual) participation
    (2) Multiple private participation
    (3) Multiple private participation including estate
    (4) Single private and single public participation
    (5) Single private and single public including legal challenge to property ownership
    (6) Multiple private and single public participation
    (7) Multiple private (including estate) and single public participation
    (8) Multiple private and multiple public participation
    (9) Multiple private and multiple public (including legal challenge)

80. Card 7

Bibliography

Cities and Intergovernmental Transfers—General

Alford, Robert. "The Comparative Study of Urban Policies," in C. F. Schnore and H. Fagin (eds.), *Urban Research and Policy, Urban Affairs Annual, Vol. 1*. Beverly Hills: Sage, 1967.

Alford, Robert, et al. "Political Conflict, Urban Structure, and the Fiscal Crisis," in Douglas Ashford (ed.), *Sage Yearbook in Politics and Public Policy*. Beverly Hills: Sage, 1977.

Allman, T. D. "The Urban Crisis Leaves Town." *Harper's*. December 1978.

Alonso, William. "Urban and Regional Imbalances in Economic Development." J. Friedman and W. Alonso (eds.), *Regional Policy*, 1975.

American Enterprise Institute Roundtable. *Future of Urban Centers*. Washington, D.C.: American Enterprise Institute, 1978.

Bahl, Roy and Larry Schroeder. "Fiscal Adjustments in a Declining State," in R. W. Burchell and D. Listokin (eds.), *Cities Under Stress: The Fiscal Crises of Urban America*. New Brunswick: Center for Urban Policy Research, 1981.

Baumol, William. "Macroeconomics of Unbalanced Growth: The Anatomy of the Urban Crisis." *American Economic Review*, 62. March 1972.

Bell, Daniel. "The Public Household." *The Public Interest*. Fall 1974.

Berry, Brian. "Urbanization and Counter-Urbanization in the United States," in Annals, *APSS*. September 1980.

Bish, Robert. *The Public Economy of Metropolitan Areas*. Chicago: Markham, 1976.

Bish, Robert and Vincent Ostrom. "Understanding Urban Government," in H. Hochman (ed.), *The Urban Economy*. New York: W. W. Norton and Company, 1976.

Bluestone, Barry and Bennett Harrison. *Capital and Communities*. Washington, D.C.: The Progressive Alliance, 1980.

Bradley, Robert B. "Focus Locus: The Crisis in Urban Political Economy." *Comparative Urban Research*. Vol. 7, No. 1, 1979.

Breckenfeld, Gurney. "Refilling the Metropolitan Doughnut," in D. Perry and A. Watkins (ed.). *The Rise of the Sunbelt Cities. Urban Affairs Annual Review*, Vol. 14. Beverly Hills: Sage, 1977.

Bryce, Herrington (ed). *Small Cities in Transition: The Dynamics of Growth and Decline*. Cambridge, MA: Ballinger, 1977.

Bunce, Harold. *An Evaluation of the Community Development Block Grant Program*. Washington, D.C.: U.S. Department of Housing and Urban Development, 1976.

Bunce, Harold L. and Robert L. Goldberg. *City Need and Community Development Funding*. Washington, D.C.: U.S. Government Printing Office, 1979.

Burchell, Robert and David Listokin (eds.) *Cities Under Stress: The Fiscal Crises of Urban America*. New Brunswick, N.J.: Rutgers University, Center for Urban Policy Research, 1981.

Burd, Gene. "The Selling of the Sunbelt: Civic Boosterism and the Media," in D. Perry and A. Watkins, *The Rise of the Sunbelt Cities. Urban Affairs Annual Review*, Vol. 14. Beverly Hills, CA: Sage, 1977.

Castells, Manuel. *The Economic Crisis and American Society*. Princeton, NJ: Princeton University Press, 1980.

_____. The *Urban Question*. Cambridge, MA: MIT Press, 1977.

Chinitz, Benjamin. *Central City Economic Development*. Cambridge, MA: Abt Books, 1978.

Cohen, Robert. "Multinational Corporations, International Finance, and the Sunbelt," in David Perry and Alfred Watkins (eds.), *The Rise of the Sunbelt Cities*. Beverly Hills, CA: Sage, 1977.

Community Economic Development Program. *The Cost of Industrial Change*. London, England: The Program, 1977.

Elkin, Stephen. "Cities Without Power. The Transformation of American Urban Regimes," in Douglas Asford (ed). *National Resources and Urban Policy*. Chicago, IL: Maaroufa, 1979.

Fainstein, Norman and Susan Fainstein. "Federal Policy and Spatial Inequality," in George Sternlieb and James W. Hughes, *Revitalizing the Northeast*. New Brunswick, N.J.: Rutgers University, Center for Urban Policy Research, 1978.

Frazier, Mark. "Privatizing the City." *Policy Review*, No. 12, Spring 1980.

Fox, Kenneth. "Uneven Regional Development in the United States." *Review of Radical Political Economics*. Vol. 10, No. 3, Fall 1978.

Friedman, John. "The Role of the Cities in National Development," in John Mueller and R. A. Gakenheimer (eds.), *American Urban Policies and the Social Sciences*. Beverly Hills: Sage, 1971.

_____. "The Spatial Distribution of Power in the Development of Urban Systems." *Comparative Urban Research*. Vol. 1, No. 3, 1973.

Gale, Stephen and Eric Moore (eds.). *The Manipulated City*. Chicago, IL: Maaroufa, 1975.

Gappert, Gary and Harold Rose (eds.). *The Social Economy of Cities*. Beverly Hills: Sage, 1975.

Goldscheid, Rudolf, "A Sociological Approach to the Problem of Public Finance," in R. Musgrave and A. Peacock (eds.). *Classics in the Theory of Public Finance*. London: MacMillan, 1954.

Gujarati, Demitar. *Pensions in New York City's Fiscal Crisis*. (Washington, D.C.: America Enterprise Institute, 1978.

Haider, Donald. "Fiscal Scarcity: A New Urban Perspective," in L. Masotti and R. Lineberry (eds.). *The New Urban Politics*. Cambridge, MA: Ballinger, 1976.

Harrison, Bennett and Edward Hill. "The Changing Structure of Jobs in Older and Younger Cities," Cambridge, MA: Harvard–MIT Joint Center for Urban Studies, March 1979.

Hill, Richard Child. "State Capitalism and Urban Fiscal Crisis in the U.S." *Journal of Urban and Regional Research*, 1977.

Hochman, Harold (ed). *The Urban Economy*. New York: W. W. Norton, 1976.

James, Franklin. "Economic Distress in Central Cities," in Burchell and Listokin (eds.), *Cities Under Stress*. New Brunswick, N.J.: Rutgers University, Center for Urban Policy Research, 1981.

_____. "Private Reinvestment in Older Housing and Older Neighborhoods." 1979 (photocopy).

Jones, E. Terrance and Donald Phares. "Formula Feedback and Central Cities: The Case of the Comprehensive Employment and Training Act." *Urban Affairs Quarterly*. September, 1978, pp. 31–54.

Jusenius, Carol and Larry Ledebur. "A Myth in the Making: The Southern Economic Challenge and the Northern Economic Decline," in E. Blaine Liner and L. Lynch (eds.). *The Economics of Southern Growth*. Durham, N.C.: Southern Growth Policies Board, 1977.

Kaplan, Robert. *Financial Crisis of Our Cities*. Washington, D.C.: American Enterprise Institute, 1976.

Lupsha, Peter. "The New Federalism: Centralization and Local Control in Perspective," in Louis H. Masotti and Robert L. Lineberry (eds.). *The New Politics*. Cambridge, MA: Ballinger, 1976.

Markusen, Ann and Terry Fastrup. "The Regional War for Federal Aid." *The Public Interest*. Fall 1978.

Markusen, Ann et al. "Who Benefits from Intergovernmental Transfers?" in Robert W. Burchell and David Listokin, *Cities Under Stress: The Fiscal Crises of Urban America*. New Brunswick, NJ: Rutgers University, Center for Urban Policy Research, 1981.

Masotti, Louis H. and Robert Lineberry (eds.). *The New Urban Politics*. Cambridge, MA: Ballinger, 1976.

Merget, Astrid E. "Disparity and Diversity: Profiles of City Finances." *Urban Data Service*, Vol. 13, No. 8, August 1981 (entire issue).

Mitchell, William. "The Shape of Political Theory to Come. From Political Sociology to Political Economy," in S. M. Lipset (ed). *Politics and the Social Sciences*. New York: Oxford University Press, 1969.

Mohl, Raymond A. and Neil Betten. "The Failure of Industrial City Planning, Gary, Indiana, 1906–1910." *Journal of the American Institute of Planners*. Vol. 38, No. 4, 1972.

Molefsky, Barry and Dennis Zimmerman. "General Revenue Sharing and Alternatives: Economic Rationales Past and Present," in Fund for Public Policy Research. *Studies in Taxation, Public Finance and Related Subjects — A Compendium*. Vol. 3, Washington, D.C.: The Fund, 1979, p. 33.

Mollenkopf, John. "Fragile Grant: The Crisis of the Public Sector in American Cities." *Socialist Review*, July–September 1976.

_____. "Paths Toward the Post-Industrial Service City," in Burchell and Listokin (eds.), *Cities Under Stress: The Fiscal Crises of Urban America*. New Brunswick, NJ: Rutgers University, Center for Urban Policy Research, 1981.

_____. "The Post-War Politics of Urban Development." *Politics and Society*. Vol. 5 (3): 1975.

Molotch, Harvey. "The City as a Growth Machine: Toward a Political Economy of Place." *American Journal of Sociology*, September 1976.

_____. "Capital Versus Neighborhood, U.S.A. *Urban Affairs Quarterly*. March 1980.

Muller, Thomas. *Growing and Declining Urban Areas: A Fiscal Comparison*. Washington, D.C.: Urban Institute, 1975.

Mushkin, Selma, ed. "Public Prices: An Overview," in S. J. Mushkin, ed., *Public Prices for Public Products*. Washington, D.C.: The Urban Institute, 1972.

Nathan, Richard. "Understanding Central City Hardship." *Political Science Quarterly*, Vol. 91, No. 1: Spring 1976.

Nathan, Richard P. and Adams, Charles, Jr. *Revenue Sharing: The Second Round*. Washington, D.C.: The Brookings Institution, 1977.

_____ and Dommel, Paul R. *Federal Aid for Cities: A Multiple Strategy*. Washington, D.C.: The Brookings Institution, 1976.

_____. "Federal–Local Relations Under Block Grants." *Political Science Quarterly*. Vol. 93, No. 3, Fall 1978, p. 421.

Nathan, Richard P. et al. *Block Grants for Community Development*. Washington, D.C.: U.S. Department of Housing and Urban Development, 1976.

_____. "Cities in Crisis: The Impact of Federal Aid." League of Women Voters. *Current Focus*. (n.d.)

Newton, Kenneth. "Feeble Governments and Private Power: Urban Politics and Policies in the United States," in Louis H. Masotti and Robert L. Lineberry (eds.). *The New Urban Politics*. Cambridge, MA: Ballinger, 1976.

Norton, Robert. *City Life-Cycles and American Public Policy* (Ph.D. Dissertation). Princeton, N.J.: Princeton University, 1977.

O'Connor, James. *The Fiscal Crisis of the State*. New York, NY: St. Martin's Press, 1973.

Ott, David and Attiat Ott. *Projections of State and Local Expenditure*. Washington, D.C.: American Enterprise Institute, 1975.

Ott, David and John Yo. *New York City's Fiscal Crisis: Can the Trend Be Reversed?* Washington, D.C.: American Enterprise Institute, 1975.

Perry, David. "The Urban Renaissance for Business," *Nation*. March 1980.

Perry, David and Alfred Watkins, (eds.). "The Rise of the Sunbelt Cities." *Urban Affairs Annual Review*, Vol. 14. Beverly Hills: Sage, 1977.

Peterson, George E. "Federal Tax Policy and the Shaping of Urban Developments," in A. Solomon (ed). *The Prospective City*. op. cit.

_____. *The Fiscal and Financial Capacity of City Governments*. (Paper prepared for the Deputy Assistant Secretary of Urban Policy, U.S. Department of Housing and Urban Development, 1979.)

_____ et al. *Monitoring Urban Fiscal Conditions*. Washington, D.C.: Urban Institute, Forthcoming.

_____. *Urban Fiscal Monitoring*. Washington, D.C.: The Urban Institute, 1978.

Piven, Frances Fox. "Cutting Up the City Pie—Who Gets What?" *The New Republic*. February 5, 1972.

Pred, Allan. "The Inter-urban Transmission of Growth: Empirical Findings vs. Regional Planning Assumption." *Regional Studies*. Vol. 8-2, 1974.

Rivkin, Jeremy and Randy Barker. *The North Will Rise Again*. Boston, MA: Beacon, 1978.

Rostow, Walt W. "A National Policy Toward Regional Change," in G. Sternlieb and J. Hughes (eds.). *Revitalizing the Northeast*. New Brunswick, NJ: Rutgers University, Center for Urban Policy Research, 1978.

_____. "Regional Change in the Fifth Kontradieff Upswing," in David Perry and Alfred Watkins (eds.). *The Rise of the Sunbelt Cities*. *Urban Affairs Annual Review*, Vol. 14. Beverly Hills, CA: Sage, 1977.

Schmid, Gregory et al. *An Alternative Approach to General Revenue Sharing: A Needs Based Formula*. Menlo Park, CA: Institute for the Future, 1975.

Schurman, Franz and Sandy Close. "The Emergence of Global City, USA." *The Progressive*. Vol. 43, No. 1, 1979.

Solomon, Arthur (ed). *The Prospective City*. Cambridge, MA: MIT Press, 1980.

Stanley, David T. *Cities in Trouble*. Columbus, OH: Academy for Contemporary Problems, 1976.

Starr, Roger. "The Dilemma of Governmental Response," in George Sternlieb and J. W. Hughes (eds.), *Post-Industrial America*. New Brunswick, NJ: Rutgers University, Center for Urban Policy Research, 1978.

Stern, James L. "The Consequences of Plant Closures." *Journal of Human Resources*. Winter 1972.

Sternlieb, George. "The City as Sandbox." *The Public Interest*. Fall 1971.

_____. "New Dimensions of the Urban Crisis," in Burchell and Listokin, *Cities Under Stress: The Fiscal Crises of Urban America*. New Brunswick, NJ: Rutgers University, Center for Urban Policy Research, 1981.

_____. "New Regional and Metropolitan Realities of America." *Journal of the American Institute of Planners*. July 1977.

_____. "Regional Market Variations: The Northeast vs. the Southwest." *Journal of the American Real Estate and Urban Economic Association*. Vol. 5, No. 1, Spring 1977.

_____. *The Tenement Landlord*. New Brunswick, NJ: Rutgers University Press, 1966.

_____ and Robert W. Burchell. *Residential Abandonment: The Tenement Landlord Revisited*. New Brunswick, NJ: Rutgers University, Center for Urban Policy Research, 1972.

_____ and James W. Hughes (eds.). *Post-Industrial America: Metropolitan Decline and Interregional Job Shifts*. New Brunswick, NJ: Rutgers University, Center for Urban Policy Research, 1975.

_____. *Revitalizing the Northeast*. New Brunswick, NJ: Rutgers University, Center for Urban Policy Research, 1978.

Surrey, Stanley. "Federal Income Tax Reform Replacing Tax Expenditures with Direct Governmental Assistance." *Harvard Law Review*. Vol. 84, No. 2, Nov. 2, 1970.

_____. "Tax Incentives as a Device for Implementing Government Policy: A Comparison with Direct Governmental Expenditures." *Harvard Law Review*. Vol. 83, No. 4, February 1970.

Thompson, Wilbur. "Aging Industries and Cities: Time and Tides of the Northeast," in George Sternlieb and James W. Hughes (eds.), *Revitalizing the Northeast*. New Brunswick, NJ: Rutgers University, Center for Urban Policy Research, 1978.

_____. "The City as a Distorted Price System." *Psychology Today*. August 1968.

_____. "Economic Processes and Employment Problems in Declining Metropolitan Areas," in George Sternlieb and James W. Hughes, *Post-Industrial America*. New Brunswick, NJ: Rutgers University, Center for Urban Policy Research, 1975.

_____. "The National System of Cities as an Object of Public Policy." *Urban Studies*. Vol. 9, No. 1, February 1972.

U.S. Comptroller General. *New York City's Fiscal Problems: A Long Road Still Lies Ahead.* Washington, D.C.: U.S. Government Printing Office, 1979.

_____. *Why the Formula for Allocating Community Development Block Grants Should be Improved.* Washington, D.C.: U.S. General Accounting Office, 1976.

U.S. Congress. House Committee on Banking, Finance and Urban Affairs. Subcommittee on the City. *City Needs and the Responsiveness of Federal Grant Programs.* 95th Congress, 2nd Session, August 1978. Washington, D.C.: U.S. Government Printing Office, 1978.

_____. *How Cities Can Grow Old Gracefully.* Washington, D.C.: U.S. Government Printing Office, 1977.

_____, Joint Economic Committee. Subcommittee on Economic Growth and Stabilization on Fiscal and Intergovernmental Policy. *The Current Fiscal Condition of Cities: A Survey of 67 of the 75 Largest Cities: A Study. 95th Congress, 1st Session, July 28, 1977.* Washington, D.C.: U.S. Government Printing Office, 1977.

_____, Senate Committee on Banking, Housing and Urban Affairs. Subcommittee on the City. *City Needs and the Responsiveness of Federal Programs.* Washington, D.C.: The Committee (n.d.).

The Growth of Intergovernmental Transfers as a Phenomenon

Adams, Charles F. and Dan L. Crippen. *The Fiscal Impact of General Revenue Sharing on Local Governments: A Report Prepared for the Office of Revenue Sharing*, U.S. Department of the Treasury. Columbus, OH: Ohio State University, School of Public Administration, 1978.

Aronson, Leanne and Carol Shapiro. *The State's Role in Urban Economic Development: An Urban Government Perspective.* Washington, D.C.: U.S. Department of Commerce, Economic Development Administration, 1978.

Bahl, Roy (ed.). *The Fiscal Outlook for Cities: Implications of a National Urban Policy.* New York, NY: Syracuse University Press, 1978.

Brammer, Dana B. "State Aid to Local Governments in the Mississippi." *Public Administration Survey.* July 1979, entire issue.

Break, George F. *Intergovernmental Fiscal Relations in the United States.* Washington, D.C.: The Brookings Institution, 1979.

Browning, Clyde. *The Geography of Federal Outlays: An Introductory and Comparative Inquiry.* Chapel Hill, NC: University of North Carolina, 1973.

Caputo, David A. "General Revenue Sharing and American Federalism: Towards the Year 2000." *Annals, American Academy of Political and Social Sciences.* May 1975, pp. 63–74.

_____. and Richard L. Cole. *Urban Politics and Decentralization: The Case of Federal Revenue Sharing.* Lexington, MA: Lexington Books, 1974

Cole, R. L. "Revenue Sharing: Citizen Participation and Social Service Aspects." *Annals, American Academy of Political and Social Sciences*, May 1975, pp. 63–74.

Comtois, Joseph D. and Jeremiah Donoghue. *Changing Patterns of Federal Aid to State and Local Governments.* Washington, D.C.: U.S. General Accounting Office, 1977.

Comtois, Joseph D. and R. J. Rosensteel. *Analysis of Intergovernmental Fiscal and Agency Issues.* Washington, D.C.: U.S. General Accounting Office, 1978.

Cotham, James C. III, and Kenneth E. Quindry (eds.). *Needs and Revenue: The Dilemma of Urban America.* Knoxville, Tenn.: Center for Business and Economic Research, The University of Tennessee, 1971.

Dickstein, Dennis. *State–Local Fiscal Relations Working Paper.* Boston, MA: Massachusetts Office of Community Affairs, Office of Local Assistance, 1977.

Dresch, Steven P. "Federalism, Tax Transfer Substitutions and the Distribution of Income," *1971 Proceedings of the Sixty-Fourth Annual Conference.* Columbus, OH: National Tax Association, 1972.

Elazar, Daniel J. "Fiscal Questions and Political Answers in Intergovernmental Finance." *Public Administration Review*, September/October, 1972.

Faith, Roger L. "Local Fiscal Crises and Intergovernmental Grants: A Suggested Hypothesis." *Public Choice.* Vol. 34 (3–4), 1979, pp. 316–331.

Firestine, Robert E. et al. "Intergovernmental Fiscal Cooperation in Growing Metropolitan Economies." *Annals of Regional Science*, November 1978, pp. 12–20.

Frieden, Bernard J. and Marshall Kaplan. *The Politics of Neglect: Urban Aid From Model Cities to Revenue Sharing*. Cambridge, MA: MIT Press, 1975.

Gabler, Richard. *Federal Grants: Their Effects on State–Local Expenditures, Employment Levels, and Wage Rates*. Washington, D.C.: U.S. Advisory Commission on Intergovernmental Relations, 1977.

──────────. *The States and Intergovernmental Aids*. Washington, D.C.: U.S. Advisory Commission on Intergovernmental Relations, 1977.

Goetz, Charles J. *What is Revenue Sharing?* Washington, D.C.: Urban Institute, 1972.

Gorham, William and Nathan Glazer (eds.). *The Urban Predicament*. Washington, D.C.: Urban Institute, 1976.

Griffin, Ed. "Revenue Sharing: Reenactment Crisis." *Southern City*. June 1979, p. 10–11 +.

Hale, George E. and Marian Lief Palley. "Federal Grants to the States: Who Governs?" *Administration and Society*. May 1979, pp. 3–27.

Haskell, M. C. "Decentralization or Concentration of Power? The Revenue Sharing Paradox." *Journal of Economic Issues*. June 1977, pp. 401–20.

Hausner, Victor A. *Coordinated Urban Economic Development: A Case Study Catalogue*. Washington, D.C.: National Council for Urban Economic Development, 1977.

Hendler, Charles I. and J. Norman Reid. *Federal Outlays in Fiscal 1978: A Comparison of Metropolitan and Nonmetropolitan Areas*. Washington, D.C.: U.S. Advisory Commission on Intergovernmental Relations, 1978.

Hilleabrand, B. F. "Counties: The Emerging Force." *Annals, American Academy of Political and Social Sciences*. November 1974, pp. 91–98.

Honey, Harold A. *State Urban Development Strategies*. Washington, D.C.: Council of State Planning Agencies, 1977.

Horton, Frank. *Federal/State/Local Cooperation*. Washington, D.C.: U.S. Government Printing Office, 1977.

Hubbell, L. Kenneth. *Fiscal Crisis in American Cities: The Federal Response*. Cambridge, MA: Ballinger Publishing Co., 1979.

Jesmer, Barry. *General Revenue Sharing: Designing a Formula Which Does Not Discourage or Distort Local Variations in Financing and Delivering Services*. Springfield, VA: NTIS, 1975.

Jiana Koplos, and Nancy Ammon. "The Growing Link Between the Federal Government and State and Local Government Financing." *Federal Reserve, St. Louis*. May 1977, pp. 13–20.

Juster, F. Thomas. *The Economic and Political Impact of General Revenue Sharing*. Washington, D.C.: U.S. National Science Foundation, 1976.

Keyserling, Leon. "Revenue Sharing—Implications for Intergovernmental Fiscal Systems." *National Tax Journal*. September 1971, pp. 313.

Kidwell, David S. and Charles A. Trzcinka. "Are All U.S. Cities Paying the Price for New York's Default?" *The Daily Bond Buyer—PSA Supplement*. November 13, 1980, pp. 28, 27.

Le Gates, Richard T. and Mary C. Morgan. "The Perils of Special Revenue Sharing for Community Development." *Journal of the American Institute of Planners*. July 1973, pp. 254–264.

Light, A. R. "State Agency Perspectives on Federalism and the Suburbs." *Social Sciences Quarterly*, September 1978, pp. 284–94.

Loucks, Edward A. "The New Federalism and the Suburbs." *Growth and Change*. October 1978, pp. 2–7.

McLure, Charles E., Jr. "Revenue Sharing: Alternative to Rational Fiscal Federalism?" *Public Policy*. Summer 1971, pp. 523–24.

Mandel, Marvin. "Revenue Sharing—Supplement or Substitute?" *State Government*. Winter 1973, pp. 16–18.

Manvel, A. D. "The Fiscal Impact of Revenue Sharing." *Annals, American Academy of Political and Social Sciences*. May 1975, pp. 36–49.

Mieszkowski, Peter and Oakland, William H. (eds.). *Fiscal Federalism and Grants-in-Aid*. Washington, D.C.: The Urban Institute, 1979.

Morris, Richard S. *Bum Rap on America's Cities: The Real Cause of Urban Decay.* Englewood Cliffs, NJ: Prentice-Hall, 1978, p. 198.

Municipal Finance Officers Association. *Revenue Sharing: An Analysis.* Washington, D.C.: The Association, 1979.

Nathan, R. P. "Federalism and Shifting Nature of Fiscal Relations." *Annals of American Academy of Political and Social Sciences.* May 1975, pp. 120–29.

_____. "The Roots and Sprouts of Revenue Sharing." *Publius: The Journal of Federalism.* Vol. 6, (4), Fall 1976.

_____. "The Uses of Shared Revenue." *Journal of Finance.* May 1975, pp. 557–65.

_____ and Charles F. Adams, Jr. *Revenue Sharing: The Second Round.* Washington, D.C.: The Brookings Institution, 1977.

_____ and P. R. Dommel. "Federal–Local Relations Under Block Grants. *Political Science Quarterly.* Fall 1978, pp. 421–42.

Netzer, Dick. "State–Local Finance and Intergovernmental Fiscal Relations." *The Economics of Public Finance.* Washington, D.C.: The Brookings Institution, 1974.

Noto, N. A. "Simplifying Intergovernmental Transfer: The Lessons of Community Development Block Grants." *National Tax Journal.* September 1977, pp. 259–67.

Oakland, William. *Financial Relief for Troubled Cities.* Columbus, OH: Academy for Contemporary Problems, 1978.

Oates, Wallace E. *The Political Economy of Fiscal Federalism.* Lexington, MA: Lexington Books, 1977.

Olympus Research Corporation. *State Responses to Central City Problems.* Prepared for the Council of State Planning Agencies. Salt Lake City, UT, 1971 (Mimeographed).

Peirce, Neal R. "Fiscal Crises Illustrate Growing Interdependence." *National Journal Reports.* February 22, 1975.

Puryear, David L. et al. "Fiscal Distress: An Imbalance Between Resources and Needs." *Occasional Papers in Housing and Community Affairs.* Vol. 4, pp. 148–168. Robert Paul Boyton (ed.), Washington, D.C.: U.S. Department of Housing and Urban Development, 1979.

Quindry, K. E. and Soule, D. M. "Revenue Sharing Between State and Local Governments: An Economic Formula." *Growth and Change.* July 1970, pp. 8–13.

Reischauer, Robert D. "General Revenue Sharing—The Program's Incentives." *Financing the New Federalism.* Washington, D.C.: Johns Hopkins University Press, 1975.

Richardson, Charles. *The State of State–Local Revenue Sharing.* Washington, D.C.: U.S. Advisory Commission on Intergovernmental Relations, 1980.

Rittenmoure, R. L. and Pluta, J. E. "Theory of Intergovernmental Grants and Local Government." *Growth and Change.* July 1977, pp. 31–37.

Rondinelli, Dennis. "Revenue-Sharing and American Cities—Analysis of the Federal Experiment in Local Assistance." *Journal of American Institute of Planners.* September 1975, pp. 319–332A.

Rutledge, P. J. "Federal–Local Relations and the Mission of the City." *Annals, American Academy of Political and Social Sciences.* November 1974, pp. 77–90.

Sacks, Seymour and Richter, Albert J. *Recent Trends in Federal and State Aid to Local Governments.* Washington, D.C.: U.S. Advisory Commission on Intergovernmental Relations, 1980.

Shannon, J. "Financing Cities: The Case for New Federalism." *Growth and Change.* October 1970, pp. 33–37.

Slavet, Joseph, et al. *Financing State and Local Services.* Lexington, MA: Lexington Books, 1975.

Stanfield, Rochelle L. "Getting the States and Regions to Help Out Their Cities." *National Journal.* October 15, 1977, pp. 1604–1605 + .

Stephens, G. Ross and Olson, Gerald W. *Pass-Through Federal Aid and Interlevel Finance in the American Federal System, 1957 to 1977,* Volume I. Springfield, VA: NTIS, 1979.

Strauss, R. P. "Overhauling the Federal Aid System: Redesigning Several Revenue Sharing and Countercyclical Aid Programs." *National Tax Journal.* September 1976, pp. 341–55.

Teitelbaum, Fred and Simon, Alice E. *Bypassing the States: Wrong Turn for Urban Aid.* Washington, D.C.: National Governors Association Center for Policy Research, 1979.

"The Intergovernmental Grant System in the U.S.A. as Seen by Local, State and Federal Officials." *Local Finance*. October 1977, pp. 14–17.

Tippet, Frank. *Trends in Fiscal Federalism 1954–1974*. Washington, D.C.: U.S. Advisory Commission on Intergovernmental Relations, 1975.

Tomer, J. F. "Revenue Sharing and Intrastate Fiscal Mismatch: A Critical View." *Public Finance Quarterly*. October 1977, pp. 445–70.

United States Advisory Commission on Intergovernmental Relations. *Significant Features of Fiscal Federalism* (Annual). Washington, D.C.: The Commission, June 1970.

_____. *General Revenue Sharing: An ACIR Re-evaluation*. Washington, D.C. Government Printing Office, 1974.

_____. *Significant Factors of Fiscal Federalism, 1979–1980*. Washington, D.C.: The Advisory Commission on Intergovernmental Relations, 1980.

_____. *State Administrators: Opinions on Administrative Change, Federal Aid, Federal Relationships*. Washington, D.C.: U.S. Government Printing Office, 1980.

_____. *The States and Distressed Communities: The 1980 Annual Report*. Washington, D.C.: U.S. Advisory Commission on Intergovernmental Relations, 1981.

_____. *State–Local Finances in Recession and Inflation: An Economic Analysis*. Washington, D.C.: The Commission, 1979.

U.S. Comptroller General. *Changing Patterns of Federal Aid to State and Local Governments, 1969–1975*. Washington, D.C.: U.S. General Accounting Office (1978).

_____. *Perspectives on Intergovernmental Policy and Fiscal Relations*. Washington, D.C.: U.S. General Accounting Office, 1980.

U.S. Congress. House Committee on Banking, Finance and Urban Affairs. Subcommittee on the City. *Revenue Sharing with the States: Hearing. . .96th Congress, 1st Session*. Washington, D.C.: U.S. Government Printing Office, 1979.

_____, House of Representatives. Committee on Government Operations. *Federal Response to Financial Emergencies of Cities. Hearings, June 23, 25, 26, 1975, 94th Congress, 1st Session*. Washington, D.C.: U.S. Government Printing Office, 1975.

_____, Joint Economic Committee. *Is the Urban Crisis Over? Hearings Before the Subcommittee on Fiscal and Intergovernmental Policy*, March, 1979. Washington, D.C.: U.S. Government Printing Office, 1979.

_____. *State and Local Government Finance and the Changing National Economy. Hearings. . .96th Congress, Second Session, July 28, 1980*. Washington, D.C.: U.S. Government Printing Office, 1980.

_____, Senate Committee on Governmental Affairs. *General Revenue Sharing—The Issues Before U.S. Hearings Before the Subcommittee on Intergovernmental Relations, July 24, September 20, and November 15, 1979*. Washington, D.C.: U.S. Government Printing Office, 1980.

_____. *Finances of Municipalities and Township Governments*. Washington, D.C.: U.S. Government Printing Office, 1979.

_____. *Local Government Finances in Selected Metropolitan Areas, 1978–1979*. Washington, D.C.: U.S. Government Printing Office, 1980.

U.S. Department of Housing and Urban Development. *Developmental Needs of Small Cities*. Washington, D.C.: The Department, 1979.

_____, Office of Policy Development and Research. *1979 Annual Report of the Financial Management Capacity Sharing Program*. Washington, D.C.: The Department, 1980.

U.S. Department of the Treasury. *Antirecessionary Payment Summaries*, Washington, D.C.: Department of the Treasury, 1975.

_____. *General Revenue Quarterly Payments, 22nd–34th Payments, 1978–1981*. Washington, D.C.: Department of the Treasury, 1978.

United States. Senate—Commission on Governmental Affairs. *General Revenue Sharing— The Issues Before Us: Hearings July 24–November 15, 1979*. Washington, D.C.: The Commission, 1979.

United States. Senate Committee on Finance. *Targeted Fiscal Assistance to State and Local Governments: Hearings, March 12–26, 1979*. Washington, D.C.: The Committee, 1979.

U.S. Office of Management and The Budget. *Federal Aid to States and Local Governments*. Washington, D.C.: Office of Management and Budget (n.d.).

Vogel, Robert C. and Robert P. Trost. "The Response of State Government Receipts to Economic Fluctuations and the Allocation of Counter-Cyclical Revenue Sharing Grants." *Review of Economics and Statistics*. August 1979, pp. 389–400.

Walker, David B. *Changing Pattern of Federal Assistance to State and Local Governments. Significant Trends in Federal Aid* (unpublished paper). July 27, 1976.

Weicher, J. C. "Aid, Expenditures, and Local Government Structure." *National Tax Journal*. December 1972, pp. 573–83.

Zimmerman, Joseph F. *Pragmatic Federalism: The Reassignment of Functional Responsibility*. Washington, D.C.: U.S. Advisory Commission on Intergovernmental Relations, 1979.

The Array of Intergovernmental Revenues

Augenbick, John. *Systems of State Support for School District Capital Expenditures*. Denver, CO: Education Commission of the States, 1977.

Barro, Stephen M. *The Impact of Intergovernmental Aid on Public School Spending*. (Ph.D. dissertation), 1974. (unpublished)

Bassi, Lauri and Fechter, Alan. *The Implications for Fiscal Substitution and Occupational Displacement Under an Expanded CETA Title VI*. Springfield, VA: NTIS, 1979.

Bendict, Marc and James P. Zais. *Incomes and Housing: Lessons from Experiments with Housing Allowances*. Washington, D.C.: Urban Institute, 1978.

Blair, B. O. and McKelvey, D. J. "Analysis of State Transit Funding Methodologies." *Transportation Research Record*, No. 589, 1977, pp. 33–35.

Blume, Lois. "Returning of Laid-Off Municipal Workers Under CETA—The Law, The Regulations, and Congressional Intent." *Adherent*. April 1976, pp. 36–56.

Bradley, Robert. "New Federalism and the Texas Urban Poor." *Texas Business Review*, March–April 1980, pp. 110–116.

Dahms, L. D. "Finding Revenue for Urban Transportation," in *Urban Transportation Economics* (Transportation Research Board Paper No. 181). Washington, D.C.: Transportation Research Board, 1978, pp. 222–224.

Dueker, Kenneth J. *Public Transportation Planning Effectiveness: Case Studies*. Iowa City, IA: University of Iowa, Institute of Urban and Regional Research, 1978.

Ferre II, Joseph S. *Financing Courthouse Facilities*. Chapel Hill, NC: University of North Carolina, Institute of Government, 1977.

Foster, Jack. *State Subsidies to Local Corrections: Final Report*. Lexington, KY: Council of State Governments, 1977.

Gatti, J. F. and Tashman, L. J. "Equalizing Matching Grants and the Allocative and Distributive Objective of Public School Financing: Reply." *National Tax Journal*, June 1978, pp. 201–202.

Government Information Services. *Federal Funding Guide*. Washington, D.C.: Government Information Services, 1982.

Hammermesh, Daniel S. and H. Pitcher. "Economic Formulas for Manpower Revenue-Sharing." *Industrial and Labor Relations*, July 1974, pp. 551–524A.

Herlihy, E. T. and Eigen, J. M. *Evaluation of Intergovernmental Responsibilities for Maintenances*. Springfield, VA: NTIS, 1979.

Hovey, Harold A. *Development Financing for Distressed Areas*. Washington, D.C.: Northeast-Midwest Institute, 1979.

Johnson, Marvin B. et al. "Equalizing Matching Grants and the Allocative and Distributive Objectives of Public School Financing: Comment and Reply." *National Tax Journal*. June 1978, pp. 197–202.

Levitan, Sar A. *Programs in Aid of the Poor for the 1980s*. Baltimore, MD: Johns Hopkins University Press, 1980.

Lookingbill, Dean et al. *Measuring the Achievement of National Urban Transportation Goals and Objectives: The Role of Metropolitan Planning Organizations*. Iowa City, IA: University of Iowa, Institute of Urban and Regional Research, 1978.

Lugar, R. G. "The Federal Government's Role in Relieving Cities of the Fiscal Burden of Low-Income Concentration." *National Tax Journal*, September 1976, pp. 286–92.

Mills, V. Raymond. "Fiscal Issues in National Transportation Policy." *Traffic Quarterly*, April 1979, pp. 311–325.

Moak, Lennox L. "Responsibilities, Financing and Management of Local Authorities in the United States." *Local Finance*, September 1976, pp. 16–30.

New York State Urban Development Corporation. *A Step-by-Step Guide to Resources for Economic Development*. Albany, NY: New York State Urban Development Corporation, 1980.

Newark, New Jersey. Department of Administration, Office of Planning and Grantsmanship. *Comprehensive Economic Development Strategy*. Newark, New Jersey: Department of Administration, 1980.

Oakland, W. H. "Incidence and Other Fiscal Impacts of State Assumption of Education Costs: Baltimore." *National Tax Journal*. March 1976, pp. 73–85.

Oakland, William. *Financial Relief for Troubled Cities*. Columbus, OH: Academy for Contemporary Problems, 1978.

Owen, Wilfred. *Transportation for Cities*. Washington, D.C.: The Brookings Institution, 1976.

Porter, Alan L. *Effects of Federal Funding on State and Local Transportation Findings* (conference paper). Atlanta, GA: Georgia Institute of Technology, School of Industrial and Systems Engineering, 1978.

Rechel, R. E. "Study on Transit Revenue Sources, Part 1," in *Urban Transportation Economics* (Transportation Board Research Paper No. 181). Washington, D.C.: Transportation Research Board, 1978, pp. 224–225.

Reischauer, R. D. "The Federal Government's Role in Relieving Cities of the Fiscal Burdens of Concentrations of Low-Income Persons." *National Tax Journal*. September 1976, pp. 293–311.

Rocheleau, Bruce and Steven Warren. "Health Planners and Local Public Finance—The Case for Revenue Sharing." *Public Health Reports*. July–August 1980.

Schafer, Robert. "Public Housing Operating Costs, Management and Subsidies," in *Operating Subsidies for Public Housing*. Boston, MA: Citizen Housing and Planning Association, 1975.

Smith, David G. "Federal Health Grants and Regional Health Politics." *Publius: The Journal of Federalism*, 1978.

Steiner, Gilbert Y. *State of Welfare*. Washington, D.C.: The Brookings Institution, 1971.

Sternlieb, George and David Listokin (eds.). *New Tools for Economic Development: The Enterprise Zone, Development Bank, and RFC*. New Brunswick, NJ: Rutgers University, Center for Urban Policy Research, 1981.

Stocker, F. D. "Diversification of the Local Revenue System: Income and Sales Taxes, User Charges, Federal Grants." *National Tax Journal*, Vol. 29, September 1976, pp. 312–321.

Taub, Leon W. *Evaluation of the National Impacts of the Local Public Works Program: Final Report* (Draft). Washington, D.C.: U.S. Department of Commerce, 1978.

Timpane, Michael (ed). *The Federal Interest in Financing School*. Cambridge, MA: Ballinger, 1978.

Tolius, David. *Northeastern State Estimates of Fiscal Relief from Welfare Reform*. New York NY: CONEG Policy Research Center, 1977.

Transportation Research Board, Washington, D.C. *Urban Transportation Economics: Proceedings of Five Workshops of Pricing Alternatives, Economic Regulations, Labor Issues, Marketing and Government Financing Responsibilities*. Springfield, VA: NTIS 1978.

Tucillo, John A. *Federal Regulations, Housing Programs, and the Flow of Urban Credit*. Washington, D.C.: Urban Institute, 1980.

U.S. Advisory Commission on Intergovernmental Relations. *Federal Aid to State and Local Governments*. Washington, D.C.: Advisory Commission on Intergovernmental Relations (n.d.)

_____. *Toward a More Balanced Transportation: New Intergovernmental Proposals*. Washington, D.C.: U.S. Government Printing Office, 1975.

U.S. Comptroller General. *Analysis of the Allocation Formula for Federal Mass Transit Subsidies*. Springfield, VA: NTIS 1979.

U.S. Department of Housing and Urban Development. *Urban Redevelopment Resources: Economic Development Programs Around the United States*. Atlanta, Georgia: Office of Program Planning, 1980.

U.S. Office of Management and Budget. *Budget of the United States Government*, Fiscal Year 1983. Washington, D.C.: U.S. Government Printing Office (1982), 1.

_____. *Budget of the United States Government, Fiscal Year 1983: Appendix*. Washington, D.C.: U.S. Government Printing Office (1982).

_____. *Catalog of Federal Domestic Assistance*. Washington, D.C.: U.S. Government Printing Office, 1980–.

_____. *Major Themes and Additional Budget Details, Fiscal Year 1983*. Washington, D.C.: U.S. Government Printing Office (1982).

Urban Systems Research and Engineering, Inc., Cambridge, Massachusetts. *Research and Evaluation Regarding the Section 8 Housing Assistance Program*. Springfield, VA: NTIS 1978.

Vaughan, Robert J. and Peter Pearse. *Federal Economic Development Programs: A Framework for Design and Evaluation*.

Verneg, Georges et al. *Federal Activities in Urban Economic Development*. Santa Monica, California: Rand, 1979.

Vincent, Phillip E. *Fiscal Responses of School Districts: Final Report*. Denver, CO: Education Commission of the States, 1978.

Walker, D. S. "Cost Allocation Forms of Aid and Fund and Administrative Structure," in *Urban Transportation Economics* (Transportation Research Board Paper No. 181). Washington, D.C.: Transportation Research Board, 1978, pp. 240–44.

Wilcox, M. C. and S. J. Mushkin. "Public Pricing and Family Income Problems of Eligibility Standards," in S. J. Mushkin (ed.), *Public Prices for Public Products*. Washington, D.C.: The Urban Institute, 1972.

Regional Competition for Intergovernmental Allocations

Alonso, William. *New National Concerns and Regional Policy*. Occasional Papers for the National Bureau of Economic Research Volume 4, No. 3, Summer 1977.

Bahl, Roy and David Puryear. "Regional Tax Base Sharing—Possibilities and Implications." *National Tax Journal*. September 1976, pp. 328–335.

Beaton, W. Patrick. *Regional Tax Base Sharing: A Critique of Current Proposals*. Charlotte, N.C.: University of North Carolina, 1978.

Biggar, Jeanne C. "The Sunning of America: Migration to the Sunbelt." *Population Bulletin*, March 1979.

Boren, David L. "The Sunbelt Myth—Blessing or Curse?" *Regional Economics and Business*, April 1980, pp. 18–21.

Brown, Lynn E. and Richard F. Syron. "Cities, Suburbs and Regions." *New England Economic Review*, January–February 1979, pp. 41–61.

Coalition of Northeastern Governors Policy Research Center and the Northeast–Midwest Institute. *The Economic Effects on the Northeast–Midwest Region of Current and Potential National Defense Expenditures*. Washington, D.C.: The Institute, 1979.

Dresch, Stephen P. and Daniel A. Updegrove. *Regional Modeling of the Industrial and Income Distributional Consequences of Secular and Policy-Induced Economic Change: Final Report*. New Haven, CT: Institute for Demographic and Economic Studies, 1978.

Dusenbury, Patricia J. *Regional Targeting*. Research Triangle Park, NC: Southern Growth Policies Board, 1979.

_____ and Thad L. Beyle. *Southern Cities and the National Urban Policy*. Research Triangle Park, NC: Southern Growth Policies Board, 1979.

Gannon, James P. "Snowbelt Blitz: Northern States Start Drive for Federal Aid for Slack Economics; but South Girds to Guard Its Interests, Leaving Carter as Man in Middle." *Wall Street Journal*. January 17, 1977.

Glendening, Parris. *Federal Impact of Regional Councils.* College Park, MD: University of Maryland, Department of Government and Politics, 1975.

Harrington, Michael J. "In Congress, An Effort to Reverse the Tide." *Empire State Report.* October–November 1976, pp. 353 and 355.

Havemann, Joel et al. "Federal Spending: The North's Loss is the Sunbelt's Gain." *National Journal.* June 26, 1976, pp. 878–91.

_____ and Rochelle L. Stanfield. "A Year Later, the Frostbelt Strikes Back." *National Journal.* 2 July 1977, pp. 1028–37.

"House Group Wants to Stem Sunbelt Flow." *Washington Post.* September 2, 1976.

"In Northeast: A Challenge to the Growing Muscle of the Sunbelt." *U.S. News and World Report.* October 18, 1976.

Jhun, U. J. and Cicarelli J. "Regionalism, Redistribution and Federal Spending." *Nebraska Journal of Economic Business.* Autumn 1978, pp. 29–36.

Jusenius, Carol L. *Documenting the "Decline" of the North and the Rise of the South (or Vice Versa). City and Regional Planning,* 1977.

_____ and Larry C. Ledebur. *A Myth in the Making: The Southern Economic Challenge and Northern Economic Decline.* Springfield, VA: NTIS, 1976.

_____. "The Northern Tier and the Sunbelt: Conflict or Cooperation?" *Challenge.* March–April 1977, pp. 44–49.

Kahn, Herman. *The Future of the U.S. and Its Regions: National Trends and Influences.* New York: Hudson Institute, 1977, p. 1975.

King, Wayne. "Federal Funds Pour into Sunbelt States." *The New York Times.* February 9, 1976, p. 24.

Mcmanus, Michael J. "The Need for a Northeast Coalition." With Appendix. *Issues Facing the Northeast* (unpublished paper), New York, NY: Fund for the City of New York, 1976.

Maffei, Barbara and John Mitrisin. *Patterns of Regional Change: The Changes, The Federal Role, and the Federal Response.* Washington, D.C.: U.S. Government Printing Office, 1977.

Martin, John F. *Regional Inequities in Federal Education Aid: The Case of ESEA Title I.* Washington, D.C.: Northeast–Midwest Institute, 1978.

Moynihan, Daniel P. "The Politics and Economics of Regional Growth." National Interest. Spring 1978, pp. 3–21.

National Economic Research Institute. *Urban Development Action Grants: A Study of Regional Influence.* Austin, Texas: The Institute, 1979.

National Governor's Association. *Understanding the Fiscal Condition of the States.* Washington, D.C.: The Association, 1976.

Newman, Monroe and Brindey J. Lewis. "Regional Resource Allocation." *Public Administration Review.* July–August 1979, p. 355–362.

Northeast-Midwest Institute. *A Case of Inequity: Regional Patterns in Defense Expenditures, 1950–1977.* Washington, D.C.: The Institute, 1977.

_____. *The Federal Balance of Payments: Regional Implications of Government Spending.* Washington, D.C.: The Institute, 1980.

_____. *Focus on Regional Cooperation—North–South Summit.* Washington, D.C.: The Institute, 1978.

_____. *A Regional Analysis of the President's Fiscal 1982 Budget.* Washington, D.C.: The Institute, 1980.

_____. *Regional Disparities in Federal Medicaid Assistance.* Washington, D.C.: The Institute, 1977.

_____. *The Regional Distribution of Public Service Jobs: A Comparison of the Present Program with Welfare Reform Options.* Washington, D.C.: The Institute, 1978.

_____. *The Regional Impact of the Cities at Chrysler.* Washington, D.C.: The Institute, 1979.

_____. *The Regional Impact of the Welfare Reform: A Comparison of H. R. 4904 with Present Law.* Washington, D.C.: The Institute, 1979.

_____. *The State of the Region: Economic Trends of the 1970s in the Northeast and Midwest.* Washington, D.C.: The Institute, 1979.

_____. *The State of the Region 1981: Economic Trends in the Northeast and Midwest.* Washington, D.C.: The Institute, 1980.

_____. *Targeting Federal Procurement to Areas of Need.* Washington, D.C.: The Institute, 1978.

_____. *Unprotected Flank: Regional and Strategic Imbalances in Defense Spending Patterns.* Washington, D.C.: The Institute, 1980.

Petersen, John E. *Frost Belt vs. Sun Belt: Special Report.* Boston, MA: First Boston Corporation, 1977.

Peterson, David. *The Relative Need of States and Regions for Federal Aid.* Research Triangle Park, NC: Southern Growth Policies Board, 1979.

Peirce, Neal R. "Northeast Governors Map Battle Plan for Fight Over Federal Funds Flow." *National Journal.* November 27, 1976, pp. 1695–1700.

_____. "The Northeast Maps Battle Plan for Economic Revival Report on the Meeting of the Newly Formed Coalition of Northeastern Governors, Saratoga Springs, New York, November 13–14, 1976," *Empire State Report* 2: 406–13. December 1976.

Rifkin, Jeremy. *The North Will Rise Again: Pensions, Power and Politics in the 1980s.* Boston, MA: Beacon Press, 1978, p. 279.

Rofuse, Robert W., Jr. *The New Regional Debate: A National Overview.* Washington, D.C.: National Governors Association, 1977.

Rones, Philip L. "Moving to the Sun: Beyond Job Control, 1968 to 1978." *Monthly Labor Review,* March 1980.

Roth, Dennis M. "Regional Employment Shifts and Wage Changes," in *Patterns of Regional Change—The Changes, the Federal Role and the Federal Response: Selected Essays.* Washington, D.C.: U.S. Government Printing Office, 1977.

Smith, Edward K., ed. "New Direction in Federal Economic Development Programs." *Explorations in Economic Research.* Summer 1977, pp. 345–460.

Southern Growth Policies Board. *The Economics of Southern Growth.* Washington, D.C.: The Board (n.d.)

_____. *Improving the Intergovernmental System.* Washington, D.C.: The Board (n.d.)

_____. *Tax Reform and Southern Economic Development.* Washington, D.C.: The Board (n.d.)

Sternlieb, George and James W. Hughes. "New Regional and Metropolitan Realities of America." *Journal of the American Institute of Planners.* July 1977.

_____ (eds.). *Post-Industrial America: Metropolitan Decline and Inter-Regional Job Shifts.* New Brunswick, NJ: Rutgers University, Center for Urban Policy Research, 1975.

Sutton, Horace. "Sunbelt vs. Frostbelt: A Second Civil War?" *Saturday Review.* April 15, 1978, pp. 28–37.

Syron, Richard. "New England's Relative Performance in the Recovery." *New England's Economic Indicators.* Federal Reserve Bank of Boston: October 1977.

Toal, William D. "The South's Share of the Federal Pie." *Monthly Review.* Federal Reserve Bank of Atlanta: April 1977.

U.S. Advisory Commission on Intergovernmental Relations. *Regional Growth, Flows of Federal Funds, 1952–76: A Commission Report.* Washington, D.C.: The Commission, 1980.

_____. *Regional Growth: Historic Perspective.* Washington, D.C.: The Commission, 1980.

U.S. Department of Housing and Urban Development. *Local Economic Development Tools and Techniques: A Guidebook for Local Government.* Washington, D.C.: U.S. Government Printing Office, 1979.

Vehorn, Charles. *The Regional Distribution of Federal Grants-in-Aid.* Columbus, OH: Academy for Contemporary Problems, 1977.

Walker, David B. "Localities and Federal Aid." *National Civic Review.* January 1979.

Wedner, Ralph. *Revitalizing the Northeastern Economy—A Survey for Action.* Springfield, VA: National Technical Information Service, 1977.

Weinstein, Bernard L. and Robert E. Firestine. *Regional Growth and Decline in the U.S.: The Rise of the Sunbelt and the Decline of the Northeast.* New York, NY: Praeger, 1978.

Weiss, Richard. *Regional Disparities in Federal Medicaid Assistance.* Washington, D.C.: Northeast-Midwest Institute, 1977.

Yoder, Marion D. *Reversing Regional Decline: Final Report*. Harrisburg, PA: Pennsylvania Department of Community Affairs, 1976.

The Impact of Intergovernmental Revenues on Local Governments

Almy, Timothy A., "City Managers, Public Avoidancy and Revenue Sharing." *Public Administration Review*. Vol. 37, No. 1, January–February 1977.

Auten, G. E. "The Distribution of Revenue Sharing Funds and Local Public Expenditure Needs." *Public Finance Quarterly*, July 1974, pp. 352–75.

Barro, Steve and Roger Vaughan. *Urban Impacts of Federal Policies*. Washington, D.C.: Rand Corporation, 1978.

Bennett, J. R. and Mayberry, E. R. "Federal Tax Burdens and Grant Benefits to States: The Impact of Imperfect Representation." *Public Choice*, 1979, pp. 257–69.

Black, Thomas et al. *UDAG Marketplace: Nine Case Studies*. Washington, D.C.: Urban Land Institute, 1979.

Bowman, John H. "Fiscal Neglect of Urban Areas by a State Government." *Land Economics*, May 1975.

Bradbury, Katharine L. et al. "Shifting Local Services to the State." *National Tax Journal*, March 1976, pp. 97–107.

Bresnick, David. "New Roles for State Officials in an Age of Fiscal Federalism." *State Government*, Spring 1980, pp. 81–83.

Brookings Institution. *Case Studies of the Impact of Federal Grants in Large Cities, 1978: Transcripts of Working Conference Proceedings, Washington, D.C., February 2, 1978*. Springfield, VA: NTIS, 1978.

Brookings Institution. *Report on Allocation of Community Development Funds to Small Cities*. Washington, D.C.: U.S. Government Printing Office, 1979.

Brown, Dick and George Phenix. *The Missing Link Between Federal Grants and Municipal Management Reforms* (draft paper). Austin, Texas: National Economic Research Institute (n.d.)

Burchell, Robert W. and David Listokin. *The Fiscal Impact of Economic Development Programs: Case Studies of Local Cost. Revenue Implications of HUD, EDA and FMHA Projects* (draft). New Brunswick, NJ: Rutgers University, Center for Urban Policy Research, 1980.

Bureau of Governmental Research and Service. *Local Government Recovery of Overhead Through Federal Grants*. Columbia, S.C.: University of South Carolina, 1978.

Butler, Daron K. *Federal General Revenue Sharing and the Finances of Texas State and Local Governments*. Austin, TX: Texas Advisory Commission on Intergovernmental Relations, 1975.

Calvin, James A. "Municipal Problems with the Federal Bureaucracy." *Urban Georgia*, April 1976.

Caputo, David A. and Richard L. Cole. "General Revenue Sharing: Its Impact on American Cities." *Governmental Finance*, November 1977, pp. 24–27 +.

Carrol, Michael A. "The Impact of General Revenue-Sharing on the Urban Planning Process—An Initial Assessment." *Public Administration Review*, March–April 1975, pp. 143–150A.

City of Philadelphia. *An Urban Strategy*. Philadelphia, PA: Office of the Mayor, 1978.

Coalition of Northeast Municipalities. *Can Community Economic Development Meet the Fiscal Needs of Municipalities? Economic Growth and Fiscal Stress in Three Northeast Cities*. Boston, MA: Coalition of Northeast Municipalities, 1980.

Community Services Administration. *Federal Outlays in Summary. Report of the Federal Government's Impact by State, County and Large City, FY 1975*. (Compiled for the Executive Office of the President.) Springfield, VA: NTIS, 1976.

U.S. Comptroller General. *How Revenue Sharing Formulas Distribute Aid: Urban–Rural Implications*. Washington, D.C.: U.S. General Accounting Office, 1980.

Copeland, Ronald M. et al. "Intergovernmental and Tax Revenues in Local Governments of South Carolina." *Business and Economic Review*, October 1979, pp. 25–30.

Cornia, Gary C. et al. *State-Local Fiscal Incentives and Economic Development.* Columbus, OH: Academy for Contemporary Problems, 1978.

Crider, Robert A. *The Impact of Recession on State and Local Finance.* Columbus, OH: Academy for Contemporary Problems, 1978.

Cuciti, Peggy L. *Federal Constraints on State and Local Governments.* Washington, D.C.: Congressional Budget Office, 1979.

_____. *Troubled Local Economies and the Distribution of Federal Dollars: Background Paper.* Washington, D.C.: U.S. Government Printing Office, 1977.

DeLeon, Richard and Richard LeGates. *Redistribution Effects of Special Revenue Sharing for Community Development* (IGS Working Paper #17). Berkeley, CA: University of California, Institute of Governmental Studies, 1976.

Dickstein, Dennis. *Report of the Governor's Task Force on Local Aid: Final Report.* Boston, MA: Massachusetts Department of Community Affairs, Office of Local Assistance, 1976.

Ehrmann, Michael M. and Douglas Ford. "CD Rehabilitation: Analysis Reveals Dramatic Growth, Successful Local Programs." *Journal of Housing*, June 1981, pp. 330–337.

Else-Mitchell, R. "The Grants Commission and Local Government." *Public Administration*, Vol. 34, No. 4, December 1975.

Follain, J. R., Jr. "Grant Impacts on Local Fiscal Behavior: Full-Information Maximum Likelihood Estimates." *Public Finance Quarterly*, October 1979, pp. 479–500.

George, Billy and Clarke, Dan. *The Impact of General Revenue Sharing on Georgia's Cities.* Atlanta, GA: Municipal Association, 1979.

Grad, F. "The Federal Role in Solid Waste Disposal," in *Evaluating the Organization of Service Delivery: Solid Waste Collection and Disposal.* New York, NY: Columbia University Graduate School of Business, Center for Government Studies, 1977.

Graham, Robert. *The Economic Impact on Local Areas of the Program of the Economic Development Administration.* Springfield, VA: NTIS, 1977.

Gramlich, Edward M. et al. *The Stimulative Effects of Intergovernmental Grants: Why Money Sticks When It Hits* (conference paper). Ann Arbor, MI: University of Michigan, Department of Economics, 1978.

Green, Kenneth H. *Potential Reactions to School Finance Reform in New York State.* Binghamton, NY: State University of New York, 1978.

Greytak, David and Bernard Jump. *The Impact of Inflation on the Expenditures and Revenues of Six Local Governments.* Syracuse, NY: Syracuse University, Metropolitan Studies Program, 1975.

Hall, John Stuart. *The Impact of Federal Aid in the City of Phoenix: A Case Study for The Brookings Institution.* Washington, D.C.: U.S. Department of Labor, 1980.

Hand, John H. "Solving the Central City Fiscal Crisis: Metropolitan Government or Intergovernmental Transfer." *Nebraska Journal of Economics and Business*, Summer 1978, pp. 49–53.

Hardy, H. M. "Budgetary Responses of Individual Governmental Units to Federal Grants: A Rejoinder." *Public Finance Quarterly*, October 1977, pp. 523–27.

Harford, J. D. "Optimizing Intergovernmental Grants with Three Levels of Government." *Public Finance Quarterly*, January 1977, pp. 99–116.

Industry Task Force on Community Revitalization. *A New Frontier for Business Opportunities. A Handbook for Private Initiative in Community Revitalization.* Washington, D.C.: Mortgage Bankers Association of America, n.d.

Isserman, Andrew M. et al. "General Revenue Sharing: Federal Incentives to Change Local Government." *American Institute of Planners*, July 1978, pp. 317–327.

Jerrett, Robert III, et al. *Job Creation and the Economic Stimulus Package.* Washington, D.C.: The Brookings Institution, 1978.

Johnson, Eric. *A Critical Review of Federal Outlays in New York* (working paper). Plattsburgh, NY: State University of New York, Technical Assistance Center, 1977.

Juster, F. Thomas. *Economic and Political Impact of General Revenue Sharing.* Ann Arbor, MI: University of Michigan, Institute for Social Research, 1977.

Kustra, Robert W. *Intergovernmental Relations Policymaking in Illinois: The Role of State Government in Urban Policymaking.* Chicago, IL: Center for Research in Urban Government. Loyola University, 1977.

Lee, Robert D., Jr. *The Differential Impacts of Total Federal Expenditures, General Revenue Sharing, and Community Development Grants Upon Local Jurisdiction in Pennsylvania: Interim Report*. University Park, PA: Pennsylvania State University, Institute of Public Administration, 1976.

_____. *The Impact of General Revenue Sharing on Local Jurisdictions in Pennsylvania: Initial Findings*. University Park, PA: Pennsylvania State University, Institute of Public Administration, 1974.

Levitan, Sar A. and Joyce K. Zickler. *Too Little But Not Too Late. Federal Aid to Lagging Areas*. Lexington, MA: Lexington Books, 1976.

Liebschutz, Sarah F. *Case Studies of the Impact of Federal Aid on Major Cities*. Washington, D.C.: The Brookings Institution, 1980.

Lovell, Catherine. *The Effects of General Revenue Sharing on Ninety-Seven Cities in Southern California. Final Report*. Riverside, CA: University of California—Riverside, Graduate School of Administration, 1975.

_____. *The Effects of New Federal Grants on Local Governments*. Riverside, CA: University of California—Riverside, Graduate School of Administration, 1978.

_____, et al. *Federal and State Mandating on Local Governments*. Riverside, CA: University of California, 1979.

_____, et al. *General Revenue Sharing in 97 Southern California Cities*. Riverside, CA: University of California Graduate School of Administration, June 1975.

Lyons, William and David R. Morgan. "The Impact of Intergovernmental Revenue on City Expenditures." *Journal of Politics*, November 1977, pp. 3–21.

Mabbutt, Richard. *Financing Local Government in Idaho: Current Patterns, Future Alternatives and Fiscal Impacts*. Boise, ID: Boise State University, Department of Political Science, 1977.

MacManus, Susan A. *The Impact of Federal Aid on the City of Houston: A Case Study for The Brookings Institution*. Washington, D.C.: U.S. Department of Labor, 1980.

McDonald, W. Scott. "Federal Grants at Work in Dallas." *Public Management*, November 1972, pp. 12–15.

Mechling, William. *Can Community Economic Development Meet the Fiscal Needs of Municipalities? Economic Growth and Fiscal Stress in Three Northeast Cities*. Boston, MA: Coalition of Northeast Municipalities, 1980.

Miller, Gerald H. *Federal Aid in Michigan: Impact of Federal Aid on State and Local Governments, Financial Magnitude and Trends: Final Report*. Lansing, MI: Department of Management and Budget, 1975.

Morgan, Jr., Daniel C. "Fiscal Neglect of Urban Areas by a State Government." *Land Economics*, May 1974, pp. 137–144.

Municipal Finance Officers Association. *State Roles in Local Government Financial Management*. Washington, D.C.: The Association (n.d.)

National Academy of Public Administration and the U.S. Advisory Commission on Intergovernmental Relations. *The State and Distressed Communities: Indicators of Significant Actions*. Washington, D.C.: NAPA, 1979.

National Council for Urban Economics. *Development Coordinated Urban Economic Development: A Case Study Analysis*. Washington, D.C.: The Council, 1978.

New York State Assembly Ways and Means Committee. *New York's Role in the Fiscal Affairs of Its Local Governments*. Albany, NY: State Legislature, 1979.

New York Temporary Commission on City Finances. *The Role of Intergovernmental Fiscal Relations in New York City*. New York: The Commission, May 1977.

Olsen, Robert. *The Effect of Advanced Federal Budgeting upon State and Local Program Delivery*. Washington, D.C.: U.S. Government Printing Office, 1979.

Olson, Gerald W. *Interlevel Payments, Pass-Through Federal Aids and State-Local System* (conference paper). Kansas City, MO: University of Missouri, Department of Economics, 1977.

Pacific Consultants. *Title XX: Comparing the Costs of Alternative Delivery Systems*. Berkeley, CA: Pacific Consultants, 1979.

Peirce, Neal R. and Jerry Hagstrom. "The Cities, Not the States, May Bear the Brunt of Revenue Sharing Cutbacks." *National Journal*, April 19, 1980, pp. 636–639.

Petersen, John E. et al. *State Roles in Local Government Financial Management*. Washington, D.C.: Government Finance Research Center, 1979, p. 56.

Pluta, Joseph E. "The Federal Economic Stimulus Package: Effect on Large Texas Cities." *Texas Business Review*, May–June 1979, pp. 89–94.

Reeb, Donald with Karsm, William, Jr. *Federal Grants: Their Impact on Cash Management of State and Local Governments*. Albany NY: Center for Governmental Research and Services, State University of New York at Albany, 1979.

Reilly, John G. and Stephen M. Gershenson. *Impact of Federal Activities on Growth and Development: A Review of the Literature*. Washington, D.C.: Booz-Allen & Hamilton, Inc., January 1976.

Reschovsky, A. "An Evaluation of Metropolitan Area Tax Base Sharing." *National Tax Journal*, March 1980, pp. 55–56.

Richtern, Albert. *Federal Grants Management: The City and County View*. Washington, D.C.: Urban Data Service, International City Management Association, 1976.

Rosenthal, Edgar. *Philadelphia City Council's Role in Setting Policy for Spending Federal Grants*. Philadelphia, PA: Economy League, Eastern Division, 1979.

Ross, John and John Shannon. *Measuring the Fiscal Blood Pressure of the States*. Washington, D.C.: U.S. Advisory Commission on Intergovernmental Relations, 1977.

Rousakis, John P. "Cities Demand a Greater Voice in Federal System." *Alabama Municipal Journal*, April 1979, pp. 11–12 +.

Sabatti, Michael John. *The Impact of Revenue Sharing upon Local Government Decisionmaking*. Chico, CA: California State University at Chico, Library, 1976.

Schmandt, Henry J.; George D. Wendel; and Allan E. Tomey. *The Impact of Federal Aid on the City of St. Louis: A Case Study for The Brookings Institution*. Washington, D.C.: U.S. Department of Labor, 1980.

Schoeplein, Robert N. *Report on the Impact of Revenue Sharing on Illinois Townships* (conference paper). Urbana, IL: University of Illinois, Department of Economics, 1976.

Scott, Paul and Robert J. MacDonald. "Local Policy Management Needs—The Federal Response." *Public Administration Review*, 1976, pp. 786–794.

Sheridan, Richard. *Analysis of the Effects Upon the States Resulting from the Elimination of General Revenue Sharing*. Columbus, OH: Ohio Legislative Budget Office, 1979.

Slack, Enid. "Local Fiscal Response to Intergovernmental Transfers." *Review of Economics and Statistics*, August 1980, pp. 364–370.

Smith, Mendon W. "Lessons from 1975's Municipal Finance Crisis." *Banking*, February 1977, pp. 87–88.

Stephens, G. Ross and Olson, Gerald W. *Policy Implications of Pass-Through Federal Aid* (conference paper). Kansas City, MO: University of Missouri, Department of Economics, 1977.

_____. *State Responsibility for Public Services and General Revenue Sharing*. Springfield, VA: NTIS, 1975.

Stern, D. "Effects of Alternative State Aid Formulas on the Distribution of Public School Expenditures in Massachusetts." *Review of Economics and Statistics*, February 1973, pp. 91–97.

Stocker, Frederick D. *A State Revenue Sharing Proposal for Ohio*, Columbus, OH: Ohio State University, Department of Economics, 1976.

Strauss, R. P. "The Impact of Block Grants on Local Expenditures and Property Tax Rates." *Journal of Public Economics*, August 1974, pp. 269–84.

Stub, Steve Band and Rittenmoure, R. Lynn. *The Impact of Federal Aid on the City of Tulsa: A Case Study for The Brookings Institution*. Washington, D.C.: U.S. Department of Labor, 1980.

Sullivan, John H. and Loren Kaye. *Bailouts, Buyouts, Takeovers: Options for Delivering State Money to Local Government*. Sacramento, CA: California Taxpayers Association, 1978.

U.S. Advisory Commission on Intergovernmental Relations. *Counter-cyclical Aid and Economic Stabilization*. Washington, D.C.: The Advisory Commission on Intergovernmental Relations, 1978.

_____. *The Federal Role in the Federal System: The Dynamics of Growth. Volume 2.*

The Condition of Contemporary Federalism: Conflicting Theories and Collapsing Constraints. Washington, D.C.: U.S. Government Printing Office, 1981.

_____. *State Community Assistance Initiatives: Innovations of the Later 70s.* Washington, D.C.: The Commission, 1979.

U.S. Comptroller General. *Assessment of New York City's Performance and Prospects Under Its 3-Year Emergency Financial Plan.* Springfield, VA: NTIS, 1977.

_____. *Impact of Anti-Recession Assistance on 52 Governments—An Update.* Enclosure C, Case Studies of 21 City Governments. Springfield, VA: NTIS, 1977.

_____. *The Long-Term Fiscal Outlook for New York City.* Springfield, VA: NTIS, 1977.

_____. *New York City's Fiscal Problems—A Long Road Still Lies Ahead.* Washington, D.C.: U.S. General Accounting Office, 1979.

U.S. Conference of Mayors. *Economic Development: New Roles for City Government: A Guidebook for Local Government.* Washington, D.C.: U.S. Department of Housing and Urban Development (1979).

U.S. Congress. Congressional Budget Office. *Changing Patterns of Federal Aid to State and Local Governments.* Washington, D.C.: U.S. Government Printing Office, 1977.

_____. *Federal Constraints on State and Local Government.* Washington, D.C.: U.S. Government Printing Office, 1979.

_____. *Troubled Local Economics and the Distribution of Federal Dollars.* Washington, D.C.: U.S. Government Printing Office, 1977.

U.S. Congress. House. Committee on Banking, Finance and Urban Affairs, Subcommittee on Economic Policy. *Effectiveness of Economic Stimulus Programs: Hearings. . .95th Congress, Second Session, February 18 and 20, 1978.* Washington, D.C.: U.S. Government Printing Office, 1978.

_____. Committee on Banking, Housing and Urban Affairs, Subcommittee on the City. *Impact of the Federal Budget on Cities.* Washington, D.C.: U.S. Government Printing Office, 1977.

_____. Select Committee on the Budget. Task Force on State and Local Government. *Impact of the Fiscal Year 1981 Budget on State and Local Government: Hearings. . .96th Congress, Second Session, February 26 and 27, 1980.* Washington, D.C.: The Committee, 1980.

U.S. Congress. Joint Economic Committee. *Special Study of Economic Change, Vol. 7. State and Local Finance: Adjustments in a Changing Economy.* Washington, D.C.: U.S. Government Printing Office, 1980.

_____. *The Current Fiscal Condition of Cities. A Survey of 67 of the 75 Largest Cities.* 95th Congress, 1st Session. Washington, D.C.: The Committee, 1977.

_____. *State and Local Budget Surpluses and the Effect of Federal Macroeconomic Policies.* Washington, D.C.: U.S. Government Printing Office, 1979.

U.S. Congress. 95th Congress, 2nd Session, House Committee on Banking, Finance and Urban Affairs. Subcommittee on the City. *City Need and the Responsiveness of Federal Grants Programs.* Washington, D.C.: U.S. Government Printing Office, 1978.

U.S. Congress. 97th Congress, 1st Session, Joint Economic Committee. *Emergency Interim Survey: Fiscal Condition of 48 Large Cities.* Washington, D.C.: U.S. Government Pringing Office, 1982.

_____. *Trends in the Fiscal Condition of Cities: 1979–81. A Staff Study.* Washington, D.C.: U.S. Government Printing Office, 1981.

U.S. Congress. Senate. Committee on Governmental Affairs. *Scope of the General Revenue Sharing Program: Hearings: March 20 and 25, 1980.* Washington, D.C.: The Committee, 1980.

U.S. Department of Commerce. "Local Business and Employment Retention Strategies." *Urban Consortium Information Bulletin,* September 1980.

_____, Economic Development Administration. *Annual Report.* Washington, D.C.: Economic Development Administration, 1966–.

_____. *Federal Activities Affecting Location of Economic Development. Final Report.* Washington, D.C.: Department of Health and Human Services, 1970–.

_____. *Food Stamps: Annual Report.* Washington, D.C.: The Department of Health and Human Services, 1970–.

U.S. Department of Housing and Urban Development. *Fifth Annual Community Development Block Grant Report.* Washington, D.C.: The Department, 1980.

_____. *UDAG Annual Report.* Washington, D.C.: U.S. Government Printing Office, 1980.

_____, Office of Community Planning and Development. *Community Development Block Grant Program. Urban Counties: The First Year Experience.* Washington, D.C.: U.S. Government Printing Office, 1977.

_____. *Pockets of Poverty: An Examination of Needs and Options.* Washington, D.C.: The Department, 1979.

_____. *UDAG National Project Summaries: Dollars and Jobs 1978-1980.* Washington, D.C.: The Office, 1980.

_____. *Urban Development Action Grant Program: First Annual Report.* Washington, D.C.: U.S. Government Printing Office, 1979.

_____. *Urban Development Action Grant Program: Second Annual Report.* Washington, D.C.: U.S. Government Printing Office, 1980.

_____, Office of Management, Division of Data Systems and Statistics. *UDAG Project Data: Coding Sheet.* Washington, D.C.: The Division, 1980.

_____. *Urban Development Action Grant Program, Quarterly Progress Report: Report Preparation Instructions.* Washington, D.C.: The Division, 1980.

_____, Office of Policy Development and Research. *Methods of Urban Impact Analysis: The President's Tax Program.* Washington, D.C.: U.S. Government Printing Office, 1979.

U.S. Department of the Treasury. *Report on the Fiscal Impact of the Economic Stimulus Package on 48 Large Urban Governments.* Washington, D.C.: U.S. Department of the Treasury, 1978.

U.S. General Accounting Office. *Criteria for Participation in the Urban Development Action Grant Program Should Be Refined.* Washington, D.C.: The Office, 1980.

_____. *Improvements Needed in Selecting and Processing Urban Development Action Grants.* Washington, D.C.: The Office, 1979.

U.S. Office of Management and Budget. "Federal Aid to State and Local Governments." *Special Analyses, Budget of the U.S. Government.* Washington, D.C.: U.S. Government Printing Office, 1974.

Vaughan, Roger J. et al. *The Urban Impacts of Federal Policies: Vol. 1, Overview.* Washington, D.C.: U.S. Department of Health, Education and Welfare, 1980.

Vernez, George et al. *Federal Activities in Urban Economic Development.* Prepared for Economic Development Administration. Santa Monica, CA: Rand Corporation, 1979.

Waldhorn, Steven A. et al. *Planning and Participation: General Revenue Sharing in Ten Large Cities.* Springfield, VA: NTIS, 1975.

Walker, David B. "The New System of Intergovernmental Relations: More Fiscal Relief and More Governmental Intrusion." *Governmental Finance,* November 1978, pp. 17-22.

Walker, Larry N. *Determinants of Revenue Sharing Usage by County Governments in Oklahoma: Fiscal Pressure, Political Partisanship and Metropolitanism.* Stillwater, OK: Oklahoma State University, Political Science Department, 1977.

_____ and Patrick Grasso. *Uses of General Revenue Sharing Funds by Local Governments in Oklahoma: or, What is New About the New Federalism.* Stillwater, OK: Oklahoma State University, Political Science Department, 1977.

White, Maurice E. "ACIR's Model State Legislation for Strengthening Local Government Financial Management." *Government Finance,* December 1979, pp. 22-26.

Williamson, Dorothy; Kenneth S. Colburn; Pamela Kacser. *The Black Community and Revenue Sharing.* Washington, D.C.: Joint Center for Political Studies, 1973.

Wright, J. Ward. *New York City and the Urban Fiscal Predicament.* Chicago, IL: Municipal Finance Officers Association, 1976.

Zimmerman, Joseph F. *Municipal Transfers of Functional Responsibilities: Interim Report.* Albany, NY: State University of New York at Albany, Graduate School of Public Affairs, 1975.

_____. *State-Local Relations: State Dominance of Local Automony?* Paper prepared for delivery at the 1980 Annual Meeting of the American Political Science Association, Washington, D.C.: August 28-31, 1980.

_____. *State Mandates on Local Governments: Final Report*. Washington, D.C.: U.S. Advisory Commission on Intergovernmental Relations, 1978.

_____. *Transfers of Functional Responsibilities*. Albany, NY: State University of New York at Albany, Graduate School of Public Affairs, 1976.

Restructuring the Intergovernmental City

Ahlbrandt, R. S., Jr. "Implications of Contracting for a Public Service." *Urban Affairs Quarterly*, Vol. 9, March 1974, pp. 337–359.

Alexander, James, Jr. "Biting the Bullet: A Checklist for Budgetary Retrenchment." *New Jersey Municipalities*, January 1981, 36, pp. 8–9.

_____. "Contracting Out and the Municipal Budget." *New Jersey Municipalities*, March 1981, 33–34, pp. 6–7.

Alternatives to Traditional Public Safety Delivery Systems: Civilians in Public Safety Services. Berkeley, CA: Institute for Local Self-Government, 1977.

Association of Bay Area Governments. *Development Fees in the San Francisco Bay Area: A Survey*. Berkeley, CA: Association of Bay Area Governments, 1980.

Ballabon, M. D. "The Self-Service Group in the Urban Economy." *Journal of the American Institute of Planners*, Vol. 38, January 1972, pp. 33–42.

Bedell, Berkley. "Give the Money to the Real Innovators: Aiding Small Business." *The New York Times*, November 29, 1981.

Bierbaum, Martin A. *The Impact of the Reagan Domestic Program on Newark, New Jersey*. Princeton, NJ: Urban and Regional Research Center, Princeton University, 1982.

Bingham, R. D. *The Adoption of Innovation by Local Government*. Lexington, MA: Lexington, 1976.

Bryce, Herrington J., (ed.), *Managing Fiscal Retrenchment in Cities*. Columbus, Ohio: Academy for Contemporary Problems, 1980.

Butler, Stuart M. *Enterprise Zones: Pioneering in the Inner City*. Washington, D.C.: The Heritage Foundation, 1980.

California Tax Foundation. *Contracting Out Local Government Services in California*. Sacramento: California Tax Foundation, 1981.

Carpenter, P. and G. R. Hall. *Case Studies in Educational Performance Contracting: Conclusions and Implications*. Washington, D.C.: Department of Health, Education and Welfare, 1971.

Clark, Terry Nichols and Lorna Crowley Ferguson. "Fiscal Strain and Private Sector Resources: How Tight Are the Linkages?" *Political Processes and Urban Fiscal Strain*. Revised January 26, 1981, pp. 1–32.

Contract Services Handbook. Washington, D.C.: Heritage Conservation and Recreation Service, 1979.

"Contracting by Large Local Governments." *International Journal of Public Administration*, Vol. 1, Summer, pp. 307–327.

"Disparity and Diversity: Profiles of City Finances." *Urban Data Service Report*, Vol. 13, No. 8, August 1981.

Fiscal Containment. Who Gains? Who Loses? The Rand Corporation, September 1978.

Fisk, Donald, Herbert Kiesling and Thomas Muller. *Private Provision of Public Services: An Overview*. Washington, D.C.: The Urban Institute, May 1978.

Florestano, P. S. "The Municipal Connection: Contracting for Public Services with the Private Sector." *Municipal Management*, Vol. 1, Fall 1978, pp. 61–71.

_____ and S. B. Gordon. "Public Versus Private: Small Government Contracting with the Private Sector." *Public Administration Review*, Vol. 40, January/February 1980, pp. 29–34.

Gurin, A. and B. Friedman. *Contracting for Services as a Mechanism for the Delivery of Human Services: A Study of Contracting Practices in Three Human Service Agencies in Massachusetts*. Waltham, MA: Brandeis University, Florence Heller Graduate School for Advanced Studies in Social Welfare, 1980.

Hawkins, Robert B., Jr., et al. *Public Benefits from Public Choice*. Sacramento, CA: Task Force on Local Government Reform, 1974.

Huth, Mary Jo. "New Hope for Revival of America's Central Cities." *Annals*, September 1980, p. 451.

Kemp, Jack. *American Renaissance*. New York: Berkeley, 1981.

Kirbin, John J. and Jeffrey I. Chapman. *Active Approaches to Local Government Revenue Generation*. Los Angeles, CA: School of Public Administration, University of California, 1980.

Kotz, Nick. "The War on the Poor. Want is Making a Comeback." *The New Republic*, March 24, 1982, pp. 19–23.

Levine, C. "Organization Decline and Cutback Management." *Public Administration Review*, Vol. 38, July–August 1978, pp. 316–325.

Levine, Charles H. (ed.). *Managing Fiscal Stress: The Crises in the Public Sector*. Chatham House Publishers, 1980.

Milliman, J. M. "Beneficiary Changes—Toward a Unified Theory," in S. J. Mushkin (ed.). *Public Prices for Public Products*. Washington, D.C.: The Urban Institute, 1972.

Morley, David, Stuart Proudfoot and Thomas Burns (eds.). *Making Cities Work: The Dynamics of Urban Innovation*. Boulder, Colorado: Westview Press, 1980.

Muller, Thomas. *Central City Business Retention: Jobs, Taxes and Investment Trends*. Washington, D.C.: U.S. Department of Commerce, June 1978.

_____. "Urban and Regional Change: The Federal Role and National Policy." Testimony prepared for the Joint Economic Committee, Congress of the United States, July 1982.

Mushkin, Selma J. (ed.). *Public Prices for Public Products*. Washington, D.C.: The Urban Institute, 1972.

Nathan, Richard P., Phillip M. Dearborn and Clifford A. Goldman. "Initial Effects of the Fiscal Year 1982 Reductions in Federal Domestic Spending," in *Reductions in U.S. Domestic Spending: How They Affect State and Local Government*. John W. Elwood (ed.), New Brunswick, N.J.: Transaction Books, 1982.

Newark, New Jersey. Mayor's Policy and Development Office, Division of Review and Planning. *Tax Abatement in Newark, New Jersey: Part I. Impact Analysis: Part II. New Directions*. Newark, NJ: Mayor's Policy and Development Office, 1978.

Newitt, Jane. "What the Northeast Was Doing Right and What Went Wrong." *American Demographics*, September 1982.

Pascal, A. H. et al. *Fiscal Containment of Local and State Government*. The Rand Corporation, September 1979.

_____ and M. Menchik. *Restraints on Taxing and Spending: Trends, Portents, Consequences*. The Rand Corporation, April 1980.

Paul, E. S. "Pricing Rules and Efficiency," in S. J. Mushkin (ed.). *Public Prices for Public Products*. Washington, D.C.: The Urban Institute, 1972.

Perry, David and Alfred Watkins. "The Urban Renaissance for Business." *The Nation*, March 1, 1980, p. 236.

Petersen, John E. "The Outlook for State and Local Government Finance." Statement before the Joint Economic Committee, Congress of the United States, July 1982.

Poole, Robert W., Jr. *Cutting Back City Hall*. New York: Universe Books, 1980.

Princeton University Urban and Regional Research Center. *Background Material on Fiscal Year 1982 Federal Budget Restrictions: A Background Document for the First Round of the Field Network Evaluation Study of the Reagan Domestic Program*. Princeton, NJ: Princeton University, Princeton Urban and Regional Research Center, 1981.

Savas, E. S. "Municipal Monopolies vs. Competition in Delivering Urban Services." *Urban Analysis*, Vol. 2, 1974, pp. 93–116.

Shannon, John. "New Federalism in the 1980s." Testimony prepared for the Joint Economic Committee, Congress of the United States, July 1982.

Sonnenblum, S. et al. *Selecting Structures for Providing Municipal Services*. Los Angeles, CA: Institute of Government and Public Affairs, University of California, 1975.

Stegman, Michael A. "Housing Block Grants: Legislation is Unlikely This Year." *Journal of Housing*, June 1981, pp. 317–324.

Sternlieb, George et al. "Growth and Characteristics of the Transfer Dependent Intergovernmental City." Submitted in concert with testimony before the Joint Economic Committee, Congress of the United States, July 1982.

Stoffel, Jennifer, "Budgets—the No. 1 Issue in 1982." *State Government News*, Vol. 25, No. 1, 1982, pp. 5-6.

Thurow, Lester C. *Zero-Sum Society: Distribution and Possibilities for Economic Change.* New York: Basic Books, 1980.

Touche Ross and The First National Bank of Boston. *Urban Fiscal Stress: A Comparative Analysis of 66 Cities.* New York: Touche Ross, 1976.

U.S. Advisory Commission on Intergovernmental Relations. *The Future of Federalism in the 1980s. Report and Papers from the Conference on the Future of Federalism, Virginia, July 25-26, 1980.* Washington, D.C.: U.S. Government Printing Office, 1981.

_____. *Local Revenue Diversification: Income Taxes, Sales Taxes and User Charges.* Washington, D.C.: U.S. Government Printing Office, 1974.

U.S. Conference of Mayors. *The Federal Budget and the Cities: A Review of the President's Budget in Light of Urban Needs and National Priorities.* Washington, D.C.: U.S. Conference of Mayors, 1982.

_____. *Report of the National Urban Conference on Federalism, November 1981, Chicago.* Washington, D.C.: U.S. Conference of Mayors, 1982.

_____. *The FY82 Budget and the Cities: A Hundred City Survey.* Washington, D.C.: U.S. Conference of Mayors, 1981.

U.S. Congress, Committee on Banking, Finance and Urban Affairs. *Effects of Budget Cuts on Cities.* Washington, D.C.: Government Printing Office, 1982.

U.S. Congress, Congressional Budget Office. *An Analysis of President Reagan's Budget Revisions for Fiscal Year 1982.* Washington, D.C.: U.S. Government Printing Office, 1981.

_____. *Analysis FY1983 Reagan Budget.* Washington, D.C.: U.S. Government Printing Office (1982).

_____. *An Analysis of the President's Budgetary Proposals for Fiscal Year 1983.* Washington, D.C.: Congressional Budget Office, 1982.

_____. *Baseline Budget Projection for Fiscal Year 1983-1987: A Report to the Senate and House Committees on the Budget—Part II.* Washington, D.C.: U.S. Government Printing Office, 1982.

_____. Budget Analysis Division. *Five Year Projections System.* Washington, D.C.: Congressional Budget Office, 1982.

_____, 96th Congress, 2nd Session. House Committee on Banking, Finance and Urban Affairs. *Urban Revitalization and Industrial Policy*, September 16 and 17, 1980.

_____, 97th Congress, 1st Session. Joint Economic Committee. Subcommittee on Monetary and Fiscal Policy. *State and Local Economic Development Strategy: A "Supply Side" Perspective.* Washington, D.C.: U.S. Government Printing Office, 1981.

_____, Joint Economic Committee. *Emergency Interim Survey: Fiscal Condition of 48 Large Cities.* Washington, D.C.: Government Printing Office, 1982.

_____, Joint Economic Committee. "State and Local Finance: Adjustments in the Changing Economy." *Special Study on Economic Change*, Vol. 7, December, 1980.

_____, Joint Economic Committee. *Trends in the Fiscal Condition of Cities: 1979-81.* Washington, D.C.: U.S. Government Printing Office, 1981.

U.S. Environmental Protection Agency. *Sewer Investment Needs by SMSA.* Washington, D.C.: U.S. Government Printing Office, 1976.

U.S. President's Commission on Housing. *The Report of the President's Commission on Housing.* Washington, D.C.: U.S. Department of Housing and Urban Development, 1982.

User Charges: Their Role in Local Government Finance. Paper delivered at the Annual Conference of the National Tax Journal.

Van Horn, Carl E. and Henry J. Raimondo. "Living with Less: New Jersey Copes with Federal Aid Cutbacks." *Public Budgeting and Finance*, forthcoming.

_____. *The Impact of Reductions in Federal Aid to New Jersey.* New Brunswick, NJ: The Center for State Politics and Public Policy, Eagleton Institute of Politics, Rutgers University, May 1982.

Vickery, W. S. "Economic Deficiency and Pricing," in S. J. Mushkin (ed.), *Public Prices for Public Products.* Washington, D.C.: The Urban Institute, 1972.

"Ways Private Firms Can Save Money for Burdened Cities." *U.S. News and World Report*, November 1975, Vol. 17, pp. 79-82.

"When the Government Lets Somebody Else Do Its Job." *National Journal*, Vol. 10, October 1977, pp. 1410–1414.

Zimmerman, J. F. "Meeting Service Needs Through Intergovernmental Agreements." *The Municipal Yearbook*. Washington, D.C.: International City Management Association, 1973.

Supporting Documents on Urban Decline

Banfield, Edward C. *The Unheavenly City Revisited: A Revision of the Unheavenly City*. Boston, MA: Little–Brown, 1974.

Berry, Brian J. L. and Quentin Gillard. *The Changing Shape of Metropolitan America: Commuting Patterns, Urban Fields, and Decentralization Processes, 1960–1970*. Cambridge, MA: Ballinger, 1977.

Carlton, Dennis W. *Why Firms Locate Where They Do: An Economic Model*. Cambridge, MA: Joint Center for Urban Studies of MIT and Harvard University, 1979.

"Fiscal Stress in Local Government." *Government Finance*, Vol. 9, No. 2, June 1980.

Harrison, Bennett and Edward Hill. *The Changing Structure of Jobs in Older and Younger Cities*. Cambridge, MA: Joint Center for Urban Studies of MIT and Harvard University, 1979.

Levine, D. J. "Receipts and Expenditures of State and Local Government, 1959–1976." *Survey of Current Business*, Vol. 58, May 1978, pp. 15–21.

Merget, Astrid E. "Disparity and Diversity: Profiles of City Finances." *Urban Data Service*, Vol. 13, No. 8, August 1981 (entire issue).

Moore, Geoffrey H. *Cyclical Consequences of Long-Run Shifts in Industrial Employment*. Newark, NJ: Center for Industrial Business Cycle Research, 1980.

New Jersey Department of Labor and Industry. *Covered Employment Trends in New Jersey*. Trenton, NJ: Bureau of Occupational Statistics and Reports, 1978.

New York City, Department of City Planning. *Economic Recovery: New York City's Program for 1977–1982*. New York: Department of City Planning, 1976.

New York City, Office of Management and Budget. Office of Economic Development. *Report on Economic Conditions in New York City, July–December 1980*. New York, NY: Office of Management and Budget, Office of Economic Development, 1981.

New York City, Office of the Mayor. *New York City's Program for 1977–1981*. New York, New York: Office of the Mayor, 1976.

Seneca, Joseph J. "New Jersey's Urban Dilemma: Decline Within Earth." *Economic Policy Papers*. Trenton, NJ: Office of Economic Policy, 1981.

Sternlieb, George and James W. Hughes, (eds.). *Revitalizing the Northeast: Prelude to an Agenda*. New Brunswick, NJ: Rutgers University, Center for Urban Policy Research, 1978.

Twentieth Century Fund. *Report of the Twentieth Century Fund Task Force on the Future of New York City*. New York, NY: Twentieth Century Fund, 1979.

U.S. Advisory Commission on Intergovernmental Relations. *Central City-Suburban Fiscal Disparity and City Distress*. Washington, D.C.: The Advisory Commission on Intergovernmental Relations, 1980.

U.S. Congress, Congressional Budget Office. *The Prospects for Economic Recovery: A Report to the Senate and House Committee on The Budget—Part I*. Washington, D.C.: Congressional Budget Office, 1982.

_____. *Real Estate Tax Shelter Subsidies and Direct Subsidy Alternatives*. Washington, D.C.: U.S. Government Printing Office, 1977.

_____. *Reducing the Federal Deficit: Strategies and Options*. Washington, D.C.: U.S. Government Printing Office, 1982.

_____. *Reducing the Federal Deficit: Strategies and Options. A Report to the Senate and House Committees on the Budget—Part III*. Washington, D.C.: U.S. Government Printing Office, 1980

_____, House Committee on the Budget. *The Congressional Budget Process: A General Explanation*. Washington, D.C.: U.S. Government Printing Office, 1981.

U.S. Department of Commerce. *Annual Housing Survey: National Sample*. Washington, D.C.: U.S. Government Printing Office, 1977.

_____. *City Employment in 1979*. Washington, D.C.: U.S. Government Printing Office, 1980.

U.S. Department of Transportation. *National Budget Inventory Survey*. Washington, D.C.: Department of Transportation, 1978.

_____, Federal Highway Administration. *Urban Mileage and Travel by Pavement Condition and Pavement Type*. Washington, D.C.: Federal Highway Administration, 1976.

Urban Institute. "Cities and Economic Development: An Interview with Larry C. Ledebur." *Urban Institute Policy and Research Report*, Vol. 11, No. 1, Spring 1981, pp. 10–13.

Vaughan, Roger. *Local Business and Employment Retention Strategies*. Washington, D.C.: U.S. Department of Commerce, 1980.

Wells, Joan A. and Laura L. Vertz. *Urban Fiscal Crisis: Another Round?* Norman, Oklahoma: Bureau of Government Research, University of Oklahoma, 1980.

Index

abandonment, 9, 10, 11, 138, 144, 145, 151, 152

Academy for Contemporary Problems, 314

AFDC (Aid to Families with Dependent Children), 121–22, 126, 170–71, 172–73, 198, 267, 278, 296, 332

aging programs, 287

Agriculture, U.S. Department of, 176, 263

Ahlbrandt, Richard, 317

aid programs, Chapter 6 *passim* (159–218); fiscal stress and, 12–13; municipal, 194–97. *See also* federal aid; grants; name of specific program; spending reductions; state aid

Aid to Families with Dependent Children. *See* AFDC

Akron, Ohio: block grants to, 184, 191; crime in, 116; distress rankings and, 27, 129, 324n4; expenditures in, 221; health care in, 102, 103, 105, 106, 208; housing in, 81; income in, 97, 99; manufacturing in, 55; services in, 73; taxes in, 234, 241; transfer payments to, 247

Albuquerque, New Mexico: loss of federal funds in, 295

Allentown, Pennsylvania: fiscal pressures in, 313

Amtrak, 289

Anaheim, California: block grants to, 184; crime in, 116, 118; distress rankings and, 27, 132, 324n4, 330; health care in, 102, 106, 108, 208; housing grants to, 184; income in, 94, 99; public assistance in, 121, 122, 126; transfer payments to, 248, 249, 253, 255

annexation, 306

Annual Housing Survey (1980), 133–43 *passim*

Anti-Recessionary Fiscal Assistance program (1976), 187, 213–17

Arizona: future of, 342

Arkansas: fiscal pressures in, 323

"Articles of Confederation," 162

Austin, Texas: capital expenditures in, 77; crime in, 112, 115, 116, 118; distress rankings and, 27, 132, 324n4, 330; health care in, 102, 106, 108; income in, 99; public assistance in, 121, 122, 126; School Lunch program in, 179; transfer payments to, 248, 253, 255

authority, budget, Chapter 8 *passim* (259–93)

automation, 4

Baltimore, Maryland: anti-recessionary assistance to, 217; block grants to, 191, 200; crime in, 112, 115, 116, 118; distress ranking of, 27, 37, 85–86, 129, 324n4, 330; future of, 342; health care in, 102, 103, 105, 106, 107; housing in, 81, 184; income in, 94, 97, 99; loss of federal funds in, 295; public assistance in, 121, 122, 126; School Lunch program in, 179; sewers in, 230; taxes in, 234, 241; transfer payments to, 247, 248, 253, 255; transportation grants to, 212

Basic Education Opportunity Grants program (BEOG), 198, 200, 332

baths, 136, 138

Baton Rouge, Louisiana: capital expenditures in, 77; crime in, 112, 115, 116, 118; distress rankings and, 27, 129, 324n4, 330; expenditures in, 221; general revenue in, 213, 239; health care in, 102, 103, 106; income in, 99; public assistance in, 121, 122; transfer payments to, 247, 248, 249, 253, 255

BEOG (Basic Education Opportunity Grants program), 198, 200, 332

Berenyi, Eileen, 317–18

blacks. *See* housing

block grants, 268, 333. *See also* aid programs; federal aid; grants-in-aid; name of specific program

bond market, 7, 236–39, 330

Boston, Massachusetts, 20, 295, 337, 340, 341

bridges, 228–29

broad-based grants, 165, 269. *See also* name of specific program

Brookings Institution, 29, 32, 36, 37, 93

budget, federal, Chapter 8 *passim* (259–93); composition of outlays of, 266–67; trends in, 263–66

Buffalo, New York: crime in, 116, 118; distress rankings and, 27, 90, 129, 324n4, 330; employment in, 47; fiscal pressures in, 307, 313; future of, 342; health care in, 102, 103, 105, 106, 107, 208; housing in, 81; income in, 97, 99; industry in, 335; infrastructure in, 230, 231; population of, 43; public assistance in, 121, 122, 126; School Lunch program in, 179; Social Security program in, 174; tax base in, 234; transfer

income security programs, 161, 170–74, 277–80;
  budget for, 263, 266; grants for, 166, 274
Indiana: fiscal pressures in, 297, 298
individuals, aid to, Chapter 6 *passim* (159–218),
  330. *See also* name of specific program
industrial/industries: base characteristics, 54–75;
  disinvestment, 4–6, 169; future of the cities and,
  333–43; high-technology, 333–40, 343; relocation, 13n3. *See also* manufacturing sector
infant mortality, 102
influenza, 104–106
infrastructure. See capital expenditures/obsoles-
  cence; public services; transportation
"Inheritor of 'Free' Property," 155–56
installations, federal: location of, 162
insurance, housing, 150–51
"Insurance Settlement Beneficiary," 156
Intercity Hardship (Brookings), 29, 36, 37
interest payments: local government and, 221
intergovernmental   cities/intergovernmentalism:
  definition of, 1, 19–21, 25, 27, 37, 85–90, 327–
  30; household decline and, 21, 25, 28; nature of,
  17–19; selection of, 19–29, 37, 39. *See also* distress measures; distressed cities; hardship
Interior, U.S. Department of, 289
International Trade Administration, 284
Interpretive Structural Modeling (ISM), 314
Intrametropolitan Hardship (Brookings), 29, 36
investments, 4, 75–85. *See also* disinvestments
ISM (Interpretive Structural Modeling), 314

Job Corps program, 198, 202, 332
Joint Economic Committee of the Congress, 295–
  96, 324n4

Kentucky: fiscal pressures in, 298
kitchens, 136

labor market: structure of, 5–6. *See also* employment; training and employment
Labor Statistics, U.S. Bureau of, 122
land and water conservation programs, 289
land grants, 162–63
landlords, 139–40, 150
Legal Services program, 287
Lewis, Carol W., 300
local government: administration of, 220–21; assistance to, 167–69, 187, 194–97, 249–56; expenditures of, 220–21, 332–33; fisc of, 43, 85; interest payments of, 221; revenues and, 231–58,
  332–33; spending reductions and, Chapter 9 *passim* (295–326). *See also* aid programs; distressed
  cities; federal aid; grants-in-aid; hardship; intergovernmental cities; state
Logalbo, Anthony T., 300
Los Angeles, California, 20, 337
"Lottery Winner," 156

Louisville, Kentucky: crime in, 115, 116; distress
  rankings and, 27, 129, 324n4; employment in,
  45; expenditures in, 221; future of, 342; health
  care in, 102, 103, 105, 106, 107; housing in, 81;
  income in, 94, 97, 99; manufacturing in, 55;
  public assistance in, 122, 126; Revenue Sharing
  program in, 213; Social Security program in,
  174; taxes in, 234, 243; transfer payments to,
  247, 248, 249, 255; transportation grants to,
  212; wholesale trade in, 73
Low-Income Housing Assistance program (1937),
  181–82, 184

Manhattan, New York, 341–42
manufacturing sector, 333–40, 341–42; employment and, 62–65; establishments in, 55–57; private investments in, 77–79; value of production
  of, 73–75. *See also* industrial disinvestment
Matz, D.B., 342
Mayors, U.S. Conference of, 303, 305, 313
means-tested programs. *See* name of specific program
Medicaid, 166, 206–208, 266, 267, 274, 287, 296,
  332
Medicare, 266, 287–89
Michigan: fiscal pressures in, 297, 298
Milwaukee, Wisconsin: crime in, 112, 116; distress
  ranking of, 27, 85, 87, 129, 324n4, 330; expenditures in, 221; health care in, 102, 105, 106; income in, 97, 99; public assistance in, 121, 122,
  126; sewers in, 230; taxes in, 234, 243; transfer
  payments to, 247, 248, 255; transportation
  grants to, 212
Minneapolis, Minnesota: crime in, 112, 116, 118;
  distress ranking of, 27, 85, 89, 129, 324n4, 330;
  expenditures in, 221; future of, 341; health care
  in, 102, 105, 106; housing grants to, 184; income
  in, 94, 97, 99; manufacturing in, 55; public assistance in, 121, 122, 126; public services in, 73;
  service industries in, 340; transfer payments to,
  247, 253, 255; wholesale trade in, 67
Minnesota: fiscal pressures in, 297, 298
Minority Business Development Agency, 285
Model Cities program, 179–80
Moody's. *See* bond market
Morrill Act (1862), 163
mortality rate, 102–106. *See also* health care programs
municipal bonds. *See* bond market
municipal government. *See* distressed cities; intergovernmental cities; local government
Mushkin, Selma, 305

Nashville-Davidson, Tennessee: crime in, 115,
  116, 118; distress rankings and, 27, 129, 324n4,
  330; health care in, 102, 105, 106; income in, 94,